Zen &
Philosophy

An Intellectual Biography of Nishida Kitarō

Michiko Yusa

University of Hawai'i Press
Honolulu

For Jory
and B. and H.

Library of Congress
Cataloging-in-Publication Data
Yusa, Michiko
Zen & philosophy :
An intellectual biography of
Nishida Kitarō / Michiko Yusa.
p. cm.
ISBN 0–8248–2402–4 (cloth : alk. paper)—
ISBN 0–8248–2459–8 (pbk. : alk. paper)
1. Nishida, Kitarō, 1870–1945.
I. Title: Zen and philosophy. II. Title.

B5244.N554 Y86 2002
181'.12—dc21
[B]   2001040662

Grateful acknowledgment is made to
Monumenta Nipponica for permission to reprint
previously published material, "Tanabe Ryūji,
Koizumi Yakumo, Preface by Nishida Kitarō.
Monumenta Nipponica 51.3 (1996) 313–16.

Designed by Deborah Hodgdon

Printed by The Maple-Vail Book
Manufacturing Group

Contents

Foreword
A Contemplative Life

It is for me an honor and a pleasant duty to preface this remarkable study. An intellectual biography is neither a mere historical account of the events of one particular person, more or less interesting as they might be, nor is it merely one more chapter in the history of ideas describing the more or less logical connection of one person's thought to ideas prevalent at a particular time and place. It is more demanding than that, and also more important. To be sure, the intellect expresses itself in ideas, and biography is concerned with the facts of a person's life. But an intellectual biography seeks to approach ideas as living entities incarnated in a living person. The connections are not only logical but also vital. A philosopher not only *has* ideas and writes about them; he *lives*. An authentic philosopher always maintains a measure of reserve about his ideas, conscious of their limitations much in the same way that he is conscious of his own physical limitations. A true philosopher is not a professor of philosophy (as Kant would have it), not a *Lesemeister*, a teacher of doctrines, but a *Lebensmeister*, a guide for life (as Eckhart puts it). To attempt an intellectual biography of this sort involves penetrating the very life of the intellect as incarnated by one of those few, as Fichte ironically phrases it, "condemned by God to be philosophers."

I say that it is an honor for me to introduce the work of Professor Michiko Yusa, because it represents the successful completion of a task as demanding as it is fascinating. At the same time, it is not without a certain sense of duty that I accept the honor, having guided the author through her master's and doctoral work, and even more so for having first drawn the attention of Professor Yusa to the importance of Nishida Kitarō. She is altogether *too* generous in naming me "the primogenitor of this work," but I gladly accept the duty of the teacher to serve one's students and welcome the chance to underline the significance of the work she has completed.

Readers of this book will be quick to recognize the devotion to detail that occupied the attentions of the author throughout the decade of its composition. I am tempted to call her book an outstanding work. Without being an expert in Japanese thought, I had a fair knowledge of Nishida's philosophy, but I must confess that this book has led me to love the man—and without love knowledge is truncated, to say the least. Professor Yusa's work blends with exquisite tact the "objective" realm of ideas with the subjective field of the personal life of the thinker. In so doing, she herself exemplifies one of the contributions of Nishida to philosophy: the overcoming of the epistemological dichotomy between objectivity and subjectivity.

Nishida is for me a living example of the struggle to rise above the split between *theōreia* and *praxis*. It is not that he drew theoretical conclusions from his concrete actions. He was no Marxist. But neither is it the case that his theories moved him directly to action. He was no idealist either. Rather his nondualistic experience, as I would put it, made him realize the falsity of the dichotomy between the two. When Cicero's Roman spirit translated the Greek *theōreia* into the Latin *contemplatio*, he did not mean to reduce the notion to a mere spinning of ideas. The *advaitic* attitude, a fundamental feature of the Oriental spirit (if I may be permitted a simplification), was nurtured in Nishida's life through the discipline of Zen. His was indeed a *contemplative life*. How else could he have kept a balance between the revolution begun by the Meiji Restoration and its unexpected escalation, led by the patriotic militarism that followed it? He embraced the Meiji spirit in opening himself fully to the philosophical influence of Western philosophy in its modern form. But he did not forfeit his Oriental wisdom so as to become a mere Japanese expert in European thought. This may be part of the reason that some of his interpretations of German idealism strike us as not quite hermeneutically accurate by Western standards. Or is this perhaps a *felix culpa?*

Of the many considerations that come to mind, I single out one. It is quite literally a "con-sideration," since what it attempts is to "put together the stars" of East and West by highlighting the paramount importance of *experience* in life, and hence also in philosophical activity. For Nishida, as it had been for the West before its so-called enlightenment, philosophy was an indispensable companion to a conscious human existence. Experience is a meeting ground for the encounter between East and West, however widely their interpretations may differ.

I see in Nishida a living example of the mutual fecundation that alone, in my opinion, can save our dominant civilization from a lethal globalization that is in effect the opposite of what Nishida meant by "unifying power." In this consideration I do not lay claim to any special authority with regard to Nishida's philosophy. Professor Yusa's text offers ample and documented detail. I wish only to elaborate briefly in my own words by way of preface to those ideas.

By and large, simplifications may be helpful but they are also dangerous. Nevertheless, the dominant culture of the West takes experience to mean an individual and *subjective* perception, or, at best, an intuition that cannot provide an *objective* basis for a lasting civilization. In the shadow of this assumption, we are told that all of us, East and West, should respect private feelings and even religious beliefs but recognize that they have little to do with the objectivity of the "real world" represented by politics, technoscience, and economics. On the contrary, for everything the East has done to cultivate happiness, its people remain economically poor and victimized by social injustice. Japan learned to swallow this assumption the hard way and paid for it with a kind of cultural schizophrenia. India offers a counterexample: schizophrenia on the one hand, chaos on the other.

Put in more academic language, the split between objectivity and subjectivity is the pit into which official philosophy has fallen, beginning with the divorce of religion from philosophy and of epistemology from ontology. Anyone who would argue that the intentions one has in constructing some technical gadget or other, say a car, influence the nature of the car is likely to be met with the polite smile we reserve for those trapped in magical, primitive, or superstitious modes of thought. And indeed, without the necessary distinctions and without reversing the *mythos* within which the modern mind understands things, the reaction is understandable.

"What has Athens to do with Jerusalem?" goes the well-known dictum of a familiar brand of Christian exclusivism. "What has Zen to do with philosophy?" is simply another form of it. Or in a milder and yet deeper way: "What has philosophy to do with religion? Or subjective experience with objective reality?" May I not be a good philosopher and a bad man? I wonder.

De nobis ipsis silemus : De re autem quae agitur . . . "Concerning ourselves we keep silent; concerning the thing itself, we ask people to think about it," wrote Francis Bacon of Verulam in the seventeenth century in the preface to his *Instauratio Magna*. A century and a half later, Immanuel Kant chose this sentence as a motto for the second edition of his *Critik der reinen Vernunft*, emphasizing yet again the primacy of objectivity, at least in the philosophical enterprise. Kant had nothing to hide regarding his life as a citizen; this was not the case with the political life of the Lord Chancellor Baron of Verulam. Roughly another century and a half later, Nishida Kitarō, well versed in modern Western philosophy, showed the same reluctance to include his personal life as part of his strenuous philosophical activity. We have Professor Yusa to thank, more than half a century later, for breaking this silence and bringing together in this *Intellectual Biography* the life and work of the most prominent philosopher of the now well-established Kyoto school of philosophy. In the process she unveils a fundamental difference between East and West much more important than the nationalist obsession with Japanese identity that plagued Japan's empire during the later years of Nishida's life. Where Bacon had defended objectivity and Kant had believed in the supremacy of the thing-in-itself, Nishida was concerned with overcoming the subject-object split in a different way than German idealism had done.

I may now return to qualify the bald statement that the "subjective" intention with which one performs an "objective" action influences both the doer and the "thing" that is done. I would not go as far as to approve the injunction of the great rabbi Akiba ben Joseph that a parchment of the Torah copied by a *goy*, a gentile, is unfit to be read in the synagogue, because I do not share his conviction of the impurity of the nonbeliever. But I do think that it expresses forcefully what is at stake. Hardly a generation earlier, Jesus of Nazareth had stressed continually that what matters most are the intentions of one's heart. Not to stray into exegetical nuances, I would only stress that overcoming the dichotomy between theory and practice is more than a theoretical subtlety. "There is no other way to carry out one's work than to think deeply on one's own," Nishida wrote to his former student Tanabe Hajime, who, in the spirit of his teacher, defined the task of philosophy as the self-realization of salvation through the transforming mediation of *zange* (repentance)—a Buddhist word that he translated as *metanoia* and understood as a leap, through grace, from self-sufficiency (*jiriki*) to transcendence (*tariki*). I conclude this consideration by simply saying that there is neither pure objectivity nor pure subjectivity. The knower and the known, the subject and the object are not only relative notions; they are two inseparable although distinguishable aspects of reality. Dualism is as lethal as monism—and *advaita* looms again on the horizon. But I should not overstep my pleasant duty as a prologist.

Professor Yusa's biography is, thus, not only a fascinating narration of a great philosopher's life but a hermeneutical key for understanding his philosophy (not always an easy read), and for situating the "place" (χώρα) of the encounter between cultures and philosophies. The pythagorean *aithēr* and the platonic *chōra* (and also, incidentally, like the Indic ākāśa), seem more suited to translate Nishida's *basho* than is the Aristotelian *topos*. Here we have a blatant example of the impoverishment of the modern philosophical tradition. Because the medieval idea of "aether" as a material fluid has long since been discarded by science, most dictionaries of philosophy shy away from even mentioning that fifth element of many pre-Socratics along with earth, water, air, and fire. The meeting of East and West cannot be reduced to an encounter between recent Western modernity and classical ancient Oriental thought. I am confident that the philosophical tradition of the Kyoto School that Nishida initiated will continue to flourish, though to say more at this point would take us beyond the reaches of the present book, since our authority does not overstep the assignment she has undertaken.

Professor Yusa's intellectual biography of Nishida seeks to intertwine the story of his family, his academic career, and his political life. Commenting on Nishida's theory of knowledge, for example, in which he insists that to know something is to love it, and that truly to love something is to know it, she notes that, at the time Nishida was writing on the subject, he had just lost one of his own daughters and was seeking to offer consolation to a friend who had suffered a similar situation a year before. The text, she tells us, demonstrates his experience of *tariki* as the act of reliance on grace and his awareness of the insufficiency of *jiriki* as mere trust in oneself. Fichte's remark that the philosophy one writes has much to do with what kind of person one is, finds rich resonance in Nishida's life. By the time one has finished reading this book, it is clear that without taking into account the experience of Zen and the historical setting of the early years of the Meiji period, there is hardly a way adequately to appreciate Nishida's contribution to philosophy.

I have already intimated the importance of this book as a case study of the mutual fecundation of cultures. The encounter of Nishida in particular, and the Kyoto school in general, with Western culture was, and still is, a starting point for a mutual fecundation. The West is much more than Enlightenment and post-Enlightenment philosophy, just as the East is much more than the Japan of the Meiji and post-Meiji era. Still, these in-depth encounters offer our times an encouraging sign of hope. It is perhaps time we took a serious look at our world's current predicament. And for this, there is much to be learned from Nishida and his biography.

R. Panikkar
Tavertet, Epiphany 2001

Acknowledgments

Without the support and kindness of many individuals and institutions, it would have been impossible to carry out the research that went into making this book. I would like to thank Western Washington University for granting me professional research leaves in 1991 and 1998. I would also like to thank the Japan Foundation for a fellowship that enabled me to do research in Japan in 1993 and 1994.

I owe special thanks to Ueda Shizuteru, professor emeritus of Kyoto University, who took a personal interest in my work and encouraged me to write *Denki Nishida Kitarō*, a biography of Nishida in Japanese. The experience of completing that book pushed me to finish the present English version. The late Professor Nishitani Keiji, who was a direct living link to Nishida, inspired me not to give up my work on Nishida Kitarō, which was personally very important for me. Raimon Panikkar, professor emeritus of University of California Santa Barbara, holds a unique place in relation to this book as the person who first suggested that I take up Nishida's thought. Master Sasaki Jōshū of the Mt. Baldy Zen Center in California was kind enough to allow me a glimpse into the fascinating world of Zen.

I am indebted to James Heisig, director of the Nanzan Institute for Religion and Culture, who facilitated my research in Japan. Graham Parkes, professor at the University of Hawai'i, and Fred Dallmayr, professor at the University of Notre Dame, took precious time to offer me invaluable suggestions for improving my text. My colleague at Western Washington University, Edward Kaplan, patiently went through many earlier versions of my manuscript. I owe him very special thanks indeed.

Yamashita Masao (retired professor, Kyoto University) and Katō Hiroyoshi (retired professor, Gakushūin University), Mr. Ōtsubo

Hideji, director of Musashi Kinenkan in Tokyo, and Mr. Inotani Kazuo, former director of Nishida Kinenkan in Unoke, supplied me with opportunities to look at rare materials and other hard-to-obtain documents. Mr. Iwanami Yūjirō, son of Iwanami Shigeo, graciously allowed me to use the fantastic book collections held at the Iwanami Company in Kanda, Tokyo. Mr. Mikami and Mr. Sasahara of Tōeisha in Kyoto graciously granted me freedom to reproduce material from the Japanese version of my biography of Nishida Kitarō.

Thanks are also due my friends. Matsunami Taiun of Daitokuji provided me with a beautiful environment in which to carry out my research in Kyoto. My most personal thanks go to Mrs. Marjory (Jory) Chadbourne, a very fine poet, who from the beginning till the end of this project, has sustained me with her boundless love. I appreciate knowing Mihoko (Okamura) Bekku, who acted as secretary to D. T. Suzuki in his last fifteen years. From time to time, she shared with me her memories of her "sensei." I had the good fortune too of coming to know Mr. Nishida Kikuhiko and the late Mr. Ueda Hisashi, both grandsons of Nishida Kitarō.

There are more individuals (many of whom are now deceased) to whom thanks are due. But I should not forget my mother and father, my two sisters and their husbands, and my other relatives. They all selflessly responded to my never-ending requests, from finding books in Japan to fixing my computer problems.

This book is dedicated to my dear friend and beloved companions and to what they stand for—love, reason, and conscience.

Introduction

Nishida Kitarō (1870–1945) defined for the Japanese what it means to philosophize. His thought was crowned with his name and came to be known as *Nishida tetsugaku*, or "Nishidan philosophy," and enjoyed high regard among his peers for its rigor and originality. His endeavors helped shape a major stream of philosophical discourse, known as the Kyoto school, which sought to go beyond merely adapting Western philosophy. His conviction of the universal validity, inherent rationality, and beauty of Japanese culture compelled him to give it a philosophical expression. Even during his lifetime, he was hailed as the representative thinker of Japan and became a cultural icon as well as a source of national pride.

Colleagues of Nishida's who were studying abroad in the 1920s and 1930s brought his thought to the attention of leading European thinkers such as Edmund Husserl and Heinrich Rickert. Nishida corresponded with the two German philosophers as well. In the late 1930s several of Nishida's essays were translated into German, but before fruitful exchanges could be undertaken, World War II erupted, and whatever discourse had been built up was buried.

More than half a century after his death, a healthy interest in Nishidan philosophy and the Kyoto school of philosophy exists among the contemporary generation of thinkers and scholars worldwide. A good number of Nishida's philosophical essays have been translated into English, German, Spanish, French, Italian, Chinese, and Korean —and the list continues to grow. Where does this "Nishidan mystique" originate?

Given the interest that Nishidan philosophy has enjoyed in Japan and elsewhere, it is curious to observe that in the late 1930s his thought was considered pro-Western and counter to the "Japanese spirit"; his physical safety was even threatened by ultranationalists. Following World War II, however, Nishidan philosophy came to be regarded as the expression of prewar "old" Japan, and thus as outmoded. Marxist and progressive thinkers even condemned it as imperialistic and nationalistic by employing the tactic of guilt by association. It was widely felt in the wake of Japan's defeat that the country had to enter a new period and that any ties with the past had to be severed.[1] In this hasty and somewhat forced cultural paradigm shift, leading Japanese intellectuals threw out the baby with the bath water.[2]

Worldwide intellectual movements after World War II attempted to deny the legacies of pre-1945 totalitarianism and ultranationalism. Martin Heidegger, for example, was targeted, and the trend did not spare Nishida from the list of the "suspicious." Nishida was branded a kind of fascist or ultranationalist, "blind" to the "demonic aspect of nationalism and imperialism." He became a convenient scapegoat for those who were inclined to look for immediate answers rather than carry out the detailed historical analyses of the times leading up to 1945 and beyond.

From the 1950s through the 1970s, it was fashionable—not just in Japan but worldwide—to embrace Marxist views if one wanted to be seen as socially engaged and intellectually conscientious. Even earlier, during the 1930s in Japan, it was held that to be an intellectual, one must be a Marxist. Although Nishida was open to such aspects of Marxism as the importance of society and action, he kept to his own path.

I offer in these pages an intellectual biography that describes Nishida's philosophical odyssey in the context of his life and that visits him in his time. This biography depicts the social-cultural-political environment in which he lived, for no thinker thinks in a vacuum. Although I hope to dispel various misconceptions about Nishida, my ultimate purpose is to make Nishida's thought more accessible to the reader by tracing its development in the concrete context of his life.

MEIJI: A UNIQUE HISTORICAL JUNCTURE

Nishida, born in 1870 (the third year of the Meiji period), grew up during a time when Western (i.e., European and North American) ideas, natural sciences, and technology were changing the traditional Japanese way of life. This dynamic historical period in which East and West came face-to-face, and sometimes collided, on an unprecedented scale stimulated creative minds. The Meiji era was a period of great intellectual activity in Japan. Internationally, Japan awoke to the expansionism of European and North American powers. Domestically, the country was undergoing changes in the political, educational, economic, technological, scientific, cultural, and religious spheres as it faced, adopted, and adapted Western models. Apart from promoting heavy industry and building up military force, the government also attempted to implement a nationalist faith by manipulating the symbols of Shinto.[3] Nishida and his friends remained critical of many changes brought about by the government's decisions.

In his youth, Nishida, like other well-educated young men of his time, was thoroughly trained in classical Chinese. This training added depth to his intellectual world, just as Westerners who are trained in Latin and Greek bring depth to their worlds. Nishida, like many of his generation, was an idealistic humanist and pushed the horizon of his world beyond the tiny archipelago of Japan. Together with his friends, he was walking an uncharted terrain, his eyes bright with curiosity.

Nishida took up philosophy because he wanted to understand the workings of the universe. A few generations earlier, Japanese intellectuals advocated "adopting the Western sciences and technology while preserving the Japanese spirit," an eclectic strategy commonly known as "Japanese in spirit, Western in technology" *(wakon yōsai)*.[4] By the time Nishida came on the stage, Japanese intellectuals were sophisticated enough to see Western tradition as a whole; they saw not only technology but also art, philosophy, and the discoveries of the natural sciences as the integral self-expression of Western civilization. To young Nishida the discipline of philosophy seemed to offer unknown promises and challenges. The clash of two fundamentally different cultures, East and West, was for him an occasion to reflect on such questions as the relationship between cognition and volition, between tradition and globalization, and the nature of history and science. He carried out his venture on his own terms and created his own system of thought. For Nishida the tension between East and West turned out to be a creative one.

ZEN AND PHILOSOPHY

The coming together of Zen Buddhism and philosophy, or Oriental *prajñā* and Western *sophia*, may constitute for some the essence of the "Nishidan mystique." Beginning in his midtwenties, Nishida underwent a formal Zen practice, which was by no means a smooth path for him. Unlike those who are mentally ready to break through the "Zen barrier," Nishida had to struggle because of his strong intellectuality and deep-rooted ego. Once liberated from things that hampered his spiritual growth, he discovered a new vantage point, both as a scholar and a man. The curious thing about Nishida's Zen practice is that even after he quit regular *zazen* (practice of sitting meditation) and *sanzen* (private interviews with a Zen master, geared toward fostering spiritual awakening), the "Zen seed" that was securely planted in him continued to grow and bring about sudden surprises at unexpected times. Because of this ongoing fermentation, Nishida became convinced that the fundamental mission of his philosophical activities was to bridge the gap between natural sciences and Zen teaching; this he confided to Mutai Risaku two years before his death.[5]

Zen opened up Nishida's mind to the vital question of his own spirituality. The practice of *kōan*—a kind of "Zen homework" designed to release the mind from the conventional opposition between subject and object—shattered his arid intellectual desire for secular fame and success and opened up a new intellectual horizon that drew its authenticity from life itself. Zen rendered his thinking flexible. He came to appreciate the import of everyday life, which he realized was the very source of his scholarly pursuits; indeed, life took precedence over his scholarly success. In his search to fulfill his spiritual destiny, he drew on a wide range of spiritual traditions, avidly reading not only Eastern thinkers but also Christian thinkers, theologians, and mystics, such as Augustine, Nicholas of Cusa, and Meister Eckhart.

Although Nishida was by nature a man of independent mind, Zen practice further fortified that spirit in him. He had many students who wished to study with him and to establish close teacher-disciple *(deshi)* relationships with him. "Not to refuse those who come to him and not to chase after those who leave him" *(kurumono wa kobamazu, sarumono wa owazu)* was Nishida's usual response. Nishitani Keiji, one of his "disciples," recalls that Nishida "aimed to inspire an independent spirit in his students so that they might go their own ways and not be fettered to their teacher's ideas. One hears frequently of Nishida's broad-mindedness in allowing his disciples to pursue their own courses of study."[6] Nishida, though considered a key figure in the establishment of the Kyoto school of philosophy, contributed to it primarily by granting his students intellectual freedom. A case in point is Tanabe

Hajime, whose declaration of independence from Nishida became the driving force behind the formation of the Kyoto school. This fact underscores that Nishida not only allowed his students to proceed in their own directions but also actually preferred that they do so. He welcomed constructive criticism of this thought from his peers and students.

Zen clearly made its mark on the content, system, and style of Nishida's thought. Nishitani Keiji, himself a profoundly enlightened Zen practitioner, observed that, through Zen, Nishida's otherwise untamed life force became his finely honed will, and through this will he purified himself. This process culminated in a union between his self and the law of the universe[7] that shaped his philosophical stance. Nishida's approach was essentially empirical. He turned his attention to the naked reality of experience itself. This empirical approach is in line with Zen teaching, which pays close attention to the here and now, to the living experience itself, before it hardens into concepts and bifurcates into subject (experiencer) and object (the experienced). Nishida acquired this knowledge of the unity of subject and object through his *zazen* meditation, which is a body-mind engagement. He came to maintain that "the separation and independence of subject and object is but an arbitrary dogma ingrained in our habit of thinking."[8] This subject-object unity was self-evident to Nishida and remained for him the fundamental epistemological conviction.

Nishida's vantage point—of the self "free of ego" (*muga*), or selflessness, which, by definitiion is free of attachment to a certain dogmatic viewpoint—enabled him to evolve his philosophical vision from that of "pure experience," to "self-consciousness," to "the *topos* (or field)," to "the absolutely contradictorily self-identical dialectical world of the one and the many." The mental-spiritual freedom of the "original self" allowed his philosophical reflections to deepen. In this sense he was an open-ended thinker.

PHILOSOPHY BEYOND ZEN

Zen was for Nishida the fountainhead and unifying force of his philosophical vision. But he realized early on in his career that it was best not to mention his Zen background, for this public knowledge had given rise to a school of interpretation that reduced his thought into a philosophy of "satori" that only a few select enlightened people could hope to understand. Many years later Nishida explained this interest to Nishitani Keiji:

> You are absolutely right to say that something of Zen is in the background of my thought. I am not an expert on Zen, but I do believe that people generally misunderstand what Zen is all about. I think the life of Zen consists in "getting at reality." It has been my dearest wish since my thirties to unite Zen and philosophy, even though that is impossible. Certainly, it is fine if *you* say [that Zen elements are present in my thought], but if ordinary uninformed people call my thought "Zen," I would strongly object, because they do not understand either Zen or my thought. They simply bundle together X and Y as the same thing, which is to misunderstand both my thought and Zen.[9]

Indeed, what distinguishes Nishida's achievement from that of his contemporaries is not his Zen practice but the serious engagement with Western thinkers, both contemporary and past, that honed his thinking. Several years of philosophical apprenticeship began about 1910. During this time he assiduously read and studied the works and methods of Western thinkers, from Plato and Aristotle to Bergson, the neo-Kantian thinkers, and Husserl. This apprenticeship gave Nishida's thought strength and toned his philosophical muscles. Agreeing with Daisetz T. Suzuki that some knowledge of Zen might be necessary to understand Nishida, Thomas Merton has pointed out that "some knowledge of existential phenomenology may serve as a preparation" as well.[10] Merton interpreted Nishida in the light of his own thorough training in Western philosophical and theological traditions. Merton's comment would have come as a personal compliment to Nishida, whose attempt was to engage in a philosophical discourse proper and not to create some eclectic blend of ideas. Nishida vigorously carried out his philosophical inquiries, which extended to the fields of modern mathematics, theoretical physics, and biology.

BIOGRAPHY AND PHILOSOPHERS

Nishida contended that a philosopher's thought should stand on its own, and that therefore a philosopher's private life had little to do with his or her thought.[11] This remark may reveal his dislike of an overtly personal display of emotions and circumstances. Nevertheless, Nishida enjoyed reading autobiographies and biographies of all sorts of men and women, philosophers, mathematicians, scientists, and educators, not only famous heroic figures but also little-known private individuals. In his teens Nishida immersed himself in the biographies of mathematicians, such as Laplace and Lagrange,[12] and he was inspired by the autobiography of Niijima Jō, the founder of Dōshisha in Kyoto. He especially devoured biographies when he was a dormitory master for a year (1901–1902) at the Fourth Higher School. He took notes on what touched him and spoke to the students at their weekly evening meetings about what he had just read. His notes contain such figures as Thomas Carlyle, Mary Lyon (a teacher at Mt. Holyoke Seminary), George Peabody (a philanthropist), John Bunyan, General Charles "Chinese" Gordon, and Yamaoka Tesshū.[13] It was in fact the autobiography of Herbert Spencer that gave Nishida the encouragement he needed to proceed in philosophy.[14] He must have read biographies of Descartes, Spinoza, and Kant, because he later recommended them to his younger colleague Tanabe Hajime.[15]

In 1922, upon receiving a copy of the autobiography of Bernard Bolzano from Miki Kiyoshi in Germany, Nishida enthusiastically introduced it to Japanese students of philosophy.[16] Years later still, Nishida enjoyed a biography of N. H. Abel, a Swedish mathematician,[17] and in the middle of World War II he was enthralled by Zsolt de Harsanyi's life of Galileo Galilei, *The Star-Gazer*.[18]

Suzuki Daisetz, his lifelong friend, makes a case for a biographical work on Nishida:

> It can be argued that one can grasp Nishida's thought simply by reading his philosophical essays. But there is much that was not expressed in words. . . . His writings are not the whole of Nishida. Unless one meets the person and spends some time with that person, one cannot grasp the "human" behind that person's thought. I believe that without knowing Nishida the person, we cannot fully grasp his thought.[19]

Suzuki depicts Nishida as someone who would initially give the people the impression of aloofness but who was actually a man of deep emotions that he concealed well. Suzuki contended that however much Nishida might have willed to engage in philosophy, no great thought would have emerged if not for these emotions.[20] We recall Fichte's adage that there is an organic unity between the kind of philosophy a person chooses and the kind of person she or he is, because "a philosophical system is not a piece of dead furniture one can acquire and discard at will; it is animated with the spirit of the person who possesses it."[21]

PRIVACY OR HISTORICAL PROPERTY?

After Nishida's death, his disciples and colleagues decided to compile his collected works. Under the leadership of Shimomura Toratarō, an editorial team was formed, comprised of Mutai Risaku, Kōsaka Masaaki, Yamanouchi Tokuryū, Watsuji Tetsurō, Amano Teiyū, and Abe Yoshishige. The team was assisted by Nagai Hiroshi, a junior colleague of Shimomura, and began publishing *Nishida Kitarō Zenshū* [Collected works of Nishida Kitarō]. One of the issues the editorial team confronted was whether to include Nishida's diary, which spanned almost half a century, from 1897 to 1945, and about 4,000 letters collected by the editors.[22] They had to reckon with Nishida's opinion that a philosopher's work has little or no connection with his private life. After deliberation, however, they reached a consensus: they would publish both his diary and the main bulk of his letters. There were ample Western precedents for this—and Nishida had become a historical figure. The team also felt that if his letters were to be published, they should be in charge of such a project, for they had known the professor personally and could read his handwriting.[23] Scholars of Nishidan philosophy today are greatly indebted to the team's decision. Nishida's diary and letters are indispensable sources for tracing his development as a thinker and a person.

A PERSONAL NOTE

I first encountered Nishida through his essay "Basho" in the spring of 1975, when I was a graduate student at the University of California at Santa Barbara. I was assigned to make a presentation on his thought in a seminar led by Professor R. Panikkar, and I have been under the spell of the "Nishidan mystique" ever since.

In the early summer of 1991, when I was doing research in Kyoto, I visited Nishida's grave at Reiun'in, a temple in the Myōshinji compound. With no introduction in hand, I rang a bell and waited for someone to respond. A young monk opened the gate and ushered me into the foyer of the main building. Soon, someone who appeared to be the head priest of the temple came out and received me. I introduced myself and said, "May I see Nishida's grave?" Thereupon the priest became irate and shouted at me: "What do you mean by 'see'? A grave is not an item on display. Did you bring flowers and incense to offer to him?" At that very moment, I realized that my attitude toward Nishida had been one of a researcher and not of a sensitive, thoughtful human being. Meanwhile, the priest disappeared without another word.

Left alone, and by then with a few tears welling up, I was about to leave the temple. As I walked out of the entrance hall, I saw the novice who had opened the gate running across the garden with a pail of water and two stalks of white lilies. Then the head priest emerged and said, "Why hurry?" He showed me into the corner of the garden where Nishida's gravestone lies, arranged the flowers in the flower stands on both sides of the gravestone, offered some incense, and began to chant the *Heart Sutra*. After he had finished this formal offering, he urged me to pray at the grave. Needless to say, I was overwhelmed by his kindness.

Afterward, he invited me into the temple and served me a bowl of green tea. Our conversation became lively. He told me that Nishida's gravesite was chosen right below the bell tower so that his spirit could hear the sound of the bell at five o'clock every evening. The priest was clearly devoted to Nishida and took great care of the grave. This small incident became a poignant reminder for me. Just as Nishida discovered the place of scholarship within the larger context of life, so must scholars be mindful not to divorce scholarship from the heart or from a humble respect for life. I cannot help but feel that because Nishida's life reminds us of this, he continues to live on and teaches those who approach him.

Conventions and Abbreviations

1. Japanese names are given in the Japanese order, family names first, followed by the given names.

2. Nishida's writings compiled in the nineteen volumes of *Nishida Kitarō Zenshū* [Collected works of Nishida Kitarō] are cited in the notes as NKZ, followed by the volume number and page number(s). Other abbreviations are as follows:

> JP *Tetsugaku Zasshi* [*The Journal of Philosophy*]
>
> JPS *Tetsugaku Kenkyū* [*The Journal of Philosophical Studies*]
>
> MKZ *Miki Kiyoshi Zenshū* [*Collected works of Miki Kiyoshi*]
>
> SDMS *Suzuki Daisetz mikōkai shokan* [*Unpublished letters of Suzuki Daisetz*]
>
> SDZ *Suzuki Daisetz Zenshū* [*Collected works of Suzuki Daisetz*]
>
> TDH *Tōkyō Daigaku hyakunenshi* [*A history of one hundred years of Tokyo University*]
>
> THZ *Tanabe Hajime Zenshū* [*Collected works of Tanabe Hajime*]

3. The Japanese system of counting the year according to the period name is translated into the Gregorian calendar year. It is still customary for the majority of Japanese to refer to the year by the traditional *nengō*: the Meiji period (1868–1912), the Taisho period (1912–1926), the Showa period (1926–1989). The current Heisei period began in 1989; thus, Heisei 13 corresponds to the year 2001.

4. Until recently the Japanese used to count one's age according to *kazoe-doshi*, a system in which a baby is one year old at birth; on the next New Year's Day, she or he becomes two. A baby born on New Year's Eve would already be two years old the next day. Unless otherwise noted, the text follows the contemporary Japanese custom, which is the same as the American and European practice for determining age.

5. Nishida's letters are cited with the number assigned in NKZ. About one hundred of Nishida's letters compiled in NKZ are misdated. The correct dates are supplied in the notes.

6. Japanese given names can have many pronunciation variants. Although utmost care has been taken to present the correct rendering, uncertain cases have required an intelligent guess.

Prologue

The winter of 1944–1945 was unusually cold. On December 14, Nishida wrote a letter to Suzuki Daisetz, his friend of sixty years:

> It snowed yesterday morning. Snow in Kamakura in December is rare, don't you think? You must take care of yourself, as you said you have a cold. It can easily develop into pneumonia, and for old folks like us that can be deadly. As for the wood for cooking and heating, we decided to cut the trees in the garden.
>
> You must live five, nay, ten more years, and write for posterity. A new age is dawning; I would imagine the new era will create all kinds of people, but I suspect that the kinds of people we have seen in our times will never be seen again.[1]

A week later he wrote a postcard to Suzuki, again, asking about his health: "How is your cold? Are you over it by now?" Nishida himself was to take the journey to eternal rest within six months of writing these letters.

By the winter of 1944, the war fought over the Pacific entered its last phase, and American planes showered bombs on major industrial centers and large cities throughout Japan. Both Nishida and Suzuki, having predicted that Japan would lose the war, had their minds fixed already on postwar recovery and reconstruction. They felt that the postwar period would bring radical changes to their country.

Nishida died on June 7, 1945, around four o'clock in the morning. He had fallen sick a few days earlier, and the doctor, sent by Iwanami Shigeo, had made a house call to find that there were no alarming symptoms. Nishida's condition suddenly deteriorated, however. Because of the air raids on the Tokyo-Yokohama area, few trains were running and the doctor was unable to rush from Tokyo to the Nishi-das in Ubagayatsu in time.

Suzuki wrote about his departed friend for the *Tokyo Shinbun:*

> Just recently, during a leisurely conversation I said, "After the war is over, why don't we visit the United States and Europe, the two of us together?" He didn't say a word but wore a faint smile on his face. I find myself planning it even now!
>
> The fact is that the East does not know the West, and the West does not know the East. This is why various conflicts occur between them.
>
> I wanted Nishida to live for four or five years longer, not merely for my sake, but for our country's, for the entire East, and ultimately for the world. But his life, which was cut short, still has enough power to cause some stir in the future. I do not believe that we will see a man like him again for a long time.[2]

Suzuki, who had lived in the United States in his twenties for about a decade and had subsequently traveled widely around the world, described Nishida as someone whose abundant imagination and critical eye had enabled him to be knowledgeable about other countries, despite his never having stepped out of Japan. Nishida, according to Suzuki, was well informed about the movements of the times and accurate in assessing global political and military situations.[3]

Nishida and Suzuki, both born in the third year of Meiji (1870), were to witness unprecedented transformations. Internationally, Japan faced the global world for the first time after following a policy of isolation from all but the Dutch and the Chinese for more than two hundred years. The Japanese were abruptly made aware that their country had to become an active member of the nineteenth-century world, which was then dominated by the European powers. On the individual level, Nishida and Suzuki grew up in times when training in Chinese literature, the honor code of *bushi* (samurai warriors), cultivation of an independent mind, and friendship based on honesty, were the air they breathed. As the Japanese exerted themselves to "modernize" their country, however, governmental bureaucracies were centralized; cultural, economic, and educational systems were standardized; party-based politics were created and then quickly degenerated. They experienced the rise of militarism, totalitarianism, and finally Japan's entry into the world war. This transition from the "feudalistic" Edo period to the modern "state" decisively and permanently changed Japan. The natural, cultural, and educational environment in which Nishida grew up had already become a relic of the past, or was about to. The devastating destruction brought by air raids and atomic bombs during the last phase of the war buried a huge part of Japan's legacy under the rubble. When we take these events into consideration, the significance of Nishida's words to Suzuki, "the kinds of people we have seen in our era will not be seen again," may strike us with unexpected force.

According to Nishida, "with a new age, a new kind of humanity is created." This can only be said by one who truly understands the nature of history. Nishida looked back on the past and fixed his gaze on the future, aware of the singularity and uniqueness of each historical epoch. History is not something that simply progresses from the past to the future; it is the expression of the spiritual and material activities of the people of a given period. Nishida would say that what is created—the human being—becomes in turn that which creates, thus contributing positively or negatively to the formation of the historical world. Herein lies the significance of the individual and the uniqueness of each culture. Education was central for Nishida because education "makes human beings,"[4] and each individual participates in the making of the world—of history.

Nishida fully grasped that Japan had become a member of the international community when it opened its ports in the late Edo period, and that Japan had responsibilities to bear and missions to carry out on the global stage. Because of his global awareness, when the Japanese government began to be run by the military in the 1930s, he became deeply worried about the future of his country. The only way he felt he could exert an influence was to engage in philosophical inquiry and articulate the essence of Japanese culture.[5] He was never an armchair philosopher, oblivious of the actual world. On the contrary, his philosophical reflections deepened as the political and social situation worsened. His respect for the historical nature of human existence convinced him that history is something "living and essential" to humanity, and for that reason, "freedom of scholarship should never be suppressed."[6] As the Ministry of Education progressively adopted measures of thought control, it only strengthened his conviction that, to preserve Japan's freedom of scholarship and thought, he needed to delve ever deeper into philosophical inquiry. The driving force of Nishida's philosophical commitment in the last years of his life came from his deep-seated concern for the preservation of national integrity and for the spiritual-cultural heritage of the Japanese people.

How did Nishida and his friends fare as Japan was swept into the vortex of world history? How was Nishida's thought shaped by and through his life experience? Following Suzuki's conviction that to know Nishida the man and to sense his underlying passion can only increase our appreciation of his thought, let us embark on the journey of tracing Nishida's life and thought.

Chapter 1

Childhood

"White Sand, Green Pine Needles"

(1870–1886)

Nishida always remembered his childhood in association with "white sandy beaches surrounded by green needles of pine trees." His place of birth, Mori, was a small village, facing the Japan Sea, about twenty kilometers northwest of the city of Kanazawa. He was born on May 19, 1870, as the oldest son of Nishida Yasunori (1834–1898) and Tosa (1842–1918), into a family that held the hereditary office of village mayor, *tomura* (literally, "ten villages"). The *tomura*, an administrative position unique to Kaga Province, oversaw the affairs of several neighboring villages.[1] This office entitled the Nishidas to bear a family name, when peasants and ordinary folks did not have family names, and to wear a set of swords, when only the samurais were allowed to bear arms (the long sword was for self-defense, and the short dagger for committing the honorable suicide). The privilege of having the family name and bearing swords meant that the Nishidas in fact enjoyed an elevated social status, close to that of samurai. Although technically members of a farmer class, the Nishidas flourished as landowners, employing a large number of peasants and workers from the village to cultivate their lands. Kitarō's grandfather, the tenth *tomura*, Nishida Aranori (d. ca. 1850), was an able administrator and a highly accomplished man of letters, especially conversant with Chinese classics. Yasunori, Kitarō's father, was also an able calligrapher and a keen educator. Under his *tomura* name, Nishida Tōemon, Yasunori ran a *terakoya* (a small private school) from 1865 to 1869 and taught calligraphy and reading to village children—twenty-five boys and six girls. Education and learning were a family tradition for the Nishidas.

Yasunori was quick-tempered, outgoing, and a man of entrepreneur mentality. He also tended to boast and philander. He had an illegitimate son from a relationship before he married Tosa. It is said that Yasunori's parents chose the strong-willed Tosa, a woman of few words, as his wife, to put an end to Yasunori's wanton lifestyle. Tosa's family, the Hayashis, also held the office of *tomura* of a rank higher than the Nishidas.[2] Tosa was introspective, often engaged in contemplation, and enjoyed reading. She was a woman of iron will, a devout Pure Land Buddhist, with a heart of gold. She never missed her daily devotion, and out of her boundless compassion she took care of homeless people who came to the village and sought her help.[3] The young Kitarō grew up imbibing his mother's generosity and her religious devotion through her milk (which he did not give up until age three or four). Kitarō was very much a mother's child and insisted that she must always be in sight. Tosa loved him unconditionally, but without ever indulging him.[4] Nishida's lifelong appreciation of Shinran, for instance, goes back to his early years, to his mother's religious devotion.

Nishida inherited from his father intensity and restlessness, and from his mother introspection and tenacity—conflicting qualities, indeed. His restlessness was manifested in his incessant visits to friends and his habit of brisk walks. Introspection and tenacity, however, characterized his philosophical style, and this quality came to his rescue at times of personal misfortune, giving him resilience. In terms of sexuality, he was aware of his father's blood in him and fastidiously kept away from involvement with women outside his marriage. The frank awareness of his sexuality gave him a no-nonsense understanding of human weaknesses and follies.

Kitarō was born in the village of Mori in a large spacious house. It had over ten large rooms, some of which were used as the *tomura*'s bureau. The house was lost in a fire, however, when Kitarō was two or three years old. The family moved to Unoke, an adjacent village, where their house stood on spacious grounds. The young boy liked the huge old tree in the yard that had a large cave inside where a family of badgers resided.[5]

Nishida's love of books was apparent from an early age. Chinese books that his grandfather read were boxed away in the second floor of the storage building (*dozō*) right next to the main house. Little Kitarō would go into the storage building, "although it was lonely and scary," up the stairs, and thumb through these books. In his childish mind he felt those "large austere characters" seemed to contain something important."[6]

Kitarō behaved the same way whenever he visited his grandparents on his mother's side, the Hayashi family.[7] The preschool boy often went there on foot, "along a brook that flowed through a field of rape flowers." These flowers were probably as tall as he was. No sooner would he get to the house than he would begin going through their collection of books, which included *Kujiki*, Ogyū Sorai's political discourse, and some volumes of *Azumakagami*.[8]

Kitarō had two older sisters, Masa (1859–1939) and Nao (1866–1883), a younger sister Sumi (1871–1955), and a younger brother, Hyōjirō (1873–1904). Kitarō got along especially well with Sumi. With a pail in his hand, he would take her to a nearby river to catch mudfish. Hyōjirō was a strong, rambunctious boy who possessed his father's outgoing character. Kitarō loved him and the two boys played together "not only as brothers but as friends, for there weren't many boys in the neighborhood." They played amid the white sand and green pine trees and enjoyed their childhood in unspoiled nature.[9] Indeed, when Nishida was growing up, most of Japan's rural areas were still untouched by heavy industry and pollution. Kitarō's favorite place was the beach about a kilometer away from their home, open to the Japan Sea. His love of the sea—captured in the image "white sand, green pine [needles]" (four Chinese characters, *haku sa sei shō*)—goes back to his early childhood.

Kitarō, born in the third year of Meiji, saw village men still wearing their hair in a topknot.[10] "Modernization" (or *bunmei kaika*) was slow to reach villages like Unoke. The first wave of modernization hit the countryside in Meiji 5 (1872), when an elementary school was established. Kitarō was two years old. Father Yasunori volunteered to be a school teacher in a nearby village of Kizu and taught calligraphy there. When Kitarō was about five years old, Yasunori set up an elementary school in Mori, which Kitarō attended.[11] The subjects taught at these schools were not so different from the days of *terakoya:* the three Rs, ethics, history, and physical education. In the following year, 1876, Yasunori closed down Mori Elementary School, moved it to Unoke, and renamed it Unoke New Elementary School. About half the village children attended the school.[12] In 1879, after the Meiji government issued a new school ordinance, Yasunori renamed this school Shinka Elementary School (*shinka* means "making anew"). As a measure to encourage learning among children, the local government of Kahoku County held an annual scholastic competition among school children, in which Kitarō participated. He scored high, got an "A" grade, and won prizes two years in a row, 1880 and 1881.[13] He was among the youngest of those who competed, and his scholastic ability proved to be far superior to that of his peers. This brought pride and honor to Yasunori. Kitarō graduated from Shinka Elementary School in March 1882, at the age of eleven. At that time, his older sister Nao helped Kitarō advance to the next step of his education.

Nao was an academically gifted young woman, then attending the Ishikawa Prefecture Girls' Normal School in Kanazawa.[14] Given the emphasis on education within the Nishida family, it was not surprising that a daughter was pursuing learning in a city away from home. Kitarō shared Nao's inborn desire for knowledge. Nao pleaded with Yasunori to let Kitarō go to Kanazawa to further his education. Yasunori was reluctant, fearing that a city-educated youth would not return to the village to become head of the family. Nao persuaded him that if Kitarō became an elementary school teacher, he would definitely come back to the village.

Nao prevailed over her father and took Kitarō with her to Kanazawa. At that time Hyōjirō also moved to Kanazawa to attend Seiren Elementary School.[15] The city of Kanazawa, the former capital of the Maeda family, opened Kitarō's eyes to a wider and larger world. Situated near the coast of the Japan Sea, about a hundred kilometers northeast of Kyoto, Kanazawa was, and still is, known as the "small Kyoto" because of its architectural and cultural elegance. The castle towers, the majestic wide cobblestone streets surrounding the castle, the beautiful garden of the Kenrokuen Park[16]—the sight of all these things must have been truly enchanting to the curious boy of twelve. The city had many hustling and bustling commercial districts. There were several famous book antiquarians, who in those days also printed and published books. Two rivers, Asano and Sai, framed the city to the north and south, offering scenic spots for walks.

Yasunori found a house for Kitarō, Nao, and Hyōjirō in Nagado-hei, a neighborhood of impressive samurai residences. Reminiscing of those olden days, Nishida wrote in 1940:

> In Kanazawa today, if you go to such sections of town as Nagamachi or Nagadohei, you will still see adobe walls and the former residences of samurai. The city air retains to this day the scent of feudal times.
>
> When I was a child, there were artisans proudly committed to their work as artists, which is by now a legacy of the past. For instance, there was a master lacquerware painter who would spend three years working on one box.[17]

The Kanazawa that the boy Kitarō saw was still basking in glorious memories of the rule of the Maeda family, very powerful feudal lords *(daimyō)* during the Edo period. The territory, or *han* (a domain ruled by a warlord), that came under the family's rule was "Kaga Province, whose revenue has one million *koku* of rice" *(Kaga hyakuman-goku).*[18] The first lord, Maeda Toshiie (1538–1599), was a perspicacious leader who knew too well that it was better to spend money to enhance cultural activities than to build up military machinery that would inevitably attract the suspicion of the Shogunate government, and which would lead the Maeda family to its possible demise. Toshiie's tactic to pour money into cultural activities became the policy embraced by the successive heads of the Maeda family. Unlike today's Japan, where cultural events and institutions tend to be concentrated in major cities, during the Edo period there were "cultural pockets" throughout the country, because the feudal lords were free to carry out their own cultural programs within their domains, and Kanazawa was one of those rich cultural centers.

Among the lords of the Maedas, especially noteworthy were the achievements of the fifth lord, Tsunanori (1643–1724), or Lord Shōun. He was a renaissance man, interested in the arts, letters, and good food; he even experimented and developed his own recipe for making exquisite tofu![19] Lord Shōun ordered several shiploads of books from China by way of Nagasaki,[20] thus building up an immense collection of Chinese books. Arai Hakuseki (1655–1725), a prominent Confucian scholar, who served the Shogunate government in Edo, was envious of the Maedas' huge collection of important books and said: "The Province of Kaga is the library of Japan" *(Kashū wa tenka no shufu nari).*[21] Under the Maeda family, learning was an important part of the upbringing of the samurai class, and Confucian learning flourished.

This emphasis on learning was still alive when Kitarō moved to Kanazawa. He first took private lessons from tutors to prepare himself for entering the Normal School. He went to Nagao Gan, principal of the Normal School, for instruction in Japanese;[22] he took Chinese from Fujita Koremasa and mathematics from Ishida Kanehisa.[23] Fujita and Ishida were also teachers at the Normal School. In those days, the professors of the Normal School were paid only a small salary, making it necessary for them to teach outside school to supplement their income.[24] The institution of private tutorials was a well-established tradition in Kanazawa.[25]

Once Yasunori consented to letting Kitarō study in Kanazawa, he felt he had to give his son the very best education possible. He sought the former *han* scholar, the distinguished Inokuchi Sei (his pennames, or *gō*, were Saikawa and Mōtoku), to tutor Kitarō in Chinese classics. Mōtoku was an unusual man. He had retired from his promising career as a Confucian scholar in Edo and returned to Kanazawa to take care of his aging mother. When not teaching, he would shut himself up in his workshop, where he would become absorbed in assembling a clock according to the specifications given in the ancient Chinese text, the *Book of Rites.* When Yasunori approached Mōtoku, the scholar was already in his seventies and was no longer taking students. But he consented to accepting Kitarō on the condition that Kitarō teach Mōtoku's grandson the book of *Mencius.* Apparently, Kitarō's classical Chinese was good enough to do that at the age of thirteen. Mōtoku's tutoring turned out to be scientific and philological. He lectured Kitarō on *The Book of Odes* (*Shikyō* in Japanese; *Shijing* in Chinese) and on the *Zuo Commentary* (*Sashiden* in Japanese; *Zuo chuan* in Chinese) of the *Spring and Autumn Annals* (*Shunjū* in Japanese; *Chunqiu* in Chinese). He also assigned Kitarō a linguistic work called *Erya* (*Jiga* in Japanese), one of the thirteen classics of the Zhou period.[26] The training Kitarō received in classical Chinese was apparently quite extraordinary. Years later, when Nishida told his university colleague, Kano Naoki (a specialist in Chinese literature), about the instruction he received from Mōtoku, Kano was amazed by the progressive insight of the old teacher in adopting the *Erya* as a textbook.[27] Mōtoku died on May 15, 1884, at the age of seventy-three, a year or so after he took on Kitarō.

Mōtoku had been a student of Yasui Sokken, a highly accomplished Confucian scholar of the late Edo period. This made Nishida a grand-disciple of Sokken, which amused Nishida years later. On one hot summer day, Amano Teiyū, a junior colleague of Nishida's at Kyoto Imperial University, called on Nishida and their conversation touched on Mori Ōgai's novel, *Yasui fujin* [Mrs. Yasui] (1914), a story about Yasui Sokken and his wife. On that day, Amano brought with him a copy of Yasui Kotarō's *Nihon jugakushi* [A history of Confucian learning in Japan]. Yasui Kotarō, grandson of Yasui Sokken, was professor of classical Chinese at the First Higher School in Tokyo. In fact, when Amano was a student at First Higher School, he took a class from Yasui. Nishida, after examining the book for a while, said, "It looks like a good book." Then he surprised Amano with the question: "Is Yasui Kotarō an ugly man?" Amano responded: "Not particularly."

Nishida asked: "Have you read Ōgai's *Yasui fujin?*" "No," replied Amano.

Thereupon Nishida told Amano to read the novel "by all means, because it is very interesting," and began to tell the gist of the story, quoting many lines verbatim:[28] Yasui Sokken was a short, ugly man; to aggravate his appearance, he lost the sight of his right eye to smallpox. Villagers mocked him, calling him "monkey." Sokken, undeterred, diligently studied Chinese classics, entered Shōheikō, the highest academic institution during the Edo period run by the Shogunate, and emerged as a greatly renowned scholar. When the question of his marriage arose, Sokken's father, knowing very well how hard it would be to arrange a marriage for his handicapped son, decided to find a girl from among the relatives who knew him. He employed a go-between, who approached Toyo, Sokken's cousin, only to be coldly rejected. Toyo's younger sister, Sayo, a sixteen-year-old of exquisite beauty, heard about the proposal, went to her mother, and asked whether she could marry him. Once married, Sayo, now Mrs. Yasui, never even gave thought to beautiful *kimono* or makeup and simply devoted herself to taking care of her husband and raising their children. A guest who visited the Yasuis one day remarked to the master of the house: "Your wife is much brighter than you." "Why do you say that?" asked Sokken, rather amused. The guest said: "Judging from the fact that she is *so* beautiful and yet married you!"

Yasui Sokken belonged to the lineage of Shushigaku (Zhu Xi learning) that went back to Hayashi Razan. The other tradition of Shushigaku in Japan originated with Fujiwara Seika. Arai Hakuseki, mentioned earlier, belonged to the Seika school. These two lineages, the Razan school and the Seika school, flourished during the Edo period. By lineage, Nishida would have belonged to the Razan-Sokken-Mōtoku line. Had he lived in the Edo period, our philosopher might have been a Confucian scholar of the Razan lineage!

In July 1883 Nishida was accepted into the preparatory division of the Ishikawa Prefecture Normal School. At that time Yasunori forged Kitarō's record of birth, giving him an August 10, 1868, birthdate, to make him old enough to be admitted into the school. Forging birth records was quite a common practice in those days. The authority of the central government was yet to seep into the daily lives of the people. In the summer of 1883, Nao graduated from the Girls' Normal School. That fall both Nao and Kitarō contracted typhoid. Tosa moved to Kanazawa to take care of her sick children. Kitarō recovered from typhoid, but Nao succumbed to it and died on November 28.[29] The sadness Nishida felt at his sister's death was deeply chiseled in his heart:

> I first experienced the death of one of my closest family members when my older sister died of illness; I was thirteen or fourteen then. At that time I learned for the first time how sad the death of a human being is; I hid myself in a place where nobody could see me and shed tears alone. Even within my childish heart, I wished from the bottom of my heart that if my death could bring her back to life, I would die in her place.[30]

Having recovered from his illness, Nishida returned to the Normal School. Despite his having missed many days of classes because of his illness, he was awarded a copy of *Kika shogaku reidai* [Elementary geometry problem book][31] on February 27, 1884, for his excellent achievement. While bedridden during his illness, Nishida had begun to reflect on the future course of his life. In August 1884 he completed the required course work of the main division of the Normal School and was certified to teach at the elementary school level,[32] but in October he withdrew from the Normal School to pursue higher learning elsewhere. At this time Kitarō encountered no resistance from his father, which suggests that the position of the Nishida family in the village had changed, and that there was no longer any compelling reason for Kitarō to return to Unoke. Besides, Tosa had moved out to Kanazawa, and the father and mother began to lead separate lives. Their marriage was virtually over.

Nishida now set his mind on entering the Ishikawa Prefecture Senmon Gakkō, a school that trained specialists in law, humanities, and natural sciences. Senmon Gakkō was *the* preparatory school for Tokyo University. Sons of the former samurai class, for whom learning was an integral part of life, gathered there, making it truly an elite school. To prepare himself for entering the Senmon Gakkō, Nishida went back to private tutors. This time he studied English under Sakuma Gisaburō, and mathematics under Kamiyama Kosaburō (1846–1921), an instructor at the Normal School, and Nishida came to know him there. While studying under Kamiyama's tutelage, Nishida got to know Kimura Hisashi,[33] a student at Senmon Gakkō. Kimura, a child prodigy, was to become an internationally known astronomer. In any case, Nishida secretly compared his scholastic aptitude with Kimura's and concluded that he was by no means inferior to Kimura, except in English.[34] Thereupon he applied himself even more to the study of English.

Nishida could not have done better than choosing Kamiyama, who was a direct disciple of Sekiguchi Hiraku (1842–1884),[35] a master mathematician, who originally trained in Japanese mathematics. At the young age of twenty-four, Sekiguchi passed the examinations and became a licensed teacher. With the arrival of Western learning, he turned to Western mathematics and became a pioneer in the field. In 1869 he was appointed teacher of Western mathematics at the *han*-operated school; later he taught at Tatsumi Middle School, Normal School, Keimei Gakkō, and Middle Normal School (which became Senmon Gakkō). In 1877 he opened Enshōsha, a training school for the teachers of mathematics. Some twenty students attended it, including Kamiyama Kosaburō, Ishida Kanehisa, and Tanaka Onokichi, all of whom became leading mathematics teachers in Kanazawa. Sekiguchi dedicated his life to the training of mathematicians and was the jewel of the town. Unfortunately, his life was cut short by typhoid; he died on April 12, 1884, at the age of forty-three. The city mourned his death and erected a memorial tower at Oyama Shrine. Kitarō heard much about this local hero. He proudly recalled the heritage of mathematics in Kanazawa:

> When we were children, there was an accomplished professor of mathematics, Sekiguchi Hiraku. He was originally a specialist in Japanese mathematics, but in the beginning of Meiji, he turned to Western mathematics and taught himself the subject. His understanding was so accurate that he was able to solve Todhunter's[36] differential and integral calculus. Our teacher [i.e., Kamiyama] was the direct disciple of Professor Sekiguchi. I hear that even before the tenth year of Meiji, Sekiguchi translated sections of Todhunter's differential and integral calculus into Japanese. This translation still exists in a draft form, which was donated to the Imperial Academy a few decades after his death. . . . The knowledge of English possessed by the Japanese at that time was quite rudimentary, and Sekiguchi could not read even mathematical English with ease. Sometimes, he had to deduce the meaning of the word from algebraic expressions. For instance, the word "set" was listed only as "to place" in an English-Japanese dictionary, and as such, it made no sense. He got the idea of "set" as a "collection" or "group of things" from the algebraic expressions themselves.[37]

Nishida's adolescence unfolded in close connection with his pursuit of mathematics. A decisive encounter in his life came on March 16, 1886, when he was introduced to Hōjō Tokiyuki, who had graduated from Tokyo University with a B.S. in mathematics in 1885 and had just returned to Kanazawa to teach at Senmon Gakkō. Nishida remembered the first encounter:

> Professor Hōjō came out to greet us in the entrance hall of his house. He said he was busy and instead handed me a mimeographed set of math problems to work on. At that time, the professor was in his early thirties, but already bold, and his conspicuously protruding Adam's apple left a lasting impression on me. Having solved the problems, I returned to his house a few days later, at which time he allowed me to come inside the house and we talked.[38]

Hōjō was also trained under Sekiguchi Hiraku. Nishida made a favorable first impression on Hōjō, who wrote in his diary on March 16, 1886: "I loved the earnestness of this boy's attitude toward learning and gave him permission to attend the monthly seminar on mathematics held on the first Wednesday."[39] Hōjō's monthly seminar was for the teachers of mathematics.[40] When Nishida attended his first meeting, the day's topic was "differential and integral calculus and determinants." It was naturally far over his head, but he was struck by the ingenuity of "determinants" because the device made it easy to solve algebraic equations.[41]

Yasunori was so proud that his son was now tutored by the "holder of a university degree" *(gakushi)* [42] that he threw a special picnic banquet in Hōjō's honor on a day when the peach blossoms were in full bloom.[43] Hōjō was to play a key role in Nishida's life, first as a teacher of mathematics, later as a guardian figure, and much more. The two were separated in age only by eleven years, but Hōjō, with his many important connections in government and in the worlds of education and business, was able to help Nishida. Hōjō remained the true "professor" for Nishida, who was deeply indebted to his "onshi" (a teacher who has had such a formative effect that one remains forever grateful, feeling that all personal success derives in part from his teachings).

Under Hōjō's influence, Nishida began to read books in mathematics that opened his eyes to the wonder of logic. He explains:

> By chance, I got hold of a copy of *Conic Sections* by Todhunter translated into Japanese. . . . I learned for the first time that various geometric figures could be put into algebraic equations, and that rather complicated geometric problems could be easily solved by using equations. Varying curved lines, for instance, can be equated with the lines of the quadratic equation defining particular cases of an ellipse. I found it very fascinating. I came to discover how interesting logic is. I think I

was sixteen or seventeen then; I can still vividly recall where I read the book and how I read it.[44]

Nishida's early training in classical Chinese *(kanbun)* and mathematics bore witness to the sophisticated standard of scholarship that flourished in Kanazawa in the 1880s. While his training in classical Chinese familiarized him with the Confucian and Daoist literatures and developed his skill in writing compositions and poetry in Chinese, his training in mathematics cultivated his analytic and synthesizing ability. He discovered the elegant simplicity of logical principles underlying any body of data.

Chapter 2

Mathematics or Philosophy?

(1886–1891)

In September 1886 Nishida, now sixteen, was admitted into the preparatory division of Ishikawa Prefecture Senmon Gakkō, when a place fell vacant. Hōjō's recommendation must have been instrumental in his acceptance. Senmon Gakkō, or Higher School of Specialized Training, was the preparatory elite school for Tokyo University in and around Ishikawa Prefecture. It was a seven-year institution, of which the first four years were devoted to the preparatory curriculum; in the last three years students specialized in their chosen field—humanities, natural sciences, or law.[1] These subjects were mainly taught in English.[2] Nishida had no problem following the preparatory courses taught at Senmon Gakkō, thanks to the private lessons he had received. Because the professors themselves were all graduates of Senmon Gakkō, the school enjoyed a congenial, family-like atmosphere; besides, the number of students enrolled in each class was small. Nishida thrived in this environment and successfully completed his first semester of study. For his academic excellence, he was awarded a prize, Goldsmith's *Vicar of Wakefield* and Lamb's *Tales from Shakespeare*. He graduated from the preparatory division with flying colors in July 1887. During his first year in the preparatory division, Nishida made friends with Mukō Kikutarō, a kind, lively, frank young man, whose "sunflower-like" disposition he adored. The two traveled together to Tokyo in the summer of 1888, when Mukō took the entrance examination for naval school. Nishida probably visited the First Higher School and the Imperial University to see what they were like.[3]

Nishida's "honeymoon days" with the Senmon Gakkō came to an end too soon, however. The government issued a series of school regulations, *Gakkōrei*, in March and April of 1886, launching a sweeping standardization of the educational system, which was identified as one of the three pillars of modernization (along with the promotion of industry and the building up of modern military forces). Before the announcement of the school reform measures, the government adopted the cabinet system in December 1885, with Itō Hirobumi[4] as the first prime minister. Itō appointed his old friend, Mori Arinori,[5] to the post of minister of education. Mori, a native of Satsuma Province (today's Kagoshima Prefecture), was, like Itō, a member of the political clique known as the *hanbatsu* (Meiji oligarchy), composed of leading figures from the former feudal provinces *(han)* that had sided with the 1868 "Restoration."

As part of the new national educational system, Mori divided Japan into five higher school blocks; in each of these blocks a higher middle school was to be opened.[6] These higher middle schools were considered the preparatory institution to the only university then in existence, the Imperial University. Ishikawa Prefecture lobbied hard to secure Kanazawa as the site of the Fourth Higher Middle School. Since Kanazawa already had the elite Senmon Gakkō and an excellent medical school, it seemed a natural choice.[7] The Fourth Higher Middle School was opened on April 18, 1887. Mori appointed the speaker of the Kagoshima Prefecture Assembly, Kashiwada Morifumi, a politician and not an educator, as the first principal of the school. From Kagoshima Kashiwada brought former police officers and similar types to fill the positions of dormitory master and other administrative positions.[8] Their intention was to "inject the *Satsuma-hayato*"[9] spirit into the Kanazawaites. Behind this harsh measure was Mori's thought that the strong lingering anti-*hanbatsu* (oligarchy) sentiment among the Ishikawaites had to be curtailed. The antioligarchy sentiment had erupted in the person of Shimada Ichirō, who, together with other like-minded young men, carried out the assassination of Ōkubo Toshimichi in Tokyo on May 24, 1878.[10] The general sentiment of the people of former Kaga Province was still very pro-Maeda, and they looked back upon the days of the Maedas' rule with profound nostalgia. To the leaders of the Meiji government, Ishikawa Prefecture had to be brought under firm state control. The semimilitaristic administration placed in the Fourth Higher Middle School reflected that resolution.

Senmon Gakkō officially closed in September 1887, and in October the entrance examination of the Fourth Higher Middle School was held, drawing students from Ishikawa, Toyama, Fukui, Niigata, and other neighboring prefectures. Out of one hundred forty-two applicants, eighty-eight were admitted into the school. Nishida was among those who successfully passed the examination and became a student in the preparatory division, which had fifteen other students.

On October 26 the formal opening ceremony of the Fourth Higher Middle School was held at the main hall of former Senmon Gakkō. Mori Arinori was then touring the Hokuriku region, and much to the dismay of those who harbored antioligarchy sentiments, Mori made a personal appearance at the opening ceremony. It was a rainy day.[11] Mori and his entourage arrived at the school at 10 A.M. and were greeted by students, each wearing a school cap (a symbolic beginning of coerced uniformity and conformity). State control of education was beginning as part of Japan's full-scale march to remake itself as a modern nation; no one was to be spared this collectivized fate. The ceremony began solemnly at 11 A.M., and Mori delivered the following congratulatory remarks:

> It is my greatest pleasure to be here today at the opening ceremony of the Fourth Higher Middle School. Your school benefits the nation as a whole as well as the students who reside in this school district.
>
> Marquis Maeda [Toshitsugu][12] and numerous other benefactors donated a huge sum of money to this school in order to purchase land and build new school buildings. The Ministry of Education promises to do anything necessary to expedite that process and bring the wish of those benefactors into reality as soon as possible.
>
> Among the five higher middle schools that were created under the ordinance, the First and Third already existed as government schools, but the others are all new. The Fourth, that is, your school, is opening before the Second and Fifth; I am especially pleased to hear that several students have been admitted into the main division, and nearly a hundred into the preparatory division.
>
> Regarding the medical division students, they are from the former Prefecture Medical School, and I need not say how excellent they are.[13]

Following these words, Mori gave a longer formal speech, in which he emphasized the important role of higher middle schools in improving the status of Japan as a member of the international community.[14]

The handling of the school property that had belonged to the Senmon Gakkō was debated at the November Ishikawa Prefecture Assembly, and it was decided that its landholdings, buildings, books, and other equipment were all be transferred to the Fourth Higher Middle School.[15] Externally, the transition went smoothly. But such was not the case with the students and professors. Nishida felt that "the family-like atmosphere of the Senmon Gakkō disappeared almost overnight when it became the nation's Fourth Higher School," and that "the school, which enjoyed an intimate warmth between teachers and students, was turned into a strictly militaristic school governed by rules."[16] This transition, from a local to a national institution, directly affected the quality of the learning experience for Nishida and his friends. As the October entrance examination brought a few formerly discrete classes together: Yamamoto (then Kaneda) Ryōkichi, Fujioka Sakutarō, Suzuki Teitarō (D. T. Suzuki), and Fukushima Junkichi became Nishida's classmates. They instantly made friends and remained friends for life. Nishida found peers who were of compatible intelligence and ambitions. He thrived in their company, spread his wings as wide as possible, and flew as high as he wanted. His creative energy was unleashed. Yamamoto, Fujioka, and Suzuki were the sons of members of the former samurai class, classified as *shizoku*, as opposed to *heimin* (common people), to which class Nishida belonged. The prestige associated with the *shizoku* class was not substantial enough to affect Nishida's making friends with his classmates; in fact Nishida was the best-off among them. In his first year, Nishida, highly motivated, worked hard on his academic subjects; there was an air of healthy competition among the boys, and the presence of Hōjō on the teaching staff was inspiring. Starting this year, a second foreign language was required, and Nishida chose German. Other required courses were Japanese, classical Chinese, English, mathematics, physics, chemistry, drawing, and physical education.

Among his classmates, Nishida was especially impressed by Yamamoto Ryōkichi, a born leader, an organizer, and a young man of action. Although a year junior to Nishida, he had already developed a clear sense of who he was, and this won Nishida's instant admiration. Yamamoto was a gifted writer and was asked from time to time to pen an editorial column by the editor of the local *Hokuriku Shinbun* (Hokuriku Newspaper). He would compose an editorial so fast that the page-boy from the newspaper, who came to give him the assignment, used to just wait there for him to finish it.[17]

Fujioka Sakutarō, blessed with native intelligence, was always the top student without particularly studying. Unfortunately, however, from childhood he suffered chronic asthma, which arrested his physical development, and he remained a frail, small-framed man. By the time Nishida got to know him, Fujioka's father was dead, and the family fortune was quite reduced. Fujioka was fond of reading novels, especially of the Edo period, and was gifted in writing stories and drawing; he used to draw figures during the class period, especially heads of men and women, and sometimes his drawing would spill into

Nishida's notebook because they were sitting right next to each other.[18] Nishida found Fujioka to be sensitive and gentle, and an excellent confidant, but not without sarcastic wit. Nishida described him as "the personification of frailty itself" and "every inch an artist."[19]

Suzuki Teitarō, better known in the West as D. T. Suzuki, was a son of the medical doctor retained by the Honda family (the Hondas worked closely with the Maeda family). When Teitarō was scarcely five years old, his father died, and the family fortunes dwindled rapidly. In fact, Suzuki was so poor that he was no longer able to pay the tuition and had to drop out of the Fourth Higher Middle School by the end of June 1888.[20] Although he had to leave school, he stayed in close contact with his friends, especially with Yamamoto. Reminiscing about his boyhood, Suzuki wrote: "One of us once said that Yamamoto was like a fleet steed and Nishida like a dumb ox. Yamamoto was indeed a prodigy and a man of letters. I do not know if Nishida was a dumb ox, but he was certainly like an ox in his single-minded plodding toward his goal—just the kind of will power and intellectual tenacity he had."[21]

Nishida, Yamamoto (Kaneda) Ryō-kichi, and Fujioka Sakutarō, with Orlando N. Benton, a teacher of English, early summer, 1888, when they were students at the preparatory division of Ishikawa Prefecture Senmon Gakkō. From Ueda Hisashi, *Sofu Nishida Kitarō.*

Nishida recognized in Suzuki an unusual quality that transcended the affairs of the mundane world. He composed two poems for Suzuki:

Having shed the desire
for worldly fame and profit
alone you seek a quiet place
to open up your heart.

Seated near the window, you read
volumes of Daoist classics. The bright moon
shines in, and a refreshing wind blows away
the dust of this mundane world. [22]

Hōjō married Kondō Masaki, a woman of cultivation and intelligence, on November 14, 1886, after a half year's engagement. Now that his home front was in order, he invited Nishida to come and live in his house as a *shosei* (student). It was quite common in those days for professors to have *shosei* living in their houses. The idea was that students would learn not only academic subjects but "how to live" from the professors. In the fall of 1887 Nishida moved in with the Hōjōs.[23] He studied mathematics every evening with Mrs. Hōjō. She would sit at her desk on one side of Professor Hōjō, while Nishida sat at his desk on the other side of the professor. Hōjō himself was seated at his own desk. Even in those days Nishida suffered from occasional insomnia, and he would toss in his futon unable to sleep; then past midnight koto music played by Mrs. Hōjō would sound in the clear night air. Nishida would soon fall asleep to the melody of the koto.[24] The world of classical elegance was still a part of the Hōjō household.

The school boasted unique teachers, Hōjō Tokiyuki topping the list. As Nishida recalled, "anyone who was taught by him was greatly inspired by him."[25] Years later, he wrote:

In those days the level of education and scholarship in Japan was still rudimentary. Textbooks were pretty much standardized. Upon finishing the English reader, we moved on to Macaulay's essays. The mathematics textbook was by Todhunter, physics by Stewart, chemistry by Roscoe, world history by Swinton, and so it went. The times were such that anyone who had read a few books by Mill and Spencer was considered a "philosopher." Holders of the university degree were few in Kanazawa, and we took great pride in being taught by them. The professor we most respected was Hōjō Tokiyuki; he taught us mathematics. Even to this day, I can still hear him saying in his lecture on solid geometry, "one and only one plane can be drawn between . . . ."

[Washington] Irving's *Sketch Book* was introduced to Japan around that time, and if I remember correctly, it was Professor Hōjō who taught it to us.[26] You see, in those days learning was not yet compartmentalized. For instance, a professor of chemistry [Imai] taught Chambera's world history to the class one grade above us.[27]

Besides Hōjō, Nishida very much respected Miyake Shōtarō (*gō*, Shinken),[28] a professor of classical Chinese. Miyake's field was the rigorous historical critical research, a discipline developed during the Qing dynasty in China, known in Japanese as *kōshōgaku* (investigations based on evidence, or "Han learning"). Although a distinguished disciple of Inokuchi Mōtoku, Miyake developed his own scholarly style. His knowledge of Chinese literature was immense. He had gone through the entire fourteen hundred volumes of *Kōsei keikai*,[29] for instance, and did research on every reference to the *Analects*, so that he was prepared to answer *any* question on the *Analects!*[30] Nishida always regretted that this extremely erudite professor left no written work and that his knowledge disappeared with his death.

Sometime in 1887, a rather scary accident happened. Hōjō was an avid fan of *"bēsu bōru"* (baseball), and he introduced the game to the students. He usually played catcher. One day, a student, M——, hit Hōjō on the head with a bat. Hōjō fell unconscious and was rushed to a hospital. The doctor told Mrs. Hōjō and Nishida that if he suffered from a fever that evening, that would be the end of him. They stayed up all night long, worried. To everyone's relief, he came through fine. When Nishida visited him in the hospital the following day, Hōjō, unable to talk, whispered to Nishida to tell M—— not to worry about what had happened.[31] The incident left Hōjō with a slight speech impediment.[32]

Nishida, under the care and guidance of Hōjō, did excellently in his first year of study. But this ideal setup had to come to an end. In 1888 Hōjō was accepted into the graduate school at the Imperial University and was also offered a teaching position at the First Higher School. The Hōjōs left for Tokyo in September 1888. In the fall Nishida advanced to the first year program of the main division.[33] Hōjō's departure at this particular juncture in Nishida's life was critical. He was required to declare his major before he enrolled in the main division. This presented him with a dilemma. Hōjō had advised him to go into mathematics, but Nishida was attracted to philosophy.[34] Now that Hōjō was no longer around to give him close advice, Nishida decided to follow his heart's desire. He explains this choice:

The time came when I had to decide on my major. Like many young men, I, too, wondered about this question. It was very hard for me to choose between mathematics and philosophy. A certain professor, whom I respected greatly, recommended that I should go into mathematics. His reasoning was that "in philosophy, not only logical ability but a poetic imagination is necessary," and he was not sure whether I had it. It was certainly reasonable advice, and I didn't have enough confidence in myself to challenge it. Yet I didn't feel like spending the rest of my life studying cut-and-dried mathematics. Although I did have some misgivings, I decided on philosophy.[35]

The required subjects for this year were Japanese, classical Chinese, English, German, history (of Britain, France, and Germany), mathematics, geology, physics, and physical education.[36] Having decided on his major, Nishida spent much of his time in the school library. There was a copy of Hegel's *Logic*, translated into English by William Wallace,[37] and a copy of Kant's *Critique of Pure Reason*, translated into English by Max Müller.[38] Nishida tried to read them, only to find them far over his head.[39]

Nishida took "philosophy" to mean "to inquire into the true reality of the universe."[40] He and Yamamoto exchanged their views concerning the existence of God, the immortality of the soul, and other philosophical problems.[41] Nishida briefly entertained positivist views, agreeing with Nakae Chōmin,[42] but he admitted to Yamamoto that "the universe is like a giant monster that defies our understanding." Yamamoto believed in the immortality of the soul and the existence of a compassionate God. Nishida demanded a logical proof from Yamamoto. Nishida was a skeptic who considered religion an outcome of human fear of death and general discontentment with life. The young Nishida was critical of theism and conventional views of religion, but something in him prevented him from becoming an outright atheist.[43]

Hōjō's departure from school left a large vacuum in the students' lives at school, and they began to complain about the declining quality of instruction. They were especially unhappy with a professor of English, "whose scholastic ability was not sufficient even in the eyes of the students,"[44] and students often protested about this professor and the school policies in general. Nishida intensely disliked the military-style gymnastic exercises *(heishiki taisō)* and did everything he could to interrupt the class.[45] In this way, Nishida and his friends were getting into trouble with the school authorities. In this atmosphere of discontent, Yamamoto quit the school at the end of December 1888.[46] He got a job teaching at the Ordinary Middle School, just established in October in Kanazawa. Yamamoto's decisive action made Nishida think about transferring to the First Higher School in Tokyo, where Hōjō was teaching. He turned to Hōjō for advice. Hōjō most likely told Nishida to exercise his patience.

On February 11, 1889, the Meiji Constitution was promulgated. To commemorate this historical moment, Nishida and his classmates went to a photography shop and posed in front of a camera.[47] (On this day also came the news of an ultranationalist's attempt to assassinate the education minister, Mori Arinori.)

For the photograph Yamamoto had draped over his arm a long sheet of calligraphy, on which he had written: "We Free Men Standing at the Top of Heaven" *(chōten ricchi jiyūjin)*. Fukushima Junkichi stood holding up a banner that read "Destroy! Destroy [the old order]!" The friends' high hopes for the new phase of Japan and their youthful defiant spirits were at their peak. These idealistic youths were steeped in patriotic zeal, wondering what they could do for their coun-

On the day of the promulgation of the Meiji Constitution, February 11, 1889. Front row, from left to right: Fujioka Sakutarō, Uchida Yūtarō, Yamamoto (Kaneda) Ryōkichi; back row, from left to right: Fukushima Junkichi, Matsumoto Bunzaburō, Nishida, and Matsui Kisaburō. From Kawasaki Akira, *Chōsui sensei ikō zokuhen*, frontispiece.

try. They did not doubt, even for a moment, their own ability to make a contribution to building a new constitutional nation.

Prompted by their idealism, Nishida and his friends organized a literary circle, *Gasonkai* (Respect the Individual Society) in May to develop their skills in writing and to hone their thinking through mutual criticism. Members of this group were Nishida, Yamamoto, Fujioka, Matsumoto Bunzaburō, Kawagoe Munetaka, Hasegawa Tei-ichirō, Oka Shinzō (or Sanjiro), and Yokoyama Shōsei. They produced essays and poems. Fujioka even wrote novels. They would get together once a week to criticize one another's writings. Each adopted a *gō* according to his fancy. Nishida first chose Chōse-sanjin (Mountain dweller who laughs at the lowly world) but soon called himself Uyokusei (literally, "winged being," or Pegasus). The image of the winged horse embodied for Nishida the spirit of freedom.[48] Yamamoto used Chōsui (Morning water), which had a reference to the River Asano ("*asa*" here means "morning"; it is also pronounced "*chō*"), while Fujioka called himself Tōho (Eastern peapod).

Although Nishida shared his friends' jubilant spirits in the days following the promulgation of the constitution, reality was not so kind to him. In July 1889 he received the report that he had failed his first year of the main division because of his poor attendance and bad classroom conduct, although academically he did fine. This news disheartened him because his family was then facing a period of uncertainty. In April a new local administrative regulation was put into effect that stripped Yasunori of his mayoral privileges. He left Unoke and moved to Kanazawa. Yasunori at first tried to live with his family at Nagadohei but soon moved into the house of his mistress. Nishida disapproved of his father's way of life and steadfastly sided with his mother.

Hōjō, aware that Nishida was in trouble at school, wrote him a long letter on July 17. Admonishing him for his myopic vision, he gave Nishida twelve points to keep in mind.[49] Nishida informed Hōjō of his academic failure in late July and asked him to help him transfer to the First Higher School. Hōjō rejected Nishida's request as "banal, cheap, and cowardly" and told him to change his mind, study for two more years at the Fourth Higher School, and enter the Imperial University.[50]

In the fall of 1889, Nishida was given a second chance to pursue his studies at school. He was placed in the science track to repeat his first year. That he was placed with the class that had been one year behind him was hard on his pride. Besides, he could not stand the smell of the hydrogen sulfide used in chemistry experiments, nor did he care for dragging heavy equipment to conduct terrain measurements.[51] Thinking that he "could learn on his own without going to school,"[52] he recklessly dropped out of school on March 31, 1890, after the end of the second term.[53] He did not have the courage, however, to tell Hōjō. Hōjō, unaware of what had happened, wrote to Nishida on May 18 and encouraged him to stay in school and respect the school rules.[54]

Partly to forget his unhappiness, Nishida poured much energy into the activities of Gasonkai. He wrote over fifty pieces, including poems and essays (in Japanese and Chinese); commentaries on books and public figures; social and political criticism; character descriptions of members of Gasonkai; and a Japanese translation of "The Last Minstrel" by Walter Scott.[55] These works reveal clearly Nishida the young man. In his essay "To My Dearest Friends!"[56] he supports the view that the pen is mightier than the sword in the civilized world and quotes from such diverse sources as the Old Testament, and essays by T. B. Macaulay[57] and Washington Irving,[58] while making references to Confucius, the Duke of Zhou, and ancient Chinese historical incidents. In his "To the Members of the Group,"[59] he proposes the practice of public speaking, an idea promoted by Fukuzawa Yukichi.[60] In his "On the Abolition of Prostitution,"[61] he laments the failure of the movement to make prostitution illegal. In his essay on Rousseau,[62] he defends the French philosopher from the charge of having precipitated the French Revolution. He comments that "to criticize a person, we must understand his or her time,"[63] revealing a fine hermeneutical awareness. He quotes a line from Emerson that perfectly captures the essence of Rousseau's courage: "It is easy in the world to live after the world's opinion; it is easy in solitude to live after our own; but the great man is he who in the midst of the crowd keeps with perfect sweetness the independence of solitude."[64]

In his poem entitled "India,"[65] Nishida calls out for the Indian people to rise up from colonial rule. In his "A Note on Yō Hikkan,"[66] he sharply criticizes the diplomatic efforts of Japanese leaders Inoue Kaoru and Ōkuma Shigenobu, who were not able to win the equal trade treaties. He attributes their inability to the government's lack of fundamental principles, such as the cultivation of personal integrity and learning, a view Nishida continued to hold throughout his life. Nishida lamented the death of Niijima Jō[67] on January 23, 1890, and wrote his tribute to him.

The essay entitled "A Walk,"[68] particularly reveals the Nishida of those years. It is a kind of monologue, recounting thoughts that came to him while taking a long walk one afternoon in Kanazawa. No sooner does he begin to reflect on the economic situation of the city than he moves on to the criticism of a cheap imitation of the popular journal *Kokumin no tomo* [Friends of the nation].[69] As he walks through the elegant Japanese garden of Kenrokuen, he is overcome by thoughts of the glorious past; as he passes by the residence of the prefecture governor, satirical comments rise in his mind on the corruption of the local officials. The twenty-year-old Nishida observed the social changes and issues of the day with a critical eye. This essay is of special interest, because during one of those walks Nishida was overcome by a revelatory experience: Reality is none other than what one experiences. This inspired him to develop the idea of "pure experience."[70] Brisk walks apparently invigorated his mind and heightened his awareness.

Soon after dropping out of school, Nishida fell ill and was forced to stay at home for a few weeks. He was getting better by June when the members of Gasonkai posed for a group photograph to memorialize its existence.[71] Fujioka, Matsumoto, Oka, Hasegawa, and Yokoyama were all graduating in July. Nishida wrote on the reverse side of this photo:

> Gasonkai is a literary group established by our own initiative. It was formed last year in May. Since then, more than a year has passed. Our writings have exceeded twenty volumes, and the number of pieces we have produced is several hundred. . . . In the near future some of us will leave [Kanazawa], and we won't be together as a group any more.[72]

Gasonkai dissolved in July 1890. Fujioka was accepted by the Imperial University but decided to take a year off to rest to strengthen his body. In September 1890, Yamamoto, Nishida, Fujioka, and Kawagoe formed another literary circle and called it Fuseimonkai (Incomplete Writing Society).[73] Upon Yamamoto's suggestion they celebrated a traditional festival day *(sekku)* of chrysanthemums on October 22.[74] This was an act of protest against the dissolution of the old and beautiful customs that were quickly disappearing under the invasive central government, which instituted new holidays with nationalistic overtones, such as the day of the founding of the nation *(kigensetsu)*.[75]

In the fall, Nishida, faithfully abiding by his commitment to learn on his own, began reading ferociously, only to injure his eyes. He was admitted to a hospital, and the doctor forbade him to read for a year. In one of his *waka* (traditional Japanese poems) he wrote:

Books by Hartmann
and Hegel are piled
at my pillowside
will I ever get
to read them? [76]

By February 1891, however, Nishida's eyes were repairing themselves thanks to the excellent treatment his doctor had provided. Yamamoto regularly visited Nishida in the hospital to keep him company.[77] Meanwhile, the literary group lacked its former vigor and dissolved itself in May 1891.

Nishida reminisced years later that he and his friends "yearned after lofty ideas of scholarship and fine arts" and "held progressive views."[78] They were thoroughly steeped in the humanistic spirit of the early Meiji, which was expressed in the political realm as the "free

Commemorative photograph of the Gasonkai, June 1890. Front row, from left to right: Fujioka Sakutarō, Kawagoe Munetaka, Matsumoto Bunzaburō; back row, from left to right: Hasegawa Teiichirō, Yamamoto (Kaneda) Ryōkichi, Oka Shinzō, and Nishida. From *Nishida Kitarō Zenshū*, vol. 18, *Geppō*.

civil rights movement" (*jiyū minken undō*). Nishida's dropping out of the Fourth Higher Middle School coincided with the issuance on October 30, 1890, of the *Imperial rescript on education (Kyōiku chokugo)*. The rescript aimed at imbuing a nationalistic spirit among school children and students, and the ritualized bowing in front of a copy of the education rescript would in time become a "sacred" school ceremony. Nishida, Fujioka, Suzuki, and Yamamoto all had left the school by then, marking them as a generation that was free from the government-imposed indoctrination program that was to develop into State Shinto.

It is well known that Uchimura Kanzō, then teaching at the First Higher School, got into trouble by choosing, because of his Christian faith, not to bow in front of the rescript at the school ceremony celebrating the beginning of the new year in January 1891. What is not so well known is that Hōjō Tokiyuki, Okada Ryōhei, and one other person at the First Higher School were behind this outright attack on Uchimura, which eventually led to the teacher's dismissal.[79] While the "Uchimura incident" was the center of heated controversy, Nishida was in a dark room in the hospital in Kanazawa, recovering from his eye injury.

Chapter 3

The Imperial University

(1891–1894)

When Nishida recovered from his eye trouble, he realized that his plan to study on his own was unrealistic. There was only one choice left for him—to take the entrance exam of the Imperial University as a "limited status" *(senka)* student. He was lucky that this option existed at all. It had been created on September 25, 1878, at the request of Katō Hiroyuki, the first president of the university, to accommodate students of diverse backgrounds.[1] While the graduates of higher schools were automatically admitted to the university, students applying through the venue of limited status had to take and pass an entrance examination, which was administered by the university professors in the fields the students had selected for study. The *senka* program was possible only because students whose academic training was sufficient enough to take the examination were relatively few.[2] There were certain restrictions binding the *senka* students. For instance, they were not allowed to concentrate on English, German, or French language studies, Japanese or Chinese literature, or Japanese or Chinese law.[3] Otherwise, they were free to pursue any subject or multiple subjects. They were not entitled to a university degree, but in 1890 the university began issuing a certificate to the *senka* students when they completed their studies.[4]

Tokyo University, established in April 1877, was then called the Imperial University, or Teikoku Daigaku (the Japanese word *"teikoku"* was Mori Arinori's neologism, a translation of the English word "imperial").[5] For Mori the state was the most central reality, and he planned to make the university into an institution that served the needs of the nation-state *(kokka)*. Mori defined in 1886 the role of the university as "to teach academic subjects and fine arts to serve the indispensable needs of the country and to carry out research in these areas."[6]

On June 11, 1891, Nishida went to Tokyo to take the entrance examination.[7] Fujioka Sakutarō traveled with him because he needed to make necessary arrangements with the university and find a boarding house.[8] Fujioka returned to Kanazawa soon. Nishida wrote to Yamamoto and Fujioka in Kanazawa on June 27: "The exam was so easy that I feel as if I had misread the questions. But, most likely, I did well. Strange that the entrance exam of the Imperial University is so easy!"[9] In the same letter he gave a detailed account of the previous Sunday, when his former higher school classmates gathered at his inn and had a great time. Suzuki Teitarō, then in Tokyo since May and studying English at Tokyo Senmon Gakkō (today's Waseda University), joined the party.[10]

Following the examination, Nishida called on Hōjō Tokiyuki.[11] At that time the professor "scolded" him, saying that "the *senka* track was for those who lagged behind in their studies" and that he should "retake the entrance exam of the university as a regular student." Nishida was at a loss.[12] Lack of a higher school diploma complicated the matter. Nishida was soon to discover that the post-Restoration social structure was already codified and that the academic system was fixed in its hierarchy, with the Imperial University at its top. It was clear that those who made it to the university were on the elite track, and those who didn't weren't. University students sported a school cap and a uniform studded with shining gold buttons—a symbol of the new meritocracy.

Having passed the entrance examination, Nishida was admitted into the Department of Philosophy in September 1891 as a senka student. By then, the legendary professor Ernest Fenollosa[13] had already left the university, but Nishida knew of his reputation as someone who "was able to read the works of the German philosophers in English translation and had a good grasp of them."[14] Fenollosa was briefly succeeded by G. W. Knox, an American, for the fall of 1886, before Ludwig Busse came from Germany in January 1887.

In the early years of the Meiji, courses in philosophy were typically taught by non-Japanese instructors, but starting around 1890 that situation began to change. Motora Yūjirō,[15] Inoue Tetsujirō,[16] and Nakajima Rikizō[17] were promoted to the rank of professor one after another. Under the leadership of Inoue Tetsujirō, German philosophy began to overshadow British philosophy. Inoue recalled:

At the university I primarily introduced German philosophy to the students and trained them thoroughly in it. . . . I and my colleagues were truly responsible for making German philosophy the main stream of philosophy in the Japanese academy. Certainly, Busse, who arrived in Japan in 1887, made some contribution in this respect.[18]

Nishida, despite his status as a *senka* student, decided to follow the core curriculum required of regular majors. He also took language courses that were elective. In his first year he took introduction to philosophy, history of philosophy, ethics, study of history, classical Chinese, English, Japanese literature, German, Latin, French, and biology. In his second year he took history of philosophy, logic, theory of knowledge, sociology, psychology, biology, ethics, German, Latin, history, comparative religions and Oriental philosophy, German literature, Japanese literature, and English. In his third year he studied aesthetics and the history of art, theory of education, ethics, psychology, comparative religions and Oriental philosophy, Indian philosophy, seminar in philosophy, German, German literature, and English.[19] His professors included Ludwig Busse, Nakajima Rikizō, Motora Yūjirō, Inoue Tetsujirō, Toyama Masakazu, Raphael von Koeber, Shimada Jūrei (or Chōrei), Kanda Naibu, Mozume Takami, Émile Heck, Karl Florenz, and Ludwig Riess.

To Nishida's delight, in the College of Humanities there was an active Philosophical Society (Tetsugakukai), established in 1884, which published its monthly journal, *Tetsugaku Zasshi* (Journal of Philosophy). Nishida wished to join the society because Matsumoto Bunzaburō and Fujioka Sakutarō were already members. Matsumoto acted as Nishida's sponsor, and his application for membership was unanimously accepted at the general meeting on October 23, 1891.[20] Another limited status student, Kimura Takatarō, was also accepted at the same time.[21] Nishida probably attended most of the society's monthly meetings. On those occasions, he must have seen and heard the leading thinkers of the Meiji Japanese intellectual world, such as Katō Hiroyuki, Ōnishi Hajime, Inoue Enryō, Miyake Yūjirō, Murakami Senshō, Shimaji Mokurai, all of whom made presentations to the society. Nishida was able to observe firsthand the landscape of the Meiji philosophical world.

It did not take too long, however, for Nishida to realize that the life of a limited status student was that of a second-class citizen. The *senka* students had fewer privileges by far than regular students. What troubled Nishida most was the library policy. *Senka* students were not

Professors and the graduates of the College of Humanities, Imperial University, July 1891. Nishida took classes from many of these professors. Front row, from left to right: Karl A. Florenz, Shimoda Chōrei (or Jūrei), Konakamura Kiyonori, Toyama Masakazu, James M. Dixon, Ludwig Busse, Ludwig Riess, Mozume Takami; second row, from left to right: Motora Yūjirō, Kotō Bunjirō, Sakaki Kiyoshi, Kanda Naibu, Nakajima Rikizō, Nojiri Seiichi, Murakami Senshō; third row, consisting of graduating students, from left to right: Kanō Kōkichi, Tachibana Masaki, Ōtsuka Yasuji, Fujishiro Teisuke, Fujii Senshō, Ogawa Ginjirō, Suga Torao, Makise Goichirō. From *Tokyo daigaku hyakunenshi—bukyokushi.*

permitted to read in the main hall of the library and had to use the desks arranged in the corridor just outside the library. In their third year regular students were permitted to browse the stacks, but *senka* students were not able to do so. Nishida also sensed that professors kept the *senka* students at arm's length. All this seemed to him unnecessary: there were only five regular students majoring in philosophy who entered the university when Nishida did. Despite his outwardly nonchalant appearance, Nishida was sensitive. Discriminatory treatment hurt him, bruised his pride, and made him feel like a "loser."[22] Professor Hōjō was right to insist that Nishida swallow his sense of shame and persevere for two years to graduate properly from the higher school. Although a sense of regret and remorse set in too late, Nishida was resilient. He learned to stand on his own, rise above the external confinements, and find a certain inner freedom. He concentrated on reading and thinking, gradually forming an independent style of philosophical inquiry (see Nishida's essay at the end of this chapter).

Nishida, in his antisocial mood, gave himself to introspection and spent many hours in the library reading. Although he was surrounded by brilliant minds, he did not actively seek out new friends. Among his classmates were such unique figures as Ōshima Yoshinaga, a notable educator,[23] and Iwamoto Tei, who became professor of philosophy at the First Higher School. Nishida was in the same German literature class as Natsume Kinnosuke (*gō*, Sōseki) and read Goethe's *Herrmann und Dorothea* under the guidance of Karl Florenz.[24] Natsume was a student of English literature, and a year ahead of Nishida. Nishida felt that Natsume, who was always impeccably dressed in a three-piece suit, was of a different breed, and the two never struck up a conversation.

In addition to feeling alienated from his fellow students, Nishida was disappointed in his university courses and in the professors who taught them. For instance, the course on classical Chinese, taught by the respected Shimada Chōrei, turned out to be a straight recitation of Chinese texts without commentary. Bewildered, Nishida asked those who were majoring in Chinese literature whether Shimada went into detailed discussions in the advanced courses. The answer was no. He could not help comparing Shimada with his former teacher, Miyake Shinken. One day, Nishida called on Shimada and told him that he was a student of Miyake. Shimada told Nishida that "Miyake is truly impressive; he orders books from China that I don't even know exist." Apparently, when a qualifying examination for middle school teachers was administered some years previously, Miyake traveled to Tokyo to take it. Shimada, his examiner, was totally stunned by Miyake's erudition, and invited him home and asked him how he learned his Chinese.[25]

Another disappointment for Nishida was "Introduction to Philosophy," a course taught by Ludwig Busse. Busse had been a disciple of Rudolf Hermann Lotze at the University of Berlin,[26] and his course seemed to Nishida nothing more than "an introduction to Lotze's philosophy." It struck Nishida that Busse, barely thirty years old, was too young to be a philosopher. His youthful and energetic lecture style only worsened Nishida's suspicions. Nishida was not ready to appreciate the professor's contributions: Busse adopted Kant's *Critique of Pure Reason* as the textbook for the course and introduced the method of historical study of philosophy to the Japanese students. It was not until two decades later, when Nishida discovered Lotze's thought, that he came to regret his failure to appreciate Busse:

> Lotze was a great thinker of the nineteenth century, who was blessed with penetrating contemplation, wide erudition, and subtle sensibility. . . . Through Busse, Lotze's philosophy was introduced to the Japanese philosophy classroom, and in a sense students of those days were Lotze's grand-disciples. To be frank, in those days I didn't have enough intellectual finesse to appreciate Lotze's work. While listening to Professor Busse, I could not help but feel dissatisfied with Lotze's compromising attitude. But later, when I read Lotze's *Logic*, my opinion of him radically changed. I came to believe that his *Logic* was a work that everyone must read for a foundation in modern logic. Even then, I didn't take up his *Metaphysics* to read for a long time. It was only last summer when I did so, and I was even more impressed by his greatness.[27]

Perhaps Nishida enjoyed the language courses more than the lecture courses because the non-Japanese professors did not pay much attention to the difference between the regular students and the *senka* students. One such professor was a French Catholic priest, Émile Heck, who arrived at the port of Yokohama in November 1891 and began teaching French at the university a week later. He spoke no Japanese and very little English. (Students inadvertently ended up learning French through total immersion.) The majority found Heck difficult to follow, which challenged Heck's temper in turn. The class, which started out with thirty students, shrank to seven or eight in the winter quarter, but Nishida, one of the survivors, felt he learned his French well because of Heck's approach.[28]

For personal comfort, Nishida turned to his close friends, Fujioka and Suzuki, and maintained his steady correspondence with Yamamoto back in Kanazawa. Nishida and Fujioka often went out to places of literary and historical interest in Tokyo. On November 8 they went to a "speech meeting"—a popular pastime among young intellectuals at the time.[29] Nishida describes his impressions in detail in a letter to Yamamoto:

> The first speaker was the great talent of Meiji, Mr. Fukuchi Gen'ichirō. He is a rough-looking man, lacking elegance; he looked almost like a mountain worker. He is heavy-boned and not tall. But he clearly had stage presence. While he collected himself, he surveyed the audience with a piercing glance, with an extraordinary air. His poise showed that he was very accustomed to public speaking. . . . his talk was a critique of Japanese literature. It was well paced, lucid, and powerful. While he

exhibited a tremendous breadth of knowledge, he mixed in humor, bringing the audience to belly laughs. He was a master speaker, his gestures eloquent. He spoke for about an hour, then left the stage accompanied by an incredible ovation from the audience.

Next, a Frenchman came out and preached Christianity. The audience booed and hooted. Because the uproar would not subside, he had to quit his talk in the middle and leave the stage. His name is Verbeck; he is apparently sixty-two years old and has lived in Japan for the last thirty years.

Then Mr. Ōuchi Seiran came on the stage and spoke. His speech was smooth and clear, like an undisturbed flow of water. The examples and metaphors he gave were to the point, and he captivated the audience.[30]

Fukuchi Gen'ichirō,[31] Guido Verbeck,[32] and Ōuchi Seiran[33] were all prominent figures of the time. It is easy to see why young intellectuals, including Nishida, found such meetings exciting. Through Fujioka, who had a wide circle of associations, Nishida got to meet Taoka Reiun,[34] for instance.

Suzuki was living nearby in a dormitory, Kuchōkan, and Nishida saw him quite frequently. Kuchōkan was a dormitory that housed the sons of the former retainers of the Maeda family and was operated by a board of directors that included the senior Ishikawaits, such as Hōjō Tokiyuki and Hayakawa Senkichirō, a successful businessman. It so happens that both Hōjō and Hayakawa were practicing Zen under Master Imakita Kōsen,[35] the abbot of Engakuji Temple in Kamakura. Through Hayakawa, Suzuki was introduced to Master Kōsen and began his Zen practice. Because Suzuki had no money to take a train or hire a *jinrikisha*, he would leave the dormitory in the evening on foot for Kamakura, where he would arrive in time for the morning *zazen* period. The long walk strengthened his legs and probably contributed to his longevity.

Suzuki soon dedicated his entire soul to Zen practice and often stayed over at Engakuji. He invited Nishida to visit him at the temple to experience Zen. Using the long Thanksgiving weekend, Nishida went to Kamakura from November 23 to 25.[36] During his stay, he got to meet Master Kōsen in person and received a *kōan*.[37] Although he felt attracted to Zen practice, it did not occur to him to take it up in earnest however. The time was not yet ripe for him. Even then, he felt envious of Suzuki, as his letter of December 18 to Yamamoto reveals: "Toward the end of last month, I visited Kamakura. . . . Suzuki is currently at Engakuji, doing *zazen*. I, who am embroiled in the secular life, should not envy him and long for that kind of life, but I do!"[38]

In his first year at the university, Nishida wrote an examination paper for Nakajima Rikizō—a sketch of Kant's moral philosophy. After surveying Kant's three major works on ethics, *Groundwork of the Metaphysics of Morals* (1785), *Critique of Practical Reason* (1788), and the unfinished *Metaphysics of Morals* (1803), Nishida attached a summary of the content of the three chapters of the *Groundwork of the Metaphysics of Morals*.[39] To illustrate the university education of the late nineteenth century Nishida contributed this essay to *Hiroki Tazō sensei tsuioku-bunshū* [A collection of essays in memory of Professor Hiroki Tazō] in 1933.

Nishida encouraged Yamamoto and Suzuki to apply for the university. In June 1892 they took the entrance examination and were accepted—attesting to the high standard of education they had received in Kanazawa. Suzuki was a *senka* student in the philosophy department, and Yamamoto a *senka* student in the College of Law. Suzuki soon lost interest in the university courses, however, and intensified his Zen practice, this time under Master Kōgaku (Shaku Sōen).[40]

Yamamoto at first thought of going into politics but switched to philosophy and concentrated on ethics, for he then knew that his calling was education. Yamamoto was in dire financial straits. Nishida consulted Matsui Kisaburō, his friend from higher school. Matsui agreed to contribute two yen a month, while Nishida contributed one yen a month toward Yamamoto's living expenses.[41] At that time Nishida's room and board cost 4.2 yen a month, and Suzuki was receiving six yen a month from his brother in Kobe, so three yen was a substantial help to Yamamoto. With his friends' help, Yamamoto was able to complete his university education. Fujioka offers a humorous description contrasting the Matsui and Nishida of those days: "While one worries about the sparse growth of his moustache, the other worries about the decline of his family fortune."[42]

Indeed, during Nishida's first year at the university, the Nishida family lost practically its entire fortune because of Yasunori's speculation and subsequent financial losses in the rice market. The family had to sell all their land in Unoke. During summer vacation in 1892, Nishida was obliged to go back to Kanazawa to seal a financial transaction with a local moneylender. It appears that Yasunori was no longer creditworthy, so Nishida had to represent the family. During this time his mother, Tosa, asked her husband for five hundred yen for

their children's education and obtained the money through her determined efforts. On September 7, 1892, Tosa left for Tokyo, taking
Hyōjirō with her. Nishida left for Tokyo on the following day. The
three rented a small house in the Koishikawa area in Tokyo. Hyōjirō
attended Seijō, a higher school that trained military officers-to-be.[43]
Tosa moved to Tokyo without her servants, which meant she had to do
all the household work herself. The situation in which Tosa put herself in Tokyo told Yamamoto poignantly of the decline of the once-
wealthy Nishida family.[44] Tosa did not complain a bit and briskly went
about her way. Nishida remained ever grateful to his mother for her
determination, dedication, and selfless support.

In the fall quarter of his second year of study, Nishida wrote a
paper in English, "Spinoza's Conception of God,"[45] most likely for
Busse, who was a specialist of Spinoza. In December 1892 Busse duly
fulfilled his term of employment and left for Germany.[46] His position
was filled by Raphael von Koeber[47] who came from Germany in June
1893. Inoue Tetsujirō had been entrusted with the task of inviting a
professor from Germany, and at first he extended an invitation to
Adolf Lasson, a German Jew, who declined the offer, however, because
of his advanced age. Lasson then asked Eduard von Hartmann to name
a candidate. Hartmann recommended Koeber, who had introduced
Eduard Hartmann's and Schopenhauer's thought in his supplement to
Albert Schwegler's *Handbook of the History of Philosophy* (1874), which
had ended with Hegel. This work made Koeber quite well known
among philosophy students in Germany.[48]

Because Inoue knew Hartmann personally and trusted his judgment, he entered negotiations with Koeber by writing: "Would you
like to come to Japan, where cherry blossoms bloom?"[49] This apparently touched a romantic chord in Koeber. The initial contract was
for three years, but Koeber ended up remaining at the university for
the next twenty-one years, teaching courses in philosophy and aesthetics. Koeber was a student of Euken and had also heard Kuno Fis-
cher lecture at the University of Heidelberg.

Koeber gave his first lecture in Japan to the Introduction to Philosophy class on September 15, 1893.[50] Nishida probably sat in on this
course. He liked Koeber much better than Busse, for he fit his image
of what a philosopher should be. Koeber was then in his midforties.
He lectured seated at a desk and spoke in soft low voice—a clear contrast to his predecessor. Koeber, originally trained as a classical pianist
at the Moscow Conservatory under Tchaikovsky, was a man of aes-

thetic cultivation as well. He was of the opinion that Christian and pre-Christian thinkers formed the background for contemporary Western philosophy. He discussed not only the Greeks and contemporary Western thinkers but also patristic philosophy, scholastic philosophy, and medieval Christian mystics.[51] Although Nishida claimed that his philosophical orientation had already been set by the time he met Koeber,[52] there is no denying that Nishida's intellectual horizon was significantly widened by Koeber's interest in Meister Eckhart, neo-Platonism, and the mystical tradition of the Christian West. Koeber's seminar on Schopenhauer's *Parerga und Paralipomena* also elevated Nishida's interest in Schopenhauer.

Nishida always remembered Koeber with a sense of respect. Koeber conveyed directly from his European upbringing and background what it meant to philosophize. He also advised Nishida that to study Western philosophy he should at least learn Latin. Nishida also learned from Koeber not to pass hasty judgment on great thinkers:

> At one time, when I was impudent enough to say critical things about Hegel's philosophy, Professor Koeber challenged me by saying *"Warum? Warum?"* [Why? Why?]. He repeated the expression, "non multa sed multum" (not quantity but quality),[53] and admonished me. Although he said these words *to me*, I think these were the words that he wanted to say to *all* the Japanese philosophy students of those days.[54]

The Latin phrase, "non multa sed multum," stuck in Nishida's mind as a reminder throughout his life.[55] When Koeber died on June 14, 1923, in Yokohama, Nishida reminisced about this unique individual:

> The incomparable nobility of Professor Koeber's spirit is best remembered not by praising his scholarly achievement but by recalling the influence that he exerted on the people around him. This influence came from his profoundly cultivated, refined personality, which was "cool and fragrant" as the waters flowing from the bamboo forest are cool, and the winds blowing through the flowers are fragrant. . . .
>
> I do not know how it was in the very beginning of the Meiji period, but by the time I became aware of what was going on, the Japanese philosophical world seemed to have been dominated by British philosophers, such as Mill and Spencer. From the third decade of the Meiji, German philosophy became a main stream, and it added depth to Japanese academic philosophy. Be that as it may, it was Professor Koeber

who single-handedly introduced classical philosophy to the Japanese academy. Every scholar who possesses an impressive scholarly style and contributes to today's Japanese academia was trained under Koeber.[56]

Indeed, Koeber was a man of charisma who exerted a decisive influence on a generation of young minds, including Fukada Yasukazu,[57] Hatano Seiichi,[58] Watsuji Tetsurō,[59] and Kuki Shūzō[60]—all of whom became Nishida's colleagues at Kyoto University. To Nishida, however, Koeber's scholarship was too aesthetically oriented and unsystematic.[61] Kuwaki Gen'yoku noted that Koeber disliked empiricism and the Anglo-Saxon philosophies of the nineteenth and twentieth centuries, and that some students were frustrated by the professor's strong bias.[62] Koeber was a bit of a hermit, an eccentric, and a possessor of sharp sarcasm. Inoue Tetsujirō recounted that Koeber's sarcasm was described by his German colleagues as *giftig* (poisonous),[63] and in fact Lafcadio Hearn, who taught at the university for some time, was frightened by Koeber's pro-Catholic remarks.[64] Anesaki noted that Koeber was not interested in things Japanese at all and did not go on any sightseeing trips during his entire stay in Japan with the exception of a brief excursion to Kamakura. Apparently, Koeber was happy being surrounded by Plato, Dante, Goethe's *Faust*, and the Bible.[65]

In the fall term of 1893 Nishida took two courses from the much-hailed professor Inoue Tetsujirō. In 1931, on the occasion of Inoue's seventy-seventh birthday, he recalled:

> Professor Inoue lectured twice a week; one [lecture] was on Indian philosophy, and the other on comparative philosophy. His lectures always began at three in the afternoon. The figure of the professor, coming in through the school gate, wearing a scarf and carrying a walking stick, is still in the back of my mind. I was self-willed, difficult to please, and didn't attend many lectures, but I did attend his course on Indian philosophy. I may still have the notes I took in these lectures. I also remember having called on him at his home several times.[66]

Although Nishida was not that impressed by Inoue's scholarship, he held him in due respect. Over the years, their relationship grew into one of cordial professionalism. Nishida also maintained contact with Nakajima Rikizō and Motora Yūjirō, even after graduation.

It was not part of the graduation requirements for *senka* students to write a thesis, but Nishida wrote his on Hume's theory of causation[67] in three parts: "Hyūmu izen no tetsugaku no hattatsu" [The development of philosophy before Hume],[68] "Hyūmu no ingahō" [On

Hume's theory of causation],[69] and "Hyūmu no ingahō hihan" [Critique of Hume's theory of causation].[70] Nishida published his thesis in the *Hokushinkai Zasshi*,[71] a journal of the student association of the Fourth Higher School, during his first year of teaching there, 1896 to 1897.

Nishida's experience at the Imperial University may not have been particularly happy, but it built his basic philosophical attitude and challenged his tenacity. There is no doubt that studying at the university expanded his intellectual horizons and exposed him to the highest levels of scholarship available in Japan. All in all, however, his university days were a time of relative isolation and introspection. When his graduation from the university was approaching in 1894, he looked for a teaching position in the Tokyo area, but no jobs were available for a graduate of the *senka* track.

The Limited Status Program at the College of Humanities at the Imperial University around 1891–1892*

When I first came from my hometown of Kanazawa to Tokyo, the area extending from Suidōbashi to the Military Armory Factory was still very quiet. Only a few small movable *yakitori*-stands stood there along with *jinrikisha* men waiting for customers. Below the cliff on the side of Hongō in the Kasugachō district were rice paddies, and you could hear frogs croaking. Even in Hongō, if you walked a bit further into the area of Komagome from the university, you went beyond the town and you met carts on the dusty road carrying human manure for fertilizing.

In those days there used to be a small wooden gate where the main entrance gate of the university now stands. I guess the gate on the Tatsuokachō side was the main one, instead of the present one. If you walked in that wooden gate, you saw the building of the Colleges of Law and Literature, which was totally demolished in the 1923 earthquake. I understand that the architect was a man called Conder,[1] who

---

* "Meiji nijūshigonen goro no Tōkyō Bunka Daigaku senka," NKZ 12:241–44.
1. Josiah Conder, an Englishman, was professor of engineering at Tokyo University, 1877–1882. See TDH, *Shiryō* 3:261.

designed the Aoyama Palace. The brick building that housed the Colleges of Law and Literature was not particularly large. Its second floor was given over to the library and the college president's office. We used to see Mr. Toyama, who wore oversize trousers, going in and out of his office, with his keys making a click-clank noise. Only the first floor was needed for the College of Law and Literature classrooms in those days.

We limited status students were really a miserable lot. Of course, it made sense from the point of view of the university administration [to treat us differently from the regular students], but we were treated with blatant discrimination. As I said, the second floor of the building was the library, and there was a large reading room in the middle of it, where one could sit and read. However, the limited status students were not allowed to read there; instead, we had to read outside the library at desks lined up in the hall. The third-year students of the regular division were permitted to go through the stacks, but of course, for us that was out of the question. Also, though it may be my biased impression, even when we called on our professors, some of them seemed to receive us perfunctorily.

I was suddenly being treated very differently from my fellow higher school students, with whom I had been equals only a short while before, and it hurt my feelings. I spent three years in a corner as it were, unnoticed by people. On the other hand, since I was able to study freely whatever I wanted to without being hindered by any [outside activities], there was a kind of inner joy to it. I savored my own pride as I rose above [my wretched circumstances]. When we were higher school students, we didn't take much German at school; therefore for the first year at the university, I mainly read German literature, accompanied by an English translation or annotations.

Professor Inoue Tetsujirō had returned to Japan a year or two earlier [from his study in Europe], and Professors Motora [Yūjirō] and Nakajima [Rikizō] were both promoted to professor. Japanese professors occupied the main chairs, but it was Ludwig Busse who mainly gave lectures on philosophy. He was only about thirty years old. In Berlin he had attended the last lectures of the aging Lotze, and he was a thorough-going Lotzean. In fact, his course "Introduction to Philosophy" was nothing but "an introduction to Lotze's philosophy." In those days, even a German professor gave lectures in English. Busse was a lively lecturer, and whenever he got excited, his German accent would intensify; instead of saying "generation after generation," he would say [using the hard G] "Generation afta Generation."

Ensconced among these foreign teachers was the renowned scholar of classical Chinese, Shimada Chōrei. He would come into the lecture hall, walk slowly to the lecture podium, and often take a cigarette case from his pocket, smoke a cigarette very leisurely, and only then start his lecture.

When I was a third-year student, Professor Koeber came. He was already in his forties at that time, and he even looked like a philosopher, a clear contrast to his predecessor. I remember he first lectured on Schopenhauer. He would lecture seated at his desk, unlike Busse [who lectured standing], and he spoke in a low tone of voice. After he came to Japan, Mr. Koeber seems to have formed the opinion that Japanese students, who studied philosophy without knowledge of the classical languages [i.e., Latin and Greek], were "superficial." One day when I visited him to inquire about the existence of a translation of Augustine in any modern European language, he asked me why I didn't learn a classical language. I said it was difficult for Japanese to learn classical languages; thereupon, he told me that my classmate Iwamoto read Greek. "You must read Latin at least," he said. But, while he was [stubborn on this subject], he offered me a cigarette. I said I didn't smoke. Then, he teased me and said, *"Ein Philosoph muss rauchen"* [a philosopher must smoke].

In the class a year ahead of me, there were such brilliant students as the two Matsumotos and Yoneyama Hosaburō. In the class two years below me, the class of [Meiji] 29, there were geniuses such as Kuwaki Gen'yoku, Anesaki [Masaharu], and Takayama Chogyū. The famous Natsume Sōseki was a year ahead of me, majoring in English literature, but I think we were in the same class taught by Florenz, and read [Goethe's] *Herrmann und Dorothea* together.

In our class, Ōshima Yoshinaga was the top student. But the one who came to assume a very unique position was Iwamoto Tei, who recently died. Iwamoto had already begun studying Greek, and in the library reading room, he was reading the works of the pre-Socratics by consulting a dictionary. He somewhat resembled Mr. Koeber. I never had the opportunity to see Iwamoto again after I graduated in 1894. I can only recall the image of Iwamoto clad in his student uniform, his hips slightly bent. I wanted to see him when I began to spend some time each year in Kamakura. In my laziness, I postponed seeing him, thinking there is "next time." In this way, I never got to see him. I cannot help but feel regretful at the recent news of his death. According to the newspaper, his funeral service was attended by several thousand mourners. He was a man of elevated soul.

In sharp contrast to my higher school days, when I did a lot of things and had many happy memories, I didn't form a close rapport with professors, nor did I make friends during my university days. Instead of socializing I went to the library every day, read books alone, and thought on my own. I learned a lot at the university, but there was no lecture that was truly informative or moving. In those days, such a thing as difficulty in finding a job after graduation for the holders of a university degree was unheard of. But with the limited status students, the situation was otherwise. For that reason, as soon as I graduated, I went back to my hometown to find a job and did not return to the capital city for more than a decade.

Chapter 4

Existential Impasse and Zen Practice

(1894–1899)

In July 1894 Nishida returned to Kanazawa, where he was promised a position as a teacher of English at the Ishikawa Prefecture Ordinary Middle School. But in September he learned that someone in the prefecture office had suggested another candidate. The official explanation was that someone trained in English had become available. Because he had just declined a job for which he had been recommended by Hōjō Tokiyuki, he was terribly disturbed by this unexpected course of events.[1] Nishida found the conduct of the officials and school administrators unconscionable and confided to Yamamoto: "I sigh at the degree of corruption of the 'real world,' into which I have stepped for the first time from *holy* academia."[2] He wrote to his friends, Fujioka Sakutarō, Matsumoto Bunzaburō, and Ueda Seiji,[3] asking them to keep their eyes open for a teaching position. The slight chance that Nishida might take over the position vacated by Kiyozawa Manshi in Kyoto just did not materialize.[4]

Nishida was obliged to spend the rest of 1894 unemployed. Although he could still subsist on a bit of money left in his name by way of inheritance,[5] he needed an income to support himself and his mother. The situation was not desperate, however. Besides, his friends were engaged in projects that were not generating an income and that did not interest them. Fujioka, after graduating from the Department of Japanese Literature, did not even think of getting a job and was working on his first book, *Nihon fūzokushi* [A history of Japanese customs], together with Hiraide Kōjirō.[6] Suzuki was busy translating into Japanese Paul Carus's book, *The Gospel of Buddha*.[7] Being encouraged by the example of his friends, Nishida resolved to "be useful to society" and decided to introduce Thomas Hill Green's thought to the

Japanese.[8] Green's *Prolegomena to Ethics*[9] was used as a textbook in Nakajima Rikizō's seminar (Yamamoto was sitting in on the seminar). Nishida found the *Prolegomena* rather hard to follow, with many ambiguous phrases.[10] But he came to feel that "Green's ideas, taken from Kant and Hegel, were not that original or novel."[11] By December he had decided that Green's argument was tedious.[12] He originally intended to write a summary of the whole book but lost interest midway through and abandoned the project after the second chapter of book 3. Thanks to Yamamoto, who was working as editor of a periodical, *Kyōiku Jiron* [Education Times], Nishida published his summary, "Gurīnshi rinri tetsugaku no taii" [The gist of Mr. Green's moral philosophy][13] in three installments in May 1895.[14]

In 1895 Nishida was hired as head teacher of the newly founded branch campus of the Ishikawa Prefecture Ordinary Middle School and assumed his duties as of April 1, with a monthly salary of forty-five yen, a standard sum for a starting teacher. He had five colleagues assisting him. The branch campus was located in Nanao, a scenic port town on the eastern coast of the Noto Peninsula, about sixty kilometers northeast of Kanazawa. It was part of his job description to recruit students to attend the school; therefore, he walked miles and miles (the sole means of transportation in the countryside in those days was one's legs), visiting little towns and villages to arouse the interest of prospective students. He was moderately successful in this effort. As head teacher, he was also required to give lectures to local educators whenever an occasion arose.

On April 29, 1895, however, the school building burned down in a fire that razed the town of Nanao; the authorities moved the school to a local Buddhist temple, and the dormitory and the administrative office to another local temple, and the classes resumed on May 6. This did not dampen Nishida's spirits, for the people of Nanao showed their sympathy and extended their utmost support to the school.

Nishida was young, motivated, and idealistic. He taught ethics, English, and history. Teaching ethics to the teenagers especially presented him with the question "how to teach." Nishida consulted Yamamoto, who was finishing his studies in pedagogy at the university:

> I find that it is useless to discuss ethical theories in the beginning. Do you happen to know of any good reference book? I wonder how Shōin[15] and Tōko[16] raised those able men. Don't you think the biography of Professor Niijima [Jō][17] is a good book for the students to read? For an effective education of boys that builds their characters, it

might be better to look into the regulations of the private schools of the past than to rely on the theories of the self-fashioned "educators" of today, might it not? Is there any book of this kind?[18]

Nishida felt that the middle school boys, ages twelve to fifteen, were too young for him to exert any significant influence on the formation of their characters. Although intellectually underchallenged, Nishida found teaching at a middle school fairly congenial. Now that his prospects looked decent, he decided to get married. In May 1895 he married Tokuda Kotomi, his maternal cousin.[19] Nishida was twenty-five years old; Kotomi had just turned twenty. Nishida and Kotomi had grown up knowing each other, and Kotomi, ever since she became conscious of Nishida, harbored romantic feelings toward him, an attraction strengthened by her great respect for him. When she was a child, she used to chase Nishida and beg him to help her read books like *The Tale of Genji*. In the summer of 1893 they had become engaged, and Kotomi accompanied Tosa to Tokyo in September, staying in the house for a few weeks to help Tosa. Kotomi's father was Tokuda Tagayasu, a painter, who was instrumental in introducing young Nishida to Hōjō Tokiyuki. Kotomi, daughter of an artist, had a fine eye for things beautiful. She later took pleasure, for instance, in selecting exquisite *kimono* materials for her daughters. The newlywed couple lived in rented rooms of a small temple, Daijōji, located in the outskirts of the town of Nanao, and lived a life of sweet intimacy. Kotomi soon became pregnant.

In August Nishida got together with Yamamoto and Fujioka, both of whom had returned to Kanazawa for the summer. Fujioka was moving to Osaka to teach at the Prefecture First Middle School. Yamamoto, having graduated from the university, was moving to Kyoto to teach at the Kyoto Prefecture Ordinary Middle School. Seeing his old friends uplifted Nishida's spirits, and he was inspired to write a book on ethics.[20] Such a book, he thought, would get him a decent teaching position in Tokyo, where he could pursue further studies. He began working on the history of ethics as soon as he returned to Nanao. He reported to Yamamoto: "I want to finish the 'History of Ethics' by next summer. I plan to include famous works of the Greek period, the Middle Ages, and German philosophers as well; I also intend to add my criticism of Sidgwick."[21] Yamamoto was critical of Nishida for working on a book on the side, for it seemed to him that Nishida was neglecting his school duties. Although Nishida welcomed Yamamoto's criticism, he pointed out the possibility of doing two things at the same time: "When I am at school, I exert myself for the school, and at home, I exert myself in my studies."[22] In fact, Nishida gave much thought to the philosophy of education; he was intent on nurturing and fostering students' independent thinking. Rather than distilling polite manners into the boys, Nishida felt it more important to raise young men of mettle and action. He subscribed to the motto: "Men must be prepared to die heroically, avoiding a lazy life of dull mediocrity."[23] This was thinking that he inherited from Hōjō and that was shared by Nishida's friends.

In November 1895 politicians who had a negative sentiment toward Kashima County, where Nanao was, voted in the Ishikawa Prefecture Assembly to close down the Nanao campus. This period of uncertainty for the schools in the prefecture was aggravated by the abrupt resignation of the principal of the Ishikawa Ordinary Middle School, Tomita Teruzō,[24] who then moved to Kyoto.[25] Nishida felt that the poor performance of students and the sorry state of the main campus was a reflection of the attitude of those who held the top positions: "The principal lacking caliber, how can he choose appropriate instructors? The main campus today is nothing but a boxful of rubbish, not even worth three pennies. Education in Ishikawa Prefecture has gone down the drain."[26] He felt that the only hope for improving education in Ishikawa Prefecture was to "organize a *sacred* board of education by gathering well-established senior Ishikawaites, . . . we, who are committed to education, must actively negotiate with the central government."[27] By June 1896 Nishida found a new position as an instructor of German at his alma mater, the Fourth Higher School, thanks to Ueda Seiji's intervention. Although German was a subject he did not feel comfortable teaching, he had no other choice.

A baby girl was born to Nishida and Kotomi on March 25, shortly before Nishida was to move to Kanazawa. It was a rather difficult birth. They named her Yayoi, a classical word for the month of March. The arrival of a new life had jolted Nishida. He confessed to Yamamoto:

> In your letter of the other day, you were wondering whether to remain free like a cloud-piercing phoenix that flies millions of miles or to choose a "peaceful life." I am sorry that I have chosen "family life." I sincerely hope that you won't fall into this "devil's den." . . .
>
> I became father to a baby girl on the 25th of this month and am bound to a secular life. I fear my energy may dissipate. When I go to Kanazawa, I'm thinking of going to Zen master Setsumon to listen to his talks.[28]

Nishida left for Kanazawa alone on April 3; about a month later Kotomi moved with the baby to Kanazawa and joined him in a rented house in Koshōmachi.[29]

Nishida's turn to Zen practice appears to be directly linked with the birth of Yayoi. Besides, Suzuki Daisetz had been encouraging him and Yamamoto to take up Zen practice. Suzuki wrote to Yamamoto:

> Words and actions of those who have mastered Zen strike me as having some unconventional quality, marked by freedom. . . . It is remarkable that Zen teaching actually sheds light on philosophical problems and that it profoundly influences my own actions. It might benefit Nishida a bit, if he takes it up.[30]

Suzuki was making progress in his practice and attained the initial awakening, *kenshō*, in the December 1895 *sesshin* (an intensive Zen practice). Nishida was not totally unfamiliar with Zen because Hōjō practiced Zen[31] and had organized a *zazen* group for students at Senmon Gakkō inviting Zen masters to the school to talk to the group. He also had Hakuin's *Orategama* printed for those who were interested in Zen.[32] Nishida had a copy that Hōjō had given him.[33]

Nishida had also learned a little about Master Setsumon. Setsumon Genshō was an unusual Zen master. Although born as the oldest son of a prosperous merchant family of Michizu in Wakayama, in his teens he set his mind on becoming a Zen monk. In his early twenties, he was trained by Master Dokuon[34] of Shōkokuji and had received the *inka* (authentication of enlightenment) from him. In his early thirties, he decided to go to Qing China for further training. Dokuon told him to look into the current state of Chan (Zen) Buddhism in China, because he shared with the Japanese Zen community the impression that the Chan practice had pretty much died out after the Ming dynasty. Setsumon stayed in China for three years, where, contrary to Dokuon's impression, he saw with his own eyes that the monastic Chan was still very much alive. Chinese Chan practice was much freer in its institutional form (there were no sects), practice (which combined *nienfo*, recitation of the holy name of Amida Buddha, and meditation), and in the daily lives of the monks (who kept to the precepts of celibacy; even eminent monks were simply clad and had an easy air about them). He also saw the strong lay support for the monasteries.[35]

When Setsumon returned to Japan, Dokuon appointed him abbot of Kokutaiji in Toyama, which, at that time, was in financial ruin. The temple buildings and imperial mausoleums, entrusted to the care of the temple, were run down. It was here, however, that Setsumon put his learnings of Chinese Chan into practice. He simplified his daily life and stuck to austere monastic rules; he organized strong lay support groups, "senshinkai" (pure mind group), in Toyama, Takaoka, Kanazawa, and Fushiki, and trained lay followers as well. Yamaoka Tesshū,[36] an accomplished calligrapher, swordsman, statesman, and a Zen master, was so impressed by Setsumon that he praised him as "the master of monastic rules [*vinaya*]." Tesshū energetically contributed to improving the temple's financial situation by drawing calligraphy pieces and donating them for sale. Setsumon's fame spread throughout the Hokuriku region, and wealthy donors revitalized the temple's economy.

In the early summer of 1893, on the occasion of the commemoration of the founding of Kokutaiji, Setsumon organized a "Hekigane," a celebration of the *Blue Cliff Record*. He invited Dokuon to head the ceremony and asked master teachers *(shike)*[37] from Shōkokuji, Tenryūji, Daitokuji, and Myōshinji to attend the ceremony. At the close of the successful celebration, Setsumon abruptly announced his resignation from the abbacy. He felt that he had done enough for the rehabilitation of the temple and that the time was ripe for him to "go down the mountain." Setsumon lived according to the Zen spirit of "dwelling in no fixed abode"[38]—the embodiment of nonattachment. On the day of his abdication, he left the temple and moved into Senshin'an, a small meditation center he had developed at the foot of Utatsu Hill in Kanazawa. He began his career as the teacher of lay Zen followers, *koji.*

Nishida was fortunate to have Setsumon freely available in Kanazawa. Following his move to Kanazawa in April 1896, he began to visit Senshin'an. Initially, he attended *teishō* (Zen master's talks) and also did some *zazen* (sitting meditation). By December 1896 he grew serious about his Zen practice. Wishing to participate in the winter *sesshin*, he went in vain to Kyoto to see Master Tekisui at Tenryūji.[39] Regarding Nishida's disappointment, Suzuki wrote to Yamamoto: "Nishida left Kyoto after a brief stay. It is too bad that he could not realize his wish this time. But he will certainly stick to his determination come this summer."[40]

Nishida began keeping his diary in 1897 (Meiji 30), perhaps out of practicing "mindfulness." He wrote a letter to Master Tekisui on February 1, 1897,[41] asking some questions. Five days later, he received a reply from Tekisui:

Venerable Tokusan said: "I have no words to say and no teaching to impart."
Mu (Nothing)!
This old monk has nothing else to tell you but that. Henceforth, I beg no more communication with you by way of letters.

February 4, signed Tekisui. [42]

Nishida treasured this letter; he later had it mounted and gave it to Hisamatsu Shin'ichi, one of his earliest students at Kyoto Imperial University.[43]

The year 1897 turned out to be eventful for Nishida and his friends. On February 3 Fukushima Junkichi died of consumption. A few days later, Daisetz left Japan for the United States to work for Paul Carus in LaSalle, Illinois. In April Yamamoto moved from Kyoto to Shizuoka as professor at the Prefecture Ordinary Middle School. Fujioka was promoted to the professor at the Third Higher School in Kyoto. While Nishida was occupied with school-related duties and was gradually becoming serious about Zen practice, he also pursued his philosophical studies and wrote a three-part essay on the existence of a priori knowledge. It was published in the school journal, *Hokushinkai Zasshi*.[44] But soon, misfortunes were to befall him. On May 9 his wife Kotomi took Yayoi and ran away from home without leaving any word.[45] To cull from Nishida's diary:

May 9 (Sunday) Kotomi left us for no reason; everyone kept vigil through the night.

May 10 (Monday) No news of Kotomi and Yayoi; didn't go to school.

May 11 (Tuesday) A letter came from the Tokudas in Urushijima [in Mattōchō]; Kotomi is at their place; went to school.

May 13 (Thursday) Kotomi returned home; father grew irate over this matter.

May 14 (Friday) Father expelled Kotomi from my house.

May 16 (Sunday) Tokuda [Tagayasu] came, spoke with father.

May 24 (Monday) Our marital separation.

It appears that Kotomi, barely twenty-two years old, was under enormous pressure. For one thing, she did not know how to deal with the strained relationship between Nishida and his father, Yasunori. Besides, the money Nishida gave her to run the household expenses was barely sufficient because Nishida was in the habit of spending money on books from Europe, or so it was rumored. Kotomi must have felt helpless and threw herself upon the mercy of her parents. Yasunori, unable to understand Kotomi's psychological state, was outraged over her behavior and expelled her from his son's house. This incident ended in the young couple's separation by parental decree. Although such an incident is unthinkable nowadays, in those days the head of the family (in this case, Yasunori) exercised absolute authority in family matters. Nishida and Kotomi were separated despite their mutual affection, and Kotomi had to go back to her parents.

Lightning struck twice. On May 31 Nishida was suddenly discharged from his teaching position at the Fourth Higher School as part of a "reorganization of the teaching staff." The school had been embroiled in a factional conflict for some time, with faculty members siding with the principal or against him.[46] A group of professors publicly denounced the policies of the principal, and this conflict became a national scandal and debated at the Diet (Japanese parliament).[47] First, the principal, Ōshima Seiji, was let go in mid-March for having taken no decisive action. In his place a high-ranking official from the Ministry of Education, Kawakami Hikoji, was appointed.[48]

Much to their dismay, Nishida and Tokunō Bun were implicated in this incident and summarily let go. Two professors of German, Ueda Seiji and Tokunaga Tomi, who quarreled constantly, were also let go at this time.[49] Nishida did not know of his dismissal until the very day of its announcement. In fact, the day before the official announcement, he and Tokunō went to welcome Ōshima Yoshinaga,[50] his former classmate from the Imperial University, who had been assigned a position at the Fourth Higher School. When Nishida asked Ōshima why he had come to Kanazawa, his friend hesitated and said: "I just can't tell you right now." Nishida many years later recalled: "It must have been an awkward situation for Ōshima, for I did not know that I was one of those who were to be let go in a few days and that he had come to fill one of the positions that we would be vacating."[51]

Within two weeks not only was he separated from his wife and daughter but he had also lost his means of livelihood. The combined shock was enough to make Nishida sick; he was flat in bed for a couple of days. This disaster, however, turned out to have a silver lining. Tokunō Bun[52] and Ueda Seiji[53] obtained teaching positions in Tokyo, and they were able to help Nishida land a position at Gakushūin in 1909. In any case, right after his dismissal Nishida wrote to Hōjō, explaining what had happened. Hōjō had been principal of the Yamaguchi Prefecture Higher School since 1896.

Amid the uncertainty about his future employment, Nishida left for Kyoto to attend the *sesshin* at Myōshinji, according to the resolution he had made the previous winter. For the first few days of his stay in Kyoto he stayed with Fujioka Sakutarō. On June 26, two days after his audience with Master Kokan,[54] he moved into Taizōin, one of the subtemples *(tacchū)* of Myōshinji. Master Kokan was known for his fierce training of disciples, as his name, "tiger-barrier," suggests. Nishida took an immediate liking to him. The first *sesshin* took place from July 1 to 7. He stayed on at Taizōin to attend another *sesshin* from August 6 to 12. During the second *sesshin* he heard from Hōjō, who informed him that a one-year position teaching German had become available. Ironically, this position had opened up as Kusaka Chōjiro was moving from Yamaguchi to the Fourth Higher School to fill one of the positions vacated by Nishida's colleagues. Nishida took the one-year position.

After completing his first full-scale intensive Zen practice, Nishida returned to Kanazawa on August 20. What comforted him was that Kotomi was allowed to return to his house on August 24; Yasunori's wrath had abated, but he had not lifted his decree of the separation of his son and daughter-in-law. The two "unofficially" resumed life as husband and wife, and during that short period of reunion she conceived their second child. The job in Yamaguchi came through officially on August 28, and Nishida left Kanazawa on September 2. Because his position was temporary, he decided to move to Yamaguchi alone. He traveled up to Kyoto with Fujioka, who had been visiting Kanazawa. After spending a few days in Kyoto, he took a train to Hiroshima, then a boat to Mitajiri (today's Bōsu), and from there traveled on land by horse-drawn carriage to Yamaguchi. Upon arriving in Yamaguchi on September 7, he immediately went to see Hōjō[55] to thank him for his unfailing support. The school term began on September 11.[56]

Yamaguchi is a town on the southwestern end of the main island of Japan. Nishida, describing it to a relative in Kanazawa, wrote: "It is small, comparable to Daishōji in size. It is surrounded by hills; a nondescript place."[57] He was at first upset about having to come to what felt like the end of the earth; besides, he missed his family terribly. It took him some time before he could appreciate the physical beauty of the place. The relative isolation prompted Nishida to turn inward and engage in self-questioning. The effect of the intensive Zen practice he had undertaken in Kyoto was still fresh in his mind. Freed from immediate family obligations and routines, he relived the carefree life of a bachelor, devoting his entire self to what he wanted to do. The question of his own spirituality and religion began to occupy him. His diary of October 4 reads: "This evening visited the Hōjōs. We talked about religion."[58] Self-examination and meditation were changing his outlook on the world around and within him. A quiet self-transformation was set in motion. He wrote to Yamamoto on November 11:

> When I first came to Yamaguchi, whatever I saw disgusted me. But I carefully practiced self-examination and reflected on the situation I was in and attained some peace of mind. I realized that things I was dissatisfied with were actually reflections of my base mind and felt ashamed of myself. I was deeply moved by the line in Matthew 6: "Which of you by taking thought can add one cubit to his stature?" So long as I keep this in mind, no complaint should arise. . . .
>
> Just recently, I felt a little relieved when I heard that the God of Matthew 6 nurtures even birds that neither sow, harvest, nor store.[59] As you know, the Bible really consoles me. I cannot help thinking that its teaching is one notch above that of the *Analects*. What's your opinion on this matter?[60]

Nishida was quick to respond to the lively presence of Christianity in Yamaguchi, where the history of Christianity went back to the time of Francis Xavier, the first Christian missionary to set foot on the Japanese soil, in 1549.[61] The warlord Ōuchi Yoshitaka gave Xavier permission to proselytize in his domain and gave him a decrepit Buddhist temple, Daidōji, to use as his church. In 1893, four years before Nishida's arrival in Yamaguchi, a French Catholic priest, Amatus Villion, who had read about Daidōji, found its original site after he saw an old map of the town;[62] the excitement was still lingering in the air. (Nishida's rented house in Komeyachō was only a few blocks away from the temporary chapel Villion had erected before leaving for his new assigned post in Hagi.)

Just as Nishida found solace in passages from the Bible, his interest in Zen became more focused. During the 1897–1898 winter break, he traveled to Kyoto and took part in the New Year *sesshin* at Myōshinji. In the inner cover of his 1898 diary he copied several passages of Zen sayings and anecdotes, one of them from *Zenkan sakushin*[63] [Negotiating Zen barriers], the episode of "Master Jimyō's taking the drill and piercing his thigh." Jimyō ("Ciming" in Chinese), determined to overcome mediocrity, practiced hard, and whenever he became sleepy during *zazen*, he pierced his thigh with a drill to stay awake. Nishida was especially aroused by Jimyō's words: "Although I was born a human, I am wasting my life, and I will die an unknown death. What is the worth of such an existence?"

In 1898 he began the new year with a private interview (*dokusan*) with Master Kokan.[64] Nishida was plagued with some deep-seated doubt about whether he would attain any breakthrough in his Zen practice. He thought about Suzuki, who attained his *kenshō* (initial awakening or a Zen breakthrough) after five years of practice, and he gained some encouragement from Suzuki's example.

Nishida took a few extra days in Kyoto, thus missing the school ceremony that marked the beginning of the new term. Hōjō was displeased with this behavior and rebuked him severely.[65] Nishida had to learn to be ever mindful. Because he was living alone in his rented house, he began to do *zazen* at home. Meanwhile, Hōjō was appointed principal of the Fourth Higher School on February 4, succeeding Kawakami Hikoji.[66] This news came as a disappointment to Nishida, who was rebuilding his sense of "home" with Hōjō around. He called on Hōjō on February 23, a few days before his former teacher's departure, to speak about his future plan's for which Hōjō expressed his support.[67] It would appear that Nishida told him that he was interested in pursuing the path of scholarship. The Hōjōs left Yamaguchi on Sunday, February 27.

In Yamaguchi Nishida attended an April *sesshin*, possibly at a local Zen temple, together with his colleagues who practiced Zen. The group included Inaba Masamaru,[68] a close friend of Kiyozawa Manshi, and Mitake Kingorō, who was practicing Zen under Master Tekisui Giboki.[69] Nishida especially trusted Inaba, whose appearance—a "flawless warm gentleman"—belied his firm will. Around that time, Yamamoto Annosuke,[70] two years junior to Nishida in the philosophy department at Imperial University, published in three installments an essay entitled "Shūkyō to risei" [Religion and reason] in the February, March, and May issues of *Mujintō*, a journal published by the Ōtani sect of Shin Buddhism. Nishida wrote a critique of Yamamoto's article, "Yamamoto Annosuke-kun no 'Shūkyō to risei' to iu ronbun o yomite shokan o nobu" [My reaction to Mr. Yamamoto Annosuke's "Religion and reason"],[71] which appeared in the June issue of *Mujintō*. Nishida felt that Yamamoto had left out the experiential content of religion, which for him was essential.

It is striking that Nishida's description of religion in this essay already delineated the view of God that he would unfold in 1945 in his final essay, "The Logic of *Topos* and the Religious Worldview," especially concerning the radical interrelationship between the finite (i.e., humanity) and the infinite (i.e., God). His essential understanding of what religion is was already shaped by this time. We read:

> There is no infinite separate from the finite; there is no absolute separate from the relative; there is no transcendent God outside this universe. Nay, the infinite that rejects the finite is but a finite, the absolute that takes its leave from the relative is contrariwise a relative, and the transcendent God that exists outside the universe is not an omniscient God. The real infinite is within the finite, the real absolute is in the relative, and the real omniscient God is in this reality.[72]

In June 1898 a son, Ken, was born to Nishida and Kotomi. Later in the summer Nishida went to Kyoto to take part in the summer *sesshin* at Myōshinji. Then, in September, Yasunori fell critically ill, and Nishida went back to Kanazawa for a fortnight.[73] Yasunori died of pneumonia on October 9 at the age of sixty-five. He and Yasunori had come a long way, but not to the point of mutual reconciliation. Yasunori died without lifting the marital separation he had imposed on his son.

Nishida welcomed the New Year in 1899 by attending the *sesshin* in Kyoto. In early February, the long-standing marital separation was formally ended thanks to the effort of Tosa and the Tokudas. A heavy psychological burden was lifted from his mind. Paradoxically, it was during this period of separation from his wife and children that he was growing into a family man, more mature and more understanding. Around this time his self-examination became sharper, as well. His diary of February 23 reads:

> Rain. Got up early and did *zazen*. I was often disturbed by the thought that I should be pursuing my study. I must admonish myself, remembering the episode of Tokusan. By the evening, although my willpower was weakened and I felt sluggish, I took a renewed look at myself and sat . . . . I should not read books hurriedly. If I carry out my studies by concentrating on what appears to be important to me, that should be enough.[74]

The episode of Tokusan (Deshan in Chinese) to which Nishida referred was a poignant reminder to him; it pointed out the discrepancy between studying about the Buddhist doctrines and actually living and practicing them. The story goes that Deshan, a scholar-monk, was well versed in the *Diamond Sutra*, on which he wrote a commentary. He proudly carried his commentary and came to a mountain pass where there was a tea hut. He dropped in to buy a snack. The proprietor was an old woman, who asked Deshan: "You say, 'refreshment' (*dianxin*). Now the *Diamond Sutra* says: 'Past mind (*xin*) can't be grasped, present mind can't be grasped, future mind can't be grasped.' Which mind does the learned monk desire to refresh?" Deshan was taken aback, unable to find a word, so the old woman sent him to Zen master Longtan (Ryōtan in Japanese). Upon his interaction with the master, Deshan realized that his learning was of no use, burnt his commentary then and there, and henceforth applied himself to Zen practice.[75]

Nishida not only dedicated himself to Zen practice but also cultivated his friendships in his own peculiar way. Living alone, he sought the warmth of company. He liked many of his colleagues and saw them after school on a daily basis. He often went on hiking and sight-seeing trips with his colleagues to waterfalls and hills; they occasionally convened at hot springs and took some other expeditions as well. These colleagues included Tobari Shinichirō (*gō*, Chikufū), a specialist in Nietzsche's thought,[76] and Togawa Akizō (*gō*, Shūkotsu), a professor of English literature who joined the faculty in the second year of Nishida's career in Yamaguchi. Togawa memorialized the Nishida of those days in an essay:

> Nishida would come to my house and call my name aloud from outside: "Togawa, are you home?" I would answer yes, and no sooner would I open the *shōji* screen door than Nishida would walk right in without any greeting. He would sit facing me and sip tea, without uttering a word. Ten, twenty minutes would pass in this way. Then he would say, "How about a walk?" I would respond, "Yes, let's," and we would head for a hill in the vicinity. Sometimes he would take a nap on the hilltop. Not knowing what to do, I would just hang around. When he awakened, no word of apology came from his lips, just a simple "Let's go back." Nishida, as usual, would not speak the whole way down the hill.[77]

Nishida was to some a quiet colleague, always thinking about something, wearing a half-tormented expression, so much so that one of his colleagues, Alfred Charlton, an Englishman who taught English, nicknamed him "Are You Happy?"

On May 20, 1899, Nishida was promoted to professor at Yamaguchi Higher School. At that time he was given a court rank of seventh junior, the lowest entering rank.[78] Such an entitlement insured professors of higher education a certain minimum salary as those who rendered significant service to the country. Hōjō Tokiyuki, then the fifth principal of the Fourth Higher School,[79] called Nishida to return to Kanazawa in June 1899. Now that his marriage had been restored, there was no longer any reason to be away from Kanazawa. He wholeheartedly accepted Hōjō's offer and left Yamaguchi on July 8. From July 10 on, he was in Kyoto for the summer intensive Zen practice at Myōshinji. He was finding it difficult to sever his attachment to his studies and the prospect of fame. His diary of August 6 reads:

> Every day my mind is in disarray, and I repent. Don't seek gain. Don't seek fame. Don't seek academic pursuits. Don't seek to satisfy the desires of the senses. Simply be diligent in the pursuit of the Way.[80]

He attended the *sesshin* that started on August 8, resolving that "my determination will not retract; my faith will not crumble."[81] He stayed on at the temple for a while even after the *sesshin* had ended. On August 25 he left Kyoto and returned home to Kanazawa. It was good to see Kotomi, Yayoi (now a girl of three), and Ken, his first son, born the year before during his absence. Nishida found a house in Hyakushōmachi, and the family, united once again, moved in. After a two-year sojourn in Yamaguchi, Nishida returned home transformed, emotionally and spiritually.

In 1937, many years later, when a young theologian, Takizawa Katsumi, got a job in Yamaguchi, Nishida wrote to him, recalling his days in Yamaguchi:

> The place lacks external stimuli, unfortunately, but it is an ideal place for one to engage in quiet reading, thinking, and to cultivate one's self. I knew the Yamaguchi of forty years ago. I wonder how it is now. I cannot help feeling nostalgic.[82]

Chapter 5

Toward *Kenshō*

An Inner Journey

(1899–1904)

The Fourth Higher School Nishida returned to was being radically reformed under the leadership of Hōjō Tokiyuki. Student conduct had deteriorated since the founding days of the school when Nishida had been a student. After Japan's victory in its war with China (1894–1895), the higher school students had "softened" their moral values; many engaged in heavy drinking, and a few even commuted to school from the demimonde.[1] Hōjō believed that students were the future of Japan and that an educator's mission was to guide them properly. In 1898, to prepare the ground for school reform, he first brought his trusted colleagues, Hori Koretaka[2] (a professor of Japanese) from a middle school in Yamaguchi, and Mitake Kingorō from Yamaguchi Higher School. In the following year, he discharged a few professors who had set bad examples for the students. In their stead, he brought in Sugimori Korema, professor of English; Toda Kaiichi, professor of economics, geography, and law; Nakame Satoru, professor of German and French; Ibaraki Seijirō, professor of English; Tanabe Ryūji, professor of English and Nishida, professor of philosophy and German. Once the teaching staff was strengthened, Hōjō went about implementing his reform measures. He discouraged the prevalent practice of students' cutting classes; he set up a "temperance society" *(sesshukai);*[3] and he introduced a mentor system, in which each student was assigned to a faculty member so that personal ties could be formed between students and professors.[4]

At first, students reacted negatively to Hōjō's reform measures, which seemed to them too intrusive. A group of students even turned their feelings into action and assaulted Hōjō on the day of a school athletic meet.[5] On the following day, Hōjō called the culprits into his office and spoke to them in a calm voice:

Up until today, I have been constantly irritated by students, because everywhere I turned, I only saw gutless students worse than rotted women. But today at this school I discovered you young men, who are fearless and high spirited. I cannot help but feel greatly delighted. The only thing I wish for you is that henceforth you channel your fearlessness and high spiritedness into your academic studies and achieve good results. [6]

End of speech. Students, dumbfounded, were most impressed by Hōjō's magnanimity, and said to one another: "The new principal is a cool guy!" Thereafter they applied themselves assiduously to their studies and many became men of considerable achievements. [7] This incident probably took place a year before Nishida's arrival, but everyone knew about it.

When classes began on September 11, Nishida quickly became immersed in school-related activities. He taught logic and German that year. School duties, on top of his family responsibilities, kept him busy. In his September 15 letter to Yamamoto, he describes the difficulty of pursuing Zen practice amid so many responsibilities, but he tried to stick to his routine of doing *zazen* both morning and evening.

I'm ashamed that I have made very little progress in my Zen practice. Although I want to, it is really hard to practice Zen when I have a job in the outside world and a wife and children at home. But from what I understand, if one continues to practice even an hour or half an hour daily with total concentration, and if one maintains this mental intensity of concentration at all times, the process of practice gradually "ripens." I also understand that it is the worst thing to stop practicing for even a day. . . . Fortunately, Master Setsumon is available at Utatsu Hill. When things settle down a bit, I intend to muster my courage and resume my practice with him. Lately, I keenly feel that nothing is more important than the salvation of my soul *(kokoro no sukui)*, so much so that even if I were to give many years to the practice of Zen without any concrete result, it is still the only thing I would like to pursue in my life. . . .

A man of old said that he who seeks the Way does not mind devoting his entire body and life to that pursuit. When even I don't know my "true self," how could my wife and children stand in the way of my practice to find my true self? I think there was a passage in the Bible in which Christ said, I didn't come to bring about peace but to break the ties between parents and children. [8] Certainly, this is something I cannot possibly grasp, nor is it something I should mention lightly, but I wonder whether this is the kind of resolution that those who practice the Way must possess. Whatever I do is with tears. Nothing seems to go easily, and I now realize what kind of hardship Daisetz had to go through.[9]

Nishida tried his best to focus on his Zen practice by reading books such as the *Orategama* and by regularly attending *zazen* and *teishō* periods at Senshin'an. Setsumon's only brother died, however, and the headship of the Michizu family fell on Setsumon. He had to renounce monkhood to tend to his family business in Wakayama and Tokyo. Despite this change in circumstances, he kept Senshin'an open and gave *sanzen* to his students whenever possible. Setsumon was more than just a Zen master, which brought him closer to Nishida and his colleagues, Ishikawa Ryūzō[10] and Mitake Kingorō, who were also practicing Zen under Setsumon.

From October 18 to 20, 1899, Prime Minister Itō Hirobumi, touring the Hokuriku region, was in Kanazawa. He came and gave a speech at the Fourth Higher School on October 19. Before Itō's arrival, Hōjō had sent him a personal letter, for Itō was famous for his lavish nightly parties filled with geisha entertainment, sake, and fine food.[11] Hōjō requested, firmly and yet in a roundabout way, that the prime minister refrain from his usual nightly entertainment, suggesting to Itō that such behavior was a singularly bad example for the higher school students. Itō, in awe of Hōjō's fierce commitment to education, "behaved himself while in Kanazawa."[12]

Such was the general atmosphere of the Fourth Higher School under Hōjō's leadership. In addition to his duties as principal, Hōjō taught more than twenty-five hours a week to make up for the work of instructors whose abilities were deemed substandard. Naturally, other professors were mobilized and devoted a considerable amount of time and energy to the school. In this kind of atmosphere, Nishida volunteered to give a talk on "philosophy and everyday life" and advised students to "read Confucius and Mencius; read great works of such thinkers as Carlyle, Emerson, and Goethe; ponder on the idea that there is truth different from scientific truths; and cultivate your philosophical and spiritual self-awareness."[13] As the school went into the winter recess, he found some time to sit down and write to Yamamoto:

Concerning Zen [practice], I cannot say much to you. Please consult Daisetz on this matter. What path are you going to follow to arrive at what you call "unity of thought?" For me Zen is the shortest path. But even with this shortest path, I still cannot attain that unity. However, it would be useless for me to turn elsewhere. So regardless of whether I attain awakening or not, I intend to continue practicing Zen for the rest of my life.[14]

The year 1900 turned out to be an eventful one for many of Nishida's closest friends: Yamamoto was offered the position of vice principal at the newly founded Kyoto Prefecture Second Middle School and moved from Shizuoka to Kyoto in April. Fujioka was appointed as assistant professor of Japanese at the Imperial University of Tokyo and moved from Kyoto to Tokyo in September. Matsumoto Bunzaburō was then at the University of Berlin, reading Vedic Sanskrit with Albrecht Weber.[15] On a wider horizon, Kiyozawa Manshi and his disciples established their "commune," Kōkōdō, in Tokyo and were launching their monthly journal, *Seishinkai* [Spiritual World]. The year 1900 was also eventful in the philosophical world: Ōnishi Hajime,[16] Toyama Masakazu, Nietzsche, Max Müller, and Sidgwick all died in that year.

For Nishida, however, it was quite an uneventful year. In March, however, his essay "Bi no setsumei" [An explanation of the beautiful],[17] was published in the school journal.[18] In it he argued that what evoked the sensation of the beautiful was no different from the sensation of egolessness *(muga)*—clearly revealing the process and the content of his Zen meditation. His short biographical sketch on Spinoza was carried in the November issue of the same school journal.[19] He was also involved in founding Sansanjuku, a private dormitory for the students. Although the atmosphere among students was still rebellious and combative, by the fall of 1900 a group of concerned students had begun to take part in the principal's reform movement. At the beginning of the fall term, a student in the medical division, Arima Shōzaburō, and a student of the law, Enoto Rikichi, approached Hōjō and asked for school assistance in setting up a *juku*, a privately run dormitory.

On October 5, Hōjō invited Mitake, Nishida, and Hori to his house for a dinner and brought up the students' request. Their discussion extended late into the night. Mitake, who was already running a private *juku* and had some experience, turned to Nishida and Hori and suggested that the three of them should assist the students. Nishida answered yes, and Hori agreed.[20] On November 3, 1900, the day of *Tenchōsetsu*—the birthday of Emperor Meiji and a holiday—the *juku* opened with Arima, Enoto, Fujita Toshihiko, and Moriya Hideaki as members. Nishida, Mitake, and Hori were present at the opening of the *juku*.

They first called the *juku* "Eijunji-juku" because they rented rooms from a Buddhist temple called Eijunji in Kodatsuno. But a year later they rented a house. Nishida mused on the significance of the thirty-third year of Meiji's corresponding to the year 1900 of the Gregorian calendar; he somewhat whimsically took the felicitous doubling of the number three, *"san,"* and named the *juku* "Sansan-juku" or "Three-three dorm," proclaiming to the world the year of its establishment.[21] The guiding spirit of the dormitory was to nurture meaningful friendships among the students. In Nishida's words:

> The reason I decided to be involved in setting up such a *juku* came from my own personal experience. It was in and through interactions with my friends when I was a higher school student that I gained a distinct sense of who I am, and the self-identity I gained then still forms the fundamental part of me to this day. . . . Thinking to myself whether I could be of any help to the students, I joined the project.[22]

Nishida, Mitake, Hori, and a few other professors, such as Sugimori Korema, Tanabe Ryūji, and Ishikawa Ryūzō, who agreed with the tenets of the *juku*, joined the students as their "older brothers."[23] Professors and students held a monthly get-together, when they played tennis, had dinner (the beef pot—sukiyaki—was the thing of the day!), and discussed all kinds of topics, ranging from the meaning of life to religion. On those days Nishida would typically return home past midnight. Students who chose to join Sansanjuku were serious and motivated and came from various academic backgrounds—law, medicine, natural sciences, and humanities. Although no professor spoke for one religion against another, the environment of the *juku* was spiritually supportive; some students became seriously interested in Christianity, while others took up Zen practice. Hōjō welcomed their interest in religion.

For the school year 1900–1901 Nishida taught German, logic, and a new subject, psychology. Teaching a new course meant he had to read up in the field, preparation that constituted an essential part of his own studies. For this reason, he eagerly sought to teach a variety of courses, especially in philosophy. Amidst demanding school-related duties, he also managed to concentrate on his Zen practice.

Nishida began 1901 at Senshin'an, where he paid homage to Master Setsumon and Bodhidharma. In his diary of January 6 he recorded Setsumon's words: "Zen practice is not a means to something else but an end in itself. The point of *sanzen*[24] consists in the very struggle of

doing it. . . . The end of *sanzen* is the attainment of release from life
and death *(shōji)*, and nothing else."[25]

Around this time Nishida intensified his criticism of his "acquisitive mind." On January 15, he wrote in his diary:

> A.M. school; P.M. reading and a walk; evening, reading and *zazen*.
> When I read a book, I feel hurried and skim through it. My desire for
> fame haunts me; my mind is not calm at all. I must take this fact seriously and reflect on it. It is my sordid mind that seeks achievements.
> How can I forget myself as Nishida and simply be devoid of false
> pretenses and be at ease?[26]

Similar introspective remarks are scattered throughout his diary during this period. He spent his days in constant self-scrutiny, sustained
by his Zen practice. He observed that if he felt hurried, it was because
his desire for fame ran ahead of him. He began to pay close attention
to the source of his disquietude, which in fact did not contribute to
solving any philosophical problem but exhausted his mind with unnecessary worries. It was painfully clear to him that his mind was "impure
and constantly agitated," and that he must overcome this.[27]

A new faculty member, Moriuchi Masaaki,[28] a graduate of the
Imperial University trained in philosophy, was to join the faculty in
April 1901. Nishida became concerned, fearing that his teaching
assignment in philosophy might be reduced. He spoke to Hōjō about
his concerns, and it was decided that Nishida would team-teach ethics
with Moriuchi to compensate for his reduced teaching load in the
other areas. Having put this worry behind him, he focused on what
gave him peace of mind *(jikoanjin)*. He reasoned that if he discarded
"the petty mind that covets fame" and resorted to what gave him
peace, it would be beneficial in terms of his pursuit of philosophical
studies. He wrote a reminder to himself on February 6: "I should pursue my thinking calmly, organize it, and bring it in tune with what
gives me peace."[29] On the following day, Fukuzawa Yukichi died.
Nishida's diary indicates the respect he felt for Fukuzawa: "He was a
man of independent mind and independent action. As I thought about
these qualities of his, and how he achieved things without depending
on others, I was inspired. That's the manly way!"[30]

On February 14, he heard from Suzuki Daisetz, who had been in
LaSalle, Illinois, since 1897.[31] Suzuki told Nishida that his "bodhisattva vow" to save all sentient beings constituted his peace of mind.
Nishida admired Suzuki's lofty resolution and reminded himself that
he must relentlessly examine himself and be mindful; he should main-

tain willpower to conquer his desires.[32] His constant self-reflection went hand in hand with his *zazen* practice. By this time he was single-mindedly committed to Zen practice and no longer looked to other religious paths, including Christianity.[33] He took part in the *sesshin* from February 24 to March 2 at Senshin'an. At this time Master Setsumon recognized the maturity of Nishida's Zen practice, and on March 17 he formally received him as his lay disciple *(koji)* and gave him the *koji* name, "Sunshin" (literally, "inch mind"). To Zen adepts, this name alludes to the Buddhist expression: "the entire universe is contained in one mustard seed"; that is, a physically small organ such as the heart (or mind) contains the vast universe. Setsumon knew well the acuity of his disciple's mind.

Zen practice was having a humanizing effect on Nishida, who had once regretted having become a family man, and who possibly turned to Zen out of his emotional confusion after the birth of his first child. Nishida now appreciated the importance of everyday life, here and now. The birth of his second son, Sotohiko, on February 4, had a grounding effect on Nishida, bringing his focus to the immediate task of boiling water and helping the midwife. Around this time, Nishida's younger brother, Hyōjirō became engaged and was soon to be married. Hyōjirō, who took after his father, was a bit of a lady's man and often reckless in his behavior. He had just fathered a daughter, Toki, out of wedlock. In addition, Hyōjirō had accumulated many debts, and settling them before the marriage was a matter of honor. Nishida loved his younger brother unconditionally and did everything to help clean up his brother's mess. He and Kotomi temporarily took custody of the newborn baby on March 15.[34] As far as he and Kotomi were concerned, raising two babies was not that different from raising one. Ishikawa Ryūzō helped Nishida clear up Hyōjirō's debts, and through this transaction Nishida and Ishikawa became good friends for life. With two newborn babies, Nishida's family had suddenly expanded. On March 25 he wrote in his diary:

> Under a dimly lit lamp, all the family members gathered and dined. The scene was inexpressibly charming. The utmost human happiness does not belong to "high places," nor does it exist in "natural scenery," but in "ordinary, everyday life" *(buji heijō)*. The moon was beautiful and bright. Took a walk at night.[35]

Nishida's Zen practice was entering a new phase. During his spring practice, he confessed to Setsumon his innermost shameful secrets and threw himself to the practice.[36] Despite his commitment, however, he felt he was making little progress. His diary for May 13 reads: "It has been several years since I began Zen practice. For each step forward, I make one step backward. I have gotten nowhere. I am terribly ashamed of myself."[37] Despite his moments of doubt, his concentrated effort began to bear fruit. He was starting to break away from his attachment to fame. As the place of scholarship in a larger perspective of life became clearer, he began to see that it was philosophy that he really wanted to pursue for the rest of his life. He felt that his calling was to become a thinker, not a man of religion. The question was how to unite scholarship and Zen practice.

After school on May 28, he was invited to the Hōjōs' home for dinner, and they talked about serious matters. Hōjō asked Nishida what he wanted to do with his life. He answered spontaneously: "I would like to pursue my studies."[38] Through his practice of Zen, Nishida was beginning to sense the possibility of carrying out a philosophical inquiry in a wholly different manner, that is, from the vantage point of the "real self." He wrote to Yamamoto about his sense of a new direction:

> I am so utterly absorbed in the question of my own spirituality that I do not have enough strength right now to break away from it and use my energy on other matters. As I thought about it late last night, the noise and clamor that university graduates and professors are making seem somewhat childish and silly.[39] There must be some spiritual reality, totally separate from prosaic scholarship and morality, one which is so solid that however much one beats it or pulls at it with whatever kind of skepticism, it won't budge.[40]

In 1901 Nishida did not go to Kyoto during the summer because Master Kokan suffered a heart attack and the doctor forbade him to give any more *sanzen*.[41] For the summer *sesshin* he went to a temple in Mikawa with his Zen friends, Mitake, Ishikawa, and a student from Sansanjuku, Ōsaka Motokichirō.[42] After participating in the *sesshin* from August 1 to 7, he sat at Senshin'an for the month of August.

Starting with the fall term, Nishida and Sugimori were assigned by Hōjō to the position of dormitory masters of Jishūryō. This school dormitory, established in October 1893, had been the center of the students' moral life. The dormitory masters were entrusted with the heavy responsibility of overseeing the lives of the students. As part of this assignment, Nishida was required to stay overnight on Saturday at the dormitory until Sunday noon. He did not like being cooped up indoors and missed his walk. But students loved having him around.

They often held "tea conversation gatherings," where Nishida led a discussion on books he had just read. It was during this time that he avidly read autobiographies and biographies, which he quite enjoyed.[43]

Students adored Nishida, although not without a sense of awe, and gave him a nickname: *Denken-sensei*, "Professor, the thinker."[44] Shimizu, a student in those days, recalls:

> Professor Nishida wore his hair closely cropped, put his hands between his vest and trousers, and appeared to be always engaged in thinking. He might have created the basis of his philosophy in this way. If a student, asked to answer his question during the class, said "I don't remember," Professor Nishida would say, "Keep on standing until you recall the answer." Yes, unreasonable. But in reality he was a very kind-hearted man, and students often went to his home for a visit. A bowlful of sweets would be served as an accompaniment to tea. It was established knowledge among us students that if we behaved politely, the professor would eat up all the sweets, so as soon as the sweets were served, we must eat them![45]

With the addition of his new responsibility as a dormitory master, Nishida spent an extremely busy September. For this year he was assigned to teach ethics, logic, psychology, German, and English. His university training must have come in handy in teaching so many varied courses. Once things simmered down a bit, he resumed his meditation. His single-minded commitment to Zen practice reached such heights that his diary for October 16 reads: "Pray, pray, by discarding everything—fame, profit and scholarship." On November 1 he wrote an essay, "Genkon no shūkyō ni tsuite" [On today's religions],[46] in which he noted the rising interest in religion in recent years in Japan after a period of antireligious sentiment that prevailed with the importation of Western sciences and rationalism. In this essay, against scholars who advocated the need for a new religion, he argued for the rejuvenation of traditional religions. He was critical, however, of the current state of Buddhism and Christianity. He felt that Buddhist monks and Christian missionaries, learned though they might be, had no power to move people because they had separated religious practice from their own lives. He had this to say to the Buddhist clerics: "Instead of studying Sanskrit, philosophy, and so forth, examine yourselves first and see whether you can give your lives to the practice and the dissemination of the Buddha's teaching"; and to the Christian missionaries: "Instead of studying theology, first examine yourselves to see whether your daily conduct and thoughts are in accordance with the true spirit of Jesus Christ."[47] In Nishida's view, religion entailed unity of faith and practice.

Nishida moved into Senshin'an on December 25, 1901, to welcome the New Year by doing *zazen*. His Zen practice began to mature in 1902. He was sympathetic to the reform movement of the True Pure Land Sect, led by Kiyozawa Manshi. In 1901 Kiyozawa and his followers inaugurated a monthly journal, *Seishinkai* [A Spiritual World], that drew much attention. Nishida was moved by Kiyozawa's essay, "Meimonsha no an'i" [Consolations for the lost],[48] in which Kiyozawa confessed that religion was necessary only for those who were lost, because "religion" essentially consisted of finite human beings meeting the infinite and thereby gaining a sense of wholeness. Nishida found Kiyozawa's relentless inner reflection consoling. Around this time, he himself was gradually sorting out the place of scholarly pursuits within life. On January 20 he wrote several reminders on the back cover of his diary. One of them reads:

> By sanzen *I inquire into the Great Way,*
> By scholarship, *I clarify the truth.*
> *I take the Way as my body, and*
> *Scholarship as my four limbs.*[49]

His diary for February 24 reads: "In the end, scholarship is meaningful only when carried out for the sake of life. Life is of the utmost importance. Scholarship without recourse to life is useless. Don't read books with a hasty mind."[50] Nishida was reading many books at this time, not only on philosophy. His colleagues organized various reading groups, which read Goethe's *Faust*, *Suikoden* [The men of the marshes; *Shuihuzhuan* in Chinese], Carlyle's works, Dante's *Divine Comedy*, and other works.

During the March spring break the position of dormitory master took Nishida and Sugimori to Okayama, Kobe, Nara, and Nagoya. They were entrusted by Hōjō to visit various school dormitories and to make a recommendation for the design of new dormitory buildings that the school was planning to add.[51] Hōjō radically transformed the school. The Ministry of Education decided that the school was on the right track, and they appointed Hōjō to a weightier position, founding president of the Hiroshima Higher Normal School (a college of education). Seizing the occasion of Hōjō's transfer, Nishida and Sugimori asked Hōjō whether they could be dismissed from their responsibility as dormitory masters. Hōjō left the matter to the new principal and left for Hiroshima on May 19. The new principal, Yoshimura Toratarō, relieved Nishida of the position in July. Sugimori and Hori Koretaka were summoned to Hiroshima by Hōjō to assist him, and they left Kanazawa in early summer.

Nishida traveled to Wakayama for his summer Zen practice with Setsumon. Mitake was already waiting for Nishida in Wakayama. Setsumon, delighted to see his students coming from afar, invited them to a dinner at his house and took an evening walk with them. In this friendly atmosphere, the *sanzen* schedule was relaxed. Some days Nishida skipped his audience with Setsumon altogether, partly because he was having a hard time with his *kōan* "*Mu*" and had nothing to say to the master. His analytical and conceptual mind stood in the way of his *kōan* practice. "What deludes me is the temptation to think,"[52] wrote Nishida in his diary. Setsumon, having seen that Nishida was stuck in his *kōan*, switched it to the "Sound of One Hand" *(sekishu)*. On this day, Mitake passed his *kōan*, which annoyed Nishida in no small degree. Nishida's diary for this day reads: "Mitake, saying something like he passed his *kōan*, proudly went home."[53]

Nishida had been working on the *kōan* "*Mu*" since his first *sesshin* at Myōshinji in 1897. This *kōan*, given to the novices and known as "Jōshū and the Dog," is the first case of the *Mumonkan* (*Wumenguan* in Chinese), a collection of *kōan*. The case is something like this: Someone asked Master Jōshū (*Zhaozhu* in Chinese) whether the dog had a Buddha nature. To this, Jōshū replied, "*Mu*" (it has not). On another occasion, to the same question Jōshū answered, "*U*" (it has). The discursive question of whether the dog has a Buddha nature presupposes a dichotomy between subject and object; thus, it does not touch the vitally living reality, whether it is a dog's or a person's. Actual vibrant living reality is *before* "it has" and "it has not."

Regarding the *kōan* the "Sound of One Hand," Suzuki Daisetz has the following recollection of his own:

> I still remember Master Kōsen's lifting up his hand from the table and saying, "Did you hear it? Did you hear the sound of one hand?" The meaning behind this was, "When both hands clap, there is a sound; what sound does one hand have? None." But at that time, I did not have an inkling. I was simply grateful to feel the living presence of the master.[54]

Nishida felt disconcerted by this switch of *kōan* and did not make much progress with the "Sound of One Hand." As August was drawing to a close, Nishida reflected and wrote in his diary:

Eating, sleeping, procreating—even animals can do these things. Ah, a human being should not end his life in this insignificant way! I must embody the beauty of the spiritual nature given to humanity, and live it out as best as I can. I must devote myself to Zen practice and scholarship by dedicating the time and energy I waste in fulfilling carnal desires and making uncalled-for visits to friends.[55]

After the summer practice in Wakayama, Nishida experienced a closer unity of Zen and scholarship and resumed his studies. He was appointed professor in charge of ethics for 1902–1903. He maintained the practice of mindfulness: "Engage in studies while taking life as the basis" (*jinsei o moto to shite gakumon subeshi*).[56] This simple formula became his fundamental self-injunction, as it clarified the once knotty place of scholarship in the context of life. He wrote a long letter to D. T. Suzuki on October 28, telling his friend about his current mental and psychological state (see letter at end of this chapter).

Nishida found that it was all right to take a more relaxed approach to his *kōan* practice because the inner fermentation, the effect of *kōan* practice itself, was taking place. The direction of his scholarship was also emerging clearly. His interest in scholarship, as he wrote to Suzuki, was not in the objective scientific analysis of religion and ethics but rather in depicting the "taste" of religious and moral experiences. In December 1902 his second daughter was born. On Nishida's request, Mitake named the baby Yūko, meaning an "exquisitely beautiful child."[57]

Once again, Nishida ushered in the new year at Senshin'an. His diary of New Year's day 1903 reads:

I sat and meditated the whole day. Even though I sit, I really cannot put my mind to it. I desire such things as studying abroad or becoming a university professor. My mind drifts away to things like that; besides, my body bothers me, and I cannot concentrate. They say that one cannot achieve anything of worth unless one considers oneself dead. Even though I try hard to imagine that I died on December 31, 1902, it just doesn't work. Men of old said to let go of everything. Unless my ego-self dies, how can I hope to attain purity and simplicity?[58]

Nishida's main concern around this time was to study abroad on a government-assisted program. (He inquired into the possibility in April 1903 and again in April 1904,[59] both times with a disappointing outcome.) Driven by his desire to establish himself as an academic, he was not yet free from the mundane desire for fame. When Hōjō visited Kanazawa on February 15, Nishida and Mitake called on him. The three had an enjoyable evening, and Hōjō and Mitake encouraged Nishida in his Zen practice. Hōjō told Nishida that all he had to do was to die to himself.[60]

On May 3 Murakami Senshō visited Kanazawa and gave a talk. Around this time, Nishida was briefly tempted to take up an academic study of Buddhism and Christianity. But he reminded himself: "It is enough for me to grasp the Great Truth and explain it by way of today's scholarship. I shouldn't entertain other unnecessary desires. He who pursues too many ends fails to achieve even one."[61]

From May 12 to 16 Nishida worked on an essay, "Jinshin no giwaku" [On the doubt in our heart],[62] in which he addressed the problem of why we question the meaning and purpose of life. "For what purpose do we live, work, and die?" is not an intellectual question in his view but a profoundly existential one; the answer is given only by such great spiritual figures as Gautama Buddha and Jesus Christ, who still offered light to anyone in doubt.

For Nishida's summer practice in 1903, Setsumon recommended Master Kōjū of Daitokuji; because Master Kokan of Myōshinji had just died on March 16. Nishida went to Kyoto on July 15, and four days later he settled in at Kohōan, a subtemple of Daitokuji, and paid homage to Kōjū Rōshi. Nishida's impression of the master was that he was "a candid, innocent man," and he resolved to "do it right this time."[63] He began his private audience with the master the following day. Still, philosophical questions disturbed his concentration. His diary for July 23 reads:

> It is wrong to practice Zen for the sake of scholarship. I must practice for the sake of my soul [*kokoro*], for the sake of my life. I shall not think about religion and philosophy until I attain *kenshō* [initial awakening].
>
> Did I come this far to Kyoto only to be idle, and return home empty handed? What merit is there in wasting my years like this?
>
> The master switched the *kōan* again; toil, toil, toil.[64]

Nishida at first felt disconcerted about the change of *kōan*,[65] but he quickly regained his concentration. On July 27 he wrote: "Ah, devils plaguing my mind! I can imagine what sort of battle Christ went through in the wilderness. Today, I struggled with delusions."[66] On the evening of August 3, he had a private audience with the master, who acknowledged that Nishida had passed his *kōan* "*Mu.*" This meant that Nishida had experienced *kenshō*, an initial breakthrough. But this experience came as something of a disappointment to him. His diary for this day reads:

> 7 A.M., listened to the talk. Evening, a private audience with the master. I was cleared of the *kōan* "*Mu*". But I am not that happy. Sugimori is going to study abroad. I have to rely on myself. It's no use counting on the others. The new *kōan:* "Stop the Peal of the Bell."[67]

Nishida's desire to study abroad was so deeply rooted that it may have become more important to him than passing his *kōan*.

Somewhat disconcerted, Nishida returned to Kanazawa and immediately wrote to Setsumon, expressing his skepticism regarding the authenticity of his *kenshō* experience. For the analytically minded Nishida, Master Kokan's tigerlike, tough training might have been more effective than Master Kōjū's gentler approach. Be that as it may, Setsumon responded to his letter on August 24, advising him not to doubt the validity of Zen teaching. He reminded him that the *kenshō* experience was only the beginning of more advanced practice and told him to forget what happened at Daitokuji and continue his Zen practice. Eventually, he promised Nishida, a greater illumination would come as a result of assiduous practice.[68] Nishida accepted Setsumon's words. The realization that he did break through the initial Zen barrier set in gradually, and Nishida began to feel better about turning to his philosophical inquiry. His letter to Yamamoto on November 29, 1903, tells us that he was back at his studies, reading Alexander's *Ethics*[69] and Ōnishi's *Ethics.*[70] Nishida was thinking about writing something on ethics, just as Ōnishi had done, and acknowledged to Yamamoto that he wished he could write like Ōnishi.[71]

Toward the end of 1903 and the beginning of 1904, Setsumon was away from Kanazawa, which obliged Nishida to usher in the new year at home with his family. His spiritual life was entering its nurturing stage. Like a tender newborn baby, he needed careful nourishing, and he found Augustine and other Christian writers gave him the needed comfort. It was at this time that he borrowed a copy of William James's *Varieties of Religious Experience* from the school library and found it gripping.[72] James's discussion of religious experience impressed Nishida as a "deep and delightful" work on the psychological study of religion.[73]

Years later, after Nishida's death, Shimomura Toratarō, thinking it odd that Nishida's experience of initial breakthrough was nothing earthshaking, asked D. T. Suzuki about it. Suzuki responded: "There are those cases, you know, especially with a man like Nishida, who has a rational logical mind. But Nishida must have grasped something. Otherwise, the kind of philosophy that he developed would never have been possible."[74] Nishida was turning to philosophy with the solid understanding of the worldview espoused by Zen Buddhism.

Nishida's Letter to D. T. Suzuki concerning Zen Practice[*]

October 28, 1902

My Dear Daisetz,

I got your interesting letter after quite a long silence. It came to me like "the sound of footsteps in a hollow valley." From time to time, I thought of writing to you, but since I didn't feel that what I had to say was anything special, I thought it foolish to regurgitate the same thing. So I have not written to you until now.

The book you mentioned, *Varieties of Religious Experience* by Professor [William] James, sounds very interesting, and I would certainly like to read it.[1] Would you please let me know the exact title, the publisher, and the price of the book? Last year, I read that acclaimed work on the philosophy of religion by Otto Pfleiderer, but it contained nothing more than coherent argumentation and abstract discussion; he does not strike me as a man who understands the taste of "religious life." However precise and accurate his "logical syllogisms" may be, his analysis gave me the impression that he was looking at an artificial flower. I gained nothing from it.

I have been teaching ethics for the past year. It is hard enough to save myself; yet here I am, teaching others the [moral] path. Please don't laugh at this picture of the blind leading the blind. I have no choice in this matter since it is my duty as a teacher to teach. I do so, swallowing my shame.

---

* Letter no. 42, NKZ 18:59–61.
1. Nishida was able to obtain a copy on 8 January 1904. Diary, NKZ 17:123.

It seems to me that "ethics" in the West is purely an intellectual pursuit. Its arguments are cogent, but no one pays attention to the "soul experience"—experience deep in the human heart. People forget the ground on which they stand. There are those who analyze and explain the constituents of bread and water, but none considers the actual taste of either. The result is an artificial construct, which has no impact on the human heart. I wish contemporary scholars of ethics would leave their scholarly research and, instead, explain the spiritual experience of the great figures of the past. That should be the factual basis for the study of ethics.

When I read Lessing's discussion on the beauty of ancient art, I found it more interesting and informative than Hartmann's aesthetics. I prefer discussions of art that directly deal with "moral experience" to ethics. But such books are rare. Lately, I have been reading Dante's *Divine Comedy*. He is one of those who had that experience. Likewise, I think Schopenhauer's theory of *reine Anschauung* [pure intuition] (which takes the will at its foundation) more interesting and deeper than Hegel's theory, which has the *Intellekt* at its core. What do you think?

You said you heard a talk on religious experience and found it interesting. So do I, since I first put my mind to it years ago. But because of the weakness of my determination, I have been embroiled in secular affairs, and I have not been able to attain any awakening. On top of all these duties, Professor Hōjō appointed me to the position of dormitory master last year, and I was busy with the responsibility of guiding the daily life and moral conduct of the entire student body. This year, however, on the occasion of Professor Hōjō's moving to Hiroshima, I resigned from this position. These days, I don't feel so hurried, and I am concentrating on *zazen* and reading books. In the beginning [of my Zen practice], I felt pressured and was irritable, but these days I have grown more focused. I manage to concentrate and work on my *kōan*. I visit Setsumon Rōshi from time to time for a private interview. Up to this year, I was studying the *kōan* "*Mu*". But just recently the Rōshi changed the *kōan* to the "Sound of One Hand." So I am now grappling with the "One Hand."

Forgive me for discussing such personal matters, but I think it useless at present to visit the Rōshi and am now concentrating solely on my *kōan*. Perhaps if I focus enough every day, I shall reach some awakening. What good is it if the Rōshi considers that I have passed a *kōan*, and yet I myself am dissatisfied? There are Zen practitioners who pass one *kōan* after another, thereby achieving seniority status. I am impressed neither by their behavior nor by what they say. What do you think on this matter? Your letter inspired my fighting spirit. Please write to me now and then on religious matters. Immersed though I am in secular life, if I do not attain awakening, I shall have no peace, even in death. May you hear what I am trying to say.

Yours,
Kitarō

Chapter 6

The Birth of a Philosopher

(1904–1907)

The Russo-Japanese War broke out on February 9, 1904.[1] By early May it claimed the life of Nishida's dear friend, Mukō Kikutarō, then a lieutenant commander in the Japanese navy.[2] Because Mukō's wife had died in December 1903, his death left their newborn baby an orphan. Brooding over Mukō's orphaned child, Nishida wrote a memoir about Mukō.[3]

Nishida's younger brother, Hyōjirō, a captain in the military who had been stationed in Tokyo since 1902, was also called to active duty as the war escalated. He returned to Kanazawa to entrust his wife, Hatsue, and their baby daughter, Toshiko, to Nishida's care and left for Hiroshima on June 29. The troops left Hiroshima by boat for Port Arthur. The Ninth Division—made up of soldiers recruited from the Hokuriku region, of which Hyōjirō was a part—was placed under the command of General Nogi Maresuke, who led the Third Army. For some time Hyōjirō had little to do at the military camp and asked Nishida to send him the book of Russian grammar he had left back home so that he could continue to learn the language. Hyōjirō participated in the first general assault that began on August 19. The battle plan was reckless; the Third Army was to break through the Russian forts on the northeastern hills that surrounded Port Arthur within three days.[4] The Russians were equipped with machine guns, while the Japanese had only single-shot rifles. In the fierce and bloody battle, Hyōjirō was killed in action near Mt. Banryū (Banlong) on August 24.[5]

The news of Hyōjirō's death was delivered to Nishida when he was visiting a beach at Kanaiwa in the company of Fujioka and Fujii Otoo.[6] Intellectually, Nishida tried to justify the death of Hyōjirō as an "honor" for the country, but emotionally it was extremely hard for him to accept it. A few months later in November he submitted to a news-paper a memoir about his brother.[7] His essay was filled with the silent cries of the bereaved. He did not recover from the death of Hyōjirō for a long time and passed the rest of the year depressed. His practical side, however, took responsibility for his brother's widow and child. He saw to it that Hatsue was remarried, and he and Kotomi adopted Toshiko and raised her as their own daughter. When Hyōjirō's body was recovered following the fall of Port Arthur, Nishida acquired a plot of land at Nodayama Cemetery and erected an imposing grave-stone, more than two meters high, with an inscription done by Miyake Shinken.

For the consolation of his soul, Nishida turned to Zen practice. He welcomed the new year at Senshin'an and stayed there until January 6. Master Setsumon's return to Senshin'an on New Year's Eve greatly comforted Nishida. The account of *zazen,* words of Zen masters, and the news of the Russo-Japanese War that was constantly streaming in filled his diary during the first days of 1905. The stormier the outside world became, the deeper he turned inward, as if to heal the psycho-logical wound inflicted on him by the death of Hyōjirō. On January 2, the day when the news of the Third Army's successful siege of Port Arthur reached Japan, Nishida, still at Senshin'an, felt mixed emotions. Although he could not help but feel good about Japan's victory, he was critical of the citywide celebration. Zen practice, in which he was firmly established by then, afforded him the objectivity to see the folly of such festivities. His diary for January 5 reads:

> *Zazen* in the morning. Since last night I've been possessed by doubt. . . . I have no choice but to proceed with full vigor in the direction I have chosen. I'm too old now to change the course of my life.
>
> *Zazen* in the afternoon. At noon there was a rally in the park to celebrate the fall of Port Arthur. I could hear people shouting "Banzai!" They are going to have a lantern procession this evening to celebrate the victory. How fickle are the human hearts that give themselves to such foolish festivities! People don't think about the many lives that were sacrificed and about the fact that the war still has a long way to go before it ends.[8]

On February 7, the day after the Third Army had arrived in Liao-yang to begin the siege of Mukden, Nishida wrote: "The most coura-geous act is to conquer oneself. There is no greater enterprise than self-reform and self-improvement. It surpasses the control of Manchuria. Zen practice and scholarship—these are my enterprise."⁹ In March 1905 he was still grieving. In response to Yamamoto, he wrote a lengthy letter:

> The heart wound inflicted on me last year is not yet healed. Please don't laugh at me as a silly grumbler. The problem of life is deep and tremendous. I don't know how it would be with a strong-minded person, but for me, who am sensitive and tender-minded, it is truly too heavy a burden. I turn more and more inward and am tormented although nobody knows it. Consequently, I feel reluctant about being actively engaged in anything.
>
> Partly because my teaching demands it, I've read almost all the well-known books on ethics; but unless I start out with metaphysics, I don't seem to get a satisfactory answer. Recently, I began my studies of the history of philosophy and epistemology, not because they are needed for a study of ethics, but because I cannot escape my metaphysical doubt. In this way, I'm becoming more and more reclusive. . . .
>
> The Russo-Japanese War is escalating, and no end is in sight. This is indeed a grievous situation for the country. If, luckily, we win the war, it goes without saying that the Japanese people will thrive. *But mere materialistic prosperity is worthless.* We must attempt to develop *the spiritual side of the people,* limited though we are in our power.¹⁰

It is noteworthy that Nishida was already more concerned with the spiritual well-being of the Japanese people than with their material prosperity.

Upon receiving this letter, Yamamoto immediately wrote to Suzuki:

> I am terribly sorry for Nishida, who told me that last year's *loss* hangs heavily over his mind and does not easily go away however hard he tries. I really want to console him, but he is a much bigger man than I, and I fear that our sympathies are mere trifling winds that blow helplessly against the trunk of a huge tree. I really don't know what to do. Have you heard from him lately?¹¹

Sukuki, who had earlier received the news of Hyōjirō's death, composed a sonnet in English and sent it to Nishida to console him:

> *O human life, what a fragile thing thou art!*
> *A drop of dew on a weather-beaten leaf,*
> *By passers' feet down-trodden; and how brief*
> *Thy glitter! too soon fated to depart*

To a region, whence perhaps didst thou first start.
The mournful thought doth follow us like thief;
Heavily oppressed we are without relief;—
Eternal Void, would thou allay our heart!
And yet ours is to strive, to weep, to bear;
Human are we, with fire in our veins burning;
To Reason's hollow talk let's not concede.
Our tears run free, the heart its woes declare!
From every grief endured life's lesson learning,
Into the depths of Mystery we read.[12]

In April 1905 Nishida took part in the April *zazen* practice at Senshin'an. He was becoming a seasoned practitioner, successfully assimilating the Zen teaching into his daily life. His diary for July 19 reads:

I am neither a psychologist nor a sociologist but an inquirer into life.[13]

Zen is music, Zen is art, Zen is physical exercise. There is nothing else that I seek for the consolation of my spirit. Daily life is no different from *sekishu*, the "sound of one hand." If I can be pure and candid like a child, there is no greater happiness on earth.

Non multa sed multum.[14]

For his summer practice, he decided to go to Kokutaiji to do *sanzen* under Master Zuiun.[15] He left for Kokutaiji on July 24, accompanying his older sister Masa.[16] Masa may have incurred some debt, for on his way to the temple, Nishida stopped with her at a village to pay back fifty yen to someone of questionable character. At that point Masa returned home, while Nishida proceeded to the temple. A few days later, the moneylender laid a charge against Nishida of fraud, saying that Nishida still owed him ten yen as interest. News of this accusation reached him on his fourth day at Kokutaiji. He had to cut his summer practice short, return home, and tend to the matter. The man who accused Nishida fled the village by night, and the charge was dropped. Nishida had long accepted that the sublime and the ridiculous were both part of life. After things settled down, he went to Senshin'an for intensive *zazen* from August 4 to 8. This was possibly the last of his formal Zen practice. He was now channeling his energy into his studies.

Actually he had resumed his philosophical studies soon after the death of Hyōjirō, for he was able to forget the psychological pains, however momentarily, while he concentrated on his work. In his attempt to organize his thoughts, he decided to put together his lecture notes in an orderly fashion. By January 1905 he was fully engaged in writing "Lectures on Psychology."[17] At this time, he also began working on his lecture notes on "Ethics."[18] From August 12, 1905, to March 1906, he worked on the second draft of "Ethics."[19] These lecture notes became the building blocks of his book, *Zen no kenkyū* [*An inquiry into the good*, published in 1911].

On the school front, Principal Yoshimura Toratarō discouraged students from getting interested in religion. He suspected that Nishida and Mitake were propagating Zen practice among students.[20] To the principal, an interest in religion was synonymous with pessimism and leading to suicide. A sensational suicide, committed by a First Higher School student, Fujimura Misao, who jumped into the Kegon Falls at Nikko out of his philosophical despair, was still fresh in everyone's mind. Yoshimura was predisposed to equate religion with such drastic actions.[21] The principal was reluctant to grant permission for the Sansanjuku to continue. In fact, in 1905 Yoshimura dismantled the autonomous student governance of the school dormitory, Jishūryō, and in its place implemented school-centered regulations. This kind of heavy-handed measure was eventually to backfire on Yoshimura; he was ousted by the student strike in 1911.

Throughout 1905 Sansanjuku was at its lowest point. Very few students were interested in its tenets, and Nishida found it difficult to recruit anyone who was of suitable mental and spiritual disposition. He wrote to Hori in Hiroshima and consulted him—and, indirectly, Hōjō —about whether he should continue the *juku*. In the end, he reached the conclusion that he should, but only by stepping aside and asking Tanabe and Ibaraki, who had the trust of the principal, to represent the *juku*. In this way, Sansanjuku survived the trying period.[22]

Toward the end of September 1905, Matsumoto Bunzaburō visited Kanazawa to attend a Buddhist memorial service for his father. He called on Nishida on October 1, and the two instantly renewed their friendship, although they had not seen each other for nearly a decade. Matsumoto had returned from his three years of study in Germany and was to assume the position of professor at Kyoto Imperial University the following summer. Nishida now gained one more strong ally in the mainstream of academia, because Fujioka was by then assistant professor at Tokyo Imperial University. A third daughter was born on October 14 to Nishida and Kotomi. Hori Koretaka named the baby Shizuko.

Nishida began 1906 as usual at Senshin'an, doing *zazen*. But his Zen practice no longer had peer support; Setsumon was rarely in town and Nishida's Zen companion, Ishikawa, had left Kanazawa the year before to take up the position of steward with the Maeda family in Tokyo. He thus stopped his formal practice.

In 1906 the Japanese academic world in the humanities experienced a second wave of expansion when the College of Humanities at Kyoto Imperial University opened its gates. Nishida felt that the time was ripe for him to make a move.[23] He considered two options: to remain at the Fourth Higher School and hope for a chance to study abroad, or to find a teaching position in Tokyo. Having learned from Hōjō that the chances of his studying abroad were slim, he decided to leave Kanazawa when the opportunity presented itself. Matsumoto Bunzaburō and Kuwaki Gen'yoku were moving to Kyoto in June, and Nishida hoped that this reshuffling might create a position for him.[24] For a while he also hoped that he might get the position at the First Higher School vacated by Fukada Yasukazu, who was sent to study abroad. Nishida wrote to Hori on March 6:

> Even if it is said that one's work begins at the age of forty, I think that I had better start preparing myself now. If I were to spend my time just reading books, it would not matter where I am because I can do that anywhere. But to accomplish a work of some merit, I think it is a handicap to be in the countryside. When I get a chance, I should like to move to Tokyo.[25]

No job in Tokyo materialized that spring. With much disappointment, he wrote to Yamamoto on March 21: "When one cannot work in the outside world, one cultivates one's inner world. A time such as this, when I cannot get an academic position that I would like, is indeed the best time for me to enrich my thought, isn't it? Therefore, I am resolute and quietly waiting for the opportunity to arise."[26] On March 25 he began working on sorting out lecture notes on "Religion."[27]

In the summer of 1906 two of his daughters, Yūko and Shizuko, came down with pneumonia.[28] While taking care of them, Nishida wrote an essay, "Jitsuzai ni tsuite" [That which is real, or On reality], in which he summarized the essentials of his thought thus far. Following that, he revised the second draft of "Ethics." In the essay "On reality" (which became part 2 of *Zen no kenkyū*), he attempts to build an ontology based on the phenomena of consciousness by starting out with the empirical, that is, experiential facts. Whatever we perceive, feel, or think is a phenomenon of consciousness, and we cannot get away from it. Even nature, which we normally think exists "outside" the phenomena of consciousness, in fact exists to us as phenomena of consciousness. Thus, there is no distinction between nature and the spirit, the thing and I. By taking the unifying power of consciousness as the fundamental feature of consciousness, Nishida points out that discrete entities, such as yesterday's I and today's I, are unified. This unifying power is also the power with which we concentrate our attention here and now. Nishida assumes a voluntarist perspective and asserts that the will is the primary characteristic of consciousness. This amounts to rephrasing the Buddhist insight that our actual world is constituted by our feelings and desires rather than by abstract concepts and theories. Moreover, these feelings and desires are not mere subjective realities but something transindividual and universal because they are mutually communicable.

Nishida goes on to assert that the phenomena of consciousness, whether cognitive, volitional, or aesthetic, unfold themselves in one and the same way—from the implicit to the actual. For instance, my desire to quench thirst is completed by my concrete action of drinking water. In the process of reality unfolding itself in this manner, there arises an opposition or contradiction from within consciousness,[29] and consciousness attains a larger unity by unifying these contradictions. The unifying power of consciousness thus necessarily contains opposition and contradiction. Reality develops itself through these dynamic movements of self-differentiation and unification.

This unifying power of consciousness is the principle (*ri, logos, ratio*) that establishes not only all the individual selves but this universe itself. In fact, our *self* is a manifestation of this cosmic unifying principle. For instance, when I see a flower, my consciousness is one with the flower; when I study the flower, I discard my subjective dogmatism, I am "selfless" and become one with the "thing," in this case, the flower. The more selfless, that is, objective, I become, the closer I am to the object of my inquiry.

This principle of the unifying power of consciousness is most evident in the world of religion, in which the most selfless one is the greatest, with the most power to move and transform others, as exemplified by such figures as Jesus Christ and Gautama Buddha. In the world of religion, the source of infinitely unifying activities is God; God is the fountainhead of all that is. Nishida maintains that if we reflect on the reality of the unifying power operating in our consciousness, we will find God's image (*imago dei*) therein. Further, God, as the ground of reality, is the unifying power that unites persons, you and me. In this way, God is love, mutual sharing, happiness, and peace.[30]

In his essay on "Ethics" (part 3 of the *Zen no kenkyū*), Nishida summarizes his view of ethics built upon his voluntarist conviction. In his view, the operation of the will is the most central reality and the clearest expression of the self. He rejects as inadequate ethical theories based on intuitionism, authority, and the a priori knowledge of reason (that is, "dianoetic" ethics), as well as hedonism. The only viable ethical theory for him is "energetism," the ethical view espoused by Plato, and especially by Aristotle, which held that good complies with, and consists in, the realization *(energeia)* of the self. We human beings ultimately live for our ideals and not for our physical needs. Therefore, we follow the voice of reason, which itself is a profoundly unifying power of consciousness. A person *(jinkaku)* is characterized by this voice of reason. This person is the "real self" that Zen Buddhism speaks of— it is not an abstract universal entity stripped of individual differences and characters. Rather, a person is the very operation of the unifying power of consciousness that fully realizes itself in each of us. Viewed as such, a person is a manifestation of the unifying power of the cosmos itself. A good action is a personal action sustained by sincerity and love. An authentic personal action is devoid of selfish calculations. We reach so lofty a height only by eradicating our petty egoism. A good action is compared to pure experience or pure activity itself, in which subject and object both disappear—I forget myself, and only my action is.

The objective world is the reflection of myself inasmuch as I am a reflection of the objective world. Nishida emphasizes the irreducibility of each individual (contrary to the common view nowadays that the Japanese society is group oriented and that Japanese individuals are required to melt into the whole). The end of a good action lies in the full realization of individuality *(kojinsei)*, which is singular and unique to each of us. "Individualism" of this kind must be sharply distinguished from selfish egoism, for each individual is a social being— whether we are male or female, each of us stands for the whole of humanity, as a member of a family, society, and state. But the state (nation or country) is not yet the ultimate end of humanity. Solidarity of humanity is. The present age (for Nishida, the post-Russo-Japanese War period) is an age of "armed peace." The role of each state is to surrender itself to the interest of global well-being by embracing the standpoint of world history, which would lead each nation to realize human solidarity. In his global and humanistic conviction, Nishida holds that each individual, as a person, must purify his or her motivations because when one's motivation reaches the highest love of humanity, then whatever one does is the most perfect action possible—this is the end each of us should strive for. Hence, true good consists in knowing one's real self and obtaining the power of subject-object unification. We can attain this power only if our selfish ego dies and our real self is born out of it. Nishida sees this as the meaning of *kenshō* experience (seeing one's true nature) in Zen Buddhism and "rebirth in Christ" in Christianity. [31]

In the fall term of 1906 Nishida gave his lectures in ethics at school based on what he had written during the summer. Students found it difficult to follow him, and many just let his words go in one ear and out the other. [32] But some asked whether they might have his lecture notes printed so that they would have a textbook. The result was a booklet, *Nishidashi jitsuzairon oyobi rinrigaku* [A discourse on reality and ethics according to Mr. Nishida]. [33]

For Sansanjuku, the pendulum swung back, and in the fall of 1906 the *juku* was thriving again after Kawai Yoshinari, a born leader, and Shinagawa Kazue, a man of considerable charisma, joined the *juku*. A judo champion, Shōriki Matsutarō, was also closely associated with the *juku* because of his friendship with Kawai and Shinagawa. Kawai's joining Sansanjuku single-handedly brought it to the attention of the entire student body, spreading the perception that it was an elite *juku* intended for a select group of students. Collegial support for the *juku* remained strong as well, with Mitake, Tanabe, Ibaraki, Uehara Kikunosuke (professor of English and history), and Nagai Shizuo (lecturer in German) on the board of advisors.

Many students that Nishida came to know through his involvement with Sansanjuku became notable figures—scholars, university professors, leading Christians, entrepreneurs, statesmen, and so forth. For instance, Kawai established the Komatsu Machinery Manufacture Company and became an influential industrialist. Shinagawa became president of the Yomiuri Entertainment Corporation in the post-World War II period and later president of the Yomiuri Newspaper Company. Shinagawa also did much to usher in the golden age of the Yomiuri Giants, a professional baseball team, as he scouted Nagashima Shigeo and Ō Sadaharu. Shōriki was president of the Yomiuri Newspaper Company and Nippon Television. Those who became influential Christians included Ōsaka Motokichirō, Akizuki Itaru, and Takakura Tokutarō. [34] Many graduates of Sansanjuku formed lasting friendships with Nishida, giving him contacts well beyond the ordinary walls of academia.

In November 1906 Nishida published "Jikakushugi" [Philosophy of self-awakening] in the school journal. [35] In this article he discusses the "awakening to one's self" as a "certain notable trend" of modern European thought, as evident in the works of such writers as Henrik Ibsen, Nietzsche, and Gerhart Hauptmann. This trend—a prevailing force for some time—struck Nishida as a force to be reckoned with. He saw that these writers considered the "self" as the most prized reality, which they tried to liberate from the oppressive yoke of tradition and religious dogma. In this sense, their view is different from "selfish individualism." Certainly the emphasis on the self is nothing new: Socrates was inspired by the Delphic oracle, "Know thyself," and Descartes arrived at his principle, cogito ergo sum. What was new with these writers is the emphasis they placed on the importance of the will. Nishida points out that these writers considered volition, rather than the intellect, the real essence of the self. He considers Schopenhauer, who initiated this line of inquiry, the precursor of this trend.

Members and supporters of Sansanjuku, June 9, 1907. The photo was taken in the backyard of Nishida's house in Kanazawa. Front row, from left to right: Mizushima Seiichi, Osatake Katashi, Okuzumi Aizō; second row, from left to right: Ibaraki Seijirō, Mitake Kingorō, Kawai Yoshinari, Shinagawa Kazue, Inoue Hide, Nishida, Nagai Shizuo; third row, from left to right: Sotogaki Hideshige, Tanabe Ryūji, Uehara Kikunosuke, Kyōgoku Etsuzō, Arai Keiji. Courtesy of Noto Insatsu Ltd., Kanazawa.

Nishida felt that the inquiry into volition could make two important philosophical contributions. First, it introduces a more balanced view of human beings that is not just theoretical and intellectual but also emotive and volitional. Second, it locates the source of morality within the individual and not in society, thus placing the individual beyond religious creeds and national affiliations, which was unthinkable during the feudalistic period. Against the horizon of Zen teaching, however, he finds a trace of egoism in this trend and concludes that "a cloud of nihilism hovers over it." While he resonates with the theme of "self-awakening" insofar as it liberates the individual from the yoke of traditionalism, he maintains his critical attitude toward individualism that remains on the level of "ego." Several, years later, in 1909, when he sent this article to Yamamoto, he explained his perspective:

> I wrote this essay as I found myself sympathizing with the philosophical trend of "awakening to oneself," but that does not mean I approve of it. I think that an authentic awakening to oneself consists of getting rid of one's own petty ego. Our self is not individualistic but sustained by the Great Self-awareness that is shared with God. I expanded on this point a bit at the end of my work on "Ethics,"[36] so please look at it.[37]

Nishida was experiencing a breakthrough in his philosophical writing. But on January 11, 1907, his second daughter, Yūko, died of bronchitis, which brought his attention back to home and family. Conveying this sad news, he wrote to Hori:

> She was just about five years old and at the most adorable period of her life. I cannot forget her sweet countenance saying "welcome home" to me, as she was in the habit of waiting for my return from school; her gentle posture as she used to sit quietly right by my side while I read books; her sweet voice with which she sang songs; and her suffering and pain from the repeated illnesses that she had to endure while so young—these images of her come back to me, each very vividly, and I cannot help but feel an excruciating pain in my abdomen. I think I came to realize a little better this time the true meaning of life through her death. Dense-headed as I am, it seems I cannot possibly understand the truth of life unless I go through so extreme a misfortune as the loss of my own beloved child.[38]

Yūko's death shook Nishida profoundly and made him realize that he had been preoccupied with his academic achievement and oblivious to the primary importance of life and his family. In the face of this heart-wrenching experience, he turned for consolation to Fujioka, who had lost his daughter Mitsuko in August the year before.[39] The loss of their daughters strengthened the bond between the two men. To ease his grief, Nishida wrote a memoir of Yūko,[40] only later to learn that Fujioka had done exactly the same thing when Mitsuko had died.[41] That extreme grief evoked the same reaction in the two men further amazed them.[42]

Yūko's death deepened Nishida's religious consciousness. After much suffering and grieving, he was able to find solace only by accepting the meaninglessness of trying to reason with himself about her death. Tosa, Nishida's mother, must have been able to console him with her strength, sustained by her faith in the grace of Amida Buddha. Nishida threw himself into the ocean of divine compassion. It was a kind of *tariki*[43] experience, a discovery of the power of the grace of God. A dimension of compassion, hitherto only intimated to Nishida, opened up and became central to his religious awareness.[44]

Now a more mature man and more understanding of the human condition, Nishida returned to his life of thinking and writing. He sent a copy of his essay "Jitsuzai" to Tokunō Bun and Fujioka in February. He knew that he had said something original in that essay. He wrote to Fujioka:

> What I sent you under separate cover is something I wrote last summer while I was taking care of my sick children. I gave my lectures in philosophy at school based on it. . . . I want to attempt to build a philosophical system with the ideas I developed therein. I would like Professors Motora and Inoue to look at it. . . . Would it be possible for you to explain these matters to them on my behalf?[45]

The essay was accepted and published in the March issue of *Tetsugaku Zasshi*.[46] It caught the attention of students of philosophy so much that Kihira Tadayoshi,[47] a graduate of the Fourth Higher School, who went on to the philosophy department at the Imperial University, and who was then assisting the editors of the journal, wrote a tribute to Nishida's work and an introduction about the author in the April issue of *Tetsugaku Zasshi*:

> In my view, Mr. Nishida's "On reality" best harmonizes Hegel's thought and the theory of pure experience, which is much discussed these days. In other words, it harmonizes intellectualism and voluntarism. . . . Mr. Nishida is widely read both in classics and contemporary works of East and West. While he would order the most recent books from abroad, he would also put books completely aside and apply him-

self to *zazen* practice. He has concentrated on his philosophical reflection in this manner ever since he graduated from the university more than ten years ago. . . . That kind of work cannot be achieved by anyone but a serious scholar. . . . Many have asked me who Mr. Nishida is—he is professor at the Fourth Higher School in Kanazawa.[48]

In March Nishida caught a bad cold that worsened into dry pleurisy. With the permission of the doctor, he traveled to Tokyo during the spring break and called on Professors Inoue and Motora on April 2. One of the main purposes of his visit to Tokyo was to see the president of Tokyo Imperial University, Hamao Arata.[49] The meeting, which took place on April 5, had been arranged by Hōjō Tokiyuki, who recommended Nishida for a university position.[50] In his realistic assessment of the situation, however, Nishida knew better than to expect any positive outcome.

On May 4, 1907, twin girls, Tomoko and Aiko, were born to Nishida and Kotomi. They were both premature, and Aiko died a month later on June 3, while Tomoko survived. In the meantime, Nishida's recovery from dry pleurisy was slow, and his illness often kept him away from teaching, especially on cold, rainy days. Nishida's repeated absences displeased Principal Yoshimura, which in turn dismayed Nishida, especially because he felt he had dedicated the best years of his life to the school. The emotional conflict began to put a strain on Nishida and strengthened his conviction that he ought to leave Kanazawa. His need for professional company was increasing as well. He thus began to look for a position that would give him more time to pursue his study and writing.[51] His letter to Fujioka Sakutarō of July 11, 1907, explains his situation:

> The reason I want to move to Tokyo is not that I want to be known to people; rather, I want to have an environment that is conducive to my study. It is certainly true that one can pursue scholarship even in the countryside, but I think it is clearly more advantageous to be in Tokyo. I need people around me who can teach me and criticize me rather than those whom I teach and who praise me. I need those who inspire me rather than those whom I inspire.
>
> Even if I publish anything here, because there are only a few who can give me any critical feedback as to what makes sense and what doesn't, I must seek out the opinions of those who are beyond my immediate environment. I think any author needs to have a company of minds who can understand and criticize his or her work. Those who live in the countryside know the shortcomings of life in the country,

and those who live in cities know the shortcomings of city life. Either way, there are trade-offs. I think that for cultivating one's thought, life in the countryside might be better, but for honing and developing it, life in the city is more desirable. It may be otherwise for a truly exceptional person, but I do need external stimuli. Such was clearly the case even with that prolific Natsume Sōseki who could not produce anything while he was in Kumamoto.[52]

Fujioka understood Nishida's point, for he himself was in Tokyo precisely because the necessary libraries for his research were all in Tokyo. In July Nishida sent an offprint of "Jitsuzai" to Suzuki in America and wrote:[53]

What I've sent you the other day is something totally "scientific." I intend to go on with my religious practice until the end of my life, but I think that my calling is scholarship. What do you think? . . . If I can, I would like to organize my thoughts into a book. I want to build my philosophy on the reality of the mind *(shinri)* instead of on abstract theory *(ronri)* on which most traditional philosophies have been based. In this connection I find William James's "pure experience" quite interesting.[54] He says he is going to write on metaphysics.[55] Is the work finished yet?[56]

The summer vacation of 1907 was for Nishida filled with pleasant encounters and reunions. Sōya Heihachi, a graduating student of Sansanjuku, invited Nishida to come and stay at his parents' house at Hashidate, a small lovely fishing village on the coast of the Japan Sea about fifty kilometers southwest of Kanazawa. Fujioka took a room at an inn at a nearby spa, and the two visited each other almost daily. Akegarasu Haya,[57] a disciple of Kiyozawa Manshi, came to visit Nishida and Fujioka for a few days. Sōya's friend and a member of Sansanjuku, Ishiguro Bunkichi,[58] also briefly joined this convivial group.

On August 3, in this idyllic setup, Nishida wrote a short essay, "Chi to ai" [Knowledge and love],[59] for *Seishinkai*.[60] (This essay was appended to part 4 of *Zen no kenkyū*.) In this essay it is apparent that the tender memory of Yūko was making Nishida a more humanistic thinker. He freely expresses his sympathy for personalism and emphasizes love as the ultimate knowledge, for love intuits the feelings of others. He maintains that for us to know a thing is to love it; and thus in loving a thing, we come to know it. One and the same thing can become the object of knowledge and love. Whatever the thing is, as an object of knowledge it is "impersonal"; as an object of love, it is "personal." The religious posture of *tariki* ("reliance on the grace of Amida Buddha") is relevant to the discussion of knowledge, for to know a thing is to love it, which is an act of discarding "self-centered reliance on the self" *(jiriki)* and putting faith in the saving grace of Amida. Viewed in this way, scholarship and morality are ultimately the illumination of the compassionate Buddha.

In early September Tanabe Ryūji moved to Tokyo to teach in the women's division of Gakushūin, further shrinking Nishida's circle of close colleague-friends. And then in mid-September, Moriuchi Masa-aki committed suicide. He had been suffering from severe depression for some time. Nishida contacted Moriuchi's former friends to raise funds for Moriuchi's immediate family members.[61] Their effort raised about three hundred yen.[62] In November he wrote a preface for Fuji-oka's forthcoming book *Kokubungakushi kōwa* [A narrative history of Japanese literature], dedicated to the memory of his deceased daughter, Mitsuko. In it, Nishida memorialized his own deceased daughter, Yūko (the text follows).[63]

In Memory of My Deceased Child*

My dear friend, Tōho, when you visited Kanazawa in the summer of 1904 with your family, your daughter, Mitsu, accompanied you. She was a vivacious, adorable girl. But two summers later, while you and your family were vacationing in Odawara, she died.[1] At that time, I did my best to console you, as I remembered the painful memory of the death of my younger brother in the battle of Port Arthur in 1904. But alas! How things have their ways of turning out! In January of this year, my second daughter, Yūko, who had just turned six years old, died.[2] It was then my turn to be consoled by you.

In the spring following Yūko's death, business took me to Tokyo, where I had not been for a decade.[3] There I enjoyed your hospitality. We have been very close friends since junior higher school. Our

---

* *"Kokubungakushi kōwa* no jo," NKZ 1:414–20. The essay was completed on 8 November 1907.

1. Letter no. 2691 to Fujioka Sakutarō, 7 August 1906, NKZ 19:675. Mitsuko died on 5 August 1906.

2. Yūko died on 11 January 1907.

3. Nishida was in Tokyo from 31 March to 6 April 1907.

reunion at that time, after a long period of not having seen each other, took place under unusual circumstances, each of us harboring a grief of the same kind. When I saw you, it was much more than just seeing a good old friend. We had consoled each other through letters, but when we actually saw each other, we simply exchanged words of condolences. I stayed with you for one week. We talked about many things, but our conversation never touched upon the subject of our deceased children.

In the morning of the day of my departure, you opened a box in which you had carefully kept your manuscripts, took out a piece of writing and handed it to me, saying that it was about the last days of Mitsu. You then said you wanted to dedicate your forthcoming book on the history of Japanese literature to her memory, and that you wanted me to contribute a preface to it. Until that morning, we had not talked about our deceased children, not because we wished to avoid the painful subject, but because we shared a misery that defied words. What words can express is, in the end, shallow and false. Absolute sincerity prevails at the moment when we, facing each other, cannot put our feelings into words. That was what happened to us. And yet, the flow of deep sympathy, which could not even be expressed by tears, let alone by words, was flowing from the bottom of your heart to mine, and mine to yours.

When I lost Yūko, I could not contain my distress, because I knew that the feeling of sadness would eventually dissipate. Unable to bear the grief, I wrote a memoir about Yūko so that I could at least memorialize her.[4] As soon as I did so, I sent it to you, for you were the only person who could understand how I felt then. How could I have known that you, who had earlier suffered the same fate, had done exactly the same thing, writing a memoir of your daughter?

I carefully placed your manuscript in my bag and returned home. One evening when I could not sleep,[5] I took it out and read each and every word. I was awed by how similar the deep feelings of the human heart are. Who says there is no constant law to the human heart? As if a billiard ball, hit in the same direction, would take the same course, my mind moved exactly as yours did.

As I look back on my life, I was about fourteen when I lost my older sister to whom I was most attached. At that time, I learned how

---

4. Nishida wrote about Yūko on 15 January.
5. 14 April 1907.

sad it was to lose a person I loved. It was impossible to contain my emotions; besides, I could not stand to see my mother mourn. Therefore, I hid myself in a place where no one would find me, and I cried my heart out. I still remember wishing in my childish heart that I had died instead of her. Recently, in the summer of 1904, in the brutal battle of Port Arthur, my one and only brother was killed deep within enemy lines; and his remains were not returned to us for some time. I suffered tremendously because it brought back the memory of my sister's death. My pain had not yet healed when my beloved Yūko died. One may say that one's feeling for one's family is always strong, but the bond between parent and child is something very special. When Yūko died, I underwent the most excruciating pain I had ever experienced. As I went through your memoir of Mitsu, I resonated with every twist and turn of your feelings because of my own experience. The child you lost was your first child, and the firstborn enjoys its parents' undivided attention. Small girls are especially adorable. How you must have suffered when you lost Mitsu—I know what a tender, loving father you are. Our children are infinitely dear to us, and that is an indubitable fact.

At the time of Yūko's death, some mourners told me and my wife that it was too bad that we lost her after she had grown up to six years old. But that has nothing to do with it. Others consoled us by saying it was fortunate that it was not a boy but a girl who had died; still others said that we were fortunate that we had other children. But how can this kind of reasoning console us? When Dostoyevsky lost his child, someone tried to comfort him by saying that he could have another. Responding to this, he said: "How can I love another child? I only want Sonia."

The love of parents is absolute. There is no room for rationalization. We are filled with the memories of the dead child and miss the child desperately. We feel sorry for the child and wish the child to be somehow restored to life. Young or old, it is true that death is the law of life. If we could rationalize by thinking that the dead are countless and that the death of our own child is but one more death among millions, there should be no logical reason for us to grieve. But even though death is the eternal law of humankind, what is sorrowful is sorrowful. Even though hunger and thirst are natural conditions of human existence, hunger and thirst are hunger and thirst. People say that the dead will not come back to life, so that we should not dwell on them but should try to forget them. This kind of reasoning brings unbearable pain to us parents. There is a saying that time heals all wounds and thus it is nature's boon. There is a grain of truth in this, but it also shows the callousness of the human heart. I don't want to forget my daughter. I want to keep her memory alive, at least as long as I live. This is a parent's earnest wish.

I remember, a long time ago, you and I used to sit right next to each other at school and read Washington Irving's *Sketch Book*. There was a line in it that read something like this: Pain tries to heal itself, but the wound inflicted by bereavement wishes to live on, secretly warming the memory of the dead. These lines come back to my mind now with added meaning. To remember our deceased children is the least we can do for them. The sorrow that arises in me the moment I recall Yūko is painful, but I do not wish that pain to go away.

A poet once said: "Our dead daughter was pretty. When we think of her, we ourselves are reduced to being children."[6] Indeed, parents' love for their children may be uninteresting to others, seemingly self-pitying and grudging. But I learned through the loss of my daughter that the real human touch is in that kind of experience. Kant said something like: "Everything has a price of its own, but human beings are priceless; we are the ends, while however precious a thing is, it is just a means. There is nothing more precious than human persons. We can compensate for the loss of a thing, but we cannot substitute anything for the life of a person, however young he or she may be." This absolute value of a person is most acutely felt when one loses one's own child.

When Goethe's child died, he is said to have kept on working, saying: "Beyond the dead." Goethe must have had some great realization. But our work, if cut off from our human feelings, has no value. Be it scholarly pursuit or running a business, we carry it out for the sake of humanity. If we talk about human feelings, nothing is more poignant than the feeling of parents' love for their children, although it is such a mundane thing. Those who merely hold lofty ideals and forget the natural beauty of human feelings paradoxically exhibit their poverty of spirit. We respect General Nogi precisely because his person shows forth through his poem:

Mountains and rivers, grass and trees, all are in devastation.
The wind blowing from ten miles away brings the smell of the freshly dead
bodies to the battle ground, which is now in my charge.

---

6. The allusion is to the poet of the Heian period, Ki no Tsurayuki, *Tosa nikki* [Tosa diary], entry of 4 February 935 C.E.

The cavalry does not proceed, and men have no strength left in them even to
utter a word.
I stand and watch the sunset outside the city wall of Jinzhou. [7]

I learned a great lesson from the wretched death of Yūko. I felt as
if a bucketful of cold water was poured on my constantly busied heart,
which had been preoccupied with gaining fame and profit, and I felt a
certain sense of cool purity. I also felt in the deep recesses of my heart
that a clear, warm light—like that of an autumn day—shone forth,
and a genuine, universal love for everyone sprang up within me. What
struck me deeply was that Yūko, until then happily talking, singing,
and playing, had all of a sudden disappeared and turned into white
bones in an urn. If life is simply that, it would indeed be meaningless.
But I think there is something profound here. The spiritual life of a
human being is far from trivial. We need the problem of death so that
we can grapple with life. Before the naked fact of death, life is but a
bubble. Only by solving the problem of death can we fully realize the
significance of life.

In extreme situations, we make a turnabout. The inconsolable grief
and sorrow with which parents mourn the death of their children turns
our heart to look for some means of consolation. When I remember
Yūko, whose life was as evanescent as morning dew on summer grass,
I feel the pain of my broken heart. But I am reminded thereby that I,
who am grieving over the death of Yūko, will someday die. Both the
lamenting and the lamented will return to earth in the mountains covered with evergreen trees; there will remain only the wind blowing
through the pine trees, amid the sounds of insects chirping. It will be
hard to tell who died first and who died later. Such is the law of life.
Death, viewed from the perspective of eternity, renders grieving
absurd.

Yūko was born, failed to grow up fully, and disappeared, leaving
no trace in the world. Such an existence may be called wretched. But,
in the face of death great heroes and babies alike hold no special privileges. They are one and the same before God. Among the paintings
attributed to Orcagna, there is a picture in which Death captures all
sorts of people, young and old, men and women, and piles up kings and
beggars all in the same heap. Glory and indignity, gain and loss, are but

---

7. Jinzhou is where one of the fiercest battles was fought during the Russo-
Japanese War.

dreams played out on the stage of human drama. In terms of worldly happiness, would it have been fortunate if Yūko had lived longer, or was it fortunate that she died when she did? The common view is that if she had lived longer, it would have been better. But do we ever know the secret of human destiny?

If we set aside noble spiritual aspirations and think about our lives merely in terms of the pursuit of happiness, we might question whether life is truly worth living. Yūko did not know sin or evil; she did not suffer from any sorrow or grief but simply played happily every day; and in her last moments she had her parents' knees as her pillow on which to die. There is a certain poetic beauty in this—her life was like a bouquet of flowers, now scattered over the ground. Even if she is not remembered or her death mourned by many, the clear memories chiseled in our hearts, and the grief that strikes us parents to the bone, must comfort her.

Are there any parents who do not suffer anguish and remorse at the death of their own child? We all torment ourselves with remorse, though too late, thinking we should have done this or that for the child. But we must renounce this kind of remorse in the larger realization that everything is fate. Fate works not only from outside but from inside. Behind all the mistakes we make, there looms an inconceivable power at work. In fact, we feel remorseful because we believe in our own powers. When, in misfortune, we come to terms with our powerlessness and take refuge in God (the Absolute) by abandoning ourselves, the sense of remorse turns into repentance. The burden of guilt is lifted from us, and the mind, freed of our self-conceit, comes to our rescue. For our shortcomings we ask forgiveness of the dead. We may even have a glimmer of that profound faith described in the *Tannishō:* "Chanting the name of Amida Buddha may be the seed of our rebirth into the Pure Land or our descent into hell. We have no way of knowing which way it will turn up."[8] In this kind of realization, we touch life eternal.

---

8. The *Tannishō* is a compilation of the sayings of Shinran by one of his disciples, Yuien. The quotation comes from section 2.

Chapter 7

"Pure Experience" and "On Religion"
(1908–1909)

Nishida began 1908 with the idea of writing a book dealing with *jitsu-zai to jinsei* (reality and life)[1] but was forced to abandon the project because of his poor health; once again he was suffering from a recurrence of pleurisy. Instead, he produced an essay, "Junsui keiken to shii, ishi, oyobi chiteki chokkan" [Pure experience, cognition, will, and intellectual intuition], which became part 1 of his *Zen no kenkyū*. In it he focused his attention on "pure experience."

As early as 1905 Nishida had been interested in the discussion revolving around "pure experience" led by William James. In his notes on psychology, Nishida observed that, concerning the relationship between the mind and the body, the traditional theories of materialism, spiritualism, dualism, and parallelism were all defective in that they failed to explain what we experience. Instead of subscribing to a certain theory, Nishida proceeded to focus on experience itself, which we can know. From this perspective, "spiritual" and "material" phenomena turn out to be different descriptions of the same experiential content, or "pure experience." Nishida found it fruitful to "discard all dogmatic hypotheses," and "approach reality based on the content of our experience."[2]

It is noteworthy that Nishida was reading Bergson's 1889 *Essai sur les données immédiates de la conscience* [Time and free will: an essay on the immediate data of consciousness] at the time when he was working on his essay on "pure experience."[3] Although Nishida might have discovered Bergson through William James, it is highly plausible that he did so on his own through his exploration of contemporary Western thinkers. In his later years, Nishida was clear about the debt he owed Bergson. On January 6, 1941, the day after Bergson died, Nishida gave an interview published in *Asahi Shinbun* that contains the following remark:

> Bergson is not as well known as Kant or Hegel in the contemporary world of philosophy. But when I was teaching at the Fourth Higher School, I personally gained a lot of insight from his idea of "données immédiates." It was only after I familiarized myself with Bergson's thought that I was able to formulate my idea of "pure experience" and publish my *Zen no kenkyū*.[4]

In his essay "Junsui keiken to shii, ishi, oyobi chiteki chokkan," Nishida advances his thesis that "pure experience" is the most encompassing reality. "Pure experience" is an experience of the present goings-on, and it is "pure" in that it has yet to split into subject and object, or into cognition, sensation, and volition. When the purity of the experience breaks up, meaning and judgment arise from our attempt to locate our experience within the context of the past, that is, within what we already know. Meaning and judgment are both pure experiences, viewed from different angles. Cognition, too, is a kind of pure experience. In this context, Nishida questions the conventional distinction between volition and cognition: volition and cognition, he argues, differ not in terms of experience but in terms of the kind (or system) of experience. It is for this reason that one and the same reality can become the object of cognition or volition.

Take, for instance, a glass of water. I can objectively analyze its mineral content as the object of my knowledge, or I may drink it, as the object of my desire to quench my thirst. In this way, volition is a more fundamental system, with closer ties than cognition to the reality of life. But in the end, the cognitive system and the volitional system are not two discrete systems but are systems organically intertwined. Examine the act of drinking wine, for example. We want to drink it (volition), and we determine its vintage and so forth (cognition), but "to taste" is also a volitional act—that is, I *want* to taste it. Even intellectual intuition, that which sees the ideal, is a pure experience in its profound state. Such is best seen in an artistic inspiration or in an effortless performance by an accomplished artist, wherein subject and object are in unity, knowledge and will are perfectly blended, and the distinction between the thing and the self vanishes. Therein, only one world, one scene, is present. This is none other than the manifestation of the "real self." Religious awareness—the knowledge of this real self—is a kind of intellectual intuition that directly grasps the profundity of life. Hence, one must say that scholarly activities and moral actions are sustained by profound religious awareness.[5]

Writing this essay was not easy for Nishida, because he was breaking new ground. He talks about the process in a letter to Tanabe Ryūji:

> These days, I'm slowly working on that philosophical essay. I intend to elaborate on what I wrote in "Jitsuzai" and make it into an essay of fifty to sixty pages long. It would be easy just to summarize and present other's views. But as I try to write something original, I feel as if I'm banging my head against the wall. I'm amazed by how dim-witted I am.[6]

When he finally completed the essay on May 5, he contacted Fujioka and asked for his help to get it published.[7] "Junsui keiken" duly appeared in the August 1908 issue of *Tetsugaku Zasshi*.[8]

Nishida's health declined in the second half of 1908, and he had to refrain from working long hours or engaging in strenuous thinking. Rather than idly passing the time, he thought he would write on "something that is not too demanding,"[9]—"on religion, instead of grappling with difficult philosophical problems."[10] Philosophical thinking clearly involved constant struggle for Nishida, but he could not be ultimately satisfied unless he grappled with "difficult" questions. In any case, he began writing his essay on religion on October 29, 1908.[11] In it he attempted to connect the reality of pure experience and God from a Zen Buddhist perspective. By 1908 he was no longer formally practicing *zazen*, partly because Setsumon Rōshi was no longer available, and partly because he had "poked his head" into scholarship.[12] The "Zen seed" implanted in him was taking root, however, and the act of thinking became for him a kind of meditation practice.

The resulting essay, "Shūkyōron ni tsuite" [On religion], was published in *Teiyū Rinrikai Rinrikōenshū* in May 1909;[13] it corresponds to the first three chapters of part 4 ("Religion") of *Zen no kenkyū*.[14] In this essay Nishida deals with the demand for religious awareness as something that is rooted in the unity of consciousness. By unity, he means the concentrating power of consciousness *(dhyāna)*—our ability to focus our mind on one thing or one idea to the point where the subject-object dichotomy disappears. Permeating the entire universe, this unifying power of consciousness is similar to what the medieval Christian thinkers called *ordo*, "cosmic order." From Nishida's perspective, when Kepler and Newton were moved by the beauty of the orderly movement of the stars and of natural phenomena, they were actually moved by the orderliness of the workings of consciousness.

Religious consciousness, thus understood, is the demand of life itself; it is humanity's deepest and most comprehensive demand. In this way, the universe is essentially a "religious reality."

Nishida defines religion as the relationship between God and humanity. God is the unifying power of consciousness that permeates the entire universe. God and humanity, though separated, must share some common traits, argues Nishida, for otherwise there would be no "relationship." The idea of God as a wholly transcendent creator is not tenable to him. Anticipating criticism of his ideas as "pantheistic," he emphasizes that even if God and humanity share some traits, a distinction between them must be retained.[15]

On the personality of God, Nishida asserts that we are not to infer the divine personality from our knowledge of human personality; rather, the situation is the other way around—it is the divine personality that makes us persons possible. That the divine consciousness is endowed with self-knowledge, free will, and love[16] makes it possible for human beings to partake of the qualities that are essential to making us "persons." Seen thus, the universe is the manifestation of God's personality. Be it the orderly movements of stars in the sky or our daily experiences, a great unifying power is at work, and this power is God. God is to be compared to the state of pure experience wherein there is no subject-object split, no I-thing dichotomy. Ultimately, God is the unifier of pure experience. As such, we cannot see or hear God, but we can see the image of God within the very workings of the unifying power of consciousness; we hear the voice of God in our conscience and reason.

In mid-June 1909 Nishida wrote "Kami to sekai" [God and the world], which was published in the July 1909 issue of *Teiyū Rinrikai Rinrikōenshū*[17] (the essay is chapter 4 of part 4 of *Zen no kenkyū*[18]). In it he furthers his previous argument that we can infer God's nature and God's relation to the world from the nature and contents of the unity of pure experience and from the unity of consciousness. God's eternity, omnipresence, omniscience, and omnipotence are all to be understood in terms of the nature of the unity of consciousness. After all, space and time are established by the unity of consciousness. God and the world are inseparable, since the unity of consciousness (God) gives rise to the contents of consciousness (the world). Moreover, unity implies differentiation. In our activity of reflection, the actual becomes conceptual, the concrete becomes abstract, and the one becomes many. But our activity of reflection actually leads itself to a deeper unity. Nishida interprets the Christian parable of the "fall" or "original sin" to suggest this very nature of "reflection." Precisely because of Adam's fall (that is, humanity's becoming self-conscious), Christ's atonement is meaningful, and the infinite love of God is attested. God and the world stand in opposition only so that a larger unity between the two can be achieved. We individuals are the "outcome" of God's self-differentiation.

On the question of evil, Nishida holds that there is nothing that is intrinsically evil, thus upholding the Buddhist conviction that the original mind—the "Buddha nature"—is pure. Nishida admits, however, that certainly there are sins, dissatisfactions, and torments in life. But without these negative things, life would be flat; therefore, we may regard them as necessary conditions for our spiritual improvement. The religious mind sees God's grace rather than contradictions in these wicked realities. Indeed, the sin repented is the most beautiful thing.

With the conclusion of these essays on religion, Nishida completed his entire manuscript of the *Zen no kenkyū*. Parts 2 (on reality) and 3 (on morality) were finished in 1906, part 1 (on pure experience) in 1908, and part 4 (on religion) at the end of June 1909. The year 1909 felt to Nishida like a harbinger of an eagerly awaited spring. Changes were in the air, and his sense of optimism was justified: a position at Gakushūin came through,[19] and on March 14 his sixth daughter, Umeko, was born. Nishida's household was now full of children, Yayoi, Ken, Sotohiko, Shizuko, Tomoko, Umeko, and Toshiko, Hyō-jirō's child. Nishida joked to Tanabe that "the poor tend to have many children."[20]

On April 1 Nishida rode a train to Kyoto to join Yamamoto[21] in welcoming back Suzuki Daisetz, who had just returned to Japan after twelve years abroad.[22] The reunion took place at Yamamoto's that evening.[23] Even though the three had kept in touch across the seas during those twelve years, seeing Suzuki was something Nishida had long been looking forward to. Yamamoto's diary entries give a sense of their reunion:

> *March 31* Suzuki came. Since his departure for the United States in Meiji 29, thirteen years have passed, but upon seeing each other, the feeling was one of welcoming back my own brother. Suzuki hasn't changed at all—he looks the same and thinks the same way.
>
> *April 1* Evening, Nishida came. Three of us reminisced about the olden days. A relaxed warm atmosphere filled the room. Nishida is a thinker and yet a practical man. Suzuki is a man of practical con-

cerns and ideas, endowed with sympathy. Both men are equally deep. . . . Suzuki's sympathy is comprehensive—he even comes up with what one should do. Nishida's sympathy is generous—leaving one free to decide on the means to take.[24]

The day after their joyous reunion, Nishida, Suzuki, and Yamamoto got together with Matsumoto Bunzaburō. Nishida also saw other former colleagues and students while in Kyoto, including Inaba Masamaru. He left for Tokyo on April 4 to see Fujioka and stayed with him for two days. He also saw Motora and Inoue Tetsujirō, updating his professional connections. Tokunō Bun, Ueda Seiji, Tanabe Ryūji, and Ishikawa Ryūzō, and many other close colleagues, now in Tokyo, came to visit him. Nishida attended a gathering on April 9 at Gakushikai, a club for the graduates of the Imperial University of Tokyo. Those present that afternoon were Inoue, Motora, Tanaka Kiichi (Ōdō), Tokunō, and Kihira Tadayoshi. His former students from the Fourth Higher School and Sansanjuku came to see him as well, and on the day of his departure these former students and colleagues from the Fourth Higher School came to the Shinbashi Station to bid him farewell. Surrounded by hosts of friends, Nishida felt he was no longer a stranger in Tokyo. Before returning to Kanazawa, he stayed overnight in Nagoya at the home of his former colleague, Fujii Otoo. Fujii was then teaching at the Eighth Higher School. Nishida returned home on April 11.

In June 1909 the position of professor of German at Gakushūin came through, thanks to the efforts of Hōjō[25] and Shimizu Tōru.[26] Ueda Seiji, who briefly taught there as an instructor of German, also facilitated this appointment.[27] Nishida had hoped to go into teaching philosophy, and there was a position available at Tokyo Imperial University—a volunteer lectureship without pay. It would have enabled him to teach metaphysics and epistemology, subjects in which he was keenly interested.[28] But he did not take up this opportunity, having felt that it was too preposterous to apply for a volunteer position.[29] Besides, he needed to earn a decent income. His Gakushūin position did not pay him a penny more than what he was earning at the Fourth Higher School. Because the cost of living would be higher in Tokyo, it was not the most ideal offer, but he accepted it, thinking that if he let this chance go there might not be another.[30] He took a chance, thinking that once he was in Tokyo, things would somehow work out.[31] Before he left Kanazawa on August 23, a minor mishap occurred. On August 7, when he was spreading his books on the rooftop to air them before packing, he slipped from a window, hurt himself, and had to be carried to a hospital for stitches. He mended in about a week. He and his family had a busy time packing and shipping household goods and books. Yayoi, by then a student at the Women's Higher School in Kanazawa, decided to complete her study in Kanazawa; she was left in Tosa's care. Toshiko, Hyōjirō's daughter, also remained in Kanazawa with Yayoi and Tosa. The rest of the family moved to Tokyo.

Chapter 8

Gakushūin in Tokyo

A Year of Transition

(1909–1910)

Nishida's gamble to move to Tokyo paid off handsomely. On the home front, he was able to rent a brand-new house in Nishi-ōkubo,[1] adjacent to the estate of Marquis Maeda Toshinari. This arrangement was made possible by Ishikawa Ryūzō, who was working for the Maeda family.[2] The house was situated in a good school district, which was a prime concern for Nishida, who wanted his children to get the best education possible. There was also a tramline nearby, providing a convenient commute to Gakushūin in Mejiro.[3]

The Peers School, Gakushūin, established in 1877, was for the sons[4] (and separately the daughters) of the Meiji aristocracy, or *kazoku*.[5] As of 1884 all *kazoku* boys were required to attend Gakushūin, which aimed to prepare them to be citizens in the modern world.[6] Gakushūin took as its model the practice of the European aristocracy, especially that of the British, whereby young men of the royal family were trained not only in learning skills but were also expected to take up military service.[7] Because of the twofold emphasis, distinguished men with military or literary careers served as president of the school.[8] The president at the time of Nishida's appointment was General Nogi Maresuke,[9] hero of the Russo-Japanese War. Nogi was appointed on the personal wish of Emperor Mutsuhito. Nogi, a man of steadfast loyalty, accepted the position.[10] It was a curious fate for Nishida to end up working with Nogi, for it was under Nogi's command that his younger brother had been killed in action. It is perhaps understandable that Nishida did not have a high opinion of Nogi as a general, although he unquestionably respected him as a man of sincerity.[11]

Nogi emphasized a spirit of *bushidō* (the warrior's code) in his training methods, which valued simplicity and mettle and detested sloth and feebleness. In his eyes the younger generation of aristocrats were spoiled, pampered in their Westernized luxurious lifestyle, and hence needed retraining. He added horseback riding as a regular physical education requirement.[12] Nogi had little sympathy for those students who were engaged in literary activities. There had been a literary fever among the students, who embraced Western ideals and extolled a lofty individualism. These students had formed various literary groups. Such graduates as Mushanokōji Saneatsu,[13] Shiga Naoya,[14] Arishima Takeo,[15] and their juniors, Arishima Ikuma,[16] Yamanouchi Hideo (or Satomi Ton),[17] and Yanagi Muneyoshi formed the Shirakaba (White Birch) Group in April 1910 and began publishing a monthly magazine, *Shirakaba*. Nogi's educational philosophy diametrically opposed the literary interests of students. Had his appointment in 1907 to Gakushūin come a few years earlier, the Shirakaba Group might never have been born—what a loss that would have been to the history of modern Japanese literature! Nogi succeeded in implementing his strict measures because he had the unquestionable support of the students' parents. Many students, however, felt Nogi's measures were too restrictive, and once they graduated from Gakushūin and entered universities, not a few dedicated themselves to the pursuit of joie de vivre—but that is another story.

Since 1906 Gakushūin had observed the beginning of the school year in April (instead of September) in conformity with the rest of the elementary and secondary schools throughout Japan.[18] Therefore, Nishida's appointment as professor came in the middle of the school year. This practice apparently was not uncommon in those days. On Saturday morning, September 11, Nishida and D. T. Suzuki, standing side by side, were introduced to the students as new instructors at the opening ceremony of the second quarter. Nishida and Suzuki were wearing the instructors' uniform, which was designed after a European military uniform, complete with a saber. On this day Nishida saw President Nogi and other professors and administrators for the first time. In the afternoon he proceeded to Hongō, called on Tokunō Bun, Motora Yūjirō, and Ueda Seiji. He dined at the Uedas' and returned home past 10 P.M.

Nishida was put in charge of the German section, succeeding Sakurai Masataka, who had moved to the Eighth Higher School in July.[19] Because students chose French or German as their second foreign language, it is not clear from the class lists who took Nishida's German and who took French. The class lists include[20] such names as third-year student Yanagi Muneyoshi;[21] second-year students Kido Kōichi,[22]

Nagayo Yoshirō,[23] Oda Nobuhiro,[24] and Harada Kumao;[25] and first-year students Ueda Misao[26] and Akamatsu Kotora.[27] Konoe Ayamaro,[28] who would become prime minister (1937–1941), had just entered the First Higher School in 1909 after graduating from the Middle School Division of Gakushūin in March 1909. Thus, Nishida did not know him at Gakushūin, although some Japanese biographers have preferred to assume otherwise.

German was not Nishida's field of expertise, and he was not particularly comfortable with his teaching assignment. Nagayo Yoshirō, one of the thirteen or fourteen students in Nishida's second-year German class, described Nishida the language teacher as someone who simply read aloud lines from the textbook he chose—Carl Hilty's[29] *On Happiness*—and translated them into Japanese as he went along. He never even once asked students to read the German text aloud or translate from it. But as he was going through the chapter on "Epictetus," he would passionately expand on passages that would move him. On these occasions, his enthusiasm was contagious.[30]

The upbringing of the *kazoku* boys, different from that of ordinary untitled boys, surely had a bearing upon their psychological makeup, and Nishida sensed this. Some years later, when his former colleague Hori Koretaka took up a position at Gakushūin, Nishida told him that students at Gakushūin felt that the school authorities did not understand them.[31] Nishida himself modified his teaching style from his Fourth Higher School days, where he had been nicknamed "Professor Schrecken" or "Terrifying Professor." He would not scold the students at Gakushūin, even if they came to class unprepared. He was experienced enough a teacher to know, however, how much or how little his students were studying, and he would occasionally admonish them. Student editors of the school magazine, *Hojinkai Zasshi* (possibly Ueda Misao and Akamatsu Kotora), memorialized Nishida the teacher in their article:

> Occasionally the professor spoke to us, raising his voice, about our laziness, our lack of focus, and our sloth; he especially insisted that our attitude toward learning was not serious enough, not sincere enough. Behind these words, we unmistakably felt his warmth. Each word of his, each action of his, carried a certain dignity and evoked in us a sense of respect and adoration for him.[32]

Nishida's intellectual and social life inside and outside the school tremendously improved. Through old friends and former colleagues, his circle of acquaintances widened quickly. As a professor of Gakushūin, he was invited to events hosted by the imperial family, such as chrysanthemum-viewing garden parties and weddings of the princesses. On these occasions, Kotomi was also invited, but because the Nishidas lacked the money to have a special "robe decorté" (a formal ceremonial dress for ladies) made for her, she politely excused herself from these occasions. After Nishida saw Emperor Mutsuhito at the cherry blossom viewing at Hama Detached Palace on April 27, 1910, he noted his impression in his diary: "His Majesty looks quite old with a white beard. Her Majesty is short."

Nishida enjoyed the company of his close and dear friends in Tokyo. Fujioka Sakutarō, an assistant professor of Japanese literature at Tokyo Imperial University, lived in a house in the Hongō area. Nishida called on him from time to time. Suzuki Daisetz was now his colleague at Gakushūin,[33] and so was Shimizu Tōru, a senior to Nishida at the Fourth Higher School and now a leading scholar of the Meiji Constitution. Tokunō Bun was a lecturer at Tokyo Imperial University and assisted the editors of *Tetsugaku Zasshi*. Ueda Seiji was then an assistant professor of German literature at Tokyo Imperial University and was about to leave for Europe for study abroad. Nishida also found his former colleagues from Yamaguchi Higher School days at Gakushūin: Koyanagi Shigeta and Alfred Charlton. Other colleagues from Yamaguchi, Togawa Shūkotsu and Tobari Chikufū, were teaching in Tokyo. He also renewed his acquaintance with the recently retired dean of the College of Humanities at Kyoto Imperial University, Kanō Kōkichi.[34] The two knew each other from when Nishida was a university student and Kanō rented Nishida's house in Kanazawa.

Many of Nishida's former students from the Fourth Higher School were in Tokyo as well, such as Horio Nariaki,[35] and the graduates of Sansanjuku, Yamazaki Naozō,[36] Ishiguro Bunkichi, Kawai Yoshinari, Shinagawa Kazue, Sōya Heihachi, Tada Heigorō, among others. On November 13, 1909, they had a get-together at Seifūtei, a restaurant in Ushigome.[37] Nishida enjoyed this reunion and returned home around midnight. Several colleagues from the Fourth Higher School were in Tokyo. They got together on March 30, 1910, at Mikawaya, a sukiyaki restaurant in Yotsuya and renewed their old ties.[38]

The former students of Sansanjuku who had become Christian, Akizuki Itaru, Takakura Tokutarō, and Tominaga Fukuji, were among those who happily renewed their ties with Nishida. They were studying with, or assisting, Uemura Masahisa at the Tokyo Theological Seminary, which he had established in 1904. Ōsaka Motokichirō,[39] once a devoted disciple of Uemura together with Akizuki and Taka-kura (the group known as "the three disciples of Uemura Masahisa from the Fourth Higher School," or *shikō no sanbagarasu*), had a falling-out with Uemura because of personality conflicts and had left Japan in 1908 to pursue his studies at the Auburn Theological Seminary in New York State.

It was Nishida who had originally recommended Uemura to his students who wanted to go into Christian missionary work. Nishida probably chose Uemura from among the Japanese Christian leaders because he was a man with a healthy sense of *samurai* spirit. Nishida must have read Uemura's writings, which were published in the *Rikugō Zasshi*, a journal Uemura and Kozaki Hiromichi started in October 1880. Uemura, dubbed as the "pope" of Japanese Christian churches, greatly contributed to the indigenization of Christianity in Meiji period Japan. In fact, Nishida had been introduced to Uemura in 1907 by his Christian colleague Mizuashi Ikujirō when Uemura visited the Fourth Higher School in Kanazawa. At the time, Nishida observed that Uemura "appear[ed] to be a man of wide reading; although he is not a gifted speaker, there is something impressive about him." [40] While in Tokyo, Nishida was invited a few times to Uemura's home together with Akizuki and Takakura. On one of these occasions they discussed mysticism, and Nishida borrowed a book on Western mysticism from Uemura. [41] Nishida also visited Kōkōdō, a house in Morikawa-chō, where the disciples of the late Kiyozawa Manshi lived together. Kiyozawa was a charismatic reformer of the True Pure Land sect, and his followers continued to live together even after the master's death on June 6, 1903. Nishida probably heard about Kōkōdō from Inaba Masamaru, his colleague at Yamaguchi Higher School. Inaba had been Kiyozawa's right-hand man in the reform movement. While still in Kanazawa, Nishida came to know Kiyozawa's disciples, Tada Kanae and Akegarasu Haya, each of whom came to Sansanjuku and gave a talk. Nishida befriended Sasaki Gesshō at Kōkōdō; Sasaki later became president of Ōtani University and was to play a major role in inviting Suzuki Daisetz as a professor there.

In this way, Nishida found many occasions to engage in discussions on matters of religion. He also contributed his essay, "On Religion," to the Gakushūin student journal, *Hojinkai Zasshi*. [42] The Maeda family had a private school, Keigijuku. [43] Nishida was invited to attend lectures given at the *juku*, where he came to know the marquis personally. [44] Soon, he was invited to participate in the running of the *juku* and to talk to the students. He gave a talk on Tolstoy [45] on February

27, and he invited Suzuki Daisetz to speak about Swedenborg on March 19, 1910.

To earn extra income, Nishida taught part-time at Nihon University from October 1909 to March 1910,[46] and then at Buzan University from April to June 1910.[47] He also renewed his old ties with Inoue Tetsujirō, Motora Yūjirō, and Nakajima Rikozō, although Nakajima was abroad most of that year. Nishida called on Inoue at his home about once a month. In addition, he rejoined the Philosophical Society and actively participated in their monthly meetings. He also regularly attended the meetings of the Psychology Society and the Teiyū Ethics Society.[48]

Amid his heavy teaching load and active social life, Nishida gradually managed to return to his philosophical inquiry. His diary for October 26 reads: "An extra came out in the evening, breaking the news that Itō Hirobumi was assassinated in Harbin. Tonight, I had a little breakthrough in my thought."[49] The assassination of the former prime minister, who had visited the Fourth Higher School in 1899, and whom Nishida met at that time, must have shaken him out of his daily routine and opened up his mind to a larger horizon. About a month later, on November 30, Itō Kichinosuke,[50] a graduate student of philosophy at Tokyo Imperial University, called on Nishida and asked him to speak at the monthly meeting of the Philosophical Society.[51] Nishida accepted the offer, for it was an excellent occasion for him to sort out his ideas and try them out on his peers. On December 19 he talked about "Junsui keiken sōgo no kankei oyobi renraku ni tsuite" [The mutual relationships and connections of pure experiences].[52] Although he was dissatisfied with his own presentation,[53] the ensuing discussion was lively, and the meeting lasted well past 9 P.M.[54] According to the established custom, his talk was printed in the February 1910 issue of *Tetsugaku Zasshi*.[55]

In his talk Nishida focused on the difference between himself and William James regarding the interpretation of the term "pure experience." He agrees with James that pure experience is the primary stuff of reality and that experience is something active and not merely passive,[56] but he feels that James takes lightly the "unifying nature" of experience, that is, its "structural" or "systematic" aspect. Nishida quotes from James's *Pragmatism* and other works that argue that experience is something finite and fragmentary and that according to how these finite and fragmentary experiences are connected, various worlds come into being. James appears to Nishida to oppose monistic thinking by regarding all truths as being shaped by their contexts and by holding that there is no absolute truth. In contrast, Nishida holds that various experiences are the developments of the *system* of consciousness itself. That is, experience is characterized by self-differentiation of self-consciousness, "the concrete universal." How consciousness operates is best seen in the nature of the number system, which unfolds infinitely. Although the relationships among numbers are infinitely conceivable, any particular number as part of the number system is unique and singular. Unlike James, Nishida maintains that there is a universal, creative, and unifying power at work at the foundation of all experiences.

The difference between James and Nishida may be attributable to temperamental differences, and more especially to their views of the "self." A biographer tells us that James's father, Henry James Sr., a man of Christian faith, considered losing "the individual self in the selfhood of God" as the highest good. William, however, was prone to psychological disorders and had to assert his individual selfhood to survive.[57] In marked contrast with James, Nishida was convinced that the source of the authentic selfhood was the true self, which is beyond one's ego-centered self, and that to attain this true self one's ego-bound self had to die.

Nishida welcomed the new year with his family, and in that afternoon he set out to the coastal town of Ōiso, where Fujioka Sakutarō was wintering, avoiding the harsh cold of Tokyo. In the evening the two friends took a walk on the beach, discussing what the category "Japanese literature" should be, and whether such works as Rai San'yō's *Nihongaishi*, written in Chinese, should be included. The next day, they spent all day talking, and on the third day they took a walk in the hills of Ōiso, where some plum blossoms were already in bloom. In the afternoon, Nishida got in a train bound for Kamakura; Fujioka saw him off at the platform.

A month later on February 3, 1910, the news that Fujioka died reached Nishida in the early afternoon while he was teaching third-year students. Tokunō Bun telephoned the school, and the message was hand-delivered to Nishida by a handyman. He immediately cancelled the class and hurried to the Fujiokas' home. Apparently nothing was unusual with Fujioka until the night before, but his condition suddenly deteriorated around 3 A.M., and he died of heart failure. "Ah, the farewell at Ōiso in the beginning of this year turned out to be the eternal farewell,"[58] wrote Nishida in his diary. From childhood on, Fujioka had been suffering from asthma and continuous bronchial problems. He died just as if a candle had simply burned its last bit of wick. At the news of his death, his colleagues and friends rushed to his house to mourn, all sharing the same grief and wish—if only Fujioka had been blessed with two more decades of life! Despite his frail health, Fujioka was a prolific writer of meticulous scholarship and was pioneering a field in the study of Japanese literature and language. He had written several books, *Nihon fūzokushi* [A history of Japanese customs];[59] *Heianchō bungakushi* [A history of Heian literature], 1905; *Kindai kaigashi* [A history of modern paintings];[60] *Kokubungakushi kōwa* [A narrative history of Japanese literature], 1908; and *Sandai Shōunkō-den* [A biography of Lord Maeda Shōun], 1907. He also wrote school textbooks on Japanese grammar, Japanese literature, and Japanese history, which were widely used.[61]

Nishida stayed at the Fujioka's for the wake. Fujii Otoo, Fujioka's close friend, traveled from Nagoya to take care of the funeral arrangements. Anesaki Masaharu,[62] professor of religion at Tokyo Imperial University, was among the mourners, and Nishida saw him for the first time. Fujioka was survived by his mother, his wife, Tatsumi,[63] three children, his younger brother, Kōji, and an aunt. Fujioka's oldest son, Yoshio, was then seven, the daughter, Aya, was four, and the youngest son, Michio, was two. Yoshio vividly remembered the day of his father's death:

> When I came home from school, the screen doors of the back room were all closed, and I heard my mother sobbing. Fearing something was wrong, I went around the rooms through the kitchen and peeped into the back room from the veranda. Dr. Irisawa, noticing me, gestured to me to come in. My mother's voice, "My dear boy, your father is dead," still rings clearly in my ears.[64]

The funeral took place on February 6 at the Shinjōji temple in Hōraichō. On that day, Fujioka's second son fell quite ill, and Nishida had to take him to a hospital. Following the funeral, there was much business to be taken care of, and Nishida's practical side saw to this. He took part in the discussion of publishing the collected works of Fujioka, who had left behind voluminous unpublished manuscripts as well as published materials. Haga Yaichi,[65] assisted by Yoshikawa Hideo, a former student of Fujioka's, and Wakimoto Sokurō,[66] Fujioka's family friend, took charge of this project.[67] Nishida also tried to find a buyer for Fujioka's huge collection of books.[68] It appears that the Ishikawa Prefecture Library in Kanazawa eventually secured this collection.[69] Nishida, together with Yamamoto Ryōkichi and Fujii Otoo, assumed full responsibility for seeing to the education of Fujioka's bereaved children. They managed to raise sufficient money among Fujioka's friends and colleagues and set up an educational fund for them. [70]

Nishida suffered tremendously from the death of his dear friend, so much so that it was not until thirty years later that he felt like writing anything about Fujioka. To talk about him soon after his death caused him too much pain. [71] A similar sentiment overtook Yamamoto Ryōkichi. [72] Nishida's essay on Fujioka, "Wakakarishi hi no Tōho" [Tōho of the younger days] [73] appeared in the April 1940 issue of *Kokugo to Kokubungaku* [Japanese Language and Literature], a special issue dedicated to the scholarship of Fujioka Sakutarō. Nishida's contribution begins with these words:

> It's already been thirty years since Fujioka died. I am not qualified to speak about Fujioka the scholar of Japanese literature.
>
> The only thing I can say is that we were close friends. We could always talk about everything frankly, and we gave each other necessary support for many years. Thirty years after your death, a commemorative volume dedicated to you is appearing, and I feel special joy, as if the honor were conferred on me. [74]

A happier memory of Tokyo for Nishida was the visit he made with Yamamoto and Suzuki to the former house of Lafcadio Hearn in Nishi-ōkubo on Saturday afternoon, March 19, 1910. They were guided by Tanabe Ryūji, who had been Hearn's student at the Imperial University. [75] Tanabe was instrumental in promoting Nishida's interest in Hearn. [76] Nishida read Hearn's various writings and found himself sympathizing with Hearn (see Nishida's essay at the end of this chapter).

By March 1910 Nishida felt increasingly confident about his health; his pleurisy had become well contained. He was ready to resume his philosophical inquiry. [77] At the same time, he harbored reservations about teaching German, [78] a quandary known to his friends. When Tomoeda Takahiko, assistant professor of ethics at Kyoto Imperial University, was appointed to study abroad, a vacancy opened up. Matsumoto Bunzaburō, dean of the College of Humanities, and Yamamoto Ryōkichi, dean of students, were in an ideal position to help Nishida land this position. As early as November 1909 Yamamoto had approached Nishida about whether he was willing to move to Kyoto. [79] Nishida was ready to make the change. He consulted Hōjō Tokiyuki, who, however, was obliged to remain neutral in this case because he had earlier recommended Nishida to Gakushūin. [80]

Nogi Maresuke generously gave Nishida the permission to leave Gakushūin, should the offer materialize. The appointment of Nishida was discussed at the faculty meeting of the philosophy department in Kyoto the following spring. However, there was one fly in the ointment. Nishida was older than the head of the department, Kuwaki Gen'yoku. Nishida himself found the problem trivial and wrote to Yamamoto:

> It does not bother me at all to hold a rank junior to Mr. Kuwaki. If I can be of any help, I will sincerely assist him and do my best for the sake of the ethics program. If I can have the luxury of time and access to books, and freely engage in study, there is nothing more that I would desire. In the worst scenario, even the position of lecturer would do. I feel uneasy continuing to teach German, a subject in which I have no self-confidence. [81]

Nishida's intention was clearly communicated to the department members, and his appointment was unanimously supported at the faculty meeting of April 22.[82] Kano Naoki recalled how that decision was reached:

> Mr. Nishida was a year ahead of me at the university. . . . I never saw him in any of my classes, but I got to know him in the library, which I used to frequent and where I would see him all the time. Sometimes we sat at the same desk, facing each other. We began to exchange words. . . . Some knew you well, others less, but many of us knew you one way or the other, and we unanimously voted to have you join us. In this way, I got to renew my old friendship with you. [83]

Just around this time, Halley's comet was visible from the earth, starting on May 19, 1910. Nishida observed it with keen interest.[84] Did he sense that his career was beginning to take off just like the shooting comet? His appointment at Kyoto Imperial University erased the stigma attached to his limited-status background. Inoue Tetsujirō, Nakajima Rikizō, and Motora Yūjirō were all present at the farewell party held in Nishida's honor on July 14, 1910, at Gakushikai. Others present at the gathering were Kanō Kōkichi, Anesaki Masaharu, Tokiwa Daijō, Nakajima Tokuzō, Togawa Shūkotsu, Ibaraki Seijirō, Hatta Miki, Ōshima Masanori, Tokunō Bun, and Kihira Tadayoshi— Nishida's friends, colleagues, and professional acquaintances.[85] Inoue Tetsujirō made a farewell speech.[86] The idea of collecting Nishida's essays for publication (this would become his first book, *Zen no kenkyū*) was brought up around that time by Tokunō and Kihira.

Nishida's family first moved to Kyoto on July 25, and he followed them on August 3. His sojourn of less than a year in Tokyo turned out to be a significant one. It brought him out of the academic isolation that he suffered in Kanazawa and helped him embark on the career of a philosophy professor at an imperial university. Some of the students he came in contact with while at Gakushūin, such as Kido Kōichi and Harada Kumao, were to occupy politically weighty positions in the 1930s and 1940s. Nishida's brief career at Gakushūin was to shape his world in unexpected directions beyond his wildest dreams.

On Lafcadio Hearn *

I did not know Professor Hearn personally, nor have I read many of his writings. I may therefore be criticized for being presumptuous in writing this preface to his biography. My excuse is that I am so over-joyed that my dear friend Tanabe Ryūji[1] has finally completed his project of writing his mentor's biography—a work he has carried out in addition to his official duties as a professor and that has taken him several years to complete. Also, I too am interested in Hearn as a person and in some of his writings, especially the short essays in *Exotics and Retrospectives* (1898) and the *Shadowings* (1900).

Hearn was a writer possessing a kind of mysticism that enabled him to see the workings of the spirit behind everything. He not only felt the pulsation of several thousand years of ancestral heritage in simple sensation and emotion, but he also saw the activities of past generations of our ancestors' spirits revealed in our simple bodily expressions.

According to Hearn, we as persons are not limited to one generation. Each of us is a composite of multiple persons coming down through the generations. Waves of life inherited from our ancestors surge up through our bodies, each body being a segment of the end-

---

* "*Koizumi Yakumo-den*, Jo," NKZ 1:410–13; originally published in Tanabe Ryūji, *Koizumi Yakumo*, 4th ed. (Tokyo: Hokuseidō Shoten, 1980), x–xii. This English translation, published in *Monumenta Nipponica* 51.3 (1996), 313–16, is reprinted with the permission of *Monumenta Nipponica*.

1. Tanabe, a beloved student of Hearn's at the Imperial University, remained a close family friend of the Koizumis even after Hearn's death. At the time of Nishida's visit to Hearn's house in 1910, Tanabe was working on a biography of Hearn.

less pillar of the spirit extending from the distant past to the present. Thus the physical body is the material manifestation of a host of spirits. Accordingly, Hearn recalled the blue skies of the pleasant summers of countless past generations in the vast indigo stream of the Gulf of Mexico. He pictured volcanic eruptions and wild flames of forest fires —as would have been witnessed by countless past generations—in the scarlet rays burning the sky of a tropical sunset. He heard whispers of the spirit of the deceased parents and grandparents in the constantly changing features of a child. And he nostalgically thought about the countless generations of the transmigration of souls in the thrill of a handshake with a woman he loved.

In Hearn's eyes, this world was not a fixed world of matter but of evolving spirit, going back to the past of the past and reaching out to the future of the future. The so-called law of the natural sciences established between changeless things provides merely their surface relationships. Behind these he saw the force of evolving spirit at work, operation between the infinite past and the infinite future.

For Hearn, even the ordinary world was colored with a deep mystical hue; for him, a poet's vision was reality. He translated a beautiful poem by Théophile Gautier, whom he very much admired, from the collection called *Émaux et camées* [Enamels and cameos]. If I may paraphrase the poem, it reads something like this:

> Two blocks of marble in the pediment of a Greek temple dreamed their dreams together. Later, they turned into the flesh of two lovers. Two pearls, which grew up in the same shell, whispered to each other at the bottom of the sea, becoming the teeth of lovers seeking each other. Two roses, rustling among the leaves under the splash of the fountain in the garden of Generalife [in Granada, Spain], became lips that loved each other. Two doves, which shared on a May evening the same nest upon a Venician cupola, became two hearts yearning for each other. And so the romantic sparkles of ancient times were newly kindled and burned between two lovers.[2]

This shows Hearn's approach.

Hearn loved to write ghost stories. They are interesting not because they are ghost stories but because they are set against a spiritual background of the kind described above. He approached Japa-

---

2. Hearn's translation appears in Elizabeth Bisland, *The Life and Letters of Lafcadio Hearn* (Boston: Houghton Mifflin, 1906), vol. 1, pp. 259–61.

nese culture and folk tales from this same perspective, uncovering a dimension of the soul hitherto unknown to the Japanese.[3]

Philosophically speaking, while Mr. Hearn's thinking comes close to animism, we certainly cannot identify it with the ordinary theory of animism. The workings of the spirit which he saw behind all things are the activities of spirits with personal histories. Hearn said that he got this idea from Spencer, but Spencer's theory of evolution merely refers to material evolution, and it holds that organisms, originally without any structure, gradually became differentiated and that distinct parts [of the body, for instance] became integrated into a unified whole. Blessed with a literary sensitivity, Hearn transformed this Spencerian view of evolution and interpreted it as an evolution of the spirit. By tying it to the Buddhist doctrine of transmigration and rebirth, he gave it a clearly poetic coloring and religious flavor. Previously, Nietzsche had given the theory of biological evolution a spiritual significance, and thereby romanticized it. Bergson, too, is this type of thinker. Hearn's thinking has some aspects which resemble Bergson's, but Hearn's is, of course, purely emotive and imaginary.

A military doctor born in Ireland fell passionately in love with a Greek beauty on the Ionian islands. Her brother hated the British and made an attempt on his life, but thanks to his lover's help he escaped. Born of these parents on the island of Leucadia (where Sappho is said to have put an end to her life by jumping into the sea), Hearn grew up in France, moved to the United States, and finally reached the shores of the Far East to become a naturalized citizen of Japan. This life is in itself a romance.

Hearn's emotional disposition, tested by the hardships of his early years, evolved into that of a sensitive author. I hear that he grew misanthropic in his later years, perhaps the result of his single-minded concentration on writing. But I believe that it is only natural for anyone to turn this way if he or she is sensitive and has to endure a lonely and sad existence for a long time. While he distanced himself from people, his innate sociability may have predisposed him to look for

---

3. See Nishida's essay, "Zakkan," NKZ 19:775, in which he states that he learned more about the essence of Japanese tradition through the writings of Hearn, a foreigner, than through the writings of the Japanese. Nishida refuted two extreme views that were current at that time: (1) the universalist view that all different global cultures develop in the same direction and (2) the chauvinistic view that every country has its own individual values that are incommunicable to others.

human affection in everything. I suspect that the reason why he heard whispers of the spirit behind all things was because of his deep-seated longing for love.

When I was living in Ōkubo a few years ago, I went with Tanabe one day to visit the house where Hearn used to live. His living quarters were preserved just as they had been when he was alive. His study faced a quiet garden surrounded by well-trimmed bushes and it was filled with books. There was an unusually high desk, an old ink bottle, a water jar, a strange-looking monocle, and various kinds of tobacco pipes. I felt the presence of his genius there, and I was filled with a strong and affectionate respect for him. To me, who grew up in the countryside, this visit will long remain a memory of my brief stay in Tokyo.

Chapter 9

Kyoto Imperial University

Early Years

(1910–1912)

Nishida moved to Kyoto. He was forty years old, and Kotomi, thirty-five years old, was pregnant for the eighth time. By the time Nishida arrived in Kyoto, the rest of his family was already settled in a house on Konoe Street, a few blocks south of the university campus. Right away, he wrote postcards to his friends in Tokyo, informing them of his new address. He then called on Yamamoto. In the evening of the same day he visited Kotomi's parents, Tokuda Tagayasu and Tei, who were living in the precinct of the Chion'in Temple. During the first week after his arrival in Kyoto, he took his family for walks to such famous places as the Golden Pavilion, the Saga area, Kiyomizu Temple, Sanjūsangendō, and Higashi-honganji, taking in the air of Kyoto. He also called on Kuwaki Gen'yoku, the head of the philosophy department. On one rainy day, instead of going out for a walk, he put his books in order. He also saw his office on campus and visited Fujii Otoo, his former colleague from the Fourth Higher School who had been teaching Japanese literature in the Department of Literature since November 1909.

Kyoto Imperial University, founded in 1897, opened its College of Humanities in 1906, with Kanō Kōkichi as the founding dean of the college. Kanō was supported by Matsumoto Bunzaburō, Kuwaki Gen'-yoku, Kano Naoki, and Tanimoto Tomeri. These founding members felt that the new college should be "thoroughly academic and dedicated to research, and yet open and liberal." [1] Because their institution was the "younger" brother of Tokyo Imperial University, they hoped to distinguish themselves by designing a unique curriculum and adopting an unconventional method of hiring professors. [2] At Tokyo Imperial University only its own graduates with promising careers in academia were considered for faculty positions; at Kyoto they chose to hire men of talents far beyond the confines of academic walls.[3] Kanō Kōkichi was probably the one who pushed this policy of "identifying talents in the wild" *(no ni iken o motomu)*. In the early days, however, Kanō felt tension with the government and resigned from the university on October 21, 1908, leaving Matsumoto Bunzaburō to succeed to the position of dean.

Without this liberal hiring policy, it would not have been possible to appoint Nishida as assistant professor, because he lacked a proper university diploma (the "limited status" diploma did not count). He was appointed assistant professor of ethics, replacing Tomoeda Takahiko, who was leaving to study abroad for several years.[4] It appears that Nishida's position was more than a temporary replacement from the beginning. There must have been an agreement that he would be retained as a permanent member of the faculty.

Before Nishida got busy preparing his lectures, he took his family to Kanazawa on August 11. It was a cherished duty to report to his mother his new appointment as assistant professor at the Imperial University. That he was finally able to "earn his bread as a philosopher" greatly gladdened his mother, Tosa, who had raised him in her unwavering conviction that "there was no one more precious in the world than a scholar." Nishida and his family stayed at the house at Chanokichō, where Tosa, Masa, Yayoi, and Toshiko were living. He made his rounds, seeing his former colleagues at the Fourth Higher School, and called on those to whom he owed special thanks, especially Kamiyama Kosaburō, his teacher of mathematics when he was still a teenager. Master Setsumon happened to be in Kanazawa, and the two picked up their friendship where they had left it.

On Saturday, August 20, Nishida arranged for a Buddhist ceremony at the Chōrakuji Temple in Unoke to commemorate the fiftieth anniversary of his grandfather's death, the thirteenth anniversary of his father's death, the twenty-seventh anniversary of his older sister Nao's death, and the seventh anniversary of the death of his younger brother, Hyōjirō. The family and relatives gathered for this occasion. In those days, when the sons of the family reached a respectable social position, they were expected to hold such a Buddhist ceremony to honor the ancestors. Having duly executed his filial duty, Nishida and his family spent several more days in Kanazawa, where he saw his former colleague Takahashi Shūji off for Tokyo—to teach, in fact, at Gakushūin. Nishida visited Sansanjuku with Mitake and got together with former and current students. He saw a few more friends and familiar faces before he returned to Kyoto on August 27. Two days later, on August 29, the news of the annexation of Korea was broken to the Japanese people.

The College of Humanities at Kyoto Imperial University was enjoying its youthful vigor and untapped potential. Matsumoto Bunzaburō, who was in charge of religious studies and Indian philosophy, was only a year older than Nishida. So was Takase Takejirō, who taught the history of Chinese thought. Kuwaki Gen'yoku, the Kantian specialist, who had just returned from his study abroad (1907–1909), was thirty-eight. Tomonaga Sanjūrō, a specialist on the rationalists, Hegel, and German idealism, then studying abroad, was thirty-nine. Matsumoto Matatarō, a specialist in psychology, was forty-five and the eldest of the group. Tanimoto Tomeri, a specialist in philosophy of education, was forty-four. Kano Naoki, who specialized in the history of Chinese civilization and literature, was forty-two. A scholar of aesthetics, Fukada Yasukazu, still abroad, was only thirty-two years old. Naitō Konan, a Sino-Japan specialist, was forty-four. A lecturer in sociology, Yoneda Shōtarō, who had studied at Columbia University in the United States and then with J. G. Tarde at the College de France in Paris, was thirty-seven. Uchida Ginzō, an economic historian, who had studied at Oxford, was thirty-eight. Ueda Bin, a poet-scholar of English literature, whose ability to master the English language Lafcadio Hearn praised as one in a million, was thirty-six. Fujishiro Teisuke, professor of German literature, who had translated the *Man'yōshū* into German with Karl Florenz at the Imperial University, was forty-two. The average age of the faculty members of the college was scarcely forty, and this factor encouraged collegial conviviality and frank and open intellectual exchanges.

After his return from Kanazawa, Nishida then focused his attention on his lecture notes. That year he was in charge of two courses, Introduction to Philosophy *(tetsugaku gairon)* and lectures in special topics in ethics *(rinrigaku)*. The curriculum was divided in such a way that students were required to take all the introductory courses related to their major fields. Generally speaking, the first-year students took the introductory courses *(futsū kōgi)*, second-year students took lectures on special topics *(tokushu kōgi)*, and third-year students took specialized seminars focused on specific texts *(enshū)*. Yamamoto Ryōkichi placed an announcement of his friend's arrival in the university student association publication, which read: "Replacing Assistant Professor of Ethics Tomoeda, who leaves for Europe in September, Assistant Professor Nishida will teach courses in ethics. Come by on Thursday morning to his Introduction to Philosophy class. Most likely you will be surprised that even classroom nine, the largest of the College of Humanities, will be packed."[5] This was a slight exaggeration, for Nishida's name was known then only among a limited number of philosophy specialists.

Nishida gave his first Introduction to Philosophy lecture on Thursday, September 22, and the lecture on ethics the following day. He walked into the classroom wearing kimono (top) and *hakama* (trousers), and a pair of old-fashioned rubber boots. His appearance struck the students as odd, for most of the professors, having studied in the West, were well groomed and gave lectures in three-piece suits. Since *geta* (wooden clogs) were not permitted on campus, probably because of the loud noise they make, it was by no means unusual for students to come to school in their kimono and Western shoes, but in the case of Nishida, it was not just an ordinary pair of shoes but a pair of old-fashioned rubber boots called "deep rubber" *(fukagomu)*. A colleague remarked half in jest that "the secret of Nishida's popularity among the students is that appearance of his!"

Amano Teiyū, a second-year student, who chose Kyoto Imperial University after graduating from the First Higher School in Tokyo so that he could study with Kuwaki Gen'yoku, noted his impression of this new assistant professor: "I had not heard the name Nishida Kitarō before, but when I saw him, I intuitively knew that there was something exceptional about him. But who was able to tell in those days that he was going to accomplish so monumental a task?"[6] Ueda Juzō, then a third-year student of aesthetics, had a much more direct personal impression of Nishida and vividly remembered his very first lecture:

It was a fine sunny day. . . . In the first hour of the lecture, Professor Nishida talked about reference books. He recommended Wundt's [*Einleitung in die Philosophie*, Introduction to Philosophy] as a book that gathered different theories and treated them objectively and fairly. He mentioned [Wilhelm] Jerusalem's [Introduction to Philosophy] as relatively small but dependable and written from the author's own point of view. He also mentioned works by [Oswald] Külpe and [Friedrich] Paulsen.

He then moved into the lecture topic proper, entitled "What kind of discipline is philosophy?" He read aloud from the notebook about half a page, his face practically touching it, then he put down his notebook and expounded to us on what he had just read. While this went on for about two hours, I felt through my pores that this very unassuming lecture was something totally different from any lecture I had ever heard; I felt humanity, warmth, and depth, coming from an entirely different dimension.

When the lecture was over, I put the lid back on my ink bottle and stood up. Amano, who sat next to me, and I spontaneously looked at each other. I don't know who started it, but anyway, we ended up talking about our impressions of those two hours. I don't remember the exact words we used, but I still clearly remember the atmosphere of that day and the impression made by the lecture hall, which had tall large windows and was flooded with the bright sunshine of early fall. On that day, I formed a deep respect for, and profound trust in, the professor. That was the beginning of a personal relationship that was to last for the next forty years.[7]

During the 1910–1911 academic year, Nishida's first year of teaching at Kyoto, he was given a light teaching load of just four hours a week. He nevertheless felt quite pressured, as his letter to Tanabe Ryūji reveals:

I've yet to get accustomed to my new place in Kyoto. I miss Tokyo. My work, for a pleasant change, is interesting, and I feel like giving much of myself to it, but I'm afraid my health is not really what it should be. I give only four hours of lectures a week, so it might sound like quite a relaxed schedule, but because we meet only four hours a week, preparation for the lectures takes an enormous effort. When I taught at Gakushūin, there was nothing to do once I came home from work. It was as if I were a blue-collar worker. Over here I feel I'm constantly chased by my work and am leading a far from relaxed life. Our friend Nakame [former colleague of the Fourth Higher School] says it is the modern way to work a lot and make a lot of money, and perhaps it might have been better for my health if I followed that modern way [instead of being engaged in philosophical reflections]. I really should take a walk for the sake of my health, but if I'm reading books, I become lazy and end up not going out. That's bad.[8]

Nishida's social calendar was full of activities, such as the farewell party for Tomoeda held at the Kyoto Hotel on September 7 and the regular monthly meeting of the Philosophy-Ethics Society, the first of which took place on October 6, and the members gave Nishida a welcome reception. Despite these engagements, however, he missed his friends in Tokyo, where he had enjoyed the luxury of the company of his choicest friends, Suzuki Daisetz and Fujioka. Nishida discovered that taking a daily walk helped him to switch his mood. He therefore began a daily routine, walking not only to the Silver Pavilion (Ginka-kuji) area but to the Hōnen'in and Nanzenji area, where the scenery is exquisite.[9] (This walk along the small canal is today known as the "philosophic path"—*tetsugaku no michi*—and has turned into a tourist attraction!) He had his old friends, Yamamoto and Fujii Otoo, and they gave him some comfort. He daily saw Kuwaki Gen'yoku and Ueda Bin at school and found them *Freidenker* (free thinkers).[10] Although he enjoyed their company, deep down he could not help feeling a sense of distance from them as a breed apart from his own. A question arising out of one of Goethe's poems captured his sentiment of those days: "How valuable would be the view of life of those who haven't had the experience of eating bread with tears?"[11] That he was a graduate of the *senka* (limited status) program still haunted him. He sought to commiserate with Tanabe who was also a *senka* student.

On November 29 Kotomi had a miscarriage (a baby boy) and had to stay in the hospital for about a week; her health seemed to deteriorate as a result of this miscarriage. No more children were born to the Nishidas after that. Following Kotomi's recovery, Nishida traveled to Kagoshima in mid-December to give invited lectures. He took this opportunity to stop at Hiroshima and Kumamoto. In Hiroshima he saw Hōjō Tokiyuki, Hori Koretaka, Nishi Shin'ichirō, Hori's colleague and friend, and others. At Kumamoto he saw his former colleagues now teaching at the Fifth Higher School. In Kagoshima he was shown the grave of Saigō Takamori and other places associated with the hero who had lost his life in the Seinan Uprising of 1877. Saigō, also known by his *gō*, Nanshū (Southern Island), was a national hero at the time of the Meiji Restoration and was someone Nishida as a child had admired and affectionately respected. Having paid homage to his hero, his heart was filled with nostalgia. He returned to Kyoto on New Year's Eve.

On February 19, 1911, Nishida and Yamamoto went to a gift shop in downtown Kyoto to look for a wedding present for Suzuki Daisetz, who was engaged to marry Beatrice Lane, a Scottish-American lady, whom he had met in New York. Beatrice was a graduate of Radcliffe College and a holder of an M.A. from Columbia University.[12] The wedding was to take place on December 12. Nishida and Yamamoto indulged in their conversations, mixed with a sense of envy for Suzuki's "youthfulness"—to fall in love and marry after forty![13]

Nishida's feeling that he was slightly alienated from his colleagues lingered on for a while. He wrote to Tanabe Ryūji on March 10, 1911, reacting to the news that Natsume Sōseki declined a doctorate that the government had decided to grant him:

> I can talk with my colleagues about things academic, but their personal backgrounds are so different from ours that I find it difficult to engage in conversations that require an emotional accord. The only refreshing news of these days is that Natsume Sōseki has declined his doctorate. We indeed need such a man.[14]

In February 1911 the Association of Doctors (Hakushikai) decided to confer doctorates on several leading intellectuals who did not hold that title. They failed, however, to consult the recipients they had chosen. Sōseki declined the doctorate as a gesture of protest against the government's assumption that it was a superior office to which ordinary Japanese citizens were expected to submit, and against the government's presumption that it could confer the title of highest academic honor more or less at will.

Sōseki, who had earned his B.A. from the Imperial University, had gone on to graduate school and had studied in London as a government-sponsored student. He taught at the First Higher School upon his return to Japan and was also a lecturer at the Tokyo Imperial University. He disliked the "ego" of the state institution, however, and he left the academic scene, relinquishing his promising career as professor of English literature. Instead, he earned his living as a writer and novelist. He was convinced that for him to accept a doctorate from the government was tantamount to giving a seal of approval to the government's attitude that "those who have the doctorate are scholars, those who don't aren't."[15] It might also have been his way of satirizing the prevailing attitudes of scholars who coveted doctorates.

Nishida must have read with especially keen interest Sōseki's "Hakushi mondai to Mādokku sensei to yo" [The doctorate incident, Professor Murdoch, and I],[16] published in the *Tokyo Asahi Newspaper*, March 6–8, 1911. In it Sōseki wrote about a letter that he received unexpectedly from his former teacher, James Murdoch,[17] who was then teaching at the Seventh Higher School in Kagoshima, and who read about Sōseki's decision in the paper. Murdoch had been Sōseki's teacher of English at the First Higher School. In his letter Murdoch praised the action of Sōseki as honorable, in the good company of such distinguished names as William Gladstone, Thomas Carlyle, and Herbert Spencer. Nishida had known Murdoch personally as a colleague in Kanazawa, when he first taught at the Fourth Higher School in 1896–1897,[18] so it was a curious coincidence for him to see Murdoch's name in association with the defiant action taken by Sōseki.

Nishida was gradually returning to his philosophical contemplation, and he chose to concentrate on Henri Bergson for the time being. Kuwaki Gen'yoku asked him to contribute an article to the college journal *Geibun*[19] at the first meeting of the Philosophy-Ethics Society that Nishida attended on October 6, 1910. Nishida's contribution, "Beruguson no tetsugakuteki hōhōron" [On Bergson's philosophical method],[20] appeared in the November issue. This essay is the first full-length article introducing Bergson's thought to the Japanese.[21] By this time Nishida had read Bergson's *Introduction à la métaphysique*, 1903; *Essai sur les données immédiates de la conscience*, 1889, along with Windelband's preface to a German translation; and *L'Évolution créatrice*, 1907. He most likely read F. L. Pogson's English translation of *Time and Free Will: An Essay on the Immediate Data of Consciousness* (1910).

Nishida agreed with Bergson's philosophical method of starting a philosophical reflection with "intuition," and with his view that the intellectual method or "intellectualism" was unable to fathom the living reality. Bergson held that intuition approaches things *from within;* the observer "becomes the thing itself." The natural scientific method of analysis approaches things *from without,* that is, from a certain fixed external standpoint to the thing observed.[22] A philosophical inquiry starts out with intuition and moves on to analysis.[23] Bergson's approach struck a sympathetic chord with Nishida's attempt to "get to the heart of the most fundamental reality." He introduced Bergson's thought as follows:

> Despite the prima facie impression that Bergson is discussing things pertaining to psychology or biology, we are eventually led to realize that he is tackling profoundly philosophical problems. His ideas are clear, but his writings are by no means easy to follow. His philosophy has something new and also depth. I find it provocative.[24]

Nishida also quoted from Windelband's preface to a German translation of *Matter and Memory:*[25]

> Ever since Descartes, French philosophy has developed a method in which one begins with the inner experiential facts, submits them to

critical examination, and arrives at a certain system of philosophy. The French tend to harmonize and come up with one system of thought while the Germans . . . divide their musings into psychology, epistemology, and [pure] philosophy; and this French proclivity is clearly evident in Bergson's thought.[26]

Linked by intellectual kinship, Nishida was fond of the works of both James and Bergson, while James and Bergson admired each other and formed a warm personal friendship. James, writing to Bergson on February 25, 1903, praised Bergson's *Matter and Memory* and wrote: "A philosophy of *pure experience*, such as I conceive yours to be, can be made to work, and will reconcile many of the old inveterate oppositions of the scholars."[27] Nishida read James's "Bergson and His Critique of Intellectualism," which introduced Bergson to the English-speaking world. Originally one of the lectures that James gave in 1908 at Manchester College, Oxford; the text was later published in *A Pluralistic Universe* (1909).[28] Nishida, impressed by James's latest book, wrote to Hori: "These essays by James seem to resemble Zen teaching."[29]

In September 1911 Nishida wrote another essay, "Beruguson no junsui jizoku" [Bergson's concept of pure duration],[30] for the Association of Educators *(Kyōiku gakujutsukai)*. This second essay is essentially a summary of Bergson's *L'Évolution créatrice.*[31] Nishida described Bergson's "pure duration" as reminiscent of the Zen expression: "The mind turns according to the external environment; it does so effortlessly and exquisitely."[32]

In these essays on Bergson, Nishida especially highlighted what Bergson meant by "intuition," that is, "to view things by becoming things themselves, by discarding the self-centered perspective, and by getting rid of the notions of gain and loss."[33] It is very possible that Nishida got the germane idea of "I think by becoming a thing, and I act by becoming a thing" *(mono to natte kangae, mono to natte okonau)* from Bergson.[34] There remains a subtle difference between Bergson's and Nishida's idea of "becoming a thing," however. To Bergson, it means to be one with the phenomenon itself, but in Nishida's terminology "a thing" refers to the "real self," which is beyond the ego.

As sympathetic as Nishida was to Bergson's philosophy, he felt that there was something in his own thinking that could not be explained by Bergson. He felt the need to sharpen his thinking by engaging himself in the contemporary discussions among neo-Kantian thinkers; he also wanted to move away from the language of pure experience, which was tinged with psychologism.[35] Thus, he turned his attention to the problem of logic.

Nishida's life in Kyoto began to unfold. Old friends and former students came to visit him whenever they were in Kyoto. Through his colleague Toda Kaiichi, he befriended Tsunetō Kyō and Kawakami Hajime, both teaching in the College of Law. Kawakami had been a student at Yamaguchi Higher School in 1897–1898, the first year Nishida taught there. Students, such as Amano Teiyū, Nishikida Yoshitomi, and Nozaki Hiroyoshi, began to call on Nishida at home as well. The college had an atmosphere that encouraged the open exchange of ideas between students and professors. Ueda Juzō recalls his first visit at the professor's house:

> I called on Professor Nishida on January 19, 1911, for the first time. . . . I was shown into the upstairs room, which was neatly cleaned and with all the *fusuma* dividers left open to create a spacious feeling. When the tea was brought only to me—perhaps a custom back home—he quietly said, "Tea for me also." Then he picked up a sack of cigarettes, turned it upside down, and let the cigarettes roll out all over the table in front of me. I was taken aback momentarily but realized right away that the gesture was his way of inviting me to smoke. I was touched by his frank kindness. That was the first time I encountered his thoughtful kindness, expressed in a rather casual manner, which I was to witness on numerous occasions since then.
>
> The purpose of my visit was to ask him to give a talk at our Aesthetics Society. At that time he said, "I'm currently engaged in mathematical problems and therefore cannot meet your request; but I intend to go into the problem of art some time, so when the time comes I shall give a talk."[36]

On January 30, 1911, a guest with a shaven head, clad in a monk's black robe, came to Nishida's house. It was Uemura Etsuzō, with whom Nishida shared lodgings during the *sesshin* in the summer of 1899 at Myōshinji when he was on his way back to Kanazawa from Yamaguchi. Uemura had continued with his Zen practice, became a monk, and was now living at Senjuin, a subtemple of Myōshinji in the Ryōanji area at the foot of Kinugasa Hill.[37] His Buddhist name was Hōrin (Treasure Woods). Utterly elated by the unexpected visit of his old Zen comrade, Nishida welcomed him with open arms. Hōrin told Kotomi that Nishida, having missed his baby daughter Yayoi, had spoken much about her to him. Kotomi, hearing this story for the first time, was thrilled to have a glimpse of a chapter of her husband's feelings. Hōrin became a close family friend.[38] He was the direct disciple of Ikegami Shōsan, the master trainer *(shike)* of monks at Myōshinji and became Nishida's link to the Rinzai Zen world in Kyoto. When Hisamatsu Shin'ichi expressed his desire to practice Zen, it was through Hōrin's introduction that Hisamatsu was able to participate in the *rōhatsu sesshin*, a December intensive training period commemorating the Buddha's enlightenment. This renewal of direct ties with the world of Zen became for Nishida an important connection through which he continued to receive "Zen nutrition."[39]

Nishida also formed a close contact with the world of True Pure Land Buddhists in Kyoto through Inaba Masamaru. As a matter of fact, on September 24, 1910 (soon after he had moved to Kyoto), he took Yamamoto and called on Inaba to introduce Yamamoto to "the most trustworthy colleague" of his Yamaguchi days. Inaba had been in Kyoto since 1900, working at the Shinshū Kyoto Junior Higher School, first as assistant to Kiyozawa Manshi, and after Kiyozawa's death as principal. Inaba was also closely involved in running Shinshū Ōtani University (renamed Ōtani University in 1922). Inaba asked Nishida to teach part-time at Ōtani University. Matsumoto Bunzaburō and Tomonaga Sanjūrō were already teaching at Ōtani University part-time, and there was a close relationship between the two academic institutions. Nishida began his teaching at Ōtani in 1911 and continued for the next decade or more, some years once a week, other years twice a week.

Inaba was a respected administrator-scholar within the Higashi-honganji sect, and he treated Nishida with utmost respect. When Tosa came to Kyoto to visit in May 1911, they were invited to the special ceremonial noh performance held at the private noh theater within the Higashi-honganji compound. When the Ōtani Alumni Association planned publication of a book, *Shūsokan* [Views of the founder], in 1911[40] to commemorate the 650th anniversary of the death of Shinran (1173–1263), Nishida was among those who were invited to contribute an essay, and he wrote "Gutoku Shinran."[41] He enjoyed a close relationship with Inaba, and later also with Sasaki Gesshō. He maintained a close professional association with Ōtani, and years later, on June 6, 1927, at the twenty-fifth anniversary of the death of Kiyozawa Manshi, he gave a guest lecture there.

On February 6, 1911, Kōdōkan, a publisher in Kanda, published Nishida's *Zen no kenkyū* [An inquiry into the good]—the word "zen" here means "good"; it is not the "Zen" of Zen Buddhism. As we saw earlier, all the essays of this book had been completed by the summer of 1909, and Nishida had entrusted the essays to Tokunō Bun and Kihira Tadayoshi before he left Tokyo. Kihira acted as the editor, while Tokunō looked for a publisher. It took some convincing on Tokunō's part, because Nishida was unknown and presented a "risk" to the publisher. Kihira gave the book the title *Zen no kenkyū*, against Nishida's wishes. He had wanted the title to contain such words as "reality" and "pure experience."

The chapter arrangement—"Pure Experience," "Reality," "Good," and "Religion"—was also Kihira's idea. Nishida had suggested the order of "Reality," "Good," "Religion," and "Pure Experience," thinking that putting the chapter on pure experience at the beginning unduly emphasized the epistemological nature of the book and might not be congruent with its title. The publication of the book gave Tosa and Kotomi enormous pleasure—they were overjoyed "beyond imagination."[42] As soon as the book was published, Nishida presented copies not only to Kihira and Tokunō but to his friends, Suzuki Daisetz, Tanabe Ryūji, Matsumoto Bunzaburō, and Sasaki Gesshō, and to his former professor Inoue Tetsujirō.

The publication of *Zen no kenkyū* had the effect of a small stone thrown into a calm pond. At first, the sound was heard among the specialists of philosophy, and the ripples created by the stone were to widen only gradually. An editor of the *Tetsugaku Zasshi* introduced the book in the book review section, as follows:

> This is a very serious work full of profound insight and much intellectual refinement. . . . It has neither that peculiar smell of translations, nor is it some kind of naive work. It is rather a product of the author's ceaseless effort at refining his thought. It is not a book to be read casually but something one must bring one's own reflection to, and think along with it. The style of writing is plain and clear, but what it tries to say is not given by mere common sense and demands that we think as we read. Failing to do so would render this book incomprehensible and flavorless.[43]

A review article by Takahashi Satomi, a graduate student of philosophy at Tokyo Imperial University, entitled "Ishiki genshō no jijitsu to sono imi" [Facts and meanings of the phenomena of consciousness] came out in the May and June issues of *Tetsugaku Zasshi*, 1912.[44] Takahashi gave the book high praise. Its publication, he felt, marked the first time since the Meiji Restoration that a Japanese thinker had offered the fruit of serious philosophical reflection. Although the book gave Takahashi confidence in the state of Japanese philosophical inquiries, his review raises questions about Nishida's view of pure experience. Is there such a thing as "pure" experience? If pure experiences are subject to "degrees" of purity, as Nishida seems to suggest, how can one distinguish between pure and nonpure experience? And if pure experience follow the pattern of incipient emergence and subsequent self-differentiation and self-development, at what stage does one find the "pure" experience in this process? Is not "pure experience" ultimately a kind of "mystical" experience that can only be had by the spiritually awakened (such as those who have achieved satori) or by geniuses, remaining inaccessible to ordinary people? How do we obtain a "meaning" out of the "fact" of experience? If all is pure experience, how does one distinguish between truth and falsehood? Takahashi, in essence, sees "pure experience" as a special kind of ultimate experience, accessible only to saints and the enlightened. Interestingly enough, this interpretation of pure experience still persists to this day among those who have not read Nishida's text closely.

Nishida wrote his response to Takahashi during the summer break of 1912. "Takahashi (Satomi) Bungakushi no seccho *Zen no kenkyū* ni taisuru hihyō ni kotau" [My response to Takahashi Satomi's criticism of my book, *An inquiry into the good*].[45] It was carried in the October 1912 issue of *Tetsugaku Zasshi*.[46] In his attempt to eradicate Takahashi's assumption that "pure experience" was some special kind of experience, he explained that strictly speaking there is no absolute "pure experience" or absolute "nonpure experience." From one point of view, however, all experiences are "pure experiences." He also pointed out that the distinction between "fact" and "meaning" arises only from a certain viewpoint, which itself is a phenomenon of consciousness, and that in pure experience fact *is* meaning, meaning *is* fact. He noted that if a fact has a meaning, that means that a fact contains its meaning within itself; it does not point to something totally unrelated to its content. Truth and falsehood arise with our judgment, precisely because our judging experience already contains some ideal paradigm. What is true and false changes depending on the different perspectives one assumes. Nishida thanked Takahashi for the public exchange, which forced him to articulate his thought better.

Zen no kenkyū initially sold a modest 750 copies or so, not an impressive figure, but within the range that would be expected for a philosophical writing. In another ten years, however, the book would become a best-seller, thanks to Kurata Hyakuzō (1891–1943), an extremely popular writer among the young. Kurata enthusiastically endorsed *Zen no kenkyū* in his *Ai to ninshiki no shuppatsu* [The departing point of love and cognition], published in 1921, which caught the attention of higher school students. Kurata praised Nishida's work in highly poetic language:

> In the arid, stagnant Japanese philosophical world, shamelessly filled with the smell of worldliness, he whose work gives us pure joy, moral support, and even a slight sense of surprise is Mr. Nishida Kitarō. His work is like the finely scented pale blue bellflowers growing out of dried-up, sterile earth in the mountain shadows. [47]

Kurata's endorsement of Nishida's work made it an instant hit, eventually elevating *Zen no kenkyū* to the rank of a "modern classic," a must for every young reader. It is ironical that Nishida himself was not that impressed by Kurata, who called on him on September 8, 1912. Kurata addressed his existential concern to Nishida in a letter, which reads: "Romantic love is the flower of life. How could I cheapen this sacred relationship between the sexes into a mundane hackneyed superficial thing? . . . I want to render love into art, into philosophy, and even into religion." [48] Although Kurata was unable to obtain from Nishida the answer he was looking for, that apparently did not diminish his appreciation of Nishida's work.

Emperor Mutsuhito died on July 30, 1912, and Crown Prince Yoshihito ascended the imperial throne, marking the end of the Meiji period and the beginning of the Taishō. It was in fact during this time that Nishida wrote his response to Takahashi Satomi. On September 13, the day of the funeral of the late emperor, General Nogi Maresuke and his wife Shizuko committed suicide to follow Emperor Meiji. Nishida's diary for this day reads: "Surprised to hear the news of General Nogi's suicide. I still vividly remember his countenance." The Nogis' act was hotly debated, and public opinion was divided, many questioning whether such a practice was a legacy of the feudalistic past and to be discouraged. Amid the resounding furor, Nishida wrote to Tanabe Ryūji, expressing his sentiments:

> Mr. and Mrs. Nogi's suicides moved me greatly. Especially having had daily contact with him, although only for a year, his image vividly comes back to me. I think it must be even more so for people like you

who had worked with him much longer. I feel we owe our apologies to such a sincere man. An event like the death of Mr. Nogi ought to greatly awaken self-reflection on the part of the Japanese people of today who are so lazy and avoid taking any responsibility for their actions. There are those who quibble with the appropriateness of Mr. Nogi's suicide, but there is really no room for that kind of argument. Nothing else moved me so deeply of late as the death of the Meiji Emperor and the suicide of the general. [49]

A month later, on October 13, Nishida attended a memorial service for the Nogis organized by the graduates of Gakushūin studying at Kyoto Imperial University. At the service Nishida saw Harada Kumao, Kido Kōichi, and Oda Nobuhiro, all of whom had entered the College of Law the previous year, and Akamatsu Kotora and Ueda Misao, who entered the university that September. They all came to Kyoto because the student quota at the College of Law at Tokyo Imperial University was full and Gakushūin students had to go elsewhere. [50] This memorial service brought Nishida and his former Gakushūin students together again.

One source says that Konoe Ayamaro arrived in Kyoto on the very day of the memorial service. After graduating from the First Higher School, Konoe had entered Tokyo Imperial University; dissatisfied with the lectures there, he decided to transfer to the University in Kyoto, where Kawakami Hajime and Yoneda Shōtaro taught. Yoneda, a young scholar in sociology, was quite popular among students. By the time Konoe arrived in Kyoto, the deadline for admission had already passed, but he sat in protest in front of the office of the dean of students, and finally was admitted to the College of Law. Nishida was asked, most likely through his connection with Marquis Maeda Toshinari, to be Konoe's sponsor *(hoshōnin)*, a responsibility that he accepted. On November 14 Konoe visited Nishida at his house and asked for academic advice. Harada and Kido followed Konoe's suit and began to invite Nishida to dinners, to an evening of music, to an early spring picnic on the Kamo River bank, and the like. Harada Kumao was especially impressed by Nishida; the more he got to know Nishida, the more he came to respect him. He was to become a devoted friend.

With the closure of the Meiji period, Nishida's philosophical reflections were also entering a new, more vigorous, phase. Beginning with the essay, "Ninshikiron ni okeru junronriha no shuchō ni tsuite" [On the claims of a purely logical theory of cognition], [51] he departs from the philosophy of pure experience and begins wrestling with the thought of neo-Kantians, such as Windelband, Rickert, Hermann Cohen, and Paul Natorp, paying close attention to Edmund Husserl as well.

In July 1912 Nishida wrote an essay, "Ronri no rikai to sūri no rikai" [Logical understanding and mathematical understanding],[52] in which he takes up the issue of the relationship between logic and mathematical numbers, a hotly debated problem among such thinkers as Henri Poincaré, Bertrand Russell, and Heinrich Rickert. Nishida agrees with Josiah Royce's view, discussed in his *The World and the Individual,* that our consciousness is a self-representative system. He also accepts Cantor and Dedekind's definition of the infinite as that which contains its self-representation within itself.[53] According to Nishida, "self-consciousness is intuitive and yet it contains within it the movement of inner development"; all forms of logical understanding are the development of the universal creative operation inherent in consciousness.[54] Nishida sees the essence of thinking in its creative imaginative unfolding, which is better attested by mathematical intuition than by logical processes.[55]

The essay, "Logical understanding and mathematical understanding" introduced to Japanese students of philosophy Rickert's thought and his 1911 essay "Das Eine, die Einheit und die Eins" [The One, Unity, and the Number One].[56] Rickert holds that there are three purely logical elements, the one *(das Eine),* the other *(das Andere),* and the unity *(die Einheit)* of the two. Nishida contends that Rickert's view is one-sided in that it is biased for the "one" and overlooks the fact that the "one" and the "other" can be switched by assuming a different perspective. In support of this view, he cites Hegel, who holds that the one and the other are both "something" *(etwas;* or, in Latin, *aliud).* Nishida goes on to characterize mathematical understanding in terms of intuition, that which grasps the totality and hence a concrete standpoint; whereas logical understanding assumes a certain standpoint and analyzes the relationship between the terms involved to create an abstract standpoint. Nishida proposes that both forms of understanding—that which intuits (or imagines) the whole (mathematical) and that which analyzes (logical)—are but two directions of the operation of the mind.[57] Intuition that grasps the whole emerges first, followed by analytical activities, which eventually reconstitute the initial idea to its concrete totality.[58] Next, Nishida questions how an infinite series of numbers is conceivable. Following Royce's discussion, he finds its source in the infinite nature of thinking itself, in our ability to make our thought the object of our thinking, a process that goes on ad infinitum.[59] He maintains that such a self-representative system—one that contains all potential movements of self-development within itself—is the very nature of thought.[60]

When Nishida finished with this essay on July 26, 1912, he was more dissatisfied than satisfied,[61] because it opened up further problems. The questions raised by this essay were to occupy him for the next several years, resulting in his next major book, *Jikaku ni okeru chokkan to hansei* [Intuition and reflection in self-consciousness], in 1917.[62] In September 1912 Nishida wrote "Ninshikironsha to shite no Anri Poankare" [Henri Poincaré as an epistemologist],[63] in which he praised Poincaré's achievement in the epistemology of natural sciences.

On December 23, 1912, the Nishidas moved to a larger house in Nakagawarachō, which was in the Tanaka district of Kyoto, northeast of the university campus. The house, which still stands to this day, is on the north side of Seifūsō, a large private estate where Saionji Kinmochi used to stay whenever he was in Kyoto. The two-story house that the Nishidas rented has a veranda on the south side of the second floor, running the full length of the house. This turned out to be Nishida's favorite place to pace up and down whenever he was engaged in thinking. Philosophy students would often see him walking back and forth along the veranda and were greatly inspired by the intensity of their professor's philosophical engagement.

This philosophical energy of Nishida's was directly communicated to his students; indeed, there was a quality to his lectures that moved students. Yamanouchi Tokuryū (né Nakagawa), who entered the university in 1911, and who later had the opportunity to study with Husserl and Heidegger in Germany, describes Nishida's lecture style:

> He was by no means eloquent, but I have never encountered in any other professor's lecture the quality that would touch the most essential core of one's being. Husserl's lectures were too long winded and wordy; Heidegger's lectures were too spirited. In contrast, Nishida's lectures were unpretentious. Yet one felt as if his words were coming from his inner soul—indeed one could call his lectures a piece of art.[64]

In the introductory courses Nishida would dictate to the students passages from his prepared notes and then elaborate on the content. He continued this style of lecture for the rest of his university career. In fact, there was a rumor among the students that each year Professor

Nishida cracked the same joke at exactly the same place in his introductory lectures.

His lectures in special topics, however, were "of a totally different kind, free of any format," recalls Yamanouchi, who tells us that "he would pace the platform back and forth and spoke as he walked."[65] It was essentially a "philosophical monologue" presented to the students. But he never failed to provide students with the latest news from abroad in the field. For instance, Mutai Risaku, who entered the university in 1915, noted that Nishida brought in a copy of Windelband's *Einleitung in die Philosophie* [Introduction to Philosophy][66] on the very first day of the class and announced to the students that he was going more or less to base his lectures on it.[67] The book had been published in 1914, just one year earlier.

Chapter 10

Consolidation of the Philosophy Department

(1913–1917)

The year 1913, the second year of Taisho, marked a personal, professional, and intellectual turning point for Nishida. He felt he was ready to tackle substantial philosophical problems, and thus on New Year's Day he began writing an essay "Shii to chokkan" [Thinking and intuition], with which he embarked on the long and winding road that saw its end in 1917 in his second book, *Jikaku ni okeru chokkan to hansei* [Intuition and reflection in self-consciousness].[1] To begin something new with the new year's arrival was something ingrained in Nishida; as we recall he began writing his seminal essay on pure experience on January 3, 1908. The sense of renewal brought about at the beginning of the year seems to have stimulated a creative urge in Nishida. He at first thought that he could tackle the problem of the relationship between "value and existence" on the one hand, and "meaning and fact" on the other, in a fairly straightforward manner and be done with it. But once he began his inquiry, one question led to the next, and he was to spend the next four years working on this set of problems. What he called the "documents of the hard battles I fought in my philosophical reflections"[2] thus commenced.

In January 1913 Tomonaga Sanjūrō returned from his study abroad in Germany. There was talk among Nishida's colleagues that it was now his turn to study abroad, for there was a tacit understanding that Nishida would be promoted to full professor because Kuwaki Gen'-yoku was expected to be Raphael von Koeber's successor at Tokyo Imperial University. When the opportunity to study abroad finally arose, however, Nishida was no longer interested in it. He explained: "Even if I went abroad to study, there would be nothing to be gained therefrom. Since I'm at the point where my thought is beginning to

University of Kyoto, philosophy department, 1913 or possibly 1914. Second row from left to right: Kuwaki Gen'yoku, Nishida, Tomonaga Sanjūrō; third row between Nishida and Tomonaga is Amano Teiyū. Other figures unknown. From *Nishida Kitarō Zenshū*, vol. 14, frontispiece.

take its shape, for me to waste a few years essentially doing nothing but sightseeing interests me little. Moreover, my going abroad would cause financial difficulties to my family."[3] In the face of Nishida's firm determination, his colleagues dropped the idea. This was the closest Nishida came to seeing Europe with his own eyes.

In March his eldest daughter, Yayoi, was accepted by the elite Tokyo Women's Higher Normal School (renamed Ochanomizu Women's University in 1949).[4] Yayoi moved to Tokyo from Kanazawa and began her college life. Yayoi's achievement gave Nishida a sense of tremendous satisfaction. He went to Tokyo to accompany Yayoi on the occasion of the school entrance ceremony held on April 10. The Philosophical Society seized this opportunity and asked Nishida to give a talk. Nishida happily obliged, and on April 6 he spoke about "History and Natural Sciences,"[5] treating the subjective dimension of historical events in relation to the creativity of individuals. He chose the topic in part because he was critical of the trend advocated by Rickert and others to draw a clear line between the natural sciences and the "sciences of history."[6] Nishida explains:

Nishida's children, most likely summer 1914. Front row, from left to right: Yayoi (age 18), Shizuko (9), Umeko (5), Tomoko (7); back row, from left to right: Ken (16) and Sotohiko (13). From Ueda Hisashi, *Sofu Nishida Kitarō.*

I thought that setting up arbitrary divisions in scholarly research had to be examined carefully. The nature of natural sciences has been very much studied since Kant, but not enough has been done in the area of Kulturwissenschaft, or cultural studies. I think this is a problem that merits a thorough investigation, and I'm greatly interested in it. [7]

Following his talk, members of the Philosophical Society hosted a dinner in his honor, where he saw his friends Suzuki Daisetz and Tokunō Bun, as well as colleagues and acquaintances, including Inoue Tetsujirō, Tanaka Ōdō, Fujii Kenjirō, Hayami Hiroshi, Hatta Miki, and younger philosophy students such as Takahashi Satomi (who wrote the review article on *Zen no kenkyū*), Itō Kichinosuke, and Miyamoto Wakichi (editors of the *Tetsugaku Zasshi*), and Tanabe Hajime. This was the first time Nishida saw Tanabe, and soon they began corresponding. (Their correspondence is the subject of chapter 11.)

In July 1913 the philosophy department in Kyoto lost Matsumoto Matatarō to Tokyo Imperial University, where he was appointed professor of psychology, succeeding Motora Yūjirō, who had died in

December 1912. On top of this, Nogami Toshio, an assistant professor of psychology, was to study abroad for a few years beginning in September 1913. Because of the unusual situation, Nishida was asked to teach Introduction to Psychology. With strong backing by Matsumoto Bunzaburō and Kuwaki Gen'yoku, Nishida was appointed full professor in the study of religion on August 12. This appointment meant promotion, but Nishida felt added pressure, and the burden of his new responsibilities seemed overwhelming. He realized that the period of his youthful apprenticeship was over. He was forty-three years old.

For the Japanese publishing world, 1913 was also a memorable year. Iwanami Shigeo began his business of buying and selling new and used books. Iwanami was a 1908 graduate of the limited status program of the philosophy department at Tokyo Imperial University, just as Nishida had been a decade and a half before. As a member of the Philosophical Society, Iwanami submitted a notice to the *Tetsugaku Zasshi*, advertising his new business:

> I have resigned from my teaching position and opened a bookstore in front of the tram stop at Kanda Minami-jinbōchō. We sell new books and magazines as well as trade used books. Presently, we are maintaining the policy of a fixed selling price for used books. We are hoping to expand our business to include the publication of books in the areas of philosophy, religion, and literature.[8]

This was the humble beginning of the Iwanami Bookstore, which was to become a phenomenal success and the most prestigious name in the Japanese publishing industry.

Iwanami, a man of wide connections, came to know Nishida and developed utmost respect for and loyalty to him. By 1915 the two men were well acquainted. Iwanami was eager to publish every book by Nishida and eventually became the sole publisher of his works. Iwanami published Nishida's *Jikaku ni okeru chokkan to hansei* in October 1917. In 1919 he brought out Nishida's collection of essays, *Shisaku to taiken* [Philosophical contemplation and life experience], which had originally been published by Senshōkan in 1915. In 1921 Iwanami reprinted *Zen no kenkyū* [An inquiry into the good], which had been out of print for quite some time after its initial publication by Kōdōkan in 1911. Nishida gained the strong backing of the powerful publisher, whose steadfast devotion to him helped shape Nishida's career and spread his fame as an influential thinker.

The year 1913 marked a significant career transition for Hōjō Tokiyuki as well. On May 9 he was appointed president of Tōhoku Imperial University, replacing Sawayanagi Masatarō. Hōjō inherited and supported Sawayanagi's liberal decision to admit women students into the university, the first three of which were admitted in September 1913.

Sawayanagi moved to Kyoto Imperial University to take over the responsibility from Kuhara Mitsuru, who was acting president after Kikuchi Dairoku left office in 1912. As soon as Sawayanagi took over the office of president, he launched an "administrative restructuring," under which pretext seven professors from the Colleges of Medicine and Humanities were let go. Apparently, Sawayanagi was complying with an order of the Ministry of Education. The reason he gave for his act was the vague statement that the seven professors were "either academically or personally unfit to teach at an imperial university." Among the seven forced to resign was Nishida's colleague, Tanimoto Tomeri. Fortunately, Tanimoto found a position at Ryūkoku University. Sawayanagi's unilateral style of decision making caused a university-wide protest movement that came to be known as "Sawayanagi Jiken" or the Sawayanagi incident.

In a letter to Tanabe Ryūji, Nishida refers to Sawayanagi's action: "He seems like an achiever all right, but there seems to be much opposition to him in the College of Law."[9] Indeed, the faculty members of the College of Law stood in solidarity against the president, criticizing him for having undermined the autonomy of the university and freedom of scholarship. They entered into direct discussion with the minister of education, Okuda Yoshito, in Tokyo and finally won the ministry's guarantee that it would no longer interfere with personnel matters affecting the university professors. Among those who took a hard-line position against president Sawayanagi and negotiated with the Ministry of Education was Nishida's colleague from his Fourth Higher School days, Toda Kaiichi. Konoe Ayamaro, then a second-year student in the College of Law, also stood by Toda.

While the university was in turmoil, the philosophy department was in its own period of uncertainty because of the imminent move of Kuwaki Gen'yoku to Tokyo. Kuwaki, the head of the department, had been a gifted organizer and also initiated many collegial activities. For instance, he hosted a monthly faculty gathering, "Kidakai" [literally, "tree-field meeting"] at his house. The faculty group occasionally went on excursions to such scenic places as Ishiyama and Kiyotaki in and around Kyoto. Students were fond of the energetic Kuwaki, and they protested against his departure. Nishida personally thought it better for Kuwaki to stay in Kyoto, where he could devote himself to his scholarly pursuits, but the allure of moving to the Imperial University was evidently too strong for Kuwaki to resist. When Kuwaki's move was duly approved by the dean of the college, Fukada Yasukazu suggested that a distinguished philosopher of religion, Hatano Seiichi, who had trained under Koeber at the Imperial University, should be invited to join the faculty. Hatano was Fukada's old friend from First Higher School days. Nishida and Tomonaga supported Fukada's suggestion, but Hatano was disinclined to move from Waseda University, which had been good to him, having given him the opportunity to study in Europe. To Hatano, moving from a private university to an imperial university seemed like an act of betrayal. Fukada and his colleagues understood Hatano's situation.

In August 1913 Fujii Kenjirō was appointed professor of ethics. To fill the philosophy of education position vacated by Tanimoto, Konishi Shigenao, who was a graduate of the philosophy department of the Imperial University in 1901, and who studied pedagogy with Johannes Volkelt at the University of Leipzig, was appointed professor. As noted earlier, Nishida was appointed professor of religious studies the same month. Fujii Kenjirō and Tomonaga took over the ethics courses from Nishida, while Nishida took on his new teaching assignments, Introduction to Psychology and Introduction to the Study of Religion.

Nishida had to go through an emotional adjustment after he was promoted to professor. His new teaching assignments also forced him to read widely outside his philosophical studies. On one October evening, overwhelmed by a sense of nostalgia, he wrote a long letter to Tanabe Ryūji, describing how he was feeling at this turning point in his life:

> We are now in the middle of autumn. This evening it is especially windy, rainy, and I cannot help but feel the lonesomeness of early fall. Hope all is well with you and your family. Provoked by the sense of loneliness, I'm reminiscing about various things from my Kanazawa days. As I look back on my life, I feel that the two most enjoyable periods of my life were spent in Kanazawa. One was when I was a student at the Fourth Higher School, when I was about twenty years old; I used to stay up late into the small hours of the morning with my bosom friends, enthusiastically discussing whatever we wanted. The other period was when I was about thirty years old and taught at the Fourth Higher

School; you and I and other colleagues did such things as climbing Mt. Iō at night with the students of Sansanjuku, daring the fog. In comparison, I'm leading a considerably dull life these days. Have I aged or is my health not so robust as it once used to be? I don't have the kind of stamina that I used to have. I cannot engage in debates for a long time, for instance, and if I teach even two hours, I get so exhausted that after I return home I have to rest for a few hours. Thus, I can neither read many books nor can I get up early in the morning to engage in philosophical thinking. I feel that I'm leading an idle life, and I don't like it, but what can I do? Let me assure you, though: I have no ailment.

Regardless of whatever one says about scholarship or art, the truth of human existence arises from the utmost sincerity that appears at the point where life brushes with death. I tell you, what recently touched me was a story in an insignificant magazine for children, *Nihon Shōnen*, about an older brother who suddenly realizes that his younger brother is missing while they are climbing a snowy mountain and goes back to look for him. Later the two are found dead, embracing each other and frozen. What a touching story! As Tolstoy said, truth is rooted in sincerity.

Uchida Setsuzō [a graduate of Sansanjuku], who has gone to the U.S. and is working there as a day worker, recently became ill and was hospitalized. He sent me a postcard bearing a picture of a child holding onto a dog's leash and being pulled by the dog. The caption reads: "Where are you going?" "I don't know. Ask the dog!" Uchida likened his life to this child, who is being pulled by a dog in what direction he does not know. I think this is the reality of fate all of us face. I don't know why I should wear the proud mask [of professor], having done nothing significant. . . .

This year I have to give lectures in religion and psychology. These are not my favorite subjects to teach, and besides, they keep me busy. I shouldn't complain, though, when I know that people recommended me [for promotion to the position of full professor]. But I cannot help but think that, if I had remained in my former position, I would have been carefree and have done what I pleased, enjoying a freer existence. When I think I must perform according to what is expected of my academic rank, I feel a bit strained. In secular eyes I was certainly promoted, but personally I don't know whether that was a blessing.[10]

In December a doctorate *(bungaku hakushigō)* was conferred on Nishida and Tomonaga Sanjūrō, probably upon the recommendation of President Sawayanagi.[11] Achieving this highest academic degree finally erased any stigma from Nishida's having been a higher school dropout and a graduate of a limited status program. Technically speaking, Nishida did not even have a university degree *(gakushi)*, let alone a higher school diploma, until then.

It may come as a surprise that Nishida felt it a burden to have to teach religion and psychology. After all, he had written so much on religion in his earlier days and returned to the subject in his last work, "Bashoteki ronri to shūkyōteki sekaikan" [The logic of *topos* and the religious worldview], completed two months before his death in 1945. The truth of the matter is that Nishida was not happy with any teaching duty that was not directly related to his current philosophical inquiry, because other subjects required so much extra reading. He complained in a letter of April 14, 1914, to Tanabe Hajime that he was unable to make progress in his philosophical inquiry: "Although I want to plough forth in my thought and continue to write on 'Jikaku ni okeru chokkan to hansei,' because my ideas are not clearly formed and . . . I have to teach psychology and religion—subjects outside my specialty—I have not been able to concentrate on my philosophical inquiry." [12]

Despite Nishida's own feelings about teaching Introduction to Religion, his lectures left an indelible impression on many of the young minds who heard them. He treated religion as an integral part of philosophical studies.[13] Hisamatsu Shin'ichi, a first-year student, was especially inspired by Nishida's lectures:

> In those days religion was a matter of life and death for me, so I naturally had a great thirst for the study of religion as expounded by Professor Nishida, a man of deep religious experience. I soaked in his lectures, which were like showers of merciful rain from heaven. I listened to his lectures with spiritual excitement and intense academic interest. So great was my anticipation that the lectures of every other week felt to me aeons apart.[14]

Years later, at the time of the compilation of *Nishida Kitarō Zenshū* [Collected works of Nishida Kitarō], Hisamatsu was put in charge of editing the volume of lectures. Hisamatsu felt that Nishida had given the "most memorable lectures that I heard in my entire life," and he relished the rarest of karmic bonds with his old teacher.

Hisamatsu's recollection of Nishida's lectures paints a vivid picture of Nishida in the lecture hall:

> The professor first dictated parts of his lecture notes and would later expound on them. He casually tied his kimono with an ordinary cotton sash and put a *hakama* on top of the sash. When it was cold he would

wear over his kimono a faded black cotton *haori* that had his family crest. His thin body was slightly stooped; he wore a pair of black shoes; he was never clean-shaven. He would raise his left shoulder a bit, place his hands behind his back, vigorously pace on the podium without a moment's pause. Sometimes he would fix his gaze upon a listener from behind his thick glasses; but often he looked downwards toward the floor while engaged in thinking. His lectures flowed forth spontaneously, as if his thoughts were springing from an inexhaustible underground spring. His Oriental appearance, a combination of stark simplicity and lofty transcendence, created a unique air about him that interacted with his profound religious experience and erudite knowledge of scholarship East and West. The audience was invariably captivated.

His lectures were profound and were often beyond the comprehension of ordinary minds. But as we listened, we were drawn into his lecture and began to think along with him. Sometimes our religious interests were aroused. What was happening to us was far beyond a mere conceptual understanding of the content of his lectures; rather our hearts were captured by what he had to say, and we found ourselves resonating with it. The only regrettable thing was that he gave these memorable lectures for only one year. He was given the history of philosophy position the following year. [15]

Hisamatsu's spiritual quest grew so intense that he thought of giving up his university study to dedicate himself entirely to the practice of Zen. Nishida, who remembered how he suffered from his own hasty decision to drop out of higher school, objected. Instead, he spoke to Uemura Hōrin, who made an arrangement for Hisamatsu to meet Ikegami Shōsan, the *shike* (master teacher) of Myōshinji. Master Shōsan allowed Hisamatsu to take part in the December *sesshin* at Myōshinji. [16] Thanks to Nishida's prudent advice not to give up his academic career, Hisamatsu was to graduate from the university, become a professor of Buddhist studies, and make especially notable contributions in the area of Zen aesthetics. Morimoto Kōji, another first-year student who heard Nishida's lectures on religion, had already become interested in Zen practice from another source, and was to choose to become a monk rather than pursue the path of scholarship. He eventually became a Zen master with the name Seinen (more commonly known as Shōnen). Nishida warmly supported Morimoto's decision but advised him to submit his graduation thesis at least, so that he had a university degree under his belt. Nishida clearly did not want his students to repeat the same mistake he had made when he was younger.

President Sawayanagi resigned on April 28, 1914, and the university remained in limbo for some time until the Ministry of Education appointed a successor. Despite the confusion he caused by firing professors, Sawayanagi was a man of simplicity and honesty and left very little animosity among the faculty members of Kyoto.

In the fall of 1914, with Kuwaki's move to Tokyo, Nishida was appointed professor of the first chair in the history of philosophy. The department was seriously understaffed for the 1914–1915 academic year, and Kuwaki's teaching assignments had to be shouldered by the rest of the department members.[17] Nishida taught eight hours a week that year. On top of Introduction to Philosophy, Introduction to Psychology, and a lecture on special topics (Contemporary German Philosophy), he taught a seminar for the students in philosophy and psychology in which he read a German translation of Bergson's *Matter and Memory*.

In the fall of 1914, when the College of Humanities Exhibition Building was completed, the history department moved into it. This created a closer rapprochement among the philosophy, ethics, education, sociology, aesthetics, and religion programs and encouraged cooperation. On November 15, 1914, the faculty members held their first colloquium—a precursor to the meetings of the Kyoto Philosophical Society. By this time, the philosophy department was in its ninth year of existence. The number of graduates was steadily increasing, and many of them held promising positions. Chiba Tanenari and Hatani Ryōtai (the first graduates of the department), Akamatsu Chijō, Takata Yasuma, and Nishida Naojirō (the second year's graduates), Kanetsune Kiyosuke, Nishikida Yoshitomi, Ueda Juzō, and Fujii Tanetarō (the third year's graduates), Amano Teiyū, Abe Seinosuke, and Ojima Sukema (the fourth year's graduates), Nozaki Hiroyoshi (the fifth year's graduate), Yamanouchi Tokuryū and Katsube Kenzō (the sixth year's graduates), Hisamatsu Shin'ichi and Takahashi Keishi (the seventh year's graduates) were all engaged in teaching and scholarly pursuits. Yamanouchi Tokuryū, for instance, then a graduate student and *joshu* (lecturer), was translating Rickert's *Gegenstand der Erkenntnis* [Object of Cognition] into Japanese as *Ninshiki no taishō.*[18] The Japanese translation was to turn out to be an enormous success, selling many more copies in Japan than the original German text sold in Germany.[19] Some of the younger generation of students looked promising as well.

Stimulated by vigorous research carried out by their professors, students and graduates of the philosophy department enjoyed a rigorous scholarly environment. Just as a philosophical society had been formed two decades before by the young and enthusiastic Inoue Enryō, Inoue Tetsujirō, and others at the Imperial University, now it was time for young scholars in Kyoto to do the same. Around 1913 or 1914, Takata Yasuma, Ueda Juzō, and Yamanouchi Tokuryū, all graduate students and lecturers, organized a "Monday Club" in which graduates of the philosophy department could present their research projects. Their energy was contagious and became the driving force behind the formation of the Kyoto Philosophical Society and its journal, *Tetsugaku Kenkyū* [Journal of Philosophical Studies]. These developments were a natural consequence of the consolidation of the philosophy department.

There were some reservations however, about the publication of the new journal, *Tetsugaku Kenkyū*. Some argued that the college journal, *Geibun*, might be jeopardized if a new journal was published. Others expressed concern about whether so specialized a journal could sustain itself economically. As Tomonaga recalled, a spirit of consensus prevailed among the faculty members, and they decided to go ahead with the new journal.[20] They felt that the day would inevitably come when philosophy would become independent of the disciplines of history and literature. They also decided that the business aspect of the journal should be left to the publisher, Hōbunkan, and that professors should contribute at least one or two articles a year, while graduates should also do their best to contribute. They also agreed that if the journal could not sustain itself after a few months of trial, then it should be terminated.

Nishida's own account runs contrary to the popular perception that it was his idea to publish this new journal:

> The publication of a new journal was not my own idea. The graduates of those days enthusiastically planned it. Since I, just like other professors, was affiliated with Tokyo University, I could publish my writings in the *Tetsugaku Zasshi*. But that was not the case with the graduates of Kyoto University. One's thought is not complete in the beginning and can benefit from others' feedback. Judging it best to have a forum of our own, in which we could present our ideas and hone them, I voted for the publication of our own journal.[21]

The Kyoto Philosophical Society was officially launched on February 27, 1916. Commemorating this special occasion, public lectures were held and a dinner reception followed. Former students, professionals in the Kansai area, and those interested in the new venture—about four hundred in number—gathered on this day.[22] As an integral part of the Kyoto Philosophical Society, professors and students, graduated or current, formed a more casual "Friday Club" (meetings were on the first Friday of each month), where students and professors engaged in a lively exchange of ideas.

The first issue of *Tetsugaku Kenkyū* was published in April 1916. Tomonaga Sanjūrō acted as editor-in-chief, and Konishi Shigenao was treasurer, but the actual burden was shared by every member of the department. Ueda Juzō, assistant to the editor, especially exerted himself. Nishida's sustained contribution to the journal greatly helped it stay in circulation.[23]

The inaugural issue carried Nishida's "Gendai no tetsugaku" [Contemporary philosophy][24] as the opening article. In it, he sketched the development of the modern philosophical world since Kant. He covered such thinkers as Fichte, Schelling, Schleiermacher, Hegel, Hermann Cohen and the Marburg School (Natorp and others), Wilhelm Windelband and the Baden School (Rickert and others), Bernard Bolzano, Franz Brentano, Alexius Meinong, Theodor Lipps, Edmund Husserl, Henri Bergson, and Max Planck. Nishida's dogged study of contemporary European thinkers was summarized in this essay. Yamanouchi Tokuryū remembered the impact this essay had on the students:

> It was quite an extensive article, in which he depicted the characteristics of contemporary philosophies. His manner of presentation was concise, sustained by his intellectual vigor. It caught our attention. Within a short span of several years, from the time he had moved from Kanazawa to Kyoto (not to forget that he was in Tokyo for a short while), it was evident that his scholarship was maturing robustly. We were impressed by his article, because it testified to the fact that he had made a radical metamorphosis from a lonely isolated thinker in the countryside to an erudite professor. It also clearly showed to us that even in presenting others' ideas, one must have one's own philosophical substance.[25]

In the fall of 1916 Nishida gave a series of special lectures on Fridays in response to the request of the Gakuyūkai (associated students). These Friday lectures on contemporary idealistic philosophies were transcribed and edited by Nishida's assistant, Yamanouchi, and published as *Gendai ni okeru risōshugi no tetsugaku* [Contemporary idealistic philosophy] in May 1917.[26]

Nishida steadily advanced his philosophical inquiries in a series he came to call "Jikaku ni okeru chokkan to hansei" [Intuition and reflection in self-consciousness]. He not only critically engaged the thoughts of neo-Kantians but also paid attention to Husserlian phenomenological movement. Mutai Risaku,[27] who entered the department in 1915, remembered that the special topic that year was the "Austrian School of Philosophy from Bolzano to Husserl," which was a continuation from the previous year. Nishida's health was less than ideal around this time, however. Mutai recalls that at the beginning of 1916, Nishida had to cancel many of his classes, and "especially on rainy days, almost always there was no class." Mutai's recollection continues:

> In his lectures on the special topic, the professor spoke about works by [Alexius] Meinong, [James] Martineau, Brentano, and Husserl, but many lectures on Husserl were canceled. By the time the professor began discussing Husserl, I was quite comfortable with the method of the analysis of consciousness unique to the thinkers of the Austrian School. I especially was attracted to the amazing freshness and precision in Husserl's analysis of experience based on the intentionality [of consciousness], and my interest in phenomenology was deepened. As I see it now, it was Professor Nishida who introduced the Austrian School and especially Husserl's phenomenology to Japanese students. By that time Husserl's *Ideen* was already published, but we could not get hold of a copy because of World War I. I had to ask someone who was able to borrow it from the department library to let me read it. At first it was very hard to understand, but as I plugged on I started to gather some ideas. I wrote my graduation thesis on phenomenology.[28]

Mutai later got the opportunity to study with Husserl in Freiburg for the winter semester of 1926 and the summer semester of 1927.[29] Yamanouchi's interest in phenomenology was also kindled by Nishida's "Gendai no tetsugaku" and his 1915–1916 lectures on Bolzano and Husserl.[30] Yamanouchi became a serious student of phenomenology and went to study with Husserl in Freiburg from 1921 to 1923. Indeed, Nishida is rightly credited with having introduced phenomenology to Japanese students of philosophy.[31]

In September 1915 Chiba Tanenari was appointed assistant professor of psychology. He began to team teach the introductory course in psychology with Nishida, which reduced Nishida's teaching responsibilities to some extent. A year later, when Nogami Toshio returned from Europe in August, Nishida was totally freed from his obligation to teach Introduction to Psychology. He finally found time to devote his undivided attention to his philosophical inquiries. He concentrated on his project, "Jikaku ni okeru chokkan to hansei," for the rest of 1916.

The lively collegial spirit among the members of the philosophy department was the hallmark of this period. The members collaborated and published a book, *Rottse* [Lotze], in May 1917 on the occasion of the centennial of the birth of Hermann Lotze. The collection includes essays on Lotze's contribution to various fields. Tomonaga covered the history of philosophy; Nogami, psychology; Nishida, metaphysics;[32] Fujii, ethics; Fukada, aesthetics; and Yoneda, social science. They were guided by the common goal of introducing Lotze's thought to the Japanese, while at the same time assessing his contemporary significance. The department's activities began to draw the attention of the Japanese academic world. The philosophy department was becoming a vibrant intellectual center.

Nishida's health, already delicate, grew considerably worse in 1917, and he had to cancel many hours of lectures. Mutai remembers this period:

> Because of his health, the professor covered a little more than half of the materials in the "Introduction to Philosophy," and we were unable to hear his discussion of the problem of existence. But I vividly remember how he spoke about Jacob Böhme and Schelling and spent some time on them. Whenever he got going with his lectures, the frail-looking professor would gain strength all of a sudden, shift his gaze from somewhere on the floor to the students, and his eyes would glisten sharply. The pace of his speech would accelerate, and his hands would gesticulate. At those times I was hardly able to take notes. He spoke about Böhme's biography in relatively great detail. I think he deeply resonated with Böhme (later I learned that his interest in Böhme was provoked by Hegel's history of philosophy).[33]

By the spring of 1917 Nishida reached a point where he could no longer proceed with the line of philosophical inquiry he had been carrying out, feeling that he had reached its end. He wanted to begin a fresh inquiry from a different angle.[34] During this period Nishida dealt with such questions as how self-consciousness operates, how the objective world and consciousness are distinguished, how thought is connected to experience, what the relationship is between time and consciousness, and other knotty epistemological questions. While he grappled with the origin of perception in relation to our physical body and spirit, he confirmed his position that the "will" was more fundamental than cognition and concluded his inquiry by upholding the position of "absolute will." In the last analysis, however, he was not able to answer fully the questions he set out to solve and admitted to himself that "after many trials and errors, my sword broken and arrows used up, one may say I have surrendered myself before the gate of mystery. But one thing is clear. I at least sincerely engaged in examining and questioning the issues from a new angle." [35]

Iwanami Shigeo wanted to publish the essays Nishida had written during this period in a single volume. Although Nishida felt it "irresponsible to readers" to publish such a record of tortuous philosophical battle, he agreed to it. On June 7, 1917, he completed his preface, [36] which reiterates what he initially set out to accomplish in this work:

> I attempted to consider reality according to the form of the "system of self-consciousness" and thereby explain the unity of value and being on the one hand and meaning and fact on the other—the important problems of contemporary philosophy. What I mean by self-consciousness is not something that belongs to the field of psychology. Rather it is the awareness of the transcendental ego, something akin to Fichte's "Tathandlung" [the self as the activity that establishes itself]. I got this suggestion from Royce's "Supplementary Essay" in volume one of *The World and the Individual*. . . . By giving new significance to the Fichtean view, I thought I could unite the thoughts of neo-Kantians and Bergson on a deeper level. [37]

Meanwhile, students wondered how Iwanami would advertise such an abstruse work. The advertisement, however, praises Nishida's philosophical integrity and achievement:

> The important philosophical problems of contemporary philosophies may be reduced to the relationship between (a) value and existence, and (b) meaning and reality. The present book is a crystallization of the philosophical effort of the author, who is probably the foremost original system-builder that Japan has seen since the importation of Western philosophy. He engages in a deep investigation of these central problems, while being sustained by his conviction that self-consciousness is a systematic whole. Because of the vigor of his thinking and the depth of his experience, his work enjoys the distinction of being the most unique, allowing no second. I am convinced that this book amply testifies to the fact that the essence of philosophical reflection does not consist in a simple logical organization of concepts. Rather, it shows that philosophical reflections are an intrinsic part of the profound process of attaining human authenticity. [38]

When *Jikaku ni okeru chokkan to hansei* was published on October 5, 1917, it drew much attention from the public as a ground-breaking work—"as the first original philosophical work accomplished by the hand of a single Japanese."[39] Shimomura Toratarō noted that Nishida's thought became thoroughly "modernized" in this work.[40] The book was introduced in the new book section of *Tetsugaku Zasshi* with the following words:

> There is no need to elaborate on the fact the author's reflection is eminently vigorous and profound. This present book . . . is not a book that teaches us what philosophy is but it is a book that reveals to us the essence of philosophical investigation. . . . Anyone interested in knowing what kind of height and depth Japanese philosophical investigation has achieved must read this book.[41]

Nishida had, by virtue of his assiduous work, solidly established his place as an original thinker within the Japanese academy.

Chapter 11

Correspondence with Tanabe Hajime

(1913–1917)

Sometime soon after their initial encounter in April 1913, Nishida and Tanabe Hajime began corresponding. Tanabe, born in 1885, entered Tokyo Imperial University in 1904 to study mathematics but switched to philosophy midcourse. Upon graduation in 1908 he was admitted to the graduate school, where he remained until June 1912. In 1913, when he met Nishida, he was teaching English at Kaisei Higher School in Tokyo; in August of that year he was appointed lecturer in the natural sciences faculty at Tōhoku Imperial University and moved to Sendai. It so happened that Hōjō Tokiyuki was then the president of Tōhoku University, and Nishida was able to draw Hōjō's attention to improving Tanabe's research environment. Nishida took a personal interest in developing Tanabe's career.

Tanabe, fifteen years younger than Nishida, looked up to him as a mentor, while Nishida appreciated Tanabe's background in the philosophy of natural sciences and especially in mathematics. Nishida was in the habit of destroying letters that came to him—once he had read them—and for this reason Tanabe's letters sent to Nishida did not survive. Tanabe, however, kept Nishida's letters (more than two hundred) up through 1945. Just from 1914 to 1917, during the time Nishida was working on *Jikaku ni okeru chokkan to hansei* [Intuition and reflection in self-consciousness], he wrote more than forty letters to Tanabe. The letters offer a glimpse behind the scenes of his second book and add a human dimension to this otherwise abstruse work. The letters to Tanabe, especially the early ones, are a remarkable piece of intellectual history. The correspondence indicates that Nishida was keenly interested in modern developments in mathematics and physics. Indeed, Tanabe must be credited with stimulating Nishida's interest in these areas. The letters also record how Nishida went about digesting Husserl's phenomenology and what sort of books he considered important.

The earliest extant letter of Nishida to Tanabe dates from January 1, 1914,[1] by which time the two were already engaged in detailed philosophical discussions. Tanabe was then working on an article, "Ninshikiron ni okeru ronrishugi no genkai—Māburukuha to Furaiburukuha no hihyō" [Limitations of logicism in epistemology: critique of Marburg and Freiburg schools].[2] Nishida welcomed Tanabe's research because he felt that the thought of the neo-Kantian Marburg school had not yet been fully introduced to Japan. Nishida himself was already familiar with the Marburg school thinkers through works such as Paul Natorp's *Allgemeine Psychologie* [General Psychology]. Nishida the teacher did not hesitate to urge Tanabe to cast his net more widely and "digest the thought of classical thinkers" such as Kant, Fichte, and Hegel, as well as more contemporary thinkers such as Wilhelm Windelband, Hermann Cohen, and Henri Bergson. He advised Tanabe "to create your own system of thought that is truly meaningful to you."

From this first letter to Tanabe it is clear that Nishida was already keenly interested in the thought of Edmund Husserl. For instance, he mentions Husserl's "Ideen," which came out in the *Jahrbuch für Philosophie und phänomenologische Forschung* [Yearbook for Philosophy and Phenomenological Research]. In that article, Nishida notes, Husserl discusses in detail the idea he had presented earlier in his 1910–1911 essay "Philosophie als strenge Wissenschaft" [Philosophy as Rigorous Science]. Nishida also informed Tanabe that Husserl's 1900 *Logische Untersuchungen—Prolegomena zur reinen Logik* [Logical Investigations —A Prolegomena to Real Logic], hitherto out of print, was available again. Nishida respected Husserl as "a rigorous thinker" and lamented that popular thinkers such as Rudolf Eucken, the Nobel laureate of 1909, received more attention in the Japanese academy than Husserl.

When Tanabe's article came out in two parts, Nishida responded to it. In his letter of April 2, 1914, he agrees with Tanabe that "there is a limitation to the logical approach to epistemology," and that "to solve epistemological problems one has to take the empirical venue." He adds, however, that to solve epistemological problems one needs to clarify (a) the nature of intuition and (b) its relationship to thought. He recommends that Tanabe reread Natorp's two books, which he had found helpful in understanding the philosophy of the Marburg school—the first volume of *Allgemeine Psychologie nach kritischer Methode* [General Psychology according to Critical Method] and *Allgemeine Psychologie in Leitsätzen zu akademischen Vorlesungen* [General Psychology in Guiding Principles for Academic Lectures]. He also suggests Hegel's *Logik*, as well as Fichte's *Zweite Einleitung* [The Second Introduction] and *Neuer Versuch* [New Essay], which he had found more interesting than Fichte's main work, *Grundlage der Wissenschaft* [The Foundation of Science]. To this list he adds Royce's supplementary essays in the first volume of *The World and the Individual*. Along with these recommendations, Nishida offers some personal advice:

> When we engage in philosophical activities, we must delve deeper and deeper, and think more and more precisely to solve any question that we have. We must dedicate the whole of our flesh and blood to that task. The discovery of truth is possible through "constant reflection," as Newton held.[3]

Nishida saw in Tanabe an able critic of his work and requested feedback from him on the essay series he was now writing under the heading of "Intuition and reflection in self-consciousness." His letter of April 14, 1914, is a response to Tanabe's reaction to section 8 of this essay, which appeared in March. Tanabe had questioned the choice of the word "subject" *(shukan)* to designate the aspect of the concrete experience.[4] Following Tanabe's query, Nishida talked with Kuwaki, who suggested "subjective cognition" *(shukaku)*. Nishida concluded that "subject" or "subjective cognition" is better than "sensation" *(kankaku)*, which was what Tanabe probably suggested. Seizing this occasion, Nishida expresses his wish that Japanese students of philosophy engage in a critical examination of basic terminology. He points out that Natorp uses the word "subject" to indicate "original experience." To complicate the matter, in medieval philosophy meaning the word "subject" was diametrically opposed to its modern usage.

Regarding the idea of "value" *(Wert)* held by the Baden school thinkers, Nishida recommends that Tanabe read such books as Rickert's *Grenzen der naturwissenschaftlichen Begriffsbildung* [The Limits of Concept Formation in Natural Sciences], Windelband's "Geschichitesphilosophie" [Philosophy of History], which is in his *Philosophie im Beginn des zwanzigsten Jahrhunderts* [Philosophy at the Beginning of the Twentieth Century], *Vom System der Kategorien* [Of the System of Categories], "Gleichheit und Identität" [Equality and Identity], and *Prinzipien der Logik* [Principles of Logic]. Nishida also tells Tanabe that the *Collected Works* of Wilhelm Dilthey are becoming available in six volumes and that he was looking forward to getting hold of the fourth volume, which is *Geistige Welt* [Intellectual World].

In response to Tanabe's report that he is spending some time overseeing the chores in the university library, Nishida advises him not to spend too much time on inessential tasks, and he shares his regrets that he had spent the most energetic years of his life teaching German. He tries to uplift Tanabe's spirits by reminding him that Tanabe's generation of scholars will eventually establish the Japanese philosophical forum and that to meet that demand they must diligently cultivate their thinking and scholarship.[5]

Sometime in early August 1914, Nishida traveled to Tokyo, where he got together with young graduates of the philosophy department, including Miyamoto Wakichi, Takahashi Satomi, Koyama Tomoe, and Shinomiya Kaneyuki, many of whom Tanabe knew. Nishida told him how delightful it was to mingle with this "progressive group of young scholars" and to hear their opinions.[6] Essentially agreeing with Tanabe's critique of the neo-Kantian thinkers, Nishida expresses his view that "they may have clarified the cognitive form but have not given enough attention to the cognitive content; and they are unable to get rid of the difficulty that Kant's *Ding-an-sich* [thing-in-itself] has raised." It was against this background, Nishida tells Tanabe, that he is carrying out his philosophical investigation of "clarifying the fundamental connection between direct experience and knowledge," which has required his reading the works of Fichte, Royce, Bergson, and more lately Husserl. Nishida indicates that Husserl's thought, although hard to fathom, may prove fruitful.

Nishida was finding a way to understanding Husserl's thought by going back to his predecessors, Brentano and Bolzano. He found Brentano's 1874 *Psychologie vom empirische Standpunkte* [Psychology from the Empirical Standpoint] full of original insight. He also read works by Bolzano, whom he found "highly original" but rather "*langweilig*" (tedious). Nishida found a small book published in 1894 by Kasimierz Twardowski,[7] *Zur Lehre vom Inhalt und Gegenstand der Vorstellungen* [Toward a Theory of Content and Object of the Representations], helpful in understanding Husserl because his thinking seemed to fall somewhere between Brentano's and Bolzano's on one hand and Husserl's on the other. He recommends Brentano's work to Tanabe, and also adds Hegel's *Logik*, part 1 of the *Encyclopedia of the Philosophical Sciences* (1817), although not an easy book to go through.[8] (The special topic Nishida chose for his fall 1914 lectures, "The Austrian School of Thought from Bolzano to Husserl," reflects his own research interest at the time).

In the summer of 1914 Tanabe was working on the essay "Sūgakuteki taishō no sonzai ni tsuite" [On the existence of mathematical objects], which reminded Nishida of his old article, "Logical understanding and mathematical understanding" (1912). Nishida thus recommended to Tanabe such books as Dedekind's 1887 *Was Sind und Was Sollen die Zahlen?* [What are numbers, and what should they be?], papers by Cantor on set theory, and Rickert's "Das Eine, die Einheit und die Eins." Nishida was then interested in mathematical theories, in part because his graduate assistant, Yamanouchi Tokuryū, was then working on set theory and its philosophical (i.e., logical) implications. Nishida believed that "there is an intersection between philosophy proper and other sciences such as mathematics and physics" and hoped that philosophers (himself included) would become more conversant with modern developments in mathematics and physics. This belief remained with Nishida throughout his life. In 1915 he asked Tanabe to recommend good books on non-Euclidian geometry, "not intended for specialists but for philosophers." He was also looking for books to help him understand group theory better.[9]

In September 1914 Tanabe's colleague mathematician Sono Masazō moved from Sendai to Kyoto to teach at the College of Natural Sciences; he also accepted a partial teaching assignment at the College of Humanities.[10] Nishida got together with Sono on November 29 and learned from him that Tanabe was depressed because he had very few students in his class on the philosophy of natural sciences and few colleagues with whom he could talk. On the following day Nishida wrote a very personal letter to Tanabe,[11] consoling him by drawing his attention to Japanese scholars' tendency to shut themselves in a narrowly confined research area and show little interest in interdisciplinary research—a tendency, unfortunately, that students shared. Thus, students' lack of interest in studying the philosophy of natural sciences was not unexpected. His letter continues:

> When you don't have a good library and have no colleagues with whom you can discuss things, naturally, you cannot assess the real worth of your own work, for it is like traveling alone in the desert. You are bound to feel uncertain. But I beg you not to dwell on the negative feelings; you must continue with your work out of your unflinching convictions. If you criticize your own idea until there is no more room for criticism, who else in the world could criticize it? The thing to keep in mind is sincere reflection and self-criticism. As Emerson said, one is only a part

of the world when one talks with others, but when one is alone one is the entire whole *(das Ganze)*. We sharpen our thinking when we return to our private corner. When you feel lonely, read biographies of Descartes, Spinoza, and Kant, and so forth.[12]

To overcome his sense of isolation, Tanabe became interested in Zen literature. Nishida had the following words of advice:

> Though I once wanted to pursue Zen, I eventually quit practicing it without having attained any understanding. Nevertheless, I think that Zen teaching is eminently worthwhile. When it comes to Zen, it is not good enough just to read books and think about this and that. . . . Once one takes up Zen, one has to pursue it all the way; otherwise it is better not to begin it at all. President Hōjō, experienced in Zen practice, is a person you might want to consult about Zen.[13]

Nishida steadily plowed ahead in his philosophical inquiry. Sections 14 and 15 of his "Intuition and reflection in self-consciousness" came out in January 1915, followed by sections 16 and 17 in March, and sections 18–20 in June 1915.

In July 1915 on receipt of Tanabe's two-part essay on the theory of natural numbers, "Shizensūron,"[14] Nishida responded, suggesting that Tanabe consult Hegel's *Logik*, Lotze's *Logik*, Sigwart's *Logik*, Bradley's *Principles of Logic*, and especially Husserl's *Logische Untersuchungen* [Logical Investigations]. By then Nishida was able to tell Tanabe how to go about interpreting Husserl's thought:

> If you begin with the thought of Bolzano and Brentano and move onto that of Twardowski, you will understand Husserl. What Bolzano said in terms of logic and Brentano in terms of psychology is united in Husserl's philosophical method. I think Husserl adopted and developed the ideas unfolded by Bolzano and Brentano.[15]

Tanabe's initial reaction to Husserl's "Philosophie als strenge Wissenschaft" [Philosophy as Rigorous Science] was that it was a kind of *Wesensschauung* (contemplation of being). Nishida cautioned Tanabe not to make a hasty judgment:

> If you base your judgment on that article alone, it will seem as if Husserl's phenomenology is a mere "Wesensschauung," but I understand that his endeavor is to discard any dogmatic view so as to look at reality from the standpoint of "pure experience." As opposed to Rickert, who divides the *Urteil* [judgment] and *Urteilen* [acts of judging] and

neglects the latter, Husserl strikes me as attempting to reflect on the relationship between the two from the standpoint of *reines Bewusstsein* [pure consciousness]. Therefore, if one were to define phenomenology merely as a study of *Wesensschauung*, it would be too broad. For example, mathematics is also a study of *Wesen* [essence], although Husserl seems to consider mathematical study as *eidetik* and distinguishes it from phenomenology. He discussed this point in detail in his "Ideen zu einer reinen Phänomenologie und phänomenologischen Philosophie" [Ideas, General Introduction to Pure Phenomenology]. . . . Husserl's phenomenology is certainly similar to reflexive psychology, but he himself says that he maintains the standpoint of pure consciousness to look at everything in a *beschreibend* [descriptive] manner.[16]

Although Nishida praised Husserl as "a great mind"[17] and told Tanabe to read his works, he never embraced Husserl's system wholeheartedly. For his taste Husserl's thought was too "static and analytical."[18] He maintained his usual critical attitude and held that "we should not be satisfied with, say, Husserl's phenomenology. We must go deeper."[19]

Six sections of "Intuition and reflection in self-consciousness" were published in two installments in the December 1915 (sections 21–23) and January 1916 (sections 24–26) issues of the *Geibun*.[20] Nishida wanted Tanabe to read section 26, in which he discussed his view of *Grenze* (limit). It appears that Nishida's interest in the problems of "continuum, differential, and infinity" was stimulated by Tanabe's works. Nishida had earlier received a copy of Tanabe's book, *Saikin no shizen kagaku* [Recent natural sciences], published by Iwanami Bookstore in November 1915. Nishida had a mixed reaction to this book.[21] In February 1916 Tanabe's essay, "Renzoku, bibun, mugen" [Continuum, differential, infinity] came out in three installments in *Tetsugaku Zasshi*,[22] and Nishida read it with great interest.

Tanabe had been engaged to Ashino Chiyo since April 1915; they were married on February 14, 1916.[23] Soon after that, however, Chiyo contracted pneumonia, and Tanabe found himself in fragile health as well. In response to Nishida's request,[24] he managed to write an article, "Fuhen ni tsuite" [On the universal],[25] for *Tetsugaku Kenkyū* and sent it off in late March.[26] In the face of Chiyo's illness, Tanabe struggled with the meaning of his philosophical engagement and was seriously considering taking up Zen practice.[27] Nishida extended heartfelt support:

It is not an easy thing to render one's philosophical engagement into a living power that sustains life, but I think genuine philosophy has to get to that point. In this respect, I think there is no one like Spinoza, who is an eminent model for us who engage in philosophy. Among the Stoics, Marcus Aurelius stands out as a man of warmth. But the Bible is even more profound and precious than the teachings of the Stoics.

I believe that there is nothing better than Zen to truly give one peace of mind. The only problem with Zen, as I understand it, is that it is rather difficult to enter its gate. It may be better to read Zen stories and such at first. A friend of mine from my childhood, Suzuki Teitarō Daisetz (professor at Gakushūin) has been practicing Zen for years. When you are in Tokyo, you may want to get in touch with him. He has recently written three books, *Zen no tachiba kara* [From the standpoint of Zen], *Zen no daiichigi* [The essential teachings of Zen], and the title of the third book escapes me for the moment.

Have you read Maeterlinck's *Wisdom and Destiny*? I would recommend it. Also, I once read Tsunashima Ryōsen's essays, "Byōkanroku" [Record of experiences during my illness] and "Kaikōroku" [Record of conversion], and Kiyozawa [Manshi]'s "Waga shinnen" [My spiritual convictions] and got much consolation out of them.

In any case the experience you have undergone this time is certainly a moment of supreme challenge for you. Genuine philosophy does not emerge out of reflective consciousness *(ishiki)* but out of totally letting go of one's ego. We believe in our small powers and have to suit our convenience. I think this is where we go wrong. The great truth of the universe is found in the words of Paul: "It is no longer I who live but the Christ that lives in me," and in the words of a Zen adept: "Letting go one's hands, which were clinging to the steep cliff, and being reborn after the experience of absolute extinction." Neither philosophy nor religion is possible separate from this reality—I'm not saying these things. Rather, I'm just repeating the words of the men of old.[28]

In the summer of 1916, when Nishida went to Nagano Prefecture to give three lectures that Iwanami Shigeo and Mutai Risaku had requested, he saw Tanabe in Suwa by pure coincidence, very briefly.[29] Tanabe dedicated the rest of 1916 to intensive writing, completing his essay "Fusū oyobi kyosū" [Negative numbers and imaginary numbers].[30] He almost completed "Hensū oyobi kansū" [Variables and functions][31] and "Sūri no ninshiki" [Cognition of numbers],[32] and he was also drafting "Jikanron" [On time].[33] Nishida, who did not hear from Tanabe for some time, was relieved to receive a letter from him and learn that both Tanabe and his wife were in good health and that Tanabe was writing. Nishida asked him to submit some of his new essays to *Tetsugaku Kenkyū;* he also reported to Tanabe that "Intuition and reflection in self-consciousness" was reaching its end point. He was thinking of finishing it in early 1917 and planned to organize philosophical problems in a different configuration and concentrate on each of them to make a more detailed analysis.[34] Sections 30, 31, and 32 were printed in the October 1916 issue of *Tetsugaku Kenkyū*; sections 33–36 were printed in the November issue; and sections 37 and 38 in the December issue.

The severe cold at the beginning of 1917 aggravated Nishida's chronic insomnia. He told Tanabe that he was trying to avoid taking sleeping pills because he was afraid of becoming addicted to them. His experiments with ginseng had turned out to be ineffective, and he had to go back on the pills.[35] At this time Tanabe was reading Theodor Lipps, a specialist on psychology and aesthetics. Nishida told Tanabe that Lipps's works, such as the 1903 *Leitfaden der Psychologie* [Primer of Psychology] and *Naturphilosophie* [Natural Philosophy], were "full of suggestions" and interesting.[36] He was then working on section 42 of "Intuition and reflection in self-consciousness" and was coming close to finishing. He asked Tanabe to point out any gross mistakes and oversights in this series of essays before the manuscript went to Iwanami Bookstore for publication. Tanabe responded right away with a list of corrections.

Tanabe, for his part, was also thinking of collecting his papers on the philosophy of mathematics and submitting them as a doctoral dissertation, to the philosophy department at either Tokyo Imperial University or Kyoto Imperial University. Nishida wholeheartedly endorsed the idea of Tanabe's submitting a doctoral dissertation and advised him:

> Certainly, getting a degree is not that important for a scholar, but it has the merit of winning the recognition of the general public, which may facilitate your further studies. . . . Regarding your question of whether to submit it to Tokyo or Kyoto, if you decide on Kyoto, I will be able to speak for your work, and I'm pretty certain that the dissertation will pass the review of the faculty committee. But when I consider your future, if your choosing Kyoto over Tokyo might possibly cause ill feelings among your seniors at Tokyo, it would not be good for you. I want you to deliberate on this point. I'm sure that not only Kuwaki but also Professor Inoue recognizes your work, and your dissertation will pass their scrutiny. The only thing with Tokyo is that the process of dissertation evaluation has been so stymied that it will take a long time for you to get the degree. I understand Yoshida Seichi's dissertation has yet to go through the review process even four or five years after its submission. I think this is a point worth considering as well. In any case,

I am for the idea that you should submit your dissertation and request a doctorate.[37]

Tanabe did eventually submit his dissertation to Kyoto. Years later, while studying abroad in Germany, Tanabe took part in Husserl's seminar in the summer semester of 1923.[38] Husserl, who had heard much about Nishida Kitarō from Yamanouchi Tokuryū and Kiba Ryōhon— both of whom were in Husserl's seminars in 1922—asked Tanabe to give him and his colleague mathematician Ernst Zermelo an exposition of Nishida's thought as developed in *Jikaku ni okeru chokkan to hansei*. Zermelo's special interest was the thought of Georg Cantor, and he was to compile Cantor's collected papers. Nishida's interest in Cantor must have caught the attention of both Zermelo and Husserl. Husserl and Zermelo would begin arguing with each other, however, so that Tanabe had to stop his presentation from time to time.[39] Thanks to Tanabe and others, Nishida and Husserl developed a direct personal contact: the two exchanged formal letters a few times between 1923 and 1931.[40] Nishida's name was starting to become familiar among the small circles of European thinkers.

Chapter 12

The Calm before the Storm

(1917–1919)

Nishida caught the flu during the cold weather at the beginning of 1917, and this unfortunately led to the recurrence of chronic pleurisy.[1] He initially planned to go to Tokyo to attend Yayoi's graduation in March but was obliged to stay at home until his health sufficiently recovered. In April, with the arrival of the warmer weather, he was finally able to travel to Tokyo. Nishida set aside some time to see and talk with Tanabe Hajime in private on April 7. On April 15 he gave a talk at the semiannual gathering of the Philosophical Society, entitled "Shushu no sekai" [Various worlds],[2] which was a summary of the conclusions he had arrived at at the end of his inquiry, "Intuition and reflection in self-consciousness." Among the audience of three hundred people was Miki Kiyoshi,[3] then a First Higher School student, accompanied by his mentor, Hayami Hiroshi. Miki wrote about his impression of the day:

> I did not understand his talk very well, which, nonetheless, made a strong impression on me. The professor appeared on the stage in his kimono. He fixed his gaze slightly downward, walked all over the stage, and spoke a few words at a time. It appeared as if he were speaking to himself to organize his thoughts rather than to the audience. Occasionally, he would stop in front of the blackboard and draw a circle or a line, but even that act was not so much to explain his thought as to look for appropriate ways to express his ideas. On that day I did not see an ordinary university professor. I saw "a thinker"![4]

Nishida returned to Kyoto on April 18 but was unable to give lectures at the university because of his poor health. His recovery was slow. His letter to Tanabe Hajime on May 9 informs him that he was finally feeling well enough to resume teaching.[5] On June 7, after completing the preface to his forthcoming book, *Jikaku ni okeru chokkan to hansei*, he began correcting the manuscript for publication. He agreed to the publication of these essays mainly because he could then adopt it as a textbook for his course in the fall, which was on "Chokkan to hansei" [Intuition and reflection]. It was a compilation of his hard-fought work of the past few years, and he was far from pleased with the manuscript. He took slight comfort in William James's words: "those who bring out many works will bring out something."[6] After he had sent the manuscript off to Iwanami on June 24, he took a complete break from his work for the summer.

He needed to let things go. Just several days earlier, on June 18, Nozaki Hiroyoshi, a philosophy student for whom Nishida had high hopes, suddenly died of a heart attack. That morning, Yayoi, who was living with her parents in Kyoto (she had graduated from Tokyo Women's Higher Normal School and had obtained a teaching position at the Women's School in Kyoto), was combing her hair, when her boxwood comb broke in two. An ominous feeling crossed her mind, for a comb's breaking was considered a bad omen. She remembered that "someone rushed into the front entrance of the house, informing us that Nozaki was felled by a heart attack early that morning. Father came down from the second floor in a state of shock, with tears in his eyes, cried 'What a terrible thing,' and rushed out. While I saw my father off, my heart was wrenched with pain."[7]

Nishida had known Nozaki for a long time, ever since Nozaki had been a student at the Fourth Higher School in Kanazawa when Nishida was still teaching there. One day, Nozaki had approached Nishida in the hallway of the higher school building to announce his intention to study philosophy. Following his parents' wish, he had first entered the College of Law at Tokyo Imperial University, only to feel dissatisfied. He eventually transferred to the philosophy department in Kyoto, where he distinguished himself as an excellent student. Nishida found a kindred spirit in Nozaki and enjoyed his company: "We shared the same field of study and the same interests. Setting aside the age difference, we formed a warm friendship." Turning directly to his memory of Nozaki, he wrote: "Whenever you read a book that moved you, you would knock on my door and share your thoughts. Sometimes our conversations extended into the night. Since I was a bit older than you, you never failed to treat me with the politeness that was due to one's elders, but deep down I secretly cherished you as an admirable friend of mine."[8]

Nozaki was developing the idea of "philosophy as confession" and left his manuscript behind, which his friends then made into a book and published with the title *Zange to shite no tetsugaku* [Philosophy as confession]. Nishida contributed a foreword as well as a postscript, in which he wrote:

> We, teachers and friends, regarded you as a young man of great talent. Not only were you endowed with the depth and acumen of mind of a very fine scholar, but you were also gifted with something profound and titanic that lurked at the bottom of your heart. A dark fate, the kind that we find in the tragedies of Sophocles, seems to have occupied the hidden recesses of your heart. While you were moved by such dark forces, you had a very clear, translucent mind. It is unavoidable for such a gifted person like you to become prey to youthful mental torments and agonies. [9]

Nozaki's death left Nishida feeling lonely, as if part of him had been torn away. It was soon after that tragedy that Miki Kiyoshi called on him at home in Kyoto on June 26, with Hayami Hiroshi's letter of introduction in hand. Miki decided to major in philosophy after having read Nishida's *Zen no kenkyū* and thought: "If doing philosophy means to engage in this kind of work, I will try that myself." He wished to study with Nishida, which his mentor Hayami thought was an excellent idea. On the day of his visit, Nishida talked to Miki about the university lectures, seminars, and so forth. In response to Miki's question on what kind of books students should read to begin their study of philosophy, he said one must read Kant and fetched his copy of *Critique of Pure Reason* from his study. [10] A few days later, he had a copy sent to Miki from the department library. [11] Yayoi remembered Miki's first visit clearly. Miki was in his rough attire and a torn school cap, which was then a fashion statement among the First Higher School students. In Yayoi's words:

> My father was seeing off the guest, telling him to come again to visit. When he came into the family room, I asked him: "Who was that person?" He said, with an expression of content on his face: "A bright young man who just graduated from the First Higher School at the top of his class. He heard my talk in Tokyo and decided to choose the philosophy department in Kyoto. Hayami of the First Higher School has nothing but praise for him, and I'm looking forward to having him as a student." Thinking how wonderful it must be for my father to have excellent students, I too was very happy. [12]

Nishida and his family spent July in Kanazawa, where he visited his aging mother and "relaxed everyday and lay on the beach all day long."[13] In August he and his family vacationed in Obama, a small beach town facing Wakasa Bay on the Japan Sea, where their cousin Akai Yonekichi and his family were living. He thoroughly enjoyed his daily walks through the wooded areas along the beach, and sometimes he even returned home with sweet crackers for his children. This created a sensation among the children, for their father—who knew only to buy notebooks, pencils, and books—was now coming home from his walks with sweets.[14] During this vacation, he was delighted to receive the news that his eldest son, Ken, had been accepted by the Third Higher School. When the summer heat abated at the end of August, the Nishidas returned to Kyoto. He reported the effect of his summer to Tanabe Hajime: "The vacation I took this summer, abandoning all work, appears to have had its effect. I am invigorated enough to face any task." He was ready to carry a full teaching load in the fall.[15]

The year 1917 turned out to be eventful. From June through September 1917 Waseda University experienced a campuswide upheaval caused by the rivalry of two factions, one siding with the current outgoing president and the other with the new president. A few professors and students were expelled from the university in September.[16] Also in September, in protest against these measures, Hatano Seiichi resigned from the university. The philosophy department at Kyoto seized this opportunity, and Fukada Yasukazu visited Tokyo on behalf of the department to invite Hatano to accept a teaching position. On November 7 Nishida wrote to Tanabe Hajime to inform him of the news: Hatano had agreed to move to Kyoto to join the department. Hatano began teaching at Kyoto Imperial University in January 1918.

The unrest at Waseda University actually opened up a position for Tanabe Hajime, who was invited back to Tokyo. He was reluctant to move to Waseda, however, because Waseda was a private institution and had a different academic temperament from what Tanabe, a graduate of the Imperial University, had been used to; besides, complicated personal relationships existed among the Waseda faculty members. Although the idea of moving back to Tokyo was enticing, in the end Tanabe decided against it. Nishida agreed with Tanabe's decision and pointed out to him the advantages of being in Sendai, where Tanabe was fully able to dedicate himself to his studies without worrying about such matters as collegial relationships. Nishida gave him these words of reassurance:

Please do not forget—although I don't have to remind you—to continue to pursue your studies in philosophy [as opposed to natural sciences]. In the past I, too, spent a period of academic isolation, when I just read books and engaged in thinking. I understand how you miss being away from the center of scholarly activities, but depending on how you look at the current situation, it might work out to your advantage if you are intent on establishing a philosophical system of your own. A man of old said: "The house offers nothing precious for those who enter it from the front gate."[17] In my opinion there is no other way to carry out one's work than to think deeply *on one's own*, identify the fundamental problems, and try to solve them with all one's might.[18]

The year 1917 was a time of transition for Hōjō Tokiyuki. In August he was asked to assume the presidency of Gakushūin. After deliberation, he accepted the position. On September 2 he resigned the presidency of Tōhoku Imperial University, and he and his family moved to Tokyo. When Nishida learned of Hōjō's departure from the university, he was disappointed for Tanabe's sake. Hōjō needed an able right-hand man to assist him at Gakushūin and approached Yamamoto Ryōkichi. Yamamoto, dean of students at Kyoto Imperial University, had been considering leaving his position for some time because, more often than not, he found himself in conflict with his colleagues. He accepted Hōjō's offer and resigned from the university on March 13, 1918.

Cautious about his health, Nishida had taken it easy for the rest of 1917 and only slowly began writing an essay, "Ishiki to wa nani o imisuru ka" [What is "consciousness"?],[19] and a short piece on the encounter between Leibniz and Spinoza, "Raipunittsu no hontaironteki shōmei" [Leibniz's "Quod ens perfectissimum existit"].[20] These essays were gathered with others to form his next book, *Ishiki no mondai* [Problem of consciousness], published in 1920.

Nishida suffered the death of another of his students, Okamoto (né Sabase) Haruhiko on January 19, 1918. Okamoto had graduated from the philosophy department the previous July. He was fond of literature and was creating his own field of specialty, a kind of philosophy of literature. Nishida first heard about Okamoto from a colleague who was teaching at the Third Higher School, who spoke of an unusual student who had just graduated, named Sabase:

He usually reads only what he likes, skips classes, and his grades have been nothing impressive. But he graduated at the top of the class in the Humanities Division. What he had to say about it was quintessentially

Sabase. "My poor grades would surely make my father unhappy, so I graduated at the top of the class, just to prove that I can do it."[21]

After graduation he entered the College of Humanities at Tokyo Imperial University, but disliking the atmosphere of Tokyo, he transferred back to Kyoto.[22] Shortly before he graduated from the university, he was adopted into the Okamoto family, whose family fortune, however, suddenly declined. It then fell on him to support the entire Okamoto family, and he took a number of part-time teaching jobs in the local schools and also earned some money translating Western literature into Japanese. The amount of work proved to be too much for his delicate constitution, and fatigue led to pleurisy, which he could not fight off. In a memoir about Okamoto, Nishida wrote:

> He was brilliant and sensitive; he was richly imaginative, endowed with a quality of genius. He majored in philosophy, but he took much delight in literature and demonstrated a remarkable talent in it. He especially liked the French impressionistic poets. He was plentifully gifted to create a new field of his own. He had one foot in philosophy and another in literature.[23]

The successive deaths of his beloved students, Nozaki and Okamoto, hit Nishida hard, taking away something of the youthfulness he exhibited in interacting with his students. He committed the cries of his heart in Chinese: "Ah, why must Heaven punish our philosophy department! A rare and gifted young man died, and another followed soon after, leaving behind this old wreck. The waters of the Higashiyama hills are dried up, and a cold north wind wantonly scatters away the fallen leaves!"[24] Okamoto's friends took charge of editing and publishing the writings he had left behind; *Okamoto Haruhiko ikō* [Manuscripts of the late Okamoto Haruhiko] was published in October 1918. In memory of Okamoto, Nishida wrote an essay, "Shōchō no shin'igi" [The real significance of symbols], in which he discussed the nature of the symbol as the union of meaning and existence.[25]

Twenty-five years after Nozaki's death, Nishida's students Mutai Risaku and Kōsaka Masaaki reedited Nozaki's book and republished it. At that time Nishida contributed a preface, in which he reminisced about students who died young. He wrote: "During the two decades when I taught in the philosophy department at the University of Kyoto, three bright minds died without fulfilling their intellectual promises—Nozaki Hiroyoshi, Okamoto Haruhiko, and Mitsuchi Kōzō.[26] Nozaki especially was close to me since he had known me

from the Fourth Higher School."[27] Nishida never forgot those students whom he cherished.

The deaths of Nozaki and Okamoto made Nishida think about
the health of his students. In his elder-brotherly concern, he wrote to
Tanabe Hajime:

> A student of the philosophy department, Nozaki, of whom I had great
> expectations, died last year, and early this year we lost a poet-genius,
> Okamoto, a graduate of our program. I'm devastated. Philosophical
> engagement is apparently not a very healthy thing to do. Make sure
> you don't push yourself too hard in your studies.[28]

In the first half of 1918 Nishida wrote a few essays, "Kankaku"
[Sensation],[29] "Kanjō" [Emotions],[30] and "Ishi" [The will].[31] In the
late spring Tanabe's dissertation passed the examination of the screen-
ing committee. The decision to grant him a doctorate was confirmed
at the faculty meeting of June 19 and was officially announced in major
newspapers in July. Nishida was then beginning to think about inviting Tanabe to join the faculty of the philosophy department,[32] for he
had always wanted to do something for Tanabe.[33]

From mid-July onward, Nishida traveled twice to Kanazawa and
stayed there as long as he could, for his mother was dying. On September 3, 1918, Tosa passed away at the age of seventy-six, with Nishida
at her bedside. Tosa had been a very important presence throughout
Nishida's life, having unfailingly stood for and by him. Her death
overwhelmed Nishida with a tremendous grief, so much so that he was
unable to think. He was then working on an essay, "Keiken naiyō no
shushunaru renzoku" [Various connections of experiential contents],[34]
but he could not think through the problem, especially toward the end
of this essay, and attached a special note saying that although the second half of the essay might appear to be a little confused, he had
wanted to record the confusion itself "as a token of my heart that suffered the death of my mother."[35]

The post-World War I economic boom in Japan created a demand
for more university graduates in the workforce. In response, the government set out to restructure the country's education system. The last
time a radical reform of the education system had taken place was in
1896 under Mori Arinori. In September 1917 the Terauchi cabinet set
up an ad hoc committee on education *(Rinji kyōiku kaigi)* and conducted research into the present state of education. The committee
filed its recommendation on June 22, 1918. Nakahashi Tokugorō,[36]

a businessman-turned-politician from Ishikawa Prefecture, was appointed minister of education in the Hara cabinet on September 29, 1918. Nakahashi's appointment came as a real surprise to Nishida and Yamamoto. Nishida initially took it as good news that an Ishikawaite had been put in charge of education, but he was not without apprehension. Nakahashi, not really versed in the area of education, would need to be supported by an able vice minister.[37] The Ministry of Education announced a new university ordinance *(daigakurei)* on December 6, which included the upgrading of private universities to full university status. The government also announced a revision of higher school ordinance *(kaisei kōtōgakkō rei)*, which radically expanded the higher school system. Upon reading the new plan of the government, Nishida could not help but be critical. He wrote to Yamamoto on December 26, 1918:

> I read minister of education Nakahashi's plan. I regret to say that his emphasis is on technical learning such as medicine, engineering, and law; he dismisses the fundamentals of education in humanities and natural sciences. I wonder whether this reform might lead to an impoverishment of letters and sciences, while the actual burden in these areas might be handed over to the private institutions. Nakahashi's plan looks to me too enterprise-oriented. Even if the government is to increase the number of higher schools, where are they to find teachers?

In the same letter, revealing his view of what the imperial family *(kōshitsu)* should be to Japan, Nishida reacted positively to the news that the imperial family was supportive of education:

> For the imperial family to donate money to education is among the finest deeds of recent years. It has to be so. I would like to see the imperial family acting as a patron of culture. The slogan, "revere the emperor" *(kin'nō)* made sense at the time of the Restoration, but the imperial family today no longer stands opposed to the Shogunate but is of the entire country of Japan. These days one hears a lot of clamor about the "uniqueness of the Japanese political system" *(kokutai)*, but no one bothers to recognize that the Japanese *kokutai* is grounded in humanity. They are content with propounding the dogma of the unbroken line of imperial succession. For me, this "unbroken line" is rather a symbol of great mercy, altruism, and partnership. I think we need to point out this aspect.[38]

According to the new university ordinance, the College of Humanities *(Bunka Daigaku)* was renamed the Faculty of Letters *(Bungakubu)* in February 1919. The change was supposed to provide more coherence to the various units of the university. In exchange, some degree of autonomy was taken away from each college.[39] In view of the projected increase in the number of students entering the universities, new chairs were added to the five imperial universities. Two new positions were added in June 1919 to the Faculty of Letters at Kyoto, one in Chinese language and literature and the other in Japanese literature.

This addition of professorial positions created two new positions on the level of assistant professor, and Nishida saw an opportunity to invite Tanabe Hajime to Kyoto. In fact, he had begun his initial inquiries as early as July 1918, asking Tanabe if he was interested in moving to Kyoto.[40] Tanabe was more than happy to do so to be Nishida's colleague, with one reservation: his appointment would take away opportunities from Kyoto Imperial University graduates. Nishida responded to Tanabe's concern:

> On this point, I, too, have deliberated as a professor in the philosophy department, but the position of assistant professor would be left vacant for quite a while if we did not make an appointment at this time, as I said in my previous letter, and this would not be good for the department. Certainly, no one can tell what the future will bring, but for the moment there is no one whom we can recommend for the position of assistant professor from among our graduates. Obviously, we need to think about the future of our graduates . . . , but I want to consider Kyoto University *not* as a parochial regional university in Kyoto but as one of the country's universities.[41]

At that time there was a discussion to establish a faculty of letters at Tōhoku Imperial University,[42] and Tanabe was offered the position of professor, if and when the university expanded its offerings. It would certainly be more prestigious for Tanabe to be promoted to professor rather than to move to Kyoto as assistant professor. Nishida did not want to apply any pressure on Tanabe, for he wanted him to make up his own mind:

> In Kyoto, I'm afraid you will have to remain in the position of assistant professor for a long time. Although you say you don't mind that, I feel sorry for you. At Tōhoku Imperial University, they are setting up the Faculty of Law and Humanities, . . . and you would certainly play an important role if you remain there. For this reason, I want you to tell me frankly what you would like to do. . . . Nothing would delight me more than if you were to decide to come to Kyoto and support our program here, but I think you may make a greater contribution to the

Japanese philosophical world if you have a position of independence and explore your own field.[43]

Tanabe declined the counteroffer in Sendai and was given permission by the president of the university to leave. The philosophy department in Kyoto voted in May 1919 to appoint Tanabe assistant professor of the history of philosophy. Sawamura Sentarō was appointed to the position of assistant professor of aesthetics as well. During this period of structural change at the university, one of the prime movers in the College of Humanities, accomplished historian Uchida Ginzō, died on July 22, 1919. By August Nishida had written "Ishi jitsugen no basho" [The place where the will is actualized],[44] "Ishi no naiyō" [The volitional contents],[45] "Kankei ni tsuite" [On relationships],[46] and "Ishiki no meian ni tsuite" [On the light and dark sides of consciousness].[47] Tanabe Hajime moved to Kyoto that August. Hatano Seiichi, who knew Tanabe from his Tokyo days, reassured Tanabe that Nishida was looking after Tanabe's career with a paternal compassion.[48]

Nishida faced some changes on the home front as well. On June 14, 1919, his eldest daughter Yayoi wedded Ueda Misao, with Yamamoto Ryōkichi acting as the matchmaker. Ueda was a former student of Nishida's at Gakushūin and was launching a successful career as a judge following his graduation from the College of Law at Kyoto Imperial University.

In July Nishida was invited to give lectures in Nara. At that time Kotomi and Sotohiko accompanied him. They enjoyed their visit to Tōdaiji and their walk into the hills of Mt. Mikasa. Nara was full of the charm of an ancient capital. Sotohiko duly passed the entrance examination to the Third Higher School that summer. Nishida spent August preparing the manuscript of his next book, *Ishiki no mondai*,[49] which was a collection of essays he had written during the past year and a half.[50]

All seemed well with his family, and Nishida's life was comfortable as he entered the ripeness of midlife. On September 14, however, when he had just finished his dinner and was about to stand up to leave the dining table, Kotomi cried out his name and suddenly fell on the floor. Two doctors were rushed to the Nishidas. Kotomi had suffered a stroke and lay unconscious. This happened right at the beginning of the new academic year, when students from Tokyo—Tanikawa Tetsuzō, Hidaka Daishirō, and Hayashi Tatsuo (limited status) —entered the philosophy department in Kyoto.

Chapter 13

Sorrows of Life and Philosophy

(1919–1922)

Kotomi regained her consciousness after the stroke, but she was completely paralyzed and became bedridden. Eight years later, Nishida confided to Yamamoto how he felt when his wife became disabled:

> Human beings exist in time. Precisely because there is the past, such a thing as "I" exists. The fact that the past is present in the present moment simultaneously constitutes that person's future. When my wife was suddenly paralyzed because of illness, I was overcome by this thought. It felt to me as if the important part of my past had vanished all at once, and with it, my future. Even when there is a merry occasion, there is no one to rejoice with. Even when there is a sad moment, there is no one to commiserate with.[1]

Following Kotomi's illness, successive illnesses struck his family. His eldest son, Ken, died in 1920 of complications from peritonitis; one daughter, Shizuko, began to suffer lung trouble in 1921; his daughters Tomoko and Umeko contracted typhoid fever in 1922, and Tomoko had to undergo a prolonged period of painful convalescence. Tanabe Hajime, who deeply sympathized with the Nishidas, described the situation as "Job-esque."[2] It is a curious coincidence that Nishida wrote to Tanabe Ryūji in October 1907—more than a decade earlier—of a premonition: "Last night lead-colored clouds filled the sky and hung low to the ground; moonlight faintly seeped through the thick clouds here and there; winds were violently blowing, making an incredible noise and twisting tree trunks. It was a horrific night. Is this the background for my life?"[3] In 1919 his daily life came to resemble this ghastly stormy night. The disasters tormented him and pushed his philosophical reflections closer to home, to the reality of life itself. He came to consider his philosophical activities as emanating from the profound "sorrows of life" *(jinsei no hiai)* [4] rather than from "astonishment" or "marvel" *(thaumazein)*, as Aristotle had it; it was to that Aristotelian definition that the younger Nishida had adhered.

Kotomi was no longer able to see to the household chores. Yayoi was married and established in her own home in Hirakata. Shizuko assumed the burden of homemaking, but the stress proved to be too much for her, and she began to suffer from lung trouble. The Nishidas had always kept a couple of maids who could at least take care of three daily meals, but that was all they were able to do. Without a mistress the household began to look dilapidated. Sotohiko observed his father of those trying days:

> Torn *fusuma* [dividing sliding doors] were not repaired, doors and *shōji* screens were stuck and would not open smoothly, and the *tatami* mats were dirty. The more chaotic his surroundings became the less father seemed to care about them. It was not that he did not notice things. Rather, he was living in a world of his own. [5]

As Nishida saw his surroundings gradually deteriorate, he realized how hard Kotomi had worked to create an environment conducive to his work and to protect him from the chores of daily life. The practical responsibilities for household chores and childrearing now fell on his shoulders.

In October, when he was still at a loss following Kotomi's stroke, a problem arose in the philosophy department. Tomonaga Sanjūrō was offered a position as principal at a higher school. Tomonaga, feeling that the department was entering a new phase with Hatano Seiichi and Tanabe Hajime on the teaching staff, thought it best to take the position. It would also open up an opportunity to the promising graduates of the department. Nishida understood Tomonaga's reasoning but persuaded him to stay, pointing out that Tomonaga's expertise was different from Hatano's, and that his presence was central to the convivial atmosphere among colleagues in the department. Nishida added his personal voice: "It would be too sad to lose a colleague with whom I have been able to be totally open and discuss things over the years." Nishida further entreated: "One might think that a person to consult with may be found in many ways, but I don't think human emotions are that simple. I'm sure there are better wives than my own, and better friends than my own. But my wife is my wife, and my friends are my friends." [6] These words, coming from Nishida, whose wife had had a stroke and who was lying in her bed, moved Tomonaga. He declined the offer of the principalship and remained a good colleague of Nishida's.

On October 13, 1919, Nishida gave a guest lecture at Ōtani University entitled "*Coincidentia oppositorum* to ai" [*Coincidentia oppositorum* and love].[7] In it he revealed the thought he was developing then, namely, that "logic is usually taken to mean something cold and impersonal, but it is fundamentally connected to human emotions." This is an idea he was to articulate in his 1936 essay, "Ronri to seimei" [Logic and life]. Nishida must have been reflecting on the relevance of his philosophizing when his own wife was incapacitated. Making a reference to Nicholas Cusanus's idea of "*coincidentia oppositorum*" (unity of opposites), Nishida saw a similar insight at work in Cantor's definition of the infinite: "the true infinite is that in which a part and the whole are identical." This supported Nishida's view of self-consciousness, in which that which is reflected is none other than that which reflects. Nishida asserted that there is *coincidentia oppositorum*—a unifying power of consciousness—at the ground of all knowledge. He also pointed out that love that transcends the thought of ego-centered gain and loss and that establishes the unity of the self and the other is a salient case of *coincidentia oppositorum*. Nishida was beginning to find that "logic" and "love" are in fact intertwined, as both share the moment of the unity of opposites. His reflections were acquiring the tone of personalism.

In December 1919, at the request of Ryūkoku University (then called Bukkyō Daigaku), Nishida gave a talk entitled "Shūkyō no tachiba" [The standpoint of religion],[8] in which he suggested that religious truth must in some ways be different from the truths established by the natural sciences. He was then meditating on the relationship between life and knowledge (or logic).

The new year of 1920 began relatively peacefully for Nishida. Yayoi and Toshiko made a short visit home. Nishida typically ushered in the new year by working on his philosophical writing. Colleagues, Tomonaga, Tanabe, and Hisamatsu Shin'ichi, were among the many well-wishers who called on him. The business in the department went as usual, and on the surface Nishida's life seemed to have gone back to normal. But on January 24 his colleague Kano Naoki's wife died after an illness. Nishida extended him deep-felt sympathy, for he knew what it meant to lose one's wife. Kano remembered Nishida's warmth:

It is facetiously said that philosophers lack common sense, but Nishida was the farthest from that kind of caricature. He was a man of common sense, though he did not show it. He also had a deep understanding of human conditions and emotions. If anyone has ever described him as a strange man,[9] it goes to show that such a person does not know Nishida. He was indeed a man of refined sensitivity and civility.[10]

In April 1920 Nishida went to Tokyo to attend a meeting with his colleagues Sakaguchi Takashi and Kano. During his stay in Tokyo, he got together with Yamamoto Ryōkichi and Suzuki Daisetz to discuss Yamamoto's situation. Hōjō had just stepped down from the presidency of Gakushūin, having been forced by an opposing faction of the faculty members. Hōjō's proposal to add the component of university to Gakushūin had been turned down, leading to his resignation. In this anti-Hōjō environment, Yamamoto had to make up his mind whether to stay on at Gakushūin or to leave. Daisetz, who was the dormitory master at Gakushūin, managed to detach himself from campus politics. But that was not the case for Yamamoto. Yamamoto decided to resign from Gakushūin. This uncertain situation turned into a perfect opportunity for Yamamoto to take time off from his work and travel abroad for a year. Hōjō persuaded his acquaintance, a businessman named Ataka Yakichi, to contribute ten thousand yen for Yamamoto's trip. Hōjō arranged to secure an official government paper that charged Yamamoto with the mission of "observing American and English education systems and visiting renowned schools."[11]

Although Suzuki was doing well at Gakushūin, Nishida had for some time been looking for an academic position for him, one that would enable him to engage in scholarly research and writing. In 1917, just after Suzuki had been appointed dormitory master at Gakushūin, Nishida wrote to Hori Koretaka that Suzuki was too good for such a position and should not be buried by insignificant assignments.[12] Nishida's effort bore fruit; he found a professorship for his friend at Ōtani University by gaining the commitment of President Sasaki Gesshō.[13] Suzuki accepted the offer and moved to Kyoto in May 1921.

Nishida returned home from Tokyo on April 15 to find that his eldest son was suffering from a high fever. Ken turned out to have peritonitis and was quickly admitted to the university hospital. To quell his sense of anxiety, Nishida listened to music on his phonograph. The opening movements of Beethoven's Fifth Symphony sounded as if dark fate were knocking on his door. Ken's peritonitis got much better by May, but the bacteria entered his bloodstream and caused inflammation of his heart. The doctors held out very little hope. Realizing that his son was dying, Nishida had to face the difficult task of telling Kotomi, who was bedridden. Naturally, Kotomi was distressed at first but soon regained her composure and told him that, from the very first day Ken was admitted to the hospital, she had already prepared herself for this. She reasoned that a long life did not necessarily mean happiness for everyone, and that she wanted the funeral service to be held at Senjuin, the temple where Uemura Hōrin was abbot. Enormously relieved by Kotomi's amazing courage and resolution, Nishida asked Hisamatsu Shin'ichi, who was then living on the Myōshinji temple compound, to take care of the funeral arrangements. Ken died on June 11 at the age of twenty-two. Hiramoto Tokujū, the successor to Ikegami Shōsan as the *shike* of Myōshinji, officiated at the funeral service.

Ken had been about to graduate from the Third Higher School and was planning to enter Kyoto Imperial University. According to his best friend, Kubo Yoshio, Ken was "uncomplicated, manly, and had the natural talent to be the boss of a pack, and therefore he would have made a name in the financial world."[14] He had been a young man of strong physical constitution who enjoyed participating in sport competitions. Nishida did not approve of his sons playing sports; he considered it a waste of time and insisted instead that they channel their energy into their studies. Nishida came to this view out of personal experience, regretting that he had wasted his time playing tennis when he was teaching at the Fourth Higher School.

Nishida was a strict father to his sons, but Kotomi's understanding of their sons' needs provided balance. She was, however, a strict mother to her daughters, while Nishida was a doting father to them. Thus Nishida and Kotomi made a good couple. While Ken was fighting for his life, a baby boy, Kaoru, was born to Yayoi and Ueda Misao on May 17. Because Nishida had placed a great deal of hope in his eldest son's future, Ken's death came as a severe blow to him. But Nishida felt he must maintain his calm in front of the infirm Kotomi. His overwhelming sadness, however, was expressed in a series of *waka* poems:

Since the day
he was carried on this road
on a stretcher
he was never to return home
my child

Even the dirty textbooks
pronunciations penciled in
are now treasures
I put them away
in a wooden box

Just about fifty days
with my heart
heavily afflicted
I trod this road
to the hospital

Having lived
healthily
till twenty-three
how could he disappear
like a dream [15]

His love for Ken took yet another expression—this one of magnanimity. He donated handsome leather-bound books to the library of the Third Higher School in Ken's memory, including six volumes of *Fichtes Werke* [Collected Works of Fichte], Windelband's *Präludien* [Preludes], and *Einleitung in die Philosophie* [An Introduction to Philosophy].

While Nishida was still feeling miserable from the loss of his son, the world around him moved on even more briskly than usual. Nishida's best friend, Yamamoto, was leaving for America and called on him in Kyoto on July 23. Yoneda Shōtarō was promoted to full professor, and the department held a farewell party for Yamanouchi Tokuryū and Uno Enkū, both of whom were leaving to study abroad in Europe. Ken's illness left behind a pile of medical bills. Ataka Yakichi offered monetary help. Although Nishida hesitated at first out of pride, he accepted the two hundred yen and with that money he decided to hire his aunt, Akai Maki, as a live-in governess for his daughters. She came to live with the Nishidas and taught Shizuko (fifteen), Tomoko (thirteen), and Umeko (eleven).

Nishida found it necessary from time to time to forget all that tormented him and turned to nature for consolation. He sent a letter to Tanabe Hajime with a poem:

Looking at the clouds
that travel above
the great sea, I spend
the whole day immersed
in thought [16]

Tanabe was convalescing at Tsuruga at that time. Nishida advised him to "forget everything, calm your mind, and recuperate. It will be good for you to roam in the mountains and seas as if you had become a complete fool. One must have that kind of mettle." He continues:

> I love the ocean. I can watch the waves all day long. Waves are the movements of infinity itself. I used to read such poems on the sea as those by Heine; his poem on the North Sea is impossible to understand unless one has seen the ocean of the northern country. . . .
>
> There is nothing more pleasant than to be embraced in the bosom of great nature. There is no talk of scholarship or moral discourse there.[17]

In 1921, as had been decided by the University Ordinance of 1918, universities and higher schools changed the beginning of the academic year from September to April to better align their academic calendar with the rest of the school system (elementary and secondary schools had changed their school year to begin in April around 1900).[18] Those students who entered the university in September of the previous year, Kōsaka Masaaki, Mitsuchi Kōzō, Kimura Motomori, Kobayashi Tai-chirō, and several others had to finish their first year of study in this shorter period of six or seven months, and things felt a little rushed for Nishida. His special lectures of 1920–1921 were on Hegel, which must have been part of his endeavor to concentrate on logic—a process that eventually led him to formulate his "logic of *topos*."

Among the first-year students who entered the philosophy department in April 1921 were Nishitani Keiji and Tosaka Jun, both from the First Higher School in Tokyo. Nishitani chose Kyoto over Tokyo after he had read Nishida's *Shisaku to taiken* [Philosophical contemplation and life experience] by chance and found an existential affinity with Nishida's thought. Tosaka, however, chose Kyoto, following in the trendsetter Miki Kiyoshi's footsteps. Yamanouchi Tokuryū, then in Paris, regularly sent Nishida and Kotomi postcards from Italy and other parts of Europe. These beautiful postcards especially delighted Kotomi.[19] In April, Tanabe Ryūji, the author of the *Koizumi Yakumo-den* [A biography of Lafcadio Hearn], got a chance to travel abroad to visit Hearn's relatives and acquaintances in the United States and Britain. (Following this productive trip, he revised his biography of Hearn in 1922.) In early July, Yamamoto Ryōkichi returned to Kobe from his trip abroad, while Naruse Kiyoshi (or Mukyoku),[20] lecturer in German literature, left for his study abroad.

Of all the happenings in 1921, the most important for Nishida was Suzuki Daisetz's move to Kyoto in May to assume the chair of professor of Buddhist Studies at Ōtani University. Before their arrival,

Nishida looked for a house for Suzuki and his wife, Beatrice. Their move to Ōtani led to the birth of an international journal of Buddhist studies in English, *The Eastern Buddhist.*[21] The journal aimed to disseminate the Mahāyāna Buddhist ideals into the daily lives of the people around the world and to counter the forces of "sordid industrialism and blatant militarism" that led to World War I.[22]

Nishida hardly had a moment of peace at home. Shizuko began to show symptoms of lung trouble (most likely tuberculosis) in July. Nishida was extremely sensitive to the health of his children because he now knew that a young person's illness could end in death. He expressed his feelings in *waka* poems:

> *In this depressing world*
> *the summer*
> *is half gone*
> *while I have many things*
> *on my mind*[23]

> *I haven't called what is red*
> *red and merely made it*
> *an object of my scrutiny*
> *and already fifty years*
> *of my life have gone by*[24]

While he always held that the starting point of philosophy was reality itself, this "reality" became more concrete in the face of the sufferings of his wife and children.

In the fall of 1921 Yamanouchi Tokuryū settled in Freiburg to study with Edmund Husserl. Martin Heidegger was also in Freiburg, assisting Husserl. Nishida wrote to Yamanouchi on November 28, 1921:

Thanks for the postcards of the University of Jena and the Heidelberg Castle beautifully adorned by flowers; and thanks also for your letter from your boarding house in Freiburg. It appears that there are many bright philosophy students from Japan gathered in Freiburg. It must be quite a sight. What sort of lecture does Prof. Husserl give? Might he give difficult lectures, saying *noema, noesis,* and so forth? I hope his lectures are substantial and not just full of detailed analyses and grand jargon to impress the audience. . . . About Heidegger, I know that he wrote his dissertation on Duns Scotus, but I haven't read it. I did take note of it because I felt that we may still learn from Duns Scotus.

How are the works by [Moritz] Geiger and [Karl] Jaspers in

Heidelberg? What are their reputations like? . . . Isn't this [Julius] Ebbinghaus that you mention perhaps the son of the psychologist, [Hermann] Ebbinghaus? I haven't yet read Rickert's *System der Philosophie* [1921]. If you treat the subject as Rickert does, I think it would be uninteresting. Lately, I don't read new works as much as I used to, but please let me know about anything that you read or hear that might be of interest to me. . . .

Nishikida [Yoshitomi][25] leaves Kobe tomorrow; he is going to Berlin. Tanabe [Hajime], too, will leave in early March. He's going either to Heidelberg or Freiburg.[26]

Nishida also wrote to Kiba Ryōhon[27] in Freiburg. Kiba had been Nishida's student from Fourth Higher School days:

How is phenomenology? Isn't it quite difficult? As opposed to Rickert's school, which solely focuses on logical structure, phenomenology contains elements of experience, and for that reason it is interesting. I just wonder, however, if it continues to take that static a course, what will become of it. Just as Goethe satirized Mendelssohn, might phenomenology end up killing the butterfly to get to its beauty?[28]

Shizuko's lung condition remained the same in 1922. The arrangement with Akai Maki as governess did not work very well, and she left the Nishidas. In her place a young graduate of the Women's Higher School was temporarily hired, but Nishida felt a more experienced college graduate was needed and consulted his colleagues in Tokyo, including Abe Jirō and Abe Yoshishige. In March the youngest daughter, Umeko, was accepted to the Kyoto Prefecture First Higher Women's School—welcome news for Nishida. In April, a graduate of Tokyo Women's College, Ueno Asako [she later married Nishida's son, Sotohiko], came recommended to Nishida. She had been governess to the children of Yanagi Muneyoshi. Although Asako was an experienced governess, it was impossible for her to tend to every detail of their daily lives. In May, Tomoko and Umeko ate strawberries contaminated with typhoid bacteria and became violently ill. They were sent to a hospital, and Umeko recovered after a while, but Tomoko's condition remained critical for a long time. Nishida visited his two daughters in the hospital every afternoon. His *waka* from this time reads:

My wife is ill
so are my children
only the summer

grass thrives
at my house[29]

Nishitani Keiji, also admitted to the hospital with the suspicion of typhoid fever, was in the same hospital, in the room right next to Nishida's daughters. Nishitani remembered that "I often heard the two daughters cry because of pain; someone told me that their conditions were quite serious. Every day, in the afternoon, I saw Professor Nishida come to the hospital, passing by along the corridor, wearing a grave expression on his face."[30]

To maintain some order at home, Nishida asked for volunteers from the Ittōen religious community to come and clean the house. As part of their religious practice, the members of Ittōen paid "house calls" to help people. The founder, Nishida Tenkō, however, believed that the volunteers should be rotated regularly so as to prevent their forming special attachments. Thus, Nishida had to devote time to training a succession of helpers.

In stark contrast to Nishida's domestic nightmares, life at the university was full of exciting events and activities. On March 5 Tanabe Hajime left for Berlin to study in Germany, and in April Hara Katsurō was elected dean of the Faculty of Letters. On April 29 the Prince of Wales (crown prince of England), who was traveling around the world, visited Kyoto Imperial University, and Nishida was among those who had an audience with him. In May Miki Kiyoshi left to study abroad in Germany, with financial support secured by Hatano Seiichi from Iwanami Shigeo. Also in the spring of 1922 repercussions from the 1919 educational reform began to be felt. Under this new system the number of higher schools was proliferating.[31] Accordingly, the number of incoming university students increased by leaps and bounds. The Faculty of Letters at Kyoto saw more than one hundred first-year students that spring.[32] The number of students who chose the philosophy department also increased dramatically, almost tripling in 1922. Nishitani Keiji's essay "Nishida, My Teacher"[33] describes the changing atmosphere of the department and Nishida's lectures of this period.

In April 1922 Yamamoto Ryōkichi got the position of vice principal of the newly founded elite school in Tokyo, Musashi Higher School. Nishida was delighted over how things had turned out for his friend.[34] Under Yamamoto's leadership Musashi Higher School began to carve out a niche as one of the finest private higher schools in the country. In November Yamamoto had some business to take care of in Kyoto, and the two friends seized the opportunity to get together. Yamamoto's visit was something Nishida badly needed to comfort his lonely heart. In appreciation of his constant friendship, Nishida wrote to Yamamoto: "It was so wonderful to spend some time with you and talk our hearts out. Your visit touched me very much, and I even thought of the line [from the *Analects*]—'Is it not pleasurable for a friend to come and visit from afar?' Both of us are over fifty—the beginning of old age, but somehow whenever I see you I feel as if I were in my twenties again!"[35]

Nishida found that adopting a wider horizon beyond the immediate situation was helpful in warding off his depression. His thoughts often flew over to Germany, where many of his younger colleagues were gathered. He was writing "more often to friends in Germany than to friends in Japan."[36] In the summer of 1922 Miki Kiyoshi, Naruse Mukyoku, Abe Jirō, Ishihara Ken, and Kuki Shūzō were among those in Heidelberg, where Heinrich Rickert was teaching.[37] Yamanouchi Tokuryū, Kiba Ryōhon, Itō Kichinosuke, Fujioka Zōroku, Koyama Tomoe, and Ishikawa Kōji were among those in Freiburg, where Edmund Husserl was teaching. Tanabe Hajime was moving to Freiburg in the fall. Chiba Tanenari was in Berlin. For Nishida to think about his colleagues abroad made him forget his gloom at home. His letter to Yamanouchi Tokuryū in Freiburg reads:

> I heard that Tanabe moved to Berlin. He told me that he went to the Kant Conference in Halle with Nishikida and got together with those of you from Japan. You may have been there, perhaps? It sounds like a lot of activities are going on in Germany with so many Japanese there. My heart is hovering over Germany rather than over Japan these days. Miki must have already arrived in Berlin. So might have Shinohara [Sukeichi]. According to the newspaper, [the German] foreign minister [Walther Rathenau] was assassinated, and I'm worried about those of you who are studying in Germany, since any domestic change could affect your safety. How is it in the southern part of Germany? Is it true that universities in the south, such as in Heidelberg, do not admit foreign students? Take especially good care of yourself. I'm doing well. My wife is in exactly the same condition as she was when you left. But unfortunately, two of my children are in the hospital because of typhoid.[38]

Japanese scholars studying in Germany invariably mentioned Nishida's name as the foremost representative thinker in contemporary Japan. Husserl, Rickert, and Heidegger were all familiar to an extent with the name Nishida Kitarō, but it appears that Nishida's thought remained opaque to the Western thinkers, mainly because of the language barrier. Takahashi Satomi, who studied with Husserl in Freiburg, 1926–27, tells us that Husserl failed to see the originality of Nishida's thought; instead, he believed that Nishida's "intuitionism" was something akin to his own and considered Nishida an adherent to *his* branch of phenomenology. Takahashi elaborates on this point: "Husserl's phenomenological pure intuition is something objective, with no element of logical reflection mixed in; whereas what Nishida meant by 'intuition' is something that is always within one's self-consciousness and something that is never separated from reflection."[39] Be that as it may, intellectual exchanges between the Japanese and European thinkers in the 1920s and 1930s were lively, and the level of discourse was considerably sophisticated.

In the summer of 1922 Sotohiko, now twenty-one years old, was thinking of going into philosophy. This worried Nishida. He asked Mutai Risaku, who was teaching Sotohiko at the Third Higher School, to dissuade his son from making that choice. Nishida also expressed his concern in letters to Sotohiko, explaining that "philosophy is a challenging field and demands even from naturally gifted students assiduous work and toil; many have to go through a period of uncertainty about their own ability and pass through critical points where they might just give up. Many fail and succumb in midcourse." He also wanted Sotohiko to know that "it is very difficult to earn one's living by philosophy—one has to be extremely gifted or else fortunate. I, too, had to teach at junior higher school and higher schools until I was forty years old. One must be mentally prepared to discard any idea of luxury and lead a simple life. There might even be times when one has not enough to clothe and feed the family." Nishida suggested to Sotohiko that he go into the natural sciences, instead of philosophy, for the following reason:

> While incomplete endeavor in literature or philosophy is useless, you see the result of your study in the area of natural sciences immediately, and the more you study the more results you obtain. In natural sciences, if you pursue your study to the depth of the problem, you can come in contact with the profound mystery of the universe. Regardless of what discipline you choose to specialize in, what counts is your earnest, sustained scholarly attitude. Your interest in the field you choose will emerge from a sincere engagement.[40]

Nishida wanted his only surviving son to have a solid profession. Eventually, Sotohiko obeyed his father's wish and majored in physics at the university. Sotohiko probably heard Einstein's lecture at Kyoto Imperial University in December 1922, and it is easy to imagine that a lecture by the world-famous physicist came as an affirmation of his choice.

Nishida's home life was starting to take a brighter turn. Mitsui Hachirōemon (or Takamine), the industrialist tycoon of the Mitsui Financial Group, wanted to thank Nishida for having sponsored his second son, Takaakira, on the occasion of his son's graduation from Kyoto Imperial University in 1920. The elder Mitsui insisted on building a new house for the Nishidas. The story goes that Mitsui felt sorry that such a famous philosopher was living in a humble rented house. Nishida accepted this generous offer and participated in designing the house. The house in Asukaichō, a few blocks north of the university campus, was completed in September 1922, and the family moved in on September 16. Ueda Juzō, Hisamatsu Shin'ichi, and Mutai Risaku helped with the move. Kotomi was carried to the new house in a kind of palanquin. On the following day Umeko returned to the new house from the hospital, but Tomoko still remained in critical condition. Nishida had made a quiet Japanese-style room where Kotomi could comfortably rest; for himself he designed a study with a fireplace that became his favorite room. The south end of the study had a French door that opened to the garden. Nishida named his study *Kosseikutsu* (clean-bone grotto), taking the name from a poem by Zen master Jakushitsu:

> *The spring water scattered by the wind sends off cool sound.*
> *Mountain peaks and the moon are before me; a beam of light is leaking*
>   *from the windows into the bamboo grove.*
> *An old man I am, I find it delightful to be in the mountains.*
> *Even if I die at the foot of a rock, my bones are clean!* [41]

Nishida began to take interest in planting trees in the garden. On a sunny October day Uemura Hōrin called on Nishida from Senjuin, and the two spent half a day discussing where to plant what kind of tree. A fir tree, a couple of pine trees, a cedar tree, and an oak tree over there; over here a Japanese maple tree, a peach tree, and a plum tree; in front of Kotomi's room her favorite camellias would go; right next to the study should be Nishida's favorite, daphne; and beyond the small man-made pond, a sultan's parasol. Hōrin knew an excellent nursery in Saga and told Nishida that he would have trees delivered from them. About two weeks later, however, Hōrin caught a cold, which turned into pneumonia, and died. Nishida, severely reminded of the impermanence of life, composed poems in memory of Hōrin:

> *You told me to come look*
> *at the turned autumn leaves*
> *now you are gone*
> *leaving behind*
> *the deepening autumn* [42]

Pine trees planted in Nishida's garden, which were a present from Hōrin, looked to Nishida as if they cast a languishing shadow, saddened by the death of their master.

Nishida, overcome by loneliness after Hōrin's death, was terribly in need of company. On one such day, Kōsaka Masaaki called on Nishida with no particular business. He recalled:

> I was shown to the study, where the professor was silently smoking his cigarette and absorbed in thought. His eyes were fixed on midair. I sat down, facing him, and remained silent. I had nothing to say to him. I remember it was a late afternoon on a cold autumn day. He didn't say a word, so I just sat silent. That several minutes of silence felt to me oppressively long—almost like eternity. Unable to stand the weight of the gloom, I said I should be going, and was about to stand up from my seat. At that moment the professor said, "You need not go yet, do you?" After that we spoke for quite a long time about this and that. [43]

Because Kōsaka was a 1920 graduate of the Fourth Higher School and a member of Sansanjuku, [44] the two probably talked about Kanazawa that evening.

At the end of 1922 Tomoko was still in the hospital. The muscles of her feet remained frozen tightly, and her intelligence was beginning to wane as a result of her prolonged illness. Looking back on the year, Nishida wrote to Yamanouchi in Freiburg:

> This was an eventful year for me, as much as it was for you. I am exhausted and feel lazy about everything. You might have already heard that Uemura Hōrin of Senjuin suffered pneumonia for several days and died at the beginning of November. About two weeks before, he had visited me and we spent half a day in leisurely conversation. I was acutely reminded of how transient human life is. [45]

Chapter 14

The Nishida-Einstein Connection

(1920–1922)

Nishida had a hand in inviting Albert Einstein to Japan in 1922. He had been interested since 1920 in Einstein's theory of gravity from a philosophical point of view and asked Tanabe Hajime for his opinion of Harrow's *From Newton to Einstein* and Slosson's *Easy Lessons in Einstein*.[1] This was a year before Einstein's nomination for a Nobel Prize in physics. Nishida also sought the professional opinion of Kuwaki Ayao,[2] a physicist and the younger brother of Kuwaki Gen'yoku (he and Kuwaki Ayao had begun corresponding sometime around 1912). Nishida wanted to know whether "Einstein's theory of gravity, which is much discussed in the world of theoretical physics lately," was too technical and difficult to understand.[3]

Yamamoto Sanehiko, president of a publishing company, Kaizō-sha, was thinking about inviting world-class Western thinkers to Japan, with the hope that such exchanges would enhance the level of Japanese scholarship as well as promote greater awareness of the outside world among the Japanese. (He invited Bertrand Russell to Japan in July 1921, and George Bernard Shaw in March 1933.) When Yamamoto called on Nishida in October 1920 to get his advice, Nishida, without hesitation, suggested Einstein as the foremost thinker of the modern European scientific community. Yamamoto followed up on this suggestion and contacted Ishihara Atsushi, a professor of theoretical physics at Tōhoku Imperial University. Ishihara had known Einstein personally from his days studying abroad at the Zurich Polytechnic. With Ishihara's help, Yamamoto drew up a contract in German. The invitation was warmly accepted by Einstein, who was then much coveted on the world lecture circuit. Yamamoto was prepared to spend a small fortune on this venture.

Einstein and his wife arrived at the port of Kobe on November 17,

1922, and were met by Ishihara Atsushi. During Einstein's tour, Ishihara not only accompanied the Einsteins as their personal interpreter but also translated Einstein's lectures into Japanese and made them accessible to the Japanese audience.[4] The Einsteins spent the first night in Japan in Kyoto. The next day they traveled to Tokyo and were happy when they could see Mt. Fuji from the train windows. In Tokyo, Einstein gave two public lectures as well as a series of special lectures that lasted for six days at Tokyo Imperial University. After Tokyo, they traveled to Sendai, Nikko, Nagoya, and arrived back in Kyoto, probably on December 9.

There is a side story. Ishihara was then a sort of *persona non grata* among the academic community because of his love affair and elopement with a beautiful poetess, Hara Asao. Because Ishihara was a married man, his action caused a huge sensation, and he was forced to resign from his professorship in July 1921. Nishida was sympathetic to Ishihara, as was Kuwaki Ayao. Nishida wrote to Kuwaki that Ishihara's resignation was "truly unexpected, and as you say we cannot sympathize with him enough. I truly believe that one day he will rise again from his present predicament."[5] Nishida did not endorse the move to ostracize Ishihara from the academy; instead, he invited him to Kyoto to give lectures on the theory of relativity so that students could be better prepared when Einstein came. Nishida's gesture annoyed his colleagues in the physics department,[6] but for him that was an inconsequential matter.

Nishida's interest in Einstein's theory of relativity became keener as he saw its philosophical implications. He explained to Kuwaki Ayao: "Einstein has gone very far in the area of physics. I think where he left off connects directly to philosophy. I suspect Mr. Einstein himself may not know the philosophical implications of his own thought, just as Newton was unaware of the philosophical implications of his theory."[7] Einstein's concern—the question of "a priori [principle] that constitutes the world of physics"—seemed to Nishida to point in the direction toward which his own thought was groping, a vague hunch that he was eventually to formulate into the idea of *topos*.

Einstein's talk at Kyoto Imperial University was scheduled for December 10, 1922. At that time Nishida specifically asked Einstein to speak about "how he came to formulate the theory of relativity." Nishida explained that such a talk would be enormously "beneficial to the students as well as to himself." Einstein, who "harbored a warm feeling of respect for Professor Nishida," responded by saying, "It is not an easy matter to talk about, but if that is the wish of the professor, I shall try." Einstein gave a lecture titled "How I Created the Theory of Relativity,"[8] which Ishihara Atsushi simultaneously translated into Japanese. The lecture was also transcribed and has been translated into English.[9]

Einstein was received by the Japanese enthusiastically—"Einstein fever" spread throughout the country. Nishida reported this public madness to Yamanouchi in Freiburg:

> Mr. Einstein came to Japan, and the Japanese people flocked around him as if to see an exhibit of an exotic animal rather than to listen to him. When he arrived at Tokyo Station [on the evening of November 18], the crowd swarmed around him as if welcoming a victorious general, and the automobile in which the Einsteins were seated could not get moving for a long time, I hear.[10]

After Kyoto, Einstein spoke in Osaka, Kobe, and Fukuoka, before leaving Japan on December 29 from the port of Fukuoka.

Chapter 15

An Inner Struggle
and a Breakthrough
(1923–1925)

Tomoko's serious condition hung heavily on Nishida's mind at the beginning of 1923. Tomoko was still in the hospital and faced the possibility of becoming lame or mad. Nishida's *waka* of this time reads:

> *Being tied down*
> *by the iron chain of fate*
> *and trampled all over*
> *I don't even know*
> *how to stand up* [1]

He kept his feelings close to himself, however, and his professional life went on as usual. Dozens of teachers from the Nagano Education Board who had been studying philosophy under Nishida's guidance came to Kyoto at the beginning of the year to hear his lectures on "Kant's Ethics." [2]

On the home front Nishida was daily tormented by the sad reality that assailed his wife and children. He expressed his emotions in *waka* poems:

> *It appears that I am*
> *attached to this life*
> *sometimes I feel I want*
> *to die and be done with it*
> *but no, not quite*

> *By resorting*
> *to poems*
> *and philosophical ideas*

I merely toy
with my mind

How heartily do
I hate my life
just as I hate
these ghastly
winter days [3]

Because Tomoko began to suffer melancholia in the hospital in early February, Nishida thought it best to bring her home. The family laid out her bedding right next to Kotomi's. This sight evoked another *waka:*

The daughter lies in bed on the right
the mother on the left
spring is around the corner
no sign that my loved ones
will get out of their beds [4]

While Nishida grappled with the pathetic reality of his life, a spiritual transformation was taking place inside him. A break came on February 20, 1923. His diary for that day contains two poems:

In my heart
is a profound depth
that the waves
of joys and sorrows
do not stir

Devil and Buddha
having fought
all night long
turn out to be but brothers
as the new day dawns [5]

Nishida realized that there was a "deeper mind" that was beyond the feelings of joys and sorrows and that embraced those feelings. This was indeed a renewed recognition of the "real self" that Nishida had thought he already knew through his Zen practice. This realization came over Nishida as a kind of satori, constituting for him an important existential breakthrough.

Ever since his move to Kyoto in 1921, Suzuki Daisetz had seen

Nishida from time to time. He knew his friend's innermost feelings and remarked that Nishida was undergoing an important spiritual transformation in 1923:

> Nishida, being pushed to the limits of his wits, had to realize that it was of no use for him to have passed several *kōan* in a prescribed fashion. He had to experience a "leap." He had his hands clinging to the cliff, let go, and was reborn.[6] . . . After that experience he gained a new eye with which to look at the world. Why should this not affect his philosophy? Indeed, the later development of his thought appears to have unfolded with this insight as an axis, the insight he gained from his experience of "letting go." He used to say to me, "My thought has reached the point where it cannot be explained by the framework of conventional philosophical language."[7]

This experience of "letting go," the "leap," had a philosophical implication, as Suzuki rightly pointed out. One may even suspect that this experience was at the heart of Nishida's signature idea of *topos* (*basho:* "place" or "field"). The deeper reality of "life" that Nishida had sensed years before through his kōan practice was now clearly coming back to him as a renewed, unshakable conviction. The "real self"—the "field of consciousness"—was the *topos* in which feelings such as joys and sorrows, likes and dislikes originate, while the bottom of one's heart (the *topos* itself) remains transcendent of these feelings, unmarred by them.

Tomoko's condition deteriorated, and she had to be readmitted to the hospital in March. As Nishida saw her bleeding, he felt helpless. A *waka* expresses his sense of desperation:

> *Am I to live*
> *in this miserable way*
> *in this world*
> *not a day of peace*
> *in the last five years*[8]

At the same time strong life energy was springing inside him, repelling these negative thoughts. This feeling of affirmation is found in another *waka*:

> *Just like the brilliant sunset*
> *over Mount Atago*
> *may the rest of my life*
> *be totally expended*
> *like a fire aflame*[9]

It became as clear as daylight that to live fully the rest of his life was the only gift that he could give to his family and to his philosophical endeavor. This realization forced Nishida to quit smoking, a habit he had not been able to rid himself of for a long time. His philosophical concentration seems to have undergone a process of purification. In his diary of May 21 he wrote: "From this very day I discard petty worries and mundane concerns. I live only in my philosophy. *Alles geopfert, alles geopfert, tiefes einflussreiches Erlebnis* [All is dedicated, all is dedicated, a profound influential experience]." [10]

Nishida had been working on essays addressing art, morality, and knowledge since 1920 and completed them at the beginning of 1923. All the essays, previously published in various journals, were compiled into a book, *Geijutsu to dōtoku* [Art and morality] and published by Iwanami Bookstore on July 23, 1923. [11] With this project completed, he began to think about writing on the subject of religion [12] and turned to an investigation of the will as the deeper reality of self-consciousness.

In April it was Nishida's turn to assume the editorship of the *Tetsugaku Kenkyū*. At that time he asked Kōsaka Masaaki to assist him because Mutai Risaku, who had been assisting Tomonaga, became busier in the spring of 1923 with his new teaching assignments. Kōsaka ably assisted Nishida; he was also in the position to observe closely the daily operation of the journal:

> In those days, professors' offices were located in a two-story wooden building, on the ground floor of which hung portraits of Descartes and other such Western thinkers. As you ascended the stairs from the entrance hall, the farthest room was Professor Nishida's office, and the one right next to it was Professor Fujii Kenjirō's. Professor Fujii was always in his office, but Professor Nishida never used his office, leaving not even a book there. A bold old man of a rather large build occupied the office instead, having brought in a desk from somewhere. He worked on balancing the books for the Philosophical Society. That was Mr. Takaraiwa, who was once a junior higher school principal, or so I heard, and became interested in philosophy. Through some connection, he settled in to spend his widowerhood as a self-appointed treasurer of the Kyoto Philosophical Society. Since the *Tetsugaku Kenkyū* was published by the Kyoto Philosophical Society, honoraria for the articles were dispensed by Mr. Takaraiwa. . . .
>
> Every year on the day of the public lectures of the Philosophical Society, we held a simple dinner gathering afterward at the student center, where the professors were also present. This was the most

enjoyable time of the year for Mr. Takaraiwa. Since he did not like Western food, he customarily had a tray of Japanese food prepared for him; he would bring in his own tray and occupy the most junior seat in the party. He always had to apologize for not having the same food as the rest, but his pride at being recognized and accorded a special place, and being in the company of the distinguished professors, including Professor Nishida, was clearly written on his face. It was a touching sight. . . . He, indeed, was a man of Meiji.[13]

I suspect that Nishida may have enjoyed Takaraiwa's invading his office without even bothering to ask for his permission!

Among the new students who entered the philosophy department in April 1923 were Shimomura Toratarō, Shima Yoshio, Usui Jishō, and Odaka Tomoo. The student enrollment in "pure philosophy" (*junsui-tetsugaku* or *juntetsu*) as distinguished from ethics, aesthetics, sociology, religious studies, and other fields, rose to a staggering twenty-five, a fivefold increase in two years. Amano Teiyū, who was then teaching at Gakushūin, was scheduled to study abroad in Heidelberg and visited Kyoto on April 27 to bid farewell to his former teachers.

Around this time Nishida had a new source of strain at home. Sotohiko and Ueno Asako, who had been living with the Nishidas as a governess, fell in love. Nishida disapproved of the romance, holding onto his fastidious position, which he embraced in reaction to his bitter experiences with his father's way of life and with his older sister Masa's licentious behavior. He asked Asako to move out of his house, and in her place he employed Monoi Hana, a graduate of the Women's English School (the present-day Tsuda Women's College). Monoi was an ideal tutor of English for his daughters. She was introduced to the Nishidas through the Ittōen religious community, of which she had been a member for a while. Although Asako left the Nishida household, the family continued to keep close contact with her. She had, in fact, already become a quasi–family member, and Nishida was able to talk to Asako about family matters. When the disastrous Kanto earthquake hit eastern Japan on September 1, 1923, Nishida was concerned about the safety of Asako's family members in Tokyo and called her back to the house to ease her anxiety.

Shortly before, on August 10, Nishida had sent a letter and a couple of books to Edmund Husserl.[14] By the time Husserl received Nishida's letter, the news of the earthquake had been internationally broadcast, and fund-raising efforts were initiated in various Western countries. Husserl's reply is reproduced in full for its historical interest.

Freiburg, September 19, 1923

Dear Professor Nishida,

I thank you very much for your kind gift, which I received a few days ago. I was very glad to get your photograph, which is familiar to me since Mr. Kiba has shown it to me before. His description of you in affectionate words formed an impression of you. I put up your photograph in my study.

I also thank you for sending me two of your books.[15] Besides them, I have a copy of your *Jikaku ni okeru chokkan to hansei*, which Mr. Kiba presented to me. Your distinguished disciple Mr. Tanabe[16] explained to me interesting things from this book. I would like to make some time in the near future to know more about your work from your countrymen who are studying over here.

I sincerely wish to return your kindness by sending you my articles. It is to my regret that I have not received even one offprint of my first article[17] that I submitted to *Kaizō* last year, and I have not the foggiest idea of what happened to the subsequent three articles that I submitted to the same journal.[18] I don't even know whether they were published or not. But I think I will be able to send you an offprint of my article that is currently in press in a German-Japanese journal.[19]

It was with a great sense of sadness, nay, with a shock shaking through the depth of my being, that I heard about the calamity of the great earthquake that ravaged your country. It pains me so much, as if it had happened to *me*, for I personally know precious young representatives of the Japanese philosophical world, and I hold a warm interest toward Japan.

I wish that the Japanese, an able people, will overcome this misfortune, and hope all the sufferings this earthquake brought about will turn out to be a blessing *sub specie aeternitatis*.

Truly yours,
E. Husserl[20]

In 1923 Nishida was asked to contribute articles to the magazine *Shisō* to help Iwanami, who had lost most of his company buildings in the earthquake. The death of Raphael von Koeber on June 4 added extra pressure, because the original purpose of the publication was to make Koeber's essays available. (Iwanami had been a devoted fan of Koeber's.) Nishida had his obligation to contribute essays to the *Tetsugaku Kenkyū* as well. Given his many worries at home, he was trying his best to keep his wits together. He did, however, tell his cousin-in-law Akai Yonekichi that he was "utterly exhausted, both physically and mentally."[21]

To welcome the new year, 1924, the members of the Nagano Philosophical Group returned to Kyoto, just as they had the year before, to listen to Nishida's lectures on Fichte's philosophy. Shizuko's condition remained the same, although she did occasionally suffer from a high fever. On January 7 Naruse Mukyoku returned to Japan from Germany, as did Tanabe three days later. Soon after her husband's return, Mrs. Tanabe called on the Nishidas to ask them whether they were interested in having the piano that Tanabe had sent her from Germany as a present. Because the Tanabes had no children, the piano was not played much. At the entreaties of his daughters, Nishida decided to buy it from the Tanabes. Shizuko fondly remembered this exciting event.

On January 12 distinguished historian and dean of the Faculty of Letters Hara Katsurō died, and Sakaguchi Takashi, another historian, was elected as the new dean. Fujioka Zōroku, who had studied with Husserl, also returned to Japan and called on Nishida on January 19. Amid these eventful days, Nishida had a dream one night: "My wife stood up on her own feet. When I awoke from my dream, I was overcome by a sense of tremendous loneliness. There was not a visitor today; it was a quiet day."[22]

In those days university professors received students on a set day of the week at home. Nishida's *menkai-bi* (open house) was on Monday evenings. The atmosphere of the open house reflected Nishida's somber mood. Shimomura remembered that Nishida used to remain silent:

> So long as we students didn't say a word, neither did he. When we said, "We will take our leave," he said, "Fine." It is not that this happened all the time, but because this impression is so strong, it feels like that was how things went always. . . . I was just a new student, but even Mr. Hisamatsu Shin'ichi, who was much senior to us, and who was much closer to the professor academically and personally, said that the Professor Nishida of those days was hard to approach.[23]

Nishitani Keiji and Tosaka Jun, who were graduating in March, began to join their seniors to call on Nishida at home on Mondays. On one of those occasions, Nishida found out that Nishitani was from Ushitsu, a small village in Ishikawa Prefecture. He had happened to visit Ushitsu thirty years ago, when he spent a year at Nanao and recruited students for the junior higher school.[24] By what chance would anyone from a remote village of Ushitsu be studying at Kyoto Imperial University and in the philosophy department? Nishida's heart was filled with the memories of the year he spent in Nanao (1895–1896). This factor led Nishida to form a special recognition for the young Nishitani, just as he had done for Kōsaka, a graduate of the Sansanjuku.

In the early spring of 1924, Nishida decided to adopt Aristotle's *Metaphysica* for his lectures on special topics and ordered the Ross translation. The selection reflected his growing interest in logic. Aristotle's definition of substance and substratum was to play an important role in Nishida's formulation of the idea of *topos*.

Around this time, Nishida was actively seeking to invite Watsuji Tetsurō to the university as a lecturer and was in frequent correspondence with him. The department was also looking into inviting Alexandre Koyré,[25] a French historian of the natural sciences, and this matter also kept him busy. On March 7 Toda Kaiichi, his longtime colleague from the Fourth Higher School days, died.

Nishida felt as if he were living in a closed world, despite all the kinds of activities around him:

Having left the world
and forgotten people
I simply live
in the deep recess
within myself [26]

But his life was far from that of a hermit. He freely received visitors, with the exception of those who came to ask for contributions to their journals—writing for journals deterred him from his train of thought, and he had decided long ago that he should be careful not to interrupt his thinking. The more he became one with the inner core of his being, the more spontaneous the expression of his emotions became.

Nishitani Keiji witnessed an interesting episode on February 25, 1924. There was already a caller when Nishitani went to Nishida's house, a student who had just graduated in law or economics. Nishitani describes the scene:

Nishida was already quite annoyed with the visitor; he was speechless, wearing an incredible expression of ire. Each word this student emitted was fiercely hit back by Nishida. What this student had to say was totally off the mark, and it irritated him beyond anything. But this student, totally unaware of the effect he was having on Nishida, finally began to say things like: "In your opinion, what kind of profession am I cut out for?" Nishida, excited with anger, shouted at him: "How do I know?" The student said: "But you often talk about 'intuition' and therefore I think you have the power to prognosticate." Nishida's anger finally erupted, he sprang out of the chair like a wild burning fire and said: "What I mean by 'intuition' is not that kind of thing. You'd better ask a fortune-teller. There is Takashima somebody in Tokyo." Then looking toward me, he said, "Wasn't there someone like that?" The "conversation" between the two continued in this manner. Utterly at a loss as to what I should say, I remained silent. Nishida tried to control his anger as best as he could and went on to explain what he meant by "intuition." But incited by the denseness of the student, he began to get excited again. I've never seen the professor get so excited with irritation before or after that evening. [27]

Gotō Ryūnosuke describes a similar episode.[28] When he was still a student, he called on Nishida on January 16, 1916.[29] Upon Gotō's words, "Professor Nishida, please tell me something interesting," Nishida said, "Why don't you go to a storyteller's hall?" Gotō liked this initial exchange with Nishida and held him in considerable respect.[30]

The phenomenon of students choosing Kyoto Imperial University over Tokyo to study with Nishida, Hatano, Tanabe, and others became a trend around 1920. Kakehashi Akihide, who entered the university in 1924, describes the atmosphere of the department of that time:

> It was generally acknowledged that the teaching staff of the philosophy department was the best in the country. Lectures on special topics by Nishida and Tanabe enjoyed an almost cultlike status as students flocked to these difficult lectures. Nishida was the professor of philosophy and Tanabe still an assistant professor. In Nishida's lectures professors not only of the philosophy department but also other departments and of the Faculties of Law and Economics were present, occupying the last row seats. Before them sat assistant professors of various colleges and departments, as well as the graduates of the philosophy department who were now teaching at various universities and schools in the Kansai area. Before them were seated students majoring in philosophy and other related fields. Not a seat was unoccupied—it was quite a sight. Tanabe's lectures were similar in that there were more outside auditors than students, and the contents of his lectures were sophisticated. We freshers did not pay attention to the contents of the lectures but were merely drunk with the atmosphere. I remember one time, while we were waiting for the lecture either by Professor Nishida or Professor Tanabe, Karaki Junzō [31] whispered into my ear: "Look at the four guardian disciples." We freshers, with a mixed sense of envy and respect, saw at a distance Kimura Motomori, Kōsaka Masaaki, Nishi-

tani Keiji, and Tosaka Jun, conversing and laughing in the garden in front of the psychology classrooms. [32]

Sotohiko wanted to marry Asako. Nishida was against this match because Sotohiko was still a student—and besides, Asako was several years older than Sotohiko. But Kotomi's entreaties prevailed over Nishida. Sotohiko and Asako became engaged, and once the decision was made, Nishida was eager to see them married as soon as possible. On June 1, 1924, a simple wedding ceremony was held at home so that Kotomi could witness it from her bed; Tanabe Hajime and Chiyo acted as the matchmakers. Following the ceremony, Nishida hosted an intimate luncheon reception at the Miyako Hotel. Besides his family members, the Tanabes attended, along with Hisamatsu Shin'ichi, Mutai Risaku and his wife, and Asako's older brother. Mutai remembered this day very well, for everyone was wrapped in happiness. At the banquet table the following conversation took place:

> Tanabe asked Hisamatsu what the family crest was on his *haori*. It looked like a pair of straw sandals crossing each other, but actually it was a pair of hawk's feathers crossing. Since the crest indeed looked like crossed straw sandals, everyone laughed. The newlyweds looked very happy. Nishida, too, was all smiles throughout the luncheon. [33]

Asako settled into her new role as mistress of the house and took charge of the household chores and the education of Nishida's daughters. Monoi Hana, who had been governess to the daughters, felt her services were no longer needed and left the Nishidas, although she remained a loyal friend of the family. Nishida felt enormously relieved to be spared from the household burdens and began to concentrate on his writing. For the rest of 1924 he worked on "Naibu chikaku ni tsuite" [On inner perception], [34] in which he discussed the problem of time and self-consciousness. In the fall he wrote "Hyōgen sayō" [The expressive operation], [35] in which his idea of *topos* is already present.

Thanks to Miki Kiyoshi and Amano Teiyū, who had been to Heidelberg to study with Heinrich Rickert, a rapport developed between Nishida and Rickert. On September 22, 1924, Nishida wrote to Rickert and sent him a copy of his *Jikaku ni okeru chokkan to hansei*, probably to thank Rickert for sending him a copy of *Das Eine, die Einheit und die Eins: Bemerkungen zur Logik des Zahlbegriffs*, in which Rickert acknowledged Nishida and Sōda Kiichirō as the two major Japanese thinkers who had made his own thought familiar in Japan. Rickert replied on October 31, 1924, with a sincere wish to maintain contact.[36]

In October Tanabe published a paper, "Genshōgaku ni okeru atarashiki tenkō" [A new turn in phenomenology],[37] which summarized the significance of phenomenology and Heidegger's criticism of it. This was the first article that introduced Heidegger's thought to the Japanese. In Freiburg, Tanabe had been personally acquainted with Heidegger, who was then assisting Husserl. Nishida read Tanabe's article with interest. Although he had been hearing about Heidegger through Miki and Tanabe, this essay by Tanabe made it clear to him what Heidegger was trying to achieve in his philosophy and led him to believe that "Heidegger will contribute to cultural studies from the phenomenological standpoint."[38]

With the arrival of 1925, Nishida felt like traveling. He went to Tokyo on January 2 to visit his friends. It was probably on the invitation of Iwanami Shigeo that Nishida stayed at the Imperial Hotel, which had been built by Frank Lloyd Wright in 1916; Nishida was thrilled and especially noted the room number, 134, in his diary. Guests who called on Nishida at the hotel included Amano Teiyū and Eugen Herrigel,[39] who had held the position of visiting professor at Tōhoku Imperial University for the past year. On January 6 he and Sōda Kiichirō were invited to a lunch hosted by sociologist Emil Lederer, a disciple of the late Max Weber. Herrigel was also among the lunch guests. Lederer was giving a seminar at Tokyo Imperial University, and Nishida brought up the possibility of Lederer's lecturing at Kyoto for the spring quarter, an invitation Lederer accepted.

On January 8 Nishida left Tokyo in the company of Iwanami Shigeo, Itō Kichinosuke, Watsuji Tetsurō, and Yamanouchi Tokuryū and spent an evening at a spa at Yugawara. The next day they went to Atami and stayed at the Atami Hotel. Nishida especially loved a walk through the park filled with plum trees and the view of the ocean from there.

Kotomi's condition suddenly deteriorated in late January, and she died on the evening of January 23. Family, friends, and colleagues came to help Nishida, who was in a state of profound shock. A private funeral service and cremation followed. In his diary Nishida wrote this *waka*:

She with whom I lived
for the last thirty years
has returned home

> *as white bones*
> *in a small urn* [40]

On January 27 a formal memorial service was held at Senjuin; Master
Ikegami Shōsan paid special tribute to the dead by leading the service. Tanabe Hajime and Hisamatsu Shin'ichi took full charge of the
funeral arrangements and related business for their grieving friend.

The futon on which Kotomi had laid for many years was folded
away and the tatami room was tidied.

> *Crimson camellia flowers*
> *from the tree we planted last autumn*
> *just outside the window*
> *are scattering*
> *without the mistress to see them.* [41]

Nishida remembered to thank Tanabe and Hisamatsu for their selfless
kindness. To Tanabe he wrote:

On January 9, 1925, at the plum
tree grove in Atami. From left
to right: Itō Kichinosuke, Yamanouchi Tokuryū, Iwanami Shigeo,
and Watsuji Tetsurō; Nishida is
seated. Courtesy of Iwanami
Yūjirō.

I'm deeply indebted to you. I don't know for what karmic connections, but I ended up bothering you once to take care of an auspicious event [Sotohiko's wedding] and, twice, inauspicious events [the funerals of Ken and Kotomi]. You have been so generous in bestowing your kindness on me. I'm always on the receiving end and don't know how to repay your kindness. Since I knew for a long time that my wife would someday die, I did not imagine I would go through an emotional state. But, presently, I feel as if I were a homeless traveler in a far-distant foreign land. I wonder where this feeling of mine will take me. [42]

Two days later, on January 30, Yamamoto came from Tokyo to console him. Stillness and motion, loneliness and active engagement were the opposing aspects of Nishida's life after Kotomi's death. People around him made a special effort to bring him out of his withdrawal. Although Shizuko had often missed classes because of her frail health, she was able to graduate from the Higher Women's School in Kyoto. This was a great relief to Nishida. Toward the end of March, as the academic year ended, he felt "refreshed" and began working on his essay "Jikaku no taikei" [The structure of self-consciousness], which he afterward renamed "Hataraku mono" [That which acts]. [43] Yoneda Shōtarō retired at the end of March, obliging Nishida to teach a religion seminar in 1925–1926. [44]

Amano Teiyū moved in April from Gakushūin to Kyoto as assistant professor. Watsuji Tetsurō's appointment also finally came through, and he moved to Kyoto to assume the position of lecturer in ethics. In mid-April, Eugen Herrigel visited Kyoto and delivered a lecture at the university, entitled "Ansätze zur Metaphysik in der gegenwärtigen deutschen Philosophie" [The contours of the metaphysics of contemporary German philosophy], that was attended by a large audience, including Nishida, Hatano, and Watsuji. [45] Because Emil Lederer was giving a series of lectures at the university, it looked as if a segment of the German academy had suddenly materialized in Kyoto. On May 17, on the occasion of the opening of Rakuyūkaikan (a faculty club building), [46] Crown Prince Hirohito graced the university campus to attend a garden party. Kabuki actor Onoe Shōnosuke performed a special play that was a resounding success. [47] Nishida had gone to the university at 8:30 A.M. that morning to attend to business. A few weeks later, Nishi Shin'ichirō came from Hiroshima and gave a lecture; the following day, Mizobuchi Shinma, Ishikawa Ryūzō and others who were connected with Nishida through the Fourth Higher School visited Kyoto, filling Nishida's social calendar.

Nishida stayed in contact with Husserl through Tanabe. For the

1924–1925 academic year Tanabe lectured on the development of phenomenology, and in 1925–1926 Tanabe's special topics lectures were on Lask's objective logic, Husserl's pure logic, and critical interpretation of phenomenology. Nishida's letter to Husserl on May 20, 1925, informs Husserl that "many able young Japanese scholars who studied with you are returning to Japan. I believe that your phenomenology will soon be well known over here. In our university, Professor Tanabe gives lectures on phenomenology, and in Tokyo at the University of Commerce Professor Yamanouchi is already giving lectures on phenomenology."[48]

In May, Mutai Risaku brought from his hometown in Shinshū a white birch tree and a pine tree, which he planted in Nishida's garden. Nishida's adopted daughter, Toshiko, who had married a navy officer and had been living in Kure, stopped by in Kyoto when her husband was transferred to Yokosuka. Ueda Juzō was chosen to study abroad, and the Philosophical Society gave him a farewell party. Two years in a row, the number of entering students in the philosophy department exceeded thirty, and the faculty discussed putting a cap on the number of entering students. In August, Nishida went to Kanazawa to entomb Kotomi's bones in the family graveyard at Mori. On his way back, the educators of Nagano Prefecture asked him to visit Shinshū, which he did. He gave a few talks there and returned to Kyoto on August 12. Not only in Kyoto but everywhere he visited, people went out of their way to show their kindness to him. He was able to forget his loneliness from time to time.

But the feeling of loneliness and the sense of loss struck Nishida deep and did not disappear for a long time. Around November of that year, a group of graduates from the philosophy department called on Nishida after the semiannual conference of the Kyoto Philosophical Society. Nishitani recalled Nishida's somber mood of that evening:

> The professor was not in his study but was seated in a Japanese-style room in front of a small desk. The color of his face was not very good, and he seems to have been in a solemn and depressed mood. As if his mood was transmitted to me, I even felt the lamp was dim. Someone asked him: "Professor, how are you these days?" In response, he said: "I feel as if I were in a deep forest." These words of his and his somber appearance somehow made a distinct impression on me. One could feel the air of desolation, melancholy, and serious withdrawal. We wanted to console the professor, and that was one of the reasons many of us, his former students, decided to get together and visit Professor Nishida at least once a year.[49]

Chapter 16

The Logic of the *Topos*

(1924–1926)

The signature idea of "Nishidan Philosophy" is that of *basho* (place, field, *topos*, or *chōra*).[1] Thus, it is worthwhile to pause for a moment to take a closer look at the inception of this idea, which is traceable to the 1924 essay, "Naibu chikaku ni tsuite" [On the inner perception],[2] and his 1925 essay, "Hyōgen sayō" [Expressive operation].[3]

In "Naibu chikaku ni tsuite," Nishida advances his criticism of the phenomenological method, which in his view fails to totally eradicate the objectifying stance. The phenomenological method only suspends the facts framed by the category of time, which is the standpoint of the "ego" and hence is not free from "inner perception."[4] As an alternative approach, Nishida focuses on the workings of self-consciousness and treats the cognitive subject as the unifying point of the actual and the transcendental, the universal and the particular.[5] The real knower transcends the world of objective knowledge, and yet the real knower is in the world of objective knowledge and works from within. Nishida found Aristotle's definition of substance *(hypokeimenon)*—"that of which the rest are predicated, while it is not itself predicated of anything else"[6]—fruitful in formulating his logical system. Taking this Aristotelian definition a step further, Nishida holds that the substance, which becomes the grammatical subject but not the predicate, must unify infinite predicates. That is to say, the subject is that which unifies all judgments and thus transcends judgment.[7]

In his next essay, "Hyōgen sayō," Nishida focuses on the matrix of beings—"a place where things exist" *(oite aru basho)* that is unchanging, while things located in it are constantly changing.[8] This "place" is "not consciously recognized by the operation of our consciousness," and in that sense it can be said it is "nothing" *(mu)*. In terms of the operation of self-consciousness, "that which we are not conscious of (i.e., consciousness as nothingness) is at work."[9] The idea of "nothingness" introduced here simply means that it cannot become the object of self-consciousness; it is something that lies beneath our surface consciousness. One may compare it to a vast ocean of unconsciousness that embraces articulated self-consciousness. For Nishida the will is negated in the depth of self-consciousness, and only intuition remains, wherein every thing appears by way of "expression." Even the self becomes an expression in intuition.[10]

In March 1925 Nishida began his next essay, "Hataraku mono" [That which acts],[11] in which he examines the connection between the workings of concept formation and those of judgment ("S is P") in terms of the universal and the particular. He takes the "subsumptive judgment" (*hōsetsu handan*) as the most fundamental form of judgment, in which the particulars are embraced by the universal.[12] In actual judgment (or in concept formation), sensory input determines itself within self-consciousness, and judgment is thus established. The universal is not just the predicate (P) of judgment, "S is P"; it is the *topos*, which embraces all the possible "subject terms" of judgment[13] and is thus the "concrete universal"—that which mirrors itself within itself.[14]

Apparently Nishida had been discussing the idea of *topos* for some time with Tanabe Hajime. In his letter of December 1925, Nishida mentions the process of the development of his logic of *topos*:

> Concerning that idea of *topos*, I cannot help but think that it is fruitful, but as I try to think precisely, things get confused, and it's tough going. I'm going to wrap up what I'm currently writing so I can get into more refined detailed analysis of what this *topos* is.[15]

The essay Nishida was working on at that time must have been part of "Basho" [*Topos*], which came out in June 1926 in *Tetsugaku Kenkyū*.[16] Against the conventional discussions of epistemology, which dwell on the separation of "the object, the content, and the operation," Nishida advances his thesis that there must be *something* that maintains the epistemological structure. If it is indeed the case that the objects of cognition mutually relate, they must form one coherent system, and furthermore the system itself must be maintained. His fundamental intuition is that things (beings) exist always in some "place," for otherwise the distinction between "being" and "nonbeing" cannot be sustained. Nishida turns to Plato's *Timaeus*, which abounds in the imagery of "place": "the becoming, that 'wherein' it becomes, and the source 'wherefrom' the becoming is copied and produced" (50d); "all that exists should exist in some spot (topōs) and occupying some place (chōra)" (52b).

Nishida employs the Japanese word *"basho"* to designate something like Plato's "receptacle" that receives the imprint of the Idea,[17] but with the qualification that "what I call *'basho'* is of course not identical with Plato's 'space,' 'receptacle,' and so forth."[18] *"Basho"* is in fact a spatial metaphor for the workings of consciousness. Just as the universal embraces the particular in the subsumptive judgment, so the *topos* embraces the self-conscious self. This is to say that the "field of consciousness" is the *topos*. We come to know what is outside us only by knowing what is within us. That is, "to know" means for consciousness to embrace what is within it. That which knows, the cognitive subjectivity, is a *topos*; it is beyond form, matter, and the operation of cognition, and it establishes the content and the operation of cognition.[19]

Nishida introduces the distinction between "relative nonbeing" (which is recognizable in space) and "real nothingness" (which is the field of consciousness).[20] If a thing appears to be lacking against some other thing (such as in movement), it is "relative nonbeing." "Real nothingness," in contrast, is that which establishes both being and nonbeing, for it is the matrix that allows the thing to be or not to be. It does not stand opposed to being but constitutes the "background" of being.[21] Nishida maintains that consciousness is productive and creative; it produces being from nothingness and embraces being while it itself is nothing.[22]

Nishida employs the language of grammatical subject and grammatical predicate to explain the dynamism of self-consciousness. He identifies consciousness as the predicate aspect and holds that the expanse of the grammatical predicate (i.e., consciousness) is wider than that of the grammatical subject (i.e., self-determination of the universal into a particular).[23] Ultimately, the predicate aspect is the will. The will cannot become the object of judgment, but insofar as we possess consciousness of the will, there has to be consciousness that "mirrors" the will.[24]

Nishida felt he was able to present the logical structure of *basho* by identifying the "transcendental predicate" as its volitional aspect.[25] In his letter to Mutai Risaku on June 8, he explains what he was trying to do with the idea of the *topos*:

This essay, "Basho," is not yet clear, but what I endeavored to do was to define consciousness logically as "that which becomes the grammatical predicate and not the grammatical subject" over against Aristotle's definition of substance as "that which becomes the grammatical subject and not the grammatical predicate."

While the grammatical subject, in its transcendence, endlessly moves in the direction of the particular, the grammatical predicate, in its transcendence, endlessly moves in the direction of the universal. When the latter direction becomes identical with the universal, we arrive at "nothingness" that embraces being, that which purely mirrors, or that which is material and yet contains what Plotinus called "the One" *(to hen)*. When the grammatical predicate transcends itself to the infinite maximum limit and loses itself, the grammatical subject reaches the apex of particularity and becomes that which sees itself.

Unfortunately, in the present paper I did not expound on these ideas in detail. Anyway, with the idea of the *topos* I feel I have reached the philosophical goal that I have been groping for. I shall try to reconstruct my previous ideas from the perspective of "basho." [26]

The first reaction to Nishida's theory of *basho* came from Sōda Kiichirō, [27] who had been affiliated with the philosophy department at Kyoto Imperial University since May 1921 and was a close associate of Nishida. Sōda's review article, "Nishida tetsugaku no hōhō ni tsuite Nishida hakushi no oshie o kou" [Asking for Dr. Nishida's clarification on the method of Nishidan philosophy], came out in the October issue of *Tetsugaku Kenkyū*. [28] Sōda praised Nishida's philosophical endeavor as one that "entered an original realm" and coined a new term, "Nishida tetsugaku" (Nishidan philosophy).

He offered a critique, nevertheless, from the standpoint of Rickertian neo-Kantianism. He questioned why Nishida gave priority to the will as opposed to cognition and why the *topos* is "nothing" *(mu)*. If the philosophical position of "real nothingness" transcending the standpoint of "relative nothingness" is possible, would it not be possible to think about "real real-nothingness"? How are the will and the intuition related in the *topos* of "real nothingness"? Metaphysics, after all, might be just "a metaphysical explanation of epistemology." If so, does not the idea of the *topos* merely "dogmatically build a metaphysical construction, going beyond the limits of logical reason"? [29] Sōda's questions showed Nishida that his idea of *basho* could not be understood from a Rickertian perspective.

Although Nishida felt that "Sōda's starting point seem[ed] to be too simplistic and dogmatic,"[30] he respected Sōda, a man of impeccable sincerity, and the set of criticisms coming from him drove Nishida to clarify his fundamental philosophical vision and method.

In his "Sōda-hakushi ni kotau" [My response to Dr. Sōda],[31] Nishida begins by first addressing what he sees as the larger issue of what knowledge is before answering Sōda's questions point by point. According to Nishida, there are two kinds of knowledge: the knowledge of objects and the knowledge of the workings of self-consciousness. Further, different modes of cognition yield different worlds. For instance, to know the other person by empathy constitutes an interpersonal world, while an external perception of things constitutes the world of nature.[32] In the knowledge of objects, self-identity means the unity of subject and object, whereas in reflexive consciousness, self-identity is that of the knower and the operation of knowing. The self-conscious knower, when forgetting himself or herself, reaches pure consciousness. This unity of the knower and the operation of knowing takes place in the *topos* of pure emptiness *(shin no mu no basho)*.[33]

Second, Nishida defends himself against the charge of having fallen into metaphysics. What Rickert considers "metaphysical" reality may in fact be viable living reality that falls within the boundaries of philosophical scrutiny. Nishida argues that free will, for instance, cannot be explained away as a merely psychological phenomenon; moreover, any will that lacks the awareness of freedom is not volitional by definition. This goes to show that volitional subjectivity transcends psychological phenomena and suggests that the latter is actually founded on the former.[34]

Third, Nishida criticizes Rickert's approach of limiting cognitive subjectivity to the formal judging subject alone[35] as "a dogmatic confinement of epistemology."[36] Rather than limiting the scope of cognitive activities from the outset, Nishida set out to investigate the nature of self-consciousness to clarify how knowledge is established. To do so does not necessarily mean one falls prey to metaphysics, unless one postulates some "substance" behind self-consciousness, which Nishida clearly rejects.[37]

Fourth, Nishida agrees with the neo-Kantians in their effort to "go back to Kant," since he recognizes the positive import of Kant's contribution, namely, that Kant looks for the unity of knowledge in intellectual self-consciousness. But Nishida felt that Kant does not fully explore the nature of self-consciousness. For instance, Kant does not discuss the connection between judgment and perception in self-consciousness.[38] For Kant, "to know" is an operation of the cognitive subjectivity that unifies the multitude of data given to the sensory perceptions. As such Kant's view is still bound by the tacit presupposition of the subject-object dichotomy, and intellectual subjectivity is objectively viewed. For Nishida, the real cognitive subjectivity is the transcendental *topos*, which in turn makes the subject-object dichotomy possible. The *topos* is the field of consciousness, and that a thing exists in the *topos* means that we know it.[39]

Although related to the fourth point, Nishida's fifth point maintains that what is given to consciousness is not just an intellectual perception but includes volitional input. If consciousness in general is the unification of the contents by form, as Kant has it, the principle of the given as well as the meaning of the knowing subjectivity must be polyvalent.[40] That is to say, the natural world is established by the unity of perception and thinking, while the cultural world is established by the conscious recognition of the will as part of consciousness. The concept of unique individuality *(kosei)*—the fundamental concept of cultural sciences—could not be established without taking into account the volitional aspect of self-consciousness. In this way, by reflecting deeper on the reality of self-consciousness, we recognize the deeper world of the objects of our knowledge. Nishida reiterates his position that perception is located within the field of the will and that the will is larger than perception. Thus, volitional experience is more concrete than perception.[41] Furthermore, in the depths of self-consciousness we encounter pure consciousness, which defies objective recognition. Nishida elaborates on this point:

> Self-consciousness is an infinite abyss; at the point where it loses its awareness as consciousness, real self-consciousness emerges. So long as we are aware of the shades or gradations of self-consciousness, we see an objective world of one kind or another, but when the self-consciousness transcends this reflexive stage, it transcends the realm of so-called knowledge and enters the realm of intuition. Therein true self-consciousness, or pure consciousness, manifests itself. Taking intuition as the limit of knowledge, I consider it true knowledge (and not a conceptual knowledge) and the fundamental condition for the establishment of knowledge itself.[42]

To explain the self-reflection of judging consciousness *(handan ishiki sonomono no jisei)*[43] Nishida poses two questions: How is the subject-object dichotomy possible? What does it mean to know? He focuses on the subsumptive judgment to explain the operation of consciousness in which the universal embraces particulars. By identifying the grammatical subject (S) of judgment with the particular and the grammatical predicate (P) with consciousness (i.e., conscious subjectivity) or the universal, "S is P" always means "S is located *in* P"; P is the *topos* of S. Judgment that the particular exists within the universal is "to know" from the standpoint of the transcendental *topos*, which becomes the predicate and not the subject.[44]

Nishida concludes his general statement by saying that various kinds of knowledge are determined by the kinds of *topos* that extend from the perception of the object to intuition. Accordingly, various worlds—the teleological world, the world of psychological phenomena, the historical world, the world of free will, and the world of pure intuition—are formed out of different aspects of cognitive subjectivity.[45]

Finally, Nishida turns to some of the specific questions raised by Sōda:

> What I mean by *topos* is not something objectively conjured up; it was not my point to discuss whether *topos* is being or nonbeing. The reason Sōda got this impression, I suspect, is that he presupposes that what I mean by *topos* is some kind of metaphysical entity. What I mean by *topos* is the universal by which the knowledge of judgment (or knowledge obtained by judgment) is established. . . . It is the reflective universal behind objective thinking. It is like the "predicate aspect" that is behind objective knowledge. That is *topos*. It roughly corresponds to Kantian "cognitive subjectivity" *(ninshiki shukan)*. But I don't consider subjectivity as the individual "unifying point" but rather the all-embracing field *(hōyōmen)*. To discuss this *topos* as being or nonbeing is the same as discussing whether the cognitive subjectivity is being or nonbeing. What I mean by "the *topos* of nothingness" *(mu no basho)* is that "it cannot be determined as a general concept."
>
> To the question of whether there might be nothingness beyond real nothingness, I have no answer. I consider the predicate aspect as the field of consciousness; the final predicate field that cannot be determined conceptually is the field of intuitive consciousness, and that which exists therein is that which sees itself, i.e., the subject-object unity. As to the question of whether there is not an intuition of intuition, I fail to understand the meaning of the question.[46]

Sōda's criticism stimulated Nishida's thinking and helped him sort out his ideas. By April 1927, when Nishida's response appeared in the *Tetsugaku Kenkyū*, however, Sōda's health was failing. His death of stomach cancer on August 11, 1927, cut short their fruitful exchanges.

Nishida put the idea of pure experience that he elaborated in *Zen no kenkyū* through rigorous self-criticism. His relentless investigation of the nature and workings of self-consciousness led him to formulate the idea of *topos*. His system of thought, now called "Nishida tetsugaku" was widely recognized as a unique and original achievement. But because he drew his inspiration from the experience of the primordial unity of subject and object—sometimes strictly identified with religious or mystical wisdom—his work began to stir vigorous criticism as well, as if his thought was a sort of esotericism. Criticism only honed Nishida's thinking. He was to develop his logic of *topos* into the dialectic of the one and the many, and the historical world and the individuals who make history. In this endeavor, he progressively embraced the dimension of personalism and existentialism on the one hand, and that of "impersonalism" and cosmocentrism on the other. Nishida's thought was to go through further twists and turns for the next several years. [47]

In the year Nishida's essay, "Basho," was published, the Taishō period came to an end, and a new era, Shōwa, began.

Chapter 17

Retirement

(1926–1929)

In Nishida's time university professors retired on their sixtieth birthday. Because his father had changed Nishida's official birth date to August 10, 1868, so that he could enter Normal School, his retirement was to come in August 1928. He welcomed early retirement. (Incidentally, 1928 was also the year of Edmund Husserl's retirement from the University of Freiburg, on March 31.)

The timing of Nishida's retirement coincided with a period of social unrest and transition from the "Taishō democracy" to the turbulent Shōwa years. Although Nishida had looked forward to his retirement and planned to devote himself to philosophical contemplation, he could not avoid the political realities that had begun to embroil the university. The year 1925 marked the beginning of the Japanese government's move to exercise overt nationalistic control over the people. In April the public peace ordinance *(chian ijihō)* was put into effect to suppress socialist and Marxist movements that were then gaining momentum. It was also in 1925 that the government suggested to each imperial university that "if the university so wishes, a military officer may be dispatched to each campus to conduct military training." Students who participated in the on-campus training were eligible to shorten the length of their mandatory military service. Attracted by the prospect of shorter service, about three hundred students wanted the training to be made available at Kyoto Imperial University. Strong objections, however, were raised by faculty members who felt that military training on campus would inevitably have a negative impact on the university as an institution. The faculty senate *(hyōgikai)* decided to accept the offer with the proviso that the training should be carried out "only for those who presently wish it, and that it shall never be forced on the students." Thus, the military training was allowed on campus during the summer recess of 1925. Once the military made its entry onto university campuses, however, it was there to stay. As time went on, on-campus military training not only became a fixture but also a compulsory requirement for all students.[1]

On December 1, 1925, a serious confrontation between university students and the Kyoto Prefecture police took place. The police launched a raid, without a search warrant, of the dormitories, private apartments, and boarding houses where members of the Social Sciences Study Group (*Shakai kagaku kenkyūkai*, hereafter SSSG) lived.[2] The SSSG, established in May 1924, drew mainly students of economics; in September of that year, it had joined the national organization, the National Union of the Social Sciences Students (*Zennihon gakusei shakai kagaku rengōtai*, known as "Gakuren"). The SSSG hosted Gakuren's second annual meeting in Kyoto in July 1925, flouting the ordinance that prohibited such a meeting. It was this meeting that led to the December raid. On January 15, 1926, the police began arresting leading members of the SSSG, alleging that the students had violated the public peace and the publishing ordinances.

The university publicly protested against this intrusion by the police. President Araki Torasaburō traveled to Tokyo with Sasaki Sōichi, dean of the Faculty of Law, and Sakaguchi Takashi, dean of the Faculty of Letters, and met with the home minister, Wakatsuki Reijirō, and Okada Ryōhei, minister of education. Araki promised to bring student unrest under control. An ad hoc committee of faculty members was formed to defuse the conflict, and Nishida was asked to join it. The committee decided that the SSSG could continue as a purely academic research group but prohibited it from engaging in actual political activities. It was also ordered to sever its ties with the national organization, Gakuren.[3]

Nishida's otherwise tranquil letter to Mutai Risaku in Heidelberg contains a reference to the student arrests:

> Everyone says Heidelberg is a charming quiet town. It is enviable that in Germany small towns like Heidelberg maintain the old academic tradition and are proud of it. Have you seen Professor Rickert yet?
>
> I intended to give all I've got to my lectures this quarter, but I was asked to be on the faculty committee to deal with the student incident; also I will have to go to Tokyo at the end of this month for a meeting.[4] With this and that, I haven't been able to give my best to the lectures. I'm looking forward to the days when I can quietly devote myself to reading and writing.[5]

The philosophy department was facing a period of significant transition because Nishida, Kano, Matsumoto, and Tomonaga were all retiring in close succession. In addition to the positions that opened up through retirements, the department was given a fifth chair in the history of philosophy. In March 1925 they appointed Amano Teiyū, then at Gakushūin, as assistant professor. Because these personnel decisions would have a long-lasting impact not only on the department but also on the Faculty of Letters, they needed to be made carefully. The professors' preferences sometimes conflicted. For instance, Nishida had to give up recommending Mutai Risaku for the position of lecturer because of Hatano's staunch opposition.[6] (Mutai landed a professorship at Taipei Imperial University instead, and, before assuming it, he was given the opportunity to study abroad.)

When Amano's appointment was made in 1925, Miki Kiyoshi was in Paris on the last leg of his European sojourn. Although Miki's name did not come up officially in the department discussions, Hatano[7] and Nishida were thinking about recommending him for a position in the department.[8] Miki returned to Japan in late November of 1925 and settled in Kyoto, even though he had some good job offers in Tokyo. There was a tacit agreement, or so it seemed, that Miki was to be appointed to one of the departmental openings. Miki was not officially a member of the teaching staff but volunteered to lead a reading group on Aristotle's *Metaphysica*, which was attended by Nishitani Keiji, Tosaka Jun, and other philosophy students. Miki, "who had just returned from studying with Heidegger," was perceived by them to have something fresh to offer.[9] Miki also enjoyed the city nightlife. He organized a group of young graduates of the First Higher School, which included Tanikawa Tetsuzō, Tosaka Jun, Kanba Toshio, and Kakehashi Akihide. They were often seen in the lively night clubs in the Shijō area. On those occasions, Miki would get into reckless discussions, evaluating professors—not only in Kyoto's philosophy department but throughout Japan—comparing them to German and French thinkers.[10] Rumors were quick to spread. Miki's behavior began to stir negative feelings among some department members. Miki's old romantic escapade with a widow thirty years senior to him, which had ended before he left for Europe, had become known to others beyond his friends. By the time a discussion of Miki's appointment to a faculty position arose, his reputation was such that there was strong opposition. Nishida too had to reconsider his recommendation. Nevertheless, he felt he could have prevented Miki from going astray. Writing about the situation to Tanabe, Nishida reflected that he was "indirectly responsible for whatever had happened to Miki" and that he was going to "see him to give him sincere words of admonition for [his own] sake."[11] The talk between Nishida and Miki took place sometime in late March during the spring break. Nishida's unexpected words devastated Miki.[12] Hatano had to relinquish his hopes for Miki as well.

Although Nishida had to give up the idea of retaining Miki at Kyoto, he, without Miki's knowledge, consulted Watsuji Tetsurō and Kōno Yoichi,[13] who had good connections with Hōsei University in Tokyo, to secure an academic position for his beloved student.[14] Miki was to accept the Hōsei position and leave for Tokyo in March 1927. Despite his unexpected setback, Miki remained active during his remaining time in Kyoto. When Mutai moved to Taipei, the teaching position he had held at the Third Higher School went to Miki,[15] who began teaching there in April 1926. In December of that year, with Kawakami Hajime and Ishikawa Kōji, Miki organized "Keizaigaku hihankai" (an economics study group), which examined Marx's writings and dialectical materialism. Nishida was invited as a guest speaker to one of their meetings.[16] At that time Nishida, in his criticism of Marxism, challenged Kawakami Hajime to "try to explain the origin of language in terms of dialectical materialism."[17]

Nishida welcomed 1927 with a curious mix of emotions. He felt that his life was coming to an end and that an unknown, new phase was ahead.[18] He began the new year reading "Of Thinking about Death" from the *Imitation of Christ* by Thomas à Kempis. The theme of this reading—the brevity of earthly existence, "here today, gone tomorrow"—seems to have been in keeping with his feelings. Nishida thus began the year filled with religious reflections.[19] He wrote to Yamamoto that he was feeling "this deep loneliness that touches the roots of human existence."[20] At the same time, when Tanabe, Hisamatsu, and Miki called on him and brought up the subject of publishing a Festschrift to honor his retirement,[21] he declined it, saying that retirement did not mean the end of his career but rather the beginning of serious philosophical work.

The conflicting emotions of his old life's coming to an end and his new life's beginning made Nishida envisage the finitude of his own existence, which seems to have started a process of spiritual purification. He found solace in the words of a Japanese medieval itinerant monk, Kūya: "I entrust all my actions to Heaven; I yield my actions to bodhisattvas."[22] Two *waka* poems written on March 23 reflect his mood:

> *Somehow I feel lonely*
> *I'm now a free man*
> *and yet I have no time*
> *to give myself freely*
> *to tears*

> *I see people while feeling uneasy*
> *about the dirty collars of my kimono*
> *how they embarrass me*
> *and my mind is occupied*
> *with this thought* [23]

He missed Kotomi, who used to take good care of him. He also remembered his days of intensive Zen practice—the "Four Vows" vividly came back to him: "Sentient beings are countless; I vow to save them all. Delusion is rampant; I vow to sever it all. Buddha's teaching is profound; I vow to master it. Buddha's path is paramount; I vow to embody it." [24]

On April 3 he attended the twenty-fifth anniversary commemoration of the death of master Kokan, under whom he practiced Zen thirty years previously. Nishida recorded the master's "death-poem" in his diary:

> *I lived my life of sixty-five years*
> *in the midst of blind human activities*
> *those burn like ravaging wild fires*
> *in the face of life and death*
> *all is clear, katsu!* [25]

On April 18 his colleague Fujishiro Teisuke died of cancer. At the twenty-fifth anniversary commemoration of the death of Kiyozawa Manshi on June 6, he gave a talk at Ōtani University, reminiscing about the leader of the Meiji spiritual reform; he praised Kiyozawa and Ōnishi Hajime as the two most prominent Japanese thinkers of the Meiji period. [26]

For Japan 1927 was a tumultuous year politically and economically. The March 15 financial crisis caused many local banks to close; funds were then consolidated in the major banks. (The financial crisis forced the closure of Sōda Kiichirō's bank; Nishida's colleague's worries may have caused his illness and death.) Diplomatic tensions arose between Japan and China, and political uncertainties led to the dissolution of the first Wakatsuki cabinet in April 1927. The succeeding

Tanaka cabinet fared no better as the ultraright wing spurred the country toward militarism and fascism.[27]

As Nishida's retirement neared, honors began to accumulate. On May 14 he was appointed a member of the Japan Imperial Academy (Gakushiin).[28] Colleagues including Matsumoto Bunzaburō, Kano Naoki, Naitō Konan, and Ogawa Takuji were already members of the academy, so for Nishida it was nothing more than joining the ranks of his old friends. Twice in May, Harada Kumao, who had just begun to work for Saionji Kinmochi[29] as his private secretary, called on Nishida, marking the beginning of their long-lasting friendship. Saionji was the last of the surviving *genrō* (senior councilors) to the emperor and was empowered to nominate prime ministers. Because Harada's job was to gather information for Saionji, Nishida had gained an invaluable political ear. Nishida, who had wanted to lead a quiet "private" life of otium cum dignitate, was going to become a public persona as a leading intellectual, the voice of a national conscience.

On June 17 Nishida received a copy of Heidegger's *Sein und Zeit* [Being and Time] from Mutai Risaku, who sent it from Freiburg as a present.[30] Mutai must have obtained this copy soon after its publication. Around this time Nishida was working on his essay "Shirumono" [That which knows].[31]

With the arrival of the summer vacation, Nishida's last as a professor, he felt physically and mentally relaxed.[32] On July 3 a great, unexpected experience of "rebirth" came over him. He drew a picture of a radiantly shining sun in his diary with a red pencil and wrote in German: "Wiedergeburt" (reborn), "aus bösem Traum erwacht" (awakened from a nightmare). Then he continued in Japanese: "Even a dead tree can grow a bud of new life. I've never known this kind of happiness in my life." On this day, he was alone at home and spent half a day peacefully. In the afternoon Miki came by to visit. The experience of gaining a new perspective on life must have been related to the spiritual purification he was undergoing. One can only wonder whether he experienced something like the "dropping of both the body and the mind" of which Dōgen speaks. In any case, Nishida broke through the bottom of the world and leaped into a new realm of freedom. He was then nearly finished with the preface to a collection of his essays, *Hataraku mono kara miru mono e*.[33] He dedicated the book to Hōjō Tokiyuki, who had just turned seventy. It was a token of special respect for his old mentor—this was the first and the last book that Nishida ever dedicated to anyone. The book was published by Iwanami Bookstore on October 15, 1927.

Around this time a book in English introducing Nishida's thought to the Western audience was published. Its author was Tsuchida Kyō-son, a 1918 graduate of Kyoto's philosophy department. The book, entitled *Contemporary Thought of Japan and China*, mentions not only Nishida but also Tanabe Hajime and Kuwaki Gen'yoku. Tsuchida gave Nishida the biggest salute by identifying him as "a philosopher always to be noticed whenever the highest type of philosophy in Japan is mentioned." But it is unclear whether Nishida agreed with Tsu-chida's characterization of his writing style as "a poetical monologue in spite of his strictly logical thinking. . . . [H]e seems like an Orien-tal puritanical monk."[34]

The philosophy department was given the fifth chair in the history of philosophy in October 1927, and Nishida assumed it by vacating the first chair to Tanabe Hajime, who was then promoted to profes-sor as of November 4. The department underwent a smooth transi-tion. Ojima Sukema succeeded Kano Naoki, Amano Teiyū succeeded Tomonaga Sanjūrō, and Ueda Juzō succeeded Fukada Yasukazu. After Nishida's retirement, the fifth chair of the history of philosophy was offered to Yamanouchi Tokuryū. Watsuji Tetsurō[35] was studying abroad from 1927 to 1928 with the understanding that he was to be promoted to professor after his return from Europe.[36] Hisamatsu Shin'ichi, Kōsaka Masaaki, Kōyama Iwao,[37] Doi Torakazu, and Shimo-mura Toratarō were appointed lecturers. Nishitani Keiji and Shima Yoshio were the upcoming younger generation of scholars, waiting in the wings of the main stage. There was also talk that Kuki Shūzō might be invited to join the department as a lecturer.[38]

The last seminars for philosophy students Nishida gave in the 1927–1928 academic year were on Aristotle's *Metaphysica* and *De Anima;* he also gave a seminar for sociology students, using Hegel's *Grundlinien der Philosophie des Rechts* [The Philosophy of Right]. His last lecture for his Introduction to Philosophy course was on February 4, 1928. His diary for that day reads: "The obligatory lecture is over as of today. I feel relieved physically and mentally. From this day on I shall withdraw from my public career, become a totally private man, and engage simply in the development of my thought."[39]

Just around the time Nishida was finishing his obligatory univer-sity lectures, Kawakami Hajime was forced to resign from his univer-sity position. Kawakami, a professor in the Faculty of Law, had been the faculty mentor for the SSSG and was an active supporter of labor movements and sympathetic to communism. Following the massive crackdown on the members of the Communist Party on March 15, 1928, by the Japanese government (the so-called 3.15 Incident), the SSSG at the university was ordered to dissolve on April 19. The minister of education took advantage of this occasion and accused Kawakami of neglecting his duties as the faculty mentor and demanded that the university president Araki Torasaburō fire Kawakami. Araki obeyed the ministry's order and gave Kawakami his notice of dismissal on April 16. At the faculty senate meeting on the same day, however, Araki expressed his wish to step down from the presidency at an appropriate time because he disapproved of his own action (he resigned on March 22, 1929). Ever since the Sawayanagi incident, it had been the university practice that no professor could be fired without the consent of the department faculty members. Kawakami, however, had no support from his colleagues and presented his letter of resignation on April 17.[40] Nishida remained sympathetic to Kawakami, however, and years later they would meet again.

In April 1928 Nishida's youngest daughter, Umeko, entered Tokyo Women's College, which was a great relief to Nishida. From April to June he had only one course to teach, a series of lectures on a special topic. He gave the bold title of "Tetsugaku no kyūkyokuteki mondai no ichikito" [An attempt to solve the ultimate problem of philosophy] to these farewell lectures. The last meeting of the Philosophical Society that Nishida attended was on May 12. Kōsaka Masaaki gave a talk on "Epistemology and metaphysics according to William James," and during the discussion someone criticized James as "commonplace." Nishida spoke up "in an unusually pointed manner in defense of James" and said to this person: "Which works by James have you read? He is far from what you describe!" Kōsaka was impressed that Nishida had never lost his deep respect for William James.[41]

Now that his obligatory teaching was behind him, Nishida felt his creative energy was unleashing itself. He wrote several articles: "Iwayuru ninshiki taishōkai no ronriteki kōzō" [The logical structure of the so-called world of cognitive objects],[42] "Jutsugoteki ronrishugi" [The logic of the predicate],[43] and "Girisha tetsugaku ni oite no aru mono" ["Being" according to Greek philosophy].[44] By June he had also finished "Jikojishin o miru mono no oite aru basho to ishiki no basho" [The *topos* where that which sees itself exists and the *topos* of consciousness][45] and "Augusuchinusu no jikaku" [Self-consciousness according to Augustine].[46]

Nishida's last lecture was on June 9, 1928. The list of courses that

Nishida taught at Kyoto Imperial University is reproduced here (see chart). Roman numeral I designates introductory courses *(futsū kōgi)*, II designates lectures on special topics *(tokushu kōgi)*, and III designates a close text reading or seminar *(kōdoku* or *enshū)*. The number of hours the course met each week appears in parentheses.

1910–1911   I. Introduction to Philosophy (2)
        II. Ethics (2)
        III. Reading in Ethics (2) (This course was most likely cancelled.)

1911–1912   I. Introduction to Philosophy (2)
        II. Ethics "Law" (2)
        III. (for ethics) John Dewey and James H. Tufts, *Ethics* (1)
        III. (for the study of religion) Hoeffding, *Religionsphilosophie* (2)

1912–1913   I. Introduction to Philosophy (2)
        II. Ethics, "Law" (2)
        III. Aristotle, *Ethics* (1)
        III. (for the study of religion) Schleiermacher (2)

1913–1914   I. Introduction to Psychology (2)
        I. Introduction to the Study of Religion (2)

1914–1915   I. Introduction to Philosophy (2)
        I. Introduction to Psychology (2)
        II. "Contemporary German philosophy" (1)
        III. (for philosophy and psychology) Bergson, *Materie und Gedächtnis* (2)

1915–1916   I. Introduction to Philosophy (2)
        I. Introduction to Psychology (2, team taught with Chiba Tanenari)
        II. "The Austrian school of philosophy from Bolzano and Brentano to Husserl" (fall quarter); "Hegel's *Logik*" (winter and spring quarters) (2)
        III. Kant, *Kritik der reinen Vernunft* (2)

1916–1917   I. Introduction to Philosophy (2)
        II. "Hegel's *Logik*" (2)
        III. Fichte, *Grundlage der gesamten Wissenschaftslehre* (2)

1917–1918   I. Introduction to Philosophy (2)
        II. "Intuition and reflection" (2)
        III. Leibniz, *Discourse on Metaphysics*, trans. by Montgomery (2)

1918–1919   I. Introduction to Philosophy (2)
        II. "Contemporary philosophy" (2)
        III. Spinoza, *Ethica* (2)

1919–1920   I. Introduction to Philosophy (2)
        II. "Aesthetic consciousness" (2)
        III. Bergson, *L'Évolution créatrice* (2)

1920–1921   I. Introduction to Philosophy (2)

II. "Hegel's *Logik*" (2)
III. Hegel, *Wissenschaft der Logik (Logik in der Enzyklopädie)* (2)

1921–1922   I. Introduction to Philosophy (2)
II. "Fundamental problem of ethics"
III. Hegel, *Wissenschaft der Logik (Logik in der Enzyklopädie)*;
Schelling, *Über das Wesen der menschlichen Freiheit* (2)

1922–1923   I. Introduction to Philosophy (2)
II. "Hegel's *Logik*" (2)
III. Hegel, *Phänomenologie des Geistes* (2)

1923–1924   I. Introduction to Philosophy (2)
II. "Problem of consciousness" (2)
III. Husserl, *Ideen*, and Lotze, *Metaphysik* (2)

1924–1925   I. Introduction to Philosophy (2)
II. "On Aristotle's *Metaphysica*" (2)
III. Lotze, *Metaphysik* (continuation of the previous year); Hegel,
Phänomenologie des Geistes (2)

1925–1926   I. Introduction to Philosophy (2)
II. No lecture on special topics
III. Hegel, *Phänomenologie des Geistes* (2)
III. (for religion) Weber, *Gesammelten Aufsätze* (2)

1926–1927   I. Introduction to Psychology (2)
II. "A Philosophical foundation of religion" (for philosophy and the
history of Western philosophy) (2)
III. Aristotle, *Metaphysica* (2)

1927–1928   I. Introduction to Philosophy (2)
II. No lecture on special topics
III. Aristotle, *Metaphysica* and *Über die Seele (De anima)* (2)
III. (for sociology) Hegel, *Grundlinien der Philosophie des Rechts* (2)

1928   II. An attempt to solve the ultimate problem of philosophy (2)

The Philosophical Society hosted a reception honoring Nishida's retirement on June 10, the day after his last lecture, at the Rakuyū-kaikan. Tanabe led the toast with "Kanpai!" ("Bottoms up"). Reporting on the day, an editor of *Tetsugaku Kenkyū* wrote: "The evening air was still cool, which gave us a feeling of loneliness. Professor Nishida reminisced and spoke about his life."[47] Nishida left for Tokyo the next day, as had been planned. During his ten-day visit, he took a day with Umeko and made a tour of the coastal places from Kamakura to Kugenuma. He was "struck by the quiet beauty of Kugenuma's scenery"—it reminded him of his home village of Unoke and he thought about living there for a while.[48]

A free man now, Nishida turned to artistic activities. He began to enjoy doing calligraphy. He also took up his old pleasure of reading world literature. He enjoyed translating Western poems into Japanese. One of them from this period is a song sung by Mignon in Goethe's novel *Wilhelm Meister*. It seems to have captured Nishida's feelings of those days:

> *Only those who know what longing is*
> *Should know my torments.*
> *Forlorn and alone,*
> *I gaze beyond the blue sky.*
> *Ah, those who know me and love me are*
> *Far away in the distance.*
> *My eyes befogged, my bowels burn.*
> *Only those who know what longing is*
> *Should know my agonies.*[49]

On August 18 Nishida received his "official notice of release" from the university. His eighteen-year-long career at Kyoto Imperial University had ended. He jotted down in his diary: "At last, I have become a masterless samurai *(rōnin)*." To be a masterless samurai for Nishida was far from being unemployed, however. After he had ample rest, he felt like summarizing the view of *topos* that he had developed so far. The result was his essay, "Eichiteki sekai" [The intelligible world],[50] in which he distinguishes three aspects of the "world"—the natural world as the determination of the judging universal, the world of consciousness as the determination of self-consciousness, and the intelligible world as the self-determination of consciousness that transcends intellectual apprehension. He further discusses the religious awareness given by the ultimate determination of the *topos* of nothingness, and the philosophical perspective as that of the religious self reflecting upon itself. Because of its bold clarity and religious profundity, this essay was well received and was eventually translated into German by Robert Schinzinger. After this essay, he wrote another, entitled "Chokkakuteki chishiki" [Intuitive knowledge].[51]

His letter to Hori Koretaka of September 20 describes his feelings at this juncture in his life:

> By some turn of events, my reputation, however undeserved, spread, as if a dog barking upon a false alarm provokes ten thousand other dogs to join in. Even if my public life appeared grand for the last ten years, I was visited from time to time by an unbearable sense of helplessness because of my domestic situation. The façade is but illusory. It is but

bubbles on the surface of the deep and dark flow of life. My work may have been the means of consoling myself. I take my retirement as a blessing. I shall live as a total recluse and engage in philosophical completion, such as it is. [52]

On October 1, a boy, an heir of the Nishida family, was born to Sotohiko and Asako. Nishida was overjoyed and took the honor of naming his grandson "Kikuhiko." Although in Japanese *kiku* means "chrysanthemums," typical autumn flowers, Nishida took the Chinese character *"ki"* ("multifarious") from his own name, Kitarō, chose the character *"ku,"* for "long-lasting," and added *"-hiko,"* a suffix for a male name. The birth of Kikuhiko had an amazing effect on Nishida's outlook on life; it was as if a sunrise erased the shadow that had plagued his home for so long.

But where there is life, there is death. Nishida's colleagues were quickly departing from this world. On January 28, 1928, Sakaguchi Takashi had died; in August a lecturer of sociology, Igarashi Shin, died at the young age of twenty-nine; on November 12, Fukada Yasukazu died after a prolonged illness. Despite the fact that Nishida had suffered pleurisy and could not give up his "unhygienic" habit of smoking, he was to live longer than most of his colleagues. Is this because he took habitual walks, stretching his legs, and vacationed at appropriate times to balance his life of intensity with relaxation?

Harada Kumao objected to Nishida's idea of spending the winter in Kugenuma, apparently because of its dampness. Instead, Harada, Iwanami, and Yamanouchi found a sunny house for Nishida at Zaimokuchō in Kamakura. [53] Nishida liked the climate there, and spending the hot summers and cold winters away from Kyoto in temperate Kamakura became an annual routine. His first stay in Kamakura, which lasted from December 1, 1928, to March 20, 1929, was an especially memorable one. He enjoyed a carefree existence, surrounded by his old friends. Suzuki Daisetz kept his workplace, Shōden'an, in the Engakuji compound and divided his time between Kyoto and Kamakura. Whenever Suzuki was in Kamakura, the two called on each other and enjoyed making calligraphy pieces. Hori Koretaka was also living in Kamakura. Hori was an expert in the rules of Chinese poetry (*kanshi*), such as the pitch and inflections, and was also a fair critic of Japanese *waka* poetry. Nishida asked him to correct his poems, and with such an ideal private tutor he felt free to compose. His walks along the beach and through the ruins of the old capital city of Kamakura were a wondrous source of poetic inspiration.

Nishida found Kamakura more rustic than Kyoto, a city "too refined for an ancient capital, and the beauty of its mountains and rivers is also tamed." Among Kamakura's many forgotten ruins, Nishida one day came upon the untended gravestone of the shōgun, Minamoto Yoritomo. The discovery inspired a *waka:*

Amid the fallen leaves
is this old gravestone
did you think this was going to be
your eternal abode
when you were among the living? [54]

The landscape of Kamakura reminded him of the dark history of Minamoto and Hōjō rule:

It feels to me as if a history of human wickedness and vices were concentrated in this small plot of land, where one's own blood relations doubted one another and killed, or were killed, by the hands of one's kinsmen. . . . overall one may say that the politics of the Hōjōs were filled with intrigues and machinations. Labyrinth-like valleys of the hills of Kamakura seem to symbolize that scheming human mind. The scenery evokes a sense of the sorrows of life, nay, it stirs our religious sentiments.[55]

Nishida also spent hours gazing upon the ocean, which to him was "infinity in motion." Here is one of his many *waka* on the ocean:

Since the time of separation
of heaven and earth
the sea has been constantly in motion
however long I look at it
I never get tired of it [56]

The beach of Kamakura took back Nishida by twenty years, to the time when he and Fujioka Tōho took a walk together on the beach of Ōiso. Overcome by a sense of nostalgia, he composed a poem in Chinese:

Gone are the dead
and what are the fates of the living?
I visit places laden with memories
flowers are in full bloom
and my feelings are heightened too [57]

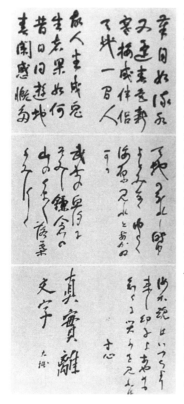

Nishida's and Suzuki's calligraphy, most likely January 1929, done in Kamakura. Five Japanese poems by Nishida are followed by D. T. Suzuki's commentary. These poems were composed in 1928 in Kamakura. The first, a poem in Chinese, reads: "Years and months are but flowing water. When we saw each other, the plum flowers that bloom in the cold of the winter were our companions. Human beings exist in between heaven and earth." The second, also in Chinese, reads: "Gone are the dead; and what are the fates of the living? I visit a place laden with memories; spring is at its height and my feelings are heightened, too." The third, a Japanese poem, reads: "Since the time of the separation of heaven from earth, the sea has been constantly in motion; however long I look at it I never get tired of it!" The fourth poem is in Japanese: "I walk in the hills of Kamakura, from an unknown trail to another, crushing the leaves once soaked in the blood of warriors." And the fifth poem in Japanese reads: "From where did your soul come, my dear grandson? I see you laugh so innocently." D. T. Suzuki's commentary caps the moment: "Reality is separate from the written words." From *Nishida Kitarō Zenshū*, vol. 10, *Furoku*.

Nishida's creative energy seems to have known no limits. He sent a collection of his poems to Hori for his corrections, with these words:

> Certainly, I have dedicated my life to a theoretical work, but I also have this wish to express the "voices of my heart" *(kokoro no koe)*, which arise from time to time when I encounter various situations and incidents in life. Occasionally I even think about wanting to write short stories by giving free rein to boundless fantasies, but, of course, it is easier said than done, and while thinking about writing something, my fantasies fade away. What I can do, however, is to attach some of my poems as an appendix to my [philosophical] works. For this reason, I ask you to delete ordinary or uninteresting poems. Trust me, your critical eye is more helpful than flattering compliments.[58]

Nishida's essay "Aru kyōju no taishoku no ji" [A retirement speech of a professor] was certainly born out of his desire to write one such "short story," an expression of the voice of his heart.

A Retirement Speech of a Professor*

It appears that the following was written by someone who heard a story from a waiter who worked at the Rakuyūkaikan. The event must have taken place quite some time ago.

On an early summer evening in the grand room of the Rakuyūkan many people gathered. Lights were brightly lit, contributing to the atmosphere of a gala celebration. The occasion appeared to be the reception for a professor who was just retiring from the university—an event quite common these days.

It was already the time of the year when it is hot and humid, but the curtains, gently dancing in the breeze coming in through the wide-open windows, gave an impression of coolness. It looked as if there were some who had not seen one another for a long time. Small groups of people formed around tables here and there, eagerly catching up with each other's news. Soon the banquet started, and in due course the dessert was served. At that time, a professor[1] who was seated across from the guest of honor, stood up and delivered a speech in a clear and articulate manner, praising the contributions of the retired professor. The guest of honor seemed a rather shy man despite his outward appearance. He stood up and mumbled a few words of thanks, which I could not hear clearly. By the time the banquet was over, people were relaxed, and a good time was had by all. Perhaps the professor, the guest of honor, felt that his earlier words of thanks had been too brief. He stood up and began to recount his life.

"As of today, my public life, which has lasted several decades, has come to an end. Just recently, I took out the *Last Essays of Elia* by Charles Lamb and read 'The Superannuated Man.' I could relate to it deeply, as it nicely captures what I now feel.

"As I look back on my life, I see that it has been quite a simple one. In the first half of it, I sat facing the blackboard. In the second half, I stood up with the blackboard behind me. I only changed my position in relation to the blackboard. This, in a nutshell, is my biography!

"But even a blade of grass that is going to be put in the fireplace tomorrow has its own history and memories. Even I, who have lived

---

* "Aru kyōju no taishoku no ji," NKZ 12:168–71. The essay appeared in *Shisō* 83 (April 1929).

1. The professor is Tanabe Hajime.

quite an ordinary life, cannot help but be awed by the sense of ever-flowing water and the destiny of human existence as I look back on the sixty years of my life.

"I was born in a poor village on the northern coast of Japan. When I was a child, I attended a village elementary school. Under the loving protection of my parents, I spent my days playing in the green pine woods and on the white sandy beach. When I was thirteen or fourteen, my older sister took me to Kanazawa, and I entered a normal school there. It was generally considered then that there was no greater scholar than a teacher of an elementary school in a village; so I entered the school that trained teachers-to-be.

"I don't know whether it was a blessing in disguise or not, but I contracted a case of deadly typhoid and was absent from the normal school for about a year. During that time, I became aware of the wider world. I quit the normal school to enter the Senmon Gakkō. When the Senmon Gakkō was renamed the Fourth Higher School, I was enrolled in it.

"The time came when I had to decide on my major. Just as many young boys wondered about this question, so did I. It was very hard for me to choose between mathematics and philosophy. A certain professor, whom I respected greatly, recommended that I should go into mathematics. His argument was that 'in philosophy, not only logical ability but a poetic imagination is necessary,' and he was not sure I had it. It was certainly reasonable advice, and I didn't have enough confidence in myself to challenge it. Yet I did not feel like spending the rest of my life studying cut-and-dried mathematics. Although I did have some misgivings, I decided on philosophy.

"My student days at the Fourth Higher School were the most enjoyable of my life. As youthful energy carried me away, I lived free as a bird, ignoring the school rules. Eventually, I dropped out of school, thinking that I could learn on my own, and that the best thing for me to do was to read any book I pleased, leaving behind the shackles of school. I stayed at home all day long, reading. But in less than a year, I badly strained my eyes, and the doctor forbade me to read. Therefore, I was forced to think again as to what I would do. I went to Tokyo and entered the College of Humanities[2] as a limited status student.

"In those days students of limited status were a miserable lot. I felt

2. At the time this was the Imperial University.

I had become a loser. As soon as I graduated from the university, I took up the position of a middle school teacher in the countryside. After that I was at Yamaguchi Higher School for a few years and finally became a teacher of German at my alma mater, the Fourth Higher School, where I taught for ten years.

"Those ten years in Kanazawa were the best years of my life. I was both physically and mentally strong then. Since I did some reading and engaged in philosophical thinking, I longed for an environment more conducive to research, but that seemed like a dream. However, when I reached around the age of 'no more doubt,'[3] I don't know by what turn of events, but I came to this university on friends' recommendations. At first, I had a one-year replacement position for a certain professor who was to study abroad,[4] but eventually I was given a permanent position and ended up spending nearly twenty years in Kyoto.

"In recent years I experienced successive family misfortunes and was worn out physically and mentally. I could not accomplish what I should have, nor did I carry out my responsibilities in full. For this reason I cannot help but feel guilty in accepting your very generous reception. I remember a passage from an English reader, which I read when I was a child. The essay was entitled 'Grave Yard.' If I remember correctly, there was a passage that read something like this: 'Whichever tombstone you look at, inscriptions read "Good Husband," "Good Wife," or "Good Child." Well then, where are the bad ones buried?' I therefore ask your forgiveness for my shortcomings, in the same way as those who had died went unpunished."

Having spoken thus, the professor sat down. Among those present, there might have been some who did not particularly care for this long and unabashed account of his personal life; others might have been secretly embarrassed by his candid speech. However, around the table arranged in a U-shape with the professor at the center, people continued their amicable conversations, reminiscing about the good old days. Eventually, the professor said he had to go somewhere far away the following day and excused himself early. Many stood up with him and walked him to the foyer of the Rakuyūkan to see him off. The professor, apparently in a very fine mood, walked out into the city street and disappeared in the dark.

---

3. The age is forty, referring to a statement by Confucius.
4. The professor is Tomoeda Takahiko

Chapter 18

Formation of the
Kyoto School of Philosophy
(1929–1932)

Nishida was enjoying his first winter in Kamakura. On February 1, 1929, he was appointed professor emeritus.[1] Visitors from the Kantō area continued to stream in to his rented house at Zaimokuchō. The popular writer, Kurata Hyakuzō, who made Nishida's *Zen no kenkyū* a best-seller, called on him twice in February, and Tanabe Juri, Odaka Tomoo, Honda Kenzō, Miyamoto Wakichi, and Ōsaka Motokichirō were among other callers. He saw Kuki Shūzō at a beachside hotel in Kamakura.

On March 2 Nishida gave a talk at the Philosophical Society at Tokyo Imperial University on "Kant and Husserl," which he later retitled "Watakushi no handanteki ippansha to iu mono" [What I call the judging universal] and published in the *Tetsugaku Zasshi*.[2] By the time Nishida wrapped up his stay in Kamakura, he had completed "Jikakuteki ippansha ni oite aru mono oyobi sore to sono haigo ni aru mono to no kankei" [That which exists in the self-conscious universal, and its relationship to what is behind it].[3]

On March 10, shortly before Nishida's departure, Iwanami took him for a drive in a chauffeured limousine; they enjoyed a ride around the Miura Peninsula, seeing such sights as the memorial where Commodore M. C. Perry had landed. Nishida left Kamakura on March 15, but before returning to Kyoto on March 20, he spent a few days in Tokyo. Hōjō Tokiyuki was seriously ill, and Nishida wanted to see his mentor for the last time. Hōjō died on April 27 at the age of seventy-two, and with his death one more chapter of Nishida's life closed.[4] He wrote an essay remembering his mentor, "Hōjō sensei ni hajimete oshie o uketa koro" [Around the time I first received instruction from Professor Hōjō].[5] In addition, friends and former colleagues decided to compile Hōjō's letters, speeches, addresses, journal entries, and other writings into a book, and Oda Shōgaku wrote a brief biography of the great educator. Yamamoto Ryōkichi took charge of collecting the material, while Nishida served as nominal editor. This tribute to Hōjō Tokiyuki, *Kakudō hen'ei* [Glimpses of greatness], was published on June 25, 1931.

In March 1929 Shizuko's lung condition, which had been touch and go, worsened. After some deliberation, Nishida decided to put her under the care of professionals at a sanatorium on Lake Biwa. In April Sotohiko got a teaching position at Kōnan Higher School as a professor of physics, and the young couple, with baby Kikuhiko, moved to Sumiyoshi. Their departure from under Nishida's roof left a big empty space at home. Nishida began to concentrate on his work to forget his loneliness. While Sotohiko and Asako had been living with him, he had moved his study upstairs so that the study could be used as the reception room. Now he moved his study back where it had been. He even moved his bed into the study and practically lived there. On May 2, he began working on the essay, "Ippansha no jikogentei" [The self-determination of the universal].⁶ The following *waka* is not really an exaggeration.

> *Reclining on this chair*
> *I write*
> *tucking myself into this bed*
> *I sleep*
> *day in, day out*⁷

He wrote to Hori: "Over here I feel hurried and unable to compose any poems. . . . These days I don't even take a walk but spend the whole day cooped up in a room doing nothing. I'm really a hermit! I'm becoming lazier and don't feel like doing anything."⁸ In fact, far from "being lazy," he was single-mindedly plowing ahead and advancing his thought, completing "Ippansha no jikogentei to jikaku" [The self-determination of the universal and self-consciousness]⁹ and "Jikaku-teki gentei kara mita ippansha no gentei" [The determination of the universal viewed from the perspective of the determination of self-consciousness].¹⁰ By October 1929 the last of this series of essays was completed,¹¹ and during the following January the essays he had written in the previous two years were collected in a single volume, *Ippansha no jikakuteki taikei* [The self-conscious structure of the universal]. Nishida's assiduous work, pushing through what happened to be an exceptionally hot summer, exhausted him completely. By the time fall arrived, he felt melancholic and needed to see his friends. He left for Tokyo in early November.

In his new collection of essays Nishida plunges into a complicated analysis of self-consciousness in its subjective, *noetic* ("grammatical predicate") and objective, *noematic* ("grammatical subject") aspects. Nishida treats consciousness in terms of self-consciousness rather than in terms of the intentionality of consciousness, as Husserl had done. In the operation of self-consciousness "the self sees the self in the self" *(jiko ga jiko ni oite jiko o miru).* The seeing self is P (the grammatical predicate), which embraces the self seen, S (the grammatical subject). In terms of their contents, P is a *topos/*field that contains all that can become the "object" of self-consciousness, whereas S is the *topos/*field of all that is: self-consciousness in its prereflected state.[12] When the seer and the seen become one, only "in the self" remains.[13] (Nishida later develops this "in the self" into the notion of the "historical body," which is "active-intuitive.") For Nishida the self-determination of the intelligible self is the prime form of the self-determination of consciousness. In it the self as the seer alone exists and the self as the seen disappears; the seer sees its own nothingness. Therein the self forgets itself, which means (as Zen Buddhism holds) that everything under the sun is none other than the self.[14] In terms of the operation of self-consciousness, whatever is given to the intelligible self is the expression *(hyōgen)* of things, and in this sense "being is expression, expression is being."[15]

In his essay, "Jikakuteki gentei kara mita ippansha no gentei," Nishida explicitly identifies "the awareness of absolute emptiness" *(zettai mu no jikaku)* with the "religious experience of 'phenomena are empty; emptiness is phenomena' *(shiki soku ze kū, kū soku ze shiki)* in which there is neither the seer nor the seen." Further identifying the Bergsonian "infinite flow of life" with the ultimate noetic direction, he sees that this infinite flow of life is "absolute nothingness" *(zettai mu)* that transcends the limitation of our cognition.[16]

With its overtly religious reference, Nishida's essay provoked sharp criticism from Tanabe Hajime. By 1929 Marxism was the intellectual fashion of the day, and it was widely contended that "unless one is a Marxist, one is not an intellectual." Nishida's diary of May 11 reads: "In the evening Tanabe and seven graduate students came over; we got into the discussion of Marx, which lasted well beyond midnight."[17] And his *waka* of September 17 reads:

> *We again discussed Marx*
> *into the small hours*
> *of the morning*
> *on account of Marx*
> *I failed to go to bed* [18]

An episode that Kōyama Iwao describes must have taken place at one of these meetings:

> Many of my seniors such as Kimura Morimoto, Kōsaka Masaaki, and Nishitani Keiji were present there. I no longer recall the exact subject matter of the discussion, but Nishida and Tanabe got engaged in an argument. At the precise moment when I thought the argument was overheating, Tanabe said to Nishida: "That's why you don't understand dialectics." Shocked by these fierce words of confrontation, I held my breath and awaited what would happen next. I stole a glance at Nishida's face. He looked a bit affronted and remained speechless for a second, but he leaned forward from his chair and said, "I didn't expect that *you* would say that." Nishida did not show any excitement and continued on with the heated discussion. [19]

Nishida appreciated the aspect of Marxism that saw society as the central concern and considered individuals to be within society, but he held that "to base everything on the material and to consider the individual as purely a reflection of society" inevitably leads to the denial of the individual, and as a result "society becomes static and stifled." He felt that Marx failed to see that society moves on precisely because of each individual's creativity and freedom. [20]

The popularity of Marxism temporarily shifted students' attention away from Nishida's philosophical endeavor. On January 25, 1930, Miki Kiyoshi, who was then teaching at Hōsei University in Tokyo and energetically advocated dialectical materialism, was invited to Kyoto to give a talk in the university lecture series. Miki was an icon among the progressive students, and his popularity was at its peak. [21] Nishida was also scheduled to give a talk on the same day about his most recent book, *Ippansha no jikakuteki taikei* [The self-conscious structure of the universal]. [22] Nishitani Keiji, who attended Nishida's lecture, remembered that particular day: "During Professor Nishida's talk, suddenly a huge passionate applause broke out from the nearby large lecture hall [where Miki was talking]. . . . Amid the general trend of the world, which was moving away from his thought, Professor Nishida continued with his philosophical investigations, indifferent to such social milieu."[23]

Whether to know the philosophical trend of the day and embrace it, to incorporate new ideas into older systems, or to engage in the pursuit of a fundamental problem of philosophy—these questions seem to have confronted every thinker in those days. Unfortunately, Miki's popularity was short-lived. In May he was arrested for allegedly giving money to the Japanese Communist Party. A charge was brought against him in July, and he was detained in the Toyotama Prison until November. While Miki was in prison, the members of the Proletariat Science Institute *(Puroretaria kagaku kenkyūjo)* denounced his interpretation of Marxism as heretical.[24] Miki, embittered by this experience, soon distanced himself from the Marxist movement.

Tanabe Hajime, who had been at odds with Nishida for some time, made public his criticism of Nishida in his May 1930 article, "Nishida sensei no oshie o aogu" [Requesting Professor Nishida's elucidation],[25] which appeared in *Tetsugaku Kenkyū*.[26] Because Tanabe was regarded as Nishida's most faithful follower, this article surprised everyone but Nishida himself, who was aware of Tanabe's criticisms. Tanabe admitted: "Each time an essay contained in this volume [*Ippansha no jikaku-teki taikei*] was published, I bothered Professor Nishida with my questions and doubts, for I was unable to follow his thought."

Tanabe's essential criticism was that Nishida "confounded" religious intuition with the ultimate philosophical perspective. Tanabe's critique concerned Nishida's philosophical method: (1) "Can philosophy systematize the religious awareness, which holds that to lose oneself is actually to find oneself?" (2) "For philosophy to assume the position of the philosophy of religion (in the sense that Plotinus's thought can be called a philosophy of religion), to postulate a final universal that is incomprehensible, and then to interpret reality as the self-determination of that universal, would lead to the negation of philosophy itself," and (3) "Self-consciousness as a philosophical principal and the absolute in the world of religion cannot be united in the concept of self-consciousness of absolute nothingness." He further made public his concern that Nishida's position might encourage *theōrein*—a quietist contemplative attitude cut off from reality. He felt that "making religion out of philosophy" contradicts the original mission of philosophy.[27]

Nishida took Tanabe's criticisms positively and welcomed the opportunity to explain and clarify his thought. He was of the opinion that open critical exchange invigorates academia and enhances the level of philosophical inquiry. He did feel, however, that Tanabe did not "yet fully comprehend the standpoint and fundamentals" of his thought.[28] He wrote his next essay, "Basho no jikogentei to shite no ishikisayō" [The operation of consciousness as the self-determination of the *topos*], to respond to Tanabe's critique.[29]

Tanabe began to develop his own path of thinking, remaining critical of Nishidan philosophy. Nishida appreciated Tanabe as one of the few who could logically follow his thought, but in the face of Tanabe's obstinacy, he complained that when, it came to the crucial point, Tanabe would draw an unexpected conclusion, one totally different from what Nishida intended. Nishida remarked that "instead of tossing the ball on this side, he tosses it on the other side and misunderstands me."[30]

Tanabe's May 1930 essay signaled his movement out from under Nishida's wing. Tosaka Jun observed that Tanabe's "declaration of independence" became the driving force behind the establishment of the Kyoto school of philosophy.[31] Tosaka, a student of both Nishida and Tanabe, published an article, "Kyōto-gakuha no tetsugaku" [On the philosophy of the Kyoto school] in 1932,[32] pointing out that Nishidan philosophy was growing into a larger phenomenon, the Kyoto school of philosophy. In his next article, "Tanabe tetsugaku no seiritsu" [Establishment of Tanabean philosophy],[33] Tosaka elaborated on his earlier observation:

> If Professor Tanabe Hajime did not go beyond Nishidan philosophy, he would have merely remained a follower of Nishidan philosophy. But Prof. Tanabe's impressive activities of recent years obviously make it clear to everyone that Nishidan philosophy has its successor. In this way Nishidan philosophy is transformed into the Kyoto school of philosophy in a sure and successful manner. I must reiterate my congratulations on the development of the Kyoto school, since Dr. Tanabe has finally established his own philosophical system: Tanabean philosophy.[34]

The term "Kyoto school of philosophy" may be variously defined. The philosophy department around the time of Nishida's retirement was full of vitality and enjoying its "golden age."[35] Nakai Masakazu argues that the Kyoto school was largely formed before Nishida's retirement. Nakai, a 1925 graduate of the aesthetics program and a teaching associate (*joshu*), also worked as assistant editor of *Tetsugaku Kenkyū* from 1926 to 1937. Writing in the 1950s, he recalls the department:

Great professors—Nishida, Fukada, Tomonaga, Hatano, Fujii, Konishi, and Matsumoto—were in the company of younger energetic assistant professors and lecturers, such as Amano Teiyū, Tanabe Hajime, Watsuji Tetsurō, Yamanouchi Tokuryū, Ueda Juzō, Ojima Sukema, Kuki Shūzō —all shining like bright stars. Students of the first generation, such as Miki Kiyoshi, Tosaka Jun, Nishitani Keiji, Kōsaka Masaaki, Kimura Motomori, and of the second generation, Shimomura Toratarō, Kōyama Iwao, Mashita Shin'ichi,[36] Danno Yasutarō,[37] and others, gathered at the houses of their professors and engaged in lively, sparkling debates. Dr. Tanabe's Saturday gathering was like a glittering seminar. As I look back on those days, I realize how happy I was, moving among those stars and nebulae.[38]

Nakai defines this "body of brilliantly scattered diversity" as the Kyoto school, which is not for him "a fixed entity, as some people like to believe, but rather it was like one gigantic comet, a shooting star with a shining tail."[39]

Regardless of how one defines the scope of the Kyoto school, the fact remains that the philosophy department in Kyoto was one of the most vigorous intellectual centers of philosophical inquiry in Japan during the 1920s and 1930s. The reason a "Tokyo school of philosophy" was never formed is in part due to Tokyo's sprawling geography. Shimomura Toratarō, who left Kyoto and moved to Tokyo in 1941, observes:

Only after I moved to Tokyo, . . . did I realize the density of the atmosphere of Kyoto. While I was still in Kyoto I thought I was leading a rather vague and uncritical existence, but after I breathed the air in Tokyo I realized that I had been rigorously trained. . . . In Kyoto I was in the ravine among gigantic hills, but in Tokyo I was in an open field. I felt a frank and generous acceptance of the city. But at the same time I sensed a lack of close relationships among people in Tokyo. There was no "center" in Tokyo. Perhaps that was why I felt that scholarly intensity was lacking in Tokyo. In Kyoto professors were unshakable, solid centers. It felt to me as if that breed of people did not exist in Tokyo.[40]

The differences between Kyoto and Tokyo persist today, informing their respective academic traditions. One can thus appreciate the happy union of geographical conditions and dedicated thinkers that brought about what came to be known as the Kyoto school of philosophy.

Chapter 19

Remarriage and Nishida's View of Women

(1927–1931)

Nishida's biggest concern around the time of his retirement was the future of his three daughters, Shizuko, Tomoko, and Umeko. "I have three daughters, all graduated from women's higher school, and the oldest is already twenty-three. I truly would like to see them married,"[1] he wrote to a former student. He felt a heavy responsibility for his daughters, especially now that Kotomi was no longer by his side. His *waka* reveals how he felt in the face of what seemed like a daunting task:

> *There are many things*
> *one should not have*
> *in this world*
> *but at the top of the list*
> *are daughters*[2]

He remembered how complicated it was just to arrange Yayoi's marriage—and at that time Kotomi was there.

Nishida turned to his close friends, colleagues, and former students for help. Half mocking himself, he wrote to Hisamatsu:

Girls are different from boys in that their fate is largely determined by their parents' decisions—although it is true that even when we make a decision that we think is best for them, it may turn out to be the wrong one, and again, we are dealing with life and don't know what tomorrow will bring. For this reason, I want to give them all my love. To this end, sometimes my thoughts run before reality, sometimes I mull things over too much, and sometimes I'm at a loss. Well, after expending all my human follies, when I calmly reflect, I cannot help but laugh at myself.

I suppose that water flows to where it flows, and human affairs take their own course. But just as the water does not always flow without making a whirl, this kind of quandary may be viewed as a beautiful pattern on the flow of human life.[3]

Former students who were consulted on this matter included Hisamatsu, Yamanouchi Tokuryū, Miyake Gōichi (graduate of 1919, then teaching at Tōhoku Imperial University), Kōsaka Masaaki (graduate of 1923), Kimura Motomori (graduate of 1923, then teaching at Hiroshima University of Arts and Sciences), and Katsube Kenzō (graduate of 1914, then teaching at Hiroshima Higher Normal School). Old friends and their families were all behind Nishida to help. Tanabe Hajime's wife, Chiyo, Yamamoto Ryōkichi's wife, Kiku, and the widowed Mrs. Hōjō Masaki each volunteered to have Nishida's daughter(s) stay at their homes and to teach them homemaking and other refinements such as the arts of flower arrangement and tea ceremony, expected of well-bred young women.

Thanks to Ide Takashi, a junior colleague of Kuwaki Gen'yoku, the engagement of Umeko to Kaneko Takezō, then a lecturer of philosophy at Tokyo Imperial University, was arranged in April 1929. Umeko was still a student at Tokyo Women's College at that time.[4] Tomoko had recovered from a life-threatening illness and grew up into a young woman of average health, but she was mentally fragile. Nishida thought "a man of warm heart, who could support her financially," would be best for her.[5] Eventually, through the good offices of Suzuki Daisetz, Kobayashi Zentei, an artist, showed interest in Tomoko, and they were married on October 19, 1930 (the marriage, however, did not last for more than a year, and Tomoko returned home). Shizuko, who had lung trouble, wanted to put off marriage for some time and instead concentrate on her painting. Nishida consented to her wish.

Meanwhile, Yamamoto Ryōkichi and his wife, Kiku, brought up the subject of remarriage to Nishida in November 1929, when he traveled to Tokyo. The Yamamotos had in mind a professor of mathematics. The idea intrigued Nishida, and he talked about it with Iwanami when they went to Nikko the following day. Iwanami understood Nishida's passionate, romantic side,[6] and took a personal interest in finding the right woman for him.

Nishida made up his mind to pursue the possibility of remarriage but sought more a woman of warmth and feelings than a woman of mere common sense.[7] He wrote to Yamamoto in December:

I've given much thought to the matter. If there is truly an ideal woman, that should constitute my supreme happiness. For the last five years, since the death of my wife, I have been totally absorbed in the duty of marrying off my daughters, leaving no time to think about myself. Now that the futures of my daughters are more or less settled, I cannot stand this deep feeling of loneliness that arises from the depths of my soul. I feel as if my mind is standing precariously at a turning point. It is as if my heart, having withstood a decade of hardship, seeks consolation. . . . A woman with considerable cultivation, who understands a life dedicated to scholarly pursuit, would be the most ideal.[8]

There was a vague possibility that a woman friend of the Watsujis was available, but this lady declined Nishida's proposal, feeling she was inadequate for him (see the letter at the end of this chapter). During the rest of 1930, little else occurred on this front.

Nishida's philosophy, however, was acquiring a distinctively personalistic dimension. He wrote the essay "Hyōgenteki jiko no jikogentei" [The self-determination of the expressive self],[9] as well as two other essays, "Basho no jikogentei to shite no ishikisayō" [The operation of consciousness as the self-determination of *topos*], and "Watakushi no zettaimu no jikakuteki gentei to iu mono" [What I call "the self-conscious determination of absolute nothingness"],[10] in which he responds to questions raised by Tanabe Hajime's 1930 article. In "Basho no jikogentei to shite no ishikisayō" Nishida explains that the knowledge of the operation of consciousness cannot be obtained by objective logic but only through the self-determination of the self-conscious individual, or the *topos*; further, that kind of determination is "intuition" or "love." In "Watakushi no zettaimu no jikakuteki gentei to iu mono," he explains that "the determination of nothingness" means "that a fact determines itself," and that "the eternal now" is conceivable as the "shape" of that kind of determination. He further articulates his idea that "all that exists exists in time; beings are temporal" and "real time is the self-determination of the eternal now."[11]

In October Tomoko was married and moved out of the house, leaving Nishida lonelier and the household more neglected.[12] Now only Nishida, Shizuko, and a new and inexperienced maid lived in the large house, which looked so abandoned and so quiet that it was burglarized one night. Nishida realized that he needed more protection[13] and asked his former student Morimoto Kōji, then practicing Zen at Shōkokuji, to come and stay at the house at night.[14]

By 1931 Nishida decided that the time had come to either find the right woman or give up the idea of remarriage.[15] For the sake of his children, he looked for a woman without children.[16] He also felt he was too old just to have "a cozy family person" around him: "I would like to meet a woman of intellectual interests, someone who has her own interests in scholarship or art. Unless the woman has some spiritual and intellectual *(geistig)* interests, she would end up being a sort of housekeeper. I would feel sorry if that happened."[17] Once the image of the kind of woman Nishida was looking for became clear, the place to find such a person naturally became obvious. Nishida thought there might be someone among the professors teaching at the Women's English School (today's Tsuda Women's College) or at the Tokyo Women's Higher Normal School (today's Ochanomizu University).

With the arrival of spring, Japanese nightingales *(uguisu)* began to visit the garden at Asukaichō. Listening to the birds' call, Nishida felt a premonition of things to come:

> *Spring has come*
> *spring must have come*
> *in the morning*
> *when an* uguisu *sings*
> *my heart throbs with hope* [18]

He felt that the long winter days were now giving way to springtime warmth. In March he made a short trip to Tokyo to attend the monthly meeting of the Japanese Academy. After his return to Kyoto on March 19, he began an essay, "Eien no ima no jikogentei" [The self-determination of the eternal now],[19] which he finished on May 16. Earlier, on a sunny May 10 Sunday, Yamanouchi, Hisamatsu, and Ueda Juzō invited Nishida to the green hills of Takao, Makino-o and Togano-o. These three young professors were forming a close friendship, and Nishida endearingly called them *sankori*—"three old foxes and badgers."

From June 1 to 6, Nishida visited Hiroshima, accepting the long-standing invitation of Kimura Motomori, who was then teaching at Hiroshima University of Arts and Sciences and Hiroshima Higher Normal School. There Nishida enjoyed a boat ride, fine food at a riverside restaurant, a visit to the Itsukushima Shrine, and an overnight stay on the beautiful island of Miyajima. He thoroughly enjoyed himself and returned to Kyoto "refreshed."[20] Following his trip to Hiroshima, he wrote "Jikanteki naru mono oyobi hi-jikanteki naru mono" [That which is temporal and that which is atemporal].[21] In this essay,

he unfolds the thesis that everything that exists is temporal and established as the self-determination of the atemporal (i.e., *topos*, or interpersonal love); everything that exists expresses itself as an individual
and social being. Society is born out of the self-determination of love
because individuals find themselves by discarding themselves in the
determination of love. [22]

It was Iwanami who brought good news to Nishida about a woman,
Yamada Koto, a professor at the Women's English School, a baptized
Christian, and a graduate of Vassar College in the United States. Iwanami convinced Nishida that she was someone he ought to meet and
arranged a meeting, which took place on September 7 in Kamakura at
a beach house that belonged to the Women's English School. Yamada
Koto, who showed up in a kimono, was a tidy, attractive woman, young
looking for her age, and her soft makeup was becoming to her. [23]
Nishida's mind was made up at once. Nishida's less than polished
appearance, however, did not give Koto a very favorable first impression.

Nishida returned to Kyoto and began writing letters to Koto, one
after another, in his effort to communicate his sincere feelings to her.
Koto had been briefly married when she was about twenty, but,
because of her poor health, she was sent home soon afterwards and was
only later informed of a one-sided divorce. Nishida's letters gradually
revived her confidence in men. She kept those letters from Nishida in
her kimono folds close to her chest and took them out from time to
time to savor his words. [24] Koto, at first rather reluctant to consider
marriage, was persuaded by Nishida's sincerity. However, she was
assistant to Hoshino Ai, the second principal of the Women's English
School, and could not leave her responsibilities right away. Nishida
and Koto talked about these matters in their letters, and finally on
October 24 "all the outstanding problems were solved." [25]

While he waited for Koto to make up her mind, he wrote another
essay, "Jiai to taai oyobi benshōhō" [Self-love, other-love, and dialec-
tics]. [26] It is easy to see that Nishida's proposal of marriage to Koto
informed his philosophical ideas:

> In contrast to what is usually held, that self-love consists of the satisfac-
> tion of one's desires, I propose to distinguish desires from love. Love
> has to be the property of the person (*jinkakuteki*). The union between
> one person and another must be characterized by the act of "I see thee
> in me, and I see myself in thee." Such a union is established as the con-
> tinuity of discrete elements (*hirenzoku no renzoku*). [27]

When Koto finally accepted his proposal, Nishida wrote to Yama-moto:

> An arrangement with a teacher at Tsuda Women's English School, forty-nine years old,[28] whom Iwanami introduced to me this past summer, is on its way. Despite her long career as a school teacher, she is quite family oriented and well rounded. She has been married once but has no child of her own, and her parents are now both dead. Iwanami inquired into her background with his usual earnestness, and so did I a little. It seems to me that she is not far off the mark.[29]

On November 21 Nishida again wrote to Yamamoto:

> She has accepted my proposal, and I will go through with it. The only thing is, she is assisting the principal of the school and has to wait for her successor, who is currently in the United States, to return in July of next year before she can resign from her position. I thought it best that we get married now and asked her to be with me as much as possible until then. Please relay this news to your wife.[30]

The idea of Koto's staying at her job clearly did not occur to either of them. Such was the general custom of those days. Nishida's poems of this period are most passionate:

Years, months,
and days have gone by
in dark despair but today
I am ecstatic
because of you

Ah, my love
you are in my heart
and I now wish
to live long
for your sake

Far apart
though we are
how I long to see you
every night
in my dreams [31]

On November 11 Nishida began working on a poetic essay, "Gēte no haikei" [The background of Goethe's poetry].[32] He saw similarities between the world of Goethe's poetry and his view of the self-determination of the eternal now: "Time flows from the eternal past to the eternal future; time is born in eternity and disappears in eternity. Everything that takes place in history is shaped over against eternity as its background." To Goethe, nature, rather than "ought," was the ultimate reality and was imbued with the "eternal feminine" *(Das ewig Weibliche)*, and thus embraced humanity and offered salvation. Nishida concluded that the worldview that underlies Oriental culture —"everything arises having no place to arise from, and everything disappears, having no place to disappear to; everything that exists is eternal in its existence"—also informed Goethe's world.[33]

Nishida left for Tokyo on December 7; he and Koto were married on the twelfth.[34] Iwanami gave an intimate party for Nishida and Koto on the thirteenth, introducing Koto to Nishida's friends, including Yamamoto. Koto joined Nishida in Kyoto on December 25. Tanabe Hajime and Chiyo as well as Sotohiko and Asako came to visit and to get to know Koto.

Koto had gone to the United States to study in 1911 with the recommendation of Tsuda Umeko, the founder of the Women's English School. She was already twenty-seven years old when she enrolled in Vassar College. She majored in psychology and was awarded her degree in 1916. In the college yearbook her classmates wrote: "To come from so far away and get into the spirit of V.C. as well as Koto has, shows the strength of mind and broad interests that we all know her to have."[35] Koto was an independent-minded, active woman, but once she married Nishida, she was totally devoted to him. In the morning she would stand behind him to hold up his kimono sleeves while he washed his face; when he had finished, she would offer him a fresh towel; at night she would give him massages to ease his muscles, stiffened from writing and thinking. One day, Koto's niece said to her: "Aunt, do you have to do that much?" to which Koto replied: "Don't you see he is a national treasure to me? There is no one like him."[36]

Koto's warmth and love melted Nishida's heart, and the home atmosphere brightened up as if a spring breeze had blown in. Because no worries now pressed on his mind, Nishida was able to concentrate on his writing to his heart's content. Six of the eleven volumes of Nishida's philosophical writings compiled in *Nishida Kitarō Zenshū* were written after his remarriage—ample testimony to how fully he was able to engage in his work once freed from daily concerns.

Just as Koto was a loving wife to Nishida, he was a loving and responsible husband to her and gave thought to Koto's life after his death. Koto was eligible for half of his pension, with which she should

"The newlyweds," Nishida and Koto in late spring of 1932, in Kamakura. From *Nishida Kitarō Zenshū*, vol. 7, frontispiece.

be able to live well, he concluded.[37] Nishida basked in his happiness with tremendous peace of mind. For the first six months of their marriage, the two lived separately in Tokyo and Kyoto, but they exchanged letters almost daily. From January 30 to February 13, 1932, Nishida gave three public lectures entitled "Sei to jitsuzon to ronri" [Life, existence, and logic][38] at Kyoto Imperial University, in which he explains how logic (i.e., philosophical thought) is not divorced from life and existence, and how what is usually considered "biological life" is actually "personal" and "dialectical" as an expression of "love" (or agape) in the "eternal now," or radical temporality. On March 17 he finished his essay, "Jiyūishi" [The free will].[39] Soon after that, on March 22, he visited Koto in Tokyo. Hoshino Ai had invited him to the Women's English School as a special guest to give a talk at the commencement ceremony.

Because Nishida's life and thought are interwoven, his view of women merits consideration. True to his family tradition, he never failed to encourage his daughters to obtain a good education. He was especially hopeful for his eldest daughter, Yayoi, and taught her the roman alphabet at home while she was still a kindergarten pupil. By the time she was in the fourth or fifth grade, he had her reading such books as *Nihongaishi* (a history of Japan by Rai Sanyō, written entirely in Chinese characters), and *Taketori monogatari* [The tale of the bamboo cutter] and *Kokinshū* [Anthology of ancient and recent poems], both written in classical Japanese.[40] When Yayoi passed the entrance examination to the Tokyo Women's Higher Normal School, he was delighted. At the end of each school holiday he always saw her off at the Shichijō station; on those occasions Yayoi could not help but keenly feel his unconditional support for her pursuit of learning:

At the end of vacation when I had to go back to school in Tokyo, it was always a time when students returned to Tokyo all at once. The entrance gate, where you had to show your ticket and have it punched, was always extremely crowded, everyone pushing and shoving everyone else. It was not easy for someone like me, who was brought up as a gentle female, to mingle with male students and pass through the entrance gate quickly. In the summer, father was always clad in a simple white cotton kimono, with a long muslin sash casually tied around his body. In that casual attire, he would walk into the crowd, carrying my luggage, and wait for me to come through the entrance gate, however long it would take. Knowing how he would prefer to steal a moment to read books and think about his ideas, I felt terribly sorry for his having to waste his time like this. If I said, "I will carry the luggage, father," he would curtly say "no." I can never forget how he stood in line before me, holding a white entrance ticket at the Shichijō station. When at last I would get inside the train and turn my face toward him over the window, or even when the whistles blew and I politely bowed my head and said, "So long," my father said not a word and would not even show any gesture of farewell. He silently stood there, watching me. During my four years of schooling in Tokyo, no one else but my father saw me off at the station.[41]

When Yayoi graduated, the next question was whether she was going to earn her living as an academic or get married. She had no confidence in her ability to support herself; besides, she came under the influence of Shimoda Jirō,[42] who upheld the traditional virtue of "good wife, wise mother." She was convinced that it was better for her to be married. From that point on, Nishida stopped recommending books to her.[43] Years later, he noted that if Yayoi had been given an opportunity, she might have become an accomplished poet or short-story writer.[44]

Among Nishida's female relatives was a niece, Takahashi Fumi, who became a scholar.[45] Fumi was born on July 26, 1901 (the same year as Sotohiko), as the second daughter of Takahashi Yoshitarō and Sumi. She graduated from Tokyo Women's College in 1925. Prompted by her desire for further learning, she applied for, and was accepted by, Tōhoku Imperial University and majored in philosophy. She wrote her thesis on "Plato's *Idea* as seen in the *Phaedo*" and graduated in 1929 with her second B.A. As the first woman of the Ishikawa Prefecture to get a B.A. from an imperial university, Fumi instantly became a role model for the young Ishikawaite women. Fumi taught at Miyagi Prefecture Women's Normal School in Sendai for a few years, then at Jiyūgakuen and at the School of Economics for Women in Tokyo. She continued her philosophical writing, and one of her articles, "Supinoza ni okeru kobutsu no ninshiki ni tsuite" [Recognition of the individual according to Spinoza],[46] was published in the May issue of *Bunka*, a journal of the Association for Humanities (Bunkakai) at Tōhoku Imperial University.

In 1936 Fumi won a scholarship of 1,000 yen offered by Iwanami Shigeo that enabled her to go to Germany to study.[47] After improving her German by attending a language school in Berlin, she moved in April 1938 to the University of Freiburg, where she studied with Martin Heidegger. In the unsettling days immediately preceding the outbreak of the Second World War, she was forced to give up her study and leave Germany. She was on the last boat that left in September 1939, evacuating the Japanese living in Germany and other northern European countries.[48] While in Freiburg, Fumi was in the company of three other Japanese scholars, one of whom was Nishitani Keiji. On one September day in 1938, she invited them over for dinner at her house in Güntalstahl where she rented a room. She cooked a Japanese meal, which the young Nishitani was never to forget; the deliciousness of the rice that he tasted in a foreign land made him think about the weight of tradition, about the Japanese "blood" that he had inherited from his ancestors.[49]

Whenever Nishida wrote to Nishitani in Germany, he would ask about Fumi and would say a word or two about her: "Since her childhood, she has always been a tomboy, and sometimes she says too much and is too saucy. But she is good-hearted."[50] Nishitani came to see Fumi as "an exceptional person, who was not afraid of things and did not care about what people around her said. Her speech and manners were sometimes bold and occasionally rough, but beneath the surface was her exceedingly gentle spirit and feminine sensitivity."[51] While in Germany, Fumi translated Nishida's 1934 essay "Keijijōgakuteki tachiba kara mita tōzai kodai no bunka keitai" [The forms of ancient cultures, East and West, seen from a metaphysical perspective] into German as "Die morgenländischen und abendländischen Kulturformen in alter Zeit vom metaphysischen Standpunkte ausgesehen" (published in *Abhandlungen der Preussischen Akademie der Wissenschaft* in 1939). After her return to Japan, Fumi translated Nishida's 1921 essay "Shinzenbi no gōitsuten" [The unity of the true, the good, and the beautiful] as "Die Einheit des Wahren, des Schönen und des Guten."[52] Fumi had contracted tuberculosis while in Germany, and, despite her fight against it, she died on June 21, 1945, cutting her promising life short at the age of forty-three.

Nishida supported a woman's having her own profession. When Shizuko decided to take up painting instead of marriage, he wholeheartedly stood by her decision. Many years before, when Beatrice Lane (Mrs. Daisetz Suzuki) was about to arrive in Japan in 1911, he had looked for a job for her, writing to his friend Tanabe Ryūji, who was teaching at the Women's Division of Gakushūin: "She has some teaching experience at the college level abroad; I understand she can speak both German and French, and her personality is very affable. I dearly wish to find a job for her. If you have some connection, would you please help her?"[53] Later, after the Suzukis had moved to Kyoto in 1921, whenever Nishida would hear of a job opening, he always thought of Beatrice.[54] In Yayoi's case, if she had not chosen marriage, he might have looked for a job rather than a husband for her.

Nishida's attitude toward women was profoundly shaped by his mother, Tosa. When Hisamatsu Shin'ichi's mother was ill, Hisamatsu, a filial son, took a leave from his teaching at the university and went home to take care of her. This tormented Hisamatsu and made him think about resigning from his teaching position. Nishida told him not to worry about "trivial things" such as his teaching and to "concentrate on looking after" his mother, because the university ought to understand that sort of human situation.[55] For Nishida, Tosa always came before his scholarly obligations. When he was in Kanazawa looking after his sick mother, he was not able to concentrate on an article that he had promised to *Geibun* and asked for Ueda Juzō's understanding.[56] Nishida imparted this sense of respect to his students; for instance, when Yamanouchi Tokuryū was in Freiburg, he wrote to him: "I hear you don't write much to your mother, Sadako. Why don't you write some letters? Women tend to feel lonely."[57]

Nishida acknowledged that women felt differently from men and resolved to "take into consideration women's feelings and perspectives,"[58] especially when it came to personal decisions, such as Yayoi's engagement and marriage. Nishida wished to understand female psychology and avidly read such authors as Ibsen, the Brontë sisters, George Eliot, and others.[59] On one occasion, Nishida requested Omodaka Hisayuki, then studying in Paris, to send him a French translation of D. H. Lawrence's *Lady Chatterley's Lover*, which was then censored and unavailable in Japan.[60] Omodaka, not knowing what kind of book it was, went to Vrin Bookstore, which specialized in technical books, and inquired of the proprietor whether he carried the book; thereupon the proprietor burst out laughing and said, "Monsieur Omodaka reads that kind of book?"[61]

Nishida always appreciated women who possessed a spirit of freedom and dignity, just as he appreciated such qualities in men and cultivated them in his own youth. A biography of Florence Nightingale elicited from him both admiration and self-criticism. He was deeply impressed by her "noble intention and ability"—and then looked into himself: "It is indeed a petty thing to dwell on my personal fame and such things. Is there anyone today in this world who works with her passion, sincerity, and empathy?"[62]

From a Letter to Watsuji Tetsurō *

Dear Mr. and Mrs. Watsuji Tetsurō,

My book, *Self-conscious structure of the universal*, has come out, and I'm sending you a copy. I am terribly sorry about the recent confusion involving Miss Ibuki, regarding my remarriage. I fear I troubled you extremely. . . .

From time to time I find myself profoundly lonely and I long for intimacy. I possess many human weaknesses and am a dreamer. I like people to see me for what I am. With Montaigne, I would like to say: "They who do not rightly know themselves may feed themselves with false approbation; not I who see myself, and who examine myself to my very bowels, and who very well know what is my due, I am content to be less commended, provided I am better known. I may be reputed a wise man in such a sort of wisdom as I take to be folly." If I have to endure my present circumstances, however, I am willing to do so and put up with loneliness.

Regarding my wish for remarriage, people find it odd only because

---

*Letter no. 595, 4 January 1930, NKZ 18:396–98.

they put emphasis on the sexual aspect of it. Must an ideal old man be put in the care of his daughter-in-law and spend the rest of his life playing with his grandchildren? I hold the view that it is perfectly fine to want to improve myself as long as I live and to pursue whatever possibilities I have. Is that such a wicked thing to desire?

I would like someone to comfort my spirit and to take care of me with a warm heart, for I am by nature lazy and tend to be melancholic. I must admit, however, that so far I have met no such person. The fact is, I haven't given enough thought to the whole thing.

If I were a Zen monk or a Catholic priest, I suppose celibacy would be important, but for me, it is not so. Although I certainly have a deep-seated longing for a religious life, a merely formal religious life that denies humanity is not something that I would embrace. I don't even think that such is the ideal human existence. What I mean by "nothing-ness" (*mu*) is closer to the warm heart that Shinran possessed, which acknowledges everyone's freedom and embraces every sinner (although I don't know whether Shinran actually put it into words in this way).

While I appreciate Eastern culture as profound and precious, I cannot deny my longing for Western culture, which is a great develop-ment of rich and free humanity. Just as I derive pleasure from Sesshū's paintings or poetry in Chinese, so I cannot help but be moved by the paintings of Rembrandt or the poetry of Goethe. Instead of deriding the old Goethe who, having fallen in love with young Ulrike von Levetzow, desired to marry her, I am touched by the greatness of his humanity. From this sort of perspective, I should say of what has hap-pened: "The dream I had was an illusion, and yet I feel for her." Of course, please don't take it realistically. . . . I'm truly sorry about what happened. Please communicate my sincere apology to Miss Ibuki. I cannot apologize enough, I know

Yours ever,
Nishida

*Even the Cat Is Dead**

Even the cat is dead.

Since the marriage of one of my daughters [Tomoko] took place suddenly, I now live in a large house with a daughter and a maid. Dur-ing the day, the area around the house is quite noisy, since there is an

---

* "Danro no soba kara" [From beside the fireplace], *The Muse* 11.6 (March 1931), 223; NKZ 12:183–84. Nishida was very fond of cats.

elementary school and a public market nearby. But at night, it is dead silent. One member of the house sleeps in the room on the second floor, the other in the Japanese room on the first floor, and the third in the kitchen—we have separate places to sleep. One does not get the feeling that the three people live under one roof.

On the day of the general cleaning last year, a tomcat wandered into our house from nowhere. Its body was a bit too long, but its fur was a beautiful tiger color, so we adopted it as our house cat. It was then merely a kitten, just about a month or two old, but has recently grown considerably—to draft age! It was quite adorable. In the morning, it would go into the empty warm bed, as we got up, and take a nap, sticking its head out of the bedding. During the day, it would stretch its body on the veranda in the autumn sun or come to play with our feet. During meals, it would either sit on top of the container that keeps the cooked rice warm, keeping a watchful eye over us while we ate, or else it would sit facing us, its back against the dining table. My daughter is a painter, and there being no common topic of conversation between us, every movement of the cat became the center of our talk, and unexpected laughter would rise from it—a small ripple in a quiet pond in the forest. The cat was fine until three days ago and was basking in the sunshine in the veranda as if he owned the place. But it must have eaten something poisonous somewhere—it became sick suddenly. We found it dead this morning under the eves.

The death of a cat—nothing special. But in my lonely household, I feel like crying: "Even the cat is dead!"

On a certain dark stormy wintry day, when King Alfred was talking with priests, a bird flew into the room from one window and the next moment out the other. I remember having read this story in some history of Britain when I was a child, and that the king and priests discussed from whence that small bird had come and to where it went, for the bird in a way symbolized human existence. That cat, too: from where did it come and to where did it disappear? It is all like a dream.

(February 17, 1931)

Chapter 20

Development of Personalist Dialectics

(1932–1934)

By December 1931 Nishida had finally found his long-sought personal happiness. In stark contrast, ominous events were beginning to cloud Japanese politics. In August 1931 former prime minister Hamaguchi Osachi died of the gunshot wound inflicted a year earlier by an assassin. On September 18 an unauthorized military démarche, known as the Manchurian incident, broke out, marking the beginning of the so-called Fifteen Years War. On December 13 the second Wakatsuki cabinet dissolved after only eight months of existence, and Inukai Tsuyoshi became prime minister. Japan was moving into a period of political turmoil at home and an aggressive military campaign abroad.

On April 16, 1932, Nishida moved to Kamakura, where he rented a house in the Ōgigayatsu area for six months. Kamakura not only offered him a warmer winter, it was much closer to Tokyo, where Koto was still working. As soon as he settled in, he began working on the essay "Watakushi to nanji" [I and thou]. In this essay Nishida develops his philosophy of the person (*jinkaku*) as a dialectical reality, going beyond the Kantian philosophy of a person as an ethical entity. He unfolds the view that each of us is sustained by a personal I-Thou relationship, in which the body is more than just a mere material reality—it is the vehicle that enables interpersonal confrontation and communication. Each personal existence is determined by the absolute other (thou): at the bottom of my existence I am directly open to and connected with thee. We are each open in the depths of our being directly to the other and to the world. In this way, each individual person is irreducible and yet a member of society, just as each temporal moment is independent and yet forms a certain "flow of time." We always exist in the environment—whether natural (biological), social, or historical. In our personal existence, the environment bears a personal significance as something with which we engage in a personal dialogue. Environmental concerns are human concerns in the "personal" world. Nishida's interest in the theological thought of Karl Barth and Friedrich Gogarten[1] informs his dialectical personalism, while the Mahāyāna Buddhist assertion of the radical interdependence and interpenetration of individuals sustains his fundamental position. Without love the world of persons is incomplete. Ultimately the "Thou," the universal, has the significance of agape. Absolute nothingness that embraces you and me is agape. You and I both exist in this historical world as its creative agents, bearing witness to *creatio ex nihilo*.[2]

On May 15 Prime Minister Inukai was shot to death at his official residence by a group of young military officers in a coup attempt. The news shook the entire country. Nishida wrote to Yamamoto: "The shooting of the prime minister by the military—it is as if there is no state control. I wonder what will be the fate of the new cabinet."[3] The so-called May 15 incident seemed more like a fluke than a part of larger things to come. Although the social unrest soon died down, it nevertheless gave the Department of Police *(keishichō)* a good excuse to establish a "higher special police force" *(tokubetsu kōtō keisatsubu)*. *Tokkō*, for short, the "thought police" had branches throughout the country to monitor social "disturbances."

Nishida's presence in Kamakura came as a boon to his former students living in the Tokyo area. Miki Kiyoshi, Tosaka Jun, Tanikawa Tetsuzō, Miyake Gōichi, and Mutai Risaku were among the callers that spring. Graduates of Sansanjuku, Kawai Yoshinari, now a successful industrialist, and Ōsaka Motokichirō, an independent theologian and Christian minister, also visited him after not having seen him for more than two decades. On June 4, at the request of Tanikawa and Miki, Nishida gave a talk at Hōsei University at its spring philosophical meeting. He attracted a huge audience, more than one thousand,[4] which he did not expect and was disconcerted by,[5] feeling that his philosophical reflections were incompatible with so public a display. Nevertheless, Nishida was becoming a "people's philosopher" over and beyond the academic walls.

Ōsaka Motokichirō was writing a religion column for the *Yomiuri Newspaper*, through his connection with his friend from the Fourth Higher School days, Shōriki Matsutarō, who was president of the Yomiuri Newspaper Company. Ōsaka got to know Miki through Nishida, and the two organized discussion meetings for the newspaper. They invited Miyamoto Shōson, Kumano Yoshitaka, Murata Shirō, Honjō Yoshimune, Kuwata Hidenobu, and Ishihara Atsushi to join the discussions with Nishida. The first session was held in June, the second in July, both at Nishida's rented house in Ōgigayatsu. When published in the newspaper, the discussions received tremendous public response.

Around the time of the discussion sessions, Nishida was working on the essay "Sei no tetsugaku ni tsuite" [On the philosophy of life],[6] a condensed version of his previous essay, "Watakushi to nanji."[7] In September he was invited to Shinshū to give lectures on the "concept of person as the foundation of reality"[8] to the group of elementary and secondary schoolteachers who had been studying philosophy with Nishida as their teacher.

Tosaka Jun, in his 1932 article on the emergence of the Kyoto school (see chapter 18), criticizes Nishida's thought as "merely an attempt to establish a transhistorical hermeneutical system that deals with meanings and interpretive categories." Tosaka argues that Nishida's notion of the "practical" does not "rid itself of ethical characteristics that are strictly applicable only to the individual" and thus remains "indifferent to the actual problems of production or politics."[9] In response to Tosaka, Nishida wrote:

> What I have written so far may appear to you to be nothing more than a hermeneutical exercise. Besides, I have yet to write about my view of "praxis" [action]. But I can say this much—it will be different from conventional views of action. Moreover, I believe it is necessary to clarify first of all fundamental concepts, such as matter, sensation, the self, consciousness, society, history, and even the concept of action, before going into the general discussion of "action". Insofar as we use these words, we are obliged to know what we mean by them.
>
> I am not a Marxist. I think Marxists tend to be one-sided *(einseitig)* and not thorough. But I will accept any reasonable points they offer. Therefore, I welcome the kind of criticism you raised in your article.
>
> I've sent you an offprint of my essay, "Sei no tetsugaku ni tsuite."
> . . . I don't think the theological references I've made therein would please you, but I hope you will recognize the fact that I did advance my own view of what a person *(jinkaku)* is.[10]

Nishida's interest in developing a philosophy of the person was part of his effort to establish a larger comprehensive dialectical logic. He was prompted to develop his dialectical logic by the criticisms of not only Tosaka and other Marxist colleagues but also Tanabe Hajime. Nishida was thus shifting his focus from the analysis of "self-consciousness" (which was bound to be centered on human subjectivity) to the nature of "expression" *(hyōgen)*, "action-intuition" *(kōiteki-chok-kan)*, and "dialectics" *(benshōhō)*. The scope of his inquiry into the interpersonal relationship of "I and thou" was none other than the horizon of the "historical world."

Sometime in July, Koto finally joined Nishida, having seen through the transfer of her school duties to her successor. After enjoying their first summer months together in Kamakura, they returned to Kyoto on September 10. On October 30, the wedding of Umeko to Kaneko Takezō took place at Marunouchi Kaikan in Tokyo. This event briefly took Nishida and Koto to Tokyo, but Nishida had to return to Kyoto quickly because he had many engagements to give lectures at Ōtani University, Dōshisha University, and Ryūkoku University.

By the fall of 1932 selection of the imperial minister *(kunai-daijin)* became a sensitive issue, and pressure from the ultranationalist camp was mounting to place Hiranuma Kiichirō[11] in the position, a move both Nishida and Yamamoto opposed. Nishida still had Harada Kumao as his direct link to the backstage of politics. Yamamoto personally knew the members of the board of directors of Musashi Higher School, which included such illustrious figures as Yamakawa Ken-jirō,[12] Okada Ryōhei, and Ichiki Kitokurō.[13] Nishida and Yamamoto were concerned about Hiranuma's rise to power, especially because imperial minister was one of two posts—the other was lord keeper of the privy seal, *nai-daijin*—independent of the cabinet system. The appointees stayed in their posts as long as possible to secure the stability of the imperial court. Nishida expressed his concern to Yamamoto:

> I've heard that the Imperial Minister Ichiki [Kitokurō] may resign soon. It will be rather difficult to find his successor. Should Ichiki resign, I think it is clear that Hiranuma will gain power. But I am totally against Hiranuma for that post. For the imperial family to be connected with the camp of reactionary ideology is incomparably the most dangerous thing. Given the present-day political climate, I think that, for the position of the lord keeper of the privy seal and the minister of imperial affairs, fair and generous-minded men, who are versed in world affairs and able to envision the distant future of the country, should be appointed.
>
> While a tentative appointment will do for prime minister, when it comes to the lord keeper of the privy seal and the imperial minister, the question is not that simple. They should by all means find outstanding men. Once they identify such men, they should implore them to dedicate themselves to the job. Otherwise, I too am worried about the

imperial family and feel sorry for the future of the country. Shimizu [Tōru] is not a bad choice, since he is an earnest man, but he is not flexible enough.[14]

In this same letter to Yamamoto, Nishida revealed his criticism of the Center for National Spiritual Culture *(Kokumin seishin bunka ken-kyūjo)*, just established on August 23 by the Ministry of Education. The mission of the center was essentially to implant nationalistic-imperialistic ideology through the education system.[15] One of the founding members of the center was Kihira Tadayoshi, who had edited Nishida's *Zen no kenkyū* years before. The relationship between Nishida and Kihira was now irrevocably strained. In face of bureaucrats meddling in the sphere of ideas, Nishida renewed his commitment to the education of promising young people:

> What the Ministry of Education tries to advocate in the name of "spiritual culture" *(seishin bunka)* is no good. From now on I intend to write as much as I can, as long as my strength lasts. I want to gather young bright students around me, and by engaging them in discussions and debates, I want to train them intellectually. If I can make even a small difference intellectually and as a scholar, I should be content.[16]

Because Nishida was often away from Kyoto, the graduates who remained in the Kyoto-Osaka area began to call on him whenever he returned to Kyoto. His daily life was filled with visitors, whose company he enjoyed. In December 1932 his latest book, *Mu no jikakuteki gentei* [The self-conscious determination of nothingness],[17] was published by Iwanami. Nishida felt that with the essays contained in this book, his "tortuous struggle," which had begun in the second half of the *Hataraku mono kara miru mono e* [From that which acts to that which sees] (1926) and continued into the *Ippansha no jikakuteki taikei* [The self-conscious structure of the universal] (1930), had come to an end.[18] He now had a good idea of how his dialectical logic was shaping up.

In his next essay, "Keijijōgaku joron" [Prolegomena to metaphysics],[19] Nishida unfolds his view that "dialectical logic is possible only from the standpoint of the active self in its social and historical context." According to Nishida, "dialectical logic" leads to the self-identity of two absolutely contradicting entities, whether the individual and the universal or the grammatical subject and the grammatical predicate. Nishida attempts to define dialectical subjectivity by clarifying the meaning of self-identity; he formulates his view of the self-identical as "an individual for whom its relationship to itself is simultaneously its relationship to the absolute other." Nishida's view of the individual is ever more firmly established: "the individual is an individual only by facing another individual," and "an individual's boundaries are determined only in relation to another individual."[20] His aim in this essay is to make clear that the determination of a truly concrete universal is the self-determination of the dialectical universal. He felt that the essay provided "a logical foundation for the mutual determination of individuals," which is none other than the "determination of the *topos.*"[21]

In 1933 the Takigawa incident (also known as the University of Kyoto incident) shook the Faculty of Law at Kyoto Imperial University. Takigawa Yukitoki, a professor of law, came under attack by ultranationalists and their political allies. In January and February 1933 Minoda Muneki[22] of the Genri Nipponsha[23]—an association of right-wing intellectuals established in 1925—accused Takigawa of propagating Marxist ideology in his textbook on penal law. This issue was brought up at the Diet, and under the pressure of ultranationalists to fire the "red professor," minister of education Hatoyama Ichirō forced Takigawa's resignation, ignoring the defense of Takigawa by the president of the university, Konishi Shigenao.[24] Nishida feared that the problem might escalate and involve the entire law faculty.[25] Indeed, on May 23 the law professors unanimously voted that they would resign en masse unless the ministry rescinded its earlier demand. Hatoyama stuck to his hard-line position; he was ready to "close down the university for the sake of an ideological issue like this one."[26] On May 26 thirteen assistant and full professors resigned, including Takigawa Yukitoki, Sasaki Sōichi, Moriguchi Shigeharu, Miyamoto Hideo, Suekawa Hiroshi, and Tsunetō Kyō. Regarding this incident, Nishida wrote to Hori Koretaka on June 5:

> The dispute at Kyoto University has gotten out of hand now. It is indeed worrisome. Although I feel sorry for Mr. Konishi, he is not a man capable of handling a crisis like this one as a university president. I cannot defend Takigawa that much, but there seem to be damning rumors circulating about him, instigated by a man called Minoda. . . . It appears that the Ministry of Education is making all sorts of excuses, with the hope that if Takigawa resigns, all will be well.[27]

The incident ignited student protests beyond the campus of Kyoto to Tokyo and Tōhoku Imperial Universities, but the home ministry adopted harsh measures to suppress them, and on June 20 the police arrested Marxist students in Kyoto. In addition, the university canceled the remaining classes and entered a long summer vacation. Students dispersed as they returned to their homes, and the inflammatory protest was effectively extinguished.

The incident is evaluated today as "the last significant battle to protect the fort of liberalism from the assaults of fascism in the early Showa period."[28] There were those, including Iwanami Shigeo and Miki Kiyoshi,[29] who saw the devastating implications of this incident even at that time. Nishida, generally unimpressed by Takigawa's conduct, is said to have maintained that "we cannot close down the university for the sake of one Takigawa."[30] An indignant Iwanami approached Tanabe Hajime and Watsuji Tetsurō to muster their support, only to receive a less than lukewarm response. Lack of reaction from the intellectual community made Iwanami extremely upset, and he told Abe Yoshishige that the intellectuals were creating a precedent of giving in to the irrational demands of the military and the ultranationalists. Iwanami submitted a letter of protest to the *Tokyo Asahi Newspaper*, defending Takigawa and his book, but the newspaper turned down the letter with the excuse that it did not contain "sufficient information."[31] As a form of protest, Iwanami published a collection of papers and position statements written by seven of the professors who had resigned from the university. Sasaki Sōichi, who edited the volume, wrote that the volume was "to commit to our memory what happened, in view of the importance of the social and cultural impact that this incident will inevitably have."[32] The book, *Kyōdai jiken* [Kyoto University incident], was published in November 1933.

On a wider horizon, 1933 saw the burning of books by the Nazis in Berlin on May 10. In protest, Miki, Hasegawa Nyozekan, and other leading Japanese journalists and intellectuals wrote letters to the press. Tanabe Hajime, who had learned of Heidegger's "Rector Address," excerpts of which had been printed in the leading German newspaper, *Vossische Zeitung*, wrote a critique of Heidegger. Tanabe's "Kiki no tetsugaku ka, tetsugaku no kiki ka" [Is it a philosophy of crisis, or is it a crisis of philosophy?][33] was carried in the *Asahi Newspaper*, October 4–6. Tanabe identifies Heidegger's stance as "Aristotelian *theōrein*"— that of a simple observer unable to affect the course of politics, in contrast to the political stance associated with Plato, which is connected to concrete actions in the political sphere. Terming Plato's stance the "philosophy born of crisis," Tanabe describes Heidegger's thought as one leading to the "crisis of philosophy," for it allows one to "interpret the political necessity of the present as a necessity of fate and tolerates only abstract philosophy." Japanese intellectuals, many of whom had spent some time in Germany as scholars abroad, generally shared this critical opinion of the cultural politics of the Nazis.

Nishida, too, commented on this worldwide phenomena that attempted to "crush high culture" in a May 28 interview conducted by Ōsaka for the *Yomiuri Newspaper*. By mentioning the lofty cultural achievements of Germans in the areas of music, theater, and philosophy (especially Kant), Nishida argues that the Nazis' cultural agenda, precisely because of its lopsidedness and political motivatation, could not destroy the genuine cultural achievements of Germans. He points out the irony of the Nazis' anti-Semitic campaign: because the two most influential modern ideological forces—capitalism and communism—are the products of Jewish thinkers David Ricardo and Karl Marx. He also notes how impoverished the world of thought would be without Bergson and Einstein.[34] A few years later, in 1936, Nishida criticized the current state of Japanese educational and scholarly policies, which were patterned after the Nazis' model. Although Germany, with its "splendid world-class cultural heritage" might be able to get by with the Nazis' educational policy for the time being, Nishida felt that the situation was quite otherwise in Japan, and he urged the Japanese to think seriously about their educational and academic policies.[35] Nishida's admiration of German cultural heritage remained with him for life. When he learned of Edmund Husserl's death in 1938,[36] he expressed his sympathy for his last years[37] and lamented the passage of a "great thinker of the early twentieth century."[38]

Through Harada Kumao, Nishida renewed his old acquaintanceship with Kido Kōichi and Konoe Ayamaro, who were then becoming prominent in the political world as the "court group" (*jūshin*), a group of aristocrats actively engaged in politics. In March 1933, when Nishida spent about ten days in Kamakura, he was invited to lunch at Konoe Ayamaro's place along with Kido, Harada, and Oda Nobuhiro. Konoe had been vice speaker of the House of Peers since 1931 and was moving ever closer to the center of parliamentary politics. Kido had served as secretary to the imperial minister since 1930 and was working for the imperial household. Oda was a member of the House of Peers. Harada, as noted earlier, had been working for Saionji Kinmochi since 1926. Konoe, Kido, and Harada, known as "Saionji's three favorites," represented the younger progressive generation of the aristocracy. They began to solicit Nishida's opinions.

If Nishida was yet to articulate it, he already knew deep down that genuine cultural achievements, including philosophy, as exemplified by Plato's and Aristotle's thought, had an eternal life of their own, and that those human achievements made humanity what it was. As he saw cultural suppression by brutal political forces, he strengthened his conviction that the contribution he could make as a thinker was in the area of pure philosophical inquiry.[39] The more insane the world grew, the clearer his mission became.

On April 3 he began writing "Watakushi to sekai" [I and the world],[40] in which he argues that the Husserlian view of *noema* (the objective content of consciousness) and *noesis* (the intentional operation of consciousness) as diametrically opposed is only a formal representation of reality intellectually conceived, and that from the standpoint of the active self, "*noesis* always contains *noema*."[41] Moreover, the "self" is something conceived as the noetic determination of the creative self-determining world. The world determines itself as the sociohistorical world, which is in constant progression. Our individual selves—as independent and free individuals—exist only in relation to the self-determination of this sociohistorical world.[42] In this essay, Nishida shifts his focus of investigation from the "self-conscious self" to the "world." He further clarifies this inquiry in his next essay, "Sōsetsu" [General discussion].[43] These essays are compiled in *Tetsugaku no konpon mondai* [The fundamental problems of philosophy], published on December 25, 1933.[44]

Ever since his first stay in Kamakura in the winter of 1928, Nishida had been looking for property to purchase there.[45] In the spring of 1933 Iwanami found a perfect house for Nishida in Ubagayatsu, on a hill only a few hundred meters away from Shichirigahama beach on the Bay of Sagami. Konoe and Harada insisted that they buy the house for Nishida as a present, and so they did.[46] Nishida and Koto spent their first summer in this house from August to mid-October. Nishida missed having a study, so he and Koto added a few rooms to the house that summer. While in Kamakura, he gave a guest lecture at Hōsei University[47] on the "World of Action"[48] and at Keiō University, probably on a similar topic.

In November he gave lectures at Ōtani University on "Genjitsu no sekai no ronriteki kōzō" [The logical structure of the actual world].[49] He was then working on an essay with the same title,[50] in which he develops his thesis that the actual world is the world of action (praxis), "where we are born, work, and die." This actual world always has "a twofold significance," corresponding to the grammatical-subject aspect and the grammatical-predicate aspect, or the objective world and the subjective world, or still again, the material aspect and the mental-spiritual aspect.[51] This world is "the many as the self-negation of the One, and it is the One as the self-negation of the many." The contours of Nishida's dialectical philosophy began to emerge.

By 1934 Nishida's view of the actual historical world expanded to embrace a global perspective. The rise to power of Hitler in Europe and domestic problems in Japan, such as the Kyoto University incident, no doubt sharpened his political awareness. On New Year's Day, 1934, he composed one of his best-known *waka* poems:

Hito wa hito
ware wa ware nari
tonikakuni
waga yuku michi o
ware wa yukunari

People are people
I am I
unperturbed
I take the path
I take [52]

This poem is today inscribed on a stone monument and placed along the "philosophic path" that stretches from the Nanzenji to the Gingakuji area along the Lake Biwa minicanal, where Nishida used to take walks. Expressed in this *waka* was his determination to proceed on his own philosophical path. It could be viewed as a statement made in response not only to Tanabe's criticism of his philosophy but also to the general trend of the Japanese philosophical world of that time. Nishida was critical of Japanese academics who were just following the European thinkers. His letter to Miyake Gōichi, who had studied with Heidegger in Freiburg, 1929–1931, expresses his concerns:

Although I respect Heidegger's work, I do not believe that his philosophy is the answer to the truly profound problems of humanity. Japanese scholars devour books by German thinkers, borrow their methods, and use them skillfully, without, however, being truly sustained by their serious philosophical reflections. If this continues to be the practice, the Japanese will forever remain emulators. How could we expect to see a philosophical system that is born out of the depth of our own lives? Japanese thinkers need to engage in the mutual exchange of their views, read what their colleagues write, and establish a *Publikum*, a public forum. A philosophical tradition is not something that is established by the work of one single individual, but it takes a community of thinkers.[53]

From January 5 to 7, Nishida gave lectures to the elementary and secondary school teachers from Shinshū on the topic "Kōi no sekai" [The world of action].[54] His conclusion argues that "Japan must consider its mission as a country in the international world, and educational goals must be set by taking in this vision of Japan's role in the global world."[55] During his stay in Kamakura from February 8 through March 14, he gave a talk at the invitation of Kuwata Hidenobu on February 22 at Japan Christian Seminary at Tsunohazu in Tokyo on the "logical structure of the actual world."[56]

On March 13, the day before he was to leave Kamakura for Kyoto, he wrote to Harada, expressing his concern that Japanese politicians were motivated by the thought of Japan's profit, not its international obligations and duties:

> For Japanese politicians to consider world affairs with the Japanese interest as the central concern certainly makes sense, but they have to think of Japan not as something that exists in itself but as a nation existing in the world. Otherwise, such a slogan as "Greater Asianism" *(dai-ajia-shugi)* makes no sense. Contrary to some schools of thought that maintain that the future of the world depends on independent countries permeated by nationalism, I rather think that it will depend on a global collaboration. I suspect that the real worries of each nation actually stem from this pressing reality. I wish Japanese politicians recognized this fact.[57]

In 1934 ultranationalistic forces began to dominate the opinion of the day, to the cost of other views. One such example is the violent attack on Ōsaka Motokichirō, who was one of those who actively objected to making Shinto the "National Faith." In late March he was abducted in a car by Imaizumi Teisuke, the head of the Society Revering Grand Shrines *(Jingū hōsaikai)*, and taken to the grand shrine at Iidabashi. A group of gangsters, hired by Imaizumi, surrounded Ōsaka, while Imaizumi forced him to kneel down on the ground facing the main building of the shrine, and then made him bow to it as a gesture of apology. When Ōsaka resisted, the hired gangsters physically forced him to take that posture and delivered karate chops to his ribs. Imaizumi and his group took him farther in a car to Meiji Jingū Gaien and inflicted on him every possible physical injury. Ōsaka suffered complications from injuries to his ribs and required several operations. He had to fight for his life and remained in intensive care for months.[58] In the fall, having heard what happened to Ōsaka, the concerned Nishida visited him in the hospital. It was becoming a dangerous world for outspoken people of conviction.

A string of movements advancing the ultranationalist agenda continued to follow. On March 22, 1934, a committee on the Japanese language decided on the official pronunciation of Japan as "Nippon" (as opposed to "Nihon"), perhaps for its more decisive sound. On June 1 the "Department of Thought Control" *(Shisōkyoku)* was established within the Ministry of Education. On June 5 the state funeral of navy admiral Tōgō Heihachirō, hero of the Russo-Japanese War, was held, pushing even further back the memory of Meiji period. On June 6 a professor and dean of the law faculty at Tokyo Imperial University, Suehiro Izutarō, was indicted for the crimes of having violated the public peace ordinance, lèse-majesté, and the constitution. Then Tosaka Jun was fired in August from his lecturer's position at Hōsei University because of his Marxist ideology. Universities no longer had enough autonomy to fight back against this kind of government intrusion.

In addition, terrorist attacks on leading statesmen and bankers continued to plague Japan in 1934. When the Saitō cabinet dissolved in July, Konoe Ayamaro was the next logical choice for prime minister. But he felt unready and escaped the nomination by leaving the country for the United States, where his eldest son was graduating from high school. While in the United States, Konoe arranged to meet with former president Herbert Hoover and returned to Japan in August.[59] When Nishida was invited to the Haradas on September 25 for lunch, Konoe, Kido, Oda, and Akamatsu Kotora were present. Konoe's visit to the United States may have come up as a conversation topic over lunch, but no account survives.

By September, Nishida had completed the essays "Benshōhōteki ippansha to shite no sekai" [The world as the dialectical universal][60] and "Keijijōgakuteki tachiba kara mita tōzai kodai no bunka keitai" [The forms of ancient cultures, East and West, seen from a metaphysical perspective].[61] In his essay on the world as the dialectical universal, he makes an important shift from an anthropocentric perspective to the perspective centered on the world. In this shift, the individual is now viewed from the perspective of the world. "The individual self is merely conceivable as the individual determination of the self-determining world,"[62] declares Nishida. His task is to make this shift of perspective without sacrificing the uniqueness and autonomy of the individual. Individual determination is linear and temporal, just as each moment is connected to the past and the future. But for individual moments to connect there has to be some sort of spatial relationship —the self-determination of Absolute Nothingness—that allows multiple individuals to interact and exist all at once. The actual world is the dialectical interplay of individuals and the universal.[63] In this dialectical world, human existence, which is caught in the "contradiction" between individual determination and universal determination, is a self-contradicting existence. Moreover, precisely because of this contradictory nature, each individual is open to the religious world, in which each hears the voice of Absolute Being, or God. Our knowledge of the contradictory nature of our existence manifests itself as a profound anxiety lurking at the bottom of our existence; by breaking through this "absolute negation," we can arrive at the absolute affirmation of life itself.[64] This approach to life, inspired by Mahāyāna Buddhism, offers Nishida a viable alternative to the philosophy of angst.

Nishida's essay, "The forms of ancient cultures, East and West, seen from a metaphysical perspective," is his attempt to formulate a cultural typology. According to Nishida's characterization, Western culture is imbued with Christian spirituality and "sustained by Being." In contrast, Oriental—and especially Japanese—culture is sustained by "the determination of Nothingness."[65] This particular way of contrasting "Christian West and Buddhist East" by way of Being and Nothingness became a locus classicus for those who, in the name of the Kyoto school of philosophy or otherwise, uphold the "supremacy" of Oriental Nothingness over Western Being. Nishida's intention, however, was far from that sort of crude taxonomy and dichotomous apologetics. Rather, his was the attempt to formulate a cultural typology from a metaphysical perspective. Nishida had always held that "each culture must maintain its uniqueness in the global society, even though it originally developed itself by interaction with other cultures. Only that way can it contribute to the formation of a truly global culture."[66] This position is radically pluralistic. Nishida insists that each particular culture has its rightful place in the world, precisely because no two cultures are alike. Nishida's attempt at establishing a cultural typology was fully worked out by Watsuji Tetsurō in *Fūdo* [Climate], published in 1935.[67] In fact Nishida and Watsuji had been discussing cultural typologies for some time. While in Kamakura, Nishida collected his essays into a book, *Tetsugaku no konpon mondai zokuhen* [The fundamental problems of philosophy, part 2], which was published on October 15, 1934, by Iwanami.

Nishida returned to Kyoto on October 5. On November 25 he gave a talk on "T. S. Eliot to dentōshugi" [T. S. Eliot and traditionalism][68] at the meeting of the English Literature Society at Kyoto Imperial University. He was invited to speak by Ishida Kenji, professor of English literature. Nishida felt that T. S. Eliot's view of history, especially of the simultaneity of "the timeless" and "the temporal," resembled his own view of the active-intuitive dialectical world. He explains that a moment moves on to another moment, but there is a "spatial" dimension to the temporal movement, and for that reason the past and the future are in some sense copresent in the present. Nishida suggests that his view of time resonates with T. S. Eliot's view of "tradition." According to Eliot, tradition is not mere "handing down" or something "inherited"; it is something won over by each generation through "great labour."[69]

In around mid-October Nishida was working on an essay, "Sekai no jikodōitsu to renzoku" [The self-identity of the world and its continuity],[70] in which he develops "the dialectical logic of the self-identity of mutually opposing subject and object"[71] and discusses how individuals, who are "many (as individuals) and yet one (as a group)," exist in the historical world by being "mediated," or embraced, by the universal. Describing this structure, Nishida calls it "the continuation of the discontinuous" *(hirenzoku no renzoku)*, in which discrete entities form a continuum thanks to the topological mediator *(bashoteki baikaisha)*.[72] This dialectical universal is not something merely material or biological but ultimately has the significance of the "Thou."[73] He saw this dialectical principle at work in the formation of each historical epoch. The idea of the dialectical interplay between particular historical moments and the Eternal Now and the idea of the significance of individual creativity came to form the main thrust of his later thought.

Chapter 21

Education and Scholarship
under Fascism

(1935–1937)

During the New Year's holiday of 1935, Nishida gave his customary series of lectures to the members of the Shinano Philosophical Society on the "logical structure of the actual world."[1] He then began a two months's stay in Kamakura on January 21. He agreed to an interview on February 26 with a journalist from Kaizōsha that was published as "Beruguson, Shesutofu, sono ta—ujitsu zatsudan" [Bergson, Shestov, and so forth—conversations on a rainy day].[2] In March he wrote a preface to Kōyama Iwao's *Nishida Tetsugaku* [Nishidan philosophy], a book that explained his philosophical system, which was published by Iwanami on April 25, 1935.[3]

Around this time, ultranationalistic factions sharpened their attack on progressive thinkers, resulting in an incident involving Minobe Tatsukichi, a professor of law at Tokyo Imperial University.[4] Minobe advocated a theory of constitutional monarchy, known as the "organ theory" *(kikan-setsu)*, that placed the emperor within the framework of the constitution of Japan. Kikuchi Takeo, an army general, attacked this theory in the House of Peers on February 18, arguing that it was blasphemous to call the "divine emperor" the "organ" of the state.[5] The road for the indictment of Minobe had already been paved two years earlier in 1933, when Minoda Muneki launched his attack in the October issue of *Genri Nippon*. Minoda assailed Minobe's theory as "that which goes against the emperor system" *(han-kokutai)*.[6] The Association of Retired Veterans backed Kikuchi and circulated pamphlets that vilified Minobe's theory. On February 25, Minobe, himself a member of the House of Peers, eloquently defended his position, but this only fueled irrational sentiments among the ultranationalists.

The head of the Seiyū Party, Suzuki Kisaburō, saw this as a perfect opportunity to overthrow the ruling party. Suzuki was able to put proposals concerning the "renovation of politics and education" and a "declaration on the national essence" on the agendas of the House of Peers and the House of Representatives, respectively. These resolutions were passed unanimously by both houses with the demand that the government "clarify the nature of the emperor system *(kokutai)*." Harada Kumao, criticizing the Seiyū Party's foolish act, lamented that "the political parties are braiding their own rope to tie themselves to the point of disability; they are digging their own graves."[7] Out of petty self-interest, the Seiyū Party precipitated the dismantling of the parliamentary system.

The Minobe incident marked the beginning of a period when "the opinion of the military swayed the spheres of politics and education,"[8] and dealt a decisive blow to the independence of academic and scientific study. Nishida, concerned with the repercussions of the Minobe incident, wrote to Hori: "I feel very sorry for Mr. Minobe. From now on, we may not be able to study civil law or carry out an objective study of the history of our country."[9] He also confided to Harada: "According to the newspapers, the military is involved in the Minobe incident. I worry about how the case will be resolved. If everything is to be handled this way, I have great apprehension about the future of our country."[10] On April 9, home minister Gotō Fumio banned Minobe's books on the constitution.

Iwanami, the publisher of Minobe's works, respected Minobe's scholarship and submitted a letter of protest to the *Tokyo Asahi Newspaper*. In this letter, Iwanami praised Minobe as a man and a scholar and argued that "there should be ample room for various kinds of patriotism within the expansive imperial spirit," and that "the real and most dangerous trend of thought is one that takes a narrow view of the *kokutai* and denounces groups of people as unpatriotic by accusing them of holding onto a skewed loyalty." Because this letter was potentially injurious to Iwanami and his business, Kobayashi Isamu, assistant to Iwanami, and Tsutsumi Tsune, manager of the company, took the extraordinary step of requesting the Asahi Newspaper Company to return Iwanami's letter to them.[11] Ruffians began to hang out around Iwanami's store, and he confessed to his close friends that he was "actually afraid . . . it would be no fun to be assaulted by them." According to Iwanami, "when rabid dogs are prowling the streets, those who can kill them should do so, but those who cannot must lock themselves up to wait for them to disappear."[12] Iwanami may have thought it wise to withdraw from the scene until emotions cooled. He left the Port of Moji on May 4, traveled through the United States and European countries, and did not return to Japan until December 13, 1935.

There is more to the story of the Minobe incident. According to Harada Kumao, the accusation raised against Minobe was only a cover. The ultranationalist faction, controlled behind the scenes by Hiranuma Kiichirō, actually sought to overthrow Ichiki, the former imperial minister, who was then speaker of the privy council.[13] Because Ichiki had been Minobe's mentor at the Imperial University (Tokyo), they had a teacher-disciple relationship. Apparently, Minobe was the scapegoat for Ichiki and other liberal constitutional thinkers.[14]

Nishida was extremely angry with the tactics of the Seiyū Party, which looked only to its own gain, losing sight of the principles of the parliamentary political system. When Takami Koremichi,[15] a former student of his from the Fourth Higher School, now a member of the Seiyū Party, called on him on April 13, he did not mince words. He wrote about the visit to Harada on May 4:

> I poured out words of criticism of Yamamoto [Teijirō, the counselor to the party],[16] as well as of the Seiyū Party. I expected Takami to refute me or defend their position, but nothing came from his lips. He listened to me intently and was impressed by what I had to say. I was truly aghast at his shallow knowledge and general ignorance. Takami is a quarrelsome sort, and it is not like him to listen to someone if he has his own opinion to voice. It appeared he had nothing to say in response to my criticism. What are we to do when matters crucial for our country are decided at the parliament by the likes of him? It is truly lamentable.[17]

The Minobe incident made Nishida think about the constitution and the nature of the state. It is possible that his reflections on these issues led to his 1941 essay entitled "Kokka riyū no mondai" [The problem of *raison d'état*].[18] Nishida was also concerned about government controls encroaching on freedom of scholarship. He wrote to Yamamoto:

> Regarding the question of the constitution, what is the army minister, Hayashi Senjūrō, going to do? Is he going to set what the newspapers call the "standard national interpretation" of the constitution? Politicians and legislators should leave whatever interpretations scholars make alone. Unless they let scholars freely engage in academic research, I don't think a logical foundation for the constitution, one sustained by true academic authority, will ever emerge.[19]

Nishida was developing his thought on "Kōiteki chokkan no tachiba" [The perspective of action-intuition].[20] The idea of action-intuition *(kōiteki chokkan)* focuses on the organic unity between mental (or the spiritual) and the physical (or the material) that constitutes our experience. According to Nishida, "we see a thing by action, and the thing we see determines us as much as we determine the thing."[21] Our experience always has a claim on our body as the organ of action: "Just as the body of an artist is the organ of art, so is the body of a scholar the organ of scholarship; the life of an artist exists in beauty and that of a scholar in truth. Even the activity of thinking does not exist separate from our physical body."[22] Nishida was developing his philosophical language, which gives due recognition to the role of the body in the self-determination of the historical world. The body, thus, is a "historical body" *(rekishiteki shintai)*.[23]

By bringing to the foreground the corporeal dimension of existence, Nishida was moving right into the heart of his philosophy of the "absolutely dialectical world," in which individuals are considered to be radically in-the-world, historical and physical. Precisely because individuals are corporeal, they are creative.[24] Nishida now asserts that in the concrete world in which we live, "we see ourselves in things"; further, "the determination of our body takes the form of our expressive operations." In such a world "things *(mono)* are not mere tools but are the carriers of meaning; they are the embodiment of objectivity."[25]

In "Kōiteki chokkan no tachiba," Nishida also advances the thesis that "historical reality must partake of the nature of *logos*,"[26] although he is yet to fully develop what *logos* is. His emphasis on *logos* (literally, "logic" or "reason") may have come out of his ongoing criticism of the irrational forces that were eroding the frail foundation of the Japanese parliamentary system. Nishida went to Kamakura for the summer, from July 26 to October 6. On August 3, still reacting to the Minobe incident, the government issued a "statement concerning the clarification of *kokutai*." Extreme nationalism was fast becoming the main stream of thought.

On September 15 Nishida and Suzuki Daisetz were invited to Harada's house in Ōiso. Harada wanted to hear what Suzuki Daisetz thought about Western rationalism and Oriental wisdom.[27] Suzuki talked about the traditional Japanese sensitivity to nature as an example of the "Japanese essence."[28] Nishida joined the conversation, asserting that "Japanese nationalists must accept the fact that Japan is *in* the wider global world, and that Japan cannot be considered in isolation but only from a comprehensive global perspective." He also added that "'nationalism' in the contemporary world should not mean merely turning back to the past."[29] Harada had the conversation recorded in shorthand by Konoe Yasuko,[30] who had been working for him as his confidential notetaker. Harada had the conversation set in type in a day or so and gave it to Saionji Kinmochi. Unfortunately, the voices of intellectuals like Nishida and Suzuki appear to have been lost in the wilderness of fanatical nationalism.

On September 18 the charge of lèse-majesté that had been filed against Minobe was dropped, but Minobe had to resign from his seat in the House of Peers.[31] In the aftermath of the Minobe incident, the Ministry of Education prepared its *Kokutai no hongi* [Fundamentals of our national polity],[32] a small "textbook" of Japanese ultranationalism that was published on March 30, 1937. The government sought to attain maximum "ideological uniformity"[33] with this tract.

From September 25 until September 29, Nishida visited Tōhoku Imperial University in Sendai, having finally found some free time to accept their standing invitation.[34] Nishida was greeted by President Honda Kōtarō.[35] Miyake Gōichi, Takahashi Satomi, Abe Jirō,[36] and Ishihara Ken were all eagerly looking forward to having him in Sendai. Nishida got to see Fujita Toshihiko, the first graduate of Sansanjuku, now a professor of biology in the medical school. While in Sendai, Nishida saw Tagajō, a ruin of the ancient northernmost fort of the Heian court; its ambience struck him as "something distinctly different in the appearance of the mountains, rivers, and the atmosphere from those of the Kansai area." He also saw Matsushima, one of the three most scenic spots in Japan, the other two being Miyajima and Amanohashidate. Nishida was most impressed by the beauty of Matsushima, which brought to his mind the famous passage by Matsuo Bashō describing the islands of Matsushima covered by pine trees, from his celebrated travelogue, *Oku no hosomichi* [A narrow road to Oku]. Inspired by the beauty of the place and the presence of the great poet, Nishida composed a *waka*:

> *The oil-lit lamp*
> *burns late into the night*
> *in a room of an inn*
> *in northern Japan*
> *I read* Oku no hosomichi" [37]

Bashō stirred his wanderlust, and he felt like going as far north as Hiraizumi to follow in the poet's footsteps, but there was not enough time for that excursion.

Nishida's brief trip to Sendai was a break from his daily routine. Upon his return to Kamakura, he was yanked back into reality. The "clarification of *kokutai*" was the media focus of the day. Nishida's faith in the parliamentary system and Japan as the constitutional state drove him to oppose the military's intervention into the realm of politics. He wrote to Harada:

> I think that what we ought to despise are those politicians who try to gain political power by taking advantage of the issue of *kokutai*. The Japanese people are not worried about the existence of the government, but they are worried about the intentions of those who are trying to drive the government into a cul-de-sac by taking away the control from the government. This isn't the time for Japan to be engaged in a civil war. . . .
>
> I, though an old scholar, am praying that the government will not misjudge the present situation and will advance far-sighted policies, sustained by the firm recognition that Japan is a member of the international community.[38]

Fascist ideologies were becoming ever more dominant. The general atmosphere was such that Nishida had to give a word of caution to Hidaka Daishirō,[39] who consulted him about a job interview he was about to have at the Third Higher School:

> As you know, these are fascist times. Those who are selflessly and deeply concerned about the future of our country should not clash with the trend of the day by upholding a purist attitude to fight against it, but should persevere in the face of the present situation and make an effort to put the country gradually back on the right course.[40]

He took it as his duty to guide his students and disciples in this uncertain world. He likewise gave a word of advice to Kōsaka Masaaki to maintain an attitude of independence as a scholar:

> The path of scholarship consists in never deceiving yourself. You must criticize your own ideas and struggle with them; never rest complacent in small achievements. When you hit a wall in your philosophical reflections, it may be helpful to read the works of others. But you must walk with your own legs, firmly touching the ground.[41]

When Nishida returned to Kyoto on October 5, Hashida Kunihiko[42] and Akizuki Itaru called upon him at his house in Asukaichō. He also began to meet with a small group of graduates. Kōsaka Masaaki,

Kōyama Iwao, Nishitani Keiji, Suzuki Shigetaka,[43] Shimomura Toratarō, Doi Torakazu,[44] Shitahodo Yūkichi,[45] and Usui Jishō[46] were regular members of the "tetsugakukai," a small, intimate version of the philosophical society. At these meetings Nishida would explain his latest ideas to the younger thinkers and receive their feedback. A collection of Nishida's new essays was compiled as *Tetsugaku ronbunshū daiichi* [Philosophical essays 1] and published on December 25, 1935, by Iwanami.

On November 18 the Ministry of Education set up a committee for the renewal of education and scholarship *(Kyōgaku sasshin hyōgikai)*. Minabe Nagaharu,[47] a graduate of the Fourth Higher School, and then vice minister of education, wanted Nishida to be on the committee. Nishida, unable to refuse Minabe's plea, accepted the appointment with the understanding that he could resign any time. He explained to Yamamoto how his appointment to the committee came about:

> I said to Minabe that I could not possibly go to Tokyo as often as the position required me, and, more important, that my opinions on education are diametrically opposed to the policies of the Ministry of Education. Having made my position thus clear, I asked him, "Do you still want me?" He said, "Yes." That's how I ended up accepting his request. . . . It is clear from the outset that even if I were to attend meetings with those men, none of my opinions would be heard. But even though I have repeatedly refused their request by laying my cards on the table, the Ministry of Education still wants me to be on the committee. Is there any further reason for me to decline their request? I'm thinking of attending a few of their meetings to see how things go. If they turn out to be futile, I shall resign.[48]

Amid discouraging signs, Nishida found that at least Watsuji Tetsurō and Tanabe Hajime were on the committee. He confided to Watsuji, however: "How can our opinion be heard among those men? I think it clear from the outset that our efforts will be in vain. Especially for me, an old man, I think the contribution I can make for the country is to complete my work and not waste even a single moment."[49] Nishida attended the first meeting of the committee on December 5. He felt that the committee was merely toying with abstract ideas. He did not attend the second meeting on December 19 but shared his opinion with Watsuji:

> They may be able to come up with some useful ideas, if they set up a subcommittee or something to discuss concrete issues. . . . I read

Kihira's proposal on the "fundamental meaning of Japanese education and learning." He says we should do away even with Darwin's theory of evolution. It reminded me of that trial wherein preachers in rural America banded together and demanded that the theory of evolution should be rejected.[50]

The committee, which was supposed to make important decisions on learning and scholarship, appeared to Nishida a "truly biased group," and this made him greatly apprehensive about the future of Japan.[51] Because no one had made constructive suggestions at the meeting, Nishida, instead of retiring from the committee in silence, wrote a statement to be read at the third meeting on January 15, 1936. He entrusted it to Konishi Shigenao, who was also a committee member. Despite the objection raised by the chairman and minister of education, Matsuda Genji,[52] the committee proceeded to hear Nishida's letter, which Konisha read aloud:[53]

To "unify the world of thought of the present and the Japan of the future by means of the Japanese spirit" [as the government is intent on doing], we need to conduct scholarly research into the history of Japan and things Japanese and to clarify their essence objectively. If the humanities [seishin kagaku][54] are to be applied, they need first to be approached from the ground up, studied carefully, and understood well. A spirit that rests only on the past and lacks a future is no longer living. Clear and superior ideas do not survive in isolation from other ideas but by nature serve to unify them. This is the only way to unify Japanese thinking, the only way for Japan to become one of the centers of world culture. However, when it comes to basic research, Japanese scholarship is still in its infancy. Even in the area of physics, where we are most advanced, we have yet to produce a Dirac[55] or a Heisenberg. In the humanities things are still worse.

    Without laying a solid foundation for scholarship in Japan, we have no more hope of firmly avoiding the infiltration of foreign ideas than the Yellow River has of becoming clear blue. To be sure, this is no easy matter, but no one with great expectations for Japan can afford to ignore it. To succeed, we need to give first-rate scholars the freedom not only to engage in basic research in their various disciplines but also to actively train such scholars. In concrete terms, I think these questions deserve the attention of a special committee, but meanwhile offer two suggestions of my own: we should increase the number of full scholarships for students who have proved their academic excellence; we should establish positions for professors who can engage full-time in research.[56]

Following this statement, Tanabe and Watsuji each spoke up in support of Nishida's position. Nishida himself resigned from the committee.

The committee filed its report on October 29, 1936, recommending the development of academic disciplines based on traditional Japanese content and method.[57] In anticipation of the committee's final report, the Ministry of Education set up a commission for the promotion of Japanese learnings *(Nihon shogaku shinkō iinkai)* on September 8 to implement the committee's recommendation.[58] They also set up a committee to review education *(Kyōiku shingikai)*,[59] which held its first meeting on December 23, 1937.

The mandate of the commission for the promotion of Japanese learning was to promote research and learning in a way that propogated the ideology of Japanese *kokutai* and Japanese spirit.[60] As part of this program, it organized a series of nationwide conferences to advance nationalistic education and research policies. The commission asked Nishida to give a public keynote address at the opening ceremony of the national philosophers' conference, scheduled for the evening of October 9, 1937, at Hibiya Park. Nishida obliged the commission and spoke about "Gakumonteki hōhō" [On the scholarly method][61] (the address appears at the end of this chapter). He wrote to Hori about the experience of that evening:

> I was totally flabbergasted by the event on the evening of the ninth. Granted, there was a microphone, but I detest that kind of "street theater." I shall never again make that kind of public appearance. In any case, I emphasized, as much as I could, that scholarship had to be respected. I went there only to give my talk and left right after it, so I don't know who else was there.[62] . . . I am no longer interested in seeing Nishi [Shin'ichirō][63] to talk with him. The world is definitely changing. I can no longer expect anything out of Konoe, either.[64]

Nishida felt that his public talk at least protested against governmental infringement on freedom of inquiry and spoke for the position that academic endeavors should be free of political agendas. He explained to Yamamoto that his intent was to encourage the Japanese people to retain the sense of rationality amid the storm of nationalists' promotion of their version of emotional and illogical "Japanese spirit."[65]

On the Scholarly Method:
A Public Talk at Hibiya Park*

Since the beginning of the Meiji period, Western cultures have been imported to Japan; by learning from them we in the East have made noteworthy progress. We still have much to learn, and it is incumbent on us to continue to develop by absorbing world cultures. Obviously, however, this does not mean that we should continue to absorb and digest Western cultures but rather that we must create a new global culture while being sustained by our Eastern heritage, which has nurtured us for thousands of years.

It was inevitable that Japan, which had closed its ports to most foreign countries for several centuries, was eager to learn and absorb modern world cultures when the people came in contact with the wider world at the beginning of the Meiji era. Recently, one hears loud denunciations of the directions taken by the Meiji government, however. I suppose the Meiji government's policies were not always flawless. But I think that we must not forget the significance of the achievements of the Meiji period. The present irresponsible criticism of the Meiji period is entirely irrational, and as such it is identical with the forces that destroyed the ancient Japanese heritage at the beginning of the Meiji era.

[Today, I would rather like to raise the question:] How is it possible for us to create a new global culture while keeping our historical heritage intact?

GLOBALIZATION OF THE "JAPANESE SPIRIT"

[To answer this question, let me first discuss what time is.] "Time" is not something that simply moves on in a linear fashion from the past to the future. If that were the case, time would have no identity of its own. Time is both linear and circular—it has a spatial dimension behind it. Time comes into being as the present determines itself. That is, the past and the future are connected at the present moment (because in "time" absolutely independent discrete entities are connected), and time, as the contradictory self-identity [of the past and

---

* "Gakumonteki hōhō," NKZ 12:385–94. Nishida gave this talk on 9 November 1937. It may be read as a criticism of the *Kokutai no hongi* [Fundamentals of our national policy]. The sentences in parentheses appear to be Nishida's later additions to his talk. Section heads are supplied by the translator.

the future, of the temporal and the spatial], moves on from that which is created to that which creates. This is where "time" comes to pass. This absolutely contradictory self-identity that remains changeless amid the constant changes may be considered the spirit of history.

Even Japan, which had been outside the stage of global history for thousands of years and developed in isolation, took its form and developed as a contradictory self-identity [i.e., as a historical entity]. During the course of development there were numerous conflicts and struggles; all sorts of changes took place from one epoch to the next. But Japan always maintained its self-identity, with its imperial family *(kōshitsu)* at the center, from which the "Japanese spirit" originates.

Japan is no longer cut off from the world history and actually stands on the global stage. The present moment for the Japanese is the global, historical present moment. The Japanese spirit of the past was relatively linear, but today it must become fundamentally spatial. A new global principle has to be born out of the depths of our historical spirit, from the depths of our heart. The "imperial way" *(kōdō)* has to become global. Today, many hold that various ills resulted from the importation of foreign thoughts. But we cannot keep foreign ideas from coming into Japan by merely upholding the particular over the universal. Rather, we must cultivate a global principle from within the depths of our heart.

What does it mean for the Japanese spirit to become thoroughly global and spatial? It means for us to become thoroughly scholarly *(gakumonteki)* and rational. We must neither repel reason by emotion nor be dogmatic. The content of the Japanese spirit must be conceptually organized by a precise scholarly method. It has to be theoretical. What I mean by the "scholarly method" is for us—temporal selves— to view ourselves by reflecting ourselves in the spatial mirror. (It means that our ego selves die and that we live as authentic individuals.) We must be thoroughly self-critical in this undertaking. For the Japanese spirit to become scholarly is for it to become objective, so that it is universally valid in everyone's eyes. This is different from becoming "cosmopolitan." This point is more often than not misunderstood.

IN CRITICISM OF FACILE CHARACTERIZATIONS OF EASTERN AND WESTERN CULTURES

These days, Eastern and Western cultures are distinguished in terms of moral teaching *(kyō)* and intellectual learning *(gaku)*. But we cannot simply label the Western culture as "intellectual learning" and be done with it. Certainly, Eastern cultures, and especially Chinese culture, were based on moral learning and lacked the discipline that we know today as "intellectual learning." I by no means slight the importance of moral learning. I just think that Eastern cultures also have, just as Western cultures do, a precious insight, but that this insight is yet to be articulated into an intellectual discipline. This is why we tend to be overwhelmed by Western cultures. Lately, we have been hearing the slogan "excess emphasis on intellectual education is no good." I, for one, believe, however, that genuine intellectual development must be considered more important than ever. In the past, genuine intellectual nurturing hardly existed in Japan's education. Often education consisted of learning by rote. The study of history, for instance, was no more than a memorization of historical facts.

It is unquestionably important for the Japanese spirit to digest Western cultures and thereby create a uniquely Japanese culture. I would also imagine that many agree with me that this process has to be scholarly. Unfortunately, it strikes me that even among the intellectuals there are some who do not understand what it means to be genuinely scholarly. People have tended to consider the "spirit" as the person who uses it, and "knowledge" as a mere "tool." A phrase such as "Japanese spirit, Chinese skills" *(wakon kansai)* [1] seems to express this way of thinking. The fact is, however, that scholarship is endowed with its own spirit. This holds true even for the natural sciences. "Scholarship" means that our spirit is alive in our scholarly pursuits. Only then is "Japanese scholarship" *(nihonteki gakumon)* possible. If mathematics can be described as British, French, German, and so forth, it is only in this sense. If scholarship is not imbued by the spirit, it is but an abstract concept. The discipline of humanities is in some way different from that of the natural sciences, but it is nevertheless established in and out of our existence in [the world of] historical objective facts. And it has to be established methodically.

For instance, Japan adopted Western jurisprudence after Meiji. But jurisprudence developed in the West has its own historical background, and we became aware of the discrepancies between the Western jurisprudence and the Japanese spirit, which has its own historical background. Hence, various problems arose. How are we to deal with

---

1. The idea was advocated by Sugawara no Michizane (844–903). This spiritual and technical eclecticism resurfaced during the Tokugawa period in the slogan: "Japanese spirit, Western technology" *(wakon yōsai).*

this kind of problem? If we were to go back to the time before Western legal thought was introduced to Japan, we would have no problem. But since that is impossible, it would seem to me that we are left with a couple of options. Either we are to graft Japanese mores (as if grafting a bamboo tree) onto the Western legal system, which has its own coherent theoretical structure, or we are to deny the Western legal system altogether because it is foreign to us. But to establish a truly Japanese jurisprudence, we must first investigate the foundation of the philosophy of history and obtain our own concept of "law." This goal cannot be attained by merely pitting Japan's uniqueness against the Western countries, or by returning to the practice of old. We must go through a "paradigm struggle" to achieve this end.

A living spirit has to have a theoretical dimension. Even a myth, if it is to possess eternal life, must have some theoretical content. Mere particularity is nothing. To take the form that was shaped in the course of history as our "spirit" and to try to enter the new period is actually to kill the generative, developing spirit. A particular stands only over another particular. Such particularity is just an [abstract] instance of the universal. What is creative must be characterized by concrete universality. If we insist on mere particularity and try to give it a theoretical foundation based on the "other," such particularity is nothing but a particularity only vis-à-vis the "other."

What does it mean for us to discover a new way of seeing and thinking that comes from the very depths of our Oriental heritage and for us to shed some new light on global history? What does it mean for us to deal with the world in a theoretical manner? Since a philosophical explanation of these questions is not only complex but would be hard to follow for a general audience, let me take an example from art to illustrate my point.

ILLUSTRATION: MULTIPLE SOURCES OF ARTISTIC CREATIVITY

Western aesthetics has generally based the standard of beauty on Greek art. That is to say, so-called classical art defined the standard of beauty. It is an anthropocentric art form—a view best supported by the theory of empathy advocated by Lipps. But Riegl came to question this idea through his study of art history. He found that Lipps's theory could not explain the geometric art of the Egyptians, for instance. In its stead, Riegl proposed the artistic will as the foundation of art—the will to give shape and form *(keiseiteki ishi)*. Riegl introduced the abstracting impulse as opposed to empathy [into the vocabulary of aesthetics]. While empathy is the joy of seeing things human in nature, abstraction is the denial of humanity, a movement toward "liberation" *(gedatsu)*. (Since I don't have the time here to go into a detailed discussion of Riegl's theory of art, let me simply refer you to the writings of Riegl and Worringer.)

My point is that "art" is more diverse than classical art, and that there are opposing directions at the foundation of art. Many Europeans tend to think that their culture is the single most advanced culture and hold that other ethnic groups, once they achieve the same "evolutionary height," will become like Europeans. This view strikes me as narrow-minded and complacent. It is because the prototype of historical cultures has to be much richer than that.

Just as Riegl managed to show us a deeper and wider concept of art by examining a variety of art forms, we must delve deeply into the foundations of Western cultures to grasp them fully, and at the same time explore even further the depths of Eastern cultures to grasp the different directions that they have taken from their Western counterparts. By so doing, I believe that we can clarify the more comprehensive and deeper significance of the cultures of humanity.

To do so is not to deny Oriental cultures from the vantage point of Western cultures or vice versa. Nor is it to subsume one into the other. Rather, it is to see Eastern and Western cultures in a new light by discovering a foundation deeper than what has been upheld. I am not a specialist in art, but I suspect that there is something even more profound than, say, Egyptian or Gothic art, at the foundation of the Oriental art which expresses the "form of the formless."

TEMPORAL MODALITY AND CULTURAL MODALITY

I have taken the example of art to illustrate my point to the general audience, but I would like to say that the same goes with philosophy and religion. We must develop a new paradigm. To elaborate on this point, let me talk a little about the relationship between "reality" and "absolute." According to Mahāyāna Buddhism, the absolute is neither something that is merely transcendent nor is it the ultimate limit of the progressive movement. "Reality *is* the absolute." But this expression is prone to misunderstanding. If we were to take it to mean that we need to exert no spiritual effort on our part to "reach" the absolute, we would be making a horrible mistake. Moreover, it would lead to the negation of all things rational.

As I mentioned at the beginning of my talk, if we consider "time" in terms of absolutely contradictory self-identity, we will discover a profoundly philosophical and religious significance in the statement that "reality is the absolute." Lately, I often hear the word *imanaka* [the very present moment]. (I understand that the word *imanaka* as used in the *senmyō* [imperial epistles] simply means "now.") If we are to characterize the Japanese spirit by this word, the ground of such attribution must go back to the insight into what time is, something similar to what I have described earlier.

As I noted briefly in the *Fundamental Problems of Philosophy* (part 2), I think that we may characterize various cultures according to how time is perceived. Within the structure of time, various cultures can be situated, their mutual relationships can be delineated, and they may be brought into a larger unity. That time is the absolutely contradictory self-identity, and that it is at once linear and circular may sound like a paradox. But time does have a spatial aspect.

Theoretical and intellectual Western cultures are predominantly spatial. Chinese culture, though not intellectual, is still spatial (that is, it is based on social decorum or ritual [*li*]). In contrast, Japanese culture can be said to be linear. This is why I describe Japanese culture as rhythmical. The Japanese political system *(kokutai)*, which centers itself on the imperial family *(kōshitsu)*, and which characteristically appeals to emotion, strikes me as a rhythmical unity. History is necessarily temporal; and if we approach the protostructure of the historical world according to the structure of time, we can identify various cultures that have different centers and see that these cultures constitute the global culture by supplementing and complementing one another.

CONCLUDING REMARKS

What I have said to you this evening is my personal view, and I expect all sorts of disagreements from among scholars. I just wanted to explain my view regarding how Japan may shed new light on global culture and contribute to it from the standpoint of Oriental culture. Moreover, this is how we may "stop the inundation by foreign ideas" —a view that many advocate these days. To define Japanese culture, we must certainly investigate the history of Japan and our historical cultural heritage. This research must be thoroughly scholarly. And the result of such research will form the foundations of our thought. But if we merely focus on the uniqueness [of Japan], it will not yield a spirit that can act with vitality on the contemporary global stage.

We must possess theories. This is a point that government officials ought to keep in mind when they formulate policies on research and education. If we are to return to Oriental culture with the view that we have fallen prey to foreign cultures since the Meiji period, we will develop a merely reactionary strategy and will not solve any real problems. Even if some claim easily that the Japanese aim to digest global culture by means of the Japanese spirit without rejecting foreign cultures, *how* that is done is not given serious consideration. In my opinion, fundamental and penetrating theoretical studies in any discipline are still feeble in Japan.

Philosophy is not oblivious of politics, nor politics of philosophy. It takes a century for educational policies to bear fruit, and therefore one should not make myopic policy decisions based on immediate political interests on matters concerning research and education. Research and education have to be sustained by a deep and noble guiding spirit. Today, there is a tendency to reject theoretical thinking altogether by uncritically labeling it as "individualism" or "liberalism." I agree with the view that the concept of nation and society should not be based simply on the freedom of the individual. But to deny the individual—or individual freedom—is nothing short of coercive despotism. Today, rationalism is carelessly denounced. What simply denies rationalism, however, is nothing but irrationalism.

The bottom line is that without individual freedom there is no creativity. The concrete principle of generation and development [of culture and history] has to allow individual freedom and creativity. (In academic research, freedom has to be guaranteed. No research is possible where we are already given foregone conclusions.)

I suspect there are few in today's intellectual world who adhere to the rationalism, the individualism, or the liberalism of the late eighteenth century. Marxism, for instance, is actually a radical negation of these views. Let me say one more thing: I think that often the study of things Japanese is equated with the Japanese spirit, and that it is forgotten that the Japanese spirit comes alive in the Japanese way of looking at things and thinking about things. We should not forget that, even if we engage in the study of foreign ideas and foreign disciplines, the Japanese spirit can manifest itself through that study. And this Japanese spirit in turn works toward things Japanese. We must not be misguided by mere outward labels.

Chapter 22

Dark Political Undercurrent
(1936–1937)

The January 1936 issue of *Shisō* acknowledged Nishida's "sustained philosophical endeavor" and gave him a "proper philosophical salute, by organizing a symposium, in the truest sense of the word," with the hope that such a tribute would "contribute to the enrichment of the Japanese intellectual world."[1] Articles were contributed by Takahashi Satomi, Mutai Risaku, Miki Kiyoshi, Kōsaka Masaaki, Honda Kenzō, Nishitani Keiji, Doi Torakazu, Yamaguchi Yusuke, Shimomura Toratarō, Hosoya Tsuneo, Kōyama Iwao, Satō Nobue, Takizawa Katsumi, and Shitahodo Yūkichi.

Nishida was in Kamakura from January 22 until March 15. On January 29 Fujioka Tōho's mother died at the advanced age of ninety-seven. This caused Nishida not only to reminisce on days gone by but also to realize that he himself—at sixty-five—was no longer young. Deeply moved by this thought, he composed a few *waka* poems:

How many more times
will I return to see
the spring ocean
I
an old man

Late at night I look up
at the star-studded sky
remembering times past
as if they were only
yesterday

I am yet to reach
my beloved mother's age

but I am already
past the age
of my revered father [2]

It snowed all over Japan in February 1936. In Tokyo and Kyoto the streets were buried under heavy snowfalls. On February 26, as if to defile the pure white snow with bloodshed, a military coup (the so-called February 26 incident) took place when a factional conflict between two camps of hot-blooded young military officers erupted into an attempt to take over the government.[3] The timing was ironical, for in the general election just six days earlier, the people voted for antimilitary politicians. Nishida reacted immediately to the violent incident in a letter to Hori:

> They committed an inexcusable atrocity. I was utterly speechless. It made me think about the French Revolution. . . .
>
> Regardless of their crime, the names of those who took part in this atrocity will not be released; they will not be subject to the criticisms of the people and will get away with no more than a few years of prison, even for the murders they committed.[4] No one knows what they will do next, now that their confidence has been boosted. This is truly the destruction of our country. In my opinion, it is the responsibility of those in power, who, because of their fear of the military, have catered to its demands. This indeed is the time for the Japanese people to wake up. Unless decisive action is taken at this time, the future of our country is grim. But I see no leadership emerging from anywhere that can tame the army. The Japanese people are truly blind. Unlike the olden days, today's Japan faces foreign powers, and this domestic incident may cost Japan its existence. I wonder what is going to happen to our country. I hear that the culprits are the third regiment stationed in Azabu.[5]

Contrary to Nishida's fears, the coup was swiftly suppressed and the leaders promptly executed. The emperor, who was extremely angry at the brutal murder of his trusted ministers (the lord keeper of the privy seal, Saitō Makoto, and the finance minister, Takahashi Korekiyo) ordered swift and decisive punishment of the leaders. A fortune among misfortunes for the emperor was that Suzuki Kantarō, former grand chamberlain, survived a gunshot wound to his chest.

In the wake of the resignation of the Okada cabinet, Hirota Kōki[6] became the next prime minister. Nishida was apprehensive about this military presence in politics:

From now on Japan will be run by the military. I suppose Prince Saionji had no other choice but to appoint Hirota Kōki as prime minister. Given how the military has mishandled political issues thus far, the future of Japan is gloomy, indeed. . . . We urgently need to place in office those truly versed in the areas of diplomacy and finance.[7]

Frequent snowfall kept Nishida from his walks in Kamakura; in addition, he did not feel like concentrating on his work. Having attended the meeting of the Japanese Association for the Promotion of Scholarship *(Nihon gakujutsu shinkōkai)*[8] twice, a monthly meeting of the Imperial Academy once, and having called on Konoe once, Nishida decided to go back to Kyoto in mid-March, cutting short his stay in Kamakura by two weeks. Before he left, Miki came to visit him a couple of times. Miki wrote in his diary of February 22: "In the afternoon, I called on Professor Nishida in Kamakura. He led me into a very interesting discussion on the problem of the body. Whenever I'm talking with him, I am inspired to engage in philosophical thinking. I, too, must carry out meaningful work."[9] Nishida had this power to inspire his students. Kōsaka Masaaki noted a similar experience: "Whenever I came home from the professor's house, I felt resuscitated, and my life's spring was flowing afresh. I found joy in being alive again. When I reflected on what the professor said, it was always the same. But that same thing felt to me always fresh."[10]

At that time, Nishida was working on the essay "Ronri to seimei" [Logic and life],[11] in which he was developing his philosophy of the body. In March he told Takizawa Katsumi that he was "concentrating on the idea of 'action-intuition' [*kōitek ichokkan*]."[12] This idea focuses on the reality of the unity of the physical and the mental-spiritual in action. Our eyes, for instance, could not exist apart from their function of "seeing," and likewise, our ears could not exist separate from their function of "hearing." That is to say, our "body" is something that has acquired its present shape through a long historical process, and in that sense our body is a "historical body." Moreover, in our creative activities, we create things "by looking at the shape of things," while we use our body as a tool to create a thing that in turn claims its own objective existence.[13]

On March 31 Nishida's niece, Takahashi Fumi, came to bid farewell before she left for Germany. He was happy for her. With the arrival of spring, the hateful snowy winter[14] and the shock of the February 26 incident was passing, and renewed hope consoled Nishida. In early June, Suzuki Daisetz, accompanied by Beatrice, left Japan for

London to attend the Congress of World Religions with Anesaki Masaharu and Kagawa Toyohiko. Because Suzuki wanted to carry out research at several British university libraries, he obtained a letter of introduction from Kano Naoki through Nishida.[15] His friends' activities kept Nishida well-informed of the world situation.

During his stay in Kamakura from July 26 to October 6, Nishida consented to two interviews with Miki. One was on "Hyūmanizumu no gendaiteki igi—Nishida Kitarō hakushi ni kiku" [The contemporary significance of humanism: an interview with Dr. Nishida Kitarō],[16] which was published in *Yomiuri Shinbun,* and the other was on "Jinsei oyobi jinsei tetsugaku" [Life and a philosophy of life], which was published in the *Nihon Hyōron.*[17] Thanks to Miki's journalistic activities, Nishida's thought was becoming known to a wider public beyond the ivory tower. The popular perception of Nishida placed him at the pinnacle of Japanese thinkers; he was thought to represent the Japanese intellectual world. Nishida's social calendar was full as well. Among those whom he saw in Kamakura were Inoue Tetsujirō, Tokunō Bun, Minobe Tatsukichi, Miura Shinshichi,[18] Oda Nobuhiro, Akamatsu Kotora, Kido Kōichi, and Okabe Nagakage,[19] not to mention Iwanami and Harada.

By 1936 Iwanami needed to reset the type of Nishida's *Zen no kenkyū.* Seizing this opportunity, Nishida wrote a new preface in October 1936. After sketching the outline of his philosophical venture thus far,[20] he noted with amazement that his first book was still being read and expressed his appreciation with an allusion to a poem by the celebrated poet Saigyō: Did I ever imagine that / In my advanced age / I should cross once again / This mountain pass of Saya-no-Nakayama? / Ah, it is all thanks to having lived a long life!" (*Toshitakete / mata koyubeshito / omoikiya / inochinarikeri / Saya no Nakayama*).

From April to May 1937, Eduard Spranger, a professor of the University of Berlin, visited Kyoto. He was sent to Japan by the Nazi government to firm up the cultural liaison between Germany and Japan and to convince the Japanese people that they shared a common historical mission with the Germans.[21] Spranger's talks on the university campus included "The Nazis' policy concerning present-day German scholarship."[22]

While Spranger was still in Kyoto, the Danish theoretical physicist, Niels Bohr, visited the university and gave a talk on May 10. Nishida attended Bohr's lecture and was enormously impressed by it. He shared his excitement with Kuwaki Ayao: "That a man of such high scholarly caliber as Bohr comes to Japan from time to time is indeed a splendid thing, as it stimulates and benefits the Japanese scholarly community."[23] A few days later, on May 15, Nishida's collection of essays, *Zoku shisaku to taiken* [Philosophical contemplation and actual experience, vol. 2],[24] was published by Iwanami.

The essay "Shu no seisei hatten no mondai" [The problem of generation and development of species],[25] on which Nishida was working from 11 April to 18 May 1937, is his response to Tanabe Hajime's criticism, which Tanabe had raised in his essay "Shu no ronri to sekai zushiki—zettai baikai no tetsugaku e no michi" [The logic of species and the schemata of the world—toward a philosophy of absolute mediation].[26] Tanabe develops his "logic of the species" *(shu no ronri)* in criticism of Nishida's "logic of *topos*" and maintains that Nishida's logic failed to explain "the nation state" *(kokka)* as a species. Years later, after World War II, Tanabe looked back on his philosophical aim of the 1930s and noted that he had tried to "mediate through negation"

Outside the main building of Kyoto Imperial University; on May 3, 1937, following the luncheon reception for Eduard Spranger, professor of the University of Berlin. In the front row, third from the left, is Spranger, and on his right is Nishida. At the far right end of the front row is Amano Teiyū. In the back row, fourth from the left, is Kuki Shūzō, and to his right is Kimura Motomori. From *Kyoto daigaku bungakubu gojūnenshi.*

the "individual," which liberalism upheld as the subject, and "race," which formed the basis of the nationalistic totalitarianism then coming into vogue. He had also tried to develop his logic of "absolute mediation," or the "logic of the species," by identifying the state, which he saw as the "practical unification of the real and the ideal," as the "species." [27]

In response to Tanabe's view of "species," Nishida advances his idea that the species are not fixed entities but are "generated and develop in the historical world." Not only do human beings transform their environment, but the environment transforms human beings; thus, "the species are born out of the world" only when *"that which is created creates that which creates."* [28] For Nishida the species are the "[trans]forming dynamism that changes any given world," thus constituting the "paradigm of the actual reality." Indeed, there is "nothing in history that was given from the beginning; rather that which is given is that which is already created—the created creates that which creates." [29] According to Nishida, if we regard nature in terms of that which is created in history, then nature and history are linked. Even in the beginning of the world, there was no material "given"; it was already a "formed" world. [30]

Nishida's view of the species is underscored by his meditation on "freedom" and "necessity" for the individuals who exist in this historical world. The historical present is "that which is thoroughly determined and yet contains its self-negation within itself and moves from present moment to present moment by transcending itself." [31] In this historical present, freedom of the individual is made possible precisely as the negation of the historical moment itself. As for the uniqueness of each culture, Nishida holds that "the world forms itself by maintaining its unique characteristics," and in that process, "each particular element gains its uniqueness" and "truly lives up to its heritage." He considers the Japanese emperor system *(kokutai)*, the "unbroken line of the imperial lineage," to be also rooted in this historical process of "generation and development." This is Nishida's criticism of the then popular "imperial philosophy" *(kōdō tetsugaku)*, which looked to the mythological origin of the imperial family and ascribed divinity to the emperor. Nishida insists that "the [imperial] restoration *(ishin)* should not mean a simple turning back to the past but rather to take an ever new series of steps forward into the future." [32]

In his next essay, "Kōiteki chokkan" [Action-intuition], [33] Nishida indirectly criticizes Tanabe, who held that we intuit through our action and that out of intuition no action could arise. Nishida focuses on the intrinsic connection between action and intuition. Action arises as we "interact" with things in this concrete historical world. Things are not something we conjure up; they are something that we actually *see* because things are historically formed and manifest themselves as such.[34] We see things "actively and intuitively."[35]

This series of essays, "Ronri to seimei" [Logic and life], "Jissen to taishō ninshiki—rekishiteki sekai ni oite no ninshiki no tachiba" [Praxis and the recognition of the object—the epistemological standpoint in the historical world],[36] "Shu no seisei hatten no mondai" [The problem of generation and development of species], and "Kōiteki chokkan" [Action-intuition] were to be compiled into the second volume of *Tetsugaku ronbunshū* [Philosophical essays].[37] Nishida's thought was becoming ever more focused on *how* we human beings exist in the historical world.

Konoe Ayamaro become prime minister on June 1, 1937, succeeding the short-lived Hayashi cabinet.[38] In the eyes of Saionji Kinmochi, Konoe was the last trump card, the only one who could check the demands of the military and avert war with China. Tall, young, and handsome, the aristocratic Konoe immediately won nationwide popular support. Nishida was apprehensive and shared his mixed feelings with Harada:

> Konoe has finally accepted the position of responsibility, hasn't he? I suppose he is the only choice at this moment. I hope he will be able to carry out his mission. As regards the area of education and research, the government may not have an alternative policy at the moment, but it will be desirable if Konoe at least demonstrates his determination and tells the world that the government will not take an aggressive, narrow-minded course. If he follows in the footsteps of Mr. Hayashi, I think it would only suppress progressive thinking.[39]

It was during Konoe's administration that Japan became engaged in a full-fledged military campaign against China. Nishida was soon concerned about the escalating momentum of irrational forces within the government, as his letter to Harada demonstrates:

> If Konoe cannot carry out what the people expected of his administration, at least I want his cabinet to leave concrete testimony that it did try (in the way the people wanted them to do). . . . I'm only hoping that he won't be swayed by a certain [ultranationalistic] faction and make a faux pas. . . . The attitude of the Ministry of Education . . . is that Japan had become too Westernized in the past and that it is now time to

correct it by putting narrow-minded nationalists (*nihonshugisha*) at the helm. The ministry lacks any firm basis on which to decide what course Japan should take in education and research in order to create a Japan that can play an important role in the international community. . . .

It would be a shame if the Konoe cabinet fails, despite its enormous popularity, simply because of its policies on education and scholarship. I wrote a letter to Konoe the other day, stating my opinions,[40] but will you please speak to him on this point? [41]

Nishida's misgivings were justified, for Konoe failed to demonstrate a firm determination to halt military actions in China. On July 7 the Japanese and Chinese armies clashed outside Beijing at the Loukou (Marco Polo) Bridge, signaling the beginning of a prolonged war between Japan and China.

On August 12 Harada introduced Nishida to Nomura Kichisaburō, a navy admiral who was then president of Gakushūin.[42] Nomura, with his extensive international experience, would be sent to the United States in 1941 as part of the last-ditch effort of the Konoe cabinet to avert war.

Nishida, worried about Konoe, called on him on September 16. He came home with a sense of profound apprehension, which he confided to Harada:

Since I really could not refer directly to the problem [of the war between Japan and China], I commented on his speech and spoke about the course of world history. I said to him that the historical trend of the world today is moving toward "state control," which, however, should not mean reverting to the despotism of the past, and that the new direction of history should embrace the affirmation of individuality. I noted that in placing the Oriental or Japanese spirit as the foundation of the country, policymakers should never neglect reason and wisdom. I also said that an Oriental culture has to have its logic and that a lack of logic has been the shortcoming of Eastern cultures. I also said that Marxism is a menace precisely because it has logic. Before I left, I handed him a letter in which I had written out these points. During the meeting, Konoe seemed to be thinking along with me, but I wonder how much he actually listens.[43]

On September 21 Nishida's son Sotohiko, a reserve second lieutenant in the air division of the army, was called to active duty. This deepened Nishida's apprehension. He feared that "the present war could be prolonged indefinitely" and hoped that a solution could be found to bring it to a swift conclusion.[44] He also felt that the government was now run by "sheer force," which unilaterally suppressed "reason." [45] Having seen Sotohiko off on his journey to a military base, Nishida went to Nagano to give a talk on September 25 and 26 to the members of the Shinano Philosophical Society on the topic "Rekishiteki shintai" [The historical body]. [46]

On October 9 Nishida gave his public lecture at Hibiya Park (see chapter 21) on "The Scholarly Method." On October 22 Kido Kōichi was appointed minister of education, replacing Yasui Eiji. [47] The news came as a relief to Nishida. He considered Kido a man of "progressive ideas" who "will make a good advisor to Konoe, who tends to be influenced by the extremist faction." [48] However, Kido's appointment was made only to solidify the Konoe cabinet, while he himself was not particularly well versed in the affairs of the Ministry of Education. [49] Nishida called on Kido on October 26 to speak about the selection of the vice minister and related matters, but Kido's tight schedule prevented any in-depth conversation. [50]

The Konoe cabinet was embroiled in complicated negotiations with the Chinese government. Nishida sensed that some ominous "dark undercurrent" was sweeping the Japanese off their feet. [51] Even before Kido's appointment as minister, the Ministry of Education had asked Nishida to be on the advisory board of its academic department. He declined the request several times, but in November the ministry asked him again. Because Kido was now heading the ministry, Nishida decided to give it a chance. He explained how this came about to Watsuji:

> I thought I should not reject the effort of the academic department from the outset by making myself unavailable. If they wanted me so badly, I should accept their request. I shall state what I think at their meeting(s) and decide thereafter whether to remain on the board. I came to this decision because the present policies of the Ministry of Education put young people at a disadvantage. If I could alter the present situation, it would be worth my while.
>
> Now that Kido is minister, I can frankly tell him what I think. Moreover, Kido is different from Konoe in that he shares our view. This may be the only opportunity for us to voice our opinion to the Ministry of Education. When I saw Kido the other day, [52] he agreed with me on each point I brought up, but he intimated to me that it was difficult for him to implement any change, given the present-day political climate. He hoped I would join the advisory board, but he also told me that he would feel sorry for me because most likely no significant change would be brought about. I imagine I will end up stepping

down from the advisory board, exerting no influence on it. I feel that a dark undercurrent is flowing that will eventually sweep us off our feet. It would be wise, perhaps, not even to attend the board meeting when I already know the end result, but I think it is my duty to go into the battlefield, even if only to be defeated.[53]

The relationship between Nishida and Tanabe Hajime had become considerably strained by November 1937. Tanabe relentlessly criticized Nishida's thought as lacking the principle of rationality. Nishida was forced to defend his position in the preface to *Tetsugaku ronbunshū daini* [Philosophical essays 2], in which he asserted that his thought was "concrete thinking, thinking from the standpoint of the historical life," which allowed the thinker to approach the world not from "outside" but as an integral part of the world. Nishida answered Tanabe's charges by stating:

We don't exist because we think, but we think because we exist. Life is not simply irrational or "direct and unmediated";[54] rather our existence must contain the rational medium, that is, logical thinking. There is no such thing as a human life that does not have a logical rational medium one way or another.[55]

Tanabe's persistent criticism eventually drove Nishida to use sharper language against him—at least within the inner circle of his former students. His letter to Mutai reads:

Tanabe's argument is precise but remains on the plane of abstraction; insofar as he is stuck in Kantian epistemology, I don't think he will be able to discuss this historical world. . . . His criticism of my thought in his essay published in October[56] strikes me as sad. It seems as if unless he thinks, he does not know whether he is alive or not.

Tanabe says that no self-consciousness can be derived from my philosophy of "that which is created to that which creates" *(tsukurareta mono kara tsukuru mono e)*. I'm currently working on a response in which I maintain that it is precisely because of this dynamism that moves "from that which is created to that which creates" that self-conscious-ness arises. In this context I am trying to clarify the nature of *expression*, which has not been given much attention thus far. Tanabe dogmati-cally defines "expression" as "the object of understanding" because he is trapped by a fixed epistemological presupposition. Expression, in my view, is *poiesis*. History-bound, physical activity is an expressive activity. "Intuition" is not something merely passive; rather, it signifies that the subjective activity is dialectically embraced by the objective thing. Historical, physical activity arises from our looking at things intuitively. The activity of judgment, too, is sustained by this fact.[57]

Although some harsh words were exchanged between Nishida and Tanabe, they actually never lost respect for one another and maintained their professional relationship.

On November 13 Karl Löwith, a former disciple of Heidegger and then a lecturer at Tōhoku Imperial University in Sendai,[58] called on Nishida, accompanied by Usui Jishō. Löwith saw Nishida at least one more time before he left Japan for the United States in 1941. At that time he was presented with a farewell gift, a mounted calligraphy piece by Nishida of a "Zen circle," with these words written alongside: "The moon of the mind is singularly round; its light swallows up all things."[59] Löwith remembered Nishida fondly. Years later, in 1960, Löwith talked about the different attitudes toward life and death held by the Japanese and Europeans and quoted Nishida's thought from the German translation of Nishida's "Forms of Ancient Cultures, East and West, Seen from a Metaphysical Perspective" to illustrate his point.[60]

Calligraphy piece, "Zen circle," and a short poem: "The moon of the mind is singularly round; its light drinks in all things." From *Nishida Kitarō Zenshū*, vol. 7, *Furoku*.

In November 1937 Nishida began the essay, "Ningenteki sonzai" [Human existence].[61] In December the project of translating a selection of Nishida's essays into German was launched by Robert Schinzinger, a professor at Kōnan Higher School and a lecturer at Kyoto Imperial University.[62] He was assisted by Kimura Motomori and Kōyama Iwao in this undertaking.[63] The idea of translating Nishida's writings into German was originally suggested by Eduard Spranger, who had visited Kyoto earlier that year in April and May. The translation-related expenses were borne by the Japanese Society for the Promotion of International Cultural Understanding (Kokusai bunka shinkōkai).[64] Schinzinger chose "Gēte no haikei" (1931) because it was relatively easy for him to follow. He gave it the title "Der metaphysische Hintergrund Goethes" [Goethe's Metaphysical Background]. After that, he translated "Eichiteki sekai" (1928) as "Die intelligibile Welt" [The Intelligible World], and finally, the latest essay by Nishida, "Zettaimujunteki jikodōitsu" (1939), with the title, "Die Einheit der Gegensätze" [The Unity of Opposites]. Schinzinger had an intriguing story to tell:

> While I was working on the translation, I frequently called on Professor Nishida at his house. Without fail, he kindly explained to me in German the places that were unclear to me. On one occasion, however, he pondered on the passage for a while and then said, "I don't know what I wanted to say." Thereafter, I switched my tactic a bit and attempted a bolder translation at places that did not make immediate sense to me.[65]

The project was completed in May 1941. These three essays were collected in *Die intelligibile Welt*, published in Berlin by Walter Gruyter in 1943 (the book soon sold out and went out of print). Unfortunately, because Japan was under a U.S. submarine blockade in 1943, mail from Germany was no longer getting through. Nishida never saw his book in German, which caused Schinzinger great disappointment.[66] After the war (and after Nishida's death), Schinzinger translated his German translation into English and published *The Intelligibility and the Philosophy of Nothingness: Three Philosophical Essays* in 1958.

Chapter 23

The Dialectical World as the Absolutely Contradictory Self-Identity

(1938–1940)

It seemed to Nishida that by 1938 the Ministry of Education had lost all guiding principles and was merely reacting to constantly changing political pressures. He spent the winter of 1938 in Kamakura. As soon as he arrived in Kamakura on January 27, he contacted Kido, minister of education, but Kido was too busy to see him. Instead, Kikuchi Toyosaburō, head of the academic department, got in touch with him. Nishida conveyed his concerns that the Ministry of Education was catering to the demands of the home ministry and the army. In this environment, irrational accusations and simplistic reasoning, clad in pseudoscientific language, were on the rise and began to assail philosophical inquiries. For instance, "liberalism" was interpreted to mean "selfish individualism" and therefore should be banned.[1]

Some officials of the Ministry of Education, annoyed by Nishida's persistent criticisms, began to accuse him in public meetings, openly demonstrating their hostility against him. Nishida suspected that their accusations were prompted by his severe criticism of the activities of the Center for National Spiritual Culture, which he had voiced to the officials of the academic department.

In February 1938 a celebration commemorating the fiftieth anniversary of the promulgation of the Meiji constitution was held in Tokyo, providing a perfect opportunity for the ultranationalists to stage their nationalistic sentiments.[2] On April 1, the national mobilization ordinance was issued by the government in preparation for the Japan-China war. Shortly before then, a book by Amano Teiyū,[3] *Dōri no kankaku* [The sense of reason], came under attack by ultranationalists. It criticized military training as a part of the school curriculum and stated that it was "hampering Japanese education" and should be abolished.[4] The sensitive matter was hushed up, with the agreement that Amano would not reprint the book.[5] When the problem was thus contained, Nishida felt relieved but asked Hidaka Daishirō, who was assisting Amano, to be vigilant because the ultranationalists could renew their attack any day.[6]

Amid these worries there was a happy interlude for Nishida. On March 14 he went to visit Kimura Hisashi, his friend from the time when they studied mathematics together under the tutorage of Kami-yama Kosaburō in Kanazawa. He and Kimura renewed their friend-ship and began to see each other regularly at the monthly meeting of the Imperial Academy. Nishida wrote of Kimura after his death:

> You told me to come and visit you because you had finally built a house in Tokyo. I called on you at your brand new house in Shinmachi in Setagaya. We went right back in time by sixty years, to the olden days, and engaged in lively conversations, with no thought of decorum or propriety. Your wife, seated at our side, laughed and said that we argued like children. . . . That was the first time I met your wife, who was already a grandmother! . . . You saw me off and told me to bring my wife with me next time.[7]

Nishida reported the visit to Yamamoto with a touch of irony: "Kimura has changed to want to see an old friend like me; it goes to show that he has aged!"[8] Mrs. Kimura, recalling the day of Nishida's visit, told him that her husband said there was nothing like old friends.[9] There was to be no "next time," however, for Nishida to visit Kimura: first Nishida was struck by illness and then Kimura died.

Earlier the same day, before visiting Kimura, Nishida had attended a meeting of the board of directors of the Showa Study Group (*Shōwa kenkyūkai*), held in Nihonbashi. Gotō Fumio,[10] Arita Hachirō,[11] Miura Tetsutarō,[12] Matsui Haruo,[13] Ōkura Kinmochi,[14] Nasu Shiroshi,[15] Takahashi Kamekichi,[16] Sasa Hiroo,[17] and Tajima Michiji[18] were present. Nishida was invited to the meeting by Gotō Ryūnosuke,[19] who asked him to speak on the characteristics of Oriental philosophy in contrast to Western philosophy, and to consider whether such a thing as "national philosophy" was conceivable.[20]

Although some Japanese intellectuals now view the Showa Study Group as some sort of "fascist group," it was actually considered too progressive and anti-*kokutai* by the ultranationalists of the pre-1945 period. Members of the Genri Nipponsha, for instance, harshly criti-cized the group.[21] The Showa Study Group had a humble origin. It was initially established as a private research firm on October 1, 1933, by Gotō Ryūnosuke, who had been a classmate of Konoe Ayamaro at the First Higher School. Gotō thought that Konoe would eventually become prime minister and that it would be desirable to be well informed on various political fundamentals, both domestic and international.[22] The study group steadily grew to a respectable size, and on October 3, 1935, it officially established itself as an independent institute dedicated to the study of contemporary political issues. Rōyama Masamichi,[23] Gotō Fumio, Igawa Tadao,[24] Ōkura Kinmochi, and Takahashi Kamekichi were among the core members of the group. One of the major aims of the group was to "oppose fascism."[25] The Shōwa Kenkyūkai, generally viewed as Konoe's think tank, began to attract many people of varied backgrounds and interests. As Konoe moved closer to the position of prime minister, however, he gradually distanced himself from those associated with the Showa Study Group because he did not want to be identified with any one particular group.[26] The Showa Study Group eventually dissolved itself on November 19, 1940, in the wake of the establishment of the Taiseiyo-kusankai ["The organization that assists the emperor in running the country"].[27]

Nishida wanted to see Kido before he left for Kyoto, but the Diet was in session, which kept Kido extremely busy. Instead, Nishida wrote him a letter on March 16, stating that if politicians truly wished for the well-being of Japan, they would have to adopt a global perspective. He urged Kido to advance a bold and progressive stance:

> The idea held these days that each country in the world has to be awakened to its ethnic and nationalistic identity may appear on the surface to deny the "global world" . . . But actually, each country has to stand on its own feet as a nation-in-the-world. I think that the word "world" has become something real and urgent. I deplore that this fact is not understood by today's Japanese nationalists.
>
> The government has to determine its policies with the understanding that today's Japan indeed faces the world. In particular, the policies affecting education—"the nation's great task of one hundred years"— must be firmly based on this foundation. I think that military men actually better understand this point and have adopted this kind of global perspective. In stark contrast, those who engage in the humanities promote a view that averts the eyes of the Japanese people from the world.[28]

After Nishida returned to Kyoto on March 22, Amano Teiyū asked him to give a talk on "Nihon bunka no mondai" [The problem of Japanese culture][29] for the Monday Lecture Series, which he was organizing at the university. Nishida gave a three-part lecture on April 25, May 2, and May 9, in which he noted: "These days, some hold the view that Japan has been steadily degenerating since the Meiji Restoration. But I personally believe that Japan bumped its head against the world for the first time in the Meiji period. . . . These days, apparently the word 'world' is a dirty word, which we are not even supposed to use!"[30] His remark drew laughter from the audience—apparently his sentiment was shared.

Because the talk was given on a university campus, Nishida may have felt he could speak critically of the ultranationalist view. But his Monday Lecture gave Minoda Muneki and his group a perfect opportunity to begin a pointed attack on Nishida. Although Minoda's attack also extended to others associated with the Kyoto school, such as Tanabe Hajime, Amano Teiyū, and Watsuji Tetsurō,[31] he began his attack by focusing on Nishida in his article, "Nishida tetsugaku no hōhō ni tsuite" [On the methodology of Nishidan philosophy], which was published in the July issue of *Genri Nippon*.[32] Even before Minoda's article was published, a rumor that Minoda was going to launch an attack on Nishida was circulating, which made Nishida think about protecting his students because younger scholars were apt to be vulnerable.[33] In his letter of June 25 to Kōsaka Masaaki, he warned him to be careful about the use of the words "world" and "universal":

> I want you to be cautious with the group that tries to catch our words to do us in. If we say "world," they accuse us of espousing "cosmopolitanism," and if we say "universal," they dub it as "abstract universal" (taking it merely in the sense of natural sciences). They merely pick on words out of context and use them as ammunition for their attack. From what I understand, they are viciously against the "atomistic" way of thinking, which places the individual above the state. Please make sure that you won't be caught by your own words.[34]

By the end of June or early July, Nishida finished his essay "Yomi-naosaretaru monadorojī" [Monadology reread], which he retitled "Rekishiteki sekai ni oite no kobutsu no tachiba" [The position of the individual in the historical world].[35] This work reveals Leibniz's importance to Nishida as he developed his idea of the irreducibility of individual in the historical world. Because the discussion was cast in highly philosophical language, it did not catch the attention of Minoda and his group.

On July 9 Nishida received a copy of *Genri Nippon*, sent to him personally by Minoda.[36] He described Minoda to Takizawa Katsumi as a man "connected with the ultranationalist camp who tries to do in the academics—an infamous fascist."[37] Minoda's attack only strengthened Nishida's commitment to fight against the ultranationalists' irrational trend of thought.[38] However, because Minoda's criticism of his thought lacked any philosophical content or focus, Nishida judged it best to ignore him. He confided this to Mutai Risaku:

> I will be seventy next year, and I feel that my stamina to engage in thinking and reading is diminishing somewhat. I dearly hope that younger generations of scholars like you will persevere to develop your thought. The man called Minoda is indeed a helpless case. I think it best not to take a mad dog seriously.[39]

Minoda and his camp continued to criticize Nishida but to no avail, and therefore, they began to shift their target to Kōsaka Masaaki and Kōyama Iwao.

Meanwhile, Kido had resigned from the post of minister of education on May 26, during a time when positions within the cabinet were being shuffled. Kido and Konoe instructed the succeeding minister, Araki Sadao (an army general), to keep contact with Nishida. When Araki called unexpectedly on Nishida at his house in Kyoto on June 6, Nishida had plenty of things to say to him. He reiterated his views on issues he had written to Kido about earlier: the world had become real for Japan; educational policies must be based consistently on the recognition that Japan was part of the global community; the government must respect scholarship.[40] Araki listened to him intently and responded by saying, "What you say makes perfect sense." But Nishida was skeptical about whether Araki would be willing to change the educational policy.[41] When he returned to Kamakura on July 25 for the summer, Nishida sought a meeting with the new minister. The two met on August 8 for an hour.[42] Nishida told Araki his concern that only those truly versed in education should make educational policies and alluded to Itō Enkichi, vice minister of education, whom Nishida and others did not think suitable for the position.[43] After the meeting Nishida felt that, although Araki was not a bad man, he lacked the awareness necessary to make "a bold change" in current educational policies.[44]

Nishida began to pay closer attention to the volatile European political situation and feared that war might break out in Europe.[45] When the Germans occupied Czechoslovakia under Hitler's order, Nishida wrote to Nishitani in Freiburg: "I am worried about your safety. Here, the war with China is escalating, without anyone knowing where it is going. The importation of books from abroad is now heavily restricted, and we can no longer obtain philosophical books from the European bookstores."[46]

On September 1 a devastating typhoon hit the Kantō area, causing ninety-nine deaths. In his reply to Hisamatsu's inquiry after his and Koto's safety, he wrote, half in jest: "Because human beings have become so bad, Noah's flood may be coming soon."[47] He was, in fact, deeply apprehensive about the global situation, and his fears were realized when the rains of the Great Flood took the form of bombs showered on major cities throughout Japan. In the fall of that year, Kobe was actually hit hard by a flood. Robert Schinzinger, who was then translating Nishida's essays into German, lost manuscripts, books, and index cards that he had made for the translation project; all that survived was the final draft, which was in the hands of his colleagues.[48]

On the evening of September 29, 1938, Nishida was supposed to have dinner with Konoe and Kido at Harada's house in Ōiso, but earlier that day the foreign minister, Ugaki Kazushige, resigned, provoking Konoe's own wish to resign. To avert this crisis, Kido and Harada enlisted the help of Ikeda Shigeaki, finance minister, and Yonai Mitsumasa, navy minister, to dissuade Konoe from resigning. Harada came home late in the evening, while Nishida and the other company, having already finished dinner, were waiting for him. Late that night, Konoe agreed to stay on as prime minister, but the incident confirmed Nishida's sense of Konoe's indecisiveness.[49] Nishida always remained sympathetic to Konoe, however. Kōsaka remembered: "Professor Nishida used to say Konoe was no good, but while saying so, he was deeply concerned about him."[50] Konoe, for his part, avoided seeing Nishida as much as possible while he was in the office of prime minister, for fear of what Nishida had to say to him.

From the middle of 1938, Beatrice Suzuki (Mrs. D. T. Suzuki) was not well, and Nishida sent Koto to call on her. Beatrice was suffering from cancer, and on Nishida's advice Daisetz chose St. Luke's in Tokyo for her treatment.[51]

Nishida and Koto returned to Kyoto on October 3, and, three days later, traveled to Kanazawa. Nishida had not visited Kanazawa for a decade and a half. His former student, Kiba Ryōhon, was now a professor at the Fourth Higher School and asked him to give a talk to the students on "The Problem of Japanese Culture."[52] While in Kanazawa, Nishida saw familiar faces—visiting with Tanaka Onokichi, for instance—and went to Unoke to pray at his family grave. In Unoke he also visited the elementary school that his father had founded years ago.

In September 1938 the leaders of the Showa Study Group set up a private boarding school, Shōwajuku, to train students for the rapidly changing international and national scenes.[53] It was open to both university students and the general public, and the fifty openings drew two hundred applicants. The *juku* opened on November 2. Nishida was asked to serve on the board of advisors. He agreed to lend his name, but he was far from impressed by the list of other advisors. He wrote to Hori that they put a title of "advisor" beside his name, but that "there are all sorts of people who are advisors. The group lacks coherence; and their claim that this is the 'Shōkasonjuku,[54] of the Shōwa period is too pretentious."[55] (The *juku* was suddenly closed down after only three years, following the October 15, 1941, arrest of Ozaki Hotsumi,[56] a member of the board, on an espionage charge.[57] The news of Ozaki's arrest took everyone connected with the Showa Study Group by surprise.)

On January 5, 1939, the Konoe cabinet dissolved, and Hiranuma Kiichirō became prime minister. At that time, Konoe became speaker of the privy council (*Sūmitsuin*), and Kido became home minister, while Araki Sadao remained the minister of education. Hiranuma was the head of the ultranationalistic organization, Kokuhonsha, which advocated an extremely nationalist "path of loyalty to the emperor" (*kōdō*). As prime minister, Hiranuma declared a "national spiritual motivation week" and addressed the Japanese people on the radio on "the correct path of the subjects of the emperor."

Nishida spent his winter as usual in Kamakura. On February 2, 1939, he finished an important essay, "Zettaimujunteki jikodōitsu" [Absolutely contradictory self-identity], which fully develops his dialectical logic to explain how individuals exist in the historical world, and what society is.[58] In this venture, he positively reevaluates the significance of Leibniz's idea of the monad, especially its "expressive" aspect, in relation to the discussion of the problem of the individual and the world.[59] From the standpoint of the dialectical world, the world in which we live is "the absolutely contradictory self-identity within which individuals mutually self-determine." In such a world, the individual, as something like a monad, assumes a double structure—the individual is that which reflects the world and is simultaneously a focal point of the world. Nishida maintains that while the Leibnizian monad is merely intellectual, the "actual monad" must be "self-forming," creative, and dynamic. Each individual is a living history, in the sense that each is creative and contributes to the formation of history. Nishida contends that were if not for the freedom and creativity of the individual, neither the "individual" nor the "world" would be possible. Nishida felt that he had clarified the core of his dialectical vision in this essay.[60]

On February 8 the Bungeishunjū Company arranged "A discussion with Nishida Kitarō,"[61] in which Miki Kiyoshi, Tanikawa Tetsuzō,[62] Satō Nobue,[63] and Hayashi Tatsuo[64] took part. Their discussion began with the current problems universities were facing, such as the restructuring of the colleges and departments, and moved on to the problem of thought control and Japan-China relations. On February 18 Nishida was invited to Harada's house at Ōiso, where he saw Nomura Kichisaburō,[65] president of Gakushūin; Ikeda Shigeaki, minister of finance; and Takagi Sōkichi, a navy captain.[66] Their conversation again touched on the issues of the Japanese spirit, the present condition of the university, and political negotiations with China.[67]

After Nishida returned to Kyoto on March 24, he began his essay, "Keiken kagaku" [Experiential science].[68] On July 18 he completed his manuscript of *Tetsugaku ronbunshū daisan* [Philosophical essays 3] and sent it to Iwanami. With the works contained in this volume, Nishida felt that he had captured the essence of his thought,[69] completing the path of philosophical inquiry that he had begun in "Ronri to seimei" (1936) by articulating the shape of "logic" as the very form of self-expression of the historical life.[70]

On July 16 Beatrice Lane Suzuki passed away. On that day Nishida wrote to Yamamoto: "I understand that there was no hope for Mrs. Daisetz. There was nothing to be done, given the nature of the illness. I worry about Daisetz—I just pray he won't be hard hit by this sad event."[71]

The educational policy advanced by the Ministry of Education under the Hiranuma cabinet bore the expected ultranationalistic bias. Local governors were appointed to the post of vice minister of education[72] and heads of departments within the ministry, lowering further the standard of Japanese education. This was discouraging to Nishida.[73] The myopic vision of these officials was eventually to lead the Japanese into an irrational all-out war effort, which Nishida was to describe as "the natural outcome of the blind pride and recklessness of those louts who do not know the world."[74] In any case, he saw the danger coming. He complained to Harada:

They have discharged officials who have common sense and appointed countrified mayors and governors, who call themselves "spiritualists," and who throw their weight around by enforcing such inane orders as boys must crop their hair short. What childish absurdity! That Japan presents itself as the leader of East Asia with these fellows at the helm is truly lamentable. [75]

Nishida's impression of the local governors was shared by Harada, who observed: "If local governors are of affable character, they tend to be more like the teachers of moral education; if their characters are bad, they truly lack refinement. Those who are well-informed [of the current world situation] are extremely rare." [76] These "spiritualists," who lacked any global perspective or insight, were increasingly responsible for policies governing Japanese education.

Nishida returned to Kamakura on July 26, 1939. On August 30 the Hiranuma cabinet dissolved in the face of a German-Russian rapprochement, and army general Abe Nobuyuki formed a new cabinet. [77] Nishida was unimpressed with the composition of this new cabinet, especially in the area of diplomacy. Abe initially served as both prime minister and foreign minister. Nishida wrote to Hori:

If powerful military men interfere with diplomacy and diplomacy degenerates into nothing, Japan may come under international criticism. It would be painful for me to watch this happen. Throughout history, a successful war effort has always been accompanied by an equally successful diplomatic effort (e.g., Bismarck's diplomacy). Prime Minister is but a cheerful old man. Please destroy this letter after reading it. These days, it is quite dangerous [to criticize the government]. [78]

As usual, Nishida did not restrain his criticism regarding the choice of the minister of education. It was very clear to Nishida that the education of children was essential to the future of Japan, as it created the next generation, the tomorrow, of the country. Politicians should not tamper with educational policy; rather, the government should appoint as vice minister of education someone well trained in the field of scholarship and learning, and capable of transcending the divisions among disciplines. If not a specialist in education, then it should be someone who could understand the technical aspects of research and learning. [79] After all, education was traditionally considered "the nation's greatest task with an impact lasting a hundred years." [80] His letter to Harada on September 1, 1939, best captures Nishida's passionate commitment to education:

To change any part of the educational system has grave consequences for the country; change has to be implemented with a farsighted vision that extends one hundred years into the future. For this reason I believe that it is better not to rush into educational reform . . . but to wait until the world is calm and people are free to express their views. It is abominable that the ministry merely chants "reform, reform," and destroys things without distinguishing rocks from gems. It will take twenty or thirty years for the present-day elementary school children to reach adulthood. For this reason, we must educate children by thinking ahead by forty or fifty years.[81]

As Nishida had seen, the Abe cabinet was weak.[82] At least they had appointed Nomura Kichisaburō to the post of foreign minister on September 25. The Ministry of Education advocated the slogan, "Abolish selfish desires and dedicate yourself to the country" *(messhi hōkō)*, which was distasteful to Nishida. He described it as "crude, empty, and destroying all things graceful and beautiful"[83] in Japan's cultural and spiritual heritage.

In Europe, Germany had invaded Poland on September 1, 1939. Nishida feared that war would spread throughout Europe and the rest of the world, despite diplomatic efforts to avert it. He wrote to Hori that "if this war turns into a worldwide war, I would think the course of history will be fundamentally altered. The world cannot remain in the present situation forever. Who can guarantee that a Noah's flood is not coming?"[84] Nishida's fear was warranted. On September 3 Great Britain declared war against Germany, and the world plunged into World War II.

At this critical juncture in world history, Nishida was gazing at the "Eternal Now" on the beach of Kamakura:

In the dusk I walk
along the beach
washed by wild waves
ah! evening primroses
are in bloom[85]

In the wake of the outbreak of war, Nishida strengthened his conviction that Japanese scholars in the field of jurisprudence and economics needed to carry out a radical, in-depth study to get Japan out of the present crises.[86] In late September, having completed his preface to the third volume of his collected philosophical essays,[87] he began to work on *Nihon bunka no mondai* [The problem of Japanese culture], which Iwanami Shigeo had asked him to write as part of the "Iwanami New Books" series.[88]

It was around this time that a navy official, Takagi Sōkichi, approached Nishida. Takagi was thinking of creating a think tank, bringing together scholars and the navy. Such a group would provide naval officers with an opportunity to meet with leading intellectuals; it also would make the navy's interest known to the intellectual community and thereby gain their support.[89] Takagi's ambition was motivated in part by power struggles between the navy and the army. He specifically sought the collaboration of the Kyoto school thinkers in the hope that they would best offer the navy "a perspective that embraced both Western scientific culture and Oriental religious philosophy."[90] Takagi called on Nishida at his house in Ubagayatsu on September 28. Nishida told him first to obtain Tanabe Hajime's permission and then to get in touch with Kōyama Iwao.[91] This is how members of the Kyoto school—Kōsaka Masaaki, Kōyama Iwao, Nishitani Keiji, Suzuki Shigetaka, and Kimura Motomori—came to collaborate with the navy's think tank.[92]

On October 3 Nishida was invited to Harada's in Ōiso for a dinner, where Konoe, Kido, Oda, Nagayo Yoshirō, Ueda Misao, and Matsudaira Yasumasa[93] gathered to "dine and listen to Dr. Nishida."[94] As usual, Nishida's schedule right before his departure for Kyoto was packed. On October 11 he was invited by Iwanami to a dinner, where he was in the company of younger intellectuals: Tsuda Sōkichi, Miura Shinshichi, Ishihara Atsushi, Takemi Tarō,[95] Tōhata Seiichi,[96] and Hani Gorō.[97] Two days later he and Koto had dinner with Miki.

Following his return to Kyoto on October 16, Nishida earnestly began working on *Nihon bunka no mondai* for Iwanami's series. Because the subject matter was not quite philosophical enough and did not particularly interest him, he initially planned to expand the talk he had given at the university a year previously and be done with it.[98] But once be began writing, he realized that he had to write a whole new book. This project forced him to rest his pen from serious philosophical writing.

Nishida also had to prepare a draft of the new year's lecture to the emperor, known as the *goshinkō;* he had accepted the nomination to present the lecture for 1941. He wrote to Mutai Risaku: "It is truly a comical sight for me to be in a frock coat and wearing a silk hat, but it is for the sake of the imperial family. Since the field of philosophy has not been represented at the new year's lecture, I accepted it."[99] Part of his reason for accepting the nomination was his sense of sympathy for the emperor, now that the country was run by bureaucrats in close association with the military.[100] Nishida drafted his lecture to the emperor while he also worked on *Nihon bunka no mondai*. This coincidence of timing seems to explain Nishida's extensive references to the imperial family *(kōshitsu)* in *Nihon bunka no mondai*. According to protocol, Nishida accompanied the current new year's lecturer to the Imperial Palace on January 22, 1940. To give himself plenty of time, Nishida and Koto left Kyoto on January 11—about two weeks earlier than usual.

My Philosophical Path *

People say I am always discussing the same problem. That may be true. Since my first book, *An Inquiry into the Good* [1911], my aim has been to approach things from the most immediate and most fundamental standpoint, and my goal has been to capture this standpoint, from which everything emerges and to which everything returns.

Granted, the expression "pure experience," which I adopted in my first book, had a psychological overtone. But at least in my mind, it was a standpoint that transcended the dichotomy of subject and object, and I tried to investigate the objective world also from that standpoint. Be that as it may, what I upheld as the standpoint of "pure experience" had to be subjected to a thorough examination, as I confronted the thoughts of the neo-Kantian thinkers of the Baden school and so forth. Out of this examination, I came to hold a position somewhat akin to the philosophy of self-consciousness espoused by Fichte (see my *Intuition and Reflection in Self-Consciousness*). But what motivated my thinking from the beginning was not the Fichtean "Ego," but something that transcended it, or something that was "prior" to it. What I meant by "intuition" was not a kind of objective reality, as was the case with Fichte up to Schelling. In my mind, "intuition" was not something that transcended the operation of consciousness; rather, it was that which establishes the operation of consciousness itself.

For a philosophical system to stand on its own, a logical system is necessary. I grappled with this problem until I found a clue in my essay, *"Topos"* ["Basho," 1926]. I was guided by Aristotle's definition

---

*Preface to the *Third Philosophical Essays*, 1939, NKZ 9:3–7.

of *hypokeimenon* in arriving at this idea. But Aristotle's logic, in which the grammatical subject holds the central place, cannot deal with the reality of the self-conscious self. The self is not something objectifiable, and yet it is something we can think about. This indicated to me that there is another mode of thinking. In contrast to Aristotelian logic, which focuses on the grammatical subject *(shugoteki ronri)*, I called the other mode of thinking the "logic of the grammatical predicate" or "predicate logic" *(jutsugoteki ronri)*. The self, as the unifier of consciousness, is not something that can be conceived as a grammatical subject. Rather, it is thinkable "topologically" *(bashoteki)* as the self-determination of the field of consciousness. If we consider judgment to be established as the self-determination of the universal, the approach that emphasizes the grammatical predicate may simply be termed "[of] predicate" *(jutsugoteki)*. Of course, this logic of "predicate" does not imply that it (i.e., logic of predicate) has no grammatical subject. Rather, according to this logic, we obtain the grammatical subject as the self-determination of the universal, and insofar as the grammatical subject is determined, we can think about things objective. I called this universal the judging universal *(handanteki ippansha)*.

When we consider the universal to be topological, there is something that transcends the universal itself as the self-determination of the universal itself; even the phenomenon of our consciousness is conceivable by this transcendent something. One may object, indeed, that for us to be able to think, there has to be some grammatically subjective thing. Certainly, it is true that we "see" things and "hear" things. The question is, do we consider these "things" in terms of the objects or as the phenomena of consciousness? Here, the universal that sustains each assumption has to be different. I termed the universal that sustains the phenomena of consciousness "the self-conscious universal" *(jikakuteki ippansha)*. But the most fundamental and comprehensive universal, from which everything emerges and to which everything returns, is something like the "expressive universal" *(hyōgenteki ippansha)*. Both the knowledge of the world of objects and the knowledge of the phenomena of consciousness are established as the self-determination of this expressive universal, as its particular self-determinations. Moreover, because the self-determination of this expressive universal transcends the grammatically subjective being *(shugoteki u)*, I called it the "logic of nothingness" *(mu no ronri)*, and because it embraces individuals within it, I called it "topological" *(bashoteki)*.

But as I had already made clear in my reply to the late Dr. Sōda [April 1927], I did not postulate various kinds of universal by simply transcending the judging universal. Rather, I took the active process of self-consciousness into consideration and asserted that the process of judgment is also conceivable in terms of the concrete unfolding of self-consciousness.

From the perspective I hold today, what I called the "self-determination of the expressive universal" should be termed the unfolding of self-consciousness of the active-intuitive *(kōiteki-chokkanteki)* and creative-productive *(poieshisuteki)* self. From this perspective we can think not only about our conscious self but also about the objective world. The unfolding of natural scientific judgment is in fact nothing other than the unfolding of self-consciousness of the creative-productive self.

In contrast to Aristotle's logic of the grammatical subject *(shugoteki ronri)* or Kant's objective logic *(taishō ronri)*, I thought about the most fundamental and concrete universal, one that can also explain the activities of the self. But the universal that allows that which is thoroughly individual to be conceivable is the universal in which the many and the one are contradictorily self-identical—that is, it is the dialectical universal *(benshōhōteki ippansha)*. This is why I said "the universal determination is the individual determination, and the individual determination is the universal determination" *(The Fundamental Problems of Philosophy* [1933]).

What I earlier called the "topos" is this dialectical universal; it is the world of contradictory self-identity. "Nothingness" *(mu)* means "absolutely contradictory self-identity" *(zettaimujunteki jikodōitsu)*. From this perspective, all that exists is "being" and "non-being" at the same time. "Absolute Nothingness" is that which is totally transcendent of everything and yet that by which everything is established. The world that fashions itself as the self-determination of this dialectical universal is the world that fashions itself historically and socially—the world from which our self is born and to which it returns. The so-called "world of nature" is also part of this historical world.

Logic is not something separate from the historical world; rather it is the formula of the expressive self-formation of historical life *(rekishiteki seimei)*. Even Aristotle's logic was not a simple formal logic; it was a historical and social logic of Greece that had Plato's philosophy in the background. As such, it was connected with the metaphysical world of the Greeks. Something similar can be said of Kant's logic. But this does not mean that logic is a product of each historical epoch, nor does it mean that there is no objective universality. Rather, each historical epoch is a unique product of concrete historical life, and as such it has its own way of looking at things and thinking about things. Each epoch may be considered a particularized formulation of concrete logic. The formulation of concrete logic has to be sought in the establishment of historical life. In my essay, "Logic and life" [1936] (compiled in *Philosophical Essays 2*), I investigated that fundamental issue. The essays contained in the present *Philosophical Essays 3* complete this line of inquiry.

As I stated above, even from the beginning of my philosophical inquiry, I did not simply think about the concrete universal by transcending the judging universal, but I took into consideration the positive reality of self-consciousness. This self-consciousness is the self-consciousness of historical life. The most fundamental self-determination of the universal is the unfolding of self-consciousness of historical life. Ever since my *Inquiry into the Good*, my main objective was to grasp the most fundamental mode of perception and cognition. Today, I call my standpoint the logic of consciousness of historical life, the logic of consciousness of the creative-productive self. As such, it is the logic of the function of history. Various topological universals that I discussed at one point or another are determined functionally and historico-spatially.

I have thus far discussed various topics, but the central problem for me has always remained one and the same. I am still hoping to engage concrete, particular issues from my own perspective. But I, who have reached the age of three score and ten, which poets of old described as "rare," must admit that the philosophical problems with which I have grappled ended up my lifelong problems.

I am not suggesting that people should take up the philosophical problems that I took up. But I would like to say this much: to simply switch the topic of one's philosophical inquiry is not synonymous with making one's thought anew. Also, that a philosophical problem touches on concrete reality does not necessarily mean that the thinker's thought is "concrete." In this present historical period, which requires us to look back on the cultural heritage nurtured by our ancestors in a global perspective, I think it is necessary that we return to the most fundamental mode of viewing and thinking in our philosophical engagements. (September 1939)

Chapter 24

History, State, and the Individual

(1940–1941)

On January 15, 1940, the Abe cabinet dissolved and Yonai Mitsumasa, an admiral, was appointed prime minister. Two days earlier, the Tsuda incident had broken out, when the home minister took issue with Tsuda Sōkichi's *Kojiki oyobi nihonshoki no kenkyū* [A study of the *Records of Ancient Matters* and the *Chronicles of Japan*]. Tsuda,[1] a leading historian, had applied his method of "empirical scientific investigation" to the *Records of Ancient Matters* and the *Chronicles of Japan*, two primary sources of early Japanese history. Ultranationalists, led by Minoda and his followers, accused Tsuda of undermining the sacred origin of Japan and going against the *kokutai*, the emperor system.[2] On February 10 the book was banned.

On March 7 Yamamoto Ryōkichi invited Nishida to record their conversation[3] at a studio of the Japan Broadcasting Corporation (NHK). The recording session was a present from the former students of Yamamoto to celebrate his seventieth birthday. Their conversation on "Sōzō" [Creativity] was transcribed soon after, but it was not made public because it contained Nishida's criticism of the suppression of individual creativity under totalitarianism.[4]

The Tsuda incident took an unexpected turn on March 8, when Iwanami Shigeo, the publisher of Tsuda's works, was indicted on the charge that he had violated the publishing ordinance, article 26. According to the ordinance, the publisher of materials that "may change the political system or confuse the interpretation of the Meiji constitution" was subject to the same charges as the author. Tsuda and Iwanami were brought to trial.[5] Nishida saw Tsuda on March 7 at a meeting of scholars (*Kokumin gakujutsu kyōkai*) and did not get the impression that anything radical would come out of the harassment.[6]

He wrote to Yamamoto that "if the power of justice is influenced to this extent by the plotting of Minoda and his clique, I think we have to give up all scholarly research. P.S. Please burn this letter."[7]

Iwanami Shigeo reacted to the charge in his characteristically flamboyant way. On the very day of the indictment, he purchased property in Atami, a hot-spring resort overlooking the Pacific Ocean. He went ahead and built a house there, where he could "rest and nurture his body in case he was to be imprisoned." Nothing but the best building materials were used, and for the bathtub they drew the local hot-spring water. There was an old oak tree on the ground, which Iwanami did not want to cut down, so he asked the architect to design the house accordingly; hence, the name of this country house, "Sekirekisō" (abode cherishing the oak tree). Iwanami found it a perfect hideaway for entertaining his guests and friends, even though he had built it as a place to rest.[8]

Nishida had put the final period to *Nihon bunka no mondai* by the end of January,[9] and the book was scheduled for publication on March 30. Although he did not directly deal with historical facts in the book, the recent Tsuda incident made Nishida worry about a possible attack from Minoda. Scholarly writings were no longer exempt from ultranationalists' criticisms.[10] On the day *Nihon bunka no mondai* was published Nishida wrote to Yamamoto:

Nihon bunka no mondai . . . is a kind of ad lib work for me and not truly polished. I know that I should have given more detailed accounts for the sake of the general reader, but I didn't have enough time to do that. Also, there is that faction, Minoda and his clique, that is trying to do us in. I had to take many precautions when choosing words, especially in places where I dealt with sensitive subjects. Because I had to waste my energy on such stupid concerns, I became quite fed up. I would imagine they will take up this book regardless of what I said and attack me. I'm also worried about what might happen to Iwanami.[11]

The book sold more than 40,000 copies within ten days of its publication, clearly demonstrating to Minoda and his group Nishida's infallible position as the "boss" of the Kyoto school.[12] Minoda wrote a critique, "Nishida tetsugaku no Nihon bunkaron ni okeru datsuraku" [Lacunae in the theory of Japanese culture in the Nishidan philosophy] in *Genri Nippon*,[13] but the vague title suggests that his critique was not sharply focused. Ironically, Nishida's careful choice of words in this book, a tactic he employed to avert Minoda's attack, backfired. Postmodern critics of the Kyoto school found it a perfectly "nationalistic" text. Perhaps this merely indicates that no one can ultimately escape the fickle tides of opinion, as François Rabelais's words suggest: "Fate carries with its tides those who obey it and drags along those who resist it." [14] This reality also engulfed Nishida, despite his thinking that he could resist such tides, as his words of advice to Katsube Kenzō show: "We must have a broad perspective and proceed in the right direction; we should neither turn our back on the novelties of the time nor blindly follow the fashion of the day." [15]

Nishida knew very well that human existence in the history-bound world is a dialectical, "contradictorily identical" existence because we are ontologically caught in the pull between the larger historical environment and our decisions and actions as individuals. We are constantly confronted with our environment—whether social, political, cultural, or natural. Nishida could not, however, ever give up his idealistic belief that individuals do make a difference; he could never negate the place reserved for "the unique, history-making individual." [16] This paradox is one of the philosophical problems Nishida left for posterity to work on, or at least to ponder.

With *Nihon bunka no mondai* out of his way, Nishida resumed his philosophical inquiry. In February he had read Søren Kierkegaard's *Krankheit zum Tode* [Sickness unto Death] (1849), in which "serious analysis of religious consciousness" inspired him to write about "the foundation of practical philosophy." [17] The result was "Jissentetsugaku joron" [Prolegomena to practical philosophy], an essay he wrote between March 18 and June 30. [18] To Nishida, Kierkegaard's analysis of "despair" reveals the absolute paradox at the foundation of human existence—that a human being is not only in relation to his or her self but is also determined by others. Kierkegaard's insight captures the core of the "absolutely contradictorily self-identical" nature of human existence. [19] Kierkegaard's introspective analysis of the affective aspect, or "pathos," of human experience, described for Nishida the volitional reality of human existence in a profound manner. Kierkegaard's view of the self as determined by the Absolute Other corresponded to Nishida's view that "there is something at the depth of our self-awareness that transcends it and makes it possible." In "Jissentetsugaku joron," Nishida's thinking reaches an existential depth that renders his dialectical philosophy more concrete. When the entire world was on the brink of plunging into war, Nishida focused his thought on the bedrock of human reality. This posture reminds us of how Nishida had spent his younger days engaged in intensive self-reflection and *zazen* during the Russo-Japanese War.

By the end of June 1940, it was clear that the Yonai cabinet was at an impasse, and Konoe was again appointed prime minister. Both Nishida and Yamamoto were extremely apprehensive about this turn of events. Nishida received a telegram from Harada, who informed him of Konoe's brief visit to Kyoto. Nishida called on Konoe on the evening of June 20 and expressed his reservations about Konoe's acceptance of the responsibilities of the office.[20] Konoe told him that the circumstances were such that he had no other choice but to accept the duty and reassured him that he would do his best to hold onto his ideals. During the course of their conversation, Konoe revealed the blueprint of his "New Order." Nishida's response was that "a new order may be established but the key point is the selection of leaders; there is no political party in charge in the new order, only a monolithic entity and the inherent danger of leaving posterity with the undesirable aftermath."[21] Several days later, Nishida lamented to Yamamoto that the cabinet was only getting worse.[22]

The second Konoe cabinet was formed on July 22, 1940. In its early days Japanese political parties dissolved themselves one after another to join the bandwagon of "Konoe's New Order," which was essentially a single-party totalitarian reconfiguration of social and political structures. The Tripartite Pact between Japan, Germany, and Italy was signed in Berlin on September 27, 1940, despite strong opposition within the government and from the emperor himself.[23] Japan was steadily proceeding on its deadly course toward world war. As the shape of the New Order and the profile of the single party, "Taiseiyokusankai," emerged more clearly, Nishida was especially critical of some of its leading members, namely, Hashimoto Kingorō, the head of the Great Japan Youth Organization, and Nakano Seigō, the president of the Oriental Association, who looked to Nazi Germany as a model.[24] These were reasons enough for Nishida to worry about the future of the country.[25] On the day of the inauguration of the Taiseiyokusan Party on October 12, he wrote to Yamamoto: "I don't know where Konoe's New Order is headed. I fear that the consequences will be far worse than those of a government run by bureaucrats."[26] He was also critical of Hashida Kunihiko, minister of education: "Hashida is merely toying with abstract ideas, such as 'Japanese learning' and 'Japanese spirit.' I agree with you that he is a puppet of the military, although I think he is slightly better than the combination of Araki and Ishiguro."[27]

Nishida continued to work as usual, undeterred by the political chaos. On October 22, he finished his essay "*Poiesis* to *praksis*" [Making and doing, or Production and action],²⁸ in which he looked into the reality of action *(praksis)*. He considered *praksis* to be our activity that ultimately establishes or creates *(poiesis)* our very selves in the world—the individual many in the contradictorily self-identical world.²⁹ He also redefined "reason" *(logos)* in relation to skill *(technē)*. The world defines itself in the interconnection of *poiesis* and *praksis:* "To be rational means for us to think becoming a thing, and for us to act becoming a thing *(mono to natte kangae, mono to natte okonau),*" in the oneness of subjectivity and objectivity.³⁰

Sometime in the fall of 1940, while Nishida was in Kamakura, a public indictment of Nishidan philosophy was staged at Kyoto Imperial University. The accusation was also directed against the philosophy department.³¹ Nishida saw the political maneuvering behind such denunciations—the times were becoming "troublesome." Once he returned to Kyoto on October 29, however, the accusation subsided. In November he was decorated with the Cultural Medal *(bunka kunshō)*, the highest honor bestowed on a Japanese citizen for making a significant contribution to the development of culture and knowledge. Nishida was in acute pain from hemorrhoids, however, and could not attend the award ceremony held in Tokyo.

As if a society that had lost its rationality also had to lose the embodiment of rationality and conscience, on November 24 the last *genrō*, Saionji Kinmochi, died at the age of ninety-one. Saionji's state funeral on December 5, 1940, was not only the funeral of good old Meiji liberalism, it also looked ominously like a rehearsal for the burial of the state, the country of Japan that had been formed after the Meiji Restoration of 1868.

In December Nishida began his next essay, "Rekishiteki keiseisayō to shite no geijutsuteki sōsaku" [Artistic creation as the history-forming operation],³² in which he unfolded his theory of artistic creation in terms of "the unity of the body and the mind" *(shinshin ichinyo)* from the standpoint of "the ordinary level" *(heijōtei)*—a heavily Zen-inspired perspective. In this work Nishida discusses Western aesthetic theories developed by Aristotle, Conrad Fiedler, Alois Riegl, and Wilhelm Worringer; he also introduces the works on "art and ritual" by Jane Harrison and Robertson Smith and refers to Malinowski's findings.³³ As 1940 came to a close, he also finalized his new year's lecture to the emperor on "Rekishi tetsugaku ni tsuite" [On the philosophy of history].³⁴

Nishida welcomed New Year's Day, 1941, by visiting the mausoleum of the Meiji emperor in Momoyama and reminisced about the

bygone era of Meiji. The day was peaceful. He continued writing
"Rekishiteki keiseisayō to shite no geijutsuteki sōsaku." On January 6
a newspaper reporter from the *Asahi Shinbun* called on Nishida to get
his comments on Henri Bergson, who had died the previous day.
Nishida paid the utmost tribute to the genial thinker and expressed his
utmost indebtedness to him.[35]

On January 11 he and Koto made their seasonal move to Kamakura. Three days later, he attended the meeting of the board of directors of Fūjukai (literally, wind-tree society)—a new scholarship foundation established by Iwanami Shigeo, who put out one million yen for
this foundation in memory of his parents.[36] Scholarships were to be
given to promising young researchers in the fields of philosophy, physics, and mathematics to promote basic science research.[37] The aim of
the Fūjukai was very much like Nishida's recommendation to the
Committee for the Renewal of Education and Scholarship he made
five years previously. On January 15 Nishida attended the meeting of
consultants to the Ministry of Education. At that time he "sharply crit-

After the new year's lecture to
the emperor, January 23, 1941.
A rare picture of Nishida in
Western attire, taken in the
garden of his son-in-law,
Kaneko Tazekō, in Tokyo.
Nishida is wearing the Cultural Medal, conferred on
him in November 1940. From
Nishida Kitarō Zenshū, vol. 10,
frontispiece.

icized the ministry for blindly following the dictates of political necessity."[38] To his surprise, there were some who actually agreed with his statement.[39]

On January 23, Nishida gave his new year's lecture[40] to Emperor Hirohito. Because the allotted time was only thirty minutes, Nishida had to rush a bit during the second half of his lecture.[41]

Because Emperor Hirohito was a specialist in biology, Nishida took an example from biology to illustrate his point: "Just as biological life continues to live mediated by the activities of the cells, so has historical society its eternal life as a global reality insofar as it is mediated by individuals." Nishida made a special reference to "totalitarianism, which negates individuals," as a thing of the past and maintained his view that returning "to the spirit of the foundation of the country" and considering "the imperial family as the axis of Japanese history" does not mean a return to ancient times but a step into an ever new age, for the "restoration of the old ways *(fukko)* must mean making anew *(ishin).*" Nishida took this opportunity as his only chance to communicate his view of history directly to the emperor. Nishida felt after his talk that it might have been a little difficult for the emperor; he might have put the emperor in an awkward position.[42] However, at the new year's poetry gathering held at the Imperial Court on January 28, the emperor presented his *waka:* "Mountain peaks after mountain peaks I see clouds hovering over them; I pray winds will rise and clear them away as soon as possible." It was an expression of his wish for world peace.[43] Perhaps, Nishida's lecture addressed the emperor's personal concerns after all.

Nishida, Yamamoto, and Suzuki, already in their seventies, remained close friends. Yamamoto suggested cutting a phonograph record of their conversation, and the date was set for February 28, 1941, with the Columbia Record Company in Tokyo. Nishida had suggested beforehand that "it would be better to talk about ordinary things, such as what we did when we were young, and not to touch on current political issues."[44] When they got together, they "jumped fifty years back in time."[45] They talked about what Suzuki was working on at that time and various other matters, including how Nishida philosophized. He talked about how difficult it was for him to accept assignments unrelated to his main focus of his thought, such as the new year's lecture to the emperor *(goshinkō).* Since such a remark could easily be construed as lèse-majesté, the recording was not made public.[46] Following the recording, the three friends proceeded to a restaurant in Ushigome and enjoyed one another's company.

Nishida, Yamamoto, and Suzuki at Restaurant Yoshino in Ushigome, Tokyo, February 28, 1941. From left to right: D. T. Suzuki, Nishida, Aihara Yoshikazu (Yamamoto's son-in-law), and Yamamoto Ryōkichi. From Yamamoto Ryōkichi, *Daisetsu ate Yamamoto Ryōkichi shokan.*

After the death of Saionji, Harada's life lost its focus. He fell victim to a stroke on March 7 but fortunately survived the attack. Nevertheless, Harada's delicate condition hung on Nishida's mind. Nishida returned to Kyoto on April 4. Soon after, on April 9, his daughter Tomoko died of general debility. Tomoko, after her brief marriage, gradually lost her will to live and spent her last seven years in a hospital. By the time she died, she had lost even her will to eat—she simply wasted away.[47] Nishida wrote to his inner circle of friends about Tomoko's death and thanked them for what they had done for her over the course of many years. Less than a month after Tomoko's death, on May 7, Nishida's junior colleague Kuki Shūzō died after a brief battle with stomach cancer. He had loved Kuki's unique aesthetic talent and deeply lamented his colleague's death.

Once life settled down again at home, Nishida began working on "Kokka riyū no mondai" [The problem of raison d'état].[48] In it he advances his view that "the state is neither the Leviathan of Thomas Hobbes,[49] nor is it the *volonté générale* (general will) that Rousseau envisaged." Nor is it "the moral norm that we conceive from the stand-point of the abstract conscious self."[50] Rather, the state is created when each race becomes a unique creative power of the historical world by harboring "global subjectivity within it." In this process "the individ-ual does not become part of the world by being separated from the state but rather by being one with it. It is because the state is the process of the individuation of the world."[51] Nishida is concerned with clarifying the difference between his view and Hegel's view of the state because they appear very similar on the surface. The key to Hegel's position is universal reason; to his own, it is the concrete universal. The most fundamental difference, Nishida points out, is that in Hegel's system "creative individuality" has no place.[52] Nishida touches on the Japanese *kokutai*, the emperor system, as "the state" in the primary sense.[53] He further distinguishes the Japanese emperor system from totalitarian states, in that the former had a religious origin and had continued to develop in a religious context to the present day.[54] After completing this essay, Nishida collected his writings from 1940 to 1941 as *Tetsugaku ronbunshū daiyon* [Philosophical essays 4] and sent the manuscript to Iwanami on August 27.

On July 16, 1941, the second Konoe cabinet dissolved in order to dismiss the fascistic foreign minister, Matsuoka Yōsuke. Two days later, the third Konoe cabinet was formed. Nishida was somewhat hopeful that Konoe would actually make use of this second chance to turn over a new leaf. He wrote to Hori: "Konoe appears to be taking his duty seriously this time, and I am very pleased. The only thing is that he lacks unwavering courage when it comes to the crucial moment of decision making, and I'm worried about it. I'm only praying that he will get Japan out of the present mess."[55] But the United States–Japan peace negotiations with President Franklin D. Roosevelt ground to a halt, and the government virtually gave its seal of approval for the mil-itary to go ahead with the war against the United States on September 6 in a meeting at which Emperor Hirohito was personally present. Konoe gave up on the situation, and on October 16 the third Konoe cabinet dissolved. Nishida wrote to Yamamoto on the eve of Konoe's final resignation:

> The news of Konoe's stepping down in the face of the crisis is truly dis-tressing. I suspect he made one too many careless moves in the past, which prevented any further maneuvers. On top of this, my heart is filled with anxiety to think that the government might resort to irra-tional military force. . . . I hear that the ministry of education switched

the graduation day for higher school students back to the regular scheduled date after all. How shallow and ignorant they are, and indeed they
have staged a terribly ugly show. [56]

Nishida wrote to Konoe, feeling sorry for the way he had to resign:
"The reason Japanese statesmen age quickly is that they do not study.
Fortunately, you will have time now that you have retired from the
position of prime minister—may I suggest that you dedicate yourself
to study?" [57] On October 18 Tōjō Hideki was appointed prime minister and organized his cabinet. Nishida reacted to this turn of events
and wrote to Hori: "We are going to have a totally military government. For unknown reasons, my limbs have been swollen, and I feel
uncomfortable." [58]

From the beginning of October, Nishida had been suffering from
rheumatism. On the day that the Tōjō cabinet was installed, Nishida
and Koto were supposed to return by day train to Kyoto from Iwanami's country house, Sekirekisō, in Atami, but Nishida's physical
condition grew so much worse that they had to take a sleeper. His
condition continued to deteriorate, and he had to be admitted to the
Kyoto Prefecture Hospital for treatment at the beginning of November. [59] It was on his hospital bed that Nishida learned about the Japanese attack of Pearl Harbor from Aihara Shinsaku. Aihara, one of his
former students, brought several newspapers with him to the hospital.
Nishida's expression was extremely grave. [60] He remained in the hospital for more than fifty days. It looked as though his condition would
improve slowly, so he decided to finish his treatment at home and left
the hospital on December 28.

A New Year's Lecture to the Emperor:
On the Philosophy of History *

1. PHILOSOPHY AS A UNIFYING DISCIPLINE

Today in the West, learning *(gakumon)* is separated into many specialized fields, but learning originally grew out of the sociohistorical

---

* Nishida presented this lecture to Emperor Hirohito on 23 January 1941. The
lecture, "Rekishi-tetsugaku ni tsuite," appears in NKZ 12:267–72, and *JPS* 347
(April 1946), 1–4. Headings are supplied by the translator.

life of human beings—out of our practical [daily] lives. Thus, it should exist for [the benefit] of practical life. Learning does not exist separate from our everyday lives. That is why the more specialized and compartmentalized learning becomes, the more we have the need for a discipline that unites these specialized fields and connects them to our daily lives. This discipline is philosophy.

In antiquity, learning was not yet divided into various fields, and philosophy was looked on as learning itself. More recently, as learning became more and more specialized, philosophy as an independent discipline that unites various divisions of learning came into being.

Thus, from the days of the Greeks to the present day, the discipline of philosophy has undergone various changes. If I may describe Greek philosophy as a philosophy of the *polis*, centering in the city life of the Greeks, medieval philosophy was a religious philosophy, centering in the European Christian life, and recent philosophy is a scientific philosophy, centering in the recent scientific culture.

Turning to the East, systems such as Confucianism, which is based on the teachings of Confucius and Mencius, and the thought of the "one hundred philosophers" have been considered philosophy. In my humble opinion, Buddhist doctrines especially contain a deep philosophical truth that is at least on a par with, if not superior to, the achievements of Western philosophy. These Oriental philosophical traditions have greatly influenced Japanese thought. The difference, however, is that in the East, philosophy did not fully develop itself as a specialized learned discipline in the same way as it did in the West. I believe that we need to put our effort [into establishing philosophy as a distinct discipline].

As I just mentioned, in the West philosophy developed as a scholarly discipline. After Galileo [Galilei] and [Isaac] Newton, philosophy came under the influence of the great development of physics in the eighteenth century, and people came to regard the world purely in terms of the natural sciences. In this spirit, cultures, which developed in history, and which are unique to each country, were considered to follow the general law [of natural sciences] like any other natural phenomenon. But in the nineteenth century, people began to reflect on their own cultural heritage and amend the view of culture simply as a natural phenomenon. I believe that history as an academic discipline arose and developed mainly in the nineteenth century, for it was then that people came to recognize the differences between the laws of the natural sciences and those of history. I think that today we are moving more toward considering the fundamental structure of the world in terms of the philosophy of history, and not according to the terms laid down by the natural sciences. Similarly, the view of the law of causation has undergone changes. I think that today's quantum theory in physics bears witness to this change in focus.

2. BIOLOGICAL LIFE AND HISTORICAL LIFE

Your Majesty, since I understand that you have an in-depth knowledge of biology, may I be permitted to take the world of biology as an example to illustrate [the point of my lecture]? Biological life is shaped in and through the interaction of the formative activities of biological species and their environment. These formative activities proceed teleologically, and I believe that they cannot be simply explained away in terms of the mechanical operation of the material laws of causation. As to how the biological species shape their environment and how the environment shapes its biological species, we need to turn to the mediating activities of the cells. Cellular activities function as the medium, the biological species create their environment, and the environment creates biological species.

Human life is also shaped through the interaction of the formative activities of the species and their environment, and in this sense it is no different from biological life. But in human life, what is created is not mere matter but has its own spirit, and it in turn provokes us human beings in a spiritual way. For instance, what the ancient people created does not solely belong to times past but are endowed with their spirit and continue to touch us moderners. Again, a thing I have made stands in front of me as if it were made by someone else [in terms of its objective existence]; likewise, a thing made by someone else stands in front of me as if it were made by me [in terms of its impact on me]. This is why we always possess a commonly shared tradition, centered in which we continue to develop our human life. Human life is different from biological life in that it is historical.

In our historical life, the past is not just the events of bygone days; rather, we have to consider that the past and the future are always copresent in the present. The historical world continues to move on from the present, which contains both the past and the future, to another present, which likewise contains the past and the future. The historical world does not unfold mechanically the way the material world does, nor does it proceed teleologically the way the biological world does. Rather, it continues to develop itself, having as its content that which is beyond time, that which is eternal. In other words, the historical world is cultural.

3. THE HISTORICAL WORLD AND NATIONALISM

Any historical world begins with a certain ethnic group of people dwelling in a certain place. They create their own environment in such a way that it suits their lifestyle, although it is also true that they are shaped by the climatic conditions of the specific region. Even those of the same ethnic origin begin to create different cultures, influenced by their different environments.

Thus, at first, various ethnic groups dwell at various places and create their own cultures, but gradually with development of a transportation network, each group enters into the world of mutual relationships. Hence, one [global] world is formed, and the history of the world unfolds accordingly. For various groups of people to enter this one world means that they enter one and the same environment. Therefore, there necessarily arise mutual struggles and conflicts among the groups, and wars are inevitable. At the same time, through this process [of globalization], the cultures of various ethnic groups are synthesized and united, and a greater development of human culture takes shape.

The renowned historian Leopold von Ranke said that cultures before the fall of Rome all flowed into the great lake called Rome, and cultures after the fall of Rome all flowed out of that great lake called Rome, and that it was through the conquest of Europe by the Romans that the European countries were brought together, and one cohesive world was formed [on European soil]. Today, however, because of the development of a global transportation network, the whole earth has become one world. Consequently, today's nationalism *(kokkashugi)* has to take into account what it means to be a nation in the global world. What I mean by "nationalism" is not that every country should retreat to itself [to the isolated idea of nation]; rather, each nation should have a place of its own in this [global] world. In other words, by "nationalism" I mean that each country ought to develop its global perspective within itself.

At the time when various ethnic groups enter into a global interaction, I suppose it is in the natural course of events that severe struggles among countries take place. I think, however, that the people who possess the most globally developed historical orientation will play the key role and bring stability to the epoch. What I mean by a nation-state that has a globally developed historical quality is a nation-state that, although subscribing to totalitarianism *(zentaishugi)*,[1] does not negate the [rights of] individuals, and whose collective life is mediated by the creative activities of individual persons. Today, it is generally thought that individualism and totalitarianism are mutually exclusive, but just as it is true that "individualism" is an idea of the past, so is a "totalitarianism" that flatly negates [any role for] individuals a thing of the past. Individuals are born of the historical society, to be sure, but as long as the historical society has the individual's creative activities as its medium [of development], that historical society has an eternal life in terms of its globally historical nature. It can be likened to how biological life continues to live on, being mediated by cellular activities.

4. THE IMPERIAL FAMILY AS THE CONTINUING THRUST OF JAPANESE HISTORY

In the history of our country, the whole and the individual usually did not stand in opposition. Rather, [history] has unfolded with the imperial family *(kōshitsu)* as its center, while the individual and the whole mutually self-negated. Certainly, there were times when the power of the "whole" overshadowed that of the individual, but each time we returned to the founding spirit of Japan *(chōkoku no seishin)*, and by maintaining the central presence of the imperial family, we took a step forward into the new era and created a new epoch. I said earlier that history moves on from the present, which contains within itself the past and the future, to another present, which likewise contains the past and the future. In the case of our country, I think that the imperial family has been playing the role of the "present" that encompasses within itself the past and the future. For this reason, I think that for us to return to the original founding spirit of Japan is not just to go back to the ancient times but to take a step forward into an ever-new era. I humbly submit that "restoration of the old ways" *(fukko)* ought to mean "thoroughgoing renewal" *(ishin)*.[2]

---

1. By *"zentaishugi,"* Nishida means something more like "holism" than "totalitarianism," which is the usual translation of this word. In *Nihon bunka no mondai*, Nishida criticizes this rough-and-ready characterization of the West as individualistic and the East as totalist, because "totalitarianism means such things as Fascism or Nazism" (NKZ 12:334–35).

2. The same idea is presented in *Nihon bunka no mondai*, NKZ 12:336.

Chapter 25

Finale

(1942–1945)

During his convalescence Nishida followed the doctor's advice to the letter, from daily shots to massage and dietary restrictions, for he had utter confidence in modern medicine. Because the muscles of his fingers were frozen so that he could hardly hold a pen, he spent a lot of time reading. He was drawn to scientific books such as Heisenberg's quantum theory[1] and Max Planck's theory of causality.[2] By the summer of 1942, when he had sufficiently recovered from his rheumatism to resume writing, it felt to him as if whatever he had read and thought during the last several months was waiting to be committed to the page.

On July 5 he began "Chishiki no kyakkansei ni tsuite, aratanaru chishikiron no jiban" [On the objectivity of knowledge—the ground of new epistemology],[3] an essay in which he addresses in one bold stroke the problems of natural scientific cognition, the differences between science and philosophy, and Eastern and Western philosophies.

While Nishida was on his way to recovery, Yamamoto Ryōkichi died on July 12 of a heart attack.[4] Suzuki Daisetz remembered Nishida's response:

> How Nishida was saddened by Yamamoto's death was too painful for anyone to see. The news of Yamamoto's death reached both of us on a hot summer day. Since Nishida was not yet fully recovered, he was patiently waiting for me at his house. Unfortunately, it was extremely hot that day, and I waited until it had become tolerably cool in the early evening to call on him. When I got there, he rushed out of his room shouting, "Yamamoto is dead!" His expression, which I still recall to this day, was grave and painful. He remained devastated for a week. His frail physical condition did not help him recover from the shock easily.[5]

Nishida sent his message of condolence with Suzuki, who attended the school memorial service for Yamamoto held at Musashi Higher School on July 18:

> My dear friend, Yamamoto, you have been my closest friend for over fifty years. After I received the telegram in the early morning on the thirteenth informing me of your death, horrendous shock overtook me. Intense feelings seized my heart, and I lay flat in bed all day with an ice bag on my forehead. I can still see you clearly in my mind. Today, I wanted to come to bid farewell to your departing soul, but my body, weakened by illness, is not fit for travel. I wanted to write about you, but my grief-stricken heart would not let the pen move. Since last fall, I have not been well, and you were deeply concerned about my condition, but alas! you have departed before me! Ah, transience of life! How can anyone count on living to see the evening of the day![6]

Yamamoto's death and the hot humid summer of Kyoto were too much for Nishida. Concerned friends made an arrangement for him to stay at Hōshun'in, on the grounds of Daitokuji temple. Tucked away in the greenery of northern Kyoto, Hōshun'in offered him some respite. But worrisome news continued to flow in. On August 22 Harada Kumao fell unconscious from a stroke. Sotohiko, who had been fighting in the Pacific and was stationed in the Philippines, was suffering from dengue fever. Fortunately, Sotohiko soon recovered, was transferred to Taiwan by the end of September, and safely returned to Japan in late October.

By October 1942 Nishida was able to lead a fairly normal life, although he was no longer able to take the long brisk walks that he enjoyed so much. He received former students and colleagues who came to visit him every day. Even Tanabe Hajime called on him unexpectedly. Since Nishida felt well enough to travel, he and Koto left for Kamakura on October 21. On November 3 Iwanami Shigeo threw a grand Thanksgiving reception, commemorating the thirtieth anniversary of his business, and invited some five hundred guests. Nishida's health did not permit him to attend so large a social event, but he sent a congratulatory message.[7] The evening was dubbed "the last supper for the liberals," for not only was this kind of luxury no longer really possible in the face of the war effort but liberal thinkers were fast losing their platform from which to speak as well.

Nishida welcomed 1943 by working on "Jikaku ni tsuite" [On self-consciousness],[8] which he finished on March 25. In this essay he treats the "self-conscious self" as originally grounded in the world. From

January 20 to January 29 he stayed at Iwanami's Sekirekisō in Atami, and on January 24 Konoe and Nagayo Yoshirō came over to join him and Iwanami for lunch.

On April 29 Nishida was invited to a gathering hosted by Iwanami, where Akashi Teruo,[9] Furuno Inosuke,[10] Ueno Naoaki, Watsuji Tetsurō, Suzuki Daisetz, Ishii Mitsuo,[11] and the mayor of the city of Kamakura talked about the present state of the war and the future of Japan. On May 12 Nishida met with Kanamori Tokujirō,[12] Kanai Shōji,[13] Tanabe Juri,[14] and Ishida Isoji. Kanamori sought Nishida's advice regarding the fundamental direction of the constitution if Japan should lose the war.[15] These gatherings indicate that concerned intellectuals were already thinking ahead to Japan's survival after the war.

In May 1943 Nishida was unexpectedly asked to share his views with military officers. Yatsugi Kazuo,[16] head of the Institute of National Strategy (*Kokusaku kenkyūkai*), wanted to solicit Nishida's help, thinking that his philosophical touch would give loftiness to a draft of a "Proclamation of the Greater East Asiatic Nations," which was to be issued at the Greater Asian Conference in November.[17] On May 19 Nishida, accompanied by Tanabe Juri, attended a dinner meeting arranged by Yatsugi. There he saw government officials and politicians, including Satō Kenryō (director of the Department of Army Affairs), Amō Eiji (former ambassador to Italy, then the head of the Department of Information), Nagai Ryūtarō (politician from the Ishikawa Prefecture), Shimomura Kainan,[18] and Ōkura Kinmochi. At this meeting Nishida is said to have openly criticized the Japanese military policies in Asia as "imperialist" and to have stated his view that Japanese overseas activities should be neither "imperialist" nor "colonialist."[19] Yatsugi asked Nishida to propose what Japan's role should be. Nishida obliged and wrote his "Sekai shinchitsujo no genri" [The principles for a new world order] the following day. Nishida's draft, however, was too sophisticated for the military men to understand. (Kanai Shōji and Tanabe Juri eventually recast Nishida's proposals in a simpler form.[20]) Despite Nishida's hope that some of his ideas might be understood by the military, Tōjō's public statement on Greater East Asia contained no part of Nishida's proposals. Disappointed, Nishida wrote to Hori: "Having read the newspapers, I grew disgusted. I compromised on my choice of words, for I thought it more important to establish the fundamental ideal, but nothing of my ideal is understood, nothing is taken up."[21] This brief encounter with the military, which produced "The Principles for a New World Order," came to an ambiguous end.[22] Nishida, dissatisfied with the way his proposals were handled, reworked them yet again after he returned to Kyoto on June 16.[23]

There is another aspect to this encounter between Nishida and the army. Ōshima Yasumasa tells us that there was pressure from some ultranationalists within the army who insisted Nishida must be arrested on account of his philosophy, which they viewed as "pro-Western" and antithetical to the Japanese emperor system. Yatsugi intervened on Nishida's behalf and established a personal acquaintance with Satō Kenryō, who had the power to stop such arrests.[24]

On July 17 Nishida returned to Kamakura, where he concentrated on preparing *Tetsugaku ronbunshū daigo* [Philosophical essays 5], which he sent off to Iwanami on September 3. During this time Ōsaka Moto-kichirō, who had recovered from the deadly attack of 1934, called on Nishida and the two spoke for a long time.[25] Nishida received visitors daily and especially enjoyed the visits of Suetsuna Joichi,[26] a professor of mathematics at Tokyo Imperial University who was introduced to him by Shimomura Toratarō in March. Suetsuna found a universal mind in Nishida, and Nishida found in Suetsuna someone who could understand his thought and respond from a mathematical perspective.[27] The two instantly formed a teacher-disciple bond.[28] In March Nishida was also visited by Yukawa Hideki,[29] a leading theoretical physicist and a junior colleague of Sotohiko. Yukawa, when a university student at Kyoto Imperial University, was an avid fan of Nishida and used to sit in on his Introduction to Philosophy course. Yukawa found that "the distance between philosophy and theoretical physics narrowed considerably"[30] whenever he was talking with Nishida.

Nishida was looking forward to the end of July, when he would be finished with "cumbersome visits by politicians" and could expect some peaceful moments to "learn more about mathematics from Suetsuna and physics from Tomonaga."[31] Tomonaga Shin'ichirō[32] was Yukawa's colleague and then Shimomura's colleague at Tokyo University of Arts and Sciences (Bunri Daigaku). When in the company of these young scholars, Nishida was able to forget that he was the target of accusations by "narrow-minded Japanese nationalists."[33] In fact, Nishida had to write a short article, "Dentō" [The tradition], that summer to respond to the charges brought to his door by Satō Tsūji, an ultranationalist advocate of a "philosophy of the imperial way,"[34] who had argued that Nishida's philosophy was "Greek" and went against the Japanese spirit.[35] In a world progressively growing more absurd, Nishida found peace of mind when he was in the company of these young men who were dedicated to their studies. He saw in them a ray of hope for the future of Japan as well. He wrote to Yanagida Kenjūrō that he was certain that "a great cosmic equilibrium will be restored someday," and that "the truth will be restored to its rightful place."[36] In the same letter, he refers to the Confucian scholars who were persecuted during the Qin Dynasty under the rule of the first emperor and the prime minister, Li Si. When things are thus put into a proper perspective, he felt, "what we are presently going through seems nothing."

Through the exchange of views with Suetsuna and others, Nishida's interest in the philosophy of natural sciences was rekindled. He began "Butsuri no sekai" [The world of physics] on September 18[37] but ended his work on the essay in mid-November because he did not have enough stamina to investigate the matter fully.[38] He was acutely aware that his intellectual tenacity was diminishing in proportion to the decline in his physical stamina. He confided to Mutai: "The task of connecting Buddhist thought and the modern scientific spirit through my logic of *topos* is what I dearly wish to accomplish—in fact, it is my final goal. But I don't feel that I have much strength left in me."[39] The death of celebrated novelist and poet Shimazaki Tōson on August 22 prompted Nishida to reflect on his own death:

> Just like the cool autumn wind of these days, I have a cool resolution in my heart this fall. As I sink into the depth of myself, I find calm infinite joy. . . . I would like to die unnoticed by the public, unlike Tōson, whose funeral has become a huge public event. I would like to go quietly and insignificantly (just as Leibniz is said to have been buried like a dog).[40]

On September 26 Nishida learned from the newspaper of the death of Kimura Hisashi.[41] As his old friends departed one by one, his heart turned to Suzuki Daisetz, the only living close friend from his childhood. They began to call on each other quite frequently. To Nishida's relief, Harada's condition was steadily improving.[42] On December 1 Nishida began writing "Ronri to sūri" [Logic and mathematical logic],[43] which he especially wanted Suetsuna to read.[44] On December 18 Iwanami arranged a meeting, where Nishida, Daisetz, Watsuji, and Takemi Tarō saw Makino Nobuaki,[45] a former lord keeper of the privy seal. On this occasion Nishida candidly informed Makino of what he had heard from Kimura Motomori on the sorry state of education. Makino then relayed what he heard from Nishida to the members of the privy council, and the reality of Japanese education came to the attention of those concerned. Minami Hiroshi,[46]

December 18, 1943, at Restaurant Hamasaku in Tokyo. From left to right: Iwanami Shigeo, D. T. Suzuki, Watsuji Tetsurō, Makino Nobuaki, Takemi Tarō, and Nishida. Courtesy of Mr. Iwanami Yūjirō.

who had considerable power in the Ministry of Education, visited Nishida to learn more about the actual problems.

The year 1944 rolled in. On January 10, Mori Jūjirō,[47] a member of the parliament, called on Nishida with an introduction from Osada Arata[48] and asked him to write on the emperor system *(kokutai)*. The topic did not interest Nishida, but Mori was not the only one who had asked Nishida's view on this matter. Therefore he wrote a kind of sketch on *kokutai*[49] on February 25.

The new year also brought Nishida a premonition of his death. On January 12 he wrote to Sotohiko: "All of you, my children, are now grown up and carrying out your respective work splendidly. I can die peacefully without any regrets."[50] He sorted out his financial affairs with Sotohiko, assisted by Kubo Yoshio, who used to be the best friend of his deceased son, Ken, and with whom Nishida still kept in touch. Nishida's main concern was to set aside enough money for Shizuko so that she could live free of worries even after his death. He then turned to his essay on religion, "Yotei-chōwa o tebiki to shite shūkyō-tetsug-aku e" [Toward a philosophy of religion with the Leibnizian notion of preestablished harmony as a guide].[51] This essay is a preliminary study for his philosophy of religion.[52] In April he wrote "Dekaruto tetsugaku ni tsuite" [On Descartes' philosophy],[53] in which he reiterates his view that philosophy begins with an inquiry into the nature of knowledge, and therefore of self-consciousness. He also criticizes those who oppose the study of philosophy as pro-Western and denigrate "reason" as a mere abstract concept.

From May 4 to June 17 Nishida returned to his house in Asukai-chō in Kyoto for the last time. Shizuko knew that this would be the last time she would see her father, and the two spent much time together talking their hearts out. Kōsaka, Kōyama, Suzuki Shigetaka, Nishitani, and Kimura Motomori gathered for the last "philosophical meeting" with the professor. Beginning in February 1944 ultranationalists led by Minoda and his group had been loudly condemning Nishida's thought as "internationalist" and "counter to the national interest," and arguing that "it should be banned." To ease the pressures coming from Minoda's faction,[54] an inquest *(shisō shingikai)* was set up within the Ministry of Education to "question and investigate" Nishida's thought.[55] Nishida was reassured in advance that nothing would come of the inquest: it was merely a foil to pacify the ultranationalists.[56] Mutai Risaku was one of the investigators, and from him Nishida gathered that "the committee will be dissolved before it will have reached any conclusion."[57] In view of the general hostility against the Kyoto school, Kōsaka and others advised Nishida to withhold his essay on *kokutai* from publication.[58] But a rumor spread that the members of the Kyoto school were hiding something from the government authorities.[59] What happened was that a copy of the essay was circulated against Nishida's wishes by Yanagida Kenjūrō[60] in the Nagano Prefecture. With this new development those close to Nishida decided that it would be best to publish it. The essay was submitted in December 1944 to the *Tetsugaku Kenkyū* with an inconspicuous title, *"Tetsugaku ronbunshū daiyon hoi"* [A supplement to the *Fourth philosophical essays*].[61] The anti–Kyoto school sentiment held by the head of the academic department delayed the confirmation of the doctoral degrees to Nishitani Keiji and Yanagida Kenjūrō.[62] It seems that there was no end to the harassment of the Kyoto school thinkers by the Ministry of Education.

Nishida and Koto left Kyoto on June 17, stayed overnight at Yayoi's house in Shizuoka, and returned to Kamakura the next day. Nishida then began his next essay, "Kūkan" [Space][63] as the war front on the Pacific was moving closer to Japan. On July 3 Nishida wrote to Kimura Motomori:

I can more or less imagine what is going on in Saipan. It seems that the situation is becoming pressing, as we had predicted from the very beginning of the war. What's happening today stems precisely from politicians who lack foresight. Who is destroying our country? Looking at Japan's current situation, I feel painfully that it is more important to create human beings *(ningen o tsukuru)* than anything else, including social systems and organizations. I just wish that the people would wake up. Everything boils down to education. If the people remain as uncritical and blind as they are now, nothing can be hoped for.[64]

Nishida had already written to Kimura in 1938 about the importance of education: "Education consists in making a human being; to make a human being is to create the world."[65] In his mind it was clear that sound education and scholarly achievement would become the pillar of the reconstruction of Japan in the postwar period. It was in this spirit that he encouraged his disciples and younger friends.

The Tōjō cabinet dissolved on July 21. The only thing Nishida could say was that "it would have been better had Tōjō resigned much earlier."[66] In any case, army general Koiso Kuniaki organized his cabinet and appointed Yonai Mitsumasa, an admiral, as minister of the navy to bring together the interests of the army and navy. Nishida wrote to Hori:

At least the new cabinet seems better than its predecessor. . . . I just hope that they can unite their effort at this critical moment. Sincere and well-informed people must lead Japan, and one billion Japanese will have to cooperate as one mind. It won't do to have undesirable ambitious characters leading "one billion Japanese as one mind."[67]

The jingoistic slogan, "one hundred million people, one mind" *(ichioku isshin)*, would soon turn into the more radical "one hundred million people gloriously die for the emperor" *(ichioku gyokusai)*.

Around July and August 1944 the air raids by the American forces began in earnest in the Kyūshū area. Nishida completed his essay "Kūkan" on August 14, and after sorting out his manuscript for the sixth volume of *Philosophical Essays*,[68] he began writing on "Seimei" [Life][69] on September 16. The quality of rationed food was deteriorating rapidly.[70] By September people's daily lives were severely affected by the lack of food. Nishida noticed that he had lost a lot of weight. His letter to Hori on September 22 reveals his immediate physical and mental condition:

As I touch my thighs, shoulders, and stomach, I feel my bones right beneath my skin. I'm a skeleton! This must be what "famine" means. Sometimes I feel that I won't live long, and sometimes I think that I ought to prepare my will, but so far, I haven't done anything. I'm continuing my daily work. What I want to commit to writing does not cease to flow forth. Considering that it is my raison d'être to write, I transcend my thoughts of life and death and devote myself to work in the mornings. I'm exhausted by the afternoon, however. I used to take long walks, but lately, because my legs are no longer strong, I just take short walks along the beach near my house, which is terribly boring! I'm spending my days randomly reading, nay perusing, books and magazines.[71]

Daisetz believed that Nishida's death was unnecessarily hastened by malnutrition due to the shortage of food during the final phase of the war. It indeed appears that way. By this time, visitors to the Nishidas were rare, too, because the transportation system, heavily impacted by the war front's encroachment on the islands of Japan proper, was no longer dependable. Toward the end of September Nishida wrote to Ueda Juzō, who had kindly employed Shizuko as a secretary for his aesthetics program: "I used to hate those flowers that they offer at the graves *(higanbana)*, because they remind me of the cemetery, but this year, I find in them muted loneliness. Is it because I'm one step closer to my own grave? Ah!"[72]

On November 24 the American air raids of Tokyo began with some seventy or eighty B29 planes. Kaneko's and Umeko's house was razed by fire on December 22, forcing them to take refuge in the house of their relatives. Toward the end of 1944 Inoue Tetsujirō died, and so did Matsumoto Bunzaburō,[73] who had always been very healthy. Nishida felt those whom he knew were hurriedly bidding farewell, one after another.

Nishida began 1945 with worries over the Kanekos, who had just lost their house in the air raid. Nishida's January 2, 1945, diary entry reads: "Wrote to Kaneko, Sotohiko, and Umeko. In this life, there is not a moment of peace when one is free from worries and hardships. Life is tragic."[74] To Iwanami, Nishida described the present world as "that of lions, tigers, and beasts; not of humanity."[75] It was a severely cold winter that year. On January 25 Nishida completed "Sūgaku no tetsugakuteki kisozuke" [Giving a philosophical foundation for mathematics],[76] and on February 4 he embarked on his last essay, "Basho-teki ronri to shūkyōteki sekaikan" [The logic of *topos* and the religious worldview].[77] The issue he addresses in this essay is his ultimate worldview, a truly significant matter to him, and something he wanted everyone he knew to read.[78]

Nishida felt a little relieved when the Kanekos found a house in Azabu, but he could not shake his thought that "life is full of uncertainty; one never knows what tomorrow will bring."[79] On February 8 Tokunō Bun died. Then, on February 14, Nishida and Koto received a telegram from Ueda Misao, informing them that Yayoi was critically ill. She died that night (see Nishida's essay at the end of this chapter). The sudden and unexpected death of Yayoi devastated Nishida. He poured out his grief to Sotohiko:

> I cannot help but dwell on memories of Yayoi. I am in the depths of infinite loneliness and sorrow. I fathered seven children, but four of them have already died, and only three of you are living. With Yūko's death, I experienced for the first time the sorrows of a parent losing one's own child, and with Yayoi's death, I have learned the sorrows of an old man who survived the death of his own child. I pray that the three of you will be kind and helpful to one another and will lead your lives filled with precious love.[80]

By March vegetables were scarce, and the situation was such that "there was no other way but to eat weeds."[81] Around that time Nishida's relatives recommended that he and Koto evacuate to a small village near Kanazawa. Nishida did not show keen interest in doing so. He was ready to die any day. Major cities in Japan were now targets of air raids; in Tokyo seven to eight hundred thousand people lost their homes in the air raids, and Nagoya and Osaka were also badly damaged. On March 17 Nishida received the news of the death of Uchida Yūtarō, another old friend of sixty years.

Sensing that Japan's defeat was near, Nishida wrote a long letter to Kōyama Iwao and asked him to share it with Kōsaka, Kimura Motomori, Nishitani, Suzuki Shigetaka, and others—his close circle of followers. They took this letter from Nishida as his "will."

> Given the present level of preparedness of the Japanese, the idea of "total war" is ill-conceived. The Japanese ought to have been trained to organize things in a much more systematic way, but no such education was given to the people in the past. It is too late now, even if the government tries to invent how to "braid a rope made out of mud." I am worried about what is going to happen at this juncture.
>
> I think this is the time for the Japanese to make a crucial decision

on whether to continue fighting or stop. If we continue to be dragged by the military government into sustaining the war effort and become unable to stand up on our own feet, I fear it will have a devastating effect on the Japanese people as a people. Under no circumstances should the Japanese people lose *spiritual confidence.* Even if we lose the war in terms of military might, we must not lose our cultural and moral confidence in the historical universality of the Japanese *kokutai* in terms of the formation of the global world. We must firmly hold onto this understanding of history and give confidence to the people regarding the future development of the Japanese people. When Konoe came over the other day, I told him my view; he was in total agreement with me. But it seems no one can do anything now, even Konoe.

To me, there is no other way but to accept the defeat of Japan and to try to instill cultural and spiritual confidence into the minds of the Japanese people. Therefore, I would like to say this to you all: you have to build a profound foundation of thought and scholarship as a starting point for the postwar Japanese recovery. In response to Konoe, who had asked a question of me on this point, I firmly told him that the Japanese people are absolutely capable of doing so. If we solely depend on might, it is certain that we will be destroyed. . . .

I am so old and don't know how much longer I will live, but I am working to establish a moral-cultural foundation for the future of the Japanese people. I'm currently writing a treatise on religion. . . . I will write as much as I can for posterity.[82]

Nishida must have had a passage from the *Analects* of Confucius in the back of his mind, in which Confucius, setting his priorities among "the essentials of sufficient food, sufficient troops, and the confidence of the people,"[83] said he would give up the troops first, then food, because "from of old, death has been the lot of all men, but a people without faith cannot survive."[84] A few days later, on March 14, Nishida wrote a long letter to Nagayo Yoshirō, assessing the cause of the present misery of the Japanese people and his hope for rebuilding Japan.[85]

Having thus left his "will" to the younger generation, Nishida dedicated the remainder of his life to writing, with the thought of bequeathing it as his legacy for the future of Japan. On April 7 the Koiso cabinet dissolved, and Suzuki Kantarō became prime minister. Soliciting the help of Tōgō Shigenori as his foreign minister, the new prime minister began his effort to bring the war to a swift conclusion. Nishida sensed that a new movement was emerging. He communicated to Kōsaka: "Japan has a great mission for the rest of Asian countries to represent a position of morality and culture. The true future of Japan is ahead of you."[86]

Nishida completed his "Bashoteki ronri to shūkyōteki sekaikan" on April 14. He was especially eager for Suzuki Daisetz to read it, and he explained his task to him:

> I want to make clear that religious reality cannot be grasped by conventional objective logic, but it reveals itself to the "logic of contradictory self-identity," or what you call "the logic of *sokuhi.*" From the standpoint of *prajñā* (wisdom), I want to discuss what a "person" is and want to connect that "person" to the actual historical world.[87]

In his April 12 letter to Hisamatsu, Nishida explained that he had grappled with "the roots of life and death" in this essay, had spent some time delineating "the uniqueness of Buddhism as distinguished from Christianity," and had "touched on the excellent points of Buddhism." He also told Hisamatsu that he was working everyday "with the determination to die" and likened the circumstances to those of "Hegel, who wrote his *Phenomenology of the Spirit* in Jena under Napoleon's gunfire."[88]

Because it was feared that air raids were now threatening Kamakura, the local government issued an order that every household must dig a bomb shelter. Koto, with the help of handymen, began digging a cave in the hill behind the house. But even during those highly tense moments, Nishida seems to have kept his own perspective and stayed several steps removed from the madness. That both Nishida and Koto were able to maintain their calm, even under the extreme scarcity of food and essential goods, has an air of indescribable elegance.

War-related news, streaming in from abroad, filled Nishida's diary during his last days: the occupation of Berlin by the Russian Red Army, the execution of Mussolini, the violent end of Hitler, the suicide of Goebbels, and the unconditional surrender of Germany. On May 1 Nishida wrote to Tomonaga Sanjūrō:

> About one hundred each of B29 and P51 fly in over us, and people have recommended that we should evacuate to the countryside for safety, but since the maid would not come with us, and it seems too much trouble for an old couple to live in Shinshū or somewhere like that, we decided to entrust our lives to Heaven. We feel calm inside.
>
> The other night, when they attacked the Tokyo-Yokohama area, we could clearly hear the sound of bombs exploding, and the sky beyond

that eastern hill covered with miscanthus glowed crimson. It is a horrible world to live in. I wonder where it is going to take us. Sometimes I think my friends who have departed are lucky in that they don't have to experience this hardship, but I also think that it is interesting to witness this kind of age. Both Germany and Italy had a miserable end, didn't they? After all, totalitarianism cannot work. Please do take good care of yourself. I would like to see you once again. My greetings to your wife. [89]

On May 19 Nishida received a letter out of the blue from Tanabe Hajime, who requested his and Konoe's help to secure the continued existence of the imperial family after the defeat of Japan. [90] Nishida immediately replied, explaining to Tanabe that no single individual was in a position of power any more to enact any idea and ended his letter with these words: "I am a useless old man; I sincerely pray for you younger people to fight hard." [91] On May 24, Fujii Otoo died. Two days later, in response to a request, Nishida translated a poem by Goethe into Japanese to offer it as an inscription to be chiseled on the side of the gravestone for Kuki Shūzō at Hōnen'in. [92] In the air raids of May 29, Iwanami's house in Koishikawa and his store were burned down. The next day, Nishida began his never-to-be-finished essay, "Watakushi no ronri ni tsuite" [Concerning my logic]. [93]

From the end of May, Nishida was unwell and took to bed. In the early morning of June 7, he died of uremia. Goethe's poem, which Nishida had offered to Kuki's grave, seemed like a fitting inscription for his own grave:

Miharukasu
yama no itadaki
kozue ni wa
kaze mo ugokazu
tori mo nakazu.
Mate shibashi,
yagate nare mo yasuman

Visible far in the distance
Are the mountain peaks.
At the trees' tip
No wind blows,
No birds chirp.
Wait a while,
You too shall rest. [94]

Engravings on Kuki's grave, a translation of
Goethe's poem, "Wandrers Nachtlied," into
Japanese. Nishida's calligraphy, May 26, 1945.
From *Nishida Kitarō ibokushū*.

*In Memory of My Eldest Daughter, Ueda Yayoi** *

Yayoi died yesterday. Last evening, Mr. Sumiyoshi, who lives down the
hill from us, came to our house to convey a telephone message from
the Kamakura post office that there was a telegram from the Uedas,
which said: "Yayoi is in a critical condition." I was very surprised.
When she came to visit us in the middle of last month and stayed with
us overnight, she did not look ill, nor have I heard since then that she
was suffering from illness. Does a telegram, saying Yayoi is "in a critical condition," mean perhaps she is dying? Even then, I held onto a
single ray of hope. In the morning, as soon as we got up, Koto made
a long-distance telephone call to Shizuoka. Misao answered the phone

---

* "Ueda Yayoi no omoide no ki," NKZ 12:261–66. There is a notation inserted
after the main title: "15 February 1945, written the day before the battleships were
sunk by bombs."

and said to Koto: "After all, it was hopeless. She suffered greatly from an illness called cholecystitis [inflammation of the gall bladder] and died yesterday." The postcard that the Uedas wrote to us the day before yesterday did not mention anything of her condition, so she must have been all right then. What a terrible thing to have happen to her!

I am overcome with an undescribable feeling of loneliness. She was born in the back room of a small temple located at the end of a town, called . . . yes, Daijōji, when I was teaching at a junior higher school in the small city of Nanao on the Noto Peninsula, soon after I got married. She was my first child. I remember that it was a rather difficult birth. I became a teacher at the Fourth Higher School soon after that, so she grew up in Kanazawa. Since she was our first child, my mother took care of her, practically raising her. Yayoi was a very bright child. While she was attending the [Kanazawa] Elementary School (auxiliary to the Normal School), she composed a *waka* poem. The teachers praised her very highly, and it became a bit of a sensation. Yayoi studied at the Women's Higher School at Anamizuchō. During her fourth year, the year of her graduation, she took an entrance examination for the Tokyo Women's Higher Normal School [today's Ochanomizu University], and she passed with flying colors and was accepted. By that time, I was teaching at Kyoto University, so as soon as she graduated from the Tokyo Women's Higher Normal School, she moved to Kyoto and taught Japanese language and literature at the Dōshisha Women's School. She later married Ueda Misao, with my closest friend, Yamamoto Ryōkichi, acting as the go-between.

Ever since I began to suffer from [rheumatism] and moved to Kamakura to live here year round, Yayoi went out of her way to take care of me out of her filial love. Bless her beautiful warm heart! She came over to our house last month on the fifteenth; she stayed overnight with Umeko and left in the early morning of the sixteenth. That was the last time I ever saw her!

At the beginning of this month, she sent me a postcard, saying that Kaoru, her eldest son, had been called to the war and departed in good health and spirits, seen off by his parents and brothers. This was her last letter to me.

My grandmother's name was something like "Yae," and because Yayoi was born in March [called *yayoi* in classical Japanese], we named her Yayoi.

After I left Nanao for Kanazawa, we were living in a house rented from Ōmi Hisaburō in Koshōmachi. At that time Yayoi was just about a month old, and my wife and I put this child, peacefully sleeping, between us.

She was loved by my mother and was very close to her. But my aged mother did not live long enough to see her marry. Yayoi must be very happy to see her grandmother in heaven, if such a thing happens.

Misao's letter, written on the day of Yayoi's death, February 14, said that because Yayoi had a stomach pain on the twelfth, he asked Dr. Imai of the Shizuoka Hospital to make a house call. The doctor said that her gall bladder was swollen and that she must absolutely take it easy and stay in bed. She followed the doctor's advice and took some medicine. Since Dr. and Mrs. Imai were close acquaintances of Yayoi in Shizuoka, the doctor came again that night, examined her, and told Misao that her heart was failing a little and her pulse was weak, and to keep a very close watch over her. Late that night, he came over once again, accompanied by two nurses. To his chagrin, the doctor found that her condition had deteriorated extraordinarily. He gave her camphor and a glucose injection, which revived her momentarily, but her condition worsened rapidly during the morning of the fourteenth. Despite all the doctor's efforts, she finally passed away at 8:45 A.M. Dr. Imai was greatly saddened and said that Yayoi was under tremendous psychological pressure. Her second son's illness last year, the injury of the third son, and the eldest son's being summoned to the war—all came in close succession and finally took their toll on her. What else can we do but pity Yayoi? Even though she was so deeply tormented and suffering with her worries, she never even once complained to us. She was always kind and cheerful.

She gave birth to four sons, which good fortune people envied. But she died without seeing the promising future of those boys. I had seven children; four have already died. When my second daughter died, I for the first time experienced how painful the death of a child was, but at my advanced age I experienced the sadness of an old man who is bereaved of his [now grownup] child, especially because it was Yayoi, who was so warmhearted, and about whom I have so many memories.

She, who moved to Kanazawa less than a month after she was born, being placed between her parents in a room on the second floor of Ōmi's, grew up, graduated from the Women's [Higher] School, entered the Tokyo Women's Higher Normal School, taught, married, gave birth to four sons, became a fully mature mistress of her household, and then suddenly disappeared. I remember having seen Haeckel's *History of Natural Creation* or something like that, which began with drawings of the development of a human embryo: an egg within the mother's womb that goes through a succession of individual and generic transformations within ten months, assuming at one time the shape of a fish and a pig at another, finally coming out as a beautiful woman. Where did Yayoi come from, and where has she gone? Should I say: "Everything about human beings is rootless, resembling the flowers on top of trees" [as a Zen saying goes]?

If Yayoi would have lived on, grown old, and enjoyed some leisure, she might have become a poet or a short-story writer.

Epilogue

When Nishida died, Koto and Nishida's youngest daughter, Umeko, were at his bedside. News of his death reached Suzuki Daisetz almost immediately, and he rushed to the Nishidas' home. Several days after Nishida's death, Daisetz recorded his memories:

> The last time I saw you, less than a month ago, you were talking with your usual ardor and candor about such things as "the ordinary mind is the way" and the self-determination of the absolute present.
>
> I thought of calling on you again soon, but I kept on procrastinating because of the train situation; the few trains that ran were tremendously crowded, and if I ended up walking home it would have been hard on me the following day. But in the morning of 7 June, the sudden news was communicated to me that you were no longer among the living.
>
> Since I had no idea how long it would take me to get there, I prepared a box lunch and went out. I managed to get on the train somehow or other. When I got off the train, I climbed up the valley of Ubagayatsu in great haste. When I saw Mrs. Nishida come out to greet me, I, who had resolved not to cry, burst into tears; to keep from collapsing, I had to hold on to the pillar of the entrance hall.
>
> Soon, I walked into the room where Nishida used to receive me. He was lying on a bed. Mr. Iwanami was already there and offered incense, while Mrs. Nishida lifted the white cloth that covered Nishida's face. He looked as if he were sleeping peacefully. But his eyes of course had lost their gaze and those lips that had talked so animatedly about mathematics, physics, and logic were now sealed. Nishida is dead.[1]

Daisetz suffered a tremendous shock from Nishida's death and stayed in bed for several days, tormented.

On the day that Nishida died, Tanikawa Tetsuzō and Watsuji Tetsurō hurried in the evening to the Nishidas' home. Suetsuna Joichi, who was then in the countryside taking care of moving books and research materials from the university library, received a telegram from Mutai Risaku on June 8, left right away and arrived in Kamakura on the ninth in the early afternoon to find that it was the day of the cremation.

Telegrams reached those in Kyoto around noon on June 8. That evening, Kōsaka Masaaki and Kimura Motomori hastily packed, took Shizuko along with them, and squeezed themselves into a jam-packed train. They traveled overnight and arrived in Kamakura just in time to join the funeral procession to the crematorium. They asked to see Nishida's face once again, and the cover of the coffin was removed. Kimura remembered: "His eyes were quietly closed, his head turned slightly to the left. The wrinkles between his eyebrows, which showed when he concentrated, seemed ever more deeply chiseled on his face. Blue and purple wild flowers were on either side of his face." [2] In those days of scarcity at the end of the war, the family had a hard time even finding enough pieces of wood to make a coffin.

Suzuki took charge of the funeral service, held at Tōkeiji temple [3] in Kita-kamakura on June 13. Risking air raids, Nishida's disciples and those who respected him gathered at his funeral. Iwanami Shigeo and Nunokawa Kakuzaemon represented Iwanami Bookstore. From among Nishida's close students Kōsaka Masaaki, Mutai Risaku, Kimura Motomori, Miyake Gōichi, Shimomura Toratarō, Tanikawa Tetsuzō, Yanagida Kenjūrō, and Kataoka Hitoshi were present. Miki Kiyoshi, had he not been imprisoned, would certainly have been among the mourners. Although Inoue Zenjō, the abbot of Tōkeiji temple, was on military duty at Sakura, he obtained special permission to take a temporary leave to perform the funeral service. Tachibana Toshiko, Hyōjirō's daughter who had been adopted and raised by Nishida as his own daughter, was also there among the family members, Koto, Sotohiko, Shizuko, Umeko, Asako, and Kaneko Takezō. Indeed, the many hardships of wartime ensured that Nishida's wish to die peacefully, unnoticed by the public, was fulfilled.

Nishida's bones and ashes were divided in three at the request of his friends and students. A third was buried in the grave of the Nishida family in Unoke, another third at Tōkeiji in Kamakura, and the last third at Reiun'in at the Myōshinji temple in Kyoto. Nishida's students in Kyoto set up a "Sunshin-kai" (a group honoring Sunshin, Nishida's Buddhist name) to commemorate their professor and erected a gravestone at Reiun'in in 1948.[4] A natural stone with a shape that reminds one of the Buddha's *parinirvāna* (final rest) was chosen—probably by Hisamatsu Shin'ichi and Ueda Juzō, men of excellent taste. From the belltower right above Nishida's grave at Reiun'in, the temple gongs tuned to the *ōjiki* scale reverberate into the air every day.[5]

Atomic bombs were dropped over Hiroshima and Nagasaki before Japan saw the end of the war on August 15, 1945. The war ultimately demanded tremendous sacrifices on the part of the people, not only the Japanese soldiers who died for the "glory" of Japan, but also those Asian people and war hostages who were killed or tortured by the Japanese army. Every Japanese in one way or another "participated" in the war, either as soldiers on the front line or as victims of air raids or as pitiful figures whose death was hastened by starvation.

Many of Nishida's friends and colleagues died either right before the end of the war or soon after. Tosaka Jun, who had been imprisoned because of his Marxist ideology, died on August 9 in prison. Soon after, Miki Kiyoshi, who was also serving a sentence for having assisted in the escape of the convicted Marxist Takakura Teru, died of a sudden illness on September 26 in a filthy prison cell. How much was lost with the deaths of these individuals became clear only gradually to postwar Japanese intellectuals.

Following the arrival of the Allied occupation forces in Japan, Konoe Ayamaro, Kido Kōichi, and Hashida Kunihiko were among those who were on the list of war criminals. Hashida, minister of education under the Tōjō cabinet, committed suicide by taking poison on September 4. Konoe, indignant at being treated with an obvious lack of respect, also committed suicide by taking poison on December 16, 1945. Kido served his prison sentence until his release in 1955. Shimizu Tōru, the last president of the privy council, could not bear to see the Meiji constitution abolished and threw himself in the ocean at Atami on September 25, 1947, becoming a martyr of the Meiji constitution.

Kimura Motomori, chosen as a member of the MacArthur Commission on Education, was to address the reorganization of the Japanese educational system. Unfortunately, overworked Kimura succumbed to a bad cold and died on his lecture trip to Shinshū on February 12, 1946, at the young age of fifty-one.

Harada Kumao, who had been hard hit by the suicide of Konoe and was worried about Kido in the Sugamo prison, died on the morning of February 26, 1946, exactly ten years after the February 26 incident. His exhausted heart simply gave up. Iwanami Shigeo, who was decorated with the Cultural Medal on February 11, 1946, had a stroke on April 20 and died five days later.

In this way, many of Nishida's closest friends and those he most trusted departed from the ranks of the living, one after another, as if to join him. Aihara Shinsaku lamented the situation: "Miki and Kimura departed in such a hurry after Professor Nishida had passed away. Had the professor lived longer, perhaps they might have lived longer."[6] This sentiment, illogical as it may seem, was not held by Aihara alone.

The expression, "the tragedy of the Kyoto school," is often heard in the context of the members' alleged cooperation with the nationalists of pre-1945 Japan,[7] but the real "tragedy" of the Kyoto school perhaps lies in the untimely deaths of Miki, Tosaka, and Kimura in the unusual circumstances of war-torn Japan, as well as in the deaths of such figures as Iwanami and Harada, who did their best to protect the sanity and conscience of the Japanese people. Was the Japanese experience just another case in world history of a country's losing its reason and surrendering to collective madness? In any case, the Japanese who faced the task of recreating a new Japan paid a very high price.

Until the end of his life, Nishida maintained his calm and a balanced perspective on the war. It is said that two months before he died, his nephew Takahashi Shichirō called on him at Ubagayatsu and urged him to move to Kizu for safety. At that time, Nishida, visibly angry at the military, harshly criticized it and said: "'One hundred million people courageously dying for the emperor' is absolutely out of the question!" He also told Maki Kenji, who called on him about two weeks before his death: "This war will bring about unexpected results to both the victorious and the defeated."[8]

On July 10, 1947, in a still devastated Tokyo, the Iwanami Bookstore began publishing *Nishida Kitarō Zenshū* [Collected works of Nishida Kitarō]. When publication of the first volume was announced, buyers formed a long line the night before, encircling the entire block where Iwanami's bookstore stood. No sooner had the store opened in the morning than all copies were sold out.[9] This was indeed a phenomenon that made newspaper headlines, revealing that the people were spiritually hungry, intellectually thirsty, and looking desperately for cultural sustenance.

More than half a century later, as we look back on the life of Nishida Kitarō, we are again reminded of his words to Suzuki Daisetz: "A new age is dawning; I imagine there will be all kinds of people, but I suspect that the kinds of people we have seen in our era will never be seen again."[10]

Notes

INTRODUCTION

1. Michiko Yusa, "Reflections on Nishida Studies."

2. Michiko Yusa, "Amerika de Nishida kenkyū o kangaeru."

3. Nishida was against this manipulation. He believed that the emperor was an ordinary human being whom one should feel sorry for because he had been deprived of his freedom. See Ueda Hisashi, *Sofu Nishida Kitarō*, 48–49 [hereafter cited as Sofu]. Also see Michiko Yusa, "Nishida and Totalitarianism," 109.

4. Ever since the Tokugawa shogunate permitted "Western learning" *(yōgaku)* to be imported in 1716, the Japanese took the expedient way of adopting useful information, such as medicine, without bothering with its cultural matrix. Such figures as Sakuma Shōzan (1811–1864) and Hashimoto Sanai (1834–1859) championed this approach. See entry "Wakon yōsai," *Tetsugaku jiten* [A dictionary of philosophy], 1535–1536.

5. Letter no. 1798 to Mutai Risaku, 27 July 1943, NKZ 19:249.

6. Nishitani Keiji, "Nishida, my teacher," in *Nishida Kitarō*, translated by Yamamoto and Heisig, 24.

7. Ibid., 27

8. *Jikaku ni okeru chokkan to hansei*, NKZ 2:53.

9. Letter no. 1738, 19 February 1943, NKZ 19:224–25.

10. Thomas Merton, "Nishida: A Zen Philosopher," 67.

11. Shimomura Toratarō, "Nishida sensei no shokanshū ni tsuite," 301.

12. "Takagi hakushi no *Kinsei sūgakushidan*," NKZ 12:235.

13. "Bibō," NKZ 13:477–91.

14. Diary, 3 July 1905, NKZ 17:147.

15. Letter no. 2372, 30 November 1914, NKZ 19:519.

16. "Borutsāno no jiden," NKZ 12:131–33; published in *JPS* 80 (November 1922), 91–92.

17. "Sūgakusha Āberu," NKZ 12:134–37; printed in *Tokyo Asahi Shinbun*, October 15 and 16, 1933.

18. Diary, 13 February 1944, NKZ 17:679.

19. Suzuki Daisetz, "Nishida no omoide," SDZ 28:378.

20. Suzuki Daisetz, *"Eien no kage* no jo," SDZ 28:491.

21. Johann Gottlieb Fichte, "Erste Einleitung in die Wissenschaftslehre" (1797), *Sämmtliche Werke*, 1:434.

22. In the end, they chose to discard perfunctory notices (such as change of address) and selected about 2,500 letters.

23. Shimomura, "Nishida sensei no shokanshū ni tsuite," 301.

PROLOGUE

1. Letter no. 2066, 14 December 1944, NKZ 19:361.

2. Suzuki Daisetz, "Nishida no omoide," SDZ 28:381–82.

3. Ibid., SDZ 28:375–77 and 381–82.

4. Letter no. 1952 to Kimura Motomori, 3 July 1944, NKZ 19:311

5. Letter no. 855 to Kimura Motomori, 2 September 1934, NKZ 18:501.

6. Letter no. 908 to Hori Koretaka, 17 March 1935, NKZ 18:523.

CHAPTER 1: CHILDHOOD

1. The *tomura* system went back to 1604. Wakabayashi Kisaburō, "Kagahan," 217.

2. Takeda Atsushi, "Nishida Kitarō nenpu, Meiji 3–Meiji 13," 182.

3. Takeuchi Yoshitomo, *Nishida Kitarō*, 6–7.

4. Shimatani Shunzō, *"Zen no kenkyū* no umareru made," *JPS* 347 (April 1946), 32.

5. Nishida Shizuko, "Chichi," 4.

6. "Dokusho," NKZ 12:228.

7. Once a distinguished *tomura*, they lost much of their fortune because they cosigned a bad loan. Takeda Atsushi, "Nishida Kitarō nenpu," 185.

8. "Azumakagami," NKZ 12:233–34.

9. "Yo no otōto, Nishida Hyōjirō o omou," NKZ 13:166–67.

10. *Danpatsurei*, or the ordinance to cut off topknots, was issued in Meiji 4 (1871).

11. Until 1896 (Meiji 29), the starting age for children to attend elementary school was not specified. Ishikawaken Kyōikushi Hensan Iinkai, *Ishikawaken kyōikushi*, 1:1272 [hereafter cited as *Ishikawaken kyōikushi*].

12. Fifty-three percent of children attended the elementary school in Ishikawa Prefecture in 1876.

13. In the competition held on September 10, 1880, Nishida was awarded a physics textbook and a *Concise History of Japan*, and in the competition of June 8, 1881, a calligraphy set.

14. The school, established in 1875, was one of the first in Japan to promote women's education. In 1883 it was annexed to the Ishikawa Prefecture Normal School as the Girls' Division.

15. "Yo no otōto, Nishida Hyōjirō o omou," NKZ 13:167.

16. This private garden of the Maeda family was opened to the public once in 1872, then permanently in May 1874. Ishibayashi Bunkichi, *Ishikawa hyakunenshi*, 23–24.

17. "Miyake Shinken sensei," NKZ 12:212.

18. One *koku* is a unit roughly equivalent to the amount of rice one individual consumes a year. Kaga Province could potentially sustain a population of one million people.

19. See Wakabayashi Kisaburō, "Kagahan," 138–43.

20. "Meiji no hajime goro, Kanazawa no furuhon," NKZ 12:210.

21. Komatsu Shūkichi, "Kagahan Meirindō no gakusei kaikaku," 334ff.

22. See *Sofu* 33 n. 49. The reading of Nagao's given name is uncertain.

23. Ishida Kanehisa (1836–1898) was a close disciple of Sekiguchi Hiraku.

24. *Ishikawaken kyōikushi*, 384–85.

25. Called *kajuku*, this practice of a school teacher's running a private *juku* was not formally discouraged until 1889 (Meiji 32). See *Ishikawaken kyōikushi*, 1276.

26. "Shoei sōhon *Jiga* go," NKZ 12:185.

27. Shimatani Shunzō, "*Zen no kenkyū* no umareru made," *JPS* 347 (April 1946), 36.

28. Amano Teiyū, "Nishida Sensei kajitsu seidan," 182–84.

29. Incidentally, on this very day the fancy Rokumeikan ("Palace of the Deer Cry") opened with a grand ball in Tokyo, marking the height of the phase of extreme Westernization of Japan.

30. "Yo no otōto Nishida Hyōjirō o omou," NKZ 13:170.

31. The author of the textbook is Sekiguchi Hiraku; the book was published in Meiji 13 (1880). See Tanaka Onokichi, *Kyōdo sūgaku*, 183.

32. See *Sofu* 20.

33. Kimura Hisashi (1870–1943) entered the Department of Astronomy at the Imperial University and became the first director of the Mizusawa Observatory in Iwate Prefecture. He discovered the Z-term and published his paper of 1902, "On the Existence of a New Annual Term in the Variation of Latitude, Independent of the Components of the Pole's Motion." He was the first recipient of the Japan's Cultural Medal in 1937.

34. Kimura Motomori, "Nishida Kitarō sensei no hanashi," 188.

35. Tanaka Onokichi, *Kyōdo sūgaku*, 181–87. Kamiyama and three other disciples lived with Sekiguchi at his private *juku*, "Enshōsha."

36. Isaac Todhunter (1820–1884); his book was used as a college textbook in England. See Tanaka Onokichi, *Kyōdo sūgaku*.

37. "Koniku sekushonsu," NKZ 12:207–08.

38. "Hōjō sensei ni hajimete oshie o uketa koro," NKZ 12:257–58.
39. Hōjō's diary, March 16, 1886, in *Kakudō hen'ei*, edited by Nishida Kitarō, 775.
40. Tanaka Onokichi, *Kyōdo sūgaku*, 191.
41. "Hōjō sensei ni hajimete oshie o uketa koro," NKZ 12: 258.
42. The number of graduates from Tokyo University was less than one hundred in the early 1880s. See *Tōkyō Daigaku hyakunenshi* [hereafter TDH], *Tsūshi*, 1:469.
43. Hōjō's diary of April 18, 1886, compiled in *Kakudō hen'ei*, 776.
44. "Koniku sekushonsu," NKZ 12:208.

CHAPTER 2: MATHEMATICS OR PHILOSOPHY? (1886–1891)

1. *Ishikawaken kyōikushi*, 303–50.
2. "Yamamoto Chōsui-kun no omoide," NKZ 12:245.
3. "Mukō shōsa o omou," NKZ 13:161–65.
4. Itō Hirobumi (1841–1909) was born in Hagi in today's Yamaguchi Prefecture and served four terms as prime minister; he later became the first speaker of the privy council.
5. Mori Arinori (1847–1889) held diplomatic positions in early Meiji. In 1882 he saw Itō Hirobumi in Paris, and the two agreed on the future course of Japan. Itō promised him the position of minister of education then.
6. The First Higher Middle School was established in Tokyo (1886), the Second in Sendai (1887), the Third in Kyoto (1886), the Fourth in Kanazawa (1887), and the Fifth in Kumamoto (1887). These "higher middle schools" were reclassified as "higher schools" in 1894.
7. *Ishikawaken kyōikushi*, 656.
8. "Yamamoto Chōsui-kun no omoide," NKZ 12:247.
9. *Satsumo-hayato* translates as "rough and tough."
10. Ishibayashi Bunkichi, *Ishikawa hyakunenshi*, 58–74.
11. "Monbu daijin gakuji junshi zuikō nikki," in *Mori Arinori Zenshū*, edited by Ōkubo Toshiaki, 1:720.
12. After the restoration, former feudal lords *(daimyō)* were given aristocratic ranks. The Maedas pledged 80,000 yen for the new school. *Ishikawaken kyōikushi*, 656.
13. *Mori Arinori Zenshū*, 1:555.
14. Ibid., 1:556–57.
15. *Ishikawaken kyōikushi*, 661.
16. "Yamamoto Chōsui-kun no omoide," NKZ 12:247.
17. Ibid., NKZ 12:247.
18. "Wakakarishi hi no Tōho," NKZ 12:223.
19. "Gasonkaiin shokun o hyōsu," NKZ 16:598.
20. See Suzuki Daisetz's letter no. 4 to Yamamoto Ryōkichi, 11 September 1888,

in *Suzuki Daisetz mikōkai shokan,* edited by Inoue Zenjō and Zen Bunka Kenkyūjo, 47–48 [hereafter cited as SDMS].

21. Suzuki Daisetz, "Nishida no omoide," SDZ 28:381.

22. "Gasonkai Uyoku bunkō," NKZ 16:604. This poem probably dates from 1889.

23. "Hōjō-sensei ni hajimete oshie o uketa koro," NKZ 12:258.

24. Ibid., 258–59.

25. Ibid., 258.

26. See Daiyon kōtō chūgakkō, *Daiyon kōtō chūgakkō ichiran* (1887), 48 [hereafter cited as *Ichiran*].

27. "Shikō no omoide," NKZ 12:164–65.

28. Miyake Shinken (1853–1933) had a library of books in Chinese containing more than 41,000 volumes that had been catalogued by Mukyūkai *(Shinken sensei kyūzōsho mokuroku).* Miyake moved to Hiroshima Higher Normal School and then to Tokyo on the request of the Maeda family to catalogue their holdings of books in Chinese. See "Miyake Shinken sensei," NKZ 12:212–15.

29. *Huangqing jingjie.*

30. "Miyake Shinken sensei," NKZ 12:214.

31. "Hōjō-sensei ni hajimete oshie o uketa koro," NKZ 12:259.

32. Tanaka Onokichi, *Kyōdo sūgaku,* 192.

33. The school had three divisions. The length of study for the main division was two years; for the preparatory division, three years; and the subpreparatory division, two years.

34. It is said that Inoue Enryō's *Tetsugaku issekiwa* [A philosophical discussion on an evening], 1886–1887, caught Nishida's attention. See Kōsaka Masaaki, "Nishida Tetsugaku," 22. Also see Kimura Motomori, "Nishida Kitarō sensei no hanashi," 188.

35. "Aru kyōju no taishoku no ji," NKZ 12:169–70.

36. *Ichiran* (1888), 11–12.

37. *Translation from the Encyclopedia of the Philosophical Science with Prolegomena* (Oxford: Clarendon Press, 1874).

38. Müller's translation is the first English edition of Kant's *Critique of Pure Reason* (London: Macmillan, 1881).

39. "Shikō no omoide," NKZ 12:166.

40. Letter no. 1 to Yamamoto Ryōkichi, ca. 1888, NKZ 18:3–5.

41. See letters no. 1 and 2 to Yamamoto Ryōkichi, ca. 1888, NKZ 18:3–7.

42. Nakae Chōmin (1847–1901) studied in France for three years beginning in 1871; on his return to Japan he introduced Rousseau's idea of the social contract. He expounded on his atomist theory in his 1886 *Rigaku kōgen* [A profound exposition of science].

43. Some Marxist thinkers lamented that Nishida's subsequent development of thought was pure "going down hill."

44. "Yamamoto Chōsui-kun no omoide," NKZ 12:247. Cf. D. T. Suzuki's letter no. 9 to Yamamoto Ryōkichi, 28 December 1888, SDMS, 68.

45. Suzuki's letter no. 6 to Yamamoto Ryōkichi, 6 October 1888, SDMS, 54.

46. The first term ended on December 24, at which time he received his grades. See *Sofu* 48.

47. "Yamamoto Chōsui-kun no omoide," NKZ 12:48; this photo is the frontispiece of *Chōsui sensei ikō, zokuhen,* edited by Kawasaki Akira.

48. It was Miyake Shinken who described Nishida and his company as lads "with wings." Nishida liked the expression and took it as his *gō* (pen name) "Tōhingi," NKZ 16:607–08.

49. Hōjō's diary of 17 July 1889, compiled in *Kakudō hen'ei,* 356.

50. Ibid., 358 (2 August 1889).

51. "Koniku sekushonsu," NKZ 12:209.

52. "Yamamoto Chōsui-kun no omoide," NKZ 12:248.

53. The school year was divided into three terms, the first term from September 11 to December 24, the second term from January 8 to March 31, and the third term from April 8 to July 10.

54. *Kakudō hen'ei,* 310–11.

55. Walter Scott (1771–1832), Scottish novelist and poet, was the author of *Ivanhoe* (1820).

56. "Yo ga saiaisuru shokun yo," NKZ 16:581–84.

57. Thomas Babington Macaulay (1800–1859) was a British essayist and historian.

58. Washington Irving (1783–1859) was an American writer.

59. "Honkai kaiin shokun yo," NKZ 16:595–96.

60. Cf. Fukuzawa Yukichi, *Gakumon no susume* [An encouragement of learning], chap. 12.

61. "Haishōron," NKZ 16:624–26.

62. "Jean Jacques Rousseau," NKZ 16:585–87.

63. Ibid., 586–87.

64. Ibid., 587. The quotation is apparently from Emerson's essay "Self-Reliance."

65. "Indokoku," NKZ 16:588–90.

66. "Yō Hikkan ki," NKZ 16:620–21.

67. Niijima Jō (1843-1890), eager to see the wider world, smuggled himself out of Japan in 1864 to America. With the patronage of American people he came to know, he enrolled in Phillips Academy in 1865 and graduated in 1867. He was baptized in 1866. He entered Amherst College in 1867, graduated in 1870 with a B.S., and studied further at Andover Theological Seminary. He returned to Japan in 1874. With the help of the Congregational missionary, J. D. Davis, he established Dōshisha in Kyoto, an institution of higher learning.

68. "Sanpo," NKZ 16:591–94.

69. The popular journal, edited by Tokutomi Sohō, was first published in February 1887.

70. "Han o oaratani ni suru ni atatte" (1936), NKZ 1:7. Abe and Ives, *An Inquiry into the Good*, xxxiii.

71. A frontispiece, SDMS.

72. Kōsaka Masaaki, "Meiji shisōshi," 418.

73. "Fuseimonkai Uyokusei sōkō," NKZ 16:637–50.

74. NKZ 16:646–47. According to the lunar calendar, September 9 was the *chōyō no sekku*, or chrysanthemum festival.

75. In 1872 the Meiji government abolished the traditional "five festivals" of January 1, March 3, May 5, July 7, and September 9 (notice the doubling of the number of the month and the day), in its attempt to bring Japan out of its "feudalistic" past and to make it a member of the modern world. Instead of the traditional festivals, such nationalistic holidays as the foundation of the nation day (February 11) and the birthday of the emperor Meiji (November 3) were instituted. These government measures gradually diluted the rich and varied Japanese folk traditions.

76. "Gūsei," NKZ 16:650.

77. Suzuki's letter no. 13 to Yamamoto Ryōkichi, 6 February 1891, SDMS, 87–88.

78. "Yamamoto Chōsui-kun no omoide," NKZ 12:247.

79. Hōjō's letter to the school authority is compiled in *Kakudō hen'ei*, 309–10. There is no record of Nishida's commenting on Hōjō's involvement in this affair.

CHAPTER 3: THE IMPERIAL UNIVERSITY (1891–1894)

1. Whenever the quota of a department was not filled, *senka* students were admitted. See TDH, *Shiryō*, 1:605, and *Tsūshi*, 1:467–68. In 1925 the dramatic increase in students' interest in this program forced its closure.

2. In 1895 the ratio of university students to elementary school pupils was less than one percent. See *Kakudō hen'ei*, 5.

3. TDH, *Tsūshi* 1:467–68.

4. Nishida asked Yamamoto to inquire after the status of his "certificate"; letter no. 18 to Yamamoto Ryōkichi, 24 October 1894, NKZ 18:29.

5. TDH, *Shiryō* 1:127. University of Tokyo was from its inception rendered in English as "Imperial University of Tokio"; Mori took the word "imperial" and coined a Japanese word, *teikoku*. See the recollection of the secretary to the minister of education, Koba Sadanaga (1859–1944), in TDH, *Shiryō* 1:125–28.

6. TDH, *Shiryō* 1:121.

7. Letter no. 17 to Yamamoto Ryōkichi, 13 June 1891, SDMS, 107.

8. SDMS, 104–05 n. 12.

9. Letter no. 4 to Yamamoto Ryōkichi and Fujioka Sakutarō, 27 June 1891, NKZ 18:11.

10. Suzuki's letter no. 17 to Yamamoto Ryōkichi, 13 June 1891, SDMS, 106–07. See also Suzuki's letters to Yamamoto no. 14 (19 March 1891), no. 15 (18 April 1891), and no. 16 (23 May 1891), SDMS, 93–108.

11. Letter no. 4 to Yamamoto Ryōkichi and Fujioka Sakutarō, 27 June 1891, NKZ 18:11.

12. "Hōjō sensei ni hajimete oshie o uketa koro," NKZ 12:260.

13. Ernest F. Fenollosa (1853–1908), a graduate of Harvard College, was invited to teach at Tokyo University in 1878 at the age of twenty-six. He remained in the position until August 1886.

14. Kaneko Takezō, "Akikaze no kōgen ni tatsu gakufu sanagarani" [Resembling my father-in-law, standing on the hill in the autumn wind], 280.

15. Motora Yūjirō (1858–1912) was a specialist in experimental psychology. He went to the United States in 1883, studied at Boston University, then at the Johns Hopkins University under the guidance of Stanley Hall. He received his Ph.D. in 1888.

16. Inoue Tetsujirō (1855–1944) was a graduate of Tokyo University. He was in Europe from 1884 to 1890, and upon his return to Japan he was immediately appointed professor of philosophy. He dominated the world of academic philosophy until his retirement in 1923.

17. Nakajima Rikizō (1858–1918) was a specialist in ethics. A graduate of Dōshisha, he studied in the United States at the Western Reserve Academy, Western Reserve University, and Yale University, where he received his Ph.D. in 1889.

18. Inoue Tetsujirō, "Meiji tetsugakukai no kaiko," 57.

19. Student Record, 1885–1897, College of Humanities, Imperial University.

20. *JP* 58 (December 1892), 1300.

21. Kimura organized the "Association of Greater Japan" *(Dainihon kyōkai)* in 1897 and advocated "New Shinto." The group published a journal, *Nihonshugi.*

22. "Aru kyōju no taishoku no ji," NKZ 12:170.

23. See *Ōshima Yoshinaga*, edited by Ōshima Sensei Kinenkai.

24. Karl Florenz (1865–1939) taught German and Sanskrit.

25. "Miyake Shinken Sensei," NKZ 12:213.

26. R. H. Lotze (1817–1881) was a German metaphysician and a forerunner of neo-Kantianism.

27. "Rottse no keijijōgaku," NKZ 1:395–96.

28. Shimatani Shunzō, "*Zen no kenkyū* no umareru made," 42 n. 2.

29. Michiko Yusa, "A Speech Meeting of November 8, 1891."

30. Letter no. 9 to Yamamoto Ryōkichi, 8 November 1891, NKZ 18:16–17.

31. Fukuchi Gen'ichirō (1841–1906) was a multitalented man. He was not only a specialist in European legal systems but also a gifted journalist. He devoted his later years to creating the Kabukiza in Tsukiji and writing kabuki plays.

32. G. H. F. Verbeck (1830–1898) was an American missionary of Dutch (not French) extraction. Nishida was misinformed on this point. Verbeck was a consultant to the high officials of the Meiji government, including Ōkuma Shigenobu, Soejima Taneomi, and Itō Hirobumi. His ideas formed the backbone of the Iwakura Mission.

33. Ōuchi Seiran (1845–1918), a Sōtō Zen monk who trained under Hara Tanzan, renounced his monastic commitment to engage in social work. He was a "socially engaged" Buddhist who established schools for the handicapped.

34. Taoka Reiun (1870–1912), an active social and cultural critic, was a *senka* student in Chinese literature.

35. Imakita Kōsen (1816–1892), advocated *koji* Zen ("Zen for lay followers") and trained disciples, such as Akizuki Satsuo, Hōjō Tokiyuki, and Hiranuma Kiichirō.

36. November 23 was a holiday *(niinamesai)* in those days.

37. Suzuki Daisetz's letter no. 22 to Yamamoto Ryōkichi, 25 November 1891, SDMS, 124.

38. Letter no. 8 to Yamamoto Ryōkichi, 18 December 1891, NKZ 18:16. Also see letter no. 11 to Yamamoto Ryōkichi, 14 April 1892, NKZ 18:19.

39. "Kanto rinrigaku" [Kant's ethics], NKZ 13:3–20.

40. Shaku Sōen (1859–1919) succeeded Imakita Kōsen. He was an unusual Zen priest, attended Keiō Gijuku (today's Keiō University), and studied Pāli in Sri Lanka.

41. Letter no. 13 to Yamamoto Ryōkichi, 15 September 1892, NKZ 18:21–22.

42. Yamamoto Ryōkichi, "Ko Matsui Kisaburō kyōju chōji" [Lamentation of the death of the late professor Matsui Kisaburō], in *Chōsui sensei ikō*, edited by Uchida Sen'nosuke.

43. "Yo no otōto Nishida Hyōjirō o omou," NKZ 13:167. Hyōjirō successfully passed the entrance examination to the Shikan Gakkō, Japan's "West Point," in 1893.

44. Yamamoto Ryōkichi, "Gojukkaiko, Nijūrokunen," in Chōsui sensei ikō, edited by Uchida Sen'nosuke, 25.

45. NKZ 16:653–57.

46. Ludwig Busse (1862–1907) earned his Ph.D. from the University of Berlin. After he returned to Germany, he taught at the Universities of Rostock, Königsberg, and Münster. He published *Philosophie und Erkenntnistheorie* (1894), *Die Wechselwirkung zwischen Leib und Seele* (1900), and *Geist und Körper, Seele und Leib* (1903). See *JP* 252 (February 1908), 220.

47. Raphael von Koeber (1848–1923) was trained as a pianist but changed his mind and pursued philosophy at the Universities of Jena and Heidelberg. World War I prevented him from returning to Europe. He was made an honorary citizen of Tokyo.

48. Inoue Tetsujirō, "Rafaeru fon Kēberu-shi o tsuikaisu," 60–64.

49. Ibid., 60–64.

50. Anesaki Masaharu, "Kēberu sensei no tsuikai," 68.

51. Kuwaki Gen'yoku, "Kēberu sensei ni tsuite," 65.

52. "Kēberu sensei," NKZ 13:177.

53. The expression suggests that a deep understanding is more important than an accumulation of superficial knowledge.

54. "Kēberu sensei," NKZ 13:177.

55. Diary, 19 July 1905, NKZ 17:148.

56. "Kēberu sensei," NKZ 13:176.

57. Fukada Yasukazu (1878–1928) graduated from the Imperial University in 1902.

58. Hatano Seiichi (1877–1950) graduated from the Imperial University in 1899.

59. Watsuji Tetsurō (1889–1960) graduated from Tokyo Imperial University in 1912.

60. Kuki (1888–1942) was a classmate of Watsuji at Tokyo Imperial University; he graduated in 1912.

61. Takahashi Satomi, "Nishida Kitarō sensei no kotoba," 165–66.

62. Kuwaki Gen'yoku, "Kēberu sensei ni tsuite," 66.

63. Inoue Tetsujirō, "Rafaeru von Kēberu-shi o tsuikaisu," 64.

64. Tanabe Ryūji, *Koizumi Yakumo*, 132–33. Koeber's sarcastic remark—that the Roman Catholic Church ought to rule the entire world and that anyone who did not belong to it ought to be burned at the stake—frightened Hearn.

65. Anesaki Masaharu, "Kēberu sensei no tsuikai," *JP* 438 (August 1923), 68–73.

66. "Inoue Sensei" [Professor Inoue], NKZ 13:184.

67. Shimomura Toratarō, "Nishida sensei no kotodomo, Unokemura kikō," 306.

68. NKZ 13:42–46.

69. NKZ 13:47–54.

70. NKZ 13:55–59.

71. *Hokushinkai Zasshi* 13:1–12.

CHAPTER 4: EXISTENTIAL IMPASSE AND ZEN PRACTICE (1894–1899)

1. Letter no. 14 to Yamamoto Ryōkichi, 19 September 1894, NKZ 18:23–25.

2. Letter no. 16, 8 October 1894, NKZ 18:27–28.

3. A year junior to Nishida at the Fourth Higher School; Ueda Seiji went on to the Imperial University and majored in German literature.

4. Letter no. 17 to Yamamoto Ryōkichi, 20 October 1894, NKZ 18:28.

5. Letter no. 19 to Yamamoto Ryōkichi, 1 December 1894, NKZ 18:32.

6. Published by Tōyōdō in Tokyo in 1895.

7. *Budda no fukuin*, published in 1895.

8. Letter no. 17 to Yamamoto Ryōkichi, 20 October 1894, NKZ 18:29.

9. Thomas Hill Green (1836–1882) was a British neo-Hegelian.

10. Letter no. 17 to Yamamoto Ryōkichi, 20 October 1894, NKZ 18:29.

11. Letter no. 18 to Yamamoto Ryōkichi, 24 October 1894, NKZ 18:30–31.

12. Letter no. 19 to Yamamoto Ryōkichi, 1 December 1894, NKZ 18:31.

13. NKZ 13:21–41.

14. *Kyōiku Jiron* 362 (May 5), 363 (May 15), 364 (May 25).

15. Yoshida Shōin (1830–1859) founded Shōkasonjuku in the village of Matsumoto near the city of Hagi. This private school produced prominent leaders of the Meiji Restoration, such as Takasugi Shinsaku and Itō Hirobumi. Shōin believed in individualized education tailored to each student's need.

16. Fujita Tōko (1806–1855) was a historian and Confucian scholar of Mito *han*; he believed that a good natural environment was necessary for nurturing good character in children.

17. Possibly *Watakushi no wakaki hibi* [My Younger Days], 1885.

18. Letter no. 20 to Yamamoto Ryōkichi, 20 May 1895, NKZ 18:33–34.

19. Born on March 21, 1875; Kotomi's mother was Tosa's younger sister.

20. Letter no. 24 to Yamamoto Ryōkichi, 18 November 1895, NKZ 18:38. Nishida was then working on "Eikoku rinrigakushi," NKZ 16:3–86. He finished the essay and sent it to Yamamoto on January 23, 1897. It was published in *Rinrigakushi*, edited by Yamamoto Ryōkichi.

21. Letter no. 22 to Yamamoto Ryōkichi, 2 October 1895, NKZ 18:36.

22. Letter no. 23 to Yamamoto Ryōkichi, 26 October 1895, NKZ 18:37.

23. Ibid.

24. Tomita, formerly a politician and the county mayor, turned educator.

25. Letter no. 24 to Yamamoto Ryōkichi, 18 November 1895, NKZ 18:38.

26. Ibid.

27. Letter no. 25 to Yamamoto Ryōkichi, 19 December 1895, NKZ 18:39–40.

28. Letter no. 26 to Yamamoto Ryōkichi, 31 March 1896, NKZ 18:41–42.

29. "Ueda Yayoi no omoide no ki," NKZ 12:261–63.

30. Letter no. 40 to Yamamoto Ryōkichi, 25 February 1896, SDMS, 197.

31. He began his practice under Setsumon in March 1886. *Kakudō hen'ei*, 774.

32. *Chōsui sensei ikō, zokuhen*, edited by Kawasaki Akira, 66. Also see Suzuki Daisetz, "Watakushi no rirekisho," SDZ 30:549.

33. "Hōjō sensei ni hajimete oshie o uketa koro," NKZ 12:260.

34. Dokuon (1819–1895) became the first chief abbot of the Rinzai Zen School; his enlightenment and virtue surpassed sectarian boundaries and was highly respected by all.

35. These are the impressions reported by D. T. Suzuki who visited China in 1934. See Suzuki Daisetz, "Shina bukkyō inshōki," SDZ 30:463–561. What Setsumon encountered in China must have been quite similar to what Suzuki saw.

36. Yamaoka Tesshū (1836–1888), received the *inka* (master's acknowledgement of

enlightenment) from Tekisui in 1880; he established Tesshūji in Shizuoka Prefecture and Zenshō'an in Ueno, Tokyo.

37. Zen masters who are officially in charge of teaching novices.

38. This phrase in variation appears in the *Diamond Sutra* 4, 10.c, and 14.e. Nishida quoted this passage in his final essay on religion, NKZ 11:423.

39. Tekisui (1822–1899), abbot of Tenryūji, was an influential figure of the Meiji Zen circle. His distinguished disciples included Gazan Shōtei and Yamaoka Tesshū.

40. Letter no. 43 to Yamamoto Ryōkichi, 7 January 1897, SDMS, 208.

41. Diary, NKZ 17:7.

42. Hisamatsu Shin'ichi, "Nishida Sensei to Zen (1)" 17–18.

43. Ibid., 18.

44. "Sentenchishiki no umu o ronzu," *Hokushinkai Zasshi*, 14–16 (February, April, June 1897). The first and the third installments correspond to NKZ 13:60–65 and NKZ 13:65–71. The second installment seems to be missing from NKZ.

45. Diary, NKZ 17:14–15.

46. This schism translated into a clash between local and central government power. See *Ishikewaken kyōikushi*, 666–68.

47. The problem became more widely known because it was written up in a journal, *Nihonjin*, by a writer using a pseudonym. See Ishibayashi, *Ishikawa hyakunenshi*, 574.

48. Kawakami forced the resignation of Paul Ehmann, whose term of employment had not expired, and in turn was fired in February 1898. Hōjō succeeded Kawakami.

49. Kishi Shigeji, "Shikō no omoide," 47.

50. Ōshima Yoshinaga taught logic and English at the Fourth Higher School.

51. "Ōshima-kun to watakushi," NKZ 19:880.

52. Tokunō Bun (1866–1945) assumed lectureship at the Imperial University; he later became professor at the Tokyo Higher Normal School of Education. Nishitani Keiji, *Nishida Kitarō*, 71.

53. Ueda Seiji became professor of German literature at Tokyo Imperial University.

54. Kokan (1839–1903) became *shike* (master teacher) in 1892 and then abbot in May 1899. *Kinsei zenrin sōhōden*, edited by Obata Buntei, 3:234–39.

55. Diary, NKZ 17:18.

56. Hōjō's diary, *Kakudō hen'ei*, 7.

57. Letter no. 31 to Hayashi Uruwashi, 18 November 1897, NKZ 18:47.

58. Diary, NKZ 17:18.

59. A full citation of the passage reads: "Behold the fowls of the air; for they sow not, neither do they reap, nor gather into barns; yet your heavenly Father feedeth them. Are ye not much better than they?" Matthew 6:26.

60. Letter no. 30 to Yamamoto Ryōkichi, 1897, NKZ 18:45–46.

61. Xavier (1506–1552), a Jesuit, was in Yamaguchi in 1549.

62. Villion (1843–1932) was in Yamaguchi 1889–1895. A. Villion, *Cinquante ans d'apostolat au Japon.* See also Ikeda Toshio, *Birion shinpu.*

63. *Zenkan sakushin,* a collection of anecdotes and famous passages from Buddhist scriptures, was intended to help Zen practitioners break through the "barriers."

64. Diary, NKZ 17:24.

65. Diary, 11 January 1898, NKZ 17:25.

66. *Kakudō hen'ei,* 878.

67. Hōjō's diary, *Kakudō hen'ei,* 361.

68. Inaba Masamaru (1865–1944) was a graduate of the Imperial University and specialized in biology and geology. He had helped found the Ōtani Ordinary Middle School before coming to Yamaguchi, where he taught from 1897 to 1900. He was actively involved in the reform movement of the Ōtani sect and became the president of Ōtani University.

69. Letter no. 34 to Yamamoto Ryōkichi, 15 September 1899, NKZ 18:51.

70. Yamamoto Annosuke was two years junior to Nishida and graduated from the philosophy department at (Tokyo) Imperial University.

71. NKZ 13:72–77.

72. Ibid., 77.

73. Nishida's letter to Inaba Masamaru, 13 October 1898. See Kitano Hiroyuki, "Nishida Kitarō shokan santsū ni tsuite," 231.

74. Diary, NKZ 17:36.

75. "Tokusan Carrying His Bundle," *Hekiganroku,* case 4. See *The Blue Cliff Record,* translated by Thomas Cleary and J. C. Cleary, 24.

76. Tobari Chikufū (1873–1955) was trained in German literature under Florenz at the Imperial University. Nishida became interested in Nietzsche's thought through Tobari.

77. Togawa Shūkotsu, "Sono koro no hitotachi," *Shizen kimagure kikō,* quoted by Shimomura Toratarō in "Wakaki Nishida Kitarō Sensei," 34.

78. See Nishida's curriculum vitae, submitted to Gakushūin. The court rank is a title of "merit"; it is a form of government acknowledgment of service rendered to the country of Japan.

79. February 1898–March 1902.

80. Diary, NKZ 17:44.

81. Ibid.

82. Letter no. 1079 to Takizawa Katsumi, 14 March 1937, NKZ 18:590.

CHAPTER 5: TOWARD KENSHŌ (1899–1904)

1. *Shikō hachijūnen,* edited by Tomatsu Nobuyasu, 43.

2. Hori Koretaka (1868–1954) was a professor of Japanese.

3. For addresses to the students see *Kakudō hen'ei,* 17–21.

4. *Shikō hachijūnen*, 43.

5. The incident most likely occurred on 3 November 1898.

6. Postscript to *Kakudō hen'ei*, 896.

7. Ibid. This episode was narrated by someone who participated in the assault.

8. Matthew 10:35–37: "For I am come to set a man at variance against his father, and the daughter against her mother, and the daughter-in-law against her mother-in-law. . . . He that loveth father or mother more than me is not worthy of me: and he that loveth son or daughter more than me is not worthy of me."

9. Letter no. 34 to Yamamoto Ryōkichi, 15 September 1899, NKZ 18:50–51.

10. Ishikawa Ryūzō (1867–1944) was one of the ten disciple swordsmen of Yamaoka Tesshū. He succeeded Tesshū to become the second headmaster of the Mutōryū School; he was also a gifted calligrapher.

11. *Kakudō hen'ei*, 26–27, 19 October 1899.

12. Hori Koretaka, "Shikō Sansanjuku ni tsuite," 229.

13. The gist of his talk is printed in the student journal, *Hokushinkai Zasshi* 25 (December 1899), 94–100.

14. Letter no. 35 to Yamamoto Ryōkichi, 20 December 1899, NKZ 18:51.

15. Matsumoto's correspondence in *JP* 157 (March 1900), 300–01, and *JP* 167 (April 1901), 85–87.

16. Ōnishi (1864–1900) was not only a liberal thinker but an accomplished poet. He was opposed to making the *Imperial Rescript on Education* the embodiment of the national ethic. Nishida respected him enormously.

17. "Bi no setsumei," NKZ 13:78–80. English translation by Steve Odin in *Monumenta Nipponica*.

18. *Hokushinkai Zasshi* 26 (5 March 1900), 1–3.

19. "Benedict Spinoza," *Hokushinkai Zasshi*, 28 (15 November 1900), 36–39.

20. Hori Koretaka, "Shikō Sansanjuku ni tsuite," 227–33.

21. "Sansanjuku yonjisshūnen kinen ni atarite," NKZ 13:126–27.

22. "Hori Koretaka-kun no 'Shikō Sansanjuku ni tsuite' o yomite," NKZ 13:124–25.

23. Ibid., 124.

24. *Sanzen* is a private interview with a Zen master, during which the master tests the student's progress on his or her *kōan* practice.

25. Diary, 6 January 1901, NKZ 17:46–47.

26. Diary, 15 January 1901, NKZ 17:47–48.

27. Diary, 1 February 1901, NKZ 17:49.

28. Moriuchi committed suicide in 1907.

29. Diary, 6 February 1901, NKZ 17:50.

30. Diary, 7 February 1901, NKZ 17:50.

31. Through Shaku Sōen's connection, Suzuki went to the United States to work for Paul Carus at the Open Court at LaSalle, Illinois.

32. Diary, 14 February 1901, NKZ 17:51.

33. Letter no. 36 to Yamamoto Ryōkichi, 19 February 1901, NKZ 18:53.

34. In 1905 Toki was adopted by Nishida's friend, Shimizu Otohachi.

35. Diary, NKZ 17:54.

36. Diary, 5 April 1901, NKZ 17:55. He was at Senshin'an from April 1 to 6.

37. Diary, NKZ 17:59.

38. Diary, NKZ 17:60.

39. Nishida is probably referring to the "New Shinto" movement advocated in 1897 by those who adhered to a chauvinistic cultural stance, including Kimura Takatarō, Inoue Tetsujirō, Motora Yūjirō, and Takayama Chogyū.

40. Letter no. 39 to Yamamoto Ryōkichi, 16 July 1901, NKZ 18:56.

41. Obata Buntei, *Kinsei zenrin sōhōden* 3:238.

42. Ōsaka became an ardent Christian.

43. "Jishūryō shakan jidai no omoide," NKZ 19:780–81. (See also my introduction, page xxi.)

44. Later Nishida was given another nickname, *Schrecken-sensei*, "Professor, the Terrifying," because he was not easy on those students who cheated or who did not come to class properly prepared.

45. Shimizu Yoshichirō, "Furui Shikō no omoide," 50.

46. NKZ 13:81–84; published in *Mujintō* (December 1901).

47. NKZ 13:83–84.

48. *Seishinkai* 2:1 (January 1902).

49. Diary, 20 January 1902, NKZ 17:99.

50. Diary, 24 February 1902, NKZ 17:74.

51. NKZ 17:76–7 and NKZ 19:721. The two new dormitory buildings were completed in 1903.

52. Diary, 7 August 1902, NKZ 17:87.

53. Ibid.

54. Quoted by Akizuki Ryōmin, *Jinrui no kyōshi, Suzuki Daisetz*, 131.

55. Diary, NKZ 17:90.

56. Diary, 9 October 1902, NKZ 17:94.

57. Letter no. 57 to Hori Koretaka, 14 January 1907, NKZ 18:78.

58. Diary, 1 January 1903, NKZ 17:101.

59. Diary, NKZ 17:108 and NKZ 17:126.

60. Diary, NKZ 17:105.

61. NKZ 13:85–89; published in *Hokushinkai Zasshi* 35 (June 1903), 1–6. For an English translation, see Jeff Shore and Fusako Nagasawa, "On the Doubt in Our Heart," *Eastern Buddhist* 17, no. 2 (1984), 7–11.

62. Diary, 11 June 1903, NKZ 17:113.

63. Diary, 19 July 1903, NKZ 17:117.

64. Diary, 23 July 1903, NKZ 17:117.

65. Diary, 25 July 1903, NKZ 17:117.

66. Diary, 27 July 1903, NKZ 17:118.

67. Diary, 3 August 1903, NKZ 17:119.

68. Setsumon's letter is reproduced in *Sofu*, 121–22.

69. Samuel Alexander, *Moral Order and Progress: An Analysis of Ethical Conceptions* (1889).

70. Published in 1897, Ōnishi wrote this work while he was a graduate student at the Imperial University of Tokyo.

71. Letter no. 51 to Yamamoto, 29 November 1903, NKZ 18:72. The letter is misdated 1905 in NKZ.

72. Diary, 8 January 1904, NKZ 17:123.

73. Letter no. 47 to Yamamoto Ryōkichi, 8 March 1905, NKZ 18:67.

74. Shimomura Toratarō, "Wakaki Nishida Kitarō sensei," 49–50.

CHAPTER 6: THE BIRTH OF A PHILOSOPHER (1904–1907)

1. Christopher Martin, *The Russo-Japanese War*. Russia declared war on 9 February and Japan on 10 February.

2. "Mukō shōsa o omou," NKZ 13:163; *Hokkoku Shinbun*, 11 and 12 May 1904.

3. "Mukō shōsa o omou," NKZ 13:161–65.

4. Ishibayashi Bunkichi, *Ishikawa hyakunenshi*, 530.

5. Letter no. 45 to Kuwabara Masahisa, 29 August 1904, NKZ 18:64.

6. Fujii Otoo (1868–1945) was an accomplished poet and scholar of Japanese literature and a close friend of Fujioka's; he was Nishida's colleague at the Fourth Higher School and later at Kyoto Imperial University.

7. "Yo no otōto Nishida Hyōjirō o omou," NKZ 13:166–70.

8. Diary, NKZ 17:130.

9. Diary, NKZ 17:134.

10. Letter no. 47 to Yamamoto Ryōkichi, 8 March 1905, NKZ 18:66–67 (emphasis added).

11. Yamamoto Ryōkichi, *Daisetsu ate, Yamamoto Ryōkichi shokan*, Yamamoto's letter no. 7 to Suzuki Daisetz, 12 March 1905, 27.

12. "A sonnet to Nishida who lost his brother in the siege of Port Arthur," Suzuki's letter no. 63 to Yamamoto Ryōkichi, 12 February 1905, SDMS, 325.

13. Nishida had finished his first draft of "Lectures in Psychology" in the early part of 1905 and was then working on the first draft of "Ethics."

14. Diary, NKZ 17:148.

15. Zuiun Gikan (1853–1935) trained under Dokuon and succeeded Setsumon as the abbot of Kokutaiji.

16. Masa (1859–1939) had been married and divorced twice. Divorce carried a social stigma in those days.

17. "Shinrigaku kōgi," NKZ 16:87–148.

18. Diary, 15 January 1905, NKZ 17:131. The end result was "Rinrigaku sōan (1)," NKZ 16:149–203.

19. "Rinrigaku sōan (2)," NKZ 16.204–66: Nishida's diary of 9 August 1905 reads: "Began working on this day."

20. Letter no. 48 to Hori Koretaka, 18 May 1905, NKZ 18:68–69.

21. Fujimura committed suicide in May 1903.

22. Letter no. 50 to Hori Koretaka, 20 September 1905, NKZ 18:71.

23. Diary, 31 January 1906, NKZ 17:164; 4 February 1906, NKZ 17:165; and 15 March 1906, NKZ 17:167.

24. Yamamoto Ryōkichi's letter to Suzuki, 14 July 1906, *Daisetsu ate*, 45.

25. Letter no. 52, NKZ 18:73.

26. Letter no. 53, NKZ 18:74.

27. NKZ 16:258–66. "Religion" was attached to the second draft of "Ethics."

28. Letter no. 2690 to Fujioka Sakutarō, 15 July 1906, NKZ 19:674.

29. For instance, we recognize the color red only in opposition to all the other colors—that is, non-reds.

30. *Zen no kenkyū*, NKZ 1:46–101.

31. Ibid., NKZ 1:102–68.

32. Shinagawa Kazue, "Omoide no ki," 58.

33. See editor's comment, NKZ 1:461–62. The printing of this text was finished on 21 April 1907, but it is possible that an earlier version was printed sometime in the fall of 1906.

34. Letter no. 96 to Hori Koretaka, 9 November 1908, NKZ 18:112–13. They all studied with Uemura Masahisa.

35. NKZ 13:90–95; published in *Hokushinkai Zasshi* 45 (19 November 1906), 4–10.

36. That is, *Zen no kenkyū*, part 3, chap. 12, NKZ 1:156–63.

37. Letter no. 111 to Yamamoto Ryōkichi, 9 June 1909, NKZ 18:125.

38. Letter no. 57, 14 January 1907, NKZ 18:78.

39. Letter no. 2691 to Fujioka Sakutarō, 7 August 1906, NKZ 19:675.

40. He wrote the memoir on 15 January 1907; NKZ 17:171.

41. Fujioka Sakutarō, "Shūenki," 26–73. He wrote his memoir on 4 September 1906.

42. "*Kokubungakushi kōwa no jo*," NKZ 1:414–15.

43. The essential tenet of Pure Land Buddhism is that one is saved only by one's unwavering faith in the grace of Amitābha (Amida in Japanese) Buddha, not by relying on one's own "power."

44. NKZ 1:418.

45. Letter no. 2695, 15 February 1907, NKZ 19:679.

46. *JP* 241 (1907), 1–64.

47. Kihira Tadayoshi (1874–1949) was a graduate of the Fourth Higher School in 1897, and graduated from the department of philosophy at Tokyo Imperial University in 1900. Later in his life he became an ardent ultranationalist and led the Center for National Spiritual Culture from 1932 to 1943. Nishida and Kihira drifted apart.

48. *JP* 242 (1907), 115–16.

49. Hamao Arata (1849–1925) was president of the Imperial University from 1893 to 1897, and again from 1905 to 1912.

50. To cull from Hōjō's diary for March 22, 1907: "Early morning I called on President Hamao and recommended Nishida to be employed at the university." And the next day: "In the train back to [Hiroshima] I read Mr. Nishida's 'On Reality.' Although I could not fully follow his argument because of the technical words in psychology he employed, overall I must say I agree with his argument." See *Kakudō hen'ei*, 408.

51. Letter no. 2702 to Fujioka Sakutarō, 22 June 1907, NKZ 19:684.

52. Letter no. 2705, NKZ 19:686–87. Sōseki taught at the Fifth Higher School from April 1896 to July 1900.

53. This letter was most likely written in 1907, not in 1906 (the year given in NKZ).

54. William James, "A World of Pure Experience," September and October 1904. Nishida asked Suzuki to send him an offprint of James's essays as soon as they appeared in the *Journal of Philosophy, Psychology, and Scientific Methods*. Suzuki was a review editor at the Open Court, and he regularly received offprints.

55. The reference is to James's *Pragmatism*. Nishida read a notice in the June 1905 *JP* (220:72) that James had turned to philosophy. Diary, 3 July 1905, NKZ 17:147.

56. Letter no. 55, 13 July 1907, NKZ 18:76.

57. Akegarasu Haya (1877–1954) asked Nishida to write the essay, "Chi to ai," for the *Seishinkai*.

58. Ishiguro was Nishida's advisee; he took up Zen practice.

59. NKZ 1:196–200.

60. The journal was published by Kiyozawa Manshi and his followers.

61. Letter no. 65 to Tanabe Ryūji, 5 October 1907, NKZ 18:85.

62. Nishida's annual salary at that time was 1,000 yen.

63. "*Kokubungakushi kōwa* no jo," NKZ 1:414–20.

CHAPTER 7: PURE EXPERIENCE AND ON RELIGION (1908–1909)

1. Diary, 3 January 1908, NKZ 17:194.

2. "Shinrigaku kōgi," NKZ 16:99–100 (emphasis added).

3. Diary, 26 February 1908: "Ordered books . . . Bergson, *Les données immédiates*," NKZ 17:197. Although it has been suggested that Nishida did not discover Bergson until later, he clearly already knew about Bergson's work in 1908. See, for instance, Shimomura Toratarō, "Nishida Kitarō and Some Aspects of His Philosophical Thought," in *A Study of Good*, translated by V. Viglielmo, 204.

4. "Yukeru Beruguson," 7 January 1941, *Asahi Shinbun*.

5. Part 1, "Junsui keiken," *Zen no kenkyū*, NKZ 1:9–45.

6. Letter no. 75 to Tanabe Ryūji, 14 March 1908, NKZ 18:95.

7. Letter no. 2707, 24 May 1908, NKZ 19:688.

8. *JP* 258 (August 1908), 20–63.

9. Letter no. 93 to Tanabe Ryūji, 20 October 1908, NKZ 18:111.

10. Letter no. 95 to Tanabe Ryūji, 28 October 1908, NKZ 18:112.

11. Diary, NKZ 17:212.

12. Letter no. 96 to Hori Koretaka, 9 November 1908, NKZ 18:113. There is no mention of *taza* (doing *zazen*) in his diary of 1907, but there are some entries related to Zen in 1908: January 12, NKZ 17:195; February 21, NKZ 17:197; October 3, NKZ 17:210; and November 28, NKZ 17:213.

13. *Teiyū Rinrikai Rinrikōenshū* 80 (1909), 48–72.

14. NKZ 1:169–89.

15. In "The logic of *topos* and the religious worldview" (1945), Nishida called his definition of religion "something like panentheism" (NKZ 11:399). Different from pantheism, his position defines all to be "in" God, but the distinction between God and humanity is strictly maintained.

16. These are the three personal characteristics discussed by J. R. Illingworth, *Personality Human and Divine* (London: Macmillan, 1907).

17. *Teiyū Rinrikai Rinrikōenshū* 82 (1909), 65–73.

18. NKZ 1:189–96.

19. The possibility of Nishida's move to Gakushūin came up in 1908; see letter no. 85 to Tanabe Ryūji, 16 July 1908, NKZ 18:103. The position became almost certain in 1909; letter no. 102 to Tanabe Ryūji, 2 February 1909, NKZ 18:119.

20. Cf. letter no. 103 to Tanabe Ryūji, 7 February 1909, NKZ 18:120.

21. Yamamoto assumed the position of dean of students at Kyoto Imperial University in 1908.

22. Suzuki headed back to Japan via Europe in 1908.

23. Diary, NKZ 17:220.

24. Ueda Hisashi, *Yamamoto Ryōkichi sensei-den*, 108.

25. Hōjō seems to have used his connection with Okada Ryōhei to help obtain this position for Nishida.

26. Shimizu Tōru was Nishida's senior at the Fourth Higher School; he was teaching at Gakushūin.

27. Ueda Seiji taught at Gakushūin from April through August 1909. See Gakushūin, *Kaikō gojūnen kinen, Gakushūinshi*, 54.

28. Letter no. 85 to Tanabe Ryūji, 16 July 1908, NKZ 18:103, and letter no. 86 to Fujioka Sakutarō, 17 July 1908, NKZ 18:105–06.

29. Letter no. 2713 to Fujioka Sakutarō, 17 June 1909, NKZ 19:693.

30. Letter no. 111 to Yamamoto Ryōkichi, 9 June 1909, NKZ 18:125.

31. Letter no. 2710 to Fujioka Sakutarō, 23 September 1908, NKZ 19:691.

CHAPTER 8: GAKUSHŪIN IN TOKYO (1909–1910)

1. Letter no. 116 to Tanabe Ryūji, 16 July 1909, NKZ 18:128. Also letter no. 118 to Tanabe Ryūji, 15 August 1909, NKZ 18:129.

2. Ishikawa taught *kendō* to Maeda Yoshinari and his peers. Tanabe Ryūji, *Nishida Kitarō no tegami*, 110.

3. Gakushūin moved its campus from Yotsuya to Mejiro (then the village of Takada) in September 1908. Gakushūin Hyakunenshi Hensan Iinkai, *Gakushūin hyakunenshi* 1:12.

4. Ibid., 1:4.

5. The Meiji aristocracy comprised the traditional courtier families, former feudal lords *(daimyō)* and their high-ranking ministers, meritorious warriors who contributed to the success of the Meiji Restoration, and scholars and statesmen who made important contributions to the newly founded state.

6. *Gakushūin hyakunenshi* 1:2.

7. Ibid., 1:5–6.

8. Ibid., 1:13.

9. Nogi was the tenth president and was in office from January 1907 until his suicide in September 1912. Ibid., 1:12.

10. Hidaka Daishirō, "Nogi Taishō to Suzuki sensei no inshō oyobi omoide," 283.

11. Kōsaka Masaaki, *Nishida Kitarō sensei no tsuioku*, 36.

12. Hidaka Daishirō, "Nogi Taishō to Suzuki Daisetsu sensei," 279–80.

13. Mushanokōji (1885–1976) was the driving force behind the Shirakaba Group.

14. Shiga (1883–1971) came under the influence of Uchimura Kanzō but never embraced Christianity.

15. Arishima Takeo (1878–1923) came under the influence of Uchimura Kanzō and was baptized in 1900. He committed love-suicide on June 9, 1923.

16. Arishima Ikuma (1882–1974), a younger brother of Takeo, was a painter. He married Harada Nobuko, the younger sister of Harada Kumao.

17. Satomi Ton (1888–1983) was a younger brother of Arishima Takeo but was adopted by the Yamauchi family.

18. In compliance with the decree of 1901 and 1902, elementary and middle schools switched their school year to begin in April. See *Gakushūin hyakunenshi* 1:487. The reason seems to be purely a matter of budgetary convenience. See Monbushōnai Kyōikushi Hensankai, *Meiji-ikō kyōikuseido hattatsushi*, 4:29–36.

19. See "List of Former Professors," in Gakushūin, *Kaikō gojūnen kinen Gakushūin-shi*, 45.

20. Besides these classes in the humanities track, Nishida also taught first-year students in the science track. Lists of students in respective classes are kept at the alumni office of Gakushūin.

21. Yanagi Muneyoshi (1889–1961), commonly known as Yanagi Sōetsu, was an aesthete, inspired by Pure Land Buddhist teaching. He looked up to Suzuki Daisetz as his mentor.

22. Kido Kōichi (1889–1977) was a grandson of Kido Kōin. He held important posts, including the minister of education, minister of welfare and health, and home minister. In 1940 he succeeded Yuasa Kurahei as lord keeper of the privy seal and closely assisted the emperor. Kido was tried at the Far Eastern Marshall Court, found guilty of war crimes, and imprisoned until 1955.

23. Nagayo Yoshirō (1888–1961) was a member of the Shirakaba Group and became a professional writer.

24. Oda Nobuhiro (1889–) was a son of Viscount Oda Nobutoshi and became a member of the House of Peers.

25. Harada Kumao (1888–1946) became the secretary of Saionji Kinmochi in 1926.

26. Ueda Misao (1890–1964) married Nishida's eldest daughter, Yayoi. He became judge of the Supreme Court.

27. Akamatsu Kotora (1890–1944) became mayor of Kyoto on April 17, 1939, and held that office for a year.

28. Konoe Ayamaro (1891–1945), popularly known as Konoe Fumimaro, was born into one of the noblest aristocratic families. He inherited the title of duke when his father, Atsumaro, died in 1904. Ayamaro committed suicide on December 16, 1945, to avoid being tried as a war criminal at the Far Eastern War Crimes Court.

29. Carl Hilty (1833–1909) was a notable Swiss thinker, scholar of jurisprudence, and statesman.

30. Nagayo Yoshirō, "Sanzetsu," 381.

31. Hori Koretaka, "Hōjō sensei no sokumen," 244.

32. "Nishida sensei no hon'in o sararuru o oshimu," *Hojinkai Zasshi* 82 (November 1910), 157–58.

33. Suzuki had been teaching English at Gakushūin since the spring semester of 1909 as a temporary replacement. He was formally appointed instructor in September 1909 and promoted to professor the following year.

34. Kanō Kōkichi (1865–1942) briefly held a position of professor at the Fourth Higher School from 1892 to 1894. He became the principal of the First Higher School in 1898 at the young age of 33. His scholarship uncovered Andō Shōeki's thought.

35. Horio lived in Nishida's house at Nagadohei as a *shosei*, 1903–1904. He went into the publishing business in Tokyo.

36. Yamazaki was then teaching at Waseda University.

37. Diary, NKZ 17:230.

38. Diary, NKZ 17:240.

39. Ishiguro Yoshitane, "Ōsaka Motokichirō shōden," 2:493–507.

40. Letter no. 68 to Tanabe Ryūji, 10 November 1907, NKZ 18:89.

41. Diary, 30 December 1909, NKZ 17:233.

42. *Hojinkai Zasshi* 80 (March 1910), 1–17. This is the same article that was published in the May 1909 issue of *Teiyūrinrikai Rinrikōenshū.*

43. The school was initially set up to educate the young Toshinari and his peers; it continued its operation even after that purpose was met. *Maeda Toshinari,* edited by Maeda Toshinari-kō Denki Hensan Iinkai, 519–21.

44. Maeda Toshinari (1885–1942) succeeded Toshitsugu, the fifteenth Lord Maeda. It is possibly through this connection with Toshinari that Nishida was asked to become Konoe Ayamaro's sponsor when the latter entered Kyoto Imperial University in 1912. Ayamaro's mother, Sawako, was the fifth daughter of the fourteenth lord, Maeda Yoshiyasu.

45. Leo Tolstoy was tremendously popular among the Japanese during the early twentieth century and influenced young people, especially Mushanokōji Saneatsu and Arishima Takeo, the leading members of the Shirakaba group.

46. Nihon University was founded in 1889 as a law school and in 1903 converted into a general university.

47. Buzan University was established in 1909 by a Shingon Buddhist sect; in 1926 it was incorporated into the newly established Taishō University.

48. First organized as an informal discussion group called Teiyū Konwakai in 1897 (Meiji 30) by Ōnishi Hajime, Anesaki Masaharu, Yokoi Tokio, and others. In 1898 the group was formalized, and in 1900 they changed the name to Teiyū Rinrikai (Teiyū Ethics Society) and began publishing their journal. See *JP* 154 (December 1899), 992–97.

49. Diary, NKZ 17:229.

50. Itō graduated from the philosophy department in June 1909 and continued on to the graduate school. He was at that time a member of the steering committee of the Philosophical Society and in 1911 became editor of *JP.* See *JP* 297 (November 1911), 98.

51. Diary, 30 November 1909, NKZ 17:231.

52. NKZ 13:96–105.

53. Diary, NKZ 17:232.

54. *JP* 275 (January 1910), 120–22.

55. *JP* 276, 43–57.

56. For Nishida the passive view of experience espoused by such thinkers as Locke, Mach, Ziehen, Münsterberg, and John Dewey—that various objects simply reflect on the mind and thereby constitute our experience—was merely a hypothesis. "Junsui keiken sōgo no kankei oyobi renraku ni tsuite," NKZ 13:97–98.

57. Gay Wilson Allen, *William James, A Biography*, 164.

58. Diary, NKZ 17:236.

59. Coauthored with Hiraide Kōjirō (Tokyo: Tōyōdō, 2 vols., 1895).

60. Reprint 1983.

61. Fujioka Kōji, "Ani no omoide," *Kokugo to Kokubungaku*, 17.4 (1940), 394.

62. Anesaki Masaharu (1873–1949) was a close friend of Takayama Chogyū and was professor of religious studies.

63. Yoshida Tatsumi (1872–1944) was a native of Kanazawa; the two were married in 1898.

64. Fujioka Yoshio, "Chichi no omoide," 391–92.

65. Haga Yaichi was briefly a colleague of Fujioka's at the Third Higher School in Kyoto from 1897 to 1898. He was professor at the Imperial University.

66. Wakimoto Sokurō (1883–1963) was the best friend of Fujioka's younger brother, Kōji, and used to dote on Mitsuko whenever he came to visit the Fujioka's. The book dedicated to Mitsuko's memory, *Kokubungakushi kōwa*, was actually transcribed by Wakimoto, while Fujioka dictated it. See preface to *Kokubungakushi kōwa*, 19.

67. Letter no. 124 to Yamamoto Ryōkichi, 9 April 1910, NKZ 18:135.

68. It was eventually housed in the Prefecture Library in Kanazawa. See Fujioka Yoshio, "Chichi no omoide," 392.

69. Ibid.

70. Thanks to their care, the boys were well educated. Yoshio became president of Saitama University and Yamanashi University, and Michio, who specialized in architecture, became professor at the Tokyo University of Industry. Aya died soon after her marriage.

71. See letter no. 825 to Yamamoto Ryōkichi, 25 December 1933, NKZ 18:489–90: "Already twenty years have passed since Tōho died. . . . I'm overcome by my emotions."

72. Yamamoto Ryōkichi, "Lamenting the death of Fujioka Sakutarō" (a tentative title given by the editor), in *Chōsui sensei ikō zokuhen*, edited by Kawasaki Akira, 122–24.

73. "Wakakarishi hi no Tōho," NKZ 12:221–27.

74. Ibid., 221.

75. On this visit see Michiko Yusa, "Nishida and Hearn," *Monumenta Nipponica* 51.3 (1996), 309–12.

76. Tanabe introduced Nishida to such authors as the Brontë sisters and T. S. Eliot.

77. Letter no. 122 to Hori Koretaka, 22 March 1911, NKZ 18:132.

78. Letter no. 110 to Tanabe Ryūji, 6 June 1909, NKZ 18:123–24.

79. Diary, 6 November, NKZ 17:230.

80. Letter no. 125 to Yamamoto Ryōkichi, 23 May 1910, NKZ 18:140.

81. Letter no. 124, 9 April 1910, NKZ 18:138.

82. Diary, 22 April 22 1910, NKZ 17:242.

83. Kano Naoki, "Nishida-kun no omoide," *JPS* 347 (April 1946), 87.

84. Nishida kept a close watch on the comet. See Diary, 25 and 29 May, NKZ 17:245.

85. NKZ 17:249–50.

86. *JP* 282 (August 1910), 146.

CHAPTER 9: KYOTO IMPERIAL UNIVERSITY (1910–1912)

1. Amano Teiyū, "Kenkyūteki, kaihōteki," 448–49.

2. For instance, Kyoto Imperial University hired Japanese scholars to occupy the chairs of Western literatures. Natsume Sōseki was invited to join the faculty but declined the offer for personal reasons. In his place, poet-scholar Ueda Bin was appointed.

3. For instance, Kōda Rohan taught for a year at the university. Naitō Konan, a reporter for the Osaka Asahi Newspaper, was recruited as a lecturer in Chinese studies and was later made a professor.

4. For Nishida's recollection of the early days of the college, see "Zuikan," NKZ 19:785–86.

5. *Ibunkaishi* 1 (1909), 91.

6. Amano Teiyū, "Kyōdai Bungakubu sanjisshūnen kansō, Meiji kara Taishō e," 106–07.

7. Ueda Juzō, "Nishida sensei," 102–03.

8. Letter no. 129, 29 September 1910, NKZ 18:142.

9. Letter no. 130 to Tanabe Ryūji, 16 October 1910, NKZ 18:143.

10. Ibid.

11. Letter no. 131 to Tanabe Ryūji, 30 October 1910, NKZ 18:143. This is actually a part of a song sung by a harp player in Goethe's *Wilhelm Meisters Lehrjahre* [Wilhelm Meister's Apprenticeship], book 2, chap. 13. Nishida quoted these lines in his letter to Fujioka Sakutarō, no. 2692, 2 November 1906, NKZ 19:676: "Wer nie sein Brot mit Tränen ass,/Wer nie die kummervollen Nächte/Auf seinem Bette weinend sass,/Der kennt euch nicht, ihr himmlischen Mächte." ("He who has never eaten his bread with tears,/He who has never sat on his bed crying/At sorrow-filled nights,/Does not know you, heavenly powers.")

12. Beatrice Lane (1878–1939) was born in Boston, the daughter of Thomas Jefferson Lane of New Hampshire, who was in the diplomatic service, and Emma Erskine Hearn, a descendent of Scottish nobility. She was interested in the teaching of Krishnamurti and the Theosophical Society. In April 1906 Suzuki, accompanying Shaku Sōen as translator, met Beatrice in New York.

13. Yamamoto Ryōkichi, "Suzuki Daisetz to daijōbukkyō no sekai shōkai," 212.

14. Letter no. 137, NKZ 18:147.

15. Natsume Sōseki, "Hakushi mondai no nariyuki (2)," 273–75. (Originally published 15 April 1911, *Tokyo Asahi Shinbun*.)

16. Natsume Sōseki, "Hakushi mondai to Mādokku Sensei to yo," 276–81.

17. Murdoch (1856–1921), a Scotsman, held a M.A. degree from Aberdeen. In 1918 he moved to Australia and became professor of Japanese history at the University of Sydney. He wrote *A History of Japan*, 3 vols. For biographical information on Murdoch, see John L. Mish's foreword, compiled in Murdoch's *History of Japan* (New York: Frederick Ungar, 1964), vol. 3, part 1, vii–xvi.

18. According to Nishida's diary, he called on Murdoch on January 30, 1897, and again on June 5, at which time Murdoch gave him two books in English as a present. See Diary, NKZ 17:7 and 17:16.

19. *Geibun* was established by the faculty of the College of Humanities and had just begun publication in April 1910, a few months before Nishida joined the university

20. NKZ 1:317–26.

21. Itō Kichinosuke, "Tetsugakukai shiryō," *JP* 300 (February 1912), 205. Itō overlooked the 1910 article by Nishida that appeared in *Geibun*.

22. "Beruguson no tetsugakuteki hōhōron," NKZ 1:318–19.

23. Ibid., 324.

24. Ibid., 318.

25. W. Windelband, Preface to *Materie und Gedächtnis* (Jena: 1908), i–xv.

26. "Beruguson no tetsugakuteki hōhōron," NKZ 1:317–18.

27. Ralph Barton Perry, *The Thought and Character of William James*, 343.

28. In his 1911 essay on Bergson, Nishida quoted Bergson's vitae almost verbatim from James text. See "Kōi" [Editor's emendation], NKZ 1:450–51.

29. Letter no. 122 to Hori Koretaka, 22 March 1910, NKZ 18:132.

30. NKZ 1:327–33.

31. Nishida relied on an English translation by Arthur Mitchell, *Creative Evolution* (New York, H. Holt, 1911).

32. "Beruguson no junsui jizoku," NKZ 1:328.

33. "Beruguson no tetsugakuteki hōhōron," NKZ 1:320.

34. Ibid., 326.

35. Preface to 1928 "Han o arata ni suru ni atatte," NKZ 1:6.

36. Ueda Juzō, "Nishida sensei," 103.

37. In 1921 Uemura was made the ninth abbot of Senjuin, a temple belonging to Myōshinji.

38. Ueda Yayoi, "Ano koro no chichi," in *Sofu*, 202.

39. Zen men seem to enjoy free and easy personal relationships. Master Setsumon dropped by out of the blue at Nishida's house in Kyoto one evening in late December 1914; by pure coincidence, Ishikawa Ryūzō came by, and the three dined together and spoke late into the night. Setsumon had just ended a period

of turbulence, quit his family business, returned to monkshood, and was looking forward to resuming the life of teaching. But the next thing Nishida heard of Setsumon was the news of his sudden death of peritonitis on 4 August 1915, at a small temple in Wakasa.

40. See Shimomura Toratarō, "Kōki" [Postscript], NKZ 1:469–70.

41. "Gutoku Shinran" [Shinran the fool], NKZ 1:407–09. For an English translation, see D. Hirota.

42. Ueda Yayoi, "Anokoro no chichi," in *Sofu*, 208.

43. *JP* 290 (April 1911), 114–16. The book review editor was probably Miyamoto Wakichi, who took Nishida as his mentor.

44. *JP* 303, 48–73; *JP* 304, 51–70.

45. NKZ 1:299–316.

46. *JP* 308, 37–57.

47. Kurata Hyakuzō, "Seimei no ninshikiteki doryoku," 307. The date of composition given for this essay is 12 November 1912, three months after Kurata visited Nishida.

48. Kurata in *Abe Jirō, Kurata Hyakuzō-shū*, 422.

49. Letter no. 159 to Tanabe Ryūji, 17 September 1912, NKZ 18:160–61.

50. *Gakushūin hyakunenshi*, 1:626.

51. NKZ 1:209–34; published in *Geibun* (August and September 1911).

52. NKZ 1:250–67; published in *Geibun* (September 1912).

53. On this point Nishida consulted extensively Josiah Royce's *The World and the Individual* (New York: Macmillan, 1899, 1901), 500–02 and passim.

54. "Ronri no rikai to sūri no rikai," NKZ 1:251.

55. Ibid., 259.

56. Published in *Logos—Internationale Zeitschrift für Philosophie der Kultur* (Tübingen), 2.1 (1911), 26–78.

57. "Ronri no rikai to sūri no rikai," NKZ 1:261–62.

58. Ibid., 262–63.

59. Ibid., 263–64.

60. Ibid., 264, 266.

61. Diary, 26 July 1912, NKZ 17:296.

62. "Ronri no rikai to sūri no rikai," NKZ 1:267.

63. "Ninshikironsha to shite no Anri Poankare," NKZ 1:397–401; published in *Geibun* (October 1912).

64. Yamanouchi Tokuryū, "Kaiko," 465.

65. Ibid., 464.

66. Tübingen: J. C. B. Mohr (P. Siebeck), 1914.

67. Mutai Risaku, "Sonokoro no Nishida sensei," 115.

CHAPTER 10: CONSOLIDATION OF THE PHILOSOPHY DEPARTMENT (1913–1917)

1. For an English translation, see *Intuition and Reflection in Self-Consciousness*, translated by Viglielmo, Takeuchi, and O'Leary.

2. "Jo" [Preface], *Jikaku ni okeru chokkan to hansei*, NKZ 2:11.

3. Diary of Yamamoto Ryōkichi, 21 February 1913, quoted in Ueda Hisashi, *Yamamoto Ryōkichi sensei-den*, 119.

4. It was the only institution of higher education for women, with the exception of Tōhoku Imperial University in Sendai (founded in 1907), which began admitting women in 1913.

5. It was retitled "Shizen kagaku to rekishigaku," *JP* 319 (September 1913), 1–33; NKZ 1:268–98.

6. Letter no. 2367 to Tanabe Hajime, 2 April 1914, NKZ 19:509.

7. Letter no. 2370 to Tanabe Hajime, 28 August 1914, NKZ 19:517.

8. *JP* 322 (December 1913), 101.

9. Letter no. 173, 14 August 1913, NKZ 18:168.

10. Letter no. 175, 3 October 1913, NKZ 18:169–71.

11. There were three ways to become a doctor in those days: (1) to go through graduate school and have a dissertation accepted, (2) to be recommended by the members of the Association for Doctors *(Hakushikai)*, or (3) to be recommended by the president of the university. Those who earned Ph.D.s overseas were customarily conferred a doctorate according to the third option. See *JP* 146 (1899), 323–24.

12. Letter no. 2368, NKZ 19:512.

13. *Shūkyōgaku*, lecture notes, NKZ 15:221–381.

14. NKZ 15:393.

15. Hisamatsu Shin'ichi, *Kōki* [Editor's postscript], NKZ 15:394.

16. Hisamatsu Shin'ichi, "Gakkyū seikatsu no omoide," 430–32.

17. Letter no. 185 to Tanabe Ryūji, 22 September 1914, NKZ 18:178.

18. Published by Iwanami, on 1 July 1916; the translation was added to the Iwanami "Bunko" (pocketbook edition) series in 1927. Nishida wrote a preface for it in May 1916, NKZ 13:188–90.

19. Heinrich Rickert, *Das Eine, die Einheit und die Eins: Bemerkungen zur Logik des Zahlbegriffs* (Tübingen: Verlag von J. C. B. Mohr, 1924), vii.

20. Tomonaga Sanjūrō, "*Tetsugaku Kenkyū* no hossoku," 106.

21. "Zuikan," NKZ 19:785–86.

22. *JPS* 1 (April 1916), 136.

23. Tomonaga Sanjūrō, "*Tetsugaku Kenkyū* no hossoku," 106.

24. *JPS* 1 (April 1916) 1–41; NKZ 1:334–68.

25. Yamanouchi Tokuryū, "*Tetsugaku Kenkyū* no hajime no koro," 275.

26. NKZ 14:3–82.

27. Mutai (1890–1974) became one of the students closest to Nishida.

28. Mutai Risaku, "Sono koro no Nishida sensei," 117–18.

29. Mutai Risaku, "Edomundo Husseru," *Shisō* 194 (July 1938), 80–81.

30. Yamanouchi Tokuryū, "*Tetsugaku Kenkyū* no hajime no koro," *JPS* 500 (September 1966), 276.

31. Y. Nitta, H. Tatematsu, and E. Shimomise, "Phenomenology and Philosophy in Japan," 8.

32. Nishida finished his "Rottse no keijijōgaku," on 5 January 1917; compiled in NKZ 1:375–96.

33. Mutai Risaku, "Sono koro no Nishida sensei," 117.

34. Letter no. 2385 to Tanabe Hajime, 31 December 1916, NKZ 19:532.

35. "Jo," *Jikaku ni okeru chokkan to hansei*, NKZ 2:11.

36. Ibid., 3–11.

37. Ibid., 3–4.

38. *JPS* 21 (December 1917), back cover.

39. *Iwanami Shoten gojūnen*, edited by Iwanami Yūjirō, 9.

40. Shimomura Toratarō, "*Jikaku ni okeru chokkan to hansei* to Roisu no self representative system—nōto," 1.

41. *JP* 369 (November 1917), 128.

CHAPTER 11: CORRESPONDENCE WITH TANABE HAJIME (1913–1917)

1. Letter no. 2366, NKZ 19:507.

2. *JP* 324 (February 1914), 1–26, and *JP* 325 (March 1914), 1–21.

3. Letter no. 2367, 2 April 1914, NKZ 19:508–12.

4. "Jikaku ni okeru chokkan to hansei," NKZ 2:54.

5. Letter no. 2368, 14 April 1914, NKZ 19:512–13.

6. Letter no. 2369, 5 August 1914, NKZ 19:513–15.

7. Twardowski (1866–1938) was a Polish philosopher whose contribution paved the way for the emergence of phenomenology and analytic philosophy.

8. Letter no. 2369 to Tanabe Hajime, 5 August 1914, NKZ 19:514.

9. Letter no. 2375, NKZ 19:525.

10. Sono (1886–1969) was a graduate of the Kyoto Imperial University. His area of specialty was the ring theory. In 1968 he was decorated with the cultural merit award *(bunka kōrōshō)*.

11. Letter no. 2372, 30 November 1914, NKZ 19:519–21.

12. Letter no. 2372 to Tanabe Hajime, 30 November 1914, NKZ 19:519. In this letter Nishida advises Tanabe to read Cohen's 1871 *Kants Theorie der Erfahrung* [Kant's Theory of Experience], which should shed light on Cohen's later work, *Die Logik der reinen Erkenntnis* [Logic of Real Knowledge], published in 1901.

13. Letter no. 2372, 30 November 1914, NKZ 19:520; Nishida mentions Zen to Tanabe once again in his letter no. 2383, 9 May 1916, NKZ 19:531.

14. *JP* 337 (March 1915), 33–85 and 338 (April 1915), 37–72.

15. Letter no. 2375, 12 July 1915, NKZ 19:524.

16. Letter no. 2376, 4 September 1915, NKZ 19:525–26.

17. Letter no. 2375 to Tanabe Hajime, 12 July 1915, NKZ 19:524.

18. Ibid.

19. Letter no. 2378 to Tanabe Hajime, 30 November 1915, NKZ 19:527.

20. During this time Nishida was also working on his essay "Gendai no tetsugaku," which was his contribution to the inaugural issue of *Tetsugaku Kenkyū* [*Journal of Philosophical Studies*]. Diary, 7 January 1916: "Finished 'Contemporary philosophy.'" NKZ 17:339.21.

21. Letter no. 2379 to Tanabe Hajime, 8 January 1916, NKZ 19:528.

22. *JP* 348, 349, and 351.

23. Letter no. 2379, 8 January 1916, NKZ 19:528.

24. The article was published in *JPS* 2 (May 1916), 37–70.

25. Letter no. 2378, 30 November 1915, NKZ 19:527.

26. Letter no. 2381 to Tanabe Hajime, 23 March 1916, NKZ 19:529–30.

27. Cf. letter no. 2454, NKZ 19:575. Tanabe never lost interest in Zen.

28. Letter no. 2383, 9 May 1916, NKZ 19:530–31.

29. Letter no. 2384 to Tanabe Hajime, 14 August 1916, NKZ 19:531–32.

30. The essay appeared in two installments in *JP* 358 (December 1916), 17–46, and *JP* 359 (January 1917), 74–103.

31. *JP* 363 (May 1917), 35–104, and *JP* 364 (June 1917), 39–65.

32. *JPS* 13 (April 1917), 1–61.

33. *JPS* 17 (August 1917), 1–49.

34. Letter no. 2385 to Tanabe Hajime, 31 December 1916, NKZ 19:532–33.

35. Letter no. 2387, 1 February 1917, NKZ 533–34.

36. Ibid.

37. Letter no. 2388, 12 February 1917, NKZ 19.534–35.

38. *Husserl-Chronik, Husserliana Dokumente*, edited by Karl Schuhmann, 269.

39. Shimomura Toratarō, *Shimomura Toratarō Chosakushū*, 12: 281–82. Also Nishitani Keiji, "Tanabe sensei no koto," 282.

40. See Husserl's letter to Nishida, dated 19 September 1923, *Shimomura Toratarō Chosakushū*, 12: 280–81. Quoted in chap. 15 at n. 20.

CHAPTER 12: THE CALM BEFORE THE STORM (1917–1919)

1. Letter no. 2393 to Tanabe Hajime, 9 May 1917, NKZ 19:538.

2. Published in *JP* 364 (June 1917), 1–17. It was added to *Jikaku ni okeru chokkan to hansei* as a "batsu" [postscript], NKZ 2:337–50.

3. Miki (1897–1945) was to become a sort of cultural icon, representing the progressive intellectuals of pre–World War II Japan. He died an untimely death in a filthy prison cell in September 1945.

4. Miki Kiyoshi, "Nishida sensei no kotodomo," *Miki Kiyoshi Zenshū* 17:295 [hereafter cited as MKZ]. This essay was originally published in *Fujin Kōron* (August 1941).

5. Letter no. 2393, 9 May 1917, NKZ 19:538.

6. Letter no. 2395, 3 June 1917, NKZ 19:539–40.

7. Ueda Yayoi, "Ano koro no chichi," compiled in *Sofu*, 201–02.

8. "Nozaki Hiroyoshi-shi chōji," written on 20 June 1917, NKZ 13:171.

9. "Batsu" [Postscript], Nozaki Hiroyoshi, *Zange to shite no tetsugaku*, NKZ 13:202.

10. Miki Kiyoshi, "Nishida sensei no kotodomo," MKZ 17.296–97.

11. Nishida's postcard addressed to Miki, 4 July 1917; compiled in *Miki Kiyoshi no shōgai to shisō*, edited by Muroi Michihiro, 14.

12. Ueda Yayoi, "Ano koro no chichi," in *Sofu*, 199.

13. Letter no. 2398 to Tanabe Hajime, 20 July 1917, NKZ 19:541.

14. Nishida Shizuko, "Chichi," 19.

15. Letter no. 2402, 5 September 1917, NKZ 19:542–43.

16. Nakanishi Keijirō, *Waseda Daigaku hachijūnenshi*, 169.

17. That is, those who have not suffered adversities in life lack the appreciation of things.

18. Letter no. 2405, 15 October 1917, NKZ 19:544–45.

19. *JPS* 22 (January 1918), 1–28; NKZ 3:5–27.

20. *Geibun* 9.1 (January 1918), NKZ 3:232–36.

21. Nishida Kitarō, "Jo," in Okamoto Haruhiko, *Sheringu no shōchō shisō*, NKZ 13:197.

22. Ibid.

23. An excerpt from Nishida's memorial essay written on 26 January 1918; NKZ 13:199.

24. Ibid.

25. *Shichō* 2.3 (March 1918); it was later compiled in his *Ishiki no mondai*. NKZ 3:78–82.

26. Unable to bear the burden of unrequited love, he committed suicide; he introduced Kierkegaard to Japanese readers.

27. "Jo," Nozaki Hiroyoshi, *Zange to shite no tetsugaku* (republication), NKZ 13:225. Nishida wrote the preface in the summer of 1942.

28. Letter no. 2411, 22 February 1918, NKZ 19:547.

29. *JPS* 27 (June 1918), 1–27; NKZ 3:28–50.

30. *JPS* 28 (July 1918), 11–42; NKZ 3:51–77.

31. *Geibun* 9.9 (September 1918); NKZ 3:83–98.

32. Nishida first mentioned this idea in his letter, no. 2419, 23 July 1918, NKZ 19:553–54, and it soon developed into a concrete possibility.

33. See letter no. 2411, 22 February 1918, NKZ 19:547–48.

34. *JPS* 35 (February 1919), 1–28, and *JPS* 36 (March 1919), 42–63; NKZ 3:99–140.

35. *Kōi* [MS variations], NKZ 3:562.

36. Nakahashi Tokugorō (1861–1934) graduated from the limited status program of the College of Law at Tokyo University in 1886, went into the graduate school, and simultaneously assumed governmental positions. He was also the president of the Osaka Commercial Vessels Company. He was minister of education for Hara and Takahashi Korekiyo, September 1918–June 1922.

37. Letter no. 235 to Yamamoto Ryōkichi, 6 October 1918, NKZ 18:204.

38. Letter no. 239 to Yamamoto Ryōkichi, 26 December 1918, NKZ 18:206–07.

39. Monbushōnai Kyōikushi Hensankai, *Meiji-ikō kyōikuseido hattatsushi*, 5:486.

40. Letter no. 2419 to Tanabe Hajime, 23 July 1918, NKZ 19:553.

41. Letter no. 2421, 10 August 1918, NKZ 19:555–56.

42. In August 1920 the College of Law and Letters was added to Tōhoku Imperial University.

43. Letter no. 2431, 7 April 1919, NKZ 19:561.

44. Hatano Seiichi's letter to Tanabe Hajime, 27 May 1919, *Hatano Seiichi Zenshū*, 6:47.

45. *Geibun* 10.4 (April 1919); NKZ 3:141–56.

46. *JPS* 38 (May 1919), 17–46, and *JPS* 39 (June 1919), 18–38; NKZ 3:157–98.

47. *Geibun* 10.6 (June 1919); NKZ 3:199–209.

48. *JPS* 42 (September 1919), 1–15; NKZ 3:210–23.

49. *Ishiki no mondai* includes an essay, "Kotai gainen" [The concept of the individual], previously unpublished in any of the journals, the date of which cannot be determined. The book was published by Iwanami Bookstore on 5 January 1920.

50. Letter no. 2445 to Tanabe Hajime, 7 August 1919, NKZ 19:569.

CHAPTER 13: SORROWS OF LIFE AND PHILOSOPHY (1919–1922)

1. Letter no. 433 to Yamamoto Ryōkichi, 9 February 1927, NKZ 18:321.

2. Ishikawa Kōji, "Doitsu seikatsu o tomo ni shita Tanabe Hajime sensei no omoide," 3.

3. Letter no. 67, 22 October 1907, NKZ 18:87–88.

4. "Basho no jikogentei to shite no ishikisayō," (June 1930), NKZ 6:116.

5. Nishida Sotohiko, "Chichi no sunda ieie," 268.

6. Letter no. 257 to Tomonaga Sanjūrō, 9 October 1919, and letter no. 258 to the same, 10 October 1910, both NKZ 18:215–18.

7. NKZ 14:295–300. The talk was published in *Mujintō* 24.11 (November 1919).

8. NKZ 14:303–09; published in the Ryūkoku University journal, *Rokujō Gakuhō* (January 1920).

9. As Nishida became famous, various legends were born, this being one of them.

10. Kano Naoki, "Nishida-kun no omoide," *JPS* 347 (April 1946), 28.

11. Ueda Hisashi, *Yamamoto Ryōkichi sensei-den*, 39.

12. Letter no. 211 to Hori Koretaka, 17 March 1917, NKZ 18:193.

13. Letter no. 267 to Yamamoto Ryōkichi, 15 March 1920, NKZ 18:223.

14. Ueda Hisashi, *Zoku sofu Nishida Kitarō*, 73.

15. "Jisen shiikashū," NKZ 12:435–36. Ken's age as traditionally counted.

16. This poem is compiled in "Jisen shiikashū," NKZ 12:435. Nishida composed it years earlier, however, while he was still teaching at the Fourth Higher School in Kanazawa. He must have been very fond of this *waka* because he shared it with Tanabe Hajime in his letter to Tanabe, 4 August 1920, NKZ 19:570.

17. Letter no. 2446, 4 August 1920, NKZ 19:570.

18. Monbushōnai Kyōikushi Hensankai, *Meiji-ikō kyōikuseido hattatsushi* 5:490–91.

19. Letter no. 311 to Yamanouchi Tokuryū, 28 May 1922, NKZ 18:246–47.

20. Naruse (1885–1958) was a specialist in German literature; he founded the Japan Goethe Association in 1931.

21. Sasaki Gesshō, Suzuki Daisetz, Beatrice Suzuki, Yamabe Shōgaku, and Akanuma Chizen formed the Eastern Buddhist Society. See "Editorial," Eastern Buddhist Society, *Eastern Buddhist* 1 (May 1921), 81.

22. Ibid., 80.

23. Diary, 29 July 1921, NKZ 17:383.

24. Ibid., 384. The poem is also collected in "Jisen shiikashū," NKZ 12:437.

25. Nishikida was among the first students to graduate from the philosophy department of Kyoto Imperial University in 1911. He became professor at Tōhoku Imperial University but died young.

26. Letter no. 302, 18:239–40.

27. Kiba graduated from Tokyo Imperial University in 1911. He was a member of Kōkōdō, a house where Kiyozawa Manshi's followers lived. He became professor at Ōtani University and later at his alma mater, the Fourth Higher School.

28. Letter no. 314 to Kiba Ryōhon, 15 July 1922, NKZ 18:248–49.

29. "Jisen shiikashū, NKZ 12:436. The notation reads: "the summer of 1922, Tomoko and Umeko, having become ill, were hospitalized."

30. Nishitani Keiji, "Kōki" [Editor's postscript], NKZ 17:722.

31. By 1926 there were thirty-four higher schools throughout Japan.

32. The number was to increase steadily each year. One hundred forty students entered the College of Letters in 1923; 236 in 1924; 304 in 1925; and 330 in 1926.

33. Nishitani Keiji, *Nishida Kitarō*, trans. Yamamoto Seisaku and J. Heisig, esp. 11–12.

34. Letter no. 309 to Yamamoto Ryōkichi, 7 April 1922, NKZ 18:245.

35. Letter no. 322, 19 November 1922, NKZ 18:259.

36. Letter no. 315 to Yamanouchi Tokuryū (in Freiburg), 7 August 1922, NKZ 18:249.

37. See Michiko Yusa, "Philosophy and Inflation: Miki Kiyoshi in Weimar Germany, 1922–1924," 45–71.

38. Letter no. 313 to Yamanouchi Tokuryū (in Freiburg), 28 June 1922, NKZ 18:248.

39. Takahashi Satomi, "Gakusha o okoraseta hanashi," 221.

40. Letter no. 318 to Nishida Sotohiko, 15 August 1922, NKZ 18:254–55. Also letter no. 317, written to Sotohiko on the same day, NKZ 18:251–54.

41. Diary, end cover of 1925, NKZ 17:425.

42. "Jisen shiikashū," NKZ 12:436. The notation reads: "3 November 1922, upon the death of my Zen friend, Hōrin"; this poem appears in the notes section of his Diary, 1922, NKZ 17:395.

43. Kōsaka Masaaki, *Nishida Kitarō sensei no tsuioku*, 13–14.

44. Kōsaka Masaaki, "Hito oyobi shisōka to shite no Nishida Kitarō sensei," 72.

45. Letter no. 326 to Yamanouchi Tokuryū (in Freiburg), 27 December 1922, NKZ 18:262.

CHAPTER 14: THE NISHIDA-EINSTEIN CONNECTION (1920–1922)

1. Letter no. 2446 to Tanabe Hajime, 4 August 1920, NKZ 19:570.

2. Kuwaki Ayao (1878–1945), graduated from the Department of Physics at Tokyo Imperial University in 1899. He was a specialist in the history of science and a professor at Kyūshū Imperial University in Fukuoka beginning in 1914.

3. Letter no. 280 to Kuwaki Ayao, 21 August 1920, NKZ 18:230.

4. Ishihara Atsushi. "Ainsutain kyōju no kōen," part 1, *Kaizō* (January 1923), 307–30, and part 2, *Kaizō* (February 1923), 28–44.

5. Letter no. 297 to Kuwaki Ayao, 21 September 1921, NKZ 18:236.

6. Letter no. 316 to Kuwaki Ayao, 11 August 1922, NKZ 18:251.

7. Letter no. 320 to Kuwaki Ayao, 26 August 1922, NKZ 18:257–58.

8. Ishihara Atsushi, "Ainsutain kyōju no kōen," part 2, *Kaizō* (February 1923), 39. Ishihara notes that the lecture at Kyoto University was held on 10 December; elsewhere he gives the date of 14 December. Judging from the rest of Einstein's itinerary, it is more likely 10 December.

9. A. Einstein, "How I Created the Theory of Relativity," translation into English from Japanese by Yoshimasa Ono, *Physics Today* 35 (August 1982), 45–47.

10. Letter no. 324 to Yamanouchi Tokuryū (Freiburg), 17 December 1922, NKZ 18:261.

CHAPTER 15: AN INNER STRUGGLE AND A BREAKTHROUGH
(1923–1925)

1. "Jisen shiikashū," NKZ 12:437. According to the notation, Nishida composed this *waka* after visiting Tomoko in the hospital in December 1922. The *waka* is recorded in the notes section of Diary 1922, NKZ 17:395.

2. Diary, 3 January 1923, NKZ 17:396. Also letter no. 327 to Yamamoto Ryōkichi, 7 January 1923, NKZ 18:263.

3. The three poems appear in Diary, 28 January 1923, NKZ 17:397.

4. Diary, 10 February 1923, NKZ 17:398.

5. Diary, NKZ 17:398.

6. This is a common expression in Zen. "Letting go of one's hold on a precipice" (*Mumonkan*, case 32) or "Going beyond the top of a pole one hundred feet high" (*Mumonkan*, case 46) designate the state of liberation from any attachment, even to enlightenment itself.

7. Suzuki Daisetz, "Nishida Shizuko hen, *Chichi Nishida Kitarō no uta*, no jo," SDZ 28:520–21.

8. Diary, 4 April 1923, NKZ 17:399.

9. Diary, 10 April 1923, NKZ 17:399.

10. Diary, NKZ 17:400.

11. NKZ 3:237–545. For an English translation see Dilworth and Viglielmo, trans., *Art and Morality*.

12. "Jo," *Hataraku mono kara miru mono e*, NKZ 4:3.

13. Kōsaka Masaaki, "*Tetsugaku Kenkyū* henshū no omoide," *JPS* 400 (February 1951), 107–08. Mr. Takaraiwa died on 16 December 1923.

14. Diary, 10 August 1923, NKZ 17:401; also 19 June 1931, NKZ 17:470.

15. They are most likely *Ishiki no mondai* (1920) and *Geijutsu to dōtoku* (1923), although *Zen no kenkyū*, 2d ed. (Iwanami Shoten, 1921), and *Shisaku to taiken*, 2d ed. (Iwanami Shoten, 1922), are possibilities.

16. By this time Tanabe had already left Freiburg for Paris.

17. "Erneuerung—Ihr Problem und Ihre Methode," *Kaizō* (March 1923), 84–92, 63–83.

18. "Kojin rinri mondai no saishin," *Kaizō* (February 1924), 2–31, and "Honshitsu kenkyū no hōhō" *Kaizō* (April 1924), 107–116. The third article that Husserl mentions may be "Furantsu Burentāno no omoide," (1919), which Itō Kichinosuke brought back to Japan. It was translated by Watsuji Tetsurō, *Kaizō* (March 1923), 86–98.

19. "Die Idee einer philosophischen Kultur: Ihr erstes Aufkeimen in der griechischen Philosophie," *Japanische-deutschen Zeitschrift für Wissenschaft und Technik* (1923), 45–51.

20. Shimomura Toratarō. "Setsumon Rōshi, Hussāru, Rikkerto no tegami," 280–81. The present translation is based on the Japanese translation, with some simplification.

21. Letter no. 346 to Akai Yonekichi, 2 December 1923, NKZ 18:273.

22. Diary, 20 January 1924, NKZ 17:405.

23. Shimomura Toratarō, "Wakaki Nishida Kitarō sensei," 9.

24. Diary, 28 January 1924, NKZ 17.406.

25. Koyré (1892–1964) was director of École Pratique des Hautes Études at the Sorbonne and was also affiliated with the Princeton Institute for Advanced Studies. His major contributions are to the study of Galileo Galilei and Isaac Newton.

26. Diary, 9 March 1924, NKZ 17:409.

27. Nishitani Keiji, "Waga shi Nishida Kitarō sensei o kataru," 22.

28. Gotō Ryūnosuke (1888–1984) was a loyal supporter of Konoe Ayamaro and founded the Showa Study Group in December 1933; he participated in organizing the first Konoe cabinet in 1937.

29. Diary, NKZ 17:340.

30. *Gotō Ryūnosuke-shi danwa sokkiroku*, edited by Naiseishi Kenyūkai, 24.

31. Karaki Junzō (1904–1980) was a literary critic and specialist in medieval Japanese literature. He entered the philosophy department in 1924 and later became a professor at Meiji University.

32. Kakehashi Akihide, "Rōgoku to guntai," 49–50.

33. Mutai Risaku, "Kyōdai rainin tōsho no Tanabe sensei," 2.

34. *JPS* 96, 102, and 103 (March, September, and October 1924); NKZ 4:76–134.

35. *Shisō* 41 (March 1925) 1–39; NKZ 4:135–72.

36. Shimomura Toratarō, *Shimomura Toratarō Chosakushū*, 283–84.

37. *Shisō* 36 (October 1924), 1–23.

38. Letter no. 2470 to Tanabe Hajime, 2 October 1924, NKZ 19:582.

39. Eugen Herrigel (1885–1955) became interested in Zen and studied archery under Master Awa Kenzō. He wrote about his experience in his *Zen and Archery* and other books.

40. Diary, NKZ 17:414.

41. Nishida's *waka*, 28 January 1925, diary, NKZ 17:415.

42. Letter no. 2459 to Tanabe Hajime, 28 January 1925, NKZ 19:577. Also see letter no. 368 to Hisamatsu Shin'ichi, 28 January 1925, NKZ 18:282.

43. NKZ 4:175–207.

44. He adopted Max Weber's *Gesammeltenaufsätze* [Collected Essays] as the textbook.

45. *JPS* 110 (May 1925), 107.

46. The construction of this building began in 1922 to commemorate the twenty-fifth anniversary of the founding of the university. *Kyoto Daigaku nanajūnenshi*, edited by Kyoto Daigaku Nanajūnenshi Henshū Iinkai, 89–90 [hereafter *Kyōdai nanajūnenshi*].

47. *Kyōdai nanajūnenshi*, 91.

48. Dokumente, Briefwechsel, *Husserliana* 6 (1994), 307.

49. Nishitani Keiji, "Waga shi Nishida Kitarō sensei o kataru," 36.

CHAPTER 16: THE LOGIC OF THE TOPOS (1924–1926)

1. Nishida's *basho* is actually closer to the Greek word *"chōra"* (the place in which a thing is) than to *"topos,"* which many translators of Nishida, including myself, have adopted. The advantage of adopting *topos* is its orthographic simplicity. Nishida himself never used the word *"topos"* in his writings except when making references to "topology." He customarily used a German word, *Platz*, in his personal notes.

2. *JPS* 96, 102, and 103 (March, September, and October 1924); NKZ 4:76–134.

3. NKZ 4:135–72; originally published in *Shisō* 41 (March 1925), 1–39.

4. "Naibu chikaku ni tsuite," NKZ 4:134.

5. Ibid., 83.

6. Ibid., 95. Cf. Aristotle, *Metaphysica*, 7.3.1–3 (1028b–1029b).

7. "Naibu chikaku ni tsuite," NKZ 4:97–98.

8. "Hyōgen sayō," NKZ 4:164.

9. Ibid., 153.

10. Ibid., 169–170.

11. NKZ 4:175–207; originally published in *JPS* 115 (October 1925), 91–130.

12. "Hataraku mono," NKZ 4:177 and passim.

13. Ibid., 186.

14. Ibid., 201.

15. Letter no. 2476 to Tanabe Hajime, 8 December 1925, NKZ 19:584.

16. "Basho," NKZ 4:208–89; *JPS* 123 (June 1926), 1–99.

17. "Basho," NKZ 4:208–09.

18. Ibid., 209.

19. Ibid., 215–16.

20. Ibid., 242–43.

21. Ibid., 220.

22. Ibid., 237.

23. Ibid., 278–79.

24. Ibid., 281.

25. "Jo", *Hataraku mono kara miru mono e*, NKZ 4:5.

26. Letter no. 404 to Mutai Risaku (in Heidelberg), 8 June 1926, NKZ 18:303–04.

27. Sōda Kiichirō (1881–1927) was a banker, economist, and scholar. He studied abroad in the United States, England, and Germany.

28. *JPS* 127 (October 1926), 1–30.

29. Ibid.

30. Letter no. 421 to Yamanouchi Tokuryū, 14 October 1926, NKZ 18:314–15.

31. NKZ 4:280–323; *JPS* 133 (April 1927), 1–40.

32. "Sōda-hakushi ni kotau," NKZ 4:298.

33. Ibid., 294–95.

34. Ibid., 299.

35. Ibid., 311.

36. Ibid., 304.

37. Ibid., 311.

38. Ibid., 305.

39. Ibid., 315–16.

40. Ibid., 307.

41. Ibid., 308–09.

42. Ibid., 309.

43. Ibid., 314.

44. Ibid., 315.

45. Ibid., 316–19.

46. Ibid., 321–22.

47. "Jo," *Mu no jikakuteki gentei* (1932), NKZ 6:10.

CHAPTER 17: RETIREMENT (1926–1929)

1. *Kyōdai nanajūnenshi*, 95–96.

2. *Kyōdai gojūnenshi*, 302; also *Kyōdai nanajūnenshi*, 96.

3. *Kyōdai nanajūnenshi*, 96–97.

4. Nishida was in Tokyo to administer examinations to higher school teachers. Nishida's letter to Tanabe Ryūji, 17 May 1926, *Nishida Kitarō no tegami*, 209.

5. Letter no. 402 to Mutai Risaku (in Heidelberg), 7 May 1926, NKZ 18:302.

6. Letter no. 2477 to Tanabe Hajime, 17 December 1925, NKZ 19:594.

7. Hatano held a high opinion of Miki, who transcribed and edited his summer lecture of 1920. It was published as *Shūkyō-tetsugaku no honshitsu oyobi sono konpon mondai* [The essence and the fundamental problems of the philosophy of religion] by Iwanami in November 1920.

8. Letter no. 2461 to Tanabe Hajime, 8 March 1925, NKZ 19:578–79.

9. Nishitani Keiji, "Waga shi Nishida Kitarō sensei o kataru," *Nishida Kitarō*, 23.

10. Kakehashi Akihide, "Rōgoku to guntai," 51–52.

11. Letter no. 2482 to Tanabe Hajime, 4 March 1926, NKZ 19:586–87.

12. Nishitani Keiji, "Waga shi Nishida Kitarō sensei o kataru," 23.

13. Kōno was a graduate of the philosophy department at Tokyo Imperial University. While he was in Kyoto, teaching at the Third Higher School, he befriended Nishida. Kōno Yoichi, "Nishida sensei no hen'ei," 191–201.

14. Letter no. 426 to Watsuji Tetsurō, 7 January 1927, NKZ 18:318; see also letters no. 428, 429, and 430, all to Watsuji Tetsurō, NKZ 18:319–20.

15. Letter no. 395 to Watsuji Tetsurō, 31 January 1926, NKZ 18:298.

16. Ishikawa Kōji, "Nishida tetsugaku to keizaigaku," 132–33.

17. This probably took place in 1927. Ibid., 133.

18. Perhaps the acute tinnitus Nishida began to suffer around this time is related to his anxiety over the changes he was facing. Diary, 25 March 1927, NKZ 17:433.

19. Nishitani Keiji, "Waga shi Nishida Kitarō sensei o kataru," 43.

20. Letter no. 433 to Yamamoto Ryōkichi, 9 February 1927, NKZ 18:321.

21. Diary, 13 February 1927, NKZ 17:431.

22. Diary, 9 March 1927, NKZ 17:432.

23. Diary, 23 March 1927, NKZ 17:433.

24. Diary, 27 March 1927, NKZ 17:433.

25. Diary, 3 April 1927, NKZ 17:434.

26. Quoted by Kondō Jungo, "Kyoshō no ne," 217–18.

27. The Tanaka cabinet went along with the military's demands and sent troops to Shandong Province in China, a policy that was to be severely criticized by the public. The cabinet dissolved in 1929.

28. Letter no. 446 to Yamamoto Ryōkichi, 15 May 1927, NKZ 18:327.

29. Saionji Kinmochi (1849–1940), born into an aristocratic family, studied jurisprudence and later went into politics. He served as minister of education, foreign minister, prime minister, and was the president of the Seiyū Party. He died on November 24, 1940, and was honored by a state funeral.

30. Letter no. 447 to Mutai Risaku (in Freiburg), 17 June 1927, NKZ 18:327; also letter no. 2516 to Tanabe Hajime, 20 June 1927, NKZ 19:600.

31. NKZ 4:324–87; *Shisō* 70 and 71 (August and September 1927).

32. Letter no. 450 to Hisamatsu Shin'ichi, 2 July 1927, NKZ 18:329.

33. He completed the manuscript on 24 July 1927. Diary, NKZ 17:439.

34. Tsuchida, Kyoson, *Contemporary Thought of Japan and China*, 74–75.

35. Watsuji began as a lecturer in March 1925 and was promoted to assistant professor in July of the same year. He became professor in 1931 and moved to Tokyo Imperial University in 1934.

36. He returned to Japan on 3 July 1928.

37. Kōyama Iwao (1905–1993) entered the philosophy department in 1925.

38. Letter no. 2544 to Tanabe Hajime, 21 December 1928, NKZ 19:609. Kuki had sent Nishida a copy of *Propos sur le Temps*; Nishida's reaction was: "He seems to be a man of Bildung [cultivation]. It would not be bad to have this kind of man as a lecturer."

39. Diary, NKZ 17:445.

40. *Kyōdai nanajūnenshi*, 97–98.

41. Kōsaka Masaaki, "Sensei to gendai no mondai" [Professor Nishida and the contemporary problems], in *Nishida Kitarō sensei no tsuioku*, 160; also 143.

42. NKZ 5:5–57; published in *JPS* 145 (April 1928), 1–60.

43. NKZ 5:58–92; published in *Shisō* 78 (April 1928), 1–34.

44. NKZ 12:102–11; published in Iwanami Kōza series, *Sekai sichō*, vol. 3 (April 1928).

45. NKZ 5:98–122; published in *JPS* 148 (July 1928), 1–30.

46. NKZ 12:112–18; published in the Iwanami Kōza Series, *Sekai shichō*, vol. 7 (July 1928).

47. *JPS* 148 (July 1928), 124.

48. Letter no. 489 to Hori Koretaka, 20 September 1928, NKZ 18:348.

49. NKZ 12:175. *The Muse* 7 (October 1928), 1. The original reads: "Nur wer die Sehnsucht kennt/ Weiss, was ich leide! / Allein und abgetrennt/ Von aller Freude, / Seh' ich ans Firmament/ Nach jener Seite. / Ach! der mich liebt und kennt/ Ist in der Weite. / Es schwindelt mir, es brennt/ Mein Eingeweide./ Nur wer die Sehnsucht kennt/ Weiss, was ich leide!"

50. NKZ 5:123–85; published in *JPS* 151 (October 1928), 1–74.

51. NKZ 5:186–261; published in *JPS* 154 (January 1929), 1–82.

52. Letter no. 489 to Hori Koretaka, 20 September 1928, NKZ 18:347–48.

53. Letter no. 499 to Nishida Asako, 11 November 1928, NKZ 18:352.

54. "Kamakura zōei," NKZ 12:173.

55. Preface to "Kamakura zōei," NKZ 12:172.

56. "Kamakura zōei," NKZ 12:173.

57. Ibid., 174.

58. Letter no. 519 to Hori Koretaka, 26 January 1929, NKZ 18:362–63.

CHAPTER 18: FORMATION OF THE KYOTO SCHOOL OF PHILOSOPHY (1929–1932)

1. *JP* 505 (March 1929), 105.

2. NKZ 14:331–39; *JP* 507 (May 1929), 44–54.

3. NKZ 5:262–352; published in *Shisō* 83, 84, and 85 (April, May, and June 1929).

4. Letter no. 556 to Hori Koretaka, 28 April 1929, NKZ 18:377; also letter no. 557 to Yamamoto Ryōkichi (same day), NKZ 18:377.

5. NKZ 12:257–60; originally published in a supplementary issue of *Shōshi* 109 (October 1929), 31–33, a magazine of the alumni association of the Hiroshima Higher Normal School.

6. NKZ 5:353–417; published in *Shisō* 88–89 (September–October 1929).

7. Diary, 21 June 1929, NKZ 17:458.

8. Letter no. 555, 24 June 1929, NKZ 17:379–80.

9. NKZ 5:419–30; published in *JPS* 163 (October 1929) 1–15. "Ippansha no

jikogentei to jikaku" constitutes the first half of "Sōsetsu" [General discussion] in NKZ.

10. NKZ 5:430–64; published in *Shisō* 90 and 91 (November and December 1929). "Jikakuteki gentei kara mita ippansha no gentei" constitutes the second half of "Sōsetsu" [General discussion] in NKZ.

11. Letter no. 579 to Yamamoto Ryōkichi, 5 October 1929, NKZ 18:385.

12. "Jikakuteki gentei kara mita ippansha no gentei," NKZ 5:453–54.

13. "Ippansha no jikogentei to jikaku," NKZ 5:409.

14. Ibid., 409.

15. Ibid., 374, 382, 383, and passim.

16. Ibid., 451.

17. Diary, NKZ 17:457.

18. "Jisen shiikashū," NKZ 12:443.

19. Kōyama Iwao, "Omoide no mitsu yotsu," 150.

20. "Jitsuzai no kontei to shite no jinkaku gainen," NKZ 14:172–74. These are lectures Nishida gave at the Shinano Tetsugakukai, 3–5 September 1932.

21. Matsuda Michio, "Shōwa shigonen no koro, Miki Kiyoshi o megutte," 142–44.

22. *Ippansha no jikakuteki taikei* was published by Iwanami on 10 January 1930. The Philosophical Society asked Nishida to talk about the ideas developed in his most recent book. He agreed and gave several lectures from 18 January (Saturday) onward.

23. Nishitani Keiji, "Waga shi Nishida Kitarō sensei o kataru," 35.

24. Matsuda Michio, "Shōwa shigonen no koro, Miki Kiyoshi o megutte," 144–48.

25. THZ 4:305–28.

26. *JPS* 170 (May 1930), 1–40.

27. Tanabe Hajime, "Nishida sensei no oshie o aogu," THZ 4:305–28.

28. Letter no. 623 to Mutai Risaku, 12 June 1930, NKZ 18:410–11.

29. *Shisō* 100 (September 1930), 1–26; NKZ 6:86–116.

30. Morimoto Kōji, "Watakushi no Nishida sensei," 12.

31. Tosaka Jun, "Kyoto gakuha no tetsugaku," *Tosaka Jun Zenshū* 3:171–76 [hereafter cited as TJZ]. Originally published in *Keizai Ōrai* (September 1932).

32. Ibid.

33. Tosaka Jun, "Tanabe tetsugaku no seiritsu," TJZ 3:177–84. This article was first published in *Shisō* 128 (January 1933), 113–24.

34. Ibid., 177.

35. Shimomura Toratarō, "Kaiko," *JPS* 500 (September 1966), 278.

36. Mashita Sin'ichi (1906-1985) was active as a Marxist while he was a student.

37. Danno Yasutarō (1902–1967) specialized in social thought. He eventually became a professor at Tokyo Imperial University.

38. Nakai Masakazu, "Kaiko jūnen, omoiizuru mama ni," *JPS* 400 (February 1951), 109.

39. Ibid., 112.

40. Shimomura Toratarō, "Kaiko," *JPS* 500 (February 1951), 277.

CHAPTER 19: REMARRIAGE AND NISHIDA'S VIEW OF WOMEN (1927–1931)

1. Letter no. 454 to Miyake Gōichi, 10 September 1927, NKZ 18:331.

2. "Jisen shiikashū," NKZ 12:442. It is dated 25 June 1927.

3. Letter no. 498, 3 November 1928, NKZ 18:351–52.

4. Umeko suffered from pleurisy, had to recuperate for a few years, and the wedding finally took place on 30 October 1932.

5. Letter no. 575 to Hori Koretaka, 8 September 1929, NKZ 18:383.

6. Nishitani Keiji, "Waga shi Nishida Kitarō sensei o kataru," 37.

7. Letter no. 584 to Yamamoto Ryōkichi, 11 November 1929, NKZ 18:387.

8. Letter no. 588 to Yamamoto Ryōkichi, 9 December 1929, NKZ 18:390.

9. Nishida began working on this essay on 14 February 1930. Published in two installments in *JPS* 172 and 173 (July and August 1930); NKZ 6:13–85.

10. NKZ 6:117–80. Probably completed in December 1930, it was published in two installments in *Shisō* 105 and 106 (February and March 1931).

11. "Jo," *Mu no jikakuteki gentei*, NKZ 6:6–7.

12. Letter no. 641 to Yamanouchi Tokuryū, 28 October 1930, NKZ 18:416.

13. Letter no. 646 to Nishida Asako, 24 November 1930, NKZ 18:418.

14. Letter no. 653 to Yamanouchi Tokuryū, 24 December 1930, NKZ 18:420.

15. Letter no. 658 to Nishida Asako, 25 January 1931, NKZ 18:423.

16. Letter no. 662 to Yamanouchi Tokuryū, 5 February 1931, NKZ 18:425; also letters no. 658, 661, and 663, NKZ 18:423–26.

17. Letter no. 663 to Yamanouchi Tokuryū, 16 February 1931, NKZ 18:425.

18. Diary, 5 March 1931, NKZ 17:465.

19. NKZ 6:181–232; published in *JPS* 184 (July 1931), 1–63.

20. Letter no. 676 to Kimura Motomori, 9 June 1931, NKZ 18:431.

21. NKZ 6:233–59; published in *Shisō* 112 (September 1931), 1–22.

22. "Jo," *Mu no jikakuteki gentei*, NKZ 6:7–8.

23. Ueda Hisashi, *Nishida Kitarō no tsuma*, 50. Koto considered wearing soft makeup part of keeping up her personal appearance, see ibid., 98.

24. Ibid., 51.

25. Diary, NKZ 17:475.

26. NKZ 6.260–99; *JPS* 191 and 192 (February and March 1932).

27. "Jo," *Mu no jikakuteki gentei*, NKZ 6:8.

28. According to the traditional way of counting one's age.

29. Letter no. 693 to Yamamoto Ryōkichi, 5 November 1931, NKZ 18:438.

30. Letter no. 697 to Yamamoto Ryōkichi, 21 November 1931, NKZ 18:439–40.

31. Diary, 1 December 1931, NKZ 17:475–76.

32. NKZ 12:138–49; originally published in *Gēte Nenpō* (December 1931) and translated by Schinzinger and others into German as "Der metaphysische Hintergrund Goethes."

33. "Gēte no haikei," NKZ 12:149.

34. The record of the exact day of his marriage is in neither his diary nor letters. A chronology compiled by Ueda Hisashi, *Nishida Kitarō no tsuma*, has 12 December as the wedding date.

35. Ueda Hisashi, *Nishida Kitarō no tsuma*, 32.

36. Ibid., 54.

37. Letter no. 786 to Nishida Shizuko, 28 August 1933, NKZ 18:475.

38. NKZ 14:343–67. The three lectures were transcribed by Kōsaka Masaaki and Nishitani Keiji.

39. NKZ 6.300–40; published in *Shisō* 120 (May 1932), 1–34.

40. Ueda Yayoi, "Ano koro no chichi," in *Sofu*, 200–01.

41. Ibid., 200.

42. Shimoda, a graduate of the Imperial University in 1896, specialized in the education of women.

43. "Ano koro no chichi," 201.

44. "Ueda Yayoi no omoide," NKZ 12:264 (see memoir at end of chap. 25).

45. Asami Hiroshi brought out three books on Fumi: *Takahashi Fumi no "Furaiburuku tsūshin"*; *Mikan no josei-tetsugakusha, Takahashi Fumi, shiryōshū*; and *Mikan no josei-tetsugakusha, Takahashi Fumi*.

46. *Bunka* 1.5 (May 1934), 55–91.

47. Abe Yoshishige, *Iwanami Shigeo-den*, 392. This was part of Iwanami's scholarship program to support young scholars, a program he began in 1934.

48. Asami Hiroshi, *Takahashi Fumi no "Furaiburuku tsūshin,"* 182–84.

49. Nishitani Keiji, "Meshi o kutta keiken," 218–24.

50. Letter no. 1111 to Nishitani Keiji (in Berlin), 12 June 1937, NKZ 18:603.

51. Nishitani Keiji, "Waga shi Nishida Kitarō sensei o kataru," 18, also 34.

52. Fumi's translation was published in *Sendai Kokusai Bunka Kyōkaishi* [Journal of the Sendai International Cultural Society] (1940), 116–66.

53. Letter no. 149 to Tanabe Ryūji, 20 November 1911, NKZ 18:152–53.

54. Letter no. 2313 to Suzuki Daisetz, 9 January 1928, NKZ 19:489.

55. Letter no. 225 to Hisamatsu Shin'ichi, 30 June 1918, NKZ 18:199.

56. Letter no. 117 to Ueda Juzō, 26 December 1913, NKZ 18:171–72.

57. Letter no. 326 to Yamanouchi Tokuryū (in Freiburg), 27 December 1922, NKZ 18:262.

58. Letter no. 218 to Tanabe Ryūji, 13 October 1917, NKZ 18:196.

59. See "Danro no soba kara," NKZ 12:182–83.

60. Diary, 21 September 1936, has a reference to this book, and on 1 November Nishida wrote: "Finished reading yesterday Lawrence, *Lady Chatterley's Lover.*" NKZ 17:544 and 17:547. Also letter no. 1055 to Shimomura Toratarō, 7 November 1936, NKZ 18:589–90.

61. Omodaka Hisayuki, "Nishida sensei no omoide," 158. Omodaka continues: "Finally, I found a copy at another bookstore and sent it to him. Seizing the opportunity, I also read the book and was truly impressed to know that the professor's philosophical depth also had roots in those areas of human experience."

62. Diary, 24 August 1901, NKZ 17:66.

CHAPTER 20: DEVELOPMENT OF PERSONALIST DIALECTICS (1932–1934)

1. Letter no. 655 to Miyake Gōichi (in Freiburg), 4 January 1931, NKZ 18:422.

2. NKZ 6:341–427; published as *Iwanami Tetsugaku Kōza*, vol. 8 (July 1932), and vol. 10 (September 1932). There is an Italian translation by Renato Andolfato, *L'Io e il Tu*. The title suggests Martin Buber's *Ich und Du*. Most likely Nishida knew something about Buber's thought through F. Gogarten. Nishida mentions Buber's work in his diary of 20 August 1934, NKZ 17:506. The diary entry indicates that Nishida had not yet read Buber's work, and it is not clear whether he ever did.

3. Letter no. 733 to Yamamoto Ryōkichi, 18 May 1932, NKZ 18:453. Saitō Makoto organized the cabinet on 26 May 1932 and held office until 8 July 1934.

4. *Hōsei Daigaku hachijūnenshi*, edited by Tanikawa Tetsuzō, 435.

5. Letter no. 739 to Watsuji Tetsurō, 12 June 1932, NKZ 18:455–56.

6. NKZ 6:428–51; published in *Risō* 34 (October 1932).

7. Letter no. 749 to Tosaka Jun, 4 October 1932, NKZ 18:460.

8. "Genjitsu no kontei to shite no jinkaku gainen," NKZ 14:133–74; lectures given 3–5 September 1932.

9. Tosaka Jun, "Kyōto gakuha no tetsugaku," 3.173–74.

10. Letter no. 749 to Tosaka Jun, 4 October 1932, NKZ 18:460.

11. Hiranuma (1867–1952) founded the *Kokuhonsha* (Fundamental National Society) in 1924; the group is considered "idealistic right wing" *(kannen uyoku)*. Hiranuma held top government positions, including minister of justice, speaker of the privy council, home minister, and prime minister.

12. *Musashi nanajūnen*, edited by Musashi Nanajūnen no Ayumi Henshū Iinkai, 3.

13. Ichiki (1867–1944), a younger brother of Okada Ryōhei, was a specialist in

jurisprudence. He was the founding principal of Musashi Higher School, 1921–1926. From 1925 to 1933 he was minister of imperial affairs and from 1934 to 1936 speaker of the privy council.

14. Letter no. 758 to Yamamoto Ryōkichi, 8 November 1932, NKZ 18:465.

15. See "Kokumin Seishin Bunka Kenkyūjo," in *Kyōikugaku jiten*, edited by Kido Mantarō, 2:803.

16. Letter no. 758 to Yamamoto Ryōkichi, 8 November 1932, NKZ 18:465.

17. Published on 20 December 1932, NKZ 6:1–451.

18. "Jo," *Mu no jikakuteki gentei*, NKZ 6:10.

19. NKZ 7:5–84. Nishida completed revising the essay on 19 January 1933.

20. "Keijijōgaku joron," NKZ 7:55.

21. "Sōsetsu," NKZ 7:183–84.

22. Minoda Muneki (1894–1946) graduated from Tokyo Imperial University in 1920. He cofounded the journal *Genri Nippon* with Mitsui Kōshi and dedicated his life to the mission of attacking those who adhered to Marxism and "German idealism."

23. The group's mission was to denounce democracy and Marxism as threats to the emperor system *(kokutai)*. See *Genri Nippon* 19.2 (February 1943), 1–2.

24. Kyoto Daigaku, "Bukyokushi, Hōgakubu," in *Kyōto Daigaku hyakunenshi*, 4–5 [hereafter cited as *Kyōto Daigaku hyakunenshi*].

25. Letter no. 776 to Yamamoto Ryōkichi, 20 May 1933, NKZ 18:471.

26. Kyōto Daigaku hyakunenshi, "Bukyokushi, Hōgakubu," 5.

27. Letter no. 777, 5 June 1932, NKZ 18:471.

28. *Kyōto Daigaku hyakunenshi*, "Bukyokushi, Hōgakubu," 10.

29. Miki and Toyoshima Yoshio organized the Alliance for the Freedom of the Arts and Sciences *(Gakugei jiyū dōmei)* in protest. "Chronology," MKZ 19:871–72.

30. Abe Yoshishige, *Iwanami Shigeo-den*, 348.

31. Ibid., 349–50.

32. *Kyōdai jiken*, edited by Sasaki Sōichi et al., 1.

33. THZ 8:3–9.

34. *Yomiuri Shinbun*, 28 May 1933, reprinted in Asami Hiroshi, "Fukkoku sanpen," 139–40.

35. Letter no. 988 to Watsuji Tetsurō, 16 January 1936, NKZ 18:555.

36. Husserl died on 27 April 1938.

37. Letter no. 1249 to Nishitani Keiji (in Freiburg), 1 July 1938, NKZ 19:33.

38. Letter no. 1247 to Mutai Risaku, 10 July 1938, NKZ 19:32.

39. Letter no. 2268 to Ōsaka Motokichirō, 7 September 1938, NKZ 19:469.

40. NKZ 7:85–172; this essay was published for the first time as part of *Tetsugaku no konpon mondai*.

41. "Watakushi to sekai," NKZ 7:143–44.

42. Ibid., 86.

43. NKZ 7:173–200. He finished this essay by August 1933.

44. For an English translation, see Dilworth, *Fundamental Problems of Philosophy: The World of Action.*

45. Letter no. 600 to Hori Koretaka, 24 January 1930, NKZ 18:400.

46. Nishida Koto, "Kamakura no ie," 250.

47. The lectures were presented on 25, 27, and 29, September 1933.

48. Tanikawa Tetsuzō, edited by *Hōsei Daigaku hachijūnenshi*, 435.

49. NKZ 14:421–509.

50. NKZ 7:217–304; this essay was published in three installments in *Shisō* 140, 141, and 142 (January, February, and March 1934).

51. NKZ 7:242.

52. Diary, NKZ 17:496.

53. Letter no. 824 to Miyake Gōichi, 29 December 1933, NKZ 18:489. For a similar letter addressed to Miyake, see letter no. 846, 7 July 1993, NKZ 18:497–98 (dated 1934 in NKZ, but more likely written in 1933).

54. NKZ 14:175–213.

55. "Kōi no sekai," NKZ 14:213.

56. Letter no. 834 to Kuwata Hidenobu, 11 February 1934, NKZ 18:493.

57. Letter no. 1082, 13 March 1934, NKZ 18:589–90. This letter is misdated as 1937 in NKZ.

58. Ishiguro Yoshitane, "Ōsaka Motokichirō shōden," 520–21.

59. Harada's son-in-law, Shōda Tatsuo (a banker), wrote Harada's biography, *Jūshintachi no shōwashi*. See 1:239–40.

60. NKZ 7:305–428; published in *JPS* 219, 220, and 221 (June, July, and August 1934).

61. NKZ 7.429–53; published in *Bungaku* 2 (September 1934) and later translated into German by Takahashi Fumi.

62. "Jo," *Tetsugaku no konpon mondai zokuhen*, NKZ 7:203.

63. Ibid., NKZ 7:204.

64. "Benshōhōteki ippansha to shite no sekai," NKZ 7:426–27.

65. "Keijijōgakuteki tachiba kara mita tōzai kodai no bunka keitai," NKZ 7:448–49.

66. Ibid., 452.

67. Ibid., 443.

68. NKZ 14:371–85.

69. "T. S. Eliot to dentōshugi," NKZ 14:379.

70. NKZ 8:7–106; published in *Shisō* 152, 153, and 154 (January, February, and March 1935).

71. "Jo" [preface] to *Tetsugaku ronbunshū daiichi*, NKZ 8:4.

72. "Sekai no jikodōitsu to renzoku," NKZ 8:25.

73. Ibid., 38–39.

CHAPTER 21: EDUCATION AND SCHOLARSHIP UNDER FASCISM (1935–1937)

1. NKZ 14:214–64.

2. NKZ 19:862–75.

3. Nishida felt that Kōyama's presentation was rather superficial. See letter no. 919 to Hori Koretaka, 29 April 1935, NKZ 18:527, and letter no. 930 to Suzuki Daisetz, 14 June 1935, NKZ 18:532.

4. Minobe Tatsukichi (1873–1948); his interpretation of the Meiji Constitution was generally accepted among the leading scholars, judges, and those who closely assisted the emperor.

5. It is said that Emperor Showa was for the "organ theory" himself, and he felt sympathetic to Minobe. Shōda Tatsuo, *Jūshintachi no Shōwashi*, 1:288–89. Also see Harada Kumao, *Saionjikō to seikyoku*, 4:238.

6. Minoda Muneki, "Minobe hakushi, *Kenpō satsuyō* no kibensakujutsuteki kokutai henkaku shisō, sono gakujutsuteki hihan to shochi yōsei," *Genri Nippon* 8 (October 1933).

7. Shōda Tatsuo, *Jūshintachi no shōwashi* 1:287.

8. Ibid., 304–05.

9. Letter no. 911 to Hori Koretaka, 21 March 1935, NKZ 18:524.

10. Letter no. 914 to Harada Kumao, 29 March 1935, NKZ 18:525.

11. Kobayashi Isamu, *Sekirekisō shujin—hitotsu no Iwanami Shigeo-den*, 181–83.

12. Abe Yoshishige, *Iwanami Shigeo-den*, 351–53.

13. Shōda Tatsuo, *Jūshintachi no shōwashi* 2:283–86; Miyazawa Toshiyoshi, *Tennō kikansetsu jiken* 2:458–82.

14. Miyazawa Toshiyoshi, *Tennō kikansetsu jiken* 2:566.

15. Ibid., 1:153–54. Takami wanted to defeat Minobe.

16. Yamamoto Teijirō (1870–1937) led the party's opposition to Minobe's "organ theory." Ibid., 1:153–54.

17. Letter no. 920 to Harada Kumao, 4 May 1935, NKZ 18:527–28.

18. NKZ 10:265–337.

19. Letter no. 925, 19 May 1935, NKZ 18:530.

20. NKZ 8.107–219; published in *Shisō* 158, 159, and 160 (July, August, and September 1935).

21. "Kōiteki chokkan no tachiba," NKZ 8:131.

22. Ibid., 174.

23. Ibid., 180.

24. Ibid., 188.

25. Ibid., 214.

26. Ibid., 217–18.

27. Shōda Tatsuo, *Jūshintachi no shōwashi* 1:295.

28. A transcription of their conversation is reprinted in ibid., 1:296–99.

29. Letter no. 985 to Harada Kumao, NKZ 18:553. The letter was most likely written around 20 September 1935.

30. Yasuko, wife of Konoe Ayamaro's half-brother, was taught the art of shorthand by her father, Mōri Takenori, Lord of Saeki in Bungo. Harada totally trusted her confidentiality. The notes she took for Harada became *Saionjikō to seikyoku* [Prince Saionji and political affairs].

31. *Sources of Japanese Tradition*, edited by Tsunoda Ryusaku, et al., 747. Also see letter no. 952 to Harada Kumao, 18 September 1935, NKZ 18:540.

32. *Kokutai no Hongi: Cardinal Principles of the National Entity of Japan*, translated by J. O. Gauntlett, and edited with an introduction by R. K. Hall.

33. *Sources of Japanese Tradition*, edited by Tsunoda Ryusaku et al., 785.

34. Letter no. 754 to Ishihara Ken, 21 October 1932, NKZ 18:463.

35. Honda Kōtarō (1870–1954) was a student of Nagaoka Hantarō. He was the sixth president of the university, 1931–1940. In 1936 he was given the cultural medal for his invention of the KS magnet ("KS" stands for the donor of the research fund, Sumitomo Kichiemon).

36. Abe Jirō (1883–1959) was a professor of aesthetics.

37. Letter no. 954 to Nishida Sotohiko, 28 September 1935, NKZ 18:541.

38. Letter no. 957 to Harada Kumao, 3 October 1935, NKZ 18:542.

39. Hidaka Daishirō (1896–1977) graduated from the philosophy department in 1922. He was then dean of students at the Third Higher School.

40. Letter no. 963 to Hidaka Daishirō, 13 October 1935, NKZ 18:545.

41. Letter no. 1046 to Kōsaka Masaaki, 30 September 1936, NKZ 18:575.

42. Hashida (1882–1945) was the younger brother of Fujita Toshihiko. He was principal of the First Higher School (1937–1940) and became minister of education in the Tōjō cabinet (1940–1943).

43. Suzuki graduated from the history department at Kyoto Imperial University in 1931. His specialty was Western history.

44. Doi Torakazu (1902–1971) was a graduate of the philosophy department in 1926 and then professor at the Third Higher School; his specialty was Nietzsche and German philosophy.

45. Shitahodo Yūkichi (1904–) graduated from the philosophy department in 1930; he was a specialist of Christian thought.

46. Usui Jishō (1900–1991) specialized in sociology and graduated from the philosophy department in 1926. He became a professor at Kyoto University.

47. Minabe Nagaharu (1886–1958) graduated from the College of Law at Tokyo Imperial University in 1911 and entered the home ministry. He was governor

of Yamanashi, Tokushima, Okayama, Miyagi, Aichi, and Ōsaka Prefectures. He was vice minister of education, August 1934–June 1936.

48. Letter no. 971 to Yamamoto Ryōkichi, 10 November 1935, NKZ 18:548.

49. Letter no. 978 to Watsuji Tetsurō, 1 December 1935, NKZ 18:551.

50. Letter no. 984 to Watsuji Tetsurō, 23 December 1935, NKZ 18:553.

51. Letter no. 987 to Yamamoto Ryōkichi, 11 January 1936, NKZ 18:554.

52. Matsuda held this post from July 1934 through January 1936.

53. "Kyōgaku sasshin hyōgikai sōkai gijiroku," edited by Ishikawa Ken, 14:363.

54. The word *"seishin kagaku"* appears to be a Japanese translation of the German term *"Geisteswissenschaften."*

55. P. A. M. Dirac taught at Cambridge University, England; he wrote *The Principle of Quantum Physics.*

56. Cited in *Kyōgaku sasshin hyōgikai sōkai gijiroku*, edited by Ishikawa Ken et al., 14:363–64.

57. The committee filed its proposal on this day. Ibid., 14:436–46.

58. *Nippon shogaku shinkō iinkai*, edited by Monbushō Kyōgakukyoku, 1.

59. It appears that there was an attempt earlier to set up a similar committee, *Bunkyō shingikai* (see letter no. 1098 to Yamamoto Ryōkichi, 16 May 1937, NKZ 18:597), but the plan was rescinded; see letter no. 1122 to Hori Koretaka, 8 July 1937, NKZ 18:609.

60. *Nihon shogaku shinkō iinkai*, 1.

61. NKZ 12:385–94.

62. Takakusu Junjirō and Kanokogi Kazunobu were other speakers.

63. Nishi Shin'ichirō (1873–1943) had been a mutual acquaintance of Hori Koretaka and Nishida, but by this time Nishi had turned into a hard-core Japanese nationalist who propounded national ethics.

64. Letter no. 1150 to Hori Koretaka, 12 October 1937, NKZ 18:621.

65. Letter no. 1170 to Yamamoto Ryōkichi, 2 December 1937, NKZ 18:630.

CHAPTER 22: DARK POLITICAL UNDERCURRENT (1936–1937)

1. The editor's postscript, *Shisō* 164 (January 1936), 262.

2. Diary, 1936, precise date unknown, NKZ 17:549.

3. The coup was attempted by the Kōdō faction, which believed that to gain control of the government they had to resort to a coup d'état. The rival Tōsei faction believed that they could achieve the same end by political means.

4. Nishida's allusion is to the light sentencing of the leaders of the May 15 incident in 1932.

5. Letter no. 1005, 27 February 1936, NKZ 18:561.

6. Hirota Kōki (1878–1948); his background was in the elite foreign services.

7. Letter no. 1009 to Hori Koretaka, 2 March 1936, NKZ 18:563.

8. *Nihon Gakujutsu Shinkōkai* was established on 28 December 1932. Unlike many other organizations established around that time, this was a group of renowned scholars and professionals who were interested purely in the encouragement of scholarship in Japan, independent of any political agenda of the day.

9. Diary of Miki Kiyoshi, 22 February 1936, MKZ 19:153.

10. Kōsaka Masaaki, *Nishida Kitarō sensei no tsuioku*, 42–43.

11. NKZ 8:273–394; it appeared in *Shisō* 170, 171, and 172 (July, August, and September 1936).

12. Letter no. 1010 to Takizawa Katsumi, 11 March 1936, NKZ 18:563.

13. "Ronri to seimei," NKZ 8:280–318, 8.362, and passim.

14. Letter no. 1018 to Hori Koretaka, 3 April 1936, NKZ 18:566.

15. Letter no. 1028 to Suzuki Daisetz, 8 May 1935, NKZ 18:569.

16. Compiled in *Miki Kiyoshi Zenshū* 17:429–504.

17. October 1936, 90–102.

18. Miura Shinshichi (1877–1947) was a specialist of Western civilization and comparative study of cultures.

19. Okabe Nagakage (1884–1970) took up a diplomatic career and was a member of the House of Peers.

20. "Han o arata ni suru ni atatte" [Upon resetting the type], *Zen no kenkyū*, NKZ 1:6–7. For an English translation of this preface, see *An Inquiry into the Good*, translated by Abe and Ives, xxxi–xxxiv.

21. Spranger stayed in Japan for about a year, during which time he gave eighty public lectures. See Karl Löwith, *Nachizumu to watakushi no seikatsu*, 184–86.

22. Letter no. 1107 to Hori Koretaka, 8 June 1937, NKZ 18:602.

23. Letter no. 1104, 2 June 1937, NKZ 18:600–01.

24. NKZ 12:1–195. Short philosophical essays, literary essays, and selected poems, written between 1926 and 1933, were compiled in this volume.

25. NKZ 8:500–40; published in *Shisō* 182 (July 1937), 1–34.

26. *JPS* 235, 236, and 237 (October, November, and December 1935).

27. Tanabe Hajime, *Shu no ronri no benshōhō*, 1–2.

28. "Shu no seisei hatten no mondai," NKZ 8:500–01.

29. Ibid., 502.

30. Letter no. 1075 to Kōsaka Masaaki, 21 March 1937, NKZ 18:588.

31. "Shu no seisei hatten no mondai," NKZ 8:511–12.

32. Ibid., 537–38. It was reiterated in his public speech, "Gakumonteki hōhō."

33. NKZ 8:541–71; published in *Shisō* 183 (August 1937), 1–25.

34. "Kōiteki chokkan," NKZ 8:542–43.

35. Ibid., 546.

36. NKZ 8:395–499; published in *JPS* 252, 253, and 254 (March, April, and May 1937).

37. Published by Iwanami on 15 November 1937.

38. Hayashi Senjūrō held office from 2 February to 4 June 1937.

39. Letter no. 1105 to Harada Kumao, 3 June 1937, NKZ 18:601.

40. On 8 June 1937; see diary, NKZ 17:558.

41. Letter no. 1115 to Harada Kumao, 23 June 1937, NKZ 18:605–06.

42. Diary, NKZ 17:561.

43. Letter no. 1138 to Harada Kumao, 18 September 1937, NKZ 18:615–16.

44. Letter no. 1148 to Mutai Risaku, 5 October 1937, NKZ 18:619–20.

45. Letter no. 1142 to Harada Kumao, 27 September 1937, NKZ 18:617.

46. NKZ 14:265–91.

47. Letter no. 1155 to Hori Koretaka, 23 October 1937, NKZ 18:623–24; also letter no. 1157 to Yamamoto Ryōkichi, 24 October 1937, NKZ 18:624. Yasui had been governor of Ōsaka-fu, 1935–1937, and was blatantly neglecting scientific studies. Yasui was devoted to Hiraizumi Kiyoshi, a professor of the history of Japanese thought at Tokyo Imperial University. Hiraizumi established the Vermilion Ray Society *(Shūkōkai)*, which gathered ultranationalistic students on campus. See TDH, *Tsūshi* 2: 493.

48. Letter no. 1153 to Harada Kumao, 22 October 1937, NKZ 18:622–23.

49. Letter no. 1159 to Yamamoto Ryōkichi, 26 October 1937, NKZ 18:625.

50. Ibid., NKZ 18:625.

51. Letter no. 1166 to Hori Koretaka, 19 November 1937, NKZ 18:628.

52. It was on 1 November 1937. See diary, NKZ 17:566. Kido was briefly in Kyoto on an official visit.

53. Letter no. 1302 to Watsuji Tetsurō, 18 November 1937, NKZ 19:54–55. This letter is misdated 1938 in NKZ.

54. Tanabe repeatedly criticized Nishida's thought as "unmediated." See letter no. 1325 to Takizawa Katsumi, 22 February 1939, NKZ 19:65.

55. "Jo," *Tetsugaku ronbunshū daini*, NKZ 8:269.

56. Nishida refers to the first installment of Tanabe's "Shu no ronri no imi o akirakani su," which appeared in *JPS* 259 (October 1937), 32–73, attacking Nishida's notion of absolute nothingness as "being" insofar as it is mentionable as a concept.

57. Letter no. 1168 to Mutai Risaku, 22 November 1937, NKZ 18:629.

58. Karl Löwith (1897–1973) had to leave the German academic world in 1933 because he was Jewish. In 1936 Kuki Shūzō facilitated his obtaining the position of lecturer at Tōhoku Imperial University, where he taught until 1941. After World War II, he was offered a chair at the University of Heidelberg and returned to Germany.

59. Karl Löwith, *Tōyō to seiyō*, 23.

60. Ibid., 21–24.

61. NKZ 9:9–68; Nishida worked on the essay from 8 November 1937 to 24 January 1938; it was published in *Shisō* 190 (March 1938), 1–50.

62. Schinzinger was lecturer of German literature at the university from March 1937 to July 1940.

63. Letter no. 1185 to Nishitani Keiji (in Freiburg), 22 January 1938, NKZ 19:7.

64. Letter no. 1189 to Kimura Motomori, 5 February 1938, NKZ 19:8.

65. Robert Schinzinger, "Nishida Tetsugaku no hon'yaku no kotonado," 236.

66. Ibid., 240.

CHAPTER 23: THE DIALECTICAL WORLD AS THE ABSOLUTELY CONTRADICTORY SELF-IDENTITY (1938–1940)

1. Letter no. 1192 to Yamamoto Ryōkichi, 6 February 1938, NKZ 19:9. Also letter no. 1193 to Yamamoto Ryōkichi, 9 February 1938, NKZ 19.10.

2. Letter no. 1195 to Harada Kumao, 11 February 1938, NKZ 19:10–11.

3. He was dean of students at Kyoto Imperial University.

4. Amano Teiyū, "Tokuiku ni tsuite," in *Amano Teiyū Zenshū*, 1:167–69.

5. Hidaka Daishirō, "*Dōri no Kankaku* ni tsuite," 1–4.

6. Letter no. 1209 to Hidaka Daishirō, 7 March 1938, NKZ 19:16–17.

7. "Kimura Hisashi-kun no omoide," NKZ 12:252–56.

8. Letter no. 1222, 5 April 1938, NKZ 19:21–22.

9. "Kimura Hisashi-kun no omoide," NKZ 12:255.

10. He was a leader of the rising bureaucrats and had a good rapport with the military.

11. Arita Hachirō (1884–1965) went into diplomacy and held the post of foreign minister for the Hirota, Konoe (first term of office), Hiranuma, and Yonai cabinets.

12. Miura Tetsutarō (1874–1972) was the president of Tōyō Keizai Shinpōsha (Tōyō Economist Newspaper Company).

13. Matsui Haruo (1891–1966) entered the home ministry and held top positions in the Department of Natural Resources.

14. Ōkura Kinmochi (1882–1968) was on the board of the Manchurian Railroad and a member of the House of Peers.

15. Nasu Shiroshi (1888–1984) was an agriculture specialist and professor at Tokyo Imperial University.

16. Takahashi Kamekichi (1894–1977) was director of the Takahashi Keizai Kenkyūjo (Takahashi Economics Research Institute).

17. Sasa Hiroo was a reporter for *Asahi Shinbunsha*, Asahi Newspaper Company.

18. Tajima Michiji (1885–1968) was the president of Shōwa Bank.

19. Letter no. 1427 to Harada Kumao, 12 March 1938, NKZ 19:105–106. This letter is misdated 1940 in NKZ.

20. Sakai Saburō, *Shōwa kenkyūkai—aru chishikijin-shūdan no kiseki*, 158.

21. Minoda Muneki, "Shōwa Kenkyūkai no gengo-majutsu," *Genri Nippon* (August 1940); Minoda Muneki, "Shōwa Kenkyūkai o kaishō subeshi," ibid. (October

1940); Mitsui Kōshi, "Shōwa Kenkyūkai no kyōgyaku-shisō o shochi subeshi," ibid. (October 1940).

22. Sakai Saburō, "Shōwa Kenkyūkaino higeki," 235.

23. Rōyama Masamichi (1895–1980), who came under the influence of Yoshino Sakuzō, was a professor of political science at Tokyo Imperial University until 1939; he resigned his post to protest the firing of Kawai Eijirō.

24. Igawa Tadao (1893–1947) was secretary of the finance ministry. In 1941 he represented the Japanese government in diplomatic negotiations with the United States.

25. Sakai Saburō, "Shōwa Kenkyūkai no higeki," 236.

26. Ibid., 237.

27. Ibid., 233.

28. *Kido Kōichi kankei bunsho,* edited by Oka Yoshitake et al., 540–41.

29. A transcript of the talk is in NKZ 14:389–417.

30. "Nihon bunka no mondai," NKZ 14:396.

31. Letter no. 1243 to Mutai Risaku 4 July 1938, NKZ 19:30.

32. In fact, Minoda had criticized Nishida a decade earlier in "Nishida hakushi no ninshikiron o hyōsu," *Genri Nippon* (October 1927), but apparently at that time his attack did not gain momentum because it made no stir and his accusation passed unnoticed.

33. Letter no. 1243 to Mutai Risaku 4 July 1938, NKZ 19:30.

34. Letter no. 1240 to Kōsaka Masaaki, 25 June 1938, NKZ 19:28–29.

35. NKZ 9:69–146; he began working on the essay sometime in April 1938; it appeared in *Shisō* 195 and 196 (August and September 1938).

36. Letter no. 1247 to Mutai Risaku, 10 July 1938, NKZ 19:33.

37. Letter no. 1248 to Takizawa Katsumi, 11 July 1938, NKZ 19:33.

38. Ibid.

39. Letter no. 1268, 3 September 1938, NKZ 19:40.

40. Letter no. 1238 to Harada Kumao, 16 June 1938, NKZ 19:27–28. Letter no. 1240 to Kōsaka Masaaki, 25 June 1938, NKZ. See also 19:28–29.

41. Letter no. 1239 to Yamamoto Ryōkichi, 21 June 1938, NKZ 19:28.

42. Letter no. 1255 to Harada Kumao, 4 August 1938, NKZ 19:35.

43. Itō held this post from 7 June 1937 to 23 December 1938.

44. Letter no. 1270 to Yamamoto Ryōkichi, 7 September 1938, NKZ 19:41.

45. Letter no. 1277 to Kōsaka Masaaki, 19 September 1938, NKZ 19:43.

46. Letter no. 1288 to Nishitani Keiji (in Freiburg), 13 October 1938, NKZ 19:49. Also see letter no. 1308 to Nishitani Keiji (in Freiburg), 13 January 1939, NKZ 19:57.

47. Letter no. 1269 to Hisamatsu Shin'ichi, 4 September 1938, NKZ 19:40–41.

48. Robert Schinzinger, "Nishida Tetsugaku no hon'yaku no kotonado," 236.

49. Cf. diary, NKZ 17:582.

50. Kōsaka Masaaki, *Nishida Kitarō sensei no tsuioku*, 35.

51. Letter no. 1292 to Suzuki Daisetz, 20 October 1938, NKZ 19:50.

52. Letter no. 1296 to Kiba Ryōhon, 3 November 1938, NKZ 19:52–53.

53. Miki Kiyoshi, "Shōwajuku sōsetsu ni tsuite" [A word on the establishment of Showajuku] *Miki Kiyoshi Zenshū*, 15:329–33.

54. On Shōkasonjuku, see chap. 4, note 15.

55. Letter no. 1295, 29 October 1938, NKZ 19:51.

56. Ozaki Hotsumi (1901–1944) was a China specialist. In 1941 the Ozaki-Sorge espionage incident came to light; he was found guilty and was executed in 1944.

57. Sakai Saburō, *Shōwa kenkyūkai*, 191.

58. NKZ 9:147–222; the essay was written from 31 October 1938 to 14 January 1939 and published in *Shisō* 202 (March 1939), 1–62.

59. Nishida's interest in Leibniz had been rekindled by Shimomura Toratarō in about 1935 and took definite form in the essay, "Rekishiteki sekai ni oite no kobutsu no tachiba" (1938). See note 35 above. Also see "Zettaimujunteki jikodōitsu," NKZ 9:155.

60. "Jo," *Tetsugaku ronbunshū daiyon*, NKZ 10:3, dated August 1941.

61. Bungeishunjū, "Nishida Kitarō o kakomu zadankai," 457–74.

62. Tanikawa Tetsuzō (1895–1989) was a professor at Hōsei University, where he was president from 1963 to 1965.

63. Satō was a professor at Hōsei University.

64. Hayashi Tatsuo (1896–1984) led the Heibonsha Encyclopedia project, 1954–1958, and had a great impact on the intellectual life in post-1945 Japan.

65. Nomura was appointed foreign minister in September 1939 and on 27 November 1940 was dispatched to the United States as ambassador. On 16 April 1941 he entered negotiations with Cordell Hull, secretary of state, to avert the war between Japan and the United States.

66. Takagi Sōkichi (1893–1979) was a naval officer, served as secretary to the navy minister, and also taught at the naval academy. In November 1939 he established a think tank that was to expand in 1940.

67. Takagi Sōkichi, *Takagi Sōkichi nikki*, 14.

68. NKZ 9:223–304; *Shisō* 207 (August 1939), 1–67.

69. "Jo," *Tetsugaku ronbunshū daigo*, NKZ 10:341, dated September 1943.

70. "Jo," *Tetsugaku ronbunshū daisan*, 9:6.

71. Letter no. 1361 to Yamamoto Ryōkichi, 16 July 1939, NKZ 19:79.

72. Ishiguro Hidehiko was vice minister from 23 December 1938 to 5 September 1944.

73. Letter no. 1343 to Yamamoto Ryōkichi, 18 April 1939, NKZ 19:72.

74. Letter no. 2147 to Nagayo Yoshirō, 14 March 1945, NKZ 19:401.

75. Letter no. 1362 to Harada Kumao, 27 July 1939, NKZ 19:79.

76. Harada Kumao, *Saionjikō to seikyoku* 5:82.

77. Ernst L. Presseisen, *Germany and Japan*, 225: "The new cabinet that finally took office under General Abe signified Japan's political dilemma. Its lack of political color was the real excuse for its existence."

78. Letter no. 1367 to Hori Koretaka, 30 August 1939, NKZ 19:81.

79. Letter no. 1369 to Harada Kumao, 1 September 1939, NKZ 19:82.

80. Nishida's letter to Kido Kōichi, 16 March 1938, *Kido Kōichi kankei bunsho*, edited by Oka Yoshitake et al., 541.

81. Letter no. 1369 to Harada Kumao, 1 September 1939, NKZ 19:82.

82. Letter no. 1370 to Hori Koretaka, 2 September 1939, NKZ 19:83. Also letter no. 1381 to Yamamoto Ryōkichi, 29 September 1939, NKZ 19:87.

83. Letter no. 1381 to Yamamoto Ryōkichi, 29 September 1939, NKZ 19:87.

84. Letter no. 1370 to Hori Koretaka, 2 September 1939, NKZ 19:83.

85. Letter no. 1372 to Hisamatsu Shin'ichi, 8 September 1939, NKZ 19:84; also letters no. 1375 and 1377.

86. Letter no. 1386 to Yamamoto Ryōkichi, 8 October 1939, NKZ 19:89.

87. Published on 15 November 1939 by Iwanami.

88. The purpose of the series was to inform the general public of contemporary social and political issues.

89. Takagi Sōkichi, *Taiheiyō sensō to rikukaigun no kōsō*, 189.

90. Ibid., 190–191.

91. Ibid., 201.

92. See Ōshima Yasumasa, "Daitōa sensō to Kyoto gakuha."

93. Matsudaira Yasumasa (1893–1957) taught at Meiji University. He was then secretary to the lord keeper of the privy seal.

94. Kido Kōichi, *Kido Kōichi nikki*, 750.

95. Takemi Taro (1904–1983) was a well-known medical doctor.

96. Tōhata Seiichi (1899–1983) was Miki Kiyoshi's brother-in-law and a scholar of political and economic implications of agriculture.

97. Hani Gorō (1901–1983) was a historian and a cultural critic. He and Miki Kiyoshi were lifelong friends.

98. Letter no. 1352 to Takizawa Katsumi, 6 June 1939, NKZ 19:76.

99. Letter no. 1406 to Mutai Risaku, 21 January 1940, NKZ 19:98.

100. Letter no. 1381 to Yamamoto Ryōkichi, 29 September 1939, NKZ 19:87.

CHAPTER 24: HISTORY, STATE, AND INDIVIDUAL (1940–1941)

1. Tsuda Sōkichi (1873–1961) was trained under Shiratori Kurakichi.

2. Abe Yoshishige, *Iwanami Shigeo-den*, 226.

3. Letter no. 1423 to Hori Koretaka, 4 March 1940, NKZ 19:104; letter no. 1424 to Yamamoto Ryōkichi, 5 March 1940, NKZ 19:105.

4. The transcription was printed in the August 1979 *Geppō* (monthly supplement) to NKZ 11, 3–8.

5. The preliminary examination began on 30 October 1940, and the guilty verdict was delivered on 21 May 1942. Tsuda and Iwanami appealed and were eventually acquitted on 4 November 1944 because the statute of limitations expired.

6. Letter no. 1429 to Hori Koretaka, 12 March 1940, NKZ 19:106.

7. Letter no. 1428, 12 March 1940, NKZ 19:106.

8. Abe Yoshishige, *Iwanami Shigeo-den*, 225–30.

9. Letter no. 1409 to Nunokawa Kakuzaemon, 30 January 1940, NKZ 19:99.

10. Letter no. 1329 to Hori Koretaka, 12 March 1940, NKZ 19:107.

11. Letter no. 1434 to Yamamoto Ryōkichi, 30 March 1940, NKZ 19:110.

12. Letter no. 1436 to Iwanami Shigeo, 8 April 1940, NKZ 19:110–11.

13. *Genri Nippon* (April 1940).

14. Quoted by Ōshima Yasumasa, "Daitōa sensō to Kyoto gakuha," 138.

15. Letter no. 1463 to Katsube Kenzō, 1 August 1940, NKZ 19:119.

16. "Jo," *Tetsugaku ronbunshū daiyon*, NKZ 10:6 (August 1941).

17. Letter no. 1411 to Hisamatsu Shin'ichi, 9 February 1940, NKZ 19:110. Also letter no. 1410 to Mutai Risaku, 7 February 1940, NKZ 19:100.

18. "Jissentetsugaku joron," NKZ 10:7–123.

19. Ibid., 20, 23.

20. Diary, NKZ 17:619.

21. Letter no. 1490 to Iwanami Shigeo, 26 September 1940, NKZ 19:129. Also letter no. 1492 to Harada Kumao, 26 September 1940, NKZ 19:129–30.

22. Letter no. 1356 to Yamamoto Ryōkichi, 26 June 1940, NKZ 19:77–78 (misdated as 1939 in NKZ). In this letter Nishida also wonders about the effectiveness of the ministry of education.

23. Ernst Presseisen, *Germany and Japan*, 266.

24. On the leadership of Taiseiyokusankai, see Akagi Suruki, *Konoe shintaisei*, 157.

25. Letter no. 1490 to Iwanami Shigeo, 26 September 1940, NKZ 19:129; letter no. 1492 to Harada Kumao, 26 September 1940, NKZ 19:129–30.

26. Letter no. 1503 to Yamamoto Ryōkichi, 12 October 1940, NKZ 19:134.

27. Letter no. 1507 to Yamamoto Ryōkichi, 25 October 1940, NKZ 19:136.

28. NKZ 10:124–76; published in *Shisō* 223 (December 1940), 1–44. Nishida adopted these Greek words from Aristotle's *Nicomachean Ethics* Book VI.

29. "*Poiesis to praksis*," NKZ 10:142–43.

30. Ibid., 156–58.

31. Letter no. 1382 to Shimomura Toratarō, 29 September 1939, NKZ 19:87 (this letter was most likely written in 1940). Also letter no. 1505 to Kimura Motomori, 22 October 1940, NKZ 19:135.

32. NKZ 10:177–264; published in *Shisō* 228 (May 1941), 1–35, and 229 (June 1941), 1–38.

33. NKZ 10: 183–210.

34. NKZ 12.267–72. Nishida sent the final draft to the Imperial Ministry on 27 December 1940.

35. "Yukeru Beruguson," 7 January 1941, *Asahi Shinbun*. See chap. 7, n. 4.

36. Abe Yoshishige, *Iwanami Shigeo-den*, 397–98: Iwanami wanted to make up for what he felt was a lack of filial piety when he was a boy. He likened the "wind blowing through trees" (*fūju*) to the sad voices of his parents. Nonprofit organization status was granted to Fūjukai on 2 November 1940 by the ministry of education.

37. *Iwanami Shoten gojūnen*, 209.

38. Letter no. 1529 to Yamamoto Ryōkichi, 16 January 1941, NKZ 19:144.

39. Letter no. 1534 to Tomonaga Sanjūrō, 25 January 1941, NKZ 19:146.

40. "Goshinkō sōan, Rekishi tetsugaku ni tsuite," NKZ 12:267–72.

41. Letter no. 1542 to Hisamatsu Shin'ichi, 3 February 1941, NKZ 19:149.

42. Letter no. 1534 to Tomonaga Sanjūrō, 25 January 1941, NKZ 19:146.

43. Shōda Tatsuo, *Jūshintachi no shōwashi* 2:234.

44. Letter no. 1550 to Yamamoto Ryōkichi, 13 February 1941, NKZ 19:153.

45. Letter no. 1561 to Yamamoto Ryōkichi, 15 March 1941, NKZ 19:157.

46. The recorded conversation was transcribed by Ueda Hisashi. "Daisetsu to Yamamoto Ryōkichi, Nishida Kitarō (2)."

47. Letter no. 1369 to Yamamoto Ryōkichi, 16 April 1941, NKZ 19:160.

48. "Kokka riyū no mondai," NKZ 10:265–337.

49. Hobbes advocated a secular monarchy governed by a social contract.

50. "Kokka riyū no mondai," NKZ 10:326–27.

51. Ibid., 327.

52. Ibid., 331.

53. Ibid., 333.

54. Ibid., 334.

55. Letter no. 1606 to Hori Koretaka, 11 September 1941, NKZ 19:175.

56. Letter no. 1622 to Yamamoto Ryōkichi, 15 October 1941, NKZ 19:181.

57. Kōsaka Masaaki, *Nishida Kitarō sensei no tsuioku*, 35–36.

58. Letter no. 1625 to Hori Koretaka, 19 October 1941, NKZ 19:182.

59. Letter no. 1629 to Hori Koretaka (dictated), 6 November 1941, NKZ 19:183.

60. Aihara was a 1927 graduate of the philosophy department at Kyoto Imperial University.

CHAPTER 25: FINALE (1942–1945)

1. *Die physikalischen Prinzipien der Quantentheoriene*, mentioned in "Chishiki no kyakkansei ni tsuite, aratanaru chishikiron no jiban," NKZ 10:344–49.

2. *Der Kausalbegriff in der Physik*, mentioned in "Chishiki no kyakkansei ni tsuite," NKZ 10:385.

3. "Chishiki no kyakkansei ni tsuite," NKZ 10:343–476; published in *Shisō* 248 and 249 (January and February 1943).

4. Diary, NKZ 17:648.

5. Suzuki Daisetz, "Nishida no omoide," SDZ 28:372–73.

6. "Yamamoto Ryōkichi-shi chōshi," NKZ 13:175.

7. "Zetsudai," NKZ 13:155.

8. "Jikaku ni tsuite," NKZ 10:477–564; *Shisō* 252 and 253 (May and June 1943).

9. Akashi Teruo (1881–1956) was a prominent banker and a financial advisor to Iwanami Shigeo.

10. Furuno Inosuke (1891–1966) founded the Dōmeitsūshinsha, a news agency that specialized in international news.

11. Ishii Mitsuo was a businessman who practiced Zen at the Engakuji temple.

12. Kanamori Tokujirō (1886–1959) was a specialist in jurisprudence and the constitution.

13. Kanai Shōji (1885–1967) was a medical doctor and politician; he served in the post of chief advisor to the Manchurian government.

14. Tanabe Juri (1894–1962) was a sociologist and specialized in the thought of August Comte and Emile Durkheim.

15. "Heiwa kenpō ni Nishida tetsugaku no seishin" [Hokkoku Newspaper article], edited by Hashimoto Hōkei, 40–42.

16. Yatsugi Kazuo (1899–1983) was a powerful politician.

17. Yatsugi Kazuo, "Nishida Kitarō hakushi to Daitōa sensō," 358. For "Joint Declaration Adopted on November 6, 1943," of the Assembly of Greater Asiatic Nations, see *The Japan Year Book, 1943–44*, edited by S. Takagaki, 1049.

18. Otherwise known as Shimomura Hiroshi (1875–1957) he served as director-general in the Taiwan government, as well as president and vice president of Asahi Newspaper Company.

19. Tanabe Juri, "Bannen no Nishida Kitarō to Nihon no unmei," 27.

20. Letter no. 1781 to Watsuji Tetsurō, 14 June 1943, NKZ 19:243.

21. Letter no. 1783 to Hori Koretaka, 18 June, 1943, NKZ 19:244. Also letter no. 1784 to Watsuji Tetsurō, 23 June 1943, NKZ 19:245. Tōjō's speech of June 16, 1943, is reprinted in *The Japan Year Book, 1943–44*, pp. 200–04.

22. For a detailed study of this contact between Nishida and the military, see Furuta Hikaru, "*Sekai shinchitsujo no genri* jikenkō," and Michiko Yusa, "Fashion and *A-letheia*: Philosophical Integrity and Wartime Thought Control." Concerning the ensuing debates on whether Nishida and the members of the Kyoto

school were "nationalists," see *Rude Awakenings*, edited by J. Heisig and
J. Maraldo; Graham Parkes, "The Putative Fascism of the Kyoto School and
the Political Correctness of the Modern Academy," 305–36; and Y. Arisaka,
"The Nishida Enigma," 81–99.

23. "Sekai shinchitsujo no genri" ("Tetsugaku ronbunshū daiyon hoi"), NKZ
12:397–416. For an English translation see Y. Arisaka, "The Nishida Enigma,"
100–105.

24. Ōshima Yasumasa. "Nishida sensei to Tanabe sensei no saigo no shoshin
kōkan," 4–5.

25. Diary, 21 August 1943, NKZ 17:670.

26. Suetsuna Joichi (1898–1970) wrote books not only on mathematics but also on
Huayan Buddhism.

27. Letter no. 1798 to Mutai Risaku, 27 July 1943, NKZ 19:249.

28. Letters no. 1756 and 1757 to Suetsuna Joichi, 1 and 2 April 1943, NKZ
19:232–35.

29. Yukawa Hideki (1907–1981) was the third son of Ogawa Takuji. He was
awarded the cultural medal in 1943 at the young age of thirty-six. His research
on the meson won the Nobel Prize in physics in 1949.

30. Yukawa Hideki, "Tabibito, aru butsurigakusha no kaisō," 5: 190–91.

31. Letter no. 1782 to Shimomura Toratarō, 15 June 1943, NKZ 19:244.

32. Tomonaga Shin'ichirō (1906–1979) was the eldest son of Tomonaga Sanjūrō.
He was a friend and colleague of Yukawa Hideki from their Third Higher
School days through Kyoto Imperial University. He was awarded a Nobel
Prize in physics in 1965.

33. Letter no. 1791 to Kumano Yoshitaka, 13 July 1943, NKZ 19:247.

34. See Minamoto Ryōen, "The Symposium on 'Overcoming Modernity,'" in
Rude Awakenings, 203. See letter no. 1833 to Takizawa Katsumi, 5 October
1943, NKZ 19:265.

35. "Dentō," NKZ 11:189–92; *Shisō* 256 (September 1943), 62–64.

36. Letter no. 1810 to Yanagida Kenjūrō, 24 August 1943, NKZ 19:254.

37. "Butsuri no sekai," NKZ 11:5–59; *Shisō* 260 (January 1944), 1–39.

38. Letter no. 1850 to Shimomura Toratarō, 14 November 1943, NKZ 19:271.

39. Letter no. 1798 to Mutai Risaku, 27 July 1943, NKZ 19:249.

40. Letter no. 1810 to Yanagida Kenjūrō, 24 August 1943, NKZ 19:254.

41. In November 1943 Nishida wrote "Kimura Hisashi-kun no omoide," NKZ
12:252–56.

42. Diary, 8 November 1943, NKZ 17:674.

43. He finished the first draft on 5 January 1944 and gave the manuscript to an
editor at the Iwanami Bookstore on 25 January. "Ronri to sūri," NKZ
11:60–113; *Shisō* 262 (March 1944), 1–36.

44. Letter no. 1885 to Suetsuna Joichi, 28 January 1944, NKZ 19:284–85.

45. Makino Nobuaki (1861–1949) was the second son of Ōkubo Toshimichi.

46. Minami Hiroshi (1869–1946), a graduate of the Fourth Higher School, was a member of the House of Peers, vice minister of education, governor general of Taiwan, and a member of the privy council.

47. Mori Jūjirō was born in 1890 in Aomori Prefecture; he became a lawyer and was an active member of the Liberal Democratic Party in the post–World War II period.

48. Osada Arata (1887–1961) was a specialist in the philosophy of education and graduated from Kyoto Imperial University in 1915.

49. Two unfinished fragments on this topic are compiled as appendixes 1 and 2, NKZ 12:416–26.

50. Letter no. 1875 to Nishida Sotohiko, 12 January 1944, NKZ 19:280.

51. "Yotei-chōwa o tebiki to shite shūkyō-tetsugaku e," NKZ 11:114–46; *Shisō* 264 (May–June 1944), 1–23.

52. Letter no. 1907 to Yanagida Kenjūrō, 9 March 1944, NKZ 19:294.

53. NKZ 11:147–88; *Shisō* 265 (July 1944), 1–30.

54. Kuroda Hidetoshi, *Shōwa genronshi e no shōgen*, 55; in the February 1944 issue of *Dokushojin* [The Reader], Nomura Shigeomi accused the Kyoto school of being "antimilitary, defeatist, and antinational," and labeled its members *kokuzoku* (national bandits).

55. Letter no. 1947 to Yanagida Kenjūrō, 19 June 1944, NKZ 19:308.

56. Kuroda Hidetoshi, *Shōwa genronshi e no shōgen*, 55–56.

57. Letter no. 1967 to Kōsaka Masaaki, 28 July 1944, NKZ 19:317–18. Also see Kuroda, *Shōwa genronshi e no shōgen*, 56.

58. Letter no. 1907 to Yanagida Kenjūrō, 9 March 1944, NKZ 19:294.

59. Letter no. 1949 to Yanagida Kenjūrō, 28 June 1944, NKZ 19:309.

60. Yanagida Kenjūrō (1893–1983), a 1925 graduate of the philosophy department, came to form a teacher-disciple relationship with Nishida in September 1936. He embraced Marxism in the post–World War II period and denounced himself for having been a follower of Nishidan philosophy.

61. Letter no. 2057 to Omodaka Hisayuki, 5 December 1933, NKZ 19:356–57. Omodaka was then helping edit this journal. Also letter no. 2058 to Kimura Motomori, 6 December 1944, NKZ 19:357.

62. Letter no. 2018 to Mutai Risaku, 23 October 1944, NKZ 19:339–40.

63. "Kūkan," NKZ 11:193–236; he began this essay on 1 July and finished it on 26 August 1944.

64. Letter no. 1952 to Kimura Motomori, 3 July 1944, NKZ 19:310–11.

65. Letter no. 1280 to Kimura Motomori, 21 September 1938, NKZ 19:45.

66. Letter no. 1966 to Hori Koretaka, 28 July 1944, NKZ 19:317.

67. Letter no. 1961 to Hori Koretaka, 21 July 1944, NKZ 19:314.

68. The proofs of this book were destroyed by the air raids of 25 February 1945, when Iwanami's print shop burned down. Nishida, having taken precautions, kept the original copy at home. Letter no. 2141 to Shimomura Toratarō, 10 March 1945, NKZ 19:396.

69. NKZ 11:289–370. Nishida abandoned this essay at midpoint. Installments were printed in *Shisō* 267 (March 1945) and 268 (August 1945).

70. Letter no. 1952 to Kimura Motomori, 3 July 1944, NKZ 19:311.

71. Letter no. 1999 to Hori Koretaka, 22 September 1944, NKZ 19:331–32.

72. Letter no. 2003 to Ueda Juzō, 27 September 1944, NKZ 19:333–34.

73. Letter no. 2085 to Hori Koretaka, 28 December 1944, NKZ 19:371.

74. Diary, NKZ 17:697.

75. Letter no. 2090, 4 January 1945, NKZ 19:374.

76. "Sūgaku no tetsugakuteki kisozuke," NKZ 11:237–84; published posthumously in *JPS* 345 (December 1944), 1–31 (the issue was actually published in September 1945).

77. "Bashoteki ronri to shūkyōteki sekaikan," NKZ 11:371–464. It was included in the seventh collection of *Tetsugaku ronbunshū* and published posthumously on 15 February 1946. There are two English translations of this work: "The Logic of *Topos* and the Religious Worldview," translated by Michiko Yusa, and in *Last Writings: Nothingness and the Religious Worldview*, translated by D. Dilworth, 47–123.

78. Letter no. 2162 to Omodaka Hisayuki, 23 March 1945, NKZ 19:408.

79. Diary, 20 January 1945, NKZ 17:698.

80. Letter no. 2128 to Nishida Sotohiko, 25 February 1945, NKZ 19:391.

81. Diary, 7 March 1945, NKZ 17:702.

82. Letter no. 2143 to Kōyama Iwao, 11 March 1945, NKZ 19:398–99.

83. *Analects* 12.7.

84. *Sources of Chinese tradition*, edited by W. T. de Bary et al., 35.

85. Letter no. 2147 to Nagayo Yoshirō, 14 March 1945, NKZ 19:401–02. For an English translation of the bulk of this letter, see Michiko Yusa, "Nishida and the Question of Nationalism," 208.

86. Letter no. 2173 to Kōsaka Masaaki, 8 April 1945, NKZ 19:413.

87. Letter no. 2144 to Suzuki Daisetz, 11 March 1945, NKZ 19:399.

88. Letter no. 2181, 12 April 1945, NKZ 19:417.

89. Letter no. 2187 to Tomonaga Sanjūrō, 1 May 1945, NKZ 19:421–22.

90. Ōshima Yasumasa, "Nishida sensei to Tanabe sensei no saigo no shoshin kōkan."

91. Letter no. 2683 to Tanabe Hajime, 20 May 1945, NKZ 19:669–70.

92. Diary, 26 May 1945, NKZ 17:709.

93. "Watakushi no ronri ni tsuite," NKZ 12:265–66; *JPS* 347 (April 1946), 5–6. For an English translation, see D. Dilworth, *Last Writings: Nothingness and the Religious Worldview*, 125–26.

94. *Wandrers Nachtlied* (Wanderer's Night Song, 1780): "Über allen Gipfeln / Ist Ruh, / In allen Wipfeln / Spürest du / Kaum einen Hauch; / Die Vögelein schweigen im Walde. / Warte nur, balde / Ruhest du auch." Taken from *Johann Wolfgang von Goethe Selected Poems*, edited by C. Middleton, 58.

EPILOGUE

1. Suzuki Daisetz, "Nishida no omoide," SDZ 28:378–79.

2. Kimura Motomori, "Nuibari," 36.

3. Suzuki had formed a close relationship with the temple because it was where Shaku Sōen was abbot at the time of his death.

4. Kataoka Hitoshi and Tsujimura Kōichi, "Sunshin-kai no koto, sono yurai, genzai, shōrai," 1–4. At the completion of the grave at Reiun'in in February 1948, a Buddhist ceremony was held to entomb a portion of Nishida's bones and ashes on 7 March 1948.

5. Ibid., 1–4.

6. Aihara Shinsaku, "Shitei," 146.

7. See Michiko Yusa, "Reflections on Nishida Studies," 287–96.

8. Kōsaka Masaaki, *Nishida Kitarō sensei no tsuioku*, 163.

9. *Iwanami Shoten gojūnen*, edited by Iwanami Yūjirō, 259.

10. Letter no. 2066, 14 December 1944, NKZ 19:361.

Glossary of Names and Terms

Abe Jirō 阿部次郎 (1883–1959)

Abe Nobuyuki 阿部信行 (1875–1953)

Abe Seinosuke 安部晴之助

Abe Yoshishige 安倍能成 (1883–1966)

ai 愛

Aihara Shinsaku 相原信作 (1905–1996)

Aihara Yoshikazu 相原良一 (1912–)

Akai Maki 赤井牧

Akai Yonekichi 赤井米吉 (1887–1974)

Akamatsu Chijō 赤松智城 (1886–1960)

Akamatsu Kotora 赤松小寅 (1890–1944)

Akanuma Chizen 赤沼智善 (1884–1937)

Akashi Teruo 明石照男 (1881–1956)

Akegarasu Haya 暁烏敏 (1877–1954)

Akizuki Itaru 秋月致

Amano Teiyū 天野貞祐 (1884–1980)

Amō Eiji 天羽英二 (1887–1968)

Anesaki Masaharu (Chōfū) 姉崎正治(嘲風) (1873–1949)

Arai Hakuseki 新井白石 (1657–1725)

Araki Sadao 荒木貞夫 (1877–1966)

Araki Torasaburō 荒木寅三郎 (1866–1942)

Arima (Sasa) Shōzaburō 有馬(佐々)章三郎

Arishima Ikuma 有島生馬 (1882–1974)

Arishima Takeo 有島武郎 (1878–1923)

Arita Hachirō 有田八郎 (1884–1965)

Asahi Shinbun 『朝日新聞』

Ashikaga Takauji 足利尊氏 (1305–1352)

Ataka Yakichi 安宅弥吉 (1873–1949)

Bashō. See Matsuo Basho

basho 場所

basho no ronri 場所の論理

bashoteki 場所的

benshōhō 弁証法

Bungakubu 文学部

Bunka『文化』

Bunka Daigaku 文科大学

bunka kunshō 文化勲章

bushi 武士

bushidō 武士道

Chiba Tanenari 千葉胤成 (1884–1972)

Daitokuji 大徳寺

Danno Yasutarō 淡野安太郎 (1902–1967)

Dōgen 道元 (1200–1253)

Doi Torakazu 土井虎賀寿 (1902–1971)

Dokuon Jōshu (Ogino) 独園承珠(荻野) (1819–1895)

dokusan 独参

Eijunji 永順寺

Emperor Meiji 明治天皇 (Mutsuhito 睦仁). See Meiji ten'nō

Emperor Shōwa 昭和天皇 (Hirohito 裕仁). See Shōwa ten'nō

Emperor Taishō 大正天皇 (Yoshihito 嘉仁). See Taishō ten'nō

Engakuji 円覚寺

Enoto Rikichi 榎戸利吉

Enshōsha 衍象舎

Ensui kyokusen『円錐曲線』

Fujii Kenjirō 藤井健治郎 (1872–1931)

Fujii Otoo (Shiei) 藤井乙男(紫影) (1868–1945)

Fujii Tanetarō 藤井種太郎 (1881–1968)

Fujimura Misao 藤村操 (1886–1903)

Fujioka (Nakatani) Aya 藤岡(中谷)綾 (1906–1927)

Fujioka Kōji 藤岡幸二

Fujioka Michio 藤岡通夫 (1908–1988)

Fujioka Mitsuko 藤岡光子 (–1906)

Fujioka Sakutarō (Tōho) 藤岡作太郎(東圃) (1870–1910)

Fujioka (Yoshida) Tatsumi 藤岡(吉田)辰巳 (1872–1944)

Fujioka Yoshio 藤岡由夫 (1903–1976)

Fujioka Zōroku 藤岡蔵六

Fujishiro Teisuke 藤代禎輔 (1868–1927)

Fujita Koremasa 藤田維正

Fujita Tōko 藤田東湖 (1806–1855)

Fujita Toshihiko 藤田敏彦 (1877–1965)

Fujiwara Seika 藤原惺窩 (1561–1619)

Fūjukai 風樹会

Fukada Yasukazu 深田康算 (1878–1928)

fukko 復古

Fukuchi Gen'ichirō 福地源一郎 (1841–1906)

Fukushima Junkichi 福島淳吉 (–1897)

Fukuzawa Yukichi 福沢諭吉 (1834–1901)

Funayama Shin'ichi 船山信一 (1907–1994)

Furuno Inosuke 古野伊之助 (1891–1966)

Fuseimonkai 不成文会

gakumon 学問

Gakushūin 学習院

Gasonkai 我尊会

Geibun 『芸文』

Genri Nippon 『原理日本』

Genri Nipponsha 原理日本社

genrō 元老

gijutsu 技術

gō 号

goshinkō 御進講

Gotō Fumio 後藤文夫 (1884–1980)

Gotō Ryūnosuke 後藤隆之助 (1888–1984)

Haga Yaichi 芳賀矢一 (1867–1927)

Hakuin Ekaku 白隠慧鶴 (1684–1768)

hakusa seishō 白砂青松

Hamaguchi Osachi 浜口雄幸 (1870–1931)

Hamao Arata 浜尾新 (1849–1925)

Han (Kan in Japanese) 漢

han 藩

hanbatsu 藩閥

Hani Gorō 羽仁五郎 (1901–1983)

Hara Asao 原阿佐緒 (1888–1969)

Hara Katsurō 原勝郎 (1871–1924)

Harada Kumao 原田熊雄 (1881–1946)

Harada Nobuko 原田信子

Hasegawa Nyozekan 長谷川如是閑 (1875–1969)

Hasegawa Teiichirō 長谷川貞一郎

Hashida Kunihiko 橋田邦彦 (1882–1945)

Hashimoto Kingorō 橋本欣五郎 (1890–1957)

Hatani Ryōtai 羽渓了諦

Hatano Seiichi 波多野精一 (1877–1950)

Hatoyama Ichirō 鳩山一郎 (1883–1959)

Hatta Miki 八田三喜 (1873–1962)

Hayakawa Senkichirō 早川千吉郎 (1863–1922)

Hayami Hiroshi 速見滉 (1876–1943)

Hayashi Magohachirō 林孫八郎 (died 1880s)

Hayashi Razan 林羅山 (1583–1657)

Hayashi Senjūrō 林銑十郎 (1870–1943)

Hayashi Tatsuo 林達夫 (1896–1984)

heijōtei 平常底

heimin 平民

Hekigan'e 碧巌会

Hekignroku 『碧巌録』

hiai 悲哀

Hidaka Daishirō 日高第四郎 (1896–1977)

Hiraide Kōjirō 平出鏗二郎

Hiraizumi Kiyoshi 平泉澄 (1895–1984)

Hiranuma Kiichirō 平沼騏一郎 (1867–1952)

Hirota Kōki 広田弘毅 (1878–1948)

Hisamatsu Shin'ichi 久松真一 (1889–1980)

Hojinkai Zasshi 『輔仁会雑誌』

Hōjō (Kondō) Masaki 北条マサキ (née 近藤)

Hōjō Tokiyori (Saimyōji) 北条時頼(最明寺) (1227–1263)

Hōjō Tokiyuki (or Tokiyoshi) 北条時敬 (1859–1929)

Hokkoku Shinbun 『北国新聞』

Hokushinkai Zasshi 『北辰会雑誌』

Honda Kenzō 本多謙三 (1898–1948)

Honda Kōtarō 本多光太郎 (1870–1954)

Honjō Yoshimune 本荘可宗

Hori Koretaka 堀維孝 (1868–1954)

Hōsei Daigaku 法政大学

Hoshino Ai 星野あい

Hōshun'in 芳春院

Hosoya Tsuneo 細谷恒夫

Ibaraki Seijirō 茨木清次郎

Ichiki Kitokurō 一木喜徳郎 (1867–1944)

ichioku gyokusai 一億玉砕

Ide Takashi 出隆 (1892–1980)

Igarashi Shin 五十嵐信 (died 1928)

Igawa Tadao 井川忠雄 (1893–1947)

Iidabashi Daimyōjin 飯田橋大明神

Ikeda Shigeaki 池田成彬 (1867–1950)

Ikegami Shōsan 池上湘山. See Shōsan Echō

Imaizumi Teisuke 今泉定助 (1863–)

Imakita (or Imagita) Kōsen 今北洪川

Inaba Masamaru 稲葉昌丸 (1865–1944)

Inokuchi Sei (Mōtoku) 井口濟(孟篤)(–1884)

Inoue Enryō 井上円了 (1858–1919)

Inoue Kaoru 井上馨 (1837–1915)

Inoue Kowashi 井上毅 (1844–1895)

Inoue Tetsujirō 井上哲次郎 (1855–1944)

Inukai Tsuyoshi 犬養毅 (1855–1932)

Ishida Isoji 石田磯次

Ishida Kanehisa 石田古周

Ishida Kenji 石田憲次 (1890–1979)

Ishiguro Bunkichi 石黒文吉

Ishihara Atsushi 石原純 (1881–1947)

Ishihara Ken 石原謙 (1882–1976)

Ishii Mitsuo 石井光雄

Ishikawa Kōji 石川興二

Ishikawa Ryūzō 石川竜三 (1867–1945)

Ishikawaken jinjō chūgakkō, Nanao bunkō 石川県尋常中学校七尾分校

Ishikawaken Senmongakkō 石川県専門学校

Ishikawaken shihangakkō 石川県師範学校

ishin 維新

Itō Enkichi 伊藤延吉

Itō Hirobumi 伊藤博文 (1841–1909)

Itō Kichinosuke 伊藤吉之助 (1885–1961)

Ittōen 一燈園

Iwamoto Tei 岩元禎 (1869–1941)

Iwanami Shigeo 岩波茂雄 (1881–1946)

Jiga (Ch. Erya) 『爾雅』

jikaku 自覚

jiko an'jin 自己安心

Jimyō (Chinese: Ciming) 慈明

Jingū hōsaikai 神宮奉斎会

jinkaku 人格

jiriki 自力

Jishūryō 時習寮

Jōshū (Zhaozhu) 趙州 (778–897)

juku 塾

junsui keiken 純粋経験

Jūshin 重臣

Kagawa Toyohiko 賀川豊彦 (1888–1960)

Kaizō 『改造』

Kakehashi Akihide 梯明秀 (1902–)

Kamiyama Kosaburō 上山小三郎 (1846–1921)

Kanai Shōji 金井章次 (1885–1967)

Kanamori Tokujirō 金森徳次郎 (1886–1959)

Kanba Toshio 樺俊雄

kanbun 漢文

Kanda Naibu 神田乃武 (1857–1923)

Kaneko Takezō 金子武蔵 (1905–1987)

Kanetsune Kiyosuke 兼常清佐 (1885–1957)

Kanō Kōkichi 狩野亨吉 (1865–1942)

Kano Naoki 狩野直喜 (1868–1947)

Kanokogi Kazunobu 鹿子木員信 (1884–1949)

kanshi 漢詩

Karaki Junzō 唐木順三 (1904–1980)

Kashiwada Morifumi 柏田盛文

Kataoka Hitoshi 片岡仁志 (1902–1993)

Katō Hiroyuki 加藤弘之 (1836–1916)

Katsube Kenzō 勝部謙造 (1885–1964)

Kawagoe Munetaka 川越宗孝 (–1891)

Kawai Yoshinari 河合良成 (1886–1970)

Kawakami Hajime 河上肇 (1879–1946)

Kawakami Hikoji 川上彦次

kazoku 華族

Keigijuku 敬義塾 (1902–1931)

Keizai Ōrai『経済往来』

kendō 剣道

Kenrokuen 兼六園

kenshō 見性

Kiba Ryōhon 木場了本 (ca. 1887–1940)

Kido Kōichi 木戸幸一 (1889–1977)

Kihira Tadayoshi 紀平正美 (1874–1949)

Kikashogakureidai『幾何初学例題』

Kikuchi Dairoku 菊池大麓 (1855–1917)

Kikuchi Takeo 菊池武夫 (1875–1955)

Kikuchi Toyosaburō 菊池豊三郎 (1892–1971)

Kimura Hisashi 木村栄 (1870–1943)

Kimura Motomori 木村素衛 (1895–1946)

Kimura Takatarō 木村鷹太郎 (1870–1931)

Kiyozawa Manshi 清沢滿之 (1863–1903)

kōan 公案

Kobayashi Isamu 小林勇 (1903–1981)

Kobayashi Taichirō 小林太一郎

Kobayashi Zentei 小林全鼎 (1893–1972)

kōdō 皇道

Kōgaku Sōen 洪嶽宗演 (1859–1919)

Kohōan 孤蓬庵

Koiso Kuniaki 小磯国昭 (1880–1950)

kōiteki chokkan 行為的直観

Koizumi Yakumo (Lafcadio Hearn) 小泉八雲（ラフカディオ・ハーン）(1850–1904)

koji 居士

kojin 個人

koji-Zen 居士禅

Kōjū Sōtaku 広州宗澤 (1840–1907)

Kokan Sōho 虎関宗補 (1839–1903)

kokka 国家

kokkashugi 国家主義

Kōkōdō 浩々洞

Kokumin seishin bunka kenkyūjo 国民精神文化研究所

Kokusaku kenkyūkai 国策研究会

kokusuishugi 国粋主義

kokutai 国体

Kokutai no hongi『国体の本義』

Kondō Masaki. See Hōjō Masaki

Konishi Shigenao 小西重直 (1875–1948)

Kōno Yoichi 河野與一 (1896–1984)

Konoe Atsumaro 近衛篤麿 (1863–1904)

Konoe Ayamaro (or Fumimaro) 近衛文麿 (1891–1945)

Konoe (Mōri) Chiyoko 近衛(毛利)千代子

Konoe Hidemaro 近衛秀麿

Konoe (Maeda) Motoko 近衛(前田)貞子

Konoe (Maeda) Sawako 近衛(前田)衍子

Konoe (Mōri) Yasuko 近衛(毛利)泰子

Kōsaka Masaaki 高坂正顕 (1900–1969)

kosei 個性

Kōsei keikai『皇清経解』

Kōsen Shōon (Imakita) 洪川宗温(今北) (1816–1892)

kōshitsu 皇室

Kōshōgaku 考証学

Kosseikutsu 骨清窟

Kōyama Iwao 高山岩男 (1905–1993)

Koyama Tomoe 小山鞆絵 (1884–1976)

Koyanagi Shigeta 小柳司氣太 (1870–1940)

Kozaki Hiromichi 小崎弘道 (1856–1938)

Kubo Yoshio 久保芳雄

Kuchōkan 久徴館

Kuhara Mitsuru 久原躬弦 (1855–1919)

Kuki Shūzō 九鬼周造 (1888–1941)

Kumano Yoshitaka 熊野義孝 (1899–)

kunai-daijin 宮内大臣

Kurata Hyakuzō 倉田百三 (1891–1943)

Kuwabara Masahisa 桑原政栄

Kuwaki Ayao 桑木或雄 (1878–1945)

Kuwaki Gen'yoku 桑木厳翼 (1874–1946)

Kuwata Hidenobu 桑田秀延 (1895–1975)

Kūya 空也 (903–972)

Kyōdai jiken 京大事件 (also Takigawa jiken)

Kyōgaku sasshin hyōgikai 教学刷新評議会

Kyōto gakuha 京都学派

Kyōto gakuren jiken 京都学連事件

Kyōto Teikoku Daigaku 京都帝国大学

Maeda Toshiie 前田利家 (1538–1599)

Maeda Toshinari 前田利為 (1885–1942)

Maeda Toshitsugu 前田利嗣 (1858–1900)

Maeda Tsunanori (Shōun) 前田綱紀(松雲) (1643–1724)

Maeda Yoshiyasu 前田慶寧 (1830–1874)

Maki Kenji 牧健二 (1892–1989)

Makino Nobuaki 牧野伸顕 (1861–1949)

Mashita Shin'ichi 真下信一 (1906–1985)

Matsuda Genji 松田源治 (1926–)

Matsuda Michio 松田道雄 (1908–1998)

Matsudaira Yasumasa 松平康昌 (1893–1957)

Matsui Haruo 松井春生 (1891–1966)

Matsui Kisaburō 松井喜三郎 (ca. 1869–1932)

Matsumoto Bunzaburō 松本文三郎 (1869–1944)

Matsumoto Matatarō 松本亦太郎 (1865–1943)

Matsuo Bashō 松尾芭蕉 (1644–1694)

Matsuoka Yōsuke 松岡洋右 (1880–1946)

Meiji Tennō (Mutsuhito) 明治天皇(睦仁) (1852–1912)

messhi hōkō 滅私奉公

Miki Kiyoshi 三木清 (1897–1945)

Minabe Nagaharu 三辺長治 (1886–1958)

Minami Hiroshi 南弘 (1869–1946)

Minamoto Yoritomo 源頼朝 (1147–1199)

Minobe jiken 美濃部事件

Minobe Tatsukichi 美濃部達吉 (1873–1948)

Minoda Muneki 蓑田胸喜 (1894–1946)

Mitake Kingorō 三竹欽五郎 (–1918)

Mitsuchi Kōzō 三土興三 (1898–1924)

Mitsui Hachirōemon (Takaakira) 三井八郎右衛門(高公) (1895–1992)

Mitsui Hachirōemon (Takamine) 三井八郎右衛門(高棟) (1857–1948)

Miura Shinshichi 三浦新七 (1877–1947)

Miura Tetsutarō 三浦鉄太郎 (1874–1972)

Miyake Gōichi 三宅剛一 (1895–1982)

Miyake Shōtarō (Shinken) 三宅少太郎(真軒) (1853–ca. 1935)

Miyake Yūjirō (Setsurei) 三宅雄二郎(雪嶺) (1860–1945)

Miyamoto Hideo 宮本英雄 (1888–1973)

Miyamoto Shōson 宮本正尊 (1893–1983)

Miyamoto Wakichi 宮本和吉 (1883–1972)

Mizobuchi Shinma 溝渕進馬

Mizuashi Ikujirō 水葦幾次郎

Monoi Hana 物井花 (also *Kimura Michiko* 木村道子)

Mori Arinori 森有礼 (1847–1889)

Mori Jūjirō 森重次郎 (1890–)

Moriguchi Shigeharu 森口繁治 (1885?–1940)

Morimoto Kōji (Seinen) 森本孝治(省念) (1889–1984)

Moriuchi Masaaki 森内政昌 (–1907)

Moriya Hideaki 守屋秀顕

Mōshi 『孟子』

Motora Yūjirō 元良勇次郎 (1858–1912)

Mozume Takami 物集高見 (1847–1928)

mu 無

muga 無我

muji 無字

Mujintō 『無尽燈』

Mukō Kikutarō 向菊太郎 (ca. 1871–1904)

Mumonkan (Wumenguan) 『無門関』

Murakami Senshō 村上専精 (1851–1929)

Murata Shirō 村田四郎 (1887–)

Musashi kōtōgakkō 武蔵高等学校

Mushanokōji Saneatsu 武者小路実篤 (1885–1976)

Mutai Risaku 務台理作 (1890–1974)

Mutōryū 無刀流

Myōshinji 妙心寺

Nagai Ryūtarō 永井柳太郎 (1881–1944)

Nagai Shizuo 永井静雄

Naganoken (Shinano) Tetsugakukai 長野県(信濃)哲学会

Nagao Gan 長尾含

Nagayo Yoshirō 長与善郎 (1888–1961)

nai-daijin 内大臣

Naitō Konan 内藤湖南 (1866–1934)

Nakae Chōmin 中江兆民 (1847–1901)

Nakagawa Hajime 中川元

Nakahashi Tokugorō 中橋徳五郎 (1861–1934)

Nakai Masakazu 中井正一 (1900–1952)

Nakajima Ichirō 中島一郎

Nakajima Rikizō 中島力造 (1858–1918)

Nakajima Tokuzō 中島徳蔵 (1864–1940)

Nakame Satoru 中目覚

Nakano Seigō 中野正剛 (1886–1943)

Naruse Kiyoshi (Mukyoku) 成瀬清(無極) (1885–1958)

Nasu Shiroshi 那須皓 (1888–1984)

Natsume Kinnosuke (Sōseki) 夏目金之助(漱石) (1867–1916)

Nihongaishi 『日本外史』

Nihon gakujutsu shinkōkai 日本学術振興会 (1932–)

Nihon hyōron 『日本評論』

Nihon Shingakkō 日本神学校

Nihon shogaku shinkō iinkai 日本諸学振興委員会

Nihon Teikoku Gakushiin 日本帝国学士院

Niijima Jō 新島襄 (1843–1890)

Nishi Shin'ichirō 西晋一郎 (1873–1943)

Nishida Aiko 西田愛子 (d. 1907)

Nishida Aranori 西田新登 (– ca. 1850)

Nishida Hyōjirō 西田憑次郎 (1873–1904)

Nishida Ken 西田謙 (1898–1920)

Nishida Kikuhiko 西田幾久彦 (1928–)

Nishida (Yamada) Koto 西田(山田)琴 (1883–1973)

Nishida (Tokuda) Kotomi 西田(得田)寿美 (1875–1925)

Nishida Masa 西田正 (1859–1939)

Nishida Nao 西田尚 (1866–1883)

Nishida Naojirō 西田直二郎

Nishida Shizuko 西田静子 (1905–1976)

Nishida Sotohiko 西田外彦 (1901–1959)

Nishida (Takahashi) Sumi 西田(高橋)隅 (1871–1955)

Nishida Tenkō 西田天香 (1872–1968)

Nishida Tomoko 西田友子 (1907–1941)

Nishida (Hayashi) Tosa 西田(林)寅三 (1842–1918)

Nishida (Tachibana) Toshiko 西田(橘)敏子 (1903–1989)

Nishida (Kaneko) Umeko 西田(金子)梅子 (1909–1996)

Nishida Yae 西田八重

Nishida Yasunori 西田得登 (1834–1898)

Nishida (Ueda) Yayoi 西田(上田)弥生 (1896–1945)

Nishida Yūko 西田幽子 (1902–1907)

Nishikida Yoshitomi 錦田義富 (1884–1927)

Nishitani Keiji 西谷啓治 (1900–1990)

Nogami Toshio 野上俊夫 (1882–1963)

Nogi Maresuke 乃木希典 (1849–1912)

Nogi Shizuko 乃木静子 (–1912)

Nomura Kichisaburō 野村吉三郎 (1877–1964)

Nozaki Hiroyoshi 野崎広義 (1889–1917)

Nunokawa Kakuzaemon 布川角左衛門

Oda Nobuhiro 織田信恒 (1889–)

Oda Shōgaku 織田小覚 (1858–)

Odaka Tomoo 尾高朝雄 (1899–1956)

Ogawa Takuji 小川琢治 (1870–1941)

Ogino Dokuon 荻野独園. See Dokuon Jōshu

Ogyū Sorai 荻生徂徠 (1666–1728)

Ojima Sukema 小島祐馬 (1881–1966)

Oka Sanjirō (or Shinzō) 岡三治郎(真三)

Okabe Nagakage 岡部長景 (1884–1970)

Okada Keisuke 岡田啓介 (1868–1952)

Okada Ryōhei 岡田良平 (1864–1934)

Okamoto (Sabase) Haruhiko 岡本(鯖瀬)春彦 (1894–1918)

Ōkubo Toshimichi 大久保利通 (1830–1878)

Okuda Yoshito 奥田義人 (1860–1917)

Ōkuma Shigenobu 大隈重信 (1838–1922)

Ōkura Kinmochi 大蔵公望 (1882–1968)

Omodaka Hisayuki 沢潟久敬 (1904–)

Ōnishi Hajime 大西祝 (1864–1900)

Onoe Shōnosuke 尾上松之助

onshi 恩師

Orategama 『遠羅天釜』

Osada Arata 長田新 (1887–1961)

Ōsaka Motokichirō 逢坂元吉郎 (1880–1945)

Ōshima Masanori 大島正徳 (1880–1947)

Ōshima Seiji 大島誠治

Ōshima Yasumasa 大島康正 (1917–)

Ōshima Yoshinaga 大島義脩 (1871–1935)

Ōuchi Seiran 大内青巒 (1845–1918)

Ozaki Hotsumi 尾崎秀実 (1901–1944)

Rai Sanyō 頼山陽 (1780–1832)

reisei 霊性

Reiun'in 霊雲院

rekishiteki shintai 歴史的身体

risei 理性

Risō 『理想』

Rongo 『論語』

rōshi 老師

Rōyama Masamichi 蠟山政道 (1895–1980)

Saigō Takamori (Nanshū) 西郷隆盛(南洲) (1827–1877)

Saigyō 西行

Saionji Kinmochi 西園寺公望 (1849–1940)

Saitō Makoto 斉藤実 (1858–1936)

Sakaguchi Takashi 坂口昂 (1872–1928)

Sakuma Gisaburō 作間義三郎

Sakurai Masataka 桜井政隆 (1879–)

samurai 侍

sanbagarasu 三羽烏

Sansanjuku 三々塾

san'yo 参与

sanzen 参禅

Sasa Hiroo 佐々弘雄

Sasaki Gesshō 佐々木月樵 (1875–1926)

Sasaki Sōichi 佐々木惣一 (1878–1965)

Satō Kenryō 佐藤賢了 (1895–1975)

Satō Nobue 佐藤信衛 (1905–)

Satō Tsūji 佐藤通次 (1901–1990)

Satomi Ton 里見弴 (1888–1983)

Sawamura Sentarō 澤村専太郎 (died 1930)

Sawayanagi jiken 沢柳事件

Sawayanagi Masatarō 沢柳政太郎 (1865–1927)

Seishinkai 『精神界』

Seiyūtō 政友党

Sekiguchi Hiraku 関口開 (1842–1884)

Sekirekisō 惜櫟荘

sekishu no onjō 隻手の音声

sekku 節句

Senjuin 仙寿院

senka 選科

Senshin'an 洗心庵

Senshinnkai 洗心会

sesshin 接心、摂心

Sessū 雪舟 (1420–1506)

Setsumon Genshō (Michizu) 雪門玄松(道津) (1850–1915)

Shaku Sōen 釈宗演. See *Kōgaku Sōen*

Shiga Naoya 志賀直哉 (1883–1971)

shike 師家

Shikō 四高

Shikyō 『詩経』

Shima Yoshio 島芳夫 (1902–1985)

Shimada Chōrei (or Jūrei) 島田重礼 (1838–1898)

Shimada Ichirō 島田一郎

Shimaji Mokurai 島地黙雷 (1838–1911)

Shimazaki Tōson 島崎藤村 (1872–1943)

Shimizu Tōru 清水澄 (1868–1947)

Shimoda Jirō 下田次郎 (1872–1938)

Shimomura Hiroshi (Kainan) 下村宏(海南) (1875–1957)

Shimomura Toratarō 下村寅太郎 (1902–1995)

Shinagawa Kazue 品川主計 (1887–1986)

Shinano Tetsugakukai 信濃哲学会

Shinmura Izuru 新村出 (1876–1967)

Shinohara Sukeichi 篠原助市 (1876–1957)

Shinomiya Kaneyuki 四宮兼之 (1884–1945)

Shinran 親鸞 (1173–1262)

shinshinichinyo 心身一如

shintaisei 新体制

Shirakaba 白樺

Shisō 『思想』

shisō shingikai 思想審議会

Shitahodo Yūkichi 下程勇吉 (1904–)

shizoku 士族

Shōkasonzuku 松下村塾 (est. 1856)

Shōriki Matsutarō 正力松太郎 (1885–1969)

Shōsan Echō (Ikegami) 湘山慧澄(池上) (1856–1928). See Ikegami Shōsan

shosei 書生

Shōwa kenkyūkai 昭和研究会

Shōwa Tennō (Hirohito) 昭和天皇(裕仁) (1901–1989)

Shōwajuku 昭和塾

shu no ronri 種の論理

shūkyō 宗教

shūkyōteki sekaikan 宗教的世界観

Shunjū Sashiden 『春秋左氏伝』

Sōda Kiichirō 左右田喜一郎 (1881–1927)

sokuhi 即非

Sono Masazō 園正造 (1886–1969)

Soshi (Zhuangzi) 『荘子』

Sōya Heihachi 増谷平八

Suehiro Izutarō 末弘厳太郎 (1888–1951)

Suekawa Hiroshi 末川博 (1892–1977)

Suetsuna Joichi 末綱恕一 (1898–1970)

Sugawara no Michizane 菅原道真 (844–903)

Sugimori Korema 杉森此馬

Sūmitsuin 枢密院

Sunshin 寸心

Suzuki Beatrice Lane Erskine 鈴木ビアトリス・レーン・アースキン (1878–1939)

Suzuki Kantarō 鈴木貫太郎 (1867–1948)

Suzuki Kisaburō 鈴木喜三郎 (1867–1940)

Suzuki Shigetaka 鈴木成高 (1907–1988)

Suzuki Teitarō (Daisetz) 鈴木貞太郎(大拙) (1870–1966)

tacchū 塔頭

Tada Heigorō 多田平五郎

Tada Kanae 多田鼎

Taisei yokusankai 大政翼賛会

Taishō Tennō (Yoshihito) 大正天皇(嘉仁) (1879–1926)

Taiyō 『太陽』

Taizōin 退蔵院

Tajima Michiji 田島道治 (1885–1968)

Takagi Sōkichi 高木惣吉 (1893–1979)

Takagi Teiji 高木貞治 (1875–1960)

Takahashi Fumi 高橋文 (1901–1945)

Takahashi Kamekichi 高橋亀吉 (1894–1977)

Takahashi Keishi 高橋敬視 (1891–1948)

Takahashi Korekiyo 高橋是清 (1854–1936)

Takahashi Satomi 高橋里美 (1886–1964)

Takahashi Shichirō 高橋七郎

Takahashi Shūji 高橋周而 (1882–1955)

Takahashi Yoshitarō 高橋由太郎

Takakura Tokutarō 高倉徳太郎 (1885–1934)

Takakusu Junjirō 高楠順次郎 (1866–1945)

Takami Koremichi 高見之通

Takarayama Yoshio 宝山良雄 (1868–1926)

Takase Takejirō 高瀬武次郎 (1858–1950)

Takata Yasuma 高田保馬 (1883–1972)

Takayama Rinjirō (Chogū) 高山林二郎(樗牛) (1871–1902)

Takemi Tarō 武見太郎 (1904–1983)

Takeuchi Yoshitomo 竹内良知 (1919–1991)

Takigawa jiken 滝川事件 (also Kyōdai jiken)

Takigawa Yukitoki 滝川幸辰 (1891–1962)

Takizawa Katsumi 滝沢克巳 (1909–1984)

Tamura Tokuji 田村徳治 (1886–1958)

Tanabe (Ashino) Chiyo 田辺(蘆野)ちよ (–1951)

Tanabe Hajime 田辺元 (1885–1962)

Tanabe Juri 田辺寿利 (1894–1962)

Tanabe Ryūji 田部隆次 (1875–1957)

Tanaka Giichi 田中義一 (1864–1929)

Tanaka Kiichi (Ōdō) 田中喜一(王堂) (1867–1932)

Tanaka Onokichi 田中鉄吉

Tanikawa Tetsuzō 谷川徹三 (1895–1989)

Tanimoto Tomeri 谷本富 (1866–1946)

Tannishō 『歎異抄』

Taoka Sayoji (Reium) 田岡佐代治(嶺雲) (1870–1912)

tariki 他力

taza 打坐

Teikoku Daigaku 帝国大学

teishō 提唱

Tenchōsetsu 天長節

Teiyū Rinrikai 丁酉倫理会

Teiyū Rinrikai Rinrikōenshū 『丁酉倫理会倫理講演集』

Tekisui Giboku 滴水宜牧 (1822–1899)

Tenjuin 天授院

tennō 天皇

Tenryūji 天龍寺

Terada Torahiko 寺田寅彦 (1878–1935)

Tetsugaku issekiwa『哲学一夕話』

Tetsugaku Kenkyū『哲学研究』

Tetsugaku Zasshi『哲学雑誌』

Tetsugakukai 哲学会

Tobari Shin'ichirō (Chikufū) 戸張信一郎(竹風) (1873–1955)

Toda Kaiichi 戸田海市 (1872–1924)

Togawa Akizō (Shūkotsu) 戸川明三(秋骨) (1870–1939)

Tōgō Heihachirō 東郷平八郎 (1847–1934)

Tōgō Shigenori 東郷茂徳 (1882–1950)

Tōhata Seiichi 東畑精一 (1899–1983)

Tōjō Hideki 東条英機 (1884–1948)

Tōkeiji 東慶寺

Tokiwa Daijō 常盤大定 (1870–1945)

Tokuda Tagayasu 得田耕 (?–1932)

Tokuda Tei 得田貞 (?–1935)

Tokujū Zenmi 徳宗禅味 (1876–1930)

Tokunō Bun 得能文 (1866–1945)

Tokusan (Deshan) 徳山 (782–865)

Tokutomi Sohō 徳富蘇峰 (1863–1957)

Tōkyō Teikoku Daigaku 東京帝国大学

Tominaga Fukuji 富永福司

Tomoeda Takahiko 友枝高彦 (1876–1957)

Tomonaga Sanjūrō 朝永三十郎 (1871–1951)

Tomonaga Shin'ichirō 朝永振一郎 (1906–1979)

tomura 十村

Tosaka Jun 戸坂潤 (1900–1945)

Toyama Masakazu 外山正一 (1848–1900)

Toyoshima Yoshio 豊島与志雄 (1890–1950)

tsubo 坪

Tsuchida Kyōson 土田杏村 (1891–1934)

Tsuda (Joshi) Eigakujuku 津田(女子)英学塾

Tsuda jiken 津田事件

Tsuda Seifū 津田青楓 (1880–1978)

Tsuda Sōkichi 津田左右吉 (1873–1961)

Tsuda Umeko 津田梅子 (1864–1929)

tsukurareta mono kara tsukuru mono e 作られたものから作るものへ

Tsunashima Ryōsen 綱島梁川 (1873–1907)

Tsunetō Kyō 恒藤恭 (1888–1967)

Uchida Ginzō 内田銀蔵 (1872–1919)

Uchida Setsuzō 内田節三

Uchida Yūtarō 内田雄太郎 (ca. 1869–1945)

Uchimura Kanzō 内村鑑三 (1861–1930)

Ueda Bin (Ryūson) 上田敏(柳村) (1874–1916)

Ueda Hisashi 上田久 (1923–1993)

Ueda Juzō 植田寿蔵 (1886–1973)

Ueda Kaoru 上田薫 (1920–)

Ueda Misao 上田操 (1890–1964)

Ueda Seiji 上田整次

Ueda Yayoi. See Nishida Yayoi

Uehara Kikunosuke 上原菊之助

Uemura Etsuzō (Hōrin) 植村悦造(宝林) (–1922)

Uemura Masahisa 植村正久 (1857–1925)

Ueno Asako 上野麻子 (1898–1996)

Ueno Naoaki 上野直昭

Ugaki Kazushige 宇垣一成 (1866–1956)

Uno Enkū 宇野円空 (1885–1949)

Usui Jishō 臼井二尚 (1900–1991)

waka 和歌

Wakatsuki Reijirō 若槻礼次郎 (1866–1949)

Wakimoto Sokurō 脇本十九郎 (1883–1963)

wakon kansai 和魂漢才

wakon yōsai 和魂洋才

Watsuji Tetsurō 和辻哲郎 (1889–1960)

Yamaguchi kōtōgakkō 山口高等学校

Yamaguchi Yusuke 山口諭助 (1901–)

Yamakawa Kenjirō 山川健次郎 (1854–1931)

Yamamoto Annosuke 山本安之助

Yamamoto (Ozawa) Kiku 山本(小沢)起久

Yamamoto (Kaneda) Ryōkichi (Chōsui) 山本(金田)良吉(晁水) (1871–1942)

Yamamoto Sanehiko 山本実彦 (1885–1952)

Yamamoto Teijirō 山本悌二郎 (1870–1937)

Yamanouchi (Nakagawa) Tokuryū 山内(中川)得立 (1890–1982)

Yamaoka Tesshū 山岡鉄舟 (1836–1888)

Yamazaki Naozō 山崎直三 (died 1933)

Yanagi Muneyoshi 柳宗悦 (1889–1961)

Yanagida Kenjūrō 柳田謙十郎 (1893–1983)

Yasui Eiji 安井英二 (1890–)

Yasui Sokken 安井息軒 (1799–1876)

Yatsugi Kazuo 矢次一夫 (1899–1983)

Yokoyama Shōsei 横山正誠

Yomiuri Shinbun 『読売新聞』

Yonai Mitsumasa 米内光政 (1880–1948)

Yoneda Shōtarō 米田庄太郎 (1873–1945)

Yoshida Seichi 吉田静致 (1872–1945)

Yoshida Shōin 吉田松陰 (1830–1859)

Yoshikawa Hideo 吉川秀雄

Yoshimura Toratarō 吉村寅太郎

Yukawa Hideki 湯川秀樹 (1907–1981)

zazen 坐禅

Zen 禅

zen 善

Zenkan sakushin 『禅関策進』

zentaishugi 全体主義

zettaimu 絶対無

zettaimujun 絶対矛盾

zettaimujunteki jikodōitsu 絶対矛盾的自己同一

zettaiu 絶対有

Zuiun Gikan 瑞雲義寛 (1853–1935)

Bibliography

NISHIDA'S WRITINGS

Nishida's writings compiled in the nineteen volumes of *Nishida Kitarō Zenshū*『西田幾多郎全集』[Collected works of Nishida Kitarō] are cited as NKZ, followed by volume and page numbers.

Collected Works

Nishida Kitarō 西田幾多郎. *Nishida Kitarō Zenshū*『西田幾多郎全集』[Collected works of Nishida Kitarō]. 19 vols. Tokyo: Iwanami, 3d ed. 1978–1980; 4th ed. 1987–1989.
———. *Nikki* 日記 [Diary]. NKZ 17:1–710.
———. *Shokanshū* 書簡集 [Letters]. NKZ 18:1–631, 19:1–768.

Books

(Dates given are those of publication.)
Geijutsu to dōtoku『芸術と道徳』[Art and morality]. 1923. NKZ 3:237–545.
Gendai ni okeru risōshugi no tetsugaku『現代に於ける理想主義の哲学』[Contemporary idealistic philosophy]. Edited by Yamanouchi Tokuryū 山内得立. Tokyo: Kōdōkan, 1917. NKZ 14:3–82 (includes works by Yamanouchi).
Hataraku mono kara miru mono e『働くものから見るものへ』[From that which acts to that which sees]. 1927. NKZ 4:1–387.
Ippansha no jikakuteki taikei『一般者の自覚的体系』[The self-conscious structure of the universal]. 1929. NKZ 5:1–481.
Ishiki no mondai『意識の問題』[Problem of consciousness]. 1920. NKZ 3:1–236.
Jikaku ni okeru chokkan to hansei『自覚に於ける直観と反省』[Intuition and reflection in self-consciousness]. 1917. NKZ 2:3–350.

Mu no jikakuteki gentei『無の自覚的限定』[The self-conscious determination of nothingness]. 1932. NKZ 6:1–451.

Nihon bunka no mondai『日本文化の問題』[The problem of Japanese culture]. 1940. NKZ 12:275–383.

Shisaku to taiken『思索と体験』[Philosophical contemplation and life experience]. 1915. 2d ed. Tokyo: Iwanami, 1919. Expanded ed., 1922. NKZ 1:203–420.

Tetsugaku no konpon mondai『哲学の根本問題』[The fundamental problems of philosophy]. 1933. NKZ 7:1–200.

Tetsugaku no konpon mondai zokuhen『哲学の根本問題続編』[The fundamental problems of philosophy, part 2]. 1934. NKZ 7:201–453.

Tetsugaku ronbunshū daigo『哲学論文集第五』[Philosophical essays 5]. 1944. NKZ 10:339–564.

Tetsugaku ronbunshū daiichi『哲学論文集第一』[Philosophical essays 1]. 1935. NKZ 8:1–266.

Tetsugaku ronbunshū dainana『哲学論文集第七』[Philosophical essays 7]. 1946. NKZ 11:287–468.

Tetsugaku ronbunshū daini『哲学論文集第二』[Philosophical essays 2]. 1937. NKZ 8:267–589.

Tetsugaku ronbunshū dairoku『哲学論文集第六』[Philosophical essays 6]. 1945. NKZ 11:1–285.

Tetsugaku ronbunshū daisan『哲学論文集第三』[Philosophical essays 3]. 1939. NKZ 9:1–335.

Tetsugaku ronbunshū daiyon『哲学論文集第四』[Philosophical essays 4]. 1941. NKZ 10:1–337.

Zen no kenkyū『善の研究』[An inquiry into the good]. Tokyo: Kōdōkan, 1911. 2d ed., Iwanami, 1921. NKZ 1:1–200.

Zoku shisaku to taiken『続思索と体験』[Philosophical contemplation and life experience, part 2]. 1937. NKZ 12:1–195.

Philosophical Writings, Essays, Lectures, and Other Writings

(Dates given are those of composition, except when a publication date is specifically noted.)

"Aru kyōju no taishoku no ji"「ある教授の退職の辞」[A retirement speech of a professor]. December 1928. NKZ 12:168–71.

"Augusuchinusu no jikaku"「アウグスチヌスの自覚」[Self-consciousness according to Augustine]. July 1928. NKZ 12:112–18.

"Azumakagami"「吾妻鏡」[On the *Chronicle of Eastern Japan*]. 21 October 1940. NKZ 12:233–34.

"Basho"「場所」[*Topos*]. By May 1926. NKZ 4:208–89.

"Basho no jikogentei to shite no ishikisayō"「場所の自己限定としての意識作用」[The operation of consciousness as the self-determination of the *topos*]. By August 1930. NKZ 6:86–116.

"Bashoteki ronri to shūkyōteki sekaikan"「場所的論理と宗教的世界観」[The logic of topos and the religious worldview]. 4 February–14 April 1945. NKZ 11: 371–464.

"Benejikutosu Supinōza"「ベネジクトス・スピノーザ」[Benedict Spinoza]. *Hokushinkai Zasshi* 28 (published 25 November 1900): 36–39.

"Benshōhōteki ippansha to shite no sekai"「弁証法的一般者としての世界」[The world as the dialectical universal]. March–June 1934. NKZ 7:305–428.

"Beruguson no junsui jizoku"「ベルグソンの純粋持続」[Bergson's concept of pure duration]. 11–15 September 1911. NKZ 1:327–33.

"Beruguson no tetsugakuteki hōhōron"「ベルグソンの哲学的方法論」[Bergson's philosophical method]. 9–14 October 1910. NKZ 1:317–26.

"Beruguson, Shesutofu, sono ta—ujitsu zatsudan"「ベルグソン、シェストフ、その他雨日雑談」[Bergson, Shestov, and so forth—Conversations on a rainy day]. Interview, 26 February 1935. NKZ 19:862–875.

"Bibō"「備忘」[Notes to myself]. Around 1902. NKZ 13:477–91.

"Bi no setsumei"「美の説明」[An explanation of the beautiful]. Published 5 March 1900. NKZ 13:78–80.

"Borutsāno no jiden"「ボルツァーノの自伝」[An autobiography of Bolzano]. October 1922. NKZ 12:131–33.

"Butsuri no sekai"「物理の世界」[The world of physics]. September–November 1943. NKZ 11:5–59.

"Chi to ai"「知と愛」[Knowledge and love]. 3 August 1907. NKZ 1:196–200.

"Chishiki no kyakkansei ni tsuite"「知識の客観性について」[On the objectivity of knowledge]. July–October 1942. NKZ 10:343–476.

"Chokkakuteki chishiki"「直感的知識」[Intuitive knowledge]. By June 1929. NKZ 5:186–261.

"Coincidentia oppositorum to ai"「Coincidentia oppositorum と愛」[*Coincidentia oppositorum* and love]. Lecture, 13 October 1919. NKZ 14:295–300.

"Danro no soba kara (2)"「暖炉の側から」[From beside the fire place, part 2]. February 1931. NKZ 12:182–84.

"Dekaruto tetsugaku ni tsuite"「デカルト哲学について」[On Descartes's philosophy]. April 1944. NKZ 11:147–88.

"Dentō"「伝統」[The tradition]. By September 1943. NKZ 11:189–92.

"Dentōshugi ni tsuite"「伝統主義に就て」[On traditionalism]. Lecture, 25 November 1934. NKZ 14:371–85. (An article on T. S. Eliot and the idea of "tradition.").

"Dokusho"「読書」[On reading books]. October 1938. NKZ 12:228–32.

"Eichiteki sekai"「叡知的世界」[The intelligible world]. August–September 1928. NKZ 5:123–85.

"Eien no ima no jikogentei"「永遠の今の自己限定」[The self-determination of the eternal now]. March–May 1931. NKZ 6. 181–232.

"Eikoku rinrigakushi"「英国倫理学史」[A history of moral philosophy in Britain]. 1895–1896. NKZ 16:3–86.

"Fuseimonkai Uyokusei sōkō"「不成文会有翼生草稿」[Writings of "Pegasus" for the Fuseimonkai]. NKZ 16:637–50.

"Gakumonteki hōhō"「学問的方法」[On the scholarly method]. Public talk, 14 October 1937. NKZ 12:385–94.

"Gasonkai Uyoku bunkō"「我尊会有翼文稿」[Writings of "Pegasus" for the Gasonkai]. May 1889–July 1890. NKZ 16:573–636.

"Gasonkaiin shokun o hyōsu"「我尊会諸君を評す」[Describing the members of the Gasonkai]. NKZ 16:597–99.

"Gendai ni okeru risōshugi no tetsugaku"「現代に於ける理想主義の哲学」[Contemporary idealistic philosophy]. Lecture, autumn 1916. NKZ 14:5–82.

"Gendai no tetsugaku"「現代の哲学」[Contemporary philosophy]. By January 1916. NKZ 1:334–68.

"Genjitsu no sekai no ronriteki kōzō"「現実の世界の論理的構造」[The logical structure of the actual world]. Lectures, November–December1933. NKZ 14:421–509.

"Genjitsu no sekai no ronriteki kōzō"「現実の世界の論理的構造」[The logical structure of the actual world]. Lectures, 7–9 January 1935. NKZ 14:214–64.

"Genjitsu no sekai no ronriteki kōzō"「現実の世界の論理的構造」[The logical structure of the actual world]. Before January 1934. NKZ 7:217–304.

"Genkon no shūkyō ni tsuite"「現今の宗教について」[On today's religions]. 1 November 1901. NKZ 13:81–84.

"Gēte no haikei"「ゲーテの背景」[The background of Goethe's poetry]. November–December 1931. NKZ 12:138–49.

"Girisha tetsugaku ni oite no arumono"「ギリシャ哲学においての『有るもの』」["Being" according to Greek philosophy]. March 1928. NKZ 12:102–111.

"Goshinkō sōan, Rekishi tetsugaku ni tsuite"「御進講草案、歴史哲学ニツイテ」[A draft of the New Year Lecture to the emperor: On the philosophy of history]. December 1940. NKZ 12:267–72.

"Gurīnshi rinri tetsugaku no taii"「グリーン氏倫理哲学の大意」[The gist of Mr. Green's moral philosophy]. October–December 1894. NKZ 13:21–41.

"Gūsei"「偶成」[An incidental poem]. Late 1890. NKZ 16:650.

"Gutoku Shinran"「愚禿親鸞」[Shinran the fool]. Circa April 1911. NKZ 1:407–409.

"Haishōron"「廃娼論」[Argument for the abolition of prostitution]. 1889–1890. NKZ 16:624–26.

"Han o arata ni suru ni atatte"「版を新にするに当つて」[Preface to *Zen no kenkyū*; On the occasion of resetting the type]. 9 October 1936. NKZ 1:6–7.

"Hataraku mono"「働くもの」[That which acts]. October 1925. NKZ 4:175–207.

"Hōjō sensei ni hajimete oshie o uketa koro"「北條先生に始めて教を受けた頃」 [Around the time when I first received instruction from Professor Hōjō]. July 1929. NKZ 12:257–60.

"Honkai kaiin shokun yo"「本会々員諸君ヨ!」[To the dear members of the Gasonkai]. 1889–1890. NKZ 16:595–96.

"Hori Koretaka-kun no 'Shikō Sansanjuku ni tsuite' o yomite"「堀維孝君の『四高三々塾について』を読みて」[Having read Mr. Hori Koretaka's "Sansanjuku of the Fourth Higher School"]. 27 November 1936. NKZ 13:124–25.

"Hyōgen sayō"「表現作用」[The expressive operation]. January 1925. NKZ 4:135–72.

"Hyōgenteki jiko no jikogentei"「表現的自己の自己限定」[The self-determination of the expressive self]. By June 1930. NKZ 6:13–85.

"Hyūmu izen no tetsugaku no hattatsu"「ヒューム以前の哲学の発達」[The development of philosophy prior to Hume]. Spring 1894. NKZ 13:42–46.

"Hyūmu no ingahō"「ヒュームの因果法」[On Hume's theory of causation]. Spring 1894. NKZ 13:47–54.

"Hyūmu no ingahōhihan"「ヒュームの因果法批判」[Critique of Hume's theory of causation]. Spring 1894. NKZ 13:55–59.

"Indokoku"「印度国」[India]. 1889–1890. NKZ 16:588–90.

"Inoue Sensei"「井上先生」[Professor Inoue]. December 1931. NKZ 13:184.

"Ippansha no jikogentei"「一般者の自己限定」[The self-determination of the universal]. May–June 1929. NKZ 5:353–417.

"Ippansha no jikogentei to jikaku"「一般者の自己限定と自覚」[The self-determination of the universal and self-consciousness]. October 1929. Retitled "Sōsetsu," part 1 of「総説」[General discussion]. NKZ 5:419–30.

"Ishi"「意志」[The will]. By August 1918. NKZ 3:83–98.

"Ishi jitsugen no basho"「意志実現の場所」[The place where the will is actualized]. By March 1919. NKZ 3:141–56.

"Ishi no naiyō"「意志の内容」[The volitional contents]. By April 1919. NKZ 3:157–98.

"Ishiki no meian ni tsuite"「意識の明暗に就いて」[On the light and dark sides of consciousness]. By August 1919. NKZ 3:210–23.

"Ishiki to wa nani o imisuru ka"「意識とは何を意味するか」[What is "consciousness"?]. By December 1917. NKZ 3:5–27.

"Iwayuru ninshiki taishōkai no ronriteki kōzō"「所謂認識対象界の論理的構造」[Logical structure of the so-called world of cognitive objects]. February 1928. NKZ 5:5–57.

"Jean Jacques Rousseau." 1889–1890. NKZ 16:585–87.

"Jiai to taai oyobi benshōhō"「自愛と他愛及び弁証法」[Self-love, other-love, and dialectics]. October–November 1931. NKZ 6:260–99.

"Jikaku ni tsuite"「自覚について」[On self-consciousness]. February–March 1943. NKZ 10:477–564.

"Jikakushugi"「自覚主義」[Philosophy of self-awakening]. November 1906. NKZ 13:90–95.

"Jikakuteki gentei kara mita ippansha no gentei"「自覚的限定から見た一般者の限定」[The determination of the universal seen as the determination of self-consciousness]. November–December 1929. Retitled "Sōsetsu"「総説」[General discussion]. NKZ 5:430–64.

"Jikakuteki ippansha ni oite aru mono oyobi sore to sono haigo ni aru mono to no kankei"「自覚的一般者に於てあるもの及それとその背後にあるものとの関係」[That which exists in the self-conscious universal, and its relationship to what is behind it]. January–March 1929. NKZ 5:262–352.

"Jikanteki naru mono oyobi hi-jikanteki naru mono"「時間的なるもの及び非時間的なるもの」[That which is temporal and that which is atemporal]. Before September 1931. NKZ 6:233–59.

"Jikojishin o miru mono no oite aru basho to ishiki no basho"「自己自身を見るものの於てある場所と意識の場所」[The *topos* where that which sees itself exists and the *topos* of consciousness]. By July 1928. NKZ 5:98–122.

"Jinshin no giwaku"「人心の疑惑」[On the doubt in our heart]. May 1903. NKZ 13:85–89.

"Jisen shiikashū"「自撰詩歌集」[Self-selected poems in Chinese and Japanese]. Up to 1935. NKZ 12:435–46.

"Jishūryō shakan jidai no omoide"「時習寮舎監時代の思出」[Memories of the times when I was a dormitory master at the Dorm Jishū]. March 1931. NKZ 19:780–81.

"Jissen to taishō ninshiki-rekishiteki sekai ni oite no ninshiki no tachiba"「実践と対象認識—歴史的世界に於ての認識の立場」[Praxis and the recognition of the object—The epistemological standpoint in the historical world]. February 1937. NKZ 8:395–499.

"Jissentetsugaku joron"「実践哲学序論」[Prolegomena to practical philosophy]. March–July 1940. NKZ 10:7–123.

"Jitsuzai no kontei to shite no jinkaku gainen"「実在の根抵としての人格概念」[The concept of person as the foundation of reality]. Lectures, 3–5 September 1932. NKZ 14:133–74.

"Jiyū ishi"「自由意志」[The free will]. Circa February 1932. NKZ 6:300–40.

"Jo"「序」[Preface] and "Batsu"「跋」[Postscript] to Nozaki Hiroyoshi 野崎広義 *Zange to shite no tetsugaku*『懺悔としての哲学』[Philosophy as repentance]. Preface, April 1920; Postscript, July 1917. NKZ 13:201–203.

"Jo"「序」[Preface] to Okamoto Haruhiko 岡本春彦 *Sheringu no shōchō shisō*『シェリングの象徴思想』[The symbolic thought of Schelling]. October 1918. NKZ 13:197–200.

"Jo, Rikkeruto, cho, Yamanouchi Tokuryū, yaku, *Ninshiki no taishō*"「序、リッケルト著、山内得立訳、『認識の対象』」[Preface to a translation of Rickert's *Object of Cognition* by Yamanouchi Tokuryū]. May 1916. NKZ 13:188–90.

"Junsui keiken sōgo no kankei oyobi renraku ni tsuite"「純粋経験相互の関係及連絡に付いて」[The mutual relationships and connections of pure experiences]. Talk, 19 December 1909; revised into article, January 1910. NKZ 13:96–105.

"Jutsugoteki ronrishugi"「述語的論理」[The logic of the predicate]. February–March 1928. NKZ 5:58–92.

"Kamakura zōei"「鎌倉雑詠」[Poems composed in Kamakura]. December 1928–March 1929. NKZ 12:172–74.

"Kanjō"「感情」[Emotions]. By June 1918. NKZ 3:51–77.

"Kankaku"「感覚」[Sensation]. May 1918. NKZ 3:28–50.

"Kankei ni tsuite"「関係に就いて」[On relationships]. May 1919. NKZ 3:199–209.

"Kanto rinrigaku"「韓図倫理学」[Kant's ethics]. Spring 1892. NKZ 13:3–20.

"Kēberu sensei no tsuikai"「ケーベル先生の追懐」[Reminiscing Professor Koeber]. June 1923. NKZ 13:176–77.

"Keijijōgaku joron"「形而上学序論」[Prolegomena to metaphysics]. January 1933. NKZ 7:5–84.

"Keijijōgakuteki tachiba kara mita tōzai kodai no bunka keitai"「形而上学的立場から見た東西古代の文化形態」[The forms of ancient cultures, East and West, seen from a metaphysical perspective]. August 1934. NKZ 7:429–53.

"Keiken kagaku"「経験科学」[Experiential science]. April–June 1939. NKZ 9:147–222.

"Keiken naiyō no shushunaru renzoku"「経験内容の種々なる連続」[Various connections of experiential contents]. By February 1919. NKZ 3:99–140.

"Kimura Hisashi-kun no omoide"「木村栄君の思出」[Memories of Mr. Kimura Hisashi]. December 1943. NKZ 12:252–56.

"Kōen no junsui ishiki"「コーヘンの純粋意識」[Pure consciousness according to Cohen]. By August 1916. NKZ 1:369–74.

"Kōi no sekai"「行為の世界」[The world of action]. Lectures, 1–5 January 1934. NKZ 14:175–213.

"Kōiteki chokkan"「行為的直観」[Action-intuition]. June 1937. NKZ 8:541–71.

"Kōiteki chokkan no tachiba"「行為的直観の立場」[The standpoint of action-intuition]. June–July 1935. NKZ 8:107–219.

"*Koizumi Yakumo-den*, Jo"「『小泉八雲伝』序」[Preface to *A biography of Koizumi Yakumo*]. March 1914. NKZ 1:410–13.

"Kokka riyū no mondai"「国家理由の問題」[The problem of *raison d'état*]. April–June 1941. NKZ 10:265–337.

"*Kokubungakushi kōwa* no jo"「『国文学史講話』の序」[Preface to *A narrative history of Japanese literature*]. November 1907. NKZ 1:414–20.

"Kokutai"「国体」[The Japanese political system]. February 1944. NKZ 12:392–416.

"Koniku sekushonsu"「コニク・セクションス」[Conic sections]. March 1939. NKZ 12:207–209.

"Kotai gainen"「個体概念」[The concept of the individual]. Circa 1919. NKZ 3:224–31.

"Kūkan"「空間」[Space]. July–August 1944. NKZ 11:193–236.

"The Last Minstrel" (translation into Japanese and Chinese of a poem by Walter
    Scott). 1889–1890. NKZ 16:635–36.

"Meiji nijūshigonen goro no Tōkyō Bunka Daigaku senka"「明治二十四五年頃の
    東京文科大学選科」[The limited status program at the College of
    Humanities at the Imperial University around 1891–1892]. October 1942.
    NKZ 12:241–44.

"Meiji no hajime goro, Kanazawa no furuhon"「明治の始頃、金沢の古本」
    [Antique books in Kanazawa in the early Meiji period]. July 1939. NKZ 12:
    210–11.

"Mignon no uta hitotsu"「Mignon の歌一つ」[A song of Mignon]. August 1928.
    NKZ 12:175.

"Miyake Shinken sensei"「三宅真軒先生」[Professor Miyake Shinken]. January
    1940. NKZ 12:212–15.

"Mukō shōsa o omou"「向少佐を憶ふ」[In memory of Lieutenant Commander
    Mukō]. May 1904. NKZ 13:161–65.

"Naibu chikaku ni tsuite"「内部知識について」[On the inner perception].
    Published March–October 1924. NKZ 4:76–134.

"Nihon bunka no mondai"「日本文化の問題」[The problem of Japanese culture].
    Lectures, April–May 1938. NKZ 14:389–417.

"Ningenteki sonzai"「人間的存在」[Human existence]. November 1937–January
    1938. NKZ 9:9–68.

"Ninshikiron ni okeru junronriha no shuchō ni tsuite"「認識論に於ける純論理派
    の主張に就て」[On the claims of a purely logical theory of cognition].
    By August 1911. NKZ 1:209–34.

"Ninshikironsha to shite no Anri Poankare"「認識論者としてのアンリ・ポアン
    カレ」[Henri Poincare as an epistemologist]. September 1912. NKZ 1:
    397–401.

"Nozaki Hiroyoshi-shi chōshi"「野崎広義氏弔詞」[In memory of Mr. Nozaki
    Hiroyoshi]. 20 June 1917. NKZ 13:171–72.

"Ōshima-kun to watakushi"「大島君と私」[Mr. Ōshima and I]. Interview, 14
    August 1937. NKZ 19:879–80.

"Poiesis to praksis"「ポイエシスとプラクシス」[Making and doing, or Production
    and action]. August–October 1940. NKZ 10:124–76.

"Raipunittsu no hontaironteki shōmei"「ライプニッツの本体論的証明」[Leibniz's
    "Quod ens perfectissimum existit"]. December 1917. NKZ 3:232–36.

"Rekishiteki keiseisayō to shite no geijutsuteki sōsaku"「歴史的形成作用としての
    芸術的創作」[Artistic creation as the history-forming operation]. April–
    June 1938. NKZ 10:177–264.

"Rekishiteki sekai ni oite no kobutsu no tachiba"「歴史的世界に於ての個物の立
    場」[The position of the individual in the historical world]. December
    1940–February 1941. NKZ 9:69–146.

"Rekishiteki shintai"「歴史的身体」[The historical body]. Lectures, 25–26 September 1937. NKZ 14:265–91.

"Rinrigaku sōan (1)"「倫理学草案」[Lecture notes on ethics, draft 1]. January 1905–August 1905. NKZ 16:149–203. "Rinrigaku sōan (2)"「倫理学草案」[Lecture notes on ethics, draft 2]. August 1905–March 1906. NKZ 16:204–266.

"Ronri no rikai to sūri no rikai"「論理の理解と数理の理解」[Logical understanding and mathematical understanding]. July 1912. NKZ 1:250–67.

"Ronri to seimei"「論理と生命」[Logic and life]. June–July 1936. NKZ 8:273–394.

"Ronri to sūri"「論理と数理」[Logic and mathematical logic]. December 1943–January 1944. NKZ 11:60–113.

"Rottse no keijijōgaku"「ロッツェの形而上学」[Lotze's metaphysics]. December 1916–January 1917. NKZ 1:375–96.

"Sanpo"「散歩」[A walk]. 1889–1890. NKZ 16:591–94.

"Sansanjuku yonjisshūnen kinen ni atarite"「三々塾四十周年記念に当りて」[At the occasion of the fortieth anniversary of Sansanjuku]. September 1939. NKZ 13:126–27.

"Sei no tetsugaku ni tsuite"「生の哲学について」[On the philosophy of life]. Circa September 1932. NKZ 6:428–51.

"Sei to jitsuzon to ronri"「生と実存と論理」[Life, existence, and logic]. Lectures, January–February 1932. NKZ 14:343–67.

"Seimei"「生命」[Life]. Unfinished; September–December 1944. NKZ 11:289–370.

"Sekai no jikodōitsu to renzoku"「世界の自己同一と連続」[The self-identity of the world and its continuity]. November–December 1934. NKZ 8:7–106.

"Sekai shinchitsujo no genri"「世界新秩序の原理」[The principle for the new world order]. "Tetsugaku ronbunshū daiyon hoi, furoku 3"「哲学論文集第四補遺附録三」[Appendix three, supplement to the *Fourth Philosophical Essays*]. May–June 1943. NKZ 12:426–34.

"Sentenchishiki no umu o ronzu"「先天知識の有無を論ず」[On the existence or nonexistence of a priori knowledge]. Published February–June 1897. NKZ 13:60–71.

"Shikō no omoide"「四高の思出」[Memories of the Fourth Higher School]. May 1927. NKZ 12:164–67.

"Shinrigaku kōgi"「心理学講義」[Lectures on psychology]. 1905. NKZ 16:87–148.

"Shinzenbi no gōitsuten"「真善美の合一点」[The unity of the true, the good, and the beautiful]. Published September 1921. NKZ 3:350–91.

"Shirumono"「知るもの」[That which knows]. February–June 1927. NKZ 4:324–87.

"Shizen kagaku to rekishigaku"「自然科学と歴史学」[Natural sciences and the study of history]. Lecture, 6 April; published August 1913. NKZ 1:268–98.

"Shōchō no shin'igi"「象徴の真意義」[The real significance of symbols]. February 1918. NKZ 3:78–82.

"Shoei Sōhon *Jiga* go"「書影宋本『爾雅』後」[A note inscribed on the personal copy of the Song edition of *Erya*]. January 1933. NKZ 12:185.

"Shu no seisei hatten no mondai"「種の生成発展の問題」[The problem of generation and development of species]. April–May 1937. NKZ 8:500–40.

"Shūkyō no tachiba"「宗教の立場」[The standpoint of religion]. Lecture, December 1919. NKZ 14:303–309.

"Shūkyōgaku"「宗教学」[Lecture notes on the study of religion]. September 1913–March 1914. NKZ 15:221–381.

"Sōda-hakushi ni kotau"「左右田博士に答ふ」[My response to Dr. Sōda]. By March 1927. NKZ 4:290–323.

"Sōsetsu"「総説」[General discussion]. September–November 1929. NKZ 5:419–81.

"Sōzō"「創造」[Creativity]. Phonogram of recorded dialogue with Yamamoto Ryōkichi. 7 March 1940. *Geppō* 月報 [Monthly supplement]. August 1979. NKZ 11:3–8.

"Spinoza's conception of God." Term paper in English. Circa 1892. NKZ 16:653–57.

"Sūgaku no tetsugakuteki kisozuke"「数学の哲学的基礎附け」[Giving a philosophical foundation for mathematics]. 23 December 1944–25 January 1945. NKZ 11:237–84.

"Sūgakusha Āberu"「数学者アーベル」[Mathematician Abel]. Published 15–16 October 1933. NKZ 12:134–37.

"Takagi hakushi no *Kinsei sūgakushidan*"「高木博士の『近世数学史談』」[Dr. Takagi's *Discussion on the history of modern mathematics*]. July 1941. NKZ 12:235–40.

"Takahashi (Satomi) Bungakushi no seccho Zen no kenkyū ni taisuru hihyō ni kotau"「高橋（里見）文学士の拙著『善の研究』に対する批評に答ふ」[My response to Takahashi Satomi's criticism of my book, *An inquiry into the good*]. August 1912. NKZ 1:299–316.

"Tetsugaku to gojin nichijō no seikatsu tono kankei"「哲学と吾人日常の生活との関係」[The relationship between philosophy and our everyday life]. Talk, 16 October 1899. Printed in Kokushinkai Zasshi『北辰会雑誌』, 25 December 1899, 95–100.

"Tōhingi"「答賓戯」[A playful response to an inquirer]. 1889–1890. NKZ 16:607–609.

"Ueda Yayoi no omoide no ki"「上田弥生の思出の記」[In memory of my daughter, Ueda Yayoi]. 15 February 1945. NKZ 12:261–64.

"Wakakarishi hi no Tōho"「若かりし日の東圃」[Tōho of younger days]. 4 January 1940. NKZ 12:221–27.

"Watakushi no handanteki ippansha to iu mono"「私の判断的一般者というもの」[What I call the judging universal]. March 1929. NKZ 14:329–64.

"Watakushi no ronri ni tsuite"「私の論理について」[Concerning my logic]. NKZ 12:265–66.

"Watakushi no zettaimu no jikakuteki gentei to iu mono"「私の絶対無の自覚的限定というもの」[What I call "The self-conscious determination of absolute nothingness"]. December 1930. NKZ 6:117–80.

"Watakushi to nanji"「私と汝」[I and thou]. June 1932. NKZ 6:341–427.

"Watakushi to sekai"「私と世界」[I and the world]. Circa April–May 1933. NKZ 7: 85–172.

"Yamamoto Annosuke-kun no 'Shukō to rise' to iu ronbun o yomite shokan o nobu"「山本安之助君の『宗教と理性』と云う論文を読みて所感を述ぶ」[My reaction to Mr. Yamamoto Annosuke's "Religion and reason"]. May 1898. NKZ 13:72–77.

"Yamamoto Chōsui-kun no omoide"「山本晃水君の思出」[Memories of Mr. Yamamoto Chōsui]. December 1942. NKZ 12:245–51.

"Yamamoto Ryōkichi-shi chōshi"「山本良吉氏弔詞」[Words of condolence at the death of Mr. Yamamoto Ryōkichi]. 18 July 1942. NKZ 13:175.

"Yo ga *saiaisuru* shokun yo"「余ガ最愛スル諸君ヨ」[To my *dearest* friends!]. 1889–1890. NKZ 16:581–84.

"Yō Hikkan ki"「洋筆管記」[A note on Yō Hikkan]. 1889–1890. NKZ 16:620–21.

"Yo no otōto, Nishida Hyōjirō o omou"「余の弟西田憑次郎を憶ふ」[In memory of my younger brother, Nishida Hyōjirō]. November 1904. NKZ 13:166–70.

"Yoteichōwa o tebiki to shite shūkyō-tetsugaku e"「予定調和を手引きとして宗教哲学へ」[Toward a philosophy of religion with the Leibnizian notion of the preestablished harmony as guide]. February–March 1944. NKZ 11: 114–46.

"Yukeru Beruguson"「逝けるベルグソン」[Bergson dead]. Interview, *Asahi Shinbun*『朝日新聞』[Asahi Newspaper], 7 January 1941.

"Zakkan"「雑感」[Miscellaneous thoughts]. Circa December 1915. NKZ 19:771–77.

"Zetsudai"「舌代」[A congratulatory message]. 3 November 1942. NKZ 13:155.

"Zettaimujunteki jikodōitsu"「絶対矛盾的自己同一」[Absolutely contradictory self-identity]. 31 October 1938–14 January 1939. NKZ 9:147–222.

"Zuikan"「随感」[Random recollections]. Interview, 14 November 1935. NKZ 19: 785–86.

Nishida's Works in Translation

Abe, Masao, and Christopher Ives, trans. *An Inquiry into the Good*. New Haven: Yale University Press, 1990.

Andolfato, Renato, trans. *L'Io e il Tu*. Padova: Unipress, 1996.

Arisaka, Yōko, trans. "The Principle of the New World Order." *Monumenta Nipponica* 51, 1 (1996): 100–105.

Dilworth, David, trans. *Fundamental Problems of Philosophy: The World of Action and the Dialectical World*. Tokyo: Sophia University, 1970.

Dilworth, David, and Valdo Viglielmo, trans. *Art and Morality*. Honolulu: University Press of Hawai'i, 1973.

Hirota, Dennis, trans. "Gutoku Shinran." *Eastern Buddhist* 28, no. 2 (1995): 242–44.

Odin, Steve, trans. "An Explanation of Beauty." *Monumenta Nipponica* 42, no. 2 (1987): 215–17.

Schinzinger, Robert, trans. *Intelligibility and the Philosophy of Nothingness*. Tokyo: Maruzen, 1958; reprint, Westport, Conn.: Greenwood Press, 1973.

Shore, Jeff, and Nagasawa Fusako, trans. "On the Doubt Our Heart." *Eastern Buddhist* 17, no. 2 (1984): 7–11.

Takahashi, Fumi, trans. "Die Einheit des Wahren, des Schönen und des Guten." *Sendai Kokusai Bunka Kyōkaishi* [Journal of the Sendai International Cultural Society], 1940: 116–66.

———. "Die morgenländischen und abendländischen Kulturformen in alter Zeit vom metaphysischen Standpunkte ausgesehen." *Abhandlungen der Preussischen Akademie der Wissenschaft* 19 (1939), 1–19. Berlin: Verlag der Akademie der Wissenschaften, in Kommission bei Walter de Gruyter, 1940.

Viglielmo, Valdo, trans. *A Study of Good*. Tokyo: Japanese Government Printing Bureau, 1960.

Viglielmo, Valdo, Takeuchi Yoshinori, and Joseph O'Leary, trans. *Intuition and Reflection in Self-Consciousness*. Albany, New York: State University of New York Press, 1987.

Yokoyama, Wayne. "Nishida Kitarō in Translation, Primary Sources in Western Languages." *Eastern Buddhist* 28, 2 (Autumn 1995): 297–302.

Yusa, Michiko, trans. "On Lafcadio Hearn." *Monumenta Nipponica* 51, no. 3 (1996): 313–16.

———. "The Logic of *Topos* and the Religious Worldview." *Eastern Buddhist* 19, no. 2 (1986): 1–29; 20, no. 1 (1987): 81–119.

SECONDARY SOURCES

1. For essays compiled in books, full bibliographical information appears under the name of the compiler or editor.

2. It is common practice in Japan for a publisher or school to publish its own books. Therefore, the author or school and the publisher may be identical.

3. *Geppō*, meaning "monthly supplement," or *Furoku*, meaning "supplement," signal a uniquely Japanese publishing practice. After the publication of an author's collected works, additional useful information may be provided by others and printed as a leaflet for insertion in one of the volumes of the *Collected Works*.

4. For a list of abbreviations refer to the "Conventions and Abbreviations" section.

5. Articles or essays in "Collected works" and anthologies are cited by volume and page number(s).

Abe Yoshishige 安倍能成. *Iwanami Shigeo-den* 『岩波茂雄伝』 [A biography of Iwanami Shigeo]. Tokyo: Iwanami Shoten, 1957.

Aihara Shinsaku 相原信作. "Sensei ni yotte yoken serareta nihonminzoku no unmei" 「先生によって予見せられた日本民族の運命」[The fate of the Japanese people foreseen by the professor]. In *Nishida Sunshin sensei hen'ei*『西田寸心先生片影』[Glimpses of Professor Nishida Sunshin], edited by Kōyama Iwao 高山岩男 and Shimatani Toshizō 島谷俊三, 40–47. Nagoya: Reimei Shobō, 1949.

———. "Shitei"「師弟」[Master and disciples]. In Shimomura, ed., NKD 142–46.

Akagi Suruki 赤木須留喜. *Konoe shintaisei to Taiseiyokusankai*『近衞新体制と大政翼賛会』[Konoe's new order and the Taiseiyokusan party]. Tokyo: Iwanami Shoten, 1984.

Akizuki Ryōmin 秋月龍眠. *Jinrui no kyōshi, Suzuki Daisetz*『人類の教師、鈴木大拙』[D. T. Suzuki as the teacher of humanity]. Tokyo: San'itsu Shobō, 1978.

Allen, Gay Wilson. *William James: A Biography*. New York: Viking Press, 1967.

Amano Teiyū 天野貞祐. *Dōri no kankaku*『道理の感覚』[The sense of reason]. *Amano Teiyū Zenshū*『天野貞祐全集』(ATZ) [Collected works of Amano Teiyū]. Vol. 1. Tokyo: Kurita Shuppankai, 1971.

———. "Kenkyūteki, kaihōteki"「研究的、開放的」[Scholarly and open]. In *Kyōto daigaku bungakubu gojūnenshi*『京都大学文学部五十年史』[Fifty years of the Faculty of Letters at Kyoto University], edited by Kyoto Daigaku Bungakubu 京都大学文学部, 448–50. Kyoto: University of Kyoto, 1956.

———. "Kyōdai Bungakubu sanjisshūnen kansō, Meiji kara Taishō e"「京大文学部三十周年感想、明治から大正へ」[The thirty years of the Faculty of Letters at Kyoto University, from Meiji to Taishō]. ATZ 1:106–08.

———. "Nishida Sensei kajitsu seidan"「西田先生夏日清談」[A conversation on a summer day with Professor Nishida]. In *Shōwa Bungaku Zenshū*『昭和文学全集』[Collection of Showa literature] 10:182–84. Tokyo: Kadokawa Shoten, 1953.

———. "Tokuiku ni tsuite"「徳育について」[On moral education]. ATZ 1:155–70.

Anesaki Masaharu 姉崎正治. "Kēberu sensei no tsuikai"「ケーベル先生の追懐」*Tetsugaku Zasshi*『哲学雑誌』438 (August 1923): 68–73.

Arisaka, Yōko. "The Nishida Enigma." *Monumenta Nipponica* 51. 1 (1996): 81–99.

Aristotle. *Aristotle's Metaphysics*. Translated by Richard Hope. New York: Columbia University Press, 1952.

———. *Nicomachean Ethics*. Translated by H. Rackham. Cambridge: Harvard University Press, 1999.

Asahi Shinbunsha 朝日新聞社, ed. *Gendai Nihon Asahi jinbutsu jiten*『「現代日本」朝日人物事典』[Asahi "who is who" in modern Japan]. Tokyo: Asahi Shinbunsha, 1990.

Asami Hiroshi 浅見洋. "Fukkoku sanpen—Yomiuri Shinbun keisai no Nishida Kitarō danwa kiji"「復刻三編―読売新聞掲載の西田幾多郎談話記事」[Three newspaper interviews given by Nishida Kitarō to the Yomiuri Newspaper]. In *Ishikawa Kōtō Senmon Gakkō kiyō*『石川高等専門学校紀要』

[Journal of Ishikawa Higher Technical School], 127–142. Kanazawa: Ishikawa Kōtō Senmon Gakkō, 1997.

———. *Mikan no josei-tetsugakusha, Takahashi Fumi* 『未完の女性哲学者、高橋文』 [A woman-philosopher who died too young—Takahashi Fumi]. Kanazawa: Hokkoku Shinbunsha, 1997.

———. *Mikan no josei-tetsugakusha, Takahashi Fumi, shiryōshū* 『未完の女性哲学者、高橋文、資料集』 [Sources, A woman-philosopher who died too young—Takahashi Fumi]. Kanazawa: Hokkoku Shinbunsha, 1997.

———. *Nishida Kitarō to Kirisutokyō no taiwa* 『西田幾多郎とキリスト教の対話』 [Dialogue between Nishida Kitarō and Christianity]. Tokyo: Chōbunsha, 2000.

———. *Takahashi Fumi no "Furaiburuku tsūshin"* 『高橋文の「フライブルク通信」』 ["Letters from Freiburg" by Takahashi Fumi]. Kanazawa: Hokkoku Shinbunsha, 1995.

Bungeishunjū 文芸春秋. "Nishida Kitarō o kakomu zadankai" 「西田幾多郎を囲む座談会」 *Bungeishunjū* (March 1939). Compiled in *Bungeishunjū ni miru Shōwashi* 『文芸春秋に見る昭和史』 [The Shōwa period seen through the *Bungeishunjū*] 1:457–74. Tokyo: Bungeishunjū, 1988.

Daiyon kōtōchūgakkō 第四高等中学校. *Daiyon kōtō chūgakkō ichiran* 『第四高等中学校一覧』 [Catalog of the Fourth Higher Middle School 1887–1894; Fourth Higher School 1897–1909]. Kanazawa: Fourth Higher Middle School, 1897–1909.

de Bary, W. T., W. Chan, and B. Watson. eds. *Sources of Chinese Tradition*. New York: Columbia University Press, 1960.

Dilworth, David. *Last Writings: Nothingness and the Religious Worldview*. Honolulu: University of Hawai'i Press, 1987.

Eastern Buddhist Society. Editorial. *Eastern Buddhist* 1 (May 1921): 80–85.

Einstein, Albert. "How I Created the Theory of Relativity." Translated into English by Y. Ono. *Physics Today* 35 (August 1982): 45–47.

Fichte, Johann Gottlieb. "Erste Einleitung in die Wissenschaftslehre" (1797). In I. H. Fichte, ed., *Fichtes sämmtliche Werke*. Vol. 1. Berlin: Veit, 1845–1846. Reprint, *Fichtes Werke*. Berlin: de Gruyter, 1971.

Fujioka Kōji 藤岡幸二. "Ani no omoide" 「兄の思出」 [Memories of my older brother]. *Kokugo to Kokubungaku* 『国語と国文学』 17, no. 4 (1940): 393–95.

Fujioka Sakutarō 藤岡作太郎. *Kokubungakushi kōwa* 『国文学史講話』 [A narrative history of Japanese literature]. Tokyo: Iwanami Shoten, 1922. Originally published by Kaiseikan (Tokyo) in 1908.

———. "Shūenki" 「終焉記」 [A record of the final days of my child]. In Ishikawa Kindai Bungakukan Kaikan Nijūgoshūnen Kinenkankōkai 石川近代文学館開館二十五周年記念刊行会, ed., *"Shūenki" to "Mihappyō jobun"* 『「終焉記」と「未発表序文」』 ["A record of the final days of my child" and "Unpublished preface"], 26–73. Kanazawa: Ishikawa Kindai Bungakukan, 1993.

Fujioka Yoshio 藤岡由夫. "Chichi no omoide"「父の思ひ出」[Memories of my father]. *Kokugo to Kokubungaku* 17, no. 4 (1940): 391–92.

Furuta Hikaru 古田光. "*Sekai shinchitsujo no genri* jikenkō"「世界新秩序の原理事件考 (1) (2)」[Investigations into the incident dealing with "The Principles for a New World Order," parts 1 and 2]. *Furoku* 付録 [Supplement], January 1979 and April 1980. NKZ 14:1–5 and NKZ 19:5–10.

Gakushūin Hyakunenshi Hensan Iinkai 学習院百年史編纂委員会, ed. *Gakushūin hyakunenshi*『学習院百年史』[A hundred years of Gakushūin]. Vol. 1. Tokyo: Gakushūin, 1981.

Gakushūin 学習院, ed. *Kaikō gojūnen kinen, Gakushūinshi*『開校五十年記念学習院史』[The first fifty years of Gakushūin]. Tokyo: Gakushūin, 1928.

———. "Kyū shokuin meibo"「旧職員名簿」[Roster of former professors and administrators]. In *Kaikō gojūnen kinen Gakushūinshi* [The first fifty years of Gakushūin], 41–60. Tokyo: 1928.

Gauntlett, J. O., trans., R. K. Hall, ed., with introduction. *Kokutai no Hongi: Cardinal Principles of the National Entity of Japan*. Newton, Mass.: Crofton, 1974.

Genri Nipponsha 原理日本社. "Genri Nipponsha kenkyū kōryō"「原理日本社研究綱要」[Research objectives of Genri Nipponsha]. *Genri Nippon*『原理日本』19 (February 1943): 1–3.

Gotō Ryūnosuke 後藤隆之助, ed. *Shōwa kenkyūkai*『昭和研究会』[The Showa Study Group]. Tokyo: Keizai Ōraisha, 1968.

Hara Takeshi 原剛 and Yasuoka Akio 安岡昭男, eds. *Nihon riku-kaigun jiten*『日本陸海軍事典』[Dictionary of Japanese army and navy]. Tokyo: Shinjinbutsu Ōraisha, 1997.

Harada Kumao 原田熊雄. *Saionjikō to seikyoku*『西園寺公と政局』[Prince Saionji and political affairs]. 9 vols. Tokyo: Iwanami Shoten, 1951.

Hashimoto Hōkei 橋本芳契, ed. "Heiwa kenpō ni Nishida tetsugaku no seishin"「平和憲法に西田哲学の精神」[The spirit of Nishidan philosophy present in the new constitution]. (Reprint of an article from *Hokkoku Newspaper*『北国新聞』, 7 June 1959). In *Dainijūnikai kinen kōza kōenshū*『第二十二回記念講座講演集』[The twenty-second lectures in memory of Professor Nishida], 40–42. Kanazawa: Nishida Kitarō Sensei Shōtokukai, 1969.

Hata Ikuhiko 秦郁彦. *Senzenki Nihon kanryōsei no seido, soshiki, jinji*『戦前期日本官僚制の制度、組織、人事』[The system, organizations, and personnel appointments of prewar Japanese bureaucracy]. Tokyo: Tokyo Daigaku Shuppankai, 1981.

Hatano Seiichi 波多野精一. *Hatano Seiichi Zenshū*『波多野精一全集』[Collected works of Hatano Seiichi]. Vol. 6. Tokyo: Iwanami Shoten, 1969.

Heibonsha 平凡社. *Tetsugaku jiten*『哲学事典』[Dictionary of philosophical terms]. Tokyo: Heibonsha, 1971.

Heisig, James W., and John C. Maraldo, eds. *Rude Awakenings: Zen, the Kyoto School, and the Question of Nationalism*. Honolulu: University of Hawai'i Press, 1994.

Hidaka Daishirō 日高第四郎. "*Dōri no Kankaku* ni tsuite"「『道理の感覚』について」[On the *Sense of reason*]. *Geppō* 月報 [Monthly supplement], March 1971. ATZ 1:1–4.

———. "Nogi Taishō to Suzuki sensei no inshō oyobi omoide"「乃木大将と鈴木先生の印象及び想い出」[Memories of General Nogi and Professor D. T. Suzuki]. In *Suzuki Daisetsu—hito to shisō*『鈴木大拙—人と思想』[D. T. Suzuki: The man and his thought], edited by Hisamatsu Shin'ichi 久松真一, Yamaguchi Susumu 山口益, and Furuta Shōkin 古田紹欽, 279–88. Tokyo: Iwanami Shoten, 1971.

Hisamatsu Shin'ichi 久松真一. "Gakkyū seikatsu no omoide"「学究生活の想い出 [Recollections of my student days]. In *Tōyōteki mu*『東洋的無』[Oriental nothingness]. *Hisamatsu Shin'ichi Chosakushū*『久松真一著作集』(HSC) [Works of Hisamatsu Shin'ichi] 1:415–34. Tokyo: Risōsha, 1970.

———. "Nishida Tetsugaku to Zen"「西田哲学と禅」[Nishidan philosophy and Zen]. In *Hasōai*『破草鞋』[A worn-out pair of sandals]. HSC 8:15–52.

Hojinkai Zasshi 輔仁会雑誌 Editorial. "Nishida sensei no hon'in o sararuru o oshimu"「西田先生の本院を去らるゝを惜む」[For Professor Nishida who left our school]. *Hojinkai Zasshi*『輔仁会雑誌』82 (November 1910): 157–58.

Hori Koretaka 堀維孝. "Hōjō sensei no sokumen"「北条先生の側面」[An aspect of Professor Hōjō]. In *Tekison, Hori sensei ikō*『荻村堀先生遺稿』[Writings of the late Professor Hori Tekison], edited by Katō Toranosuke 加藤虎之亮, 237–55. Tokyo: Hori Sensei Ikō Kankōkai, 1956.

———. "Shikō Sansanjuku ni tsuite"「四高三々塾について」[On the Sansanjuku of the Fourth Higher School]. In *Tekison, Hori sensei ikō*,『荻村堀先生遺稿』[Writings of the late Professor Hori Tekison], edited by Katō Toranosuke 加藤虎之亮, 237–55. Tokyo: Hori Sensei Ikō Kankōkai, 1956.

Husserl, Edmund. "Die Idee einer philosophischen Kultur: Ihr erstes Aufkeimen in der griechischen Philosophie" [The Idea of Philosophical Culture: Its Early Appearance in Greek Philosophy]. *Japanische Deutschen Zeitschrift für Wissenschaft und Technik* (1923): 45–51.

———. "Erneuerung—Ihr Problem und Ihre Methode" (German original). "Kakushin, sono mondai to sono hōhō"「革新—その問題とその方法」[Renewal, its problem and the method] (Japanese translation). *Kaizō*『改造』(March 1923): 84–92; 63–83.

———. "Furantsu Burentāno no omoide"「フランツ・ブレンタノの思ひ出」[Memories of Franz Brentano]. Translated by Watsuji Tetsurō 和辻哲郎. *Kaizō*『改造』(March 1923): 86–98.

———. "Honshitsu kenkyū no hōhō"「本質研究の方法」[The method of the study of essence]. *Kaizō*『改造』(April 1924): 107–16.

———. "Kojin rinri mondai no saishin"「個人倫理問題の再新」[Renewal of the problem of individual ethics]. *Kaizō*『改造』(February 1924): 2–31.

Ibunkaishi 以文会誌 [Ibunkai Journal]. Kyoto: Kyoto Imperial University Student Association. 1 (1909).

Ikeda Toshio 池田敏雄. *Birion shinpu*『ビリオン神父』[Father Villion]. Tokyo: Chūō Shuppansha, 1965.

Inoue Tetsujirō 井上哲次郎. "Meiji tetsugakukai no kaiko"「明治哲学界の回顧」[Recollections of the philosophical world of the Meiji period]. In *Tetsugaku shisō*『哲学思想』[Philosophical thoughts], edited by Shimomura Toratarō 下村寅太郎 and Furuta Hikaru 古田光, 53–71. Tokyo: Chikuma Shobō, 1965.

———. "Rafaeru fon Kēberu-shi o tsuikaisu"「ラフアエル・フォン・ケーベル氏を追懐す」[Remembering Mr. Raphael von Koeber]. Tetsugaku Zasshi 『哲学雑誌』438 (August 1923): 60–64.

Inoue Zenjō 井上禅定 and Zen Bunka Kenkyūjo 禅文化研究所, eds. *Suzuki Daisetz mikōkai shokan*『鈴木大拙未公開書簡』[Unpublished letters of Suzuki Daisetz]. Kyoto: Zen Bunka Kenkyūjo, 1989.

Ishibayashi Bunkichi 石林文吉. *Ishikawa hyakunenshi*『石川百年史』[A history of the last one hundred years of Ishikawa prefecture]. Kanazawa: Ishikawaken Kōminkan Rengōkai, 1972.

Ishiguro Yoshitane 石黒美種. "Ōsaka Motokichirō shōden"「逢坂元吉郎小伝」[A brief biography of Ōsaka Motokichirō]. In *Ōsaka Motokichirō Chosakushū* 『逢坂元吉郎著作集』[Works of Ōsaka Motokichirō], edited by Ishiguro Yoshitane, 2:493–541. Tokyo: Shinkyō Shuppansha, 1972.

Ishihara Atsushi 石原純. "Ainsutain kyōju no kōen"「アインスタイン教授の講演」[Professor Einstein's lectures]. *Kaizō*『改造』, January 1923, 307–30; February 1923, 28–44.

Ishikawa Ken 石川謙 et al., eds. "Kyōgaku sasshin hyōgikai sōkai gijiroku"「教学刷新評議会総会議事録」[Minutes of the general meetings of the committee for the renewal of education and scholarship]. In *Kindai Nihon kyōikuseido shiryō*『近代日本教育制度資料』[Sources for recent educational systems in Japan]. Vol. 14. Tokyo: Kōdansha, 1957.

Ishikawa Kōji 石川興二. "Doitsu seikatsu o tomo ni shita Tanabe Hajime sensei no omoide"「ドイツ生活を共にした田辺元先生の思い出」[Recollection of Professor Tanabe Hajime with whom I shared some days in Germany]. *Geppō* 月報 [Monthly supplement], December 1963. THZ 2:2–4.

———. "Nishida tetsugaku to keizaigaku"「西田哲学と経済学」[The Nishidan philosophy and economics]. NKD 130–35.

Ishikawaken Kyōikushi Hensan Iinkai 石川県教育史編纂委員会, ed. *Ishikawaken kyōikushi*『石川県教育史』[A history of education in Ishikawa prefecture]. Vol. 1. Kanazawa: Ishikawaken Kyōiku Iinkai, 1974.

Itō Kichinosuke 伊藤吉之助. "Tetsugakukai shiryō (1)" [Chronogical record of the Philosophical Society, part 1]. *Tetsugaku Zasshi*『哲学雑誌』300 (February 1912): 195–247.

Iwanami Yūjirō 岩波雄二郎, ed. *Iwanami Shoten gojūnen*『岩波書店五十年』[The fifty years of Iwanami Bookstore]. Tokyo: Iwanami Shoten, 1963.

Kakehashi Akihide 梯明秀. "Rōgoku to guntai"「牢獄と軍隊」[Prison and army]. In

Kaisō no Tosaka Jun『回想の戸坂潤』[Remembering Tosaka Jun], edited by Tanabe Hajime 田辺元 et al., 35–72. Tokyo: Keisō Shobō, 1976.

Kaneko Takezō 金子武蔵. "Akikaze no kōgen ni tatsu gakufu sanagarani"「秋風の高原に立つ岳父さながらに」[Resembling my father-in-law, standing on the hill in the autumn wind]. NKD 276–82.

Kano Naoki 狩野直喜. "Nishida-kun no omoide"「西田君の憶ひ出」[Memories of Nishida]. *Tetsugaku Kenkyū*『哲学研究』347 (April 1946): 27–29.

Kataoka Hitoshi 片岡仁志 and Tsujimura Kōichi 辻村公一. "Sunshin-kai no koto, sono yurai, genzai, shōrai"「寸心会のこと―その由来、現在、将来」[About the Sunshin-kai, its origin, its present, and its future]. *Furoku* 付録 [Supplement], January 1970. NKZ 16:1–4.

Kawasaki Akira 川﨑明, ed. *Chōsui sensei ikō, zokuhen*『晁水先生遺稿、続編』[Writings of the late Professor Yamamoto]. Vol. 2. Tokyo: Musashi Kōtōgakkō Yamamoto Sensei Kinenkai, 1966.

Kido Kōichi 木戸幸一. *Kido Kōichi nikki*『木戸幸一日記』[Diary of Kido Kōichi]. 2 vols. Tokyo: Tokyo Daigaku Shuppankai, 1980.

Kido Mantarō 城戸幡太郎, ed. *Kyōikugaku jiten*『教育学辞典』[Dictionary of education and pedagogy]. 5 vols. Tokyo: Iwanami Shoten, 1936–1939.

Kimura Motomori 木村素衛. "Nishida Kitarō sensei no hanashi"「西田幾多郎先生の話」[Casual discussions with Professor Nishida Kitarō]. *Kokoro*『心』(January 1964): 187–90.

———. "Nuibari"「縫針」[A sewing needle]. *Shisō*『思想』270 (October 1945): 29–37.

Kimura Tadashi 木村匡. "Monbu daijin gakuji junshi zuikō nikki"「文部大臣学事巡視随行日記」[Diary of an official who accompanied the minister of education on his trip to visit various schools]. In *Mori Arinori Zenshū*『森有礼全集』[Collected works of Mori Arinori], edited by Ōkubo Toshiaki 大久保利謙, 1:714–30. Tokyo: Senbundō, 1972.

Kishi Shigeji 岸重次. "Shikō no omoide"「四高の思い出」[Fond memories of the Fourth Higher School]. In *Shikō hachijūnen*『四高八十年』[Eighty years of the Fourth Higher School], edited by Tomatsu Nobuyasu 戸松信康, 47–48. Kanazawa: Kanazawa Daiyon Kōtōgakkō Dōsōkai, 1967.

Kitano Hiroyuki 北野裕通. "Nishida Kitarō shokan santsū ni tsuite"「西田幾多郎書簡三通について」[Three unpublished letters of Nishida Kitarō]. *Sōai Daigaku kenkyū ronshū*『相愛大学研究論集』10 (March 1994): 221–32.

Kiyozawa Manshi 清沢満之. "Meimonsha no an'i"「迷悶者の安慰」[Consolations for the lost]. In *Meiji Bungaku Zenshū*『明治文学全集』[Collection of Meiji period literature] 46:227–28. Tokyo: Chikuma Shobō, 1977.

Kobayashi Isamu 小林勇. *Sekirekisō shujin―hitotsu no Iwanami Shigeo-den*『惜櫟荘主人――一つの岩波茂雄伝』[The master of Sekirekisō: A biography of Iwanami Shigeo]. Tokyo: Iwanami Shoten, 1963.

Komatsu Shūkichi 小松周吉. "Kagahan Meirindō no gakusei kaikaku"「加賀藩明倫堂の学制改革」[Revision of the education system of Kaga domain's school, Meirindō]. In Kagahan shakai *keizaishi no kenkyū*『加賀藩社会経済史の研

究』[A study of the socioeconomic history of Kaga province], edited by
　　Wakabayashi Kisaburō 若林喜三郎, 333–66. Tokyo: Meicho Shuppan,
　　1980.

Kondō Jungo 近藤純悟. "Kyoshō no ne"「巨鐘の音」[The sound of a great bell]. In
　　Kiyozawa Manshi『清沢満之』, edited by Ōtani Daigaku 大谷大学, 215–26.
　　Kyoto: Kanshōsha, 1928.

Kōno Yoichi 河野與一. "Nishida sensei no hen'ei"「西田先生の片影」[A glimpse of
　　Professor Nishida]. NKD 191–201.

Kōsaka Masaaki 高坂正顕. "Hito oyobi shisōka to shite no Nishida Kitarō sensei"
　　「人及び思想家としての西田幾多郎先生」[Professor Nishida Kitarō: A
　　man and a thinker]. In *Nishida Kitarō to sono tetsugaku*『西田幾多郎とその
　　哲学』[Nishida. Kitarō and his philosophy], edited by Amano Teiyū 天野
　　貞祐, Hisamatsu Shin'ichi 久松真一, Kōsaka Masaaki 高坂正顕, Nishitani
　　Keiji 西谷啓治, Shimomura Toratarō 下村寅太郎, and Kōyama Iwao 高山
　　岩男, 71–109. Kyoto: Tōisha, 1985.

———. *Meiji shisōshi*『明治思想史』[A history of thought in the Meiji period]. In
　　Kōsaka Masaaki Chosakushū『高坂正顕著作集』(KMC) [Writings of
　　Kōsaka Masaaki]. Vol. 7. Tokyo: Risōsha, 1969.

———. *Nishida Kitarō sensei no tsuioku*『西田幾多郎先生の追憶』[Memories of
　　Professor Nishida Kitarō]. Tokyo: Kunitachi Shoin, 1948.

———. *Nishida Tetsugaku*『西田哲学』[Nishidan philosophy]. KMC 8 (1965).

———. "*Tetsugaku Kenkyū* henshū no omoide"「『哲学研究』編輯の思い出」
　　[Recollections of those days when I was editing the *Journal of Philosophical
　　Studies*]. *Tetsugaku Kenkyū*『哲学研究』400 (February 1951): 106–08.

———. *Nishida Kitarō sensei no shōgai to shisō*『西田幾多郎先生の生涯と思想』[Life
　　and thought of Professor Nishida Kitarō]. KMC 8 (1965): 5–234.

Kōyama Iwao 高山岩男. "Omoide no mitsu yotsu"「思い出の三つ四つ」[A few
　　recollections]. NKD 147–50.

Kurata Hyakuzō 倉田百三. "Seimei no ninshikiteki doryoku"「生命の認識的努力」
　　[The cognitive effort of life]. A section of *Ai to ninshiki no shuppatsu*『愛と
　　認識の出発』[The departing point of love and cognition]. In Abe Jirō and
　　Kurata Hyakuzō, *Abe Jirō, Kurata Hyakuzō-shū*『阿部次郎、倉田百三集』
　　[Selected writings of Abe Jirō and Kurata Hyakuzō]. *Gendai Nihon Bungaku
　　Zenshū*『現代日本文学全集』[Collection of Modern Japanese Literature]
　　74:306–17. Tokyo: Chikuma Shobō, 1956.

Kuroda Hidetoshi 黒田秀俊. *Shōwa genronshi e no shōgen*『昭和言論史への証言』[A
　　testimony on the history of freedom of expression in the Shōwa period].
　　Tokyo: Kōbundō, 1966.

Kuwaki Gen'yoku 桑木厳翼. "Kēberu sensei ni tsuite"「ケーベル先生に就て」
　　[About Professor Koeber]. *Tetsugaku Zasshi*『哲学雑誌』438 (August
　　1923): 65–67.

Kyoto Daigaku 京都大学. *Kyōto Daigaku hyakunenshi*『京都大学百年史』[One
　　hundred years of the history of Kyoto University]. Kyoto: Kyoto Daigaku,
　　web version, 1999.

Kyoto Daigaku Bungakubu 京都大学文学部, ed. *Kyōto Daigaku bungakubu gojūnenshi* 『京都大学文学部五十年史』 [Fifty years of the Faculty of Letters, Kyoto University]. Kyoto: Kyoto Daigaku Bungakubu, 1956.

Kyoto Daigaku Nanajūnenshi Henshū Iinkai 京都大学七十年史編集委員会, ed. *Kyōto Daigaku nanajūnenshi* 『京都大学七十年史』 [Seventy years of Kyoto University]. Kyoto: Kyoto University, 1967.

Löwith, Karl. *Nachizumu to watakushi no seikatsu* 『ナチズムと私の生活』 [Nazism and my life]. Translation of *Mein Leben in Deutschland vor und nach 1933* by Akima Minoru 秋間実. Tokyo: Hōsei University Press, 1990.

———. *Tōyō to seiyō* 『東洋と西洋』 [The Orient and the Occident]. Translated by by Satō Akio 佐藤明雄 into Japanese. Tokyo: Miraisha, 1990.

Maeda Toshinari-kō Denki Hensan Iinkai 前田利為公伝記編纂委員会, ed. *Maeda Toshinari* 『前田利為』 [Maeda Toshinari]. Kanazawa: Yoshida Insatsu, 1986.

Martin, Christopher. *The Russo-Japanese War*. London: Abelard-Schuman, 1967.

Matsuda Michio 松田道雄. "Shōwa shigonen no koro, Miki Kiyoshi o megutte" 「昭和四、五年のころ―三木清をめぐって」 [Around 1929–1930, concerning Miki Kiyoshi]. In his *Zaiya no shisōkatachi* 『在野の思想家たち』 [Thinkers outside the universities], 141–65. Tokyo: Iwanami Shoten, 1977.

Merton, Thomas. "Nishida: A Zen Philosopher." In his *Zen and the Birds of Appetite*, 67–70. New York: New Directions, 1968.

Middleton, Christopher, ed. *Johann Wolfgang von Goethe: Selected Poems*. Boston: Suhrkamp/Insel, 1983.

Miki Kiyoshi 三木清. *Miki Kiyoshi Zenshū* 『三木清全集』 (MKZ) [Collected works of Miki Kiyoshi]. 20 vols. Tokyo: Iwanami Shoten, 1966–1986.

———. "Hyūmanizumu no gendaiteki igi—Nishida Kitarō hakushi ni kiku" 「ヒューマニズムの現代的意義―西田幾多郎博士に訊く」 [The contemporary significance of humanism: An interview with Dr. Nishida Kitarō]. MKZ 17:492–504.

———. "Jinsei oyobi jinsei tetsugaku" 「人生及び人生哲学」 [Life and a philosophy of life: Interview with Nishida Kitarō]. *Nihon Hyōryon* 『日本評論』 (October 1936): 90–102.

———. "Nenpu" 「年譜」 [Chronology]. MKZ 19:851–89.

———. "Nishida sensei no kotodomo" 「西田先生のことども」 [About Professor Nishida]. MKZ 17:296–97.

———. "Shōwajuku sōsetsu ni tsuite" 「『昭和塾』創設について」 [A word on the establishment of Showajuku]. MKZ 15:329–33.

Minamoto Ryōen. "The Symposium on 'Overcoming Modernity.'" In *Rude Awakenings: Zen, the Kyoto School, and the Question of Nationalism*, edited by James W. Heisig and John C. Maraldo, 197–229. Berkeley: University of California Press, 1991.

Minoda Muneki 蓑田胸喜. "Gengo majutsu no gūzō to shite no Nishida tetsugaku" 「言語魔術の偶像としての西田哲学」 [Nishidan philosophy as the icon of linguistic magic]. *Genri Nippon* 『原理日本』 17 (February 1941): 22–32.

———. "Minobe hakushi, *Kenpō satsuyō* no kibensakujutsuteki kokutai henkaku shisō, sono gakujutsuteki hihan to shochi yōsei"「美濃部博士『憲法撮要』の詭弁詐術的『国体変革』思想—其学術的批判と処置要請」[An academic criticism and a demand for chastisement of the sophistry that undermines the national essence found in Dr. Minobe's *Explication of the Constitution*]. *Genri Nippon*『原理日本』8 (October 1933): entire issue.

———. "Nishida hakushi no ninshikiron o hyōsu"「西田博士の認識論を評す」[A critique of Dr. Nishida's epistemology]. *Genri Nippon*『原理日本』3 (October 1927): 6–13.

———. "Nishida Tetsugaku no Nihon bunkaron ni okeru datsuraku"「西田哲学の日本文化論における脱落」[Lacunae in the theory of Japanese culture in the Nishidan Philosophy]. *Genri Nippon*『原理日本』16 (1940): 25–38.

———. "Nishida tetaugaku no hōhō ni tsuite"「西田哲学の方法に就て」[Regarding the methodology of Nishidan philosophy]. *Genri Nippon*『原理日本』14 (July 1938): 3–22.

———. "Shinri no kamen, Nishida tetsugaku no gironsei ni tsuite"「真理の仮面—西田哲学の戯論性に就て」[A mask of truth; concerning the intended use of dramatic effect in Nishidan philosophy]. *Genri Nippon*『原理日本』15 (April 1939): 4–15.

———. "Shōwa Kenkyūkai no gengo-majutsu"「昭和研究会の言語魔術」[The linguistic magic displayed by the Showa Study Group]. *Genri Nippon*『原理日本』16 (August 1940): 1–25; 16 (September 1940): 2–18.

———. "Shōwa Kenkyūkai o kaishō subeshi"「昭和研究会を解消すべし」[The Showa Study Group ought to be dissolved]. *Genri Nippon*『原理日本』16 (October 1940): 10–14.

Mitsui Kōshi 三井甲之. "Shōwa Kenkyūkai no kyōgyaku-shisō o shochi subeshi"「昭和研究会の凶逆思想を処置すべし」[The dangerous thought of the Showa Study Group must be punished]. *Genri Nippon*『原理日本』16, 10 (October 1940): 2–9.

Miyazawa Toshiyoshi 宮沢俊義. *Tennō kikansetsu jiken*『天皇機関説事件』[The "imperial organ theory" incident]. 2 vols. Tokyo: Yūhikaku, 1970.

Monbushō Kyōgakukyoku 文部省教学局, ed. *Nippon shogaku shinkō iinkai*『日本諸学振興委員会』[A commission for the promotion of Japanese learnings]. Tokyo: Governmental Printing Bureau, 1938.

Monbushōnai Kyōikushi Hensankai 文部省内教育編纂会. *Meiji-ikō kyōikuseido hattatsushi*『明治以降教育制度発達史』[A history of the development of the education system since the Meiji period]. Vols. 4–5. Tokyo: Kyoikushiryō Chōsakai, 1938–1939.

Mori Arinori 森有礼. "Daiyon kōtōchūgakkō kaikōshiki shukuji, enzetsu"「第四高等中学校開校式祝辞、演説」. In *Mori Arinori Zenshū*『森有礼全集』, edited by Ōkubo Toshiaki 大久保利謙, vol. 1, 555–57. Tokyo: Senbundō, 1972.

Morimoto Kōji 森本孝治. "Watakushi no Nishida sensei"「私の西田先生」[My Professor Nishida]. NKD 6–12.

Murdoch, James. *A History of Japan*. 3 vols. New York: Frederick Ungar, 1964.

Muroi Michihiro 室井美千博, ed. *Miki Kiyoshi no shōgai to shisō*『三木清の生涯と思想』[Life and thought of Miki Kiyoshi]. Tatsuno, Hyōgo Prefecture: Kajōkan, 1998.

Musashi Nanajūnen no Ayumi Henshū Iinkai 武蔵七十年のあゆみ編集委員会, ed. *Musashi nanajūnen no ayumi*『武蔵七十年のあゆみ』[Seventy years of Musashi Higher School]. Tokyo: Nezu Ikueikai, 1994.

Mutai Risaku 務台理作. "Edomundo Husseru" エドムンド・フツセル [Edmund Husserl]. *Shisō*『思想』194 (July 1938): 78–86.

———. "Kyōdai rainin tōsho no Tanabe sensei" 京大来任当初の田辺先生 [Professor Tanabe, around the time of his arrival at Kyoto University]. *Geppō*「月報」[Monthly supplement], October 1963. THZ 4:1–3.

———. "Sono koro no Nishida sensei"「その頃の西田先生」[Professor Nishida of those days]. NKD 114–20.

Nagayo Yoshirō 長与善郎. "Sanzetsu"「三絶」[The three great men]. In *Satomi Ton, Nagayo Yoshirō-shū*『里見弴、長与善郎集』[Writings of Satomi Ton and Nagayo Yoshirō]. Vol. 50 of *Nihon Gendai Bungaku Zenshū*『日本現代文学全集』[Collection of Japanese contemporary literature], 378–99. Tokyo: Kōdansha, 1963.

Naiseishi Kenyūkai 内政史研究会, ed. *Gotō Ryūnosuke-shi danwa sokkiroku*『後藤隆之助氏談話速記録』[Records of conversations with Mr. Gotō Ryūnosuke]. Tokyo: Naiseishi Kenkyūkai, 1968.

Nakai Masakazu 中井正一. "Kaiko jūnen, omoiizuru mama ni" 回顧十年―思ひ出づるまゝに [Random recollections of ten years ago]. *Tetsugaku Kenkyū*『哲学研究』400 (February 1951): 108–12.

Nakamura Hajime 中村元 and Takeda Kiyoko 武田清子, eds. *Kindai Nihon tetsugaku shisōka jiten*『近代日本哲学思想家辞典』[Dictionary of modern Japanese philosophers and thinkers]. Tokyo: Tokyo Shoseki, 1982.

Nakanishi Keijirō 中西敬二郎. *Waseda Daigaku hachijūnenshi*『早稲田大学八十年誌』[Records of eighty years of Waseda University]. Tokyo: Waseda Daigaku Shuppanbu, 1962.

Natsume Sōseki 夏目漱石. "Hakushi mondai no nariyuki (2)"「博士問題の成行（二）」[How the "doctorate-incident" has unfolded, part 2]. In *Natsume Sōseki Zenshū*『夏目漱石全集』[Collected works of Natsume Sōseki], 8: 273–75. Tokyo: Kadokawa, 1975.

———. "Hakushi mondai to Mādokku sensei to yo"「博士問題とマードツク先生と余」[The "doctorate-incident," Professor Murdoch, and I]. In *Natsume Sōseki Zenshū*,『夏目漱石全集』[Collected works of Natsume Sōseki], 8: 276–81. Tokyo: Kadokawa, 1975.

Nichigai Associates 日外アソシエーツ, ed. *Japan Who was Who 1983–1987*. Tokyo: Nichigai Associates, 1988.

Nishida Kitarō Ibokushū Henshū Iinkai『西田幾多郎遺墨集編集委員会』. *Nishida Kitarō ibokushū*『西田幾多郎遺墨集』[A collection of Nishida Kitarō's calligraphy pieces]. Kyoto: Tōeisha, 1977.

———. *Nishida Kitarō Zenshū*『西田幾多郎全集』[Collected works of Nishida Kitarō]. 3d and 4th eds, 19 vols. Tokyo: Iwanami Shoten 1978–1989.

Nishida Kitarō 西田幾多郎, ed. *Kakudō hen'ei*『廓堂片影』[Glimpses of greatness]. Tokyo: Kyōiku Kenkyōkai, 1931.

Nishida Koto 西田琴. "Kamakura no ie"「鎌倉の家」[Our house in Kamakura]. NKD 249–51.

Nishida Shizuko 西田静子. "Chichi"「父」[My father]. In *Waga chichi, Nishida Kitarō*『わが父、西田幾多郎』[Our father, Nishida Kitarō], edited by Nishida Shizuko and Ueda Yayoi, 3–36. Tokyo: Kōbundō Shobō, 1948.

Nishida Sotohiko 西田外彦. "Chichi no sunda ieie"「父の住んだ家々」[Houses where my father lived]. NKD 261–73.

———. "Chichi"「父」[My father]. NKD 251–61.

Nishitani Keiji 西谷啓治. "Kōki"「後記」[Editor's postscript to Nishida's diary]. NKZ 17:711–28.

———. "Meshi o kutta keiken"「飯を喰った経験」[The experience of having eaten cooked rice]. In his *Kaze no kokoro*『風のこころ』[The mind of the wind], 218–24. Tokyo: Shinchōsha, 1980.

———. *Nishida Kitarō, sono hito to shisō*『西田幾多郎、その人と思想』[Nishida Kitarō: The man and his thought]. Tokyo: Chikuma Shobō, 1985.

———. *Nishida Kitarō*. Translated by Yamamoto Seisaku and James W. Heisig. Berkeley: University of California Press, 1991.

———. "Tanabe sensei no koto"「田辺先生のこと」[Regarding Professor Tanabe]. In *Tanabe Hajime, shisō to kaisō*『田辺元、思想と回想』[Tanabe Hajime: His thought and our recollections], edited by Takeuchi Yoshinori 武内義範, Mutō Kazuo 武藤一雄, and Tsujimura Kōichi 辻村公一, 281–86. Tokyo: Chikuma Shobō, 1991.

———. "Waga shi Nishida Kitarō sensei o kataru"「わが師西田幾多郎先生を語る」[Talking about my mentor, Professor Nishida Kitarō]. In his *Nishida Kitarō, sono hito to shisō*, 3–44.

Nitta Yoshihiro, Tatematsu Hirotaka, and Shimomise Eiichi. "Phenomenology and Philosophy in Japan." In *Japanese Phenomenology*, edited by Nitta and Tatematsu. *Analecta Husserliana* 8:3–17. Dordrecht: D. Reidel, 1979.

Obata Buntei 小畠文鼎. *Kinsei zenrin sōhōden*『近世禅林僧寶傳』[Biographies of Zen monks of the recent past]. 3 vols. Kyoto: Shibunkaku, 1938; reprinted 1973.

Oka Yoshitake 岡義武 et al., eds. *Kido Kōichi kankei bunsho*『木戸幸一関係文書』[Papers and documents related to Kido Kōichi]. Tokyo: Tokyo Daigaku Shuppankai, 1966.

Okada Akio 岡田章雄 et al., eds. *Nihon no rekishi*『日本の歴史』[History of Japan]. 8 vols. Tokyo: Yomiuri Shinbunsha, 1959.

Ōkubo Toshiaki 大久保利謙, ed. *Mori Arinori Zenshū*『森有礼全集』[Collected works of Mori Arinori]. 3 vols. Tokyo: Senbundō, 1972.

Omodaka Hisayuki 沢潟久敬. "Nishida sensei no omoide"「西田先生の思い出」[Memories of Professor Nishida]. NKD 156–60.

Ōshima Sensei Kinenkai 大島先生記念会, ed. *Ōshima Yoshinaga sensei-den* 『大島義脩先生伝』[A biography of Professor Ōshima Yoshinaga]. Tokyo: Private publication, 1939.

Ōshima Yasumasa 大島康正. "Daitōa sensō to Kyoto gakuha—chishikijin no seiji-sanka ni tsuite" 「大東亜戦争と京都学派、知識人の政治参加について」 [The Great Asian War and the Kyoto School—The participation of the intellectuals in politics]. *Chūōkōron* 『中央公論』(August 1965): 125–43.

———. "Nishida sensei to Tanabe sensei no saigo no shoshin kōkan" 「西田先生と田辺先生の最後の書信交換」[The last exchange of letters between Professor Nishida and Professor Tanabe]. *Furoku* 付録 [Supplement], April 1980. NKZ 19:1–5.

Ōtaka Toshio 大高利夫, ed. *Jinbutsu refarensu jiten* 『人物レファレンス事典』[A reference dictionary of who is who]. Tokyo: Nichigai Associates, 1983.

Parkes, Graham. "The Putative Fascism of the Kyoto School and the Political Correctness of the Modern Academy," *Philosophy East and West* 47 (July 1997): 305–36.

Perry, Ralph Barton. *The Thought and Character of William James* (Briefer Version). New York: Harper and Row, 1964.

Plato. *Timaeus*. Translated into English by R. G. Bury. New York: G. P. Putnam's Sons, 1929. Presseisen, Ernst L. *Germany and Japan: A study in totalitarian diplomacy, 1933–1941*. The Hague: Martinus Nijhoff, 1958.

Rickert, Heinrich. *Das Eine, die Einheit und die Eins: Bemerkungen zur Logik des Zahlbegriffs*. Tübingen: Verlag von J. C. B. Mohr, 1924.

Risōsha 理想社, ed. *Kyōiku jinmei jiten* 『教育人名辞典』[Dictionary of educators]. Tokyo: Risōsha, 1962.

Royce, Josiah. *The World and the Individual*. New York: Macmillan, 1901.

Sakai Saburō 酒井三郎. "Shōwa Kenkyūkai no higeki" 「『昭和研究会』の悲劇」 [The tragedy of the Showa Study Group]. *Bungeishunjū* 『文芸春秋』 (October 1964): 234–45.

———. *Shōwa Kenkyūkai—aru chishikijin-shūdan no kiseki* 『昭和研究会、ある知識人集団の軌跡』[Showa Study Group: A record of a certain group of intellectuals]. Tokyo: Chūōkōronsha, 1992.

Sasaki Sōichi 佐々木惣一, ed. *Kyōdai jiken* 『京大事件』[The Kyoto University incident]. Tokyo: Iwanami Shoten, 1933.

Schinzinger, Robert ローベルト・シンチンゲル. "Nishida Tetsugaku no hon'yaku no kotonado" 「西田哲学の翻訳のことなど」[On translating the philosophical works of Nishida]. NKD 235–40.

Schuhmann, Karl, ed. *Husserl-Chronik, Husserliana Dokumente* Band 1. Den Haag: Martinus Nijhoff, 1977.

———, ed. *Husserliana*, Band 3, *Dokumente, Briefwechsel*, Teil 6. Dordrecht: Kluwer, 1994.

Shimatani Toshizō 島谷俊三. "*Zen no kenkyū* no umareru made" 「『善の研究』の生まれるまで」[Years preceding the appearance of *An inquiry into the good*]. *Journal of Philosophical Studies* 『哲学研究』347 (April 1946): 30–48.

Shimizu Yoshichirō 清水与七郎. "Furui Shikō no omoide"「古い四高の思い出」
[Recollections of the Fourth Higher School of olden days]. In *Shikō
hachijūnen*『四高八十年』[Eighty years of the Fourth Higher School],
edited by Tomatsu Nobuyasu 戸松信康, 50. Kanazawa: Kanazawa Daiyon
Kōtōgakkō Dōsōkai, 1967.

Shimomura Toratarō 下村寅太郎, ed. *Nishida Kitarō: Dōjidai no kiroku*『西田幾多郎
―同時代の記録』(NKD) [Nishida Kitaro: Records by his
contemporaries]. Tokyo: Iwanami Shoten, 1971.

―――. *Nishida tetsugaku to Nihon no shisō*『西田哲学と日本の思想』[Nishidan
philosophy and the Japanese thought]. Vol. 12 of *Shimomura Toratarō
Chosakushū*『下村寅太郎著作集』(STC) [Works of Shimomura Toratarō].
Tokyo: Misuzu Shobō, 1990.

―――. "J. Roisu no yukari"「J. ロイスのゆかり」[Regarding J. Royce]. STC 12:
298–303.

―――. "*Jikaku ni okeru chokkan to hansei* to Roisu no self representative system―
nōto"「『自覚に於ける直観と反省』とロイスの self-representative system
―ノート」[A note on *Intuition and Reflection in Self-Consciousness* and
Royce's self-representative system]. *Furoku* 付録 [Supplement], March
1980. NKZ 18:1–5.

―――. "Kaiko"「回顧」[Reminiscences]. *Journal of Philosophical Studies*『哲学研究』
500 (September 1966): 276–78.

―――. "Nishida Kitarō and some aspects of his philosophical thought." In *A study of
good*, translated by Valdo Viglielmo, 191–217. Tokyo: Japanese Government Printing Bureau, 1960.

―――. "Nishida sensei no kotodomo, Unokemura kikō"「西田先生のことども、宇
ノ気村紀行」[Things about Professor Nishida, My journey to the village
of Unoke]. STC 12:304–07.

―――. "Nishida sensei no shokanshū ni tsuite"「西田先生の書翰集について」[A
note on the collection of letters of Professor Nishida]. In NKD 301–04.

―――. "Setsumon Rōshi, Hussāru, Rikkerto no tegami"「雪門老師、フッサール、
リッケルトの手紙」[Letters from Master Setsumon, Husserl, and Rickert].
STC 12:278–87.

―――. "Wakaki Nishida Kitarō sensei"「若き西田幾多郎先生」[The Young
Professor Nishida Kitarō]. STC 12:4–91.

Shimonaka Kunihiko 下中邦彦, ed. *Nihon jinmei daijiten, gendai*『日本人名大事典、
現代』[Dictionary of who is who in Japan―modern period]. Tokyo:
Heibonsha, 1979.

Shimonaka Yasaburō 下中弥三郎, ed. *Daijinmei jiten*『大人名事典』[Who is who].
Tokyo: Heibonsha, 1955.

Shinagawa Kazue 品川主計. "Omoide no ki"「想い出の記」[Recollections]. In
Shikō hachijūnen『四高八十年』[Eighty years of the Fourth Higher
School], edited by Tomatsu Nobuyasu 戸松信康. 56–58. Kanazawa:
Kanazawa Daiyon Kōtōgakkō Dōsōkai, 1967.

Shinchōsha Jiten Henshūbu 新潮社辞典編集部, ed. *Shinchō Nihon jinmei jiten*『新潮

日本人名辞典』[Shinchō who is who (Japanese)]. Tokyo: Shinchōsha, 1991.

Shinmura Izuru 新村出. *Kōjien*『広辞苑』[Kōjien dictionary]. Tokyo: Iwanami Shoten, 1974.

Shōda Tatsuo 勝田龍夫. *Jūshintachi no shōwashi*『重臣たちの昭和史』[A history of the Showa period as lived by the "court-group"]. 2 vols. Tokyo: Bungei-shunjū, 1981.

Sōda Kiichirō 左右田喜一郎. "Nishida tetsugaku no hōhō ni tusite—Nishida hakushi no oshie o kou"「西田哲学の方法に就いて—西田博士の教を乞う」[Asking for Dr. Nishida's elucidation on the method of Nishidan philosophy]. *Journal of Philosophical Studies*『哲学研究』127 (October 1926): 1–30.

Suzuki Daisetz 鈴木大拙. *Suzuki Daisetz Zenshū*『鈴木大拙全集』(SDZ) [Collected works of Suzuki Daisetz]. 32 vols. Tokyo: Iwanami Shoten, 1968–1971.

———. *"Eien no kage* no jo"「『永遠の影』の序」[Preface to *The eternal image*—A collection of letters from Nishida to Yamamoto Ryōkichi]. SDZ 28:490–93.

———. "Nishida no omoide"「西田の思ひ出」[Memories of Nishida]. *Shisō* 270 (October 1945): 2–11. SDZ 28:369–82.

———. "Nishida-kun no omoide futatsu mitsu"「西田君の思ひ出二つ三つ」[A few recollections of Nishida]. SDZ 28:417–21.

———. "Nishida Shizuko hen, *Chichi Nishida Kitarō no uta*, no jo"「西田静子編、『父西田幾多郎の歌』の序」[Preface to Nishida Shizuko, ed., *Japanese poems by my father Nishida Kitarō*]. SDZ 28:519–22.

———. "Shina bukkyō inshōki"「支那仏教印象記」[My impressions of Chinese Buddhism]. SDZ 30:463–561.

———. "Watakushi no rirekisho"「私の履歴書」[My curriculum vitae]. SDZ 30: 585–622.

Takagaki, Sekijiro, ed. *The Japan Year Book, 1943–44.* Tokyo: The Foreign Affairs Association of Japan, 1943. (Further edited and republished by the Interdepartmental Committee for the Acquisition of Foreign Publications, U.S. Government Printing Office, 1945.)

Takagi Sōkichi 高木惣吉. *Taiheiyō sensō to rikukaigun no kōsō*『太平洋戦争と陸海軍の抗争』[The Pacific War and the rivalry between the navy and the army]. Tokyo: Keizai ōraisha, 1982.

———. *Takagi Sōkichi nikki*『高木惣吉日記』[The diary of Takagi Sōkichi]. Tokyo: Mainichi Shinbunsha, 1985.

Takahashi Satomi 高橋里美. "Gakusha o okoraseta hanashi"「学者を怒らせた話」[Occasions when I angered eminent scholars]. *Takahashi Satomi Zenshū*『高橋里美全集』(TSZ) [Collected works of Takahashi Satomi]. 7:209–23. Tokyo: Fukumura Shuppan, 1973.

———. "Ishiki genshō no jijitsu to sono imi"「意識現象の事実とその意味」[Facts and meanings of the phenomena of consciousness]. *Tetsugaku Zasshi*『哲学雑誌』303 (May 1912): 48–73; 304 (June 1912): 51–70.

———. "Nishida Kitarō sensei no kotoba"「西田幾多郎先生の言葉」[Professor Nishida Kitarō's words]. TSZ 7:159–70.

Takeda Atsushi 竹田篤. *Nishida Kitarō*『西田幾多郎』[Nishida Kitarō]. Tokyo: Chūōkōronsha, 1979.

———. "Nishida Kitarō nenpu, Meiji 3–Meiji 13"「西田幾多郎年譜、明治3－明治13」[Chronology of Nishida Kitarō, 1870–1880]. *Risō*『理想』536 (January 1978): 178–91.

Takeuchi Yoshitomo 竹内良知. *Nishida Kitarō*『西田幾多郎』. Tokyo: Tokyo Daigaku Shuppan, 1977.

Tanabe Hajime 田辺元. *Tanabe Hajime Zenshū*『田辺元全集』(THZ) [Collected works of Tanabe Hajime]. 15 vols. Tokyo: Chikuma Shobō, 1963–1964.

———. "Kiki no tetsugaku ka, tetsugaku o kiki ka"「危機の哲学か、哲学の危機か」[Is it a philosophy of crisis, or is it a crisis of philosophy?]. 1933. THZ 8:3–9.

———. "Nishida sensei no oshie o aogu"「西田先生の教えを仰ぐ」[Requesting Professor Nishida's elucidation]. THZ 4:305–28.

———. *Shu no ronri no benshōhō*『種の論理の弁証法』[The dialectics of the logic of species]. Osaka: Akitaya, 1947.

———. "Shu no ronri no imi o akirakani su"「種の論理の意味を明かにす」[Clarification of the meaning of the logic of species]. *Tetsugaku Kenkyū*『哲学研究』259 (October 1937): 32–73.

Tanabe Hajime et al. *Kaisō no Tosaka Jun*『回想の戸坂潤』[Remembering Tosaka Jun]. Tokyo: Keisō Shobō, 1976.

Tanabe Juri 田辺寿利. "Bannen no Nishida Kitarō to Nihon no unmei"「晩年の西田幾多郎と日本の運命」[Nishida Kitarō of his last years and Japan's destiny]. In *Daijūnikai Nishida sensei kinen kōenshū*『第十二回西田先生記念講演集』[The twelfth conference in memory of Professor Nishida], 1–46. Kanazawa: Nishida Kitarō Sensei Shōtokukinenkai, 1962.

Tanabe Ryūji 田部隆次. *Koizumi Yakumo*『小泉八雲』[A biography of Lafcadio Hearn]. 4th ed. Tokyo: Hokuseidō, 1992.

———. *Nishida Kitarō no tegami*『西田幾多郎の手紙』[Letters of Nishida Kitarō]. Tokyo: Saitō Shoten, 1947.

Tanaka Onokichi 田中鉄吉. *Kyōdo sūgaku*『郷土数学』[The tradition of mathematics in Kanazawa]. Kanazawa: Ikezen Shoten, 1937.

Tanikawa Tetsuzō 谷川徹三, ed. *Hōsei Daigaku hachijūnenshi*『法政大学八十年史』[Eighty years of Hōsei University]. Tokyo: Hōsei Daigaku, 1961.

Togawa Shūkotsu 戸川秋骨. "Sono koro no hitotachi"「その頃の人達」[People of those days]. In his *Shizen kimagure kikō*『自然・気まぐれ・紀行』[Free and easy travelog in nature]. Quoted by Shimomura Toratarō in "Wakaki Nishida Kitarō Sensei" [The young Professor Nishida]. STC 12:33–34.

Tokunō Bun 得能文. "Shūkyō to risei ni tsuite Yamamoto, Nishida nikun ni shissu"「宗教と理性に就て山本西田二君に質す」[My questions to both

Yamamoto and Nishida concerning religion and reason]. *Mujintō*『無尽燈』 3 (June 1898): 10–16.

Tokyo Daigaku Hyakunenshi Henshū Iinkai 東京大学百年史編集委員会, ed. *Tōkyō Daigaku hyakunenshi*『東京大学百年史』[A history of one hundred years of Tokyo University]. *Tsūshi*『通史』[Overall History], vol. 1–2; Bukyokushi 『部局史』[History of Colleges and Departments], vol. 1; *Shiryō*『資料』 [Sources and Data], vols. 1–3. Tokyo: Tokyo Daigaku, 1984.

Tokyo Teikoku Daigaku 東京帝国大学. *Tokyo Teikoku Daigak gojūnenshi*『東京帝国 大学五十年史』[Fifty years of Tokyo Imperial University]. Vol. 1. Tokyo: Tokyo Teikoku Daigaku, 1932.

Tomatsu Nobuyasu 戸松信康, ed. *Shikō hachijūnen*『四高八十年』[Eighty years of the Fourth Higher School]. Kanazawa: Kanazawa Daiyon Kōtōgakkō Dōsōkai, 1967.

Tomonaga Sanjūrō 朝永三十郎. "*Tetsugaku Kenkyū no hossoku*"「『哲学研究』の発 足」[The launching of the *Journal of Philosophical Studies*]. *Tetsugaku Kenkyū* 400 (February 1951): 105–106.

Tosaka Jun 戸坂潤. *Tosaka Jun Zenshū*『戸坂潤全集』(TJZ) [Collected works of Tosaka Jun]. Tokyo: Keisō Shobō, 1966.

———. "Kyoto gakuha no tetsugaku"「京都学派の哲学」[The Kyoto school of philosophy]. TJZ 3:171–76.

———. "Tanabe tetsugaku no seiritsu"「田辺哲学の成立」[The establishment of Tanabean philosophy]. TJZ 3:177–84.

Tsuchida, Kyōson. *Contemporary thought of Japan and China*. New York: Knopf, 1927.

Tsunoda, Ryusaku, W. T. de Bary, and K. Donald, eds. *Sources of Japanese Tradition*. New York: Columbia University Press, 1971.

Uchida Sen'nosuke 内田泉之助, ed. Chōsui sensei ikō『晃水先生遺稿』[Writings of the late Professor Chōsui]. Tokyo: Musashi Kōkō, Ko-Yamamoto Sensei Kinenkai Jigyōkai, 1951.

Ueda Hisashi 上田久. *Nishida Kitarō no tsuma*『西田幾多郎の妻』[Nishida Kitarō's wife]. Tokyo: Nansōsha, 1986.

———. *Sofu Nishida Kitarō*『祖父西田幾多郎』[Grandfather Nishida Kitarō]. Tokyo: Nansōsha, 1978.

———, transcriber. "Daisetsu to Yamamoto Ryōkichi, Nishida Kitarō"「大拙と山 本良吉、西田幾多郎」[Daisetz, Yamamoto Ryōkichi, and Nishida Kitarō]. *Zen Bunka*『禅文化』135 (January 1990): 137–41.

———. *Yamamoto Ryōkichi sensei-den, Shiritsu nananensei Musashi Kō togakkō no sōseisha*『山本良吉先生伝、私立七年制武蔵高等学校の創成者』[A biography of Professor Yamamoto Ryōkichi—The founder of the private seven-year Musashi Higher School]. Tokyo: Nansōsha 1993.

———. *Zoku sofu Nishida Kitarō*『続祖父西田幾多郎』[Grandfather Nishida Kitarō, vol. 2]. Tokyo: Nansōsha, 1983.

Ueda Juzō 植田寿蔵. "Nishida sensei"「西田先生」[Professor Nishida]. NKD 102–08.

Ueda Yayoi 上田弥生. "Ano koro no chichi"「あの頃の父」[Father of those days].
　　In *Waga chichi, Nishida Kitarō*『わが父、西田幾多郎』[Our father, Nishida
　　Kitarō], edited by Nishida 西田静子 and Ueda Yayoi 上田弥生, 37–58.
　　Tokyo: Kōbundō Shobō, 1948. Compiled in Ueda Hisashi 上田久, *Sofu
　　Nishida Kitarō*『祖父西田幾多郎』[Grandfather, Nishida Kitarō], 199–209.

Ueno Kenchi 上野賢知, ed. *Shinken sensei kyūzōsho mokuroku*『真軒先生旧蔵書目録』
　　[Catalog of the collection of books by Professor Shinken]. Tokyo:
　　Mukyūkai, 1933.

Viglielmo, Valdo. "Nishida Kitarō: The Early Years." In *Tradition and Modernization
　　in Japanese Culture*, edited by Donald H. Shively, 507–62. Princeton:
　　Princeton University Press, 1971.

Villion, Amatus. *Cinquante ans d'apostolat au Japon* [Fifty years of apostolic work in
　　Japan]. Hong Kong: Imprimerie de la Société des Missions Étrangères, 1923.

Wakabayashi Kisaburō 若林喜三郎. "Kagahan"「加賀藩」In *Monogatari hanshi*『物
　　語藩史』[History of feudal fiefdoms told as stories]. Edited by Kodama
　　Kōta 児玉幸多 and Kitajima Masamoto 北島正元. Vol. 4. Tokyo: Jinbutsu
　　Ōraisha, 1956.

Yamada Takamichi 山田孝道, ed. *Zenshū jiten*『禅宗辞典』[Dictionary of Zen
　　Buddhism]. Tokyo: Kokusho Kankōkai, 1915.

Yamamoto Annosuke. 山本安之助. "Shūkyō to risei"「宗教と理性」[Religion and
　　reason]. *Mujintō*『無尽燈』3 (February 1898): 1–6; 3 (March 1898): 11–16;
　　3 (May 1898): 1–12.

Yamamoto Ryōkichi 山本良吉. *Daisetsu ate, Yamamoto Ryōkichi shokan*『大拙宛、山本
　　良吉書簡』[Yamamoto Ryōkichi's letters to Daisetz]. Companion volume
　　to Inoue Zenjō 井上禅定 et al., eds., *Suzuki Daisetsu mikōkai shokan*『鈴木
　　大拙未公開書簡』[Unpublished letters of Suzuki Daisetz]. Kyoto: Zen
　　Bunka Kenkyūjo, 1989.

———. "Fujioka hakushi no omoide"「藤岡博士の思出」[Memories of Dr.
　　Fujioka]. *Kokugo to Kokubungaku*『国語と国文学』17, no. 4 (1940): 400–05.

———. "Gojukkaiko, nijūrokunen"「五十回顧『二十六年』」[Reflection on the past
　　fifty years with the special significance of "twenty-six years"]. In *Chōsui
　　sensei ikō*『晁水先生遺稿』[Writings of the late Professor Chōsui], edited
　　by Uchida Sen'nosuke 内田泉之助, 12–28. Tokyo: Musashi Kōkō, Ko-
　　Yamamoto Sensei Kinenkai Jigyōkai, 1951.

———. "Ko Matsui Kisaburō kyōju chōji, omoidebanashi"「故松井喜三郎教授弔
　　辞、思出話」[Lamentation of the death of the late professor Matsui
　　Kisaburō, and some anecdotes by way of remembrance]. In *Chōsui sensei ikō*
　　『晁水先生遺稿』[Writings of the late Professor Chōsui], edited by Uchida
　　Sen'nosuke 内田泉之助, 281–93. Tokyo: Musashi Kōkō, Ko-Yamamoto
　　Sensei Kinenkai Jigyōkai, 1951.

———. "Suzuki Daisetz to daijōbukkyō no sekai shōkai"「鈴木大拙と大乗仏教の世
　　界紹介」[Suzuki Daisetz and the world of Mahayana Buddhism]. In *Chōsui
　　sensei ikō*『晁水先生遺稿集』[Writings of the late Professor Yamamoto],
　　edited by Uchida Sen'nosuke, 209–16. Tokyo: Musashi Kōkō, Ko-
　　Yamamoto Sensei Kinenkai Jigyōkai, 1951.

———. "Untitled"「無題」[Lamenting the death of Fujioka Sakutarō]. In *Chōsui sensei ikō zokuhen*『晁水先生遺稿続編』[Writings of the late Professor Yamamoto, vol. 2], edited by Kawasaki Akira 川崎明, 122–24. Tokyo: Musashi Kōkō Yamamoto Sensei Kinenkai, 1966.

———, ed. *Rinrigakushi*『倫理学史』[A history of ethics]. Tokyo: Toyamabō, 1897.

Yamanouchi Tokuryū 山内得立. "Kaiko"「回顧」[Reminiscence]. In *Kyoto Daigaku bungakubu gojūnenshi*『京都大学文学部五十年史』[Fifty years of the Faculty of Letters at Kyoto University], edited by Kyoto Daigaku Bungakubu 京都大学文学部, 464–66. Kyoto: University of Kyoto, 1956.

———. "*Tetsugaku Kenkyū* no hajime no koro"「『哲学研究』の初めの頃」[The early years of the *Journal of Philosophical Studies*]. *Journal of Philosophical Studies*『哲学研究』500 (September 1966): 275–76.

Yatsugi Kazuo 矢次一夫. "Nishida Kitarō hakushi to Daitōa sensō"「西田幾多郎博士と大東亜戦争」[Dr. Nishida Kitarō and the Greater East Asian War]. In his *Shōwa dōranshishi*『昭和動乱私史』[Personal account of the turbulent Showa period]. 3 vols. Tokyo: Keizai Ōrai, 1973.

Yukawa Hideki 湯川秀樹. "Tabibito, aru butsurigakusha no kaisō"「旅人、ある物理学者の回想」[A traveler: Recollections of a physicist]. In *Yukawa Hideki Jisen-shū*『湯川秀樹自選集』[Self-selected writings of Yukawa Hideki]. 5: 5–239. Tokyo: Asahi Shinbunsha, 1971.

Yusa, Michiko 遊佐道子. "Amerika de Nishida kenkyū o kangaeru"「アメリカで西田研究を考える」[Pondering in America on the state of Nishida studies]. Shisō『思想』857 (1995): 221–35.

———. "Contemporary Buddhist Philosophy." In *A Companion to World Philosophies*, edited by Eliot Deutsch and Ron Bontekoe, 564–72. Oxford: Blackwell Publishers, 1997.

———. *Denki Nishida Kitarō*『伝記：西田幾多郎』[A biography of Nishida Kitarō]. Supplementary vol. 1, *Nishida Tetsugaku Senshū*『西田哲学撰集』[Selected Works of Nishidan Philosophy]. Kyoto: Tōeisha, 1998.

———. "Fashion and *A-letheia*: Philosophical Integrity and Wartime Thought Control." *Hikaku Shisō Kenkyū*『比較思想研究』(Tokyo) 16 (1989): 281–94.

———. "From *Topos* to Environment: A Conversation with Nishida Kitarō." In *The Future of Religion: Postmodern Perspectives*, edited by Christopher Lamb and Dan Cohn-Sherbok, 112–27. London: Middlesex University Press, 1999.

———. "Nishida and Hearn." *Monumenta Nipponica* 51, no. 3 (1996): 309–12.

———. "Nishida and the Question of Nationalism." *Monumenta Nipponica* 46, no. 2 (1991): 203–09.

———. "Nishida and Totalitarianism: A Philosopher's Resistance." In *Rude Awakenings: Zen, the Kyoto School, and the Question of Nationalism*, edited by James W. Heisig and John C. Maraldo, 107–31. Honolulu: University of Hawai'i Press, 1994.

———. "Philosophy and Inflation: Miki Kiyoshi in Weimar Germany, 1922–1924," *Monumenta Nipponica* 53, no. 1 (1998): 45–71.

————. "Reflections on Nishida Studies," *Eastern Buddhist* 28, no. 2 (1995): 287–96.

————. "A Speech Meeting of November 8, 1891: A Religion-Ideological Landscape of Mid-Meiji Japan." *Journal of Selected Papers in Asian Studies* 1, no. 1 (1998): 40–51.

Index